CAMBRIDGE STUDIES IN EARLY MODERN HISTORY

The Changing Face
of Empire

CAMBRIDGE STUDIES IN EARLY MODERN HISTORY

*Edited by Professor J. H. Elliott, The Institute for Advanced Study, Princeton,
Professor Olwen Hufton, University of Reading, and Professor H. G. Koenigsberger,
King's College, London*

The idea of an 'early modern' period of European history from the fifteenth to the late eighteenth century is now widely accepted among historians. The purpose of the Cambridge Studies in Early Modern History is to publish monographs and studies which will illuminate the character of the period as a whole, and in particular focus attention on a dominant theme within it, the interplay of continuity and change as they are represented by the continuity of medieval ideas, political and social organisation, and by the impact of new ideas, new methods and new demands on the traditional structures.

The Changing Face of Empire

Charles V, Philip II and Habsburg Authority, 1551–1559

M. J. RODRÍGUEZ-SALGADO

Lecturer in International History
London School of Economics and Political Science

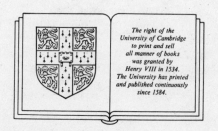

The right of the
University of Cambridge
to print and sell
all manner of books
was granted by
Henry VIII in 1534.
The University has printed
and published continuously
since 1584.

CAMBRIDGE UNIVERSITY PRESS

Cambridge

New York   New Rochelle   Melbourne   Sydney

Published by the Press Syndicate of the University of Cambridge
The Pitt Building, Trumpington Street, Cambridge CB2 1RP
32 East 57th Street, New York, NY 10022, USA
10 Stamford Road, Oakleigh, Melbourne 3166, Australia

First published 1988

Printed in Great Britain at the University Press, Cambridge

British Library cataloguing in publication data
Rodríguez-Salgado, M. J.
The changing face of empire: Charles V,
Philip II and Habsburg authority,
1551–1559. – (Cambridge studies in early modern history).
1. Austria – History – Ferdinand I,
1521–1564   2. Spain – History – House of Austria, 1516–1700
1. Title
940.2   DB65.3

Library of Congress cataloguing in publication data
Rodríguez-Salgado, M. J.
The changing face of empire.
(Cambridge studies in early modern history)
Bibliography.
1. Holy Roman Empire – History – Charles V, 1519–1556.
2. Charles V, Holy Roman Emperor, 1500–1558.
3. Philip II, King of Spain, 1527–1598.   1. Title.   II. Series.
DD179.R62 1988   943′031   87-32647

ISBN 0 521 30346 X

To David Loades and
Helmut Koenigsberger

Contents

Contents

Contents

Plates

Maps

Tables

Acknowledgements

Throughout its long transition from idea to book, Professors Helmut Koenigsberger and David Loades have encouraged and supported my efforts. I am immensely grateful to them. Dr Hamish Scott proved an admirable critic of both structure and style, much improving the text in the process. All three are to be commended as well as warmly thanked for their fortitude in reading this, and making many valuable suggestions. I was fortunate to find friends to discuss my work with and who helped to polish ideas and prose; a special thanks to Dr Maarten Ultee, who turned many a baroque phrase into clear English, and to Dr Jane Dawson, Simon Adams and Bruce Lenman with whom I have often discussed the period. My thanks also to Professor Geoffrey Parker and Dr Peter Marzall who were generous with their advice and support when I started my research. Research and writing take a heavy toll of friends and finances and I have been lucky to find both over the years. I owe a great deal to María Pilar Saenz de Buruaga, Angel Cajal, Simone Macdougall, Claire and Richard Munday, Margaret Bogie, Poh Cheng Meng and Juan Ramón Rodríguez Salgado. Nor can I forget to express my gratitude to the staff of the Archivo General de Simancas, who have been unfailingly courteous, helpful and friendly over the years. Finally, my thanks to the Universities of Hull, St Andrews and Newcastle upon Tyne who have supported my research with grants over the years.

Abbreviations

ADE	Archivo Documental Español, published by the Real Academia de la Historia.
FR	Vols. 1–9 *Negociaciones con Francia 1559–1567* (Madrid 1950–4)
Carranza	Vol. 18, *Fray Bartolomé Carranza. Documentos Históricos* (Madrid 1962)
AGS	Archivo General de Simancas
CJH.	Consejo y Juntas de Hacienda
CMC	Contaduría Mayor de Cuentas
E.	Estado
GA.	Guerra Antigua
PR.	Patronato Real
SP.	Secretarias Provinciales
A Med.	Archivo de los duques de Medina Celi. All the references are to *caja 7, legajo 249, numbers 11 and 12*, except for the letter from Philip II to Feria, 28 December 1558 which is in *caja 91, legajo 341, number 49*. The letters are identified by date in the text.
BL	British Library, London
BM	British Museum, London
mss.	Manuscripts
Add.	Additional Manuscripts
BNM mss.	Biblioteca Nacional, Madrid. Manuscripts collections.
BPR	Biblioteca del Palacio Real, Madrid
Codoin	*Colección de documentos inéditos para la historia de España* (112 vols., Madrid 1842–95)
CSP	*Calendar of State Papers*
D.	*Domestic* ed. R. Lemon (London, 1865)
Sp.	*Spanish,* ed. R. Tyler et al. (London, 1862–1964)
V.	*Venetian,* ed. R. Brown et al. (London, 1864–98)
DP	F. Díaz Plaja, *La historia de España en sus documentos. El Siglo XVI* (Madrid, 1958)
IVDJ	Instituto de Valencia de Don Juan, Madrid
RPPB	J. M. B. C. Kervijn de Lettenhove, *Rélations politiques des Pays-Bas et de l'Angleterre sous le règne de Philippe II* (11 vols., Brussels, 1882–1900)

Abbreviations

SIHM	H. de Castries et al., *Les sources inédites de l'histoire du Maroc. Premiere sèrie: Dynastie Sa'dienne* (Paris, 1905–). The collection is further subdivided into countries; the names of the countries and volumes are given.
Vertot	R. Aubert de Vertot d'Aubeuf, *Les Ambassades de Messieurs de Noailles en Angleterre* (Leyden, 1763)
VDK	G. Turba (ed.) *Venetianische Depeschen vom Kaiserhofe (Dispacci di Germania)* (vol. II, Vienna, 1892, vol. III, Vienna, 1895)

Note on currencies

The accounts of both Charles V and Philip II were calculated in a bewildering variety of coinage and monies of account. At first sight it would seem reasonable to transpose them all into a common coin or money of account, but there are a number of serious problems that render such a process inadvisable. First, documents seldom give sufficient information about the value of the currency involved. Even in the case of generic names like the *livre*, it is usual to omit vital details such as the provenance, the type (coin or money of account), or the value at the time. Second, despite the existence of some official exchange rates issued both by the sovereign and the major financial markets, there is no reliable table that can be used nor is it possible to say what the rate was at a given moment. This is of some importance since the 1550s saw constant, sudden and sharp fluctuations of exchange rates. The third major difficulty relates to the habit of including fictitious exchange rates in many of the loan contracts between the crown and financiers. This was a form of hidden interest very frequently used. I have left accounts in the money given, with the exception of sums in *maravedis*, which have been turned into ducats. I opted here to follow the procedure of the officials in Castile. The maravedi is such a small unit that it makes calculations more difficult, and the sums obtained appear out of all proportion to the rest.

The most frequently used currencies and monies of account were as follows:[1]

(1) *Ducats (ds)* – The Spanish ducat was a money of account officially valued at 375 maravedis or at 11 *reales* and 1 maravedi. The Italian ducat was a gold coin but in the documents dealt with in this work the term is used without qualification; the values given, however, show that almost invariably it was the Spanish ducat that was meant.

(2) *Escudos (es)* – This was a gold coin, similar to the *écu au soleil* of France and the *scudo* of Italy. Most accounts use the official valuation of the Spanish realms, that is 350 maravedis or 10 reales, 10 maravedis.

In England, the official value of the French and Imperial *crown* was 6 shillings and 4 pence sterling. However, the pensions and grants made by Philip to the English during 1554–8 were calculated at 5 shillings to the crown, or $6\frac{1}{2}$ pence to the real. The official valuation of the ducat was 6 shillings, 8 pence sterling.[2]

(3) *Reales (rs)* – Foreign exchange rates more often than not used the real, a Spanish silver coin for purposes of calculation, but it is seldom encountered in the loan contracts or statements of account used by the governments of Charles V or Philip II. The official value of the real was 34 maravedis.

(4) *Petit livre* of Flanders, or *Florin (fl)* – There were 20 *sols* of 12 *deniers* to each Flemish pound. The official valuation used by the sovereign's accounts during these years was of 20 *patars* (in Spanish *placas, ps*) which was a small silver coin, or 40 *gros* (in Spanish *gruesos, gs*), a unit of account as well as a coin, or 6 *carolus gulden*, a gold coin until 1541 when it was minted in silver. The Flemish (or Holland) pound or florin was the monetary unit used in the formal requests by the sovereign to the provincial governments. The exchange rates between the florin and the Spanish currencies were highly unstable during this decade. By 1563 the value of the florin was officially cited as 275 maravedis, or 7 reales, 27 maravedis.[3] In England, its official value was 3 shillings, 4 pennies sterling.[4]

ROUGH EQUIVALENTS?

Braudel calculated the escudo at twice the value of the florin, and used this computation to give his comparative equivalents of the accumulated debts in Spain and the Netherlands.[5] The evidence for this was taken from the Antwerp exchange rates, where the escudo accounts bear out these calculations.[6] Others, unfortunately, do not. At times the difference is not great. For instance, the accounts of one of the paymasters of Philip's army in the Netherlands, Jerónimo Curiel, valued the florin at 200 maravedis and the escudo at 360 maravedis in 1556.[7] But the most frequent valuation I have found in the documents cited here is that of florins of 36 patars. This would make the escudo and florin much closer in value. It would be wrong, therefore, to take the market value as the sole guideline.

---

[1] The information for Spanish currencies has been gleaned from documents cited in the text. More information about the Netherlands can be obtained from R. Ehrenberg, *Capital and Finance in the Age of the Renaissance. A Study of the Fuggers and Their Connections* (London, 1928) esp. p. 272; F. Braudel, 'Les emprunts de Charles-Quint sur la place d'Anvers', in *Charles-Quint et son temps* (Centre National de la Recherche Scientifique. Paris, 1959), p. 195; H. Buckley, 'Sir Thomas Gresham and foreign exchange', *Economic Journal* (1924), p. 596, n. 3; J. D. Tracy, *A Financial Revolution in the Habsburg Netherlands. Rente and rentiers in the County of Holland, 1515–1565* (London, 1985), p. 30 n. 6.
[2] C. E. Challis, *The Tudor Coinage* (Manchester–New York, 1978) pp. 216–18; D. M. Loades, *The Reign of Mary Tudor* (London, 1979), pp. 208–9; AGS. CMC 1 ep. 1184 ff.64–5.
[3] J. Pérez de Moya, *Reglas para co(n)tar sin pluma etc.* Included in J. de Oriega, *Tratado de Aritmetica* (Granada, 1563), p. 245.
[4] Loades, *Mary Tudor*, p. 208.
[5] 'Les emprunts', p. 195.
[6] See for example IVDJ 68m 309/6.
[7] AGS CJH 27 f. 91.

Introduction

Before his death, Ferdinand of Aragon warned his grandson, the future Charles V, not to follow the impulses of youth and embroil himself in a struggle for supremacy with France. Despite the vast inheritance that fortune had so unexpectedly bestowed upon him – the accumulated possessions of four different states – Ferdinand knew from bitter experience that France would prove more than a match for his successor. He predicted that the struggle would be long and costly, becoming an all-consuming preoccupation. It would prevent Charles from fighting against the Muslims, which was the primary task of a Christian prince, and a vital necessity for a king of Spain. If conflict did break out, Ferdinand declared that it would initiate 'an eternal war within Christendom'.[1]

He was not far off the mark. Four decades later, large areas of Charles's vast empire had been devastated by the almost continual wars against France and other enemies. The financial and political structure of his states was in chaos. Charles faced widespread internal unrest; all his states faced bankruptcy, and virtually all areas under his control were threatened with invasion. Wisely, he admitted defeat, abandoned power and sought solace, and perhaps penance, in monastic retreat. He left his son Philip the unenviable – and some believed, impossible – task of saving the empire.

This book focuses on the crucial period of transition during the 1550s when the emperor experienced physical, mental and political collapse. It analyses the impact of the long years of war and the gradual decline of the monarch, tracing the emergence of Philip II and the division of the Habsburg lands. The work begins with a voyage: Philip II's reluctant journey to Spain in 1551 just as the last major war between Charles V and the French monarch was beginning. It ends with another, similar situation, as Philip impatiently awaited a fair wind to sail back to Spain, having concluded peace with Henry II. He was no happier now than before at the prospect of returning to his homeland. Nor did his subjects greet his return with unqualified joy. By then both Aragon and Castile were gripped by rebellion.

This study seeks to revise and challenge many long-cherished misconceptions

[1] J. M. Doussinague, *El testamento político de Fernando el Católico* (Madrid, n.d.) p. 210.

about Charles V, Philip II and their relations with the lands they ruled. The aura of near sanctity that still clings to the figure of Charles hardly fits the ageing, inept leader, desperately holding on to power and refusing to take responsibility for his mistakes. Alternating between fits of depression and rage the emperor takes on a more human, if less heroic form. As for Philip, invariably portrayed as a timid man, awed by his father and adhering to all that was Spanish, he emerges as an aggressive leader, constantly at odds with his father and the Spanish realms.

Apart from some necessary revisionism, three broad questions have determined this analysis of the 1550s. First, the desire to examine how the vast multi-national empire of the Habsburgs functioned; why it was able to withstand the transfer of power from Charles to Philip II and Ferdinand I, and to what extent Philip's empire differed from that of his father. The second major preoccupation is with finance. The unprecedented length of the conflicts put intolerable strains upon the empire – but how were the wars funded? What methods were used, and what were the repercussions? I was intrigued to know more about the first so-called state bankruptcy of 1557. Lastly, there was the important matter of Philip's return to Spain in 1559 and the peace with France, long considered the most significant events of his reign. Was 1559 a turning point? The definitive settlement of the Habsburg–Valois struggle and beginning of a 'Spanish' monarchy? The answers to many questions were rather surprising. The transfer of power turned out to be far more complex and acrimonious than had been suspected; the exploration of finances revealed a fascinating epoch of rapidly-changing conditions – and no bankruptcy. As for the peace, it will be seen that it was soon threatened and seen as a respite rather than an end. Philip's return to Spain was more of a victory for the Netherlands than for the Spanish realms.

Since the internal and international spheres are studied in relation to each other, and the empire is taken as a whole, the reader will find the coverage uneven, with rapid shifts from one state to another and one theme to the next. But the advantages of presenting the overall view which the rulers and their advisers had to consider, seemed to the author to outweigh the disadvantages. In between Philip's two voyages, which were scarcely eight years apart, the world, and not just the leaders, had changed substantially. The balance of power had altered significantly; the boundaries of Europe and North Africa had been redrawn. It is curious that despite the dramatic nature of the events which fill this decade and their momentous importance, the period has attracted relatively little attention.

PERSONALITIES

As a prelude to the detailed analysis of the 1550s, it would be as well to be acquainted with the leading characters. In the sixteenth century the conflicts of powerful individuals were as important as the clash of the mighty realms over which they held sway. When sovereigns ruled as well as reigned, their personalities and aspirations are vital to an understanding of events. So too are their advisers, consorts and deputies.

Charles V (1500–58) held the highest status in Christendom; he is also the central figure in this decade.[2] By 1550 he had reached the pinnacle of power. After his defeat of the German princes in 1547 and after the death of Francis I, his chief rival, it seemed as if his two major enemies had been vanquished. He spoke and behaved as if there was nothing he could not achieve if he set his mind to it. Perhaps he had come to believe his own propaganda. Immensely arrogant and grasping, Charles nevertheless appeared to epitomize chivalric notions of the warrior-king to some of his contemporaries. They were often awed by his power, though seldom by his presence. He was capable of exuding *bonhomie* and his vices often put him on a level most common men could relate to. His gluttony was proverbial, his dislike of paper work and preference for action both in the field and in the bedroom gave him a very human touch in younger days. But in the 1550s, the darker side of his character predominated. The political perspicuity with which his supporters at the time and since have endowed him is hard to see after 1552. Stubborn, unwilling to yield to advice that did not accord with his own preconceptions and desires, he still showed physical courage and determination not to let go of power, even if this led to greater destruction.

He had never liked making decisions – he admitted that until he was thirty he had allowed his chancellor Gattinara to take the lead. After 1551 indecision, acute depression and long periods of self-imposed isolation were his most marked characteristics. He withdrew from public life and state affairs, especially in the prolonged crisis of 1553–4. Throughout this decade, he relied very heavily, at times exclusively on his sister, Mary of Hungary. From the closing months of 1552 there were long intervals when she, not the emperor, ruled. His frustration as he was forced to make way for his son and brother introduce a note of pathos, augmented by the derision in which he was held after his retirement in the monastery of Yuste. The peace he sought often evaded him; he was prone to moments of towering rage.

[2] There are hundreds of books dealing with Charles's reign: his popularity was much helped by the fact that at least three countries claimed him as their own, namely Spain, the Netherlands and Germany. But few of the biographies are noteworthy. K. Brandi, *The Emperor Charles V* (English edn., London 1939, Harvester Press–Krauss reprint, 1980) is still the weightiest and most useful although seriously neglecting Spain and the southern front. More recently, M. Fernández Alvarez, *Charles V* (London, 1975) redressed the balance in favour of Spain. H. G. Koenigsberger has written an admirably brief introduction to the reign in 'The empire of Charles V in Europe', in the New Cambridge Modern History vol. II, reprinted in his *The Habsburgs and Europe, 1516–1660* (London, 1971), pp. 1–62. But the best guides to Charles's complex character and actions are his own letters and memoirs. The latter survive in a Portuguese copy and were published in a bilingual text by A. Morel-Fatio (ed.) *Historiographie de Charles-Quint, 1e partie, suivi des mémoires de Charles-Quint* (Paris, 1913). A Spanish version is available in the excellent collection of the emperor's letters edited by M. Fernández Alvarez, *Corpus documental de Carlos V* (5 vols., Salamanca, 1971–81). These should be complemented by the letters published by K. Lanz, *Correspondenz des Kaisers Karl V* (3 vols., Leipzig, 1846). Most accounts of Charles's life, however, pass from his victory over the German princes in 1547 to his retirement with scarcely a pause.

Plate 1 Charles V

But the anger that caused abject fear and the fall of powerful men was now no more than the tantrums of an irascible old man.

By contrast, Mary of Hungary (1505–58) retained her full faculties to the end and her indomitable will was scarcely diminished by her retirement.[3] This strong, indeed overpowering woman was also noted for her proud bearing and manly deportment. Widowed soon after her marriage to the unfortunate Lewis II of Hungary, she experienced a period of political and personal neglect which undoubtedly influenced her subsequent enjoyment of and determination to wield power. Aged only twenty-six when her brother summoned her to take over the government of the Netherlands during his absence from the area, she established her regime rapidly and soon commanded a mixture of respect and fear. Her decisiveness and her capacity for political control made her an invaluable partner for Charles. She believed in strong government and found it difficult to tolerate interference or resistance either from the area she governed or from her brother and nephew, whom she was bound to serve. She was without a doubt a most difficult person to handle, and a dangerous foe.

Whereas a painter might be tempted to use bold brushstrokes to portray Mary of Hungary, he might consider a fine pencil more suitable to depict Juana (1535–73), the youngest of Charles's surviving children.[4] Her features were rather delicate and her beauty widely acknowledged. But the two women had a great deal in common. More than once Juana was described as 'masculine' by her contemporaries; a tribute to her strength of character and capacity to govern. Her decisiveness was evident in childhood. By the age of nineteen she was both a widow and a mother: her husband João died as a result of a riding accident some days before the birth of their son Sebastian in January 1554. A few months later she would assume the government of the Spanish realms. The fact that she was a woman, as much as her youth and complete lack of political experience, led most observers to assume that she would be a mere figure-head, subservient to her advisers and male relatives. They had not reckoned on her intelligence, vigour and pride. From the start she attended meetings of the major councils regularly, and once she had become familiar with her post and the problems of the realms, she took a leading part in discussions and decisions. Her ability to influence and even control the councils was amply proved during 1558 when she led the challenge to her brother's policies and refused to accept the new style of government he had devised in an attempt to strengthen his power and curb hers.[5]

[3] J. de Iongh, *Mary of Hungary. Second regent of the Netherlands* (London, 1958) although this is a rather romanticised view of Mary, parts of which are questionable, the biography brings out well her powerful character and the influence she had over Charles. The regency is covered in pp. 139–272. E. Albèri, *Le relazioni degli ambasciatori Veneti al Senato durante il secolo decimocesto* (15 vols., Florence, 1839–63), ser. 1, vol. 3, pp. 208–9 for a brief description of her.
[4] Albèri, *Relazioni*, ser. 1, vol. 3, p. 249; vol. 5, p. 121.
[5] The conflict with Philip will be amply explored in chapters 7 and 8.

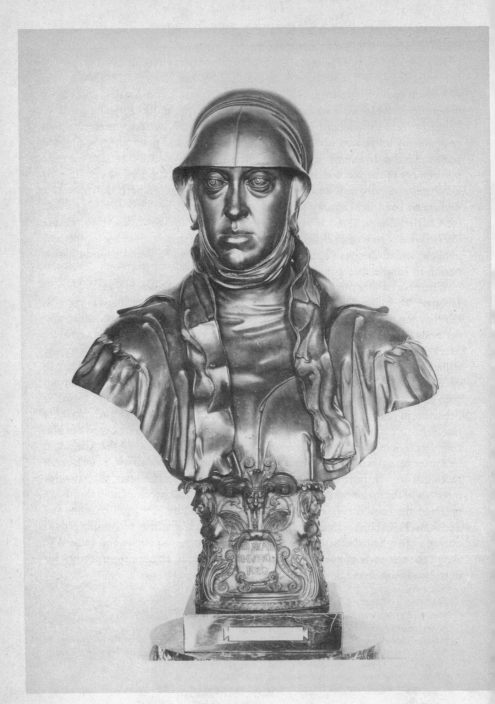

Plate 2 Mary of Hungary

The strength and personality of some of these Habsburg women often make their male kinsmen pale by comparison. Philip II (1527–98) is a monarch frequently accused of being great by circumstance and utterly undistinguished in character. Bigotry and suspicion are the most frequently cited characteristics.[6] This stark picture is inaccurate. In his youth Philip had been reserved and even cold towards friend and foe alike. He carefully cultivated an image that was highly prized in the Spanish court – Juana and their uncle Ferdinand did likewise, and were all much admired for their almost unnatural capacity for restraint. The control of emotion, particularly in public, and the ability to take reverses with stoic calmness were the salient features of what was termed *sosiego*. Yet all were capable of establishing very deep, even passionate, emotional bonds with spouses, children and friends. Restraint should not be mistaken for absence of feeling. Outside Spain, these mannerisms were considered alien and distasteful, and were usually interpreted as a mixture of haughtiness, aloofness and lack of courtesy. During Philip's long visit to the Netherlands and the Holy Roman Empire 1548–50, he was made acutely conscious that his reserve and control had created an unfavourable impression. His eagerness to establish himself and gain power prompted him to change, as did the political and personal maturity he gained during his spell as regent of the Spanish realms from 1551–4.

When he next emerged on the international stage he was unanimously acclaimed as a man of exquisite tact and graciousness. Whilst he retained an obsessive concern with honour and was intensely proud, he learnt to set aside his pride when political expediency demanded. In 1557 the Venetian ambassador was extolling the need for peace in Italy and told Philip that he 'was one of the greatest, or rather the greatest' prince. Philip 'interrupting me said, "I am no greater than the others, nor will I be so, but choose to acknowledge all the Italian potentates as friends"'.[7] In other words, Philip had learnt the art of diplomacy. Yet behind the newly expressed affability lay a man who was extremely ambitious, aggressive, and driven by inexorable willpower to achieve his goals, whatever the cost to his realms.

It is commonly thought that Philip was both indecisive and overawed by his father. Neither claim will stand up to detailed examination. He soon revealed his penchant for requesting as many opinions as possible on important issues, and liked

---

6 As in the case of Charles, accounts of Philip's life during these years are sketchy and inadequate. Many historians behave as if the reign did not really begin until 1559. The two most recent biographies in English are no exception although very valuable in other ways. P. Pierson, *Philip II of Spain* (London, 1975) is a straightforward account, whilst G. Parker, *Philip II* (London, 1979) gives a far more personal portrait. F. Braudel, *The Mediterranean and the Mediterranean world in the age of Philip II* (2nd edn., 2 vols, Paris, 1966; English trans., London, 1972) contains much information about other areas too. L. Cabrera de Córdoba, *Felipe II* is still invaluable for many details. H. G. Koenigsberger has written a useful introduction to the king's government in 'The statecraft of Philip II, *European Studies Review*, 1 (1971), pp. 1–21. Other works will be cited in the text and included in the bibliography.
7 CSP. V, vol. 6 (11), p. 1146.

Plate 3 Princess Juana

to weigh up the advice of his leading counsellors for as long as he could, but this is not to say that he lacked the capacity to make decisions or impose his will, however unpopular it might be. Philip followed the precepts of good kingship because he felt it was his duty to do so. He was conscientious, hard-working, of average intelligence and wide-ranging interests. He had his passions too – he loved hunting, tournaments, music, collecting books and fine art. But his pleasures were moderate; prudence and restraint as well as a love of order pervaded his life, and these elements lack the colourfulness of excess.

As for his relations with Charles, there was a great deal of conflict between them. Philip repeatedly opposed his father's internal and international policies. At times, they were involved in acrimonious disputes, and there was little contact between them after 1556, although they began to draw closer together in the last year of the emperor's life, when he alone seemed to sympathise with Philip's determination to win the war with France despite the appalling toll of lives and resources. Both men were acutely conscious of the need to present a united front, so they kept their quarrels out of the public eye; consequently, contemporaries failed to appreciate Philip's growing influence and until 1557 many foreign observers considered Philip a weak, timid and ineffectual prince, under the control of his well-known father. However, it was only in 1559, as he wrestled with seemingly impossible problems that the more familiar traits of Philip's character emerge – his caution increased, and it is possible to trace the beginning of the anxious, providentialist ruler who dominated Europe thereafter.

Next in status is Ferdinand (1503–64), ruler of the Habsburg lands in central Europe, king of the Romans from 1531.[8] Ferdinand always lived in the shadow of his more powerful and aggressive older brother. For most of his life he acted as Charles's deputy in the Holy Roman Empire, partly out of necessity since his own resources were insufficient to deal with the many internal and external threats to his lands, especially the advance of the Ottoman Turks. But also because he was of a gentle and quiet disposition, prone to being bullied and cajoled by Charles and Mary. At times he appears timid; he was always reserved and gracious. Like Philip, he was moderate in everything, and this proved an invaluable asset in an empire torn by confessional and political strife. He knew how to compromise and was a skilled negotiator. Always happiest when he was with his family, he was determined to advance his numerous children and obtain a just partition of the Trastámara and Habsburg inheritances denied by Charles (pp. 34–5, 110). This was one trait that Charles seriously underestimated.

His eldest son, Maximilian of Austria (1527–76), was entirely different.[9] He was a man of violent passions and temperament. Shrewd, calculating and headstrong, he

---

[8] Albèri, *Relazioni*, ser. 1, vol. 3, pp. 145–7; P. S. Fichtner, *Ferdinand I of Austria* (New York, 1982).
[9] Albèri, *Relazioni*, ser. 1, vol. 3, pp. 151–3; R. Rodríguez Raso (ed.), *Maximiliano de Austria, gobernador de Carlos V en España. Cartas al emperador* (Madrid, 1963), pp. 12–13.

Plate 4 Philip II

Plate 5 Duke of Savoy

alternated between fits of morose inactivity and furious action. It was said at the time that not even Ferdinand quite trusted him, although he evidently loved his son deeply. The difficult situation in which he saw himself tended to bring out the violent traits in his character, although it also taught him the virtue of compromise. He vehemently rejected the client status which Ferdinand had so meekly accepted from the elder branch of the family and was instrumental in stiffening his father's resolve to free himself from them.

Lower in rank, but related to the royal family was Emanuele Filiberto, duke of Savoy.[10] He was a prince in his own right, a general and councillor of state for both Charles and Philip. His father had been dispossessed of most of his Italian lands since the 1530s as a result of a French invasion, and Emanuele Filiberto had been raised largely in Charles's court. The wars of the 1550s gave him ample opportunity to demonstrate his considerable military skills. He was a fiery and colourful character; a notorious womaniser constantly embroiled in disputes. He was also a man of considerable intelligence, but his inability to restrain his temper proved a serious drawback on a political level. His youth and Italian background led to considerable opposition and disobedience within the army units he was appointed to command, and later, when he was given charge of the Netherlands. Far from tackling the situation calmly and tactfully, he tended to respond to these challenges with 'a great deal of passion' thus exacerbating them. But then the situation in the Netherlands would have tried the patience of a saint – and he was far from that.

Below these individuals both in rank and importance, there was a whole host of counsellors and governors without whom policies could not have been devised, let alone executed. A few deserve some attention at the outset since they played a leading part in government during the 1550s. It is striking how many of these were either Spanish or Italian. During the second half of his reign Charles had increasingly made use of these rather than German or Netherlands administrators who had dominated his court at first.

Apart from Mary of Hungary, his most prominent adviser was Antoine Perrenot de Granvelle (1517–86), bishop of Arras and later Cardinal Granvelle.[11] His family was from the Franche-Comté rather than from the Netherlands, where he spent most of his life. His father had been extremely close to Charles and was widely recognised as one of the most influential men at court.[12] He introduced his son to state affairs early and found in him an apt successor. The younger Granvelle was soon perceived to be a man of extraordinary abilities; highly intelligent, a good

---

[10] Albèri, *Relazioni*, ser. 1, vol. 3, p. 351; G. Claretta, *Il Duca di Savoia, Emanuele Filiberto, e la corta di Londra, 1554-5* (Pinerolo, 1892); P. Egidi and A. Segre, *Emanuele Filiberto Vol. II, 1558-1580*, (Turin, 1928).

[11] M. van Durme, *El Cardenal Granvela (15-17-1586)* (Spanish edn., Barcelona, 1957); Albèri, *Relazioni*, ser. 1, vol. 3, pp. 245, 381.

[12] J. A. Escudero, *Los secretarios de estado y del despacho (1474-1742)* (4 vols., Madrid, 1976) includes a brief analysis of the elder Granvelle's part in the administration, vol. 1, pp. 82-99.

linguist and an able negotiator. He was thoroughly acquainted with internal and international affairs and lacked neither charm nor grace. He struck both friendly and hostile observers as an urbane and cultured man. But he was also cunning, ruthless, immensely arrogant, and, as even his able and sympathetic biographer van Durme admits, he was driven by 'insatiable ambition'.[13] He did not hesitate to stoop to the lowest forms of flattery in order to curry favour and for most of this decade he was constantly having to do so.

It was a difficult time for him. At first we find him struggling to retain Charles's favour. Then, as the emperor's power waned, he successfully established a close working partnership with Mary of Hungary which brought him to the pinnacle of power. They dominated the court and government during Charles's last years. Ironically it was this very success that caused his subsequent fall from grace, albeit temporarily. Philip resented his influence and opposed many of the policies he advanced. On his accession he relegated Granvelle to a secondary role, but he could not afford to lose one of the most experienced counsellors in the Netherlands. Gradually the king came to appreciate his value and loyalty, and even to trust him, though he never liked him. Granvelle proved more successful with Philip's regents, becoming a favourite of both the duke of Savoy and later Margaret of Parma.

Like Granvelle, Fernando Alvarez de Toledo, duke of Alba (1507–82), started his military and political career in the emperor's service.[14] The two men took part in all major international negotiations during this period. Abrasive and abrupt though he was, Alba's military experience made him invaluable in these years of constant warfare. His value was considerably increased by his capacity for making decisions; whilst he lagged considerably behind Granvelle in intelligence, he often made up for this with clear-cut advice and energetic activity. Charles as much as Philip valued these qualities, and the latter in particular shared many of the duke's conceptions about religion and politics, a fact that explains their continued cooperation despite many personal quarrels. Alba was immensely avaricious, ambitious and, as so many other courtiers, capable of the most extreme obsequiousness to gain favour. But during the 1550s he overplayed his hand. He would have done well to have taken his own advice to Juan Manrique de Lara in 1555, and tone down the offensive, condescending missives to Philip. For a time, the prince tolerated Alba's patronising and sometimes disrespectful letters – mild by comparison to some of the abuse he hurled in Charles's direction. Yet as soon as he could, Philip retaliated, stripping Alba of his power in Italy and keeping him out of

---

[13] Van Durme, *Granvela*, p. 142.
[14] The most recent and the only English language biography of this major figure is by W. S. Maltby, *Alba. A biography of Fernando Alvarez de Toledo, third duke of Alba, 1507–1582* (Berkeley–London, 1983). A number of Alba's letters have been published by the duke of Alba, *Epistolario del III duque de Alba, don Fernando Alvarez de Toledo* (3 vols., Madrid, 1952).

Plate 6 Duke of Alba

court and employment for a time.[15] The duke learnt his lesson. After this his correspondence with Philip, as well as his attitude, changed considerably. Humility and subservience helped him back into favour, but without the chance of war, it is questionable whether he would have survived politically.

One of the reasons why Alba was more successful than Granvelle initially was because he changed his allegiance from Charles to Philip early – it had been accomplished during the duke's stay at the Spanish court in 1553. The gamble paid off handsomely when Charles abdicated and so speeded up Philip's rise to power. Alba's ambition was to become the royal favourite and monopolise power. When he was in favour, both he and his supporters claimed that he alone controlled important business and patronage. This had made him suspect to Charles, and led to graver problems with Philip for whom a monopoly of advice or power by any individual was anathema.[16] The note he scribbled in a letter – 'I do not want these matters to be dealt with so exclusively by one person'[17] was indicative of his life-long determination to share out information and power. Philip approved of individuals developing a speciality but he always insisted that other counsellors should consider even highly technical issues.

Alba has long been presented as the leader of one faction at Philip's court, constantly struggling against the faction of his arch-rival Ruy Gómez de Silva. This view of the situation was first promulgated by the Venetian ambassadors who resided in the Habsburg courts, and it has since become a dogma of Spanish historiography.[18] The matter was not quite so simple. Ruy Gómez de Silva (1516–73), prince of Eboli and later duke of Pastrana, was without a doubt Philip's closest friend and counsellor, and had been since an early age. Descended from minor Portuguese nobility, he had come to court to serve as a page in the household of the empress Isabel and there he made the acquaintance of the young prince. Throughout his life he would remain both a personal friend and a close political associate, although there were times when he was out of favour.[19] The prince's generosity towards Ruy Gómez during the 1550s and dependence on his advice, created the impression that he would become a favourite with all that the term implied – monopoly of advice, restricting access to the monarch, and manipulating patronage. Ruy Gómez vehemently repudiated this, and acted as if he meant it. More importantly, Philip believed that this was the case. Whatever advantage he

---

[15] The letter to Manrique de Lara is in Alba, *Epistolario*, vol. 1, pp. 364–5. Examples of the way he chided Philip or exceeded his remit, ibid., vol. 1, p. 70, pp. 318–20. The Italian venture may be followed in pp. 140ff.

[16] See the remarks by Ruy Gómez de Silva in April, 1552, AGS E.89, fol. 129, and by Francisco de Vargas in AGS E.84, fol. 20.

[17] AGS E.141, fol. 185.

[18] See for example Albèri, *Relazioni*, ser. 1, vol. 5, p. 70.

[19] Unfortunately there is no biography of this important character. The early years of friendship between him and Philip were touched upon by J. M. March in the first volume of *Niñez y juventud de Felipe II* (2 vols., Madrid, 1941–2). Albèri, *Relazioni*, ser. 1, vol. 3, p. 381; vol. 5, p. 65.

took of his special relationship with the king, it was done in a most circumspect manner.[20] His rivalry with Alba was taken as a matter of course since they were the most powerful personages at court, and Alba was known to oppose any form of power-sharing. However, for much of the 1550s they cooperated because it was imperative to present a common front against the court and courtiers of Charles V. After 1556 their mutual dislike was apparent but it did not prevent them from working together in the council or on the missions that Philip entrusted to them.

Ruy Gómez was a soft-spoken, deferential man with an almost uncanny ability to hide his feelings and cover his tracks. He was the soul of discretion and we know next to nothing about his conduct or opinions. He exuded charm though without ostentation, had fine manners and was thought most agreeable by his contemporaries. In the claustrophobic atmosphere of the court a pleasant personality was clearly at a premium. Nobody ever accused him of great intelligence, but he was a good listener and tried hard to grasp the essence of major issues, and this sufficed. Philip chose him to carry out all the delicate and important missions of this period: in Portugal (1553), with Charles in 1554–5 and 1557, with Juana in 1557 and 1559, and in the peace negotiations with the French in 1556 and 1558–9. It is interesting and very revealing to compare the tone of his correspondence (what little has survived) with different officials. The dignified and guarded missives to Alba are totally different from the chatty and sometimes vicious correspondence he exchanged with Eraso.

Clearly affability, discretion and the ability to adapt oneself to the person being addressed were invaluable assets; vital indeed for the success of courtiers and officials who could not call upon rank and wealth to secure their position. Francisco de los Cobos (died 1547), that most successful of administrators and favourites said as much in his interesting instructions to his band of protégés. They had certainly been instrumental in assuring his rise from poverty and obscurity to become the most important figure of Charles V's administration. Cobos trained a whole group of men to be loyal, circumspect, and – at least when giving advice to the sovereign – truthful and honest. His trainees dominated the empire's administration after his death.[21] Ironically, one of the secretaries Cobos considered insufficiently competent to achieve a high position was Francisco de Eraso, a man from the lower ranks of the nobility, who entered the administration under his tutelage during the early 1540s. Eraso was to become the most powerful and successful of all Cobos's men.[22] He was

---

[20] AGS E.89, fol. 129; AGS E.84, fol. 20.

[21] H. Keniston, *Francisco de los Cobos* (Pittsburg, 1960), esp. p. 339; Escudero, *Los secretarios*, vol. 1 pp. 77–99; J. A. Fernández Santamaría, *The state, war and peace: Spanish political thought in the Renaissance, 1516–1559* (Cambridge, 1977), pp. 284–90 includes a summary of Fadrique Furió Ceriol's vision of an ideal counsellor.

[22] Unfortunately there is no biography of this fascinating man. Something may be gleaned from Keniston, *Cobos*, pp. 289, 311, 337–43; Escudero, *Los secretarios*, vol. 1, pp. 104ss, although he underestimates his power in the early 1550s, and pp. 181–6. Alberi, *Relazioni*, ser. 1, vol. 3, p. 248, vol. 5, pp. 65, 67.

unquestionably intelligent, hardworking, and developed extraordinary competence over a very broad spectrum of state affairs, becoming an expert on matters as diverse as finance and the Inquisition. No one could doubt that he was cunning; but it would also appear that he was unprincipled beyond the lax boundaries of his time. Eraso earned an unenviable reputation for corruption and viciousness in a court that was no stranger to either. One contemporary commented on his astonishing ability to 'speak a man fair to his face' and say the contrary as soon as his back was turned. He also had a habit of never fully agreeing or disagreeing with anyone.[23] Yet he seems to have possessed a fascinating and – to some at least – attractive personality which endeared him to Charles and Philip. There were times during this troubled decade when Charles refused to see anyone or transact any business, but he would make an exception of Eraso. True to character, the clever secretary used this extraordinary position to buy the favour and protection of Philip. At the point when he seemed closest to the emperor therefore, Eraso was serving another master, and Philip rewarded this richly when he came to power. Irrespective of his less attractive traits, both Charles and Philip were convinced of his loyalty and he amply proved his usefulness.[24]

Two other secretaries merit special mention: Juan Vázquez de Molina and Gonzalo Pérez (*c.* 1500–66). Juan Vázquez had been groomed by Cobos as his successor, but this goal was only partly achieved. Vázquez came to be considered so invaluable for the effective running of the Castilian administration that he was constrained to remain in the realm during the extended absences of the monarchs. Moreover, his character did not seem to be in any way exceptional. An efficient administrator, he lacked the personality to become a confidant of the men and women in power. Only with Maximilian of Austria, co-regent of the Spanish realms 1548–51, does he seem to have gained a certain ascendancy, enough to prompt Charles to issue a warning against allowing Vázquez to monopolise patronage.[25] Gonzalo Pérez was in every sense a more outstanding personality.[26] He fits the picture of the ideal secretary. Philip clearly found him very congenial and trusted

---

[23] The comments on Eraso's character are from letters of M. Oertel, one of the agents of the powerful banking house of Fugger, R. Ehrenberg, *Capital and Finance in the age of the Renaissance. A study of the Fuggers and their connections* (London, 1928), p. 114.

[24] Instances of how Philip used Eraso to obtain decisions and favours from Charles in AGS E.808, fol. 140; AGS E.89, fol. 120. As soon as he took over from his father, Philip reorganised the administration and appointed Eraso as secretary with responsibility for important aspects of government; AGS E.114, fols. 27–31 for the announcement of these changes.

[25] Cit. in R. Carande, *Carlos V y sus banqueros* (3 vols., Madrid, 1943–67), vol. 3 (Madrid, 1967), p. 551. Keniston, *Cobos*, pp. 118, 289, 335–6, gives more details of the secretary's life and character; also Escudero, *Los secretarios*, vol. 1, pp. 100–7, 133–4. As can be seen from such documents as AGS E.89, fols. 122 and 320, most Castilian affairs, and particularly patronage were in his hands. After Charles V's return to Spain, he relied on Juan Vázquez for his information; the two men were in regular correspondence and there is little doubt that he was the only one Charles really trusted.

[26] A. González Palencia, *Gonzalo Pérez, secretario de Felipe II* (2 vols., Madrid, 1946); Escudero, *Los secretarios*, vol. 1, pp. 109–14, 123–33. Albèri, *Relazioni*, ser. 1, vol. 3, pp. 235, 248.

him with a great deal of confidential information. It was not until after their return to Spain in 1559 that Pérez played a vital role in government, however. When Philip reorganised the secretariat, he shared out the highest posts between Eraso and Pérez. The latter continued to be used more frequently as a private secretary: he summarised matters of state, letters, etc. and read them aloud to Philip. As with all courtiers, he accepted bribes and was intensely ambitious and proud. But the side Philip saw was the modest and quiet demeanour of a selfless secretary.

It is striking – and very revealing of the nature of court life – that of all the people who played a major role in the government during the 1550s, only two earned praise for their generosity, lack of corruption and absence of ambition. Equally noticeable is the fact that they were both considered to be of less than average intelligence. Moreover, both acted mainly as Philip's personal aides and confidants. The two were Gómez Suárez de Figueroa, count (later duke) of Feria (*c.* 1520–71), and don Antonio de Toledo, prior of León (died *c.* 1577). Little need be said about Toledo since his importance politically appears to be negligible. He was a kindly, generous man of limited mental abilities and impeccable loyalty. One Venetian envoy called him a well-endowed idiot, but this is undoubtedly a gross exaggeration.[27] Feria did have an important political role both at court and in England. He was a gentle, warm, likeable and extremely generous man, very discreet yet blunt and honest when giving advice. He was unquestionably and unswervingly loyal to Philip. The king was to address some of his most open and personal letters to Feria during these years.[28]

The importance of these men and women was greatly enhanced by the political instability prevalent during this decade. To reduce conflicts among the royal family, secretaries and courtiers tended to be used to transmit unpopular suggestions or decisions. For example, in November 1553 Juan Vázquez showed Philip a letter he had written to Eraso and asked him if he would prefer to send it as his own. In this instance, Philip decided that the contents would be best left as the expression of Vázquez's opinions in a private letter from one secretary to another. However, since he thought that something on the situation in the Indies needed to be said, he wrote a paragraph on the issue which Vázquez incorporated word for word into what one would think was purely his letter to Eraso.[29] The Spanish secretary was in turn a vehicle for communication and influence to Charles. Similarly, the plan to appoint Juana to the regency of the Spanish realms was first mooted in the nominally private correspondence between Ruy Gómez and Eraso. The reason for this was to avoid implicating Philip (with whom the proposal clearly originated) since it was suspected that Charles would oppose it – as indeed he did. But he did not impute

[27] Albèri, *Relazioni*, ser. 1, vol. 3, p. 246.
[28] M. J. Rodríguez-Salgado and S. Adams, 'The count of Feria's dispatch to Philip II of the 14 November 1558' in *Camden Miscellany XXVIII* (Camden, 4th ser., vol. 29, pp. 302–34), esp. 306–7 and notes therein. A brief discription of the prior de León in this period, in Albèri, *Relazioni*, ser. 1, vol. 3, p. 246.   [29] AGS E.100, fols. 183–4.

the proposal to his son; both men allowed their advisers to take the blame.[30] Additionally, these courtiers had the task of filtering information and recommendations from others. Counsellors and correspondents of all states used them to ensure that the king was fully apprised of their opinions. Often they sent their advice or requests in full to a favourite or secretary known to have access and influence with the king, addressing the briefest of notes to the monarch who was informed that further information would be forthcoming from a named courtier or administrator. In May 1555, for example, Alba entrusted Ruy Gómez with such a task 'in order not to tire your majesty'.[31] Such considerations apart, there is little doubt that those relying on these tactics believed that verbal communication was more effective than a letter.

There was no ideological or 'party' line to weld together such diverse and intensely competitive courtiers. The predominant view was that the best policy took full account of prevailing circumstances. Flexibility was of the essence in a multinational empire where all major decisions had to be made bearing in mind the situation in all the states. There were no prizes for consistency; the reverse was true. Consequently, whilst individuals could cooperate to promote a particular policy and might stand together on a number of issues, they were likely to find themselves in opposition over other matters. Partly as a result of this, alliances between courtiers were impermanent unless reinforced by genuine friendship or long-term shared interests. The 1550s was a period of unusually bitter strife among the Habsburg elites since all sought patronage but found it increasingly difficult to identify its source. For instance, should a German noble wanting employment and favour make his suit to Charles (emperor in name until 1558), to Ferdinand (*de facto* emperor since 1554 and to assume the title in 1558), to Maximilian, his successor, or to Philip, who was the largest military employer? The problem was no simpler in the Netherlands with Mary of Hungary, Charles, and later the duke of Savoy and Philip. Even in Spain the regent and viceroys vied with the king for control of patronage and offered alternative sources of preferment.

This insecurity intensified the natural rivalry of leading courtiers and created some curious alliances, best illustrated by sketching the career of Francisco de Eraso. A protégé of Cobos and Juan Vázquez in the 1540s, Vázquez turned against him after 1548 when he realised how greatly Eraso had grown in power. The duke of Alba took over as his protector then and remained closely allied with him until 1555, when he promoted Rodrigo de Dueñas, whom both Vázquez and Eraso regarded as a threat to their position in the Castilian administration. The two secretaries then patched up their differences and destroyed Dueñas, but henceforth Alba and Eraso became enemies, helped by a conflict over revenues from a wealthy abbey which Eraso wanted and Alba secured for Bernardino de Mendoza. Alba and Ruy Gómez worked closely together, whatever their inner doubts, since they needed to oppose

---

[30] See pp. 86–7.   [31] Alba, *Epistolario*, vol. 1, p. 120.

the influence of Granvelle and Mary of Hungary until 1555 at least. Gradually, Ruy Gómez drew closer to Eraso, who in turn had acquired a new, bitter enemy in Granvelle. Philip used Eraso to spy upon Granvelle until he arrived in the Netherlands and the latter found out. Even without this added cause, his jealousy of Eraso's influence over Charles and Philip would have made enemies of these two men. Granvelle and Alba then linked forces, united in their common hatred of Eraso and their determination to oust both the secretary and Ruy Gómez from power.[32] Life at court was made up of countless such clashes and reconciliations. Intense manoeuvring and complex plots, personal antipathy, hatred and ambition lie behind the seemingly lifeless process of decision making. The rulers and governors had this, as well as internal problems and international issues to cope with, and the pressure sometimes proved too great for them to bear. Nevertheless, these same troublesome courtiers were their friends, companions and supporters; without them the sovereigns could not have retained power over the vast, amorphous empire.

GOVERNMENT BY PROXY

The person of the monarch was the sole unifying factor in the empire. Under the influence of his grand chancellor Gattinara, Charles may well have entertained notions of creating a genuinely supra-national state in the 1520s, bound by unitary aims and pooling of resources as necessary. Such a concept ran contrary to deeply engrained traditions. The empires of Charles V and Philip II were, with few exceptions, the result of a natural process of inheritance. Marriage rather than conquest had advanced the house of Austria. The implications of this are important. Firstly, it meant that the essential independence of each state was recognised, and the duties of each unit in relation to the rest were, as has been said, quite limited. The monarch was also bound to observe the several customs, privileges and structures of each state. He was also invested with each individual title, and even when physically absent, the fiction of his constant presence was maintained by the appointment of viceroys, governors or lieutenants, who exercised his functions under his supervision. There were certain Christian ideals to which all the states of the empire subscribed too, notably the duty to wage war against the infidel and heretic. But in practice, these were interpreted in different ways and required distinct policies. For instance, it was impossible to persuade someone in Cádiz harassed beyond endurance by North African corsairs, that the best way to counter

[32] Relations between Eraso and Juan Vázquez may be followed in AGS E.89, fol. 129; E.103, fols. 4 and 5, E.90, fols. 147–8, AGS PR.55, fol. 33, E.141, fol. 137, Keniston, *Cobos*, p. 289. Eraso's return to Spain with Philip in 1559 ended Vázquez's career. Eraso–Alba relations, AGS E.103, fols. 6–7, Alba, *Epistolario*, vol. 1, pp. 234–7, Malty, *Alba*, p. 88, and pp. 140–1 below; Eraso–Granvelle, AGS E.100, fols. 171–2; C. Weiss, *Papiers d'état du Cardinal de Granvelle* (9 vols., Paris, 1841–52), vol. 5, pp. 683–6.

Muslim pressure was by supporting and subsidising the Christian advance along the Hungarian border. The relative proximity of the Italian and Spanish realms did not prevent conflicts of this sort either. Charles V's attack against Tunis was dismissed by the Spaniards as an 'Italian' venture which in no way alleviated the problems of Spain.

There was one basic principle that was both generally accepted and frequently appealed to: that all the lands of a sovereign had a duty to help him if he was in personal danger, and to support any part of his empire that was under direct attack. However, responsibility to supply aid should last only for the duration of the crisis. Despite long absences, which always debilitated royal authority, Charles and Philip successfully overcame some of the limitations imposed upon them by tradition. Charles stretched the principle of emergency aid almost to breaking point. He presented all campaigns in terms of defensive actions destined to combat pressing dangers, thus marshalling the resources of all his lands for his wars against France, the Ottomans and the German princes. He also made it appear as if loyalty to the sovereign was to be measured solely in terms of financial contributions to the wars. Furthermore, he expected his deputies to draw upon the resources of each state, putting forward his justifications and supporting his actions despite the opposition which such measures evoked. Philip followed suit, but by the time he assumed control over his portion of the empire, these tactics had produced widespread resentment and resistance. Having acted as a regent himself, he was conscious of the bitter opposition which his father's policies had provoked, but this did not prevent him from adopting similar tactics, since these had amply proved their worth. Without them, the rulers would scarcely have been able to adopt an active foreign policy.

A few preliminary remarks about the role of the regents and governors are necessary to set the numerous conflicts that fill these pages in context. They all had a dual function to fulfil. They were appointed to represent the sovereign and execute his commands; but they were also expected to protect the subjects under their jurisdiction. Ironically, they were frequently constrained to protect them from the exactions of the monarch and not just from external enemies. Too much eagerness to defend the interests and press upon the monarch the desired policies of an area could cause these deputies to fall from favour; too little attention to the problems of the area, or failure to be seen to defend them, might provoke complaints and unrest.

The instructions issued by the sovereigns encapsulate the ambiguous nature of the role of royal substitute. There were always two sets of instructions: the first was an official appointment and public statement that the person chosen would now represent the full powers of the sovereign and must be obeyed as if he or she was the sovereign in person. The deputy was expected to exercise the functions of the sovereign, the most important being the impartial administration of justice, protection of the defenceless, needy and the church, and the provision of adequate defence and efficient government for the realm. It was essential to maintain the fiction that the monarch was never absent, since only a rightful sovereign had power over his/her subjects. Consequently, there was no suggestion in the first set of documents that the substitute was in any way limited in his/her exercise of sovereign functions. The second set of instructions was the effective appointment and would outline the restrictions under which these officials would have to act. The status, age and sex of the governor or regent affected the range of powers that would be granted, as did their previous experience and character.

All regents and governors were hemmed in by considerable legal and financial restrictions, thus enabling the absent monarch to retain ultimate control of all important functions and power. For example, in June 1551, Philip was empowered to govern the Spanish realms, but he was not allowed to adjudicate territorial disputes (these had to be allowed to follow the due process of law); he could not ennoble individuals and he had no power over Spanish revenues other than to ensure that ordinary expenditure was covered. It was usual for ordinary expenses to have revenues earmarked for them in advance, so that even here he had little room for manoeuvre. He could not contract any debts or arrange loans unless specifically ordered to do so. He had no right to make appointments, but a duty to give his opinion about suitable candidates for high office (clerical, financial and judicial). He had powers of appointment to some minor offices, but even these could not be invoked without involving the councils which normally dealt with that specific sphere of government. The same applied to crown officials in towns or fortifications. In Aragon, his powers were even further limited by the numerous privileges (*fueros*) of these realms.[33]

There were constant conflicts over finance between the monarch and his regents and governors. Almost every letter they exchanged contained either a request for money or a complaint about the level of financial contributions being demanded. These officials sent frequent and pitiful cries of exhaustion as well as complaints about the misuse of funds. As early as 1520 Spanish rebels had vociferously called for retrenchment, a return to sound finances, and an end to the use of Spanish money for foreign ventures. Throughout the 1530s, the empress Isabel (from Spain) and Mary of Hungary (from the Netherlands) issued desperate warnings about the excessive demands Charles was making upon these states and the deep resentment of his policies. These letters persuade the reader that they sincerely believed that open rebellion would inevitably break out soon. Similar stories filled the pages of the viceroys and governors in the Italian states. Riots in Milan during the late 1530s gave substance to the claims that excessive financial burdens and dissatisfaction with imperial rule led to violence. By 1543 Mary was convinced that the financial burden borne by the Netherlands would lead to their immediate collapse. She reiterated this grim message in her correspondence through 1546–50. During these years Philip too was writing from Spain lamenting the impoverish-

[33] AGS PR.26, fol. 114.

ment of the realms and warning of impending catastrophe.[34] A reading of this correspondence might convince the unwary that any or all of these areas were indeed on the verge of financial and political collapse, but this impression is patently not true, as can be shown by their continued survival. This is not to say, however, that the regents were fabricating lies. Rather they were calling for the sovereign's presence and seeking a way to cope with, and reduce, the constant stream of financial requests. Heavy fiscal burdens caused trouble, and these individuals had a duty to avert dangerous situations by all means available.

However admirable and sympathetic a deputy proved, no state liked to be without the sovereign. Decisions were made far more speedily with him present, and were likely to reflect the reality of the situation. Continuous absences tended to distance the monarch from the aspirations and fears of a state, as well as from the changing circumstances of an area. Above all, if the monarch was present, the chances of advancement and reward were much increased. The sovereign was the fount of honour and key to patronage; access to him was a vital requirement for successful suits. It was also an honour to have the monarch present. All states sought constantly to tempt the monarch to come, by fair means or foul. Regents and governors normally accepted the task to make representations to their overlord, requesting his immediate return. The most frequent device to draw the absent monarch back was to make the situation at home appear so desperate that only his immediate return and personal supervision could stem the collapse of royal power. These tactics were also an effective way of enhancing the prestige of the regents, who thus appeared to be effectively retaining control despite terrible difficulties and dangers.

These letters of gloom were also a stylised form of bargaining, as can be illustrated by the exchange between Charles and Philip in 1552. As governor of the Spanish realms and aware of the prevailing discontent, Philip tried to persuade his father that the Spanish realms could not afford to finance the next Italian war. Charles responded with a touching plea, explaining that he simply could not avoid becoming involved in the conflict (this was not true), and stating that he was in a desperate situation. Indeed he said that he had never faced so great a threat from France. A few lines further down, he inadvertently let slip that he did not have the slightest clue as to how large the French army would be. Charles was demanding one million (ducats?) from Castile. Having made his complaints and received no satisfaction, Philip shared the burden between Castile and Aragon, and sent loans

---

[34] Examples of this correspondence may be found in the collection edited by M. Fernández Alvarez, *Corpus*; letters exchanged by Charles and Isabel have also been published by J. M. Jóver Zamora, *Carlos V y los españoles* (Madrid, 1963); those of Mary, cited by M. Baelde, 'Financial policy and the evolution of the demesne in the Netherlands under Charles V and Philip II (1530–60)', in H. J. Cohn (ed.), *Government in Reformation Europe* (London, 1971), pp. 203–24; for Milan see F. Chabod, *Lo stato e la vita religiosa a Milano nell'epoca di Carlo V* (Turin, 1971), pp. 106–15.

and subsidies both to the Italian and northern fronts which came close to the sum demanded.[35]

Bargaining aside, these letters indicate genuine fear and concern on the part of the regents and governors. The early modern world was only just learning to come to terms with the problems of rapid and massive inflation, and large international debts. For centuries governments had recourse to short-term loans both to fill the gap between grants of taxation and its collection, and also to fund extraordinary events such as weddings or war. All states had experienced major deficits, but borrowing on a large scale had been restricted to periods of crisis or sudden demand – usually war. The loans contracted were normally short-term and at high interest. They were usually repaid quickly by raising extraordinary revenue and/or selling crown lands and property. The prevailing belief was that they must be discharged in full. However, since Charles V's reign had been one of almost uninterrupted war, by the 1550s every one of his states was carrying a hefty debt, much of it contracted at high interest, ostensibly for a short time. Many loans had to be renegotiated and payment was frequently delayed because the quantities being loaned exceeded what even the collective revenues of his vast empire could raise or manage. This meant that interest payments rose alarmingly, and in consequence, contemporaries tended to regard the problem of the government's deficit as one of excessive interest rates. Plans to save the empire from bankruptcy increasingly revolved around the issue of creating a serviceable long-term debt at low rate of interest. This was a new departure and not just in the Habsburg empire but in states such as France, faced with similar problems. Others, such as England, continued to believe that state debts must be rapidly repaid in full.

The extent to which Charles had mortgaged or sold his patrimony was spectacular, and generally considered unprecedented. Gradually, ordinary revenues and not just extraordinary ones, were earmarked for the repayment of loans and could not be collected by the state again until the debt had been discharged. Since current revenues proved insufficient to service the debt, future revenues were anticipated and the anxiety of the governors grew. They were acutely conscious of their diminished capacity to cope with future crises and afraid of the cumulative impact of all these measures. By the 1550s most of the states within Charles's empire were experiencing serious financial dislocation and reporting signs of unrest and deep dissatisfaction with his policies.

Having spent much of his life reading accounts of impending disaster, Charles had become immune to them. He did not consider them accurate assessments of the situation. Since Philip had acted as a regent, he could be expected to be somewhat more sympathetic, but this was not the case. He clearly knew all about crying wolf; consequently he showed a remarkable facility for ignoring complaints, especially from the area he had governed, Spain. Both father and son failed to perceive that

---

[35] AGS E.90, fols. 7–8, AGS E.89, fols. 52–6, AGS E.98, fol. 200.

during the 1550s, the wolf really did come, although each state was to perceive and experience the crisis at a different time. At the heart of all these tensions, conflicts and challenges to the monarch's authority was the inexorable pressure of continuous warfare.

HONOUR AND WAR

There were many reasons why war should have been so much in vogue during this period, but one of the most important was the emphasis men placed on acquiring honour and reputation. Honour, wrote the French soldier Blaise de Monluc, was 'to be purchased at what price soever'.[36] It was – according to Ferdinand of Austria – the most important thing a man possessed.[37] His contemporaries concurred. Philip himself wrote that a king was nothing without honour and reputation and he was often to stress that 'the dignity and reputation of princes is of no less importance to them than their states'.[38] Pursuit of honour and reputation took equal priority with defence and the extermination of God's enemies in the propositions made by Charles to the representative assemblies of his states. All princes expected their subjects to share this viewpoint and subscribe willingly to the policies which made the acquisition or restoration of honour and reputation a priority. As Charles stated to the leading representatives of the Holy Roman Empire, 'our honour and dignity is your honour and dignity'.[39] The monarch's standing did indeed serve as a reflection of the status of his realms in the international sphere.

Most contemporaries believed that the easiest way to gain honour and reputation was through war. Few would have disagreed with the statement made by Robert Thorne to Henry VIII, to the effect that all princes had a natural urge to extend their lands irrespective of the cost, and that any monarch who opted not to fight or expand was to be considered a weakling, lacking 'the noble courage and spirit of all others'.[40] The glorification of war was based on a shrewd assessment of the profits it could bring, ranging from lands to booty and reputation. But it was also a reflection of the dominant culture which associated virtue and nobility with arms.

These views co-existed with Christian ideals that counselled the need for peace among Christians and war against infidels and heretics. The constant wars among France, Spain, England and the Holy Roman Empire from the closing decades of the fifteenth century had provoked a powerful reaction among educated elites against war and led to the publication of numerous eloquent discourses vaunting the

---

[36] Monluc, B. de, *The Habsburg–Valois wars and the French wars of religion*, I. Roy (ed.) (London, 1971), p. 37.   [37] Fichtner, *Ferdinand I*, p. 167.   [38] CSP V. vol. 6 (ii), p. 1143.
[39] Cit. J. Vicens Vives, 'Imperio y administración en tiempo de Carlos V', in *Charles Quint et son temps* (Paris, 1959), p. 12. Charles's propositions to the cortes of Castile have been published by F. Laiglesia (ed.), *Estudios históricos* (3 vols., Madrid, 1918), vol. 1, e.g. p. 363 (1524), p. 400 (1537).
[40] His address was printed by R. Hakluyt, *Voyages and documents*, ed. J. Hampden (London, 1965), p. 15.

value of peace. The most important leaders of the movement were Erasmus and Juan Luis Vives. With the advent and expansion of Protestantism, the advocates of peace found new supporters. But it would not be accurate to regard this as nascent pacifism. The word peace was always qualified. The paeans of praise were intended to ensure that princes restricted their aggression rather than curtailed it altogether. For all these writers it was imperative to continue and indeed intensify the conflict against the enemies of the faith. Men as diverse as Blaise de Monluc and Juan Martínez Silíceo, a tutor of Philip and later archbishop of Toledo, could only wonder at the failure of Charles V and Francis I to take note of the devastation they caused in Christendom, and the encouragement they gave to Protestants, who multiplied while 'good Christians' were slaughtered. Both concluded that such lack of perception must be due to supernatural causes – God's inscrutable design was Monluc's choice; witches and demons were blamed by Silíceo. The advocates of peace were eager to persuade princes that honour was best sought in wars that advanced the 'true faith' as they defined it. Many attempted to associate war solely with traditional Christian notions and in a sense, de-secularise it by denigrating chivalric traditions and goals.

As internal troubles multiplied and contemporaries perceived that many problems were caused by increased expenditure on war against fellow Christians, the call for peace found a ready echo among the most diverse groups. But it was hard to make much headway against centuries of tradition and deeply engrained perceptions. As Silíceo pertinently remarked, each state could boast of many individuals and institutions specifically designed to persuade or force antagonists to abandon their conflicts, yet there was no arbiter to ensure that princes would desist from further disputes.[41] In the sixteenth century, there were two supra-national institutions; both had assumed the role of peace-makers in the past. But by this time, neither the pope nor the emperor had sufficient moral or political authority to be acceptable arbiters in international disputes. Indeed, both the papacy and the emperor were frequent perpetrators of aggression against their neighbours.

Silíceo was also correct in his conclusion that princes had a different concept of peace from that of the common man. Although Erasmus, Vives and their supporters might declare that peace must be sought for its own sake; at a political level, the term peace was always strictly defined and never used without adequate qualification. There was 'good peace' – a term usually associated with such concepts as firm, secure, or long-lasting peace. And there was 'bad peace' – a term denoting the suspension of hostilities with unfavourable conditions, invariably under duress, and regarded as a short-term expedient. A good peace, as the following account will amply demonstrate, meant in practice a treaty that enabled one ruler to secure the territorial or other advantages that had been at stake in the conflict. In other words,

---

[41] Silíceo's interesting discourse dated 3 February, 1544, has been printed in March, *Niñez*, vol. 1, pp. 75–8, esp. pp. 77–8. B. de Monluc, *The Habsburg–Valois wars*, p. 37.

it was the successful culmination of a period of aggression and it implied that only one of the combatants could emerge with any degree of satisfaction. There was always a winner and a loser.

All these concepts of war, peace and honour had their roots in Christian traditions, much too ancient and complex to be dealt with at any length here.[42] However, it is important to discuss briefly the even more complex notion of 'just war' before making sense of the debates that will concern us in later chapters. The most frequent definitions of a just war which will be encountered are: first, a conflict which the pope declared to be just or holy; second, a war in defence of the patrimony; third, a war intended to secure a firm peace. Each of these categories was vague and open to debate and further qualification. For example, to what extent did the pursuit of dynastic rights which had lain dormant for some time constitute defence of the patrimony? Dynastic rights were eternal, and might be reawakened even after a formal renunciation had been incorporated into a peace treaty. But should the likes of Charles and Francis (or their successors for that matter) still be fighting to claim lands which their predecessors had lost two or three centuries previously? The claims and counter claims to Naples, Navarre, Milan and the old Burgundian lands stretched back for generations, yet they were pursued with an avidness and tenacity that belied the passage of time.[43] Dynastic rights were almost limitless in the hands of rulers like Francis and Charles who were the culmination of centuries of powerful dynastic unions. In turn, the heavy reliance on dynasticism ensured that the physical conflict between them should concentrate on certain areas – Milan and Naples, for example, or the Burgundian lands in the north. However, other areas were invaded when military strategy required it. The French monarchs had a stronger dynastic claim to Milan but Charles and Philip needed it to link their empire and eventually retained it. When Henry II had a chance to seize the duchy in

[42] Fernández-Santamaría, *Spanish political thought*, esp. chapter 5, pp. 120–60. This includes a useful bibliography for those wishing to pursue these concepts. See also M. H. Keen, *The law of war in the late middle ages*, (London, 1965); M. Fernández Alvarez, *Política mundial de Carlos V y Felipe II* (Madrid, 1966); M. Bataillon, 'Charles-quint bon pasteur, selon Fray Cipriano de Huelga', *Bulletin Hispanique* 50 (1948), pp. 398–406; P. Mesnard, 'L'expérience politique de Charles Quint et les enseignements d'Erasme' in *Fêtes et cérémonies aux temps de Charles Quint*, ed. J. Jacquot, Vol. 2: *Les fêtes de la Renaissance* (Paris, 1960), pp. 45–56.

[43] For the Burgundian inheritance see L. Febvre, *Philippe II et la Franche-Comté* (Paris, 1912), pp. 43–51; R. Vaughan, *Valois Burgundy* (London, 1975); Charles's passionate desire to recover these lands can best be illustrated by his letter to Ferdinand in 1521, cited by Mesnard, 'L'expérience politique', p. 54, and in his 1548 instruction to Philip, Laiglesia, *Estudios*, vol. 1, p. 109; *DP*, p. 340. For Naples, see A. Ryder, *The kingdom of Naples under Alfonso the Magnanimous* (Oxford, 1976). Chapter 1 takes up the story to the reign of Alfonso, it can then be followed in Menéndez Pidal (ed.), *Historia de España* (Madrid, 1966–9), vol. XVII(ii), pp. 189–98, 582ss., and in greater detail if desired, through the various works of Doussinague, cited in the bibliography. Ferdinand was formally invested with the realm by the Pope in 1504, and again 1511, see J. M. Doussinague, *La política internacional de Fernando el Católico* (Madrid, s.d.), esp. pp. 372–81. For Navarre, *DP*, pp. 101–11. Milan, Menédez Pidal, *Historia de España*, vol. XVII(ii), pp. 323ss.; again 530ss. J. M. Doussinague, *El testamento político*, esp. pp. 44–6, 56 and n. 1, p. 20.

1557 he preferred instead to march straight to Naples, despite the fact that his claim was very weak whilst that of the Habsburgs was indisputably stronger. Henry was following both a strong desire to acquire honour from a spectacular conquest and the tradition set by his immediate ancestors. French troops had taken control of Naples twice in recent times – 1494 and 1500 – and he wished to emulate their exploits. His father had tried to do the same.

The question of pre-emptive strikes was as troublesome then as now. The line between aggression and defence was so finely drawn in many instances that it was thought best to avoid pre-emptive war altogether. The risk of being accused of unjustified aggression was too great. Philip faced an even graver problem, how to justify a war, and a pre-emptive one at that, against the papacy. These issues mattered a great deal because all combatants needed to justify the actions in terms acceptable to the ideological sensitivities of the period. In order to secure the approval of contemporaries and avoid accusations of unjust and unprovoked aggression, it was important – indeed essential – to avoid beginning a conflict. Often, despite the commencement of hostilities and constant clashes, war was not formally declared precisely because the combatants were eager to wait until an incident occurred which could be construed as aggression by the other side. One of the reasons Christian princes vied with each other to obtain the pope's support was because his involvement automatically gave powerful moral validation, irrespective of the aims or history of the conflict. It was the need to prove the justice of a cause that made dynastic rights so essential – they were, after all, eminently flexible.

But neither side was immune to the pressures of peace. At the turn of the century, the Spaniards and the French had decided to end their costly dispute over Naples and concentrate on the struggle against Islam. They agreed to a partition of the realm. But the French, who were able to send more troops, were naturally tempted to use their strength to seize the whole realm in 1500. The Spaniards complained loudly of their perfidy and counter-attacked in force. They began by calling for a return to parity, yet as soon as they were in a position to do so, they annexed the whole realm. The partition agreement could not have worked in any case, because the negotiators had overlooked one essential factor: the most important source of revenue in Naples came from the tolls on migrant flocks of sheep. The patterns of transhumance cut across the political boundaries of the partition. The experience convinced both sides that there was no such thing as a peaceful solution to their conflict. Moreover, the incident was used frequently afterwards as unshakeable proof that the principle of partition itself was invalid and based on unsound reasoning.[44]

The propaganda of the period made frequent use of arguments such as the fear of encirclement. The French were constantly harping on the need to weaken or

---

[44] See note 43, p. 27 and p. 332.

destroy Charles and Philip whose territories and ambitions threatened to encircle France. Even those wars they unleashed were therefore defined as defensive. For their part, the Habsburgs claimed that French aggression had repeatedly prevented them from fulfilling their Christian duty, which was to fight the enemies of the faith. War against France was justified as a necessary prelude, a clearing of the way which would leave them free to do what they wanted, and what they were enjoined to do by the Church. There was an element of truth in all this, but much of it was bluff. Whenever Charles was persuaded to consider seriously the prospect of eliminating the conflict with France through compromise and partition, he rejected the notion. Involvement in the ideologically worthier wars against Muslims in the Maghreb, for example, or against Protestants in the Holy Roman Empire, would not bring quite the same prestige as the battles against France.

Like his father, Philip was to regard war against France as infinitely more prestigious than that against Islam. Despite his upbringing in Spain, Philip was utterly unsympathetic to the traditions of Spanish expansion southwards. If anything he pursued honour and prestige more avidly than Charles, especially during his first years in power. In his mind and policy, notions of supremacy and defence became inseparably fused. Threatened by the French and their allies, Philip argued that unless he fought and vanquished them, his empire would be destroyed. For him, the wars against France and the papacy were defensive actions, which had the additional advantage of bringing considerable prestige. Early-modern monarchs were all good at reconciling ideological dictates and ambition; Philip was no exception.

Since the search for prestige was all important it is not surprising that the sixteenth century should have construed certain conflicts as having greater honorific value than others. It was not the cost or size of a campaign which determined the rating given by contemporaries to each war, although these factors were taken into account. Whenever a reigning monarch took the field, the campaign was immediately invested with high prestige value, even if the scale and target were not of primary importance. Usually the most important campaign of any monarch's career was his first. In recent years, there has been a tendency to underestimate just how vital it was for early modern rulers to prove themselves in the field of battle; but, as can be seen here, the first campaign was actually a matter of the utmost concern to them. It was planned with great care and was viewed as the major indicator of future success or failure. It set the tone for the reign and determined the status accorded to a ruler in the international league at the start of his career. Subjects and monarchs alike would make an extraordinary effort to ensure the successful outcome of a 'first campaign'.

As was suggested earlier, the degree of honour and reputation the individual prince possessed was more than a personal virtue: it was the very barometer of greatness, and it could fluctuate wildly. Reputation could be won and lost with equal speed on the battlefield. Yet it must be retained or recovered at any cost.

Cardinal Santa Cruz had warned Charles: 'As soon as a prince loses but one grade of reputation, friends will become mistrustful, enemies will be encouraged, and in the natural course of events, he will be reduced to the lowest grade'. The bishop of Lugo, who preserved a copy of this advice, thought it important enough to send it on to Philip in 1556.[45] But there was more to honour than military success or tangible advantages such as the size of territorial possessions or number of subjects and wealth. The comparisons made at the time of the imperial election in 1519 usefully illustrate what contemporaries valued most when assessing the relative importance of each power. Charles was acknowledged the greater in terms of territorial possessions than his French rival, but this was not thought very important. France could make up in quality what it lacked in quantity. Whilst not free of the problems of distance and diversity (linguistic, legal and political), it was more compact, easier to rule and the crown enjoyed powers of taxation that Charles could not match in any of his lands. The greatest weight was given to the personal qualities of the individual monarchs. Francis was unquestionably superior to his enemy: he was still young yet already experienced in government. He had proved his military prowess in Italy, and he could boast numerous allies. Charles was inexperienced and untried. He had not yet shown that he had the capacity to marshal the resources of his various realms in order to fund a war, nor had he proved himself in the field of battle. These factors were not unconnected to the fact that he had few friends he could call upon. Acquiring another ally or securing a valuable match were two other means of increasing the honour ratings substantially. Charles feverishly set about searching for allies, with only partial success. The pope's conclusion in 1519 was challenged by few: Francis was the greater of the two. The fact may well have worked against him in the end, since the imperial electors had no wish to invest so powerful a man and neighbour with even greater power. The understandable desire to maintain their independence led other powers to change constantly from one side to the other, preventing either of them from gaining a clear ascendancy.

Once Charles had acquired the coveted imperial title, he demanded recognition as the greatest power in Christendom, only to find the French obdurate in resisting such a claim. France and her supporters maintained that the wealth and fertile lands of the kingdom, coupled with the ancient lineage of her kings and the title of being the oldest protector of the Church, gave her the right to claim primacy in Christendom. After 1519 anti-imperial writings proliferated in France. The title of Holy Roman Emperor was dismissed as an empty symbol; a minor title because it was elective and therefore at the mercy of a few petty princelings. By fighting Charles and Philip for several decades, both Francis I and Henry II proved their willingness to impose by force of arms the high-blown claims for supremacy and

---

[45] AGS E.114, fol. 130, copy sent by Lugo, 23 September, 1556.

greatness so ably put by their poets and diplomats. In the words of du Bellay, written in the aftermath of the French defeats at St Quentin, they wished to prove that whilst other kings might have a semblance of greatness ('grands d'apparence') and gain a temporary advantage over France, they could not match her wealth and power: 'rien n'est après Dieu si grand qu'un roy de France'.[46]

What were these two states fighting for – was it parity, supremacy, or hegemony? In their terms, were they merely seeking to emulate each other and be called equals; or to become the most powerful prince in Christendom; or did they seek *monarchia*? Probably the easiest answer is to say that each power sought supremacy and accused the other of seeking hegemony. The term *monarchia* had been used in the past to denote an ideal situation in which one power dominated Christendom and used its overwhelming position to enforce peace. It is in this sense that some poets still used the term when praising Charles, for example. But by the sixteenth century the word had acquired unacceptable connotations: it was associated with the unjust domination of one state over others. Hegemony implied the usurpation of sovereign authority. It is in this guise that princes used it against one other, particularly in the propaganda issued during the long struggle between Spain and France. If successful, it could act as a potent rallying call, drawing other princes to link arms against whoever dared to aim for so powerful a position within Christendom.

In the early modern world neither supremacy nor hegemony could be won in Christendom without control of Italy. The reasons for this are complex. On the one hand, there were powerful traditions which associated Italy with supremacy, in particular the memories of the Roman empire. The cultural sophistication of the area, the economic strength of Northern Italy and its fertile lands, were other aspects which drew the 'barbarians' (as the Italians called outsiders such as the French and Spaniards) to Italy. The fact that the papacy was once more resident in Rome reinforced its supra-national identity and focused attention on the peninsula. Given the importance of securing the pope's alliance or forestalling his attachment to the enemy camp, it was natural that major states should meddle in Italian affairs as a way of putting pressure on the papacy. As a result of this combination of practical advantages and associated ideas it was widely assumed that whoever controlled Italy would become the greatest power in Christendom. Gattinara declared that Italy was the sole base from which the world could be dominated. Most of his contemporaries endorsed his vision that it was the most

---

[46] Cit. François, 'L'idée de l'empire', in *Charles Quint et son temps*, (CNRS, Paris, 1959), p. 34. The most recent account of the imperial election may be found in R. J. Knecht, *Francis I* (Cambridge, 1982), pp. 25–32; Brandi, *Charles V*, pp. 21–114; M. Mignet, 'Une élection à l'Empire en 1519. Première rivalité de François 1er et de Charles-Quint', *Revue de Deux Mondes*, 2nd ser., XXIV (1854), pp. 209–64, and 'Rivalité de Charles-Quint et de François 1er', *Revue de Deux Mondes*, 2nd ser., XXVIII, (1858), II, pp. 257–305.

important part of the world – this was far from being merely the proud boast of the Italians.[47]

When Francis heard that his rival had obtained the imperial title, he expressed his conviction that Charles would immediately seek to expel the French from Italy.[48] It was here, they all believed, that the long struggle between their dynasties would be decided. In order to strengthen their position in the peninsula both sides were prepared to buy the alliances of petty Italian princelings, even with the hand of royal princes and princesses. Successive dukes of Ferrara, Savoy and Parma found wives from the royal houses of France, Spain, Portugal and the Holy Roman Empire. Popes secured immortality for their families by arranging similar matches. The unstable situation in Italy, which was divided into numerous weak prin-cipalities, also encouraged the expansionist, aggressive monarchies of France, the Empire and Spain.[49]

Despite the wide measure of agreement between the emperor and his son over the priorities of foreign policy during much of this period, it is important to stress that Philip deliberately rejected certain elements that had characterised his father's foreign relations. The reason is clear, but it has not been generally appreciated. Charles enjoyed considerable renown in his own time but many of his con-temporaries did not endorse the image of an upright and moral leader which he consistently portrayed in his own propaganda. Charles was an indefatigable propagandist. Even his private letters to his wife read like political speeches; he missed no opportunity to justify his actions. Ultimately, he was rather more successful at persuading posterity than his contemporaries, who critically noted the excesses and greed that marked his successful expansion. Charles was regarded as a restless, acquisitive, aggressive prince who often ignored dynastic rights and ignored morality if it suited him.[50] The point is of some importance, since it

---

[47] Gattinara called it 'le vrai siège et sceptre pour dominer tout le monde', cit. H. Vanderlinden, 'La politique méditerranéenne de Charles V', *Académie Royale de Belgique. Bulletin de la Classe des Lettres et des Sciences Morales et Politiques*, XIV (1928), pp. 11–23, p. 13. G. Jiménez de Quesada, *El Antijovio*, ed. R. Torres Quintero (Bogotá, 1952) called it the 'principalissima provincia del Christianismo', p. 23. [48] Mignet, 'Une election', p. 249.

[49] The best account of the situation in Italy at the turn of the century is still G. Mattingly, *Renaissance diplomacy* (London, 1963 edn.). According to I. Wallerstein, *The modern world-system* (2 vols., London, 1974 & 1980), vol. I, pp. 170–1, the struggle over Italy was due to the economic primacy of the Northern Italian city-states and was an attempt by Charles and Francis to control the 'European world economy'. Undoubtedly, the wealth of the area influenced their choice, but this does not explain why the wars began before and continued after the reigns of these monarchs. More importantly, it misses the fact that the real prize, as far as they were concerned, was Naples rather than Lombardy. Much has been written about the innately voracious and aggressive nature of the so-called 'new monarchies' of Spain, France and England, a good introduction to these views can be found in A. J. Slavin (ed.) *The 'new monarchies' and representative assemblies* (London, 1964). Insufficient attention has been paid to the fluid and intensively competitive international situation in many of these accounts.

[50] The Italian historian Giovio wrote a trenchant but not inaccurate account of Charles at the time which was rejected in the most violent terms by one of Charles's warmest supporters, see the interesting book by G. Jiménez de Quesada, *El Antijovio*.

predisposed a good many people to regard Philip as a chip of the old block. Henry II warned the English: 'He will not forget to follow his father's teachings, that is, to seize all the states he enters on the pretence of helping them'. Although Henry did not furnish any proof, he would doubtless have expected the French ambassador to do so by citing such cases as Milan, Utrecht, Siena and Piacenza, where the emperor had sent troops ostensibly in aid of existing rulers or claimants and never left.[51] Philip and his advisers were certainly aware of the more unsavoury aspects of the emperor's reputation and eager to distance themselves from it. They quite consciously set out to devise a foreign policy – especially after 1554 – that would enable Philip to promote an image of morality and strength. Their priorities were: first, to show that he was capable of defending his realms against all enemies, and that he would do so even if it meant war and pre-emptive strikes against all the major powers; second, that he would not annex or invade territories to which he had no dynastic claims; third, that even if he had strong dynastic claims and good opportunities to support them, he would set them aside rather than undermine or challenge similar claims of loyal allies. Above all Philip cultivated an image of peace. He sought to persuade his contemporaries that he was a satiated power and wanted only to concentrate on consolidating his authority at home and countering the threat from Islam.[52]

THE DISPUTED INHERITANCE

The power as well as the weakness of Charles V was encapsulated in the grandiloquent prefaces of many state documents; in a typical Spanish formula he was

Charles, by the grace of God emperor *semper augusto*, king of Germany; and doña Juana, his mother, and the same Charles, by that same grace, kings of Castile, León, Aragon, the two Sicilies, Jerusalem, Navarre, Granada, Toledo, Valencia, Galicia, the Mallorcas, Seville, Sardinia, Córdoba, Corsica, Murcia, Jaén, the Algarve, Algeciras, Gibraltar, the Canary islands, the Indies, islands and terra firma of the Ocean Sea; counts of Barcelona; lords of Biscay and Molina; dukes of Athens and Neopatria; counts of Roussillon and Cerdagne; marquises of Oristano and Gozo; archdukes of Austria; dukes of Burgundy and Brabant; counts of Flanders, Tyrol, etc.'[53]

Despite the glittering array of titles, Charles could only exercise power in his own right over those parts of his inheritance that he claimed through his paternal grandparents, that is over the Burgundian and Habsburg lands not already

---

[51] R. Aubert de Vertot d'Aubeuf, *Les Ambassades de Messieurs de Noailles en Angleterre* (Leyden, 1763), vol. II, p. 183, Henry II to Noailles, 28 September, 1553; pp. 183–90, translation of a pamphlet which publicised these views.

[52] This will become evident in the following chapters, but a useful guide to the various priorities may be found in Alba, *Epistolario*, vol. I, p. 206.

[53] This is part of AGS PR.26, fol. 114. There are variants.

transferred to Ferdinand. The Trastámara inheritance belonged to his mother alone: she was the *reina propietaria*, literally, the proprietory monarch of these lands. Doña Juana had been declared officially insane and incapable of exercising power over these lands firstly by her husband, Philip of Burgundy, later by her father, Ferdinand of Aragon – who had at first rejected the accusation – and subsequently by her own son. When Ferdinand died, Charles simply declared himself to be the ruler of her vast lands. But this unilateral declaration was dubious in law. He was, in effect, a mere guardian of his mother's possessions whilst she was incapacitated. At most, he might be considered a regent. Consequently those whom he appointed as deputies to govern the Spanish, Italian or American possessions could not be officially termed regents, although they were invariably referred to as such and the term will be used throughout this book. All appointments, offices, titles, summonses for the representative assemblies and other such matters had to be made in the joint names of Juana and Charles; he had no direct power or proprietorship until his mother's death in February 1555, by which time he had already relinquished his rights to part of the inheritance.

The matter was of considerable importance since it raised the issue of the succession. If Charles were to die before his mother, who had the right to assume regency powers over her states? Common law and practice within the Spanish realms clearly favoured the rights of the eldest surviving son of the incapacitated person. In other words, as Charles's brother, Ferdinand had a much stronger – some might even say incontestable – claim to all the Spanish, Italian and American lands than Philip. Or, to be more precise, a right to control them until such a time as doña Juana died, when the inheritance would unquestionably belong to Philip. The issue became even more complex, but remained essentially the same, when Charles decided to abdicate.

No one had intended these four separate states to be joined or controlled by one person. High mortality had disposed of all intervening claimants, leaving Charles as the eldest male heir of a vast conglomeration of lands. Yet it would be wrong to regard him as the sole heir. When it became evident that Charles would inherit the rights of the four families, his grandparents decided that their patrimonies would have to be partitioned between Charles and Ferdinand. There were abundant precedents for this; the various dynasties had divided their lands in the past. Maximilian I wanted the younger boy to be given the Austrian lands and be elected Holy Roman Emperor, leaving Charles with the Hispanic and Italian possessions as well as the New World. Both pope Leo X and Margaret of Austria (Maximilian's daughter and governor of the Netherlands during Charles's minority), supported this plan. But Ferdinand of Aragon wanted his grandson and namesake to inherit the Spanish realms, or else to be given an Italian principality comprising both Naples and Milan – although the latter had not yet been conquered by the Spanish. Unable to come to an agreement, both men drew up their different plans for the future. Ferdinand of Aragon could only dispose freely of his Aragonese possessions of course, both in Iberia and Italy, so he drew up a partition of these. On his deathbed he was persuaded to retract these arrangements and recommendations. It seems that both he and his advisers were afraid that such a partition would lead to war between the two brothers. Similar fears made Maximilian I abandon his own plans just before he died. Both men decided that it would be best if the partition was made by agreement between the two brothers themselves.

Charles inherited all the lands of his grandparents on the understanding that he must negotiate a mutually satisfactory partition with his brother. No time scale was specified and the only guidelines were the two irreconcilable proposals that had been drawn up by Maximilian I and Ferdinand of Aragon. Fearing that his brother might make a bid for control of the Spanish realms, Charles's advisers removed young Ferdinand from Spain and sent him to the Habsburg lands in central Europe. Not unnaturally, it was assumed that they had accepted Maximilian's partition plan. As soon as the emperor died, however, Charles scotched these expectations by preventing Ferdinand from being put forward as a candidate to the vacant imperial throne, and himself seizing the most exalted title in Christendom. From later evidence, it would appear that Charles promised his brother handsome compensation for what was unquestionably a major sacrifice, but we have no way of knowing exactly what was promised. When a partition was finally decreed in 1520–1, it was both without the full consultation promised to Ferdinand and certainly well below the most reasonable expectations. Ferdinand was allocated only seven Austrian duchies. This was not in keeping either with the intent or the spirit of the partition which any of the grandparents had visualised, and Ferdinand refused to consider it as a final settlement, a point which Charles accepted grudgingly. The issue of partition affected the relations of the two brothers throughout their lives; its impact was to be felt for much longer.

For some years Ferdinand sought to gain the duchy of Milan, which bordered on his Austrian lands and would enable him to create a compact state along vital trade and military routes linking Italy and the Holy Roman Empire. It was this very obvious strategic advantage that made Charles reject the plan. Yet, in 1523–5 when he required help, Charles promised Ferdinand Milan as well as Pfirt and Hainaut in exchange for support against France and as compensation for governing the Holy Roman Empire during Charles's absence. As soon as the spectacular victory of Pavia made it possible for Charles to dispense with his brother's support, he retracted his promises.[54] One year later, Charles was presented with what he considered to be a golden opportunity to satisfy his brother at no cost to himself. The death of Lewis II of Hungary at the battle of Mohacs in 1526 left the thrones of Hungary and Bohemia vacant. Charles, aided by his sister Mary, secured the election of Ferdinand to both. It would seem that he regarded this as ample compensation for the lands he should have transferred to his brother. Ferdinand

---

[54] Fichtner, *Ferdinand I*, pp. 15–18, 36–9.

might have been more inclined to agree had Charles then given him support against both the rebels and Ottoman troops who challenged his title to Hungary. The conflict with the mighty and aggressive Muslim state made these two realms as much a liability as an asset. Ferdinand was one of many who felt betrayed time and again as Charles refused to lend his forces for the battle against Ottoman encroachment.[55]

The question of partition was very much alive when Charles decided to obtain the election of Ferdinand to the title of King of the Romans in 1531. His behaviour prior to this and the debates which broke out later strongly suggest that he was motivated primarily by the need to buttress Ferdinand's position in the Holy Roman Empire, so that he could govern these lands more effectively during the emperor's frequent absences. Since it was customary for those elected to this title to succeed to the imperial throne, however, Ferdinand believed that a partition of the inheritance along the lines suggested by Maximilian I had been finally accepted by the emperor and would materialise, albeit a generation later than it should have done.

Reluctant as he was to give Ferdinand a fair share of the inheritance, Charles appreciated the need to divide this amorphous empire. By 1539 it had been decided by the emperor and his wife Isabel that the Netherlands must be separated from the rest of the patrimony. They were determined to give it to their eldest daughter María, unless another son was born in the future.[56] The rebellion of Gent appeared to confirm the wisdom of this decision. Most observers drew the conclusion that it was impossible to reconcile the interests of such different and distant lands as the Netherlands and Spain, and impossible to rule over both. The revolt highlighted the difficulties of dealing with trouble in one end of the vast empire whilst resident in another part. It also seems to have persuaded a number of leading counsellors that it would be impossible to retain the Netherlands unless the monarch was permanently in residence there. As Ferrante Gonzaga put it in 1544, if the provinces rebelled against Charles, who had been born and bred there, at a time when a member of the royal family was ruling the area firmly and efficiently in his absence, what hope was there for Philip? Born and bred in Spain, utterly unknown to the Flemings, laden with so many commitments that he would be unlikely to reside in the Netherlands for long, Philip was also handicapped by the small number of siblings and close relatives he might dispose of and appoint to govern in his absence. It was considerations such as these that decided a number of Charles's counsellors,

[55] Fichtner, *Ferdinand I*, follows the battle for Hungary, esp. in pp. 46–8, 58–65, 81–4, 95–7, 101, 118–39. A very brief summary in G. Zeller, *Histoire des relations internationales II: Les temps modernes, I. De Christophe Colomb à Cromwell* (Paris, 1953), pp. 159–62. H. Hantsch, 'Le problème de la lutte contre l'invasion turque dans l'idée politique générale de Charles Quint', in *Charles Quint et son temps* (Paris, 1959), pp. 51–60.
[56] Laiglesia, *Estudios*, vol. 1, pp. 31–9, Charles's instructions to Philip, 5 November, 1539.

and ultimately the emperor himself, to separate the Netherlands and the Spanish states.[57]

The decision to endow María with the Netherlands was not unconnected with the struggle between Charles and Ferdinand, since she was betrothed to Maximilian. It was envisaged that the two would marry and take possession of an autonomous state in the Low Countries. Once again, Charles had resorted to delaying tactics, refusing to give his brother immediate concessions, but offering future compensation for his family. Nevertheless, Charles was not a man to allow such pledges to stand in the way of political advantages. María was offered in marriage to other princes at various times, and both Milan and the Netherlands were assigned in these negotiations as potential dowries. When she was finally allowed to marry Maximilian in 1548, however, no territorial grant was made. She was assigned a cash dowry which Charles failed to pay in full. Maximilian and Ferdinand must have been bitterly disappointed.

Their anger was certainly aroused when Charles announced his decision to sever the legal and official links between the Netherlands and the Holy Roman Empire. Using his imperial powers, he established an independent state in 1548 with all his inherited and newly conquered territories in the area, including the imperial fiefs of Utrecht and Gelderland. Instead of handing the new state over to his nephew and daughter, Charles summoned Philip from Spain and ordered that he should be sworn in as his successor. Maximilian felt that he had been cheated out of lands he had grown accustomed to consider as his own future possessions. Moreover, as a potential successor to the imperial crown, he also resented the diminution of imperial power and territory. Charles thought he could keep Maximilian quiet and occupied by appointing him jointly with María, as regents of the Spanish realms during Philip's absence. The appointment was hardly sufficient compensation for the status and honour which the two would have gained if they ruled over an independent northern state.

Charles was fortunate to have such a patient and moderate brother. It was entirely due to this that an open rift between them was averted for so long. As time passed the world forgot about the intended partition, but not Ferdinand or his family. In 1548, intimations of mortality, depression or even dreams of a life without responsibilities led Charles to consider once again the matter of partition. Since doña Juana still enjoyed robust health, he decided that it was essential to clear any obstacle to Philip's succession in the Trastámara empire. As Philip was now by his father's side and under close scrutiny by contemporary observers, he was to become associated with, and even blamed for, the subsequent family rift. It must be

[57] The debates over the feasibility of retaining the Netherlands flared up in 1544 when Charles asked his counsellors whether it was better to give up Milan or the Netherlands in order to secure an enduring peace with France. See F. Chabod, '¿Milán o los Paises Bajos? Las discusiones en España sobre la "alternativa" de 1544', in *Carlos V 1500–1558,* Homenaje de la Universidad de Granada (Granada, 1958), p. 359.

stressed, however, that there is no evidence that he prompted the emperor's action, nor is it at all clear that he took part in the planning of the meeting and strategy. Charles wished to ensure that his son would automatically succeed him to the whole Trastámara inheritance and asked Ferdinand for a formal renunciation of his rights to assume the regency. Ferdinand was willing to comply, but he demanded compensation. Once again he asked to be given Milan. Charles was no more reconciled to this now than in the past and Philip would have been very unhappy if such a grant had been made. Charles had invested him with the title to Milan in 1541, although he had retained full power over the duchy and may not have intended the grant to be binding. In 1554 Charles gave his son Milan again, behaving as if no previous concession had been made.[58] But this did not prevent Philip from considering it his own.

Inevitably, the discussion moved to other areas of the multiple inheritance. Who raised the question of the imperial succession remains a mystery, but it soon became the dominant issue. At the time rumours circulated that Maximilian had publicly declared his intention to reverse Charles's ruling on the Netherlands and reimpose imperial control over the provinces as soon as he became emperor. This would undoubtedly have threatened Philip's position there. Few missed the wider implications of such talk. Milan, Siena, and Piacenza (to mention but the most important) were also imperial fiefs. Future emperors might follow Charles's example and depose or invest rulers there at will. Suddenly, Philip's possession of both the Netherlands and the central and northern Italian states looked tenuous. His position would be in jeopardy unless he wielded imperial power.

Charles summoned Ferdinand for formal talks in 1550 and deliberately excluded Maximilian, who was in Spain at the time. Almost from the start the issue of the imperial succession dominated the negotiations. Charles demanded that Ferdinand should give up his claim to the imperial succession and help Philip to obtain the coveted title instead. Ferdinand was justifiably angry and deeply upset by this. Maximilian's reaction was far more violent, and with good reason. Ferdinand had opted to follow family tradition and, as early as 1543, he had already announced his decision to partition his lands between his three sons. Maxmilian knew that he would inherit a much smaller state than his father's; without the imperial title which he was all but certain of receiving if Ferdinand succeeded Charles, he would be reduced to the status of a petty princeling. Besides, he was still smarting over his wife's dowry. Frightened that his father would be bullied and exploited as he had been in the past, Maximilian hastily left Spain without licence and insisted that his opinion should be considered in the partition debates. It was just as well; Ferdinand found it hard to overcome his usual subservience to Charles and would do almost anything to avert rows, emotion and harassment. Besides, he was being forced to face not just his bullying brother, but his infinitely more formidable sister, Mary of

[58] See pp. 102–4.

Hungary. He was in desperate need of support from someone. The rows between the two brothers became so bitter that they soon refused to speak to each other. Mary and Granvelle acted as go-betweens, although neither was impartial in the matter. On the contrary, they were there to support and implement Charles's will.

Under the circumstances, it is not surprising that the debates should have ended with Ferdinand's capitulation in March 1551. True, the ensuing settlement was regarded as a compromise by Charles, but if implemented, it would have fatally undermined the position of Ferdinand's successors. Ferdinand claimed afterwards that he had not revealed the details of the family treaty to anyone, not even his son, and there is no reason to doubt him. However, enough details were leaked to ensure that Maximilian and other alert observers grasped the main lines of the compromise.

The major clauses of the treaty are well-known and need little comment. It was agreed that Ferdinand was to succeed to the imperial title, but once in power, he would seek to persuade the seven electors to choose Philip (and not Maximilian as might have been expected) as King of the Romans, thus effectively securing the appointment of the former as the next emperor. Philip in turn would secure the succession for Maximilian or his son, so that the title would alternate between the two branches of the family. Ferdinand and his heirs would always take control of the empire during the absence of Philip or his successors. Similarly – and this clause was to be of some importance later – Philip and his heirs would exercise imperial rights over the Italian fiefs unless the emperor himself was present in the area. The agreement was to be sealed by the match between Philip and one of Ferdinand's daughters, and it was explicitly stated that failure by either party to meet any one of the conditions stipulated would invalidate the whole settlement.[59]

It was ominous that the one issue upon which Ferdinand staunchly refused to compromise was the future of the Trastámara inheritance. If Charles were to die before his mother therefore, conflict between Ferdinand and Philip was inevitable. Should he choose to retire, the succession crisis would simply come earlier, but it might be easier to arrange the transfer of power too since it would allow Philip time to secure *de facto* power over these lands. Charles had alienated his brother without effectively resolving any of the pressing problems of the still unfinished partition of the empire.

Long years of insecurity and crises of considerable magnitude thus preceded the accession of both Philip and Maximilian and the experience undoubtedly left its mark. The tenacity Philip displayed to retain all the lands that he believed belonged to him – above all the Netherlands – cannot be understood without reference to the anxiety he experienced before finally taking control of the Trastámara and Burgundian states. Nor can the attitude of the Netherlanders and the ambivalent

---

[59] AGS PR.57, fols. 121(e), (f), (h). See pp. 77–8 for the subsequent problems over the marriage clause, and pp. 131, 145, 165–7 for the ensuing difficulties over Italy.

stance of successive emperors towards this state be comprehended unless the insecurity and expectations of closer fusion with the so-called 'Austrian' Habsburgs are taken into account.

Above all, it is essential to realise that the empire as it emerged from the confused wrangling between the two brothers, made little sense. The lands that Philip finally inherited had few geographical or political links. By attaching the Netherlands to the southern realms Charles had created an indefensible empire, and he was aware of the fact. Before his death he attempted once more to sever the bonds between the Burgundian and Trastámara lands by attaching the northern states to England (p. 81). The failure of this plan left the Netherlands exposed, surrounded by two powerful and covetous neighbours. The French monarchs had dynastic claims to large parts of the area; the future emperors would have the right to reclaim the lands that had once belonged to imperial jurisdiction. Without imperial power, the military structure that had enabled Charles to defend and expand his territories was also endangered. His major recruiting grounds and the bulk of his troops were from German and Italian imperial lands; communications between his far-flung states were dependent on free passage through imperial fiefs. In particular, the formal links with the Tyrol and the north Italian states were severed, emphasising again the isolation of the Netherlands and the Franche-Comté in relation to the rest of the empire. Braudel long ago familiarised us with the problems of distance which beset Philip's empire.[60] The delay between an order and an event made government extremely difficult. Such problems were not new, but they were certainly exacerbated by the peculiar geographical and political structure of the multi-national state that emerged after 1556. Bereft of imperial support, the northern states were extremely vulnerable, but the need to provide aid for these areas in turn weakened the southern lands. The prospect of defending this scattered empire was daunting, even if it was smaller than the awesome conglomeration over which Charles had ruled. Moreover, the problems of reconciling the interests of areas as diverse and powerful as Spain and the Netherlands were to prove insuperable.

[60] F. Braudel, *The Mediterranean*, vol. 1, pp. 355–74.

The years of adversity, 1551–3

As the new decade dawned, Charles V was in a buoyant mood. His annexation of
Piacenza had been sanctioned by the papacy, and he boasted to his son that his
recent acquisitions had created more defensible states both in Italy and the
Netherlands. He had also increased his reputation greatly as a result of his victory
over the German Protestant princes in 1547. His power was awesome and it
appeared all the greater since there was no one challenging him. The world was
relatively peaceful. The wars with France had ended with the treaty of Crépy in
1544. When Henry II came to power three years later, Charles was a little uneasy,
knowing that the young king hated him and had never forgiven him the ignominy of
his captivity in Spain.[1] Moreover, like all new monarchs he would have to launch a
military campaign sooner or later. As the years passed, Charles relaxed his guard
and became somewhat contemptuous of Henry, thinking him a lesser man than his
father. It was a mistake he lived to regret. While Charles basked in the glow of his
latest victories in Italy, Henry was deftly spinning a complex web of intrigue and
rebellion that would soon entrap its careless victim. To posterity it seems ironic that
such a major tragedy should have been unleashed by a seemingly petty conflict over
an Italian duchy. This chapter will examine how the Italian war started, and why,
within two years, the emperor's power and lands were devastated.

FORBIDDEN FRUIT: PARMA AND PIACENZA

Plans for the reintegration of these duchies into the state of Milan had been
seriously discussed since at least 1520. Memories of the considerable financial
contributions they had made – about one fifth of the state's revenue in 1463 – made
it imperative to recover them as the assets of Milan were relentlessly stripped by the
emperor to fund his continuous wars. Both the emperor and the pope claimed
sovereignty over these areas. In 1545 Charles had agreed to invest the pope's son,
Pier Luigi Farnese, with the duchies in exchange for Paul III's support. Two years
later rebellion broke out and Pier Luigi was assassinated. Ferrante Gonzaga, the
imperial governor of Milan, immediately led his troops into the area and seized
Piacenza. The speed with which this was accomplished led to immediate allegations

---

[1]   Cloulas, *Henri II* (Paris, 1985), pp. 40–55.

of collusion between the emperor and the rebels, which were indignantly denied by Charles. His account of Gonzaga's actions, however, did nothing to dispel suspicion. He claimed that the rebels had placed themselves under his protection and Gonzaga had responded in order to establish imperial rights over the area before the pope could counter this move.[2] Had it all been quite as innocent as this, Charles would surely have handed over the duchy to Pier Luigi's successor, Ottavio Farnese, instead of which he held on to it and tried to invade Parma as well. As emperor, Charles had the duty to prevent unjust deprivations of imperial fiefs; as Ottavio's father-in-law, family ties should have predisposed him to protect and favour the new duke.[3]

Two powers quickly challenged Charles over Piacenza: the pope and the king of France. Francis I had been tempted by the earlier conflicts between the pope and the emperor to hope that one day the duchies might fall to France. At one stage he requested them both, as well as Milan and Montferrat, as the price for supporting the papacy. In June 1547 Orazio Farnese, third son of Pier Luigi, was betrothed to Henry II's illegitimate daughter, Diane, and sent to be educated at the French court. Henry demanded that both duchies should be given to Orazio. After two years of deadlock and with the threat of French intervention, Charles and Paul decided to compromise. Paul agreed to endorse Charles's possession of Piacenza, if he in turn would give the pope control of Parma and agree to compensate both Ottavio and Orazio. On his deathbed Paul repented of his betrayal of his grandsons. He declared Ottavio the rightful heir to both duchies and his successor, pope Julius III, confirmed this judgement in February 1550. Indeed this issue had won him the election: he had secured the all-important votes of the Farnese faction in the *Curia*, headed by cardinal Alessandro, by promising to restore Ottavio to his titles.

Unfortunately for the Farnese, Julius was committed to reconvening the Council of Trent and he could not do this without the emperor's support. Charles made his backing conditional on being granted the rights to both Parma and Piacenza. Rightly fearing for his remaining lands, Ottavio Farnese placed himself under French protection. In April 1551, after the pope had demanded that he surrender Parma, he made public his alliance with Henry and his determination to oppose both pope and emperor. Julius III declared him a rebel and his states forfeit and formally requested the aid of his 'beloved son' Charles V to eliminate this 'troublesome prince'.[4] The emperor could not have asked for a more advantageous

---

[2] Morel-Fatio, *Mémoires*, p. 332; DP, pp. 333–4, Chabod, *Lo stato*, pp. 79–84. See also the curious attempt by R. Tyler to whitewash Charles in his biography, *The emperor Charles the fifth* (London, 1958), p. 276.

[3] Ottavio was married to Charles's illegitimate daughter, Margaret.

[4] L. Romier, *Les origines politiques des guerres de religion* (2 vols., Paris, 1913–14), vol. I pp. 212–15, 229–31, 241–2; Cloulas, *Henri II*, pp. 174–7, 182, pp. 300–2; F. J. Baumgartner, 'Henry II and the Papal conclave of 1549', *Sixteenth Century Journal*, XVI, no. 3 (1985), pp. 301–14, especially pp. 302, 306, 312–13.

situation. He could now invade Parma with papal protection; he was ostensibly only a supporter, not the main belligerent in this war. He took care to place Ottavio under imperial ban too, charging him with being a restless man who constantly disturbed the peace of Italy – a description that fitted Charles rather better than the luckless Ottavio.[5]

The vast scale of the military preparations in the imperial camp demonstrates Charles's determination to seize Parma. He summoned a special council meeting in Augsburg, on 30 April 1551, to plan the campaign. It was generally agreed that to fund a campaign this large Spanish subsidies would be vital. The councillors were worried, however, because the Spanish realms were showing 'a great deal of confusion'. They considered the situation so grave that it required the presence of either Charles or Philip to calm the troubled realms and galvanise their resources. After Maximilian's recent departure only the ineffective María was left as head of the regency government, and Maximilian had announced his intention of withdrawing her services as well as his own in view of the family rows over the succession. Since Charles had no desire to return to Spain, he ordered his son to embark immediately and collect the large subsidies required.[6]

Philip was extremely unhappy about this. He begged to be allowed to participate in this war. Charles told him that the conflict was not prestigious enough. He was acutely conscious that Philip had not yet taken part in a major campaign and needed to prove his military prowess, but both the emperor and his council were adamant that he must wait. Charles explained that he was acting technically only as an ally of the pope; this meant that, however costly or prolonged, the conflict was a minor one in terms of prestige. If Henry intervened and led his troops in person, then the war would be of the required level of prestige, but there was as yet no indication that he would do so. Philip departed; by September 1551 he was back in Spain and at the head of his last regency government. By then there were signs of war everywhere. French troops were on their way to Italy in May; by August Henry decided to open another front along the Piedmont–Milan border to divide imperial forces. Skirmishes had also taken place along the Netherlands border. The pope too had armed, helped by a loan of 100,000 ds which Charles ordered Philip to send from Spain that July. The imperial ambassador in France, Simon Renard, a protégé of Granvelle, warned from May onwards that unless both sides pulled out of Parma a general war would soon break out.

Neither Charles nor Granvelle believed that Henry was capable of launching a

---

[5] AGS E. 308 s.f. Charles to Philip, 25 March 1552.
[6] The minutes of the *consulta* are in AGS E. 446 s.f.; see pp. 37–9 for details of the family quarrel. The regency of Maximilian and María can be studied in the documents published by Rodríguez Raso, *Maximiliano*, and Fernández Alvarez, *Corpus*, vol. 3; J. C. Calvete de Estrella wrote a detailed account of Philip's visit to the Netherlands, published in Antwerp, 1552, *El Felicissimo Viaie d'el mvy alto y mvy poderoso Principe Don Phelippe . . . desde España a sus tierras de la baxa Alemana. . . . (Antwerp, 1552).*

general war that year. The reasons Granvelle gave for their confidence are instructive. He pointed out that Henry would need Grison and other Swiss troops as well as Germans to fight, and this would take time and money. The season was well advanced. Above all, he could not see how Henry would dare to strike without allies, particularly in the Holy Roman Empire. Fortunately, Charles had 'pacified' this area and so removed the prospect of being attacked in the north while he was in Italy. They were all so certain of this that Charles ordered the troops manning key points in the Holy Roman Empire to move southwards and support the invasion of Parma.[7] Should problems arise in this area, it was assumed that Ferdinand would deal with them as he had done in the past. These errors of judgement cost the emperor Parma, and very nearly his life.

REBELLION IN THE HOLY ROMAN EMPIRE, 1548–52

It is highly significant that in his memoirs Charles juxtaposed the concessions he made to the German princes in 1548 to the outbreak of trouble in Parma and Piacenza. This suggests that he consciously chose to give Italy priority and missed the chance to impose a more enduring settlement in the Holy Roman Empire. Doubtless he was deterred from pursuing the matter due to the great complexity of the situation. The religious dissent that led to Protestantism had never been solely a theological issue. Charles had repeatedly patched up relations with the German princes and allowed them a measure of religious toleration. Each time he did so he was also acknowledging their power to circumscribe his political activities. Since earlier edicts allowing recognition of the Protestants had not solved the rift within the Church, Charles opted to leave the religious issue to the Council of the Church, whenever that should reconvene, and the Protestants agreed, glad to have won yet another breathing space and official toleration. Nevertheless, the emperor sought to capitalise on his victory over rebel princes by imposing changes of the judicial structure of the empire that would give him and his successor greater power over the loose federation of states. He also put forward plans for the formation of a Catholic league that would furnish him with a permanent military force in the Holy Roman Empire.

Neither Catholic nor Protestant princes liked the extension of imperial authority. They were alienated by this, by the emperor's creation of an independent state in the Netherlands, and by rumours of the 1551 family compact. The accord would have deprived the seven electors of their special position in Christendom since it was a major step towards making the title hereditary. Moreover, Maximilian's bitterness and opposition to Charles led him to draw closer to the German princes

---

[7] Preparations: Braudel, *The Mediterranean*, vol. 2, pp. 917–18; Romier, *Les origines*, vol. 1 pp. 259–60; Granvelle–Renard correspondence, Weiss, *Granvelle*, vol. 3, pp. 573–5; AGS E. 84 fol. 374, AGS E.K. 1469 fol. 44.

and may well have encouraged their decision to challenge Charles's authority. Later he was suspected of having incited the rebellion, and his demands that the emperor should publicly deny these accusations met with little response, suggesting that Charles himself thought there was some substance behind them.[8] Tension increased further in 1551 as the Council of Trent reconvened. Charles ordered the Protestants to send their representatives and many thought that their final hour had come. They prepared to defend their freedom of worship and independence by force of arms. Nevertheless, since the rebels included both Protestants and Catholics in their ranks, their propaganda did not make much use of theological argument. They concentrated on accusations that Charles had tried to pervert traditional privileges and make the Holy Roman Emperor a hereditary title. They further claimed to be acting to uphold the authority of the Holy Roman Empire, much weakened by Charles who had annexed imperial territories such as Milan, Siena, Piombino, Piacenza, Utrecht, Friesland and Cambrai, in order to increase the power of his dynasty. They also mentioned the separation of the Netherlands from the Imperial Circle. The fact that they also alienated imperial lands to buy French support weakened but did not destroy their argument – Henry had asked for Cammerich, Toul, Metz and Verdun in exchange for help.

Henry watched these developments closely and let it be known that he was prepared to support the rebels. Disaffected princes had approached him in February 1551 and three months later discussions for an alliance were well underway; by the autumn the rebels had a signed undertaking from Henry that he would help them.[9] The general awareness that Charles was totally absorbed in Italian affairs furnished his opponents with further encouragement.

Although he was fully informed of these developments, Charles refused to take them seriously. He was convinced that Maurice of Saxony, the leading German prince, would remain loyal to him. He had rewarded Maurice handsomely for his defection from the Protestant league in the last war and could not believe that he would risk these substantial gains so soon. Having underrated Henry as well as Maurice, he ignored the increasingly alarmist warnings of Mary of Hungary. But he never could ignore her for long. Eventually he decided to allay her fears by telling loyal German lords to hold their troops in readiness in case of trouble. There was no urgency in his request. Only when these routine calls met with widespread refusals or polite evasions did he appreciate that the situation was dangerous. It was not until Henry had taken Toul, Metz and Verdun that Charles accepted the need to respond to the unrest.

In a fascinating report to Philip, written from Innsbruck in March 1552, Charles outlined his options.[10] Charles conceded that he needed to act quickly to save the

[8] AGS E. 649 fol. 79; Fichtner, *Ferdinand I*, pp. 187–90, 208.
[9] Brandi, *Charles V*, p. 603ss; Cloulas, *Henri II*, pp. 306–10; earlier contacts between France and the princes R. J. Knecht, *Francis I*, pp. 223–4.
[10] AGS E. 90 fols. 7–9; instructions to Juan Manrique de Lara, 29 March.

situation. Since enemy troops had marched into Lorraine and were on the western borders of the empire, he could not take the usual route north to the Netherlands. He dismissed the suggestion to go south to Italy because he believed that this would be interpreted as flight and severely dent his reputation and honour. Making a stand in either Ulm or Augsburg was out of the question since the rebels might be strong enough to take them. Besides, relations with Ulm were poor and both cities had suffered the ravages of his troops in the last war; Charles was not at all sure that they would receive him. He could not afford the dishonour of being refused or losing either city. The only safe, sensible and honourable course of action was really to head for Vienna, Ferdinand's capital. But with the sounds of the family rows still reverberating in his mind, doubts of Ferdinand's loyalty surfaced. Charles would not place himself at the mercy of his brother. Unwilling to risk honour or make any concessions to the rebels, Charles concluded that the best policy was inactivity. He would wait where he was until he was sent aid from his Spanish and Italian realms. Even after he was appraised of Maurice of Saxony's determination to capture him, Charles refused to move, paralysed by a mixture of pride and fear. His attempts to buy time by calling on Ferdinand to mediate were unsuccessful since he was unwilling to give any concessions. Finally, only the desperate pleas of his terrified entourage persuaded him to flee from Innsbruck the night before the rebels entered the city in triumph.[11] The imperial camp was in complete disarray; the emperor's reputation had been shattered by his ignominious flight.

IN SEARCH OF A LOST REPUTATION

The most obvious and immediate result of the débâcle at Innsbruck was the total neglect of the Italian front. From being a priority it was relegated to the background, indeed ignored. The consequences were dire since Henry had successfully tapped discontent here as well. He is a much underrated monarch. It is a tribute to his skills that he coordinated the multiple rebellions and invasions so closely. He arranged for the Ottoman fleet to attack the Mediterranean lands; he encouraged Ottoman activity in Eastern Europe; he sought English friendship; he was behind the rebellion of the prince of Salerno in Naples and that of Siena. In July 1552 imperial troops were driven out of the strategic republic and, although Salerno's rebellion failed, he fled the realm and joined the French forces. He was to play a key role in galvanising the Ottomans and North African corsairs to attack Italy.[12]

Cries of help poured in from the emperor's Italian possessions, but Charles turned a deaf ear and refused to answer letters or send money. Ferrante Gonzaga,

[11] AGS E. 90 fols. 7–9; Fichtner, *Ferdinand I*, pp. 192–3; Brandi, *Charles V*, pp. 606–11.
[12] AGS E. 1042 fol. 3 for Salerno's defection; his role in Ottoman attacks, AGS E. 478 fol. 93; E. 477 s.f. *Avisos* from Marco Duer, 17 July 1552. Siena, pp. 113–14

commander of the Piedmont–Milan front was short of funds and despaired of getting help, so he signed a local truce with the French in August 1553. The emperor was beside himself with anger when he heard, and Mary of Hungary was no less violent in her condemnation of Gonzaga. The reason is clear: it was imperative to keep the war in Italy going in order to divert France and prevent Henry from concentrating his forces on an attack against the Netherlands.[13] This was all very well for the Netherlands, but the Italian commanders cogently argued that if they were to continue fighting, they must be given the resources. Gonzaga was forced to repudiate the truce, more out of the need to keep his men busy and avert conflict with the civilian population than out of subservience to the emperor. Along with many others in Italy, he turned to Philip. Numerous letters and several special envoys were sent requesting financial and military help and, above all, Philip's presence. Unless the prince came to take control, they argued, the Italian front would collapse.[14]

None of this mattered much to Charles now. After Innsbruck he set himself two goals which he thought entirely compatible: to pacify the Holy Roman Empire and to recover his honour and reputation. He needed his brother to extricate himself from his predicament, however. How else could he disarm the rebels and gain time to arm himself? Ferdinand was willing to mediate, not simply to stall for time. Charles had not expected this sign of independence and was indignant when Ferdinand, exasperated by the emperor's refusal to compromise, announced in July 1552 that he would abandon his thankless task and go to deal with the Ottoman threat along the Hungarian border instead. Despite Charles's dismissal of this as a 'misguided' policy, Ferdinand could not be persuaded to stay. Charles had no option but to compromise with the rebels. At least that was how both sides described their agreement to do nothing more until the next imperial diet met and they could fully discuss their grievances. The rebels were not punished; many, like Maurice of Saxony, chose to follow Ferdinand to the Hungarian front. The emperor was both thankful to be rid of them and concerned at his brother's growing influence within the empire.[15]

For the time being he concentrated on organising the campaign. Bereft of his brother's help and unable to rally much help or support from the empire itself, Charles made an impassioned plea to his realms during 1552–3. Their response was rapid and most gratifying. By the autumn of 1552 Charles had gathered an army of some 70,000 men. According to one enthusiastic observer, with these men he would be able to terrify France and half the world besides.[16] His achievements fell far short

13 AGS E. 1203 fol. 74; E. 1204 fols. 119, 120; E. 1202 fol. 110.
14 AGS E. 1204 fol. 76; E. 1205 fols. 66, 67; E. 1203 fol. 6; E. 1202 fol. 129.
15 Brandi, *Charles V*, pp. 606, 611–15; Fichtner, *Ferdinand I*, p. 200; AGS E. 90 fol. 79.
16 Figures differ considerably in all accounts, but 60–80,000 seem to be the most frequently cited; see J. Finot, 'Le siège de Metz en 1552 et les finances de Charles Quint', *Bulletin du Comité des Travaux Historiques et Scientifiques. Section d'Histoire et de Philologie* (Paris, 1897), pp. 260–70; he includes a review of numbers, pp. 261–3.

of this. Having eliminated his conflict temporarily with the major leaders of the revolt, he could not attack them. He could have – many thought he should have – directed his forces against the margrave Albert Albiciades, who had not been party to these negotiations and had continued to devastate imperial territories. But Charles at first ignored him and marched round Munich, Augsburg, Ulm and Alsace in a show of strength which undoubtedly deterred further aggression but did little else. Charles seems to have perceived the futility of his gesture towards the end of the campaigning season when his commanders were already discussing disbandment and winter quarters. He offered Albert Albiciades a pardon if he joined him, and with these additional troops he felt strong enough to attempt a feat that would 'satisfy both honour and reputation'.[17] In effect this required him to fight the French. But since Charles wanted to avoid accusations of having abandoned the Holy Roman Empire and once again sacrificed its interests to the war against France, he decided to attack one of the imperial territories recently invaded by France – Metz.

Mary of Hungary was appalled. The imperial generals were aghast. Unanimously they asked the emperor to desist, calling his attention to the lateness of the season and the strong fortifications of the city. He would not listen. Not even when a fierce attack of gout prevented him from being at the head of the army as he wanted. His generals were so convinced that the siege would fail they tried to persuade him to leave Alba in charge of the army, so that Charles would be spared the dishonour. Charles adhered to his absurdly optimistic view of the situation to the very end. He ignored the advice; he ignored the warnings of a French counter-attack against the Netherlands. The day before the siege was hastily lifted and the ragged army dispatched urgently to defend Hesdin, he wrote to Philip confidently predicting its success. Nothing could illustrate more poignantly the emperor's inability to assess his position rationally. His obsession with the recovery of his reputation had blinded him.[18]

Much as contemporaries might have admired Charles's determination to remain with his troops despite the deprivations and inclement weather, they took even greater note of continuing reports of his ill-health, poor judgement and indecision. This second major defeat further reduced the emperor's standing. Enemies mocked him, claiming that the siege had been a feint. It was reported that Charles had been so frightened of his enemies that he had gathered this vast army merely to escort him out of the Holy Roman Empire and take him into the safety of Flanders.[19] Although Charles continued to plan his return to the Holy Roman Empire as late as 1554, his hasty departure after the failure of the Metz campaign effectively signalled the surrender of power to Ferdinand.

[17] AGS E. 90 fols. 97–8, Eraso to Philip, 27 September 1552. The Metz campaign can be followed in Brandi, *Charles V*, pp. 616–22; Finot, 'Le siège de Metz'.
[18] AGS E. 90 fols. 82–92, Charles to Philip, 28 December 1552; E. 90 fols. 97–8 Eraso to Philip.
[19] AGS E. 90 fols. 97–8.

Alarmed by reports of his father's physical and mental health and still eager to take the field, Philip responded to the news from Germany by gathering money and troops and preparing his immediate departure for the front. He hastened to inform officials and allies that duty and honour required him to help Charles in this time of crisis. In fact, as he quickly realised, 'it would make a bad impression and undermine my honour if I were to leave his Majesty alone at this juncture'.[20] Mary of Hungary dispatched a special envoy to Spain urging her nephew to leave for the Netherlands at once before everything collapsed.[21] The one person who most definitely opposed Philip's journey was Charles. When he first learnt of Philip's plans in September 1552 he sent don Juan de Figueroa to Spain with strict orders for Philip to remain where he was. He argued that there was not enough time for Philip to levy troops, raise money, fit out ships and get to Germany before the campaigning season was over. Since he would arrive late he would only have time to take part in desultory post-seasonal activities such as burning and looting enemy posts; this was not commensurate with Philip's honour.[22] He repeated his arguments in subsequent letters.

The prince reluctantly obeyed. When his father used the troops and money he had diligently raised in order to besiege Metz, he must have been extremely bitter. The siege would have served admirably as his first campaign. There is no doubt that Charles deprived him of a chance to fight because he was determined to recover his reputation. If Philip came and succeeded where his father had failed it would have dented it even further. Moreover, it would have presented him with the problem of who should govern the Spanish realms. In view of the need to press them for large subsidies it would have to be either Philip or Charles. In human terms, the emperor's determination to prove that he was still capable of handling the situation and restoring his own honour is comprehensible. But in the tense and dangerous situation some considered it disastrous.

As soon as the emperor arrived back in Brussels with the tattered remnants of his army he faced a barrage of protest from Mary. She told her brother in no uncertain terms that they could not prevent widespread rebellion in the Netherlands without Philip's help and presence. As usual, she persuaded Charles of the wisdom of her view. It is quite likely that she even dictated the letter he sent Philip in the first week of April 1553 which ordered his urgent departure for the Netherlands. The tone and message differ substantially from a dispatch he had sent only a few days earlier. Countermanding his earlier order for Philip to remain in Spain, Charles now appended his signature to this message: 'It is evident that (your presence here) is most necessary. We need someone who can command the loyalty and obedience of

---

[20] AGS E. 92 fol. 106 Philip to Prince Doria. Some, like the bishop of Cuenca, had written urging him to go, AGS E. 89 fol. 319.

[21] I could not find her written instructions, but the contents of the mission can be gleaned from AGS E. 85 fol. 322 and E. 97 fols. 53–63.

[22] AGS E. 90 fols. 109–11, the instructions are dated 18 September.

these states during the war, in which I can no longer participate'.[23] Philip's heart must have leapt at this tantalising hint that he would take part in the campaign and might even lead it. The letter was cleverly composed, balancing threats and promises. Behind its contents lies Mary's conviction that they would achieve nothing without large quantities of money, and her realisation that they would need to coax Philip to provide it even if he did not approve of their policies. From this point onwards, Charles and Mary exploited Philip's desire to play an active role in the war as well as his fear of losing parts of his patrimony. On this occasion they flattered as well as frightened him by stressing that the situation in the Netherlands would get out of hand unless he took control. They demanded that he should come with enough money to finance the next campaign and to pay all debts assigned to the states-general of the Netherlands. Philip was also ordered to cover all the costs of his journey and arrange for regular payments to his household, since the Netherlands would not be able to finance his expenses. Philip must have been staggered both by the magnitude of the demands and the time span allowed him: he was told to do all this and arrive in Brussels by September 1553 at the latest.

FINANCING THE WARS, 1551–3

One of the unwritten principles governing relations between Charles's lands was the duty to help each other if invaded and the monarch if his power was seriously challenged or his person in danger. Hence the generous response of all his realms when Charles faced rebellion in Germany. It was always understood that the area which stood to benefit most from a conflict, however, must pay the largest share of the costs. Although successive monarchs sought to persuade their lands that they would all stand or fall together and must therefore play an equal part in all ventures and conflicts, they failed to make much headway. Looking first at the Italian wars, it is evident that Milan would have benefited most from the conquest of Parma, indeed no one else would gain directly from it. It seems appropriate therefore to begin this review of finance by examining the contributions of Milan and the other Italian states.

The Italian wars

Problems of quantification are at once apparent. Milan was ravaged by soldiers of both sides; it was forced to pay numerous contributions to army units encamped there and suffered untold devastation. Neither the local contributions nor the damage can be properly accounted or even estimated. Only the contributions of the ducal government and outside subsidies can be assessed. The governors of the duchy had met the incessant demands of the troops by negotiating loans with

---

[23] AGS E. 98 fols. 136–40; compare it with AGS E. 90 fols. 89–92.

merchant bankers, both local and international. These loans were secured by ordinary and extraordinary revenues, both current and future. By 1551 Milanese revenues had been so heavily mortgaged that no financier would lend on their security.[24] The situation has been summarised in Table 1, p. 52. Expenditure far outstripped the yield from both ordinary and extraordinary revenues, some of which had been anticipated two years in advance to service the debt. The special tax levied for the war (*mensuale*) could not cover the escalating costs. By 1553 its annual yield hardly sufficed to maintain the army for two months. After 1551 Milan could not subsist without the more or less regular subsidies from Naples and Spain – see Table 2, p. 53.

Aware that Milan could not make much direct contribution to the war, Charles argued that Parma was absolutely vital for the defence of the southern Italian realms, in particular Naples. The Neapolitans were used to this sort of argument and had become accustomed to making substantial contributions to all Italian campaigns. They reluctantly complied with some of his demands, sending 130,000 es at the beginning of the war. Aside from direct subsidies they soon found themselves having to pay for loans negotiated by Charles in the north, but assigned to Neapolitan revenues without consultation. This was the case with a contract for 50,000 ds secured on revenues which the viceroy had earmarked for urgent administrative expenses and fortifications. At the time there were rumours of invasion by the 400 ships of the Franco–Muslim fleet in which the prince of Salerno was serving. The Neapolitans needed all the money they could raise for their own defence. The viceroy, don Pedro de Toledo, an intemperate man at the best of times, told Charles he was mad to deprive the realm of what little finance it possessed. His anger grew when he realised that the emperor had negotiated loans on the security of the still unvoted Neapolitan subsidies. The realm was already restive, subject to grave external dangers and news that the sovereign intended to take the money out of Naples was likely to provoke the deputies. They might even refuse to vote the taxes. Toledo was both frustrated and angry. He assured all who would listen that Naples was being ruined by Charles and was on the verge of total collapse.[25]

Nevertheless when news of the emperor's plight and narrow escape from Innsbruck reached Naples there was an immediate response. Don Pedro González de Mendoza was probably not the only noble who spontaneously sent the emperor money.[26] The Neapolitan parliament met and voted an extraordinary grant of 800,000 ds in April 1552 to help Charles. It was this money, not as is often said, the generosity of the Fugger bankers, that saved Charles. Toledo dispatched 200,000 ds almost immediately – Charles acknowledged their receipt at the beginning of May. A further 200,000 ds followed soon after, with an additional 50,000 ds being sent to

---

[24] AGS E. 90 fols. 7–8.   [25] AGS E. 1044 fols. 23, 81; E. 1042 fol. 3.
[26] AGS E. 1044 fol. 42. He apologised for not having more than 14,000 es to give. It was a sizeable sum.

Table 1. *Finance: Milan*

Year	Needed/spent	Ordinary revenues (p.a.)	Ordinary expenditure (p.a.)	Mensuale/Extraordinary Revenue (p.a.)	Alienated revenues	Unsecured debt	Deficit
1536[A]		200,000 es		c. 300,000 es			
1547[A]							
1550[A]		128,000 es		270,000 es	all for 1550 ordinary revenue 1551		
1551[B]	500,187 es				all 1552 and 1553	210,000 es	
1553[C]	412,000	152,000	129,234	260,000 es	most of 1554		for 1553: 37,324/143,324 for 1554: 168,363/282,346
End 1553[D]	11,907 es per month army	140,000		260,000 es			
January 1554[E]					all to 1556		

[A] Chabod, *Lo stato*, pp. 118–21.
[B] AGS E 84 fol. 348, E. 503 fol. 45.
[C] Chabod, *Lo stato*, pp. 121–2. The higher figures are probably the most accurate.
[D] AGS E 1202 fol. 130, note at peak campaigning periods, the cost of the army would be c. 160,000 es per month. E 1209 fol. 11.
[E] AGS E 508 fols. 11, 12, 13.

Table 2. *Naples: Contribution for Piedmont–Milan*

1537	
1543	unspecified sums
1544	
1551	89,000 es
1552	100,000 es
1553	80,000 es
1554	100,000 es

Reference: Chabod, *Lo stato*, p. 128.

the Piedmont–Milan front. The rest was mostly spent patching up the defences of Nice and Siena, both areas for which Naples had been made responsible. Hardly any money was retained to strengthen the realm's own defences.[27] Much as they resented the emperor's policies, there were still powerful bonds of loyalty uniting the Neapolitans to their sovereign.

Subsidies had to be paid, and with the additional burden of debt, Naples was to feel the effect of the wars severely. It was estimated that expenditure for 1552 would near one million ducats, not counting unfunded debts of 270,000 ds. Toledo could not cover even a small part of this, so he resorted to dubious measures which successfully helped him to overcome the immediate financial crisis, but which contributed to the extension and intensification of unrest in the realm. He increased the hearth tax, assigning it for defence expenditure. He suspended (temporarily) all payments of grants, gifts, salaries and loans assigned to the main Neapolitan tax, the *aduana de las pecoras*. The salaries of all royal officials were also suspended, and the city of Naples was pressed to lend 7,000 ds. Most extraordinary of all was his edict to requisition one third of all the silver in the realm. He did not disclose details of his methods, but it seems that this expedient yielded substantial results, and Toledo enthusiastically advised that it should be employed again in a future crisis. Finally, in return for credit, he granted a monopoly of grain sales to a financial consortium, knowing that they would use the concession to keep grain prices high. It is scarcely conceivable that Naples would have remained seething with discontent but avoid outright rebellion had it not been for the immediate threat of Ottoman and French attacks.

There was little Sicily could do to help. The island had contributed to the war effort in the Netherlands and Germany during the 1540s, but most of its revenues were required for defence, Sicily being one of the most exposed of all the emperor's lands. Moreover, it often had to play host to the emperor's fleets and this entailed a heavy burden in terms of quartering and supplying soldiers and sailors. By 1552 a

---

[27] AGS E. 1042 fols. 5, 135; E. 1043 fols. 3, 28; E. 89 fols. 52–6.

chronic shortage of money had brought the vital building project of small look-out towers initiated by Ferrante Gonzaga in 1535 to a halt. In January 1552 the viceroy, Juan de Vega, told Charles that unless they received immediate subsidies the fleet would not be able to put to sea and the galleys Charles had ordered would never be built. Soon afterwards, with news of the approaching Franco–Muslim fleet he warned the emperor: 'we have reached a point where, unable to carry out burdens any longer, we have been forced to drop some of them'.[28] Here, as in Naples, stories of the emperor's near capture resulted in a generous subsidy. The Sicilian parliament voted an extraordinary grant of 150,000 ds, and at least a third of this was quickly sent to him.[29] The experiences of the two realms are similar in another way: for both, the extraordinary subsidies to help Charles were the last important contributions they were to make to the northern wars. Henceforth, their subsidies would be spent in Italy; even so, by 1552 the defensive and offensive expenditure of the Italian lands had to be subsidised.

The Netherlands

Infinitely more prosperous than the Italian states, the Netherlands had nevertheless experienced financial difficulties a great deal earlier. During the 1520s there had been a shortfall of some 500,000 fl per annum. As can be appreciated from a glance at Table 3, there was a sharp rise in government debts during the following decade, from 400,000 fl in 1531, to 1.3 million fl in 1539.[30] The financial system could not function with such massive deficits. Inevitably a permanent shortfall was becoming a regular feature, but it was essential to pay off most of the debt quickly if bankruptcy was to be avoided. Royal assets were plundered to manage the debt, and many loan repayments were assigned to the demesne revenues. But the large-scale wars of the early 1540s could not be funded with the old financial structures. In the late 1530s and early 1540s the financial system of the Netherlands was substantially altered. Until then, the bulk of the crown's revenue came from ordinary and extraordinary subsidies, the *aides* or *beden* which the provincial states granted individually or as a collectivity. Until the 1530s many of these taxes were estimated and allocated according to quota systems drawn up at the turn of the century.

---

[28] AGS E. 1120 fol. 3; S. Bono, *I corsari Barbareschi* (Turin, 1964), p. 207.

[29] AGS E. 648 fol. 12.

[30] Details of the Netherlands finances: Ehrenberg, *Fuggers*, pp. 248–9; C. Hirschauer, *Les Etats d'Artois de leurs origines à l'occupation française 1340–1640* (2 vols., Paris–Brussels, 1923), vol. 1, pp. 123, 146, 160; H. de Schepper, 'La organización de las "finanzas" públicas en los Paises Bajos reales 1480–1700. Una reseña', *Cuadernos de Investigación Histórica*, 8 (1984), pp. 7–33; J. D. Tracy, *A financial revolution* (London, 1985); Baelde, 'Financial policy and the evolution of the demesne in the Netherlands under Charles V and Philip II (1530–1560)', in H. J. Cohn (ed.), *Government in Reformation Europe* (London, 1971), pp. 203–24. There is a brief introduction to government debts in the Cambridge Economic History of Europe, vol. 5, pp. 358–75, and to annuities issued by cities, pp. 303–6.

Table 3. Finances of the Netherlands (in pounds Flemish)

Date	Revenues	Expenditure	Sale of annuities	Loans	Interest on loans	Deficit	Alienated revenues
1531	1,229,292 [with extra subsidies?]	1,645,270				415,878	
1539	279,931	1,421,735				1,141,804	
1545	282,654	1,703,789				1,421,135	
1551		needed 1,000,000		1,000,000		1,300,000	
1552			300,000 [600,000]	255,000	141,300	1,350,000	2.5 million
1554			1,230,000	3,071,000	285,982	5,621,000	
1555					424,765	7,000,000	
1556					1,357,287		

Based on figures cited by M. Baelde, 'Financial policy', pp. 204, 217, 220, 223. Ehrenberg, *The Fuggers*, pp. 272–3, 279. The total deficit for 1555 is endorsed by Baelde and F. Braudel, 'Les emprunts', p. 195.

Naturally these bore increasingly less relation to the effective distribution of wealth in the area. In Flanders the quotas of 1517 were not revised until 1631; in Holland, the assessments of 1515 did not change throughout the Habsburg period.[31] Worse still from the point of view of the government, large areas had been able to avoid assessment altogether for a variety of reasons. The clergy and many nobles could claim exemption from direct taxation, although the monarchs still obtained their contributions with papal agreement in the case of the former, and service or forced loans in the case of the latter. As the century progressed, the amount of the grants being retained by the provinces to meet local administrative and other expenses grew considerably.

Charles and Mary did not just want an extension of these traditional grants – they wanted to break away from subsidies voted and distributed by traditional quotas altogether. They were eager to extend other taxes such as excises, customs dues and taxes on land. The flourishing urban centres of the Netherlands were well acquainted with these forms of taxation, but they had seldom been imposed on rural areas or over entire provinces. What the government did in the early 1540s was to force most of the provinces to accept these forms of taxation. Partly because they were novel in some areas, and also because a number of expedients were imposed simultaneously, these reforms gave the appearance of a new structure and have been called the *nieuwe middelen*, or new system. It is a convenient term. Most provinces gave their assent to two or more of the following taxes during these years: one hundredth penny on exports (1 per cent); tenth penny on profits from commerce (10 per cent); excises on beer and wine; a tenth penny on income from annuities and from real estate. Furthermore, the states also agreed to anticipate much of this revenue by issuing bonds or annuities.[32]

The new system was advantageous to the government in a number of ways. It increased the yield from taxation. These taxes could be applied to areas exempt from traditional dues and indeed they extended the number of people affected considerably, particularly the excise and land taxes. They were easier to collect, less complex to manage. Above all they were invaluable for funding large loans. The states were repeatedly asked to issue annuities and assign regular payment of interest and repayment of capital on these taxes, much as the cities did when they wanted to raise money for local expenditure. The government applied a compulsory purchase scheme – each province or city would be asked to anticipate a certain amount of revenue by issuing bonds. They would then select individuals and

---

[31] Schepper, 'Las "finanzas" públicas en los Paises Bajos', p. 10; J. D. Tracy, 'The taxation system of the county of Holland during the reigns of Charles V and Philip II, 1519–1566', *Economisch-en-Sociaal-Historisch Jaarboek*, vol. 48 (1985), pp. 71–117, esp. 72.

[32] See Tracy's very clear account in *A financial revolution*, p. 90. He firmly dates these changes to 1542–4; Schepper in 'Las "finanzas" públicas en los Paises Bajos', p. 10, opts for 1536–7. Other writers range between these. The discrepancy is probably due to the different timing in each province.

institutions and assign a quota of the bonds. It was a refinement on the forced loan.

These measures aroused considerable opposition in the Netherlands. Although this was only to be expected, the government was ill prepared when the city of Gent rebelled in 1539. Charles was forced to return to the Netherlands in all haste to crush this and other opposition. The harsh repression was intended to serve as a deterrent, and it was successful. When war broke out again in 1542 the new system was fully operational and enabled Charles to fund the conflict.

At the heart of the successful exploitation of the Netherlands revenues lay the development and refinement of the *renten* or *rentes*, bonds or annuities. Sovereigns had issued and sold government bonds in the past, assigning payment of interest and capital on regular demesne revenues. Those intended as short-term investments had a modest but fair return of 1:16 or 1:12 deniers (6.67 per cent and 8.3 per cent respectively). Life annuities (*lijf-renten, rentes viagères*) might last one or two lives, and the yield was usually lower, between 4–6 per cent. Perpetual annuities were rare and carried very low interest. They tended to be gifts or rewards from the sovereign rather than sold. All types of bonds grew in popularity. Merchant bankers, individuals, institutions, all purchased them even without compulsion. Apart from government bonds, cities and provincial states could also organise their issue, often for the same reason as the monarch – the need to raise a large sum quickly. Urban areas met such expenses as grain purchases in time of famine or when asked to anticipate the yield of a subsidy by issuing bonds. Confidence was of the essence, so the provision of reliable collateral was very important. Cities tended to be regular and prompt in their payments; the provincial states, usually run by the same people, developed an equally efficient form of management. Government bonds, unless assigned regular revenues such as those from the demesne, were more risky and invariably had to be given additional security before they would attract buyers. For a time the general receivers (financial officials in charge of revenue collection in each province) were a popular security. As the scale of lending increased and the amount of revenue being handled by these officials decreased, other sources had to be found. Soon the government pressed individuals and institutions, including cities and the states, to provide collateral. By the 1540s and 1550s they were being asked to issue annuities in their own names, but effectively on the government's behalf. The government would draw up a contract with the states or cities with details of its payment terms, but the institution would take full charge of the issue and management of the bonds.

The closer cooperation of central government and provincial institutions could not have been secured without a price. Similarly, it is hard to believe that the brutality shown at Gent sufficed to staunch opposition to other aspects of the new system. The provinces learnt to profit from the crown's needs as they had in the past. Although Hainaut and other states had permanent financial officers in the fifteenth century, most provinces did not develop regular local or provincial administrations for finance until after the 1540s. Zeeland had such a body by 1544,

Flanders in 1545 and so on.[33] The pre-eminence of provincial, as opposed to central government receivers was clear by the 1550s. They dealt with most major sources of revenue whilst the central government gradually had to relinquish control of different sources of revenue.[34] This gradual and uneven transfer of power over revenues surely accounts for the fluctuating fortunes of sales of bonds guaranteed by the central government receivers and the general receiver. They had been popular in the past, but as the amounts they handled diminished, they were not considered reliable security.[35] What appears at first sight to have been a victory for the central government was thus a considerable long-term success for the forces of particularism.

When Charles decided to launch his great campaign for Parma he demanded money from the states of the Netherlands – quickly and in very large quantities. He imposed a forced loan and ordered the provincial states to issue bonds using the quota system as in the past. He also requested extraordinary subsidies from the states. He pressed certain provinces to sell annuities for over 300,000 fl with 4–6 per cent interest in their own names. He borrowed 300,000 fl from the Fugger bankers, offering repayment with government bonds bearing annual interest of 10 per cent. He seized the 500,000 fl which Mary had raised to pay off pressing debts and deal with payments due at the November fair. She had to summon the council of finance in order to devise some hasty expedients that would enable them to meet their dues at the fair. Their solution was to sell annuities of 12 per cent for up to 400,000 fl. The issue would be in the name of the receiver general.[36]

The unrest caused by these measures was so great it requires some explanation. There was much resentment at being forced to pay so much money for a distant Italian enterprise. The Netherlanders were not interested in Parma; most of them would not even have known where it was. As can be seen from Table 3, they had also enjoyed a period of relative financial stability. Mary of Hungary had used the additional revenues after the war to reduce the state debt. All of a sudden, that level escalated beyond the bounds of previous experiences. When the real crisis came in 1552, Charles's ability to respond was considerably diminished. The Netherlanders were sullen, and had already been pressed for such large contributions they were not responsive to further demands.

In view of the urgency with which the emperor needed money after the outbreak of rebellion, the Netherlands government once again resorted to the forced sale of annuities. Revenues were being mortgaged further and further in advance. In some instances, the same people asked for the forced loan of 1551 were selected for the purchase of bonds. This was one of the reasons Holland opposed the system of compulsory purchase. Another was that all elites found these government orders

---

[33] Schepper, 'Las "finanzas" públicas en los Paises Bajos', p. 12.
[34] The process has been studied in Holland, by Tracy, 'The taxation system', pp. 86–8.
[35] Ehrenberg, *Fuggers*, pp. 114, 248.   [36] Baelde, 'Financial policy', p. 219.

distasteful. The Dutch representatives argued that bonds were a popular form of investment and could be sold on the open market, rather than by force – their arguments prevailed after 1552.[37] From this moment onwards the Netherlands were subjected to an unprecedented series of demands for subsidies and loans. In Artois, for example, they were asked to make their largest ever grant in 1552 (100,000 fl); in January 1553 they were asked for 150,000 fl, and further demands followed in April and August of that year, and again in March and September 1554.[38] This was at a time when the area was having to provide quarters for a large number of troops and was subject to attack. To meet these demands, the states had to impose additional taxes on beer, wine and other consumables, as well as on real estate and cultivated lands. The accounts of the county of Holland, recently studied by Tracy, reveal an even more dramatic rise in demands and debts. Only once in the period between 1546 and 1551 did they consent to give the sovereign more than 100,000 fl as an ordinary subsidy. In 1552 subsidies and issues of annuities amounted to 300,000 fl. The following year they were up to a staggering 550,000 fl.[39]

Inevitably the provincial states themselves resorted to novelties in order to cope with the unprecedented level of demand. In Hainaut for instance, they issued perpetual annuities for the first time to attract a different group of investors.[40] The worst affected by all this was the state debt itself. The impact of the Parma and Metz campaigns and the rebellion can be seen in Table 3 – debts catapulted from 1.3 million to 5.6 million florins. The annual deficit had risen to just over 3 million during 1553.

Although the situation was extremely grave, it would have been far worse if Mary of Hungary had not succeeded in seizing control of the financial machinery of the empire. From 1552 Mary negotiated a seemingly inexhaustible string of loans and freely assigned their repayment to other states, particularly Spain. Philip was quick to respond, complaining to his father against this unwarranted assault on the autonomy of the Spanish realms. The regent of one state had no power to commandeer the resources of another. Charles had no sympathy. He told Philip to comply with Mary's contracts.[41] Her success in raising huge loans for him during these years earned his gratitude and admiration. He came to see his sister's loans as the only barrier between himself and disaster; he was not much concerned with the political or financial implications for his states.

Whilst Mary had every reason to congratulate herself on having devised such an effective way to help Charles yet protect the lands she governed, she failed to cushion them completely from the effects of her brother's chronic indebtedness.

---

[37] Tracy, *A financial revolution*, p. 129.

[38] Hirschauer, *Artois*, vol. I, pp. 133, 137, 157, 237–9. The total of these demands was 360,000 fl, but only 230,000 fl were granted.

[39] Tracy, 'The taxation system', Table on p. 108.

[40] M. A. Arnauld, 'Les rentes d'état en Hainaut au 16e et 17e siècle', *Annales du Cercle Archaeologique du canton de Soigniers*, VIII (1942), pp. 169–70.   [41] AGS E. 90 fol. 87.

Many of the loans she negotiated and assigned to Spain had to be given additional security on Netherlands revenues. When the burden of debt proved too great for the Spanish realms and they failed to meet the conditions negotiated, some of the creditors called in their collateral. There was panic at the beginning of 1554 when Philip seized money assigned for repayment of loans to the Schetz banking firm. Mary had pressed several provincial states to give security and the Schetz looked set to ask for it. She assured Philip that the provincial states could not afford to pay these sums. Indeed, if they were asked they might stop lending themselves for this vital service to the crown and the system that had enabled them to raise such large sums would collapse. In the course of the dispute Mary unwittingly revealed that these loans had been raised to cover defence expenditure in the Netherlands. Of course at a time of war such expenses could be said to have formed part of the general war budget and therefore a legitimate charge on the emperor's other realms. But that was hard for the Spanish government to accept. After all, they were also under attack, continuously, from Islamic enemies as well as the French, yet they could not afford to provide adequate defences because so much of their money was being taken northwards. It was easy to conclude that the Netherlands were now drawing upon Spanish resources to cover basic expenditure which they should have met from their own funds.[42]

The incident illustrates the growing interdependence of the two areas. In the short-term, shifting part of the financial burden from the Netherlands to Spain was beneficial to the former. But it created a dangerous situation for the future. The survival of the northern states came to depend ever more closely on Spain, and the Spaniards were to exploit this in order to dominate the empire. However, it would not do to anticipate this trend. For most of this decade the Netherlands managed to avert catastrophe by pushing an ever growing burden of debt upon the Spanish realms.

Spanish finances

For the sake of accuracy, this section should be entitled Castilian finances, since the Aragonese realms were so protected by their privileges that they were able to resist tax demands. They voted just enough money to cover basic expenditure. Castile had its privileges and representative assembly (the cortes) whose main function was to determine the level of taxation. The eighteen towns which sent representatives could be awed and bribed by the crown. But they were often able to resist royal demands. It is seldom appreciated that much of the additional finance found in Castile during the 1550s did not come from ordinary and extraordinary taxation granted by the cortes, but from expedients outside their control. These included the mines, bullion shipments from the New World, and the alienation of royal demesne and the lands of the military orders.

[42] AGS E. 808 fols. 108, 110, 114.

The financial situation in 1551 had given cause for concern, both in Augsburg and locally. Philip had been in power scarcely three months before Ruy Gómez told Eraso that Spain could not fund the Parma war as Charles had hoped. 'There is no money here, nor do we have the means with which to acquire it', he wrote.[43] Somehow they did. Although it is impossible to give more than an impressionistic picture of their total contributions, Table 4, (p. 62) shows the frequent dispatch of substantial subsidies for the Italian front, for Germany and the Netherlands. Spanish subsidies were crucial to the emperor at the siege of Metz; without them he would have been unable to mount the attack.[44] Tables 5 and 7 also illustrate how the Castilian government responded to the crisis, increasing the amount of revenues mortgaged in advance for management of the debt by an alarming rate.

As in the Netherlands, the manipulation of government bonds became a vital tool, although the systems differed greatly. Initially Spanish monarchs had issued annuities (*juros*) as grants and rewards, usually in perpetuity and therefore heritable, or for the lifetime of the individual (*juros perpetuos, juros de por vida*, respectively). They were assignations on sound sources of revenue. Gradually they came to be sold in order to anticipate revenue; these bonds were redeemable (*juros al quitar*) and usually short-term. The buyer received a fixed interest until the crown repaid the capital. As pressure mounted, annuities were also issued to secure loans; in the 1550s they were also used as collateral, with dire consequences. Hence the alarming extension of mortgaged or alienated revenues. All might still have been well if the crown had retained control of the market in government bonds; but gradually it lost ground to the financiers. As the need for credit intensified, the government was forced to allow merchant bankers to deal in government bonds. In one instance, during March 1553, the regent had to suspend the sale of government annuities until the merchant bankers had sold theirs. There was a danger of the market being flooded and the financiers demanded priority because they needed to recover their capital quickly. Initially, when bonds were offered as security, the revenues designated would remain in the hands of the government, held in reserve and only handed over to the merchant bankers if the crown failed to meet its obligations. Later the bankers would demand that they be given control of these too until they secured the right to take up the revenues and deal in them. They undertook to pay the government the interest due on these bonds, and return them or others of equal value when their debt had been settled.[45]

---

[43] AGS E. 89 fol. 127.
[44] Finot, 'Le siège de Metz', pp. 266–8. Note that a large proportion of the cost was also met (ironically) with the last payments of the ransom which Francis I had to give in order to secure the return of his sons after he had broken the conditions of the treaty of Madrid.
[45] AGS E. 90 fol. 1; E. 97 fols. 53–63. A brief introduction to the many-sided *juro* can be found in A. Castillo Pintado, 'Los juros de Castilla. Apogeo y fin de un instrumento de crédito', *Hispania*, 89 (1963), pp. 43–70, and in the works cited in note 51.

Table 4. *Loans negotiated abroad for payment in Spain and direct subsidies*

1 *Milan, 1550–55*[A]	
1551	267,000 es
1552	745,000 es
1553	418,000 es
1554	420,000 es
1555	800,000 es
2 *Genoa and other Italian markets*[B]	
July 1551–October 1552	2,237,280 ds
	[plus 240,000 ds sent]
3 *The Netherlands*	
30 August 1551–1 January 1553[C]	790,664 ds ⎫
by March 1552[D]	800,000 ds ⎬ *c.* 800,000 ds
	⎭

Direct subsidies from Spain	
early 1552[E]	200,000 ds
1 September 1552[E]	500,000 ds
January – 30 August 1553[G]	sent or assigned 4,000,000 ds
End 1553[H]	400,000 ds
February 1554[I]	600,000 ds?

By September 1554[J] it was estimated that Spain had provided
c. 11,000,000 ds in loans and subsidies since 1551

[A] Chabod, *Lo stato*, pp. 132–3. See also Table 7 for 1555.
[B] AGS E 98 fol. 94, note these figures differ from those of Carande, *Carlos V y sus banqueros*, III, pp. 472–9.
[C] AGS E 93 fol. 95 (13 March 1553), this figure did not include interest.
[D] AGS E 90 fols. 7–8 (24 March 1552).
[E] AGS E 84 fols. 143–6.
[F] Fernández Alvarez, *Corpus*, III, pp. 471–2.
[G] AGS E 98 fol. 263, note Carande, *Carlos V y sus banqueros*, III, gives 1,052, 188 ds for January–September 1553, and 2,340,033 for the whole year.
[H] AGS E 98 fol. 352. This was the money raised to avoid the suspension of payments.
[I] Philip ordered 600,000 ds to be taken from the Indies fleet for his journey; Charles had demanded 1,000,000 ds. Note that Philip spent 221,519 ds on his preparations for the journey. AGS E 103(2) fol. 92, E 103 fol. 369.
[J] AGS E 103 fol. 369.

The Genoese merchant bankers were the most skilful manipulators of government bonds. They appreciated that here, as in other areas, there was an almost insatiable demand for annuities, particularly those bearing annual interest rates of 10 per cent or 7.14 per cent. As the crown's credit faltered in Castile, investors were deterred from buying government bonds. This, as much as the power of the financiers, forced the crown to let control slip from its grasp, since many people preferred to buy their bonds from a banking house that could offer guarantees of regular interest payments. The Castilian government had one great advantage initially over its counterpart in the Netherlands – it had regular sources of taxation, fixed for long periods of time. The preference for these may be illustrated with a contract dating from the early part of 1552. Payment was assigned partly to the *subsidio* of 1553, and on a shipment of bullion expected soon from Peru. Despite the fact that the *subsidio* – the most important ecclesiastical subsidy, usually granted for three years – had not yet been confirmed for 1553, the banker did not request additional security, but the bullion shipment had to be backed by government bonds of 7.14 per cent and 12.5 per cent.[46] This is ironic; bullion shipments soon became the most coveted form of repayment, although they continued to be considered risky assignations and needed to be backed with additional collateral, usually on regular taxation.

In a major policy review held by Charles and his counsellors during February 1552, it was accepted that the Spanish realms were as exhausted financially as the others. But Spain had access to bullion, and specie was what the financial world wanted most; therefore they concluded that Spain must take on additional burdens and debts.[47] Sound coinage, efficient management of financial fairs and the smooth running of commerce all required large quantities of bullion in circulation. Consequently all governments had legislation strictly circumscribing the export of specie. Mary of Hungary, aware that access to the bullion shipments from the New World was the most attractive offer she could make to international bankers, persuaded Charles to lift the strict controls on the export of specie out of Spain. By March 1553 they had issued export licences to the value of 1.9 million ducats, a staggering sum. Philip was quite convinced that the Castilian economy would collapse, particularly as Mary allowed the most powerful banking houses to organise the shipments of their bullion from any Spanish port, thus evading all government supervision. Naturally, they were tempted to abuse the privilege, buy up all the specie they could and sell it at a premium in foreign markets. The effect of this would be to increase the amount of credit available to enemy as well as friendly princes.[48]

Despite these cogent arguments, Mary continued to give licences. When

---

[46] AGS E. 90 fol. 1; E. 97 fols. 53–63.   [47] AGS E. 89 fol. 276.
[48] AGS E. 98 fols. 88–93; E. 89 fol. 276; E. 92 fol. 185; examples of loans with licence clauses can be examined in E. 90 fol. 87, E. 98 fol. 59.

Table 5. *The financial situation in Castile, 1551–4*

Year	Ordinary revenues	Extraordinary expedients	Revenues/Money available	Revenues/Money needed	Mortgaged revenues	Expenditure	Annual deficit	Total debt
1551[A]			611,000 ds in hand			1.4 million ds ordinary	1 million ds	
1552[B]		Forced loan 272,760 ds	none from 1552		all 1552, 1553, 1554 and part 1555			3,135,000 ds [3,162,943 ds]
March 1553[C]				4,810,443	all Indies revenue until 1557 and 'many others', 1,647,500 ds			
September 1553[D]			none	900,000 ds	most of 1554, 1555 and 1557	4 million ds assigned/sent for war during January–August 1553. 300,000 interest rates for loans		
May 1554[E]			1.1 million ds	4.5 million ds			3.3 million ds	

September 1554[F] 2.9 million

ordinary 2.8 million ds

Dec. 1554[G] to cover ordinary expenditure 888,000   up to and including 1560   4,329,435 ds

1554–60[H] 2,860,318 ds   7.9 million ds   4.4 million assigned   2.5 million not assigned

[A] AGS E 90 fol. 7–8; E 84 fol. 352; E 84 fol. 353.
[B] AGS E 89 fols. 52–6; AGS E 90 fols. 7–8.
[C] AGS E 98 fols. 88–93; E 98 fol. 98, fol. 99.
[D] AGS E 98 fol. 263.
[E] AGS E 103(2) fol. 104.
[F] AGS E 103 fol. 35; E 103(2) fol. 362.
[G] AGS E 103(2) fol. 362, fol. 365; E 103 fol. 399; Laiglesia, *Estudios*, II, pp. 130–1.
[H] AGS E 103(2) fol. 362, fol. 365; E 103 fol. 399.

pressure from Philip increased and the Spanish government showed signs of refusing to honour the licences, she allowed compensation clauses to be introduced into the contracts. For example, on a loan for 600,000 ds with export licences to cover the whole amount – some contracts allowed for the value of capital and interest – it was stipulated that if the Spanish officials did not comply with the condition they would have to pay 60,000 ds compensation. The Castilian officials were so bitterly opposed to the licences they advised Philip to pay the enormous penalty.[49] These concessions had two major repercussions: first, they increased the hostility between the regency governments in Spain and the Netherlands; second, they created a vicious circle. The emperor was consuming so much money that he encouraged both Mary and Philip to procure it. But he failed to appreciate that the two regents were negating each other's efforts. Mary was supplying him by negotiating loans assigned for payment on Spain; these were dependent on export licences. Philip was trying to supply his father with direct subsidies, and he could not collect enough money if the merchant bankers exported it. Already by the autumn of 1552 the shortage of specie in the Spanish realms was making it difficult for the regency government to meet its obligations in the financial fairs. Philip and the council of finance had to consider the possibility of delaying the October fair that year; the arrival of new contracts from Brussels which committed them to pay a further 770,000 ds convinced them that there was no other option.[50] As this incident shows, the problems of finding money were greatly magnified by the lack of control of borrowing in the Netherlands and other markets. No government could adequately cope with unexpected demands for immediate payment of what amounted to a quarter of the annual revenue.

But what of the financiers? How did they manage to survive the crown's repeated failure to meet its debts? Whilst a detailed study of the gains and losses of the merchant bankers cannot be offered here, it is important to establish a rough notion of how much they were able to secure from the impecunious emperor, otherwise their seemingly inexhaustible ability to provide credit will remain beyond comprehension.[51] The first point to note is that the financiers traded both with their own capital and with monies invested with them. They could also raise loans on the financial markets and fairs at a fraction of the cost at which they lent to the crown. On average they paid 4–12 per cent on loans, and the higher figures were very unusual. Between the late summer and autumn of 1552, interest rates paid by the

[49] AGS E. 92 fol. 185.   [50] AGS E. 92 fol. 187; E. 90 fol. 146.

[51] There have been some important studies of individual banking houses which enable the reader to trace the impact of Habsburg financial irregularities on them; Ehrenberg's study of *The Fuggers* is still excellent value; more recently, H. Lapeyre has taken the Ruiz, albeit for a slightly later period – *Simon Ruiz et les 'asientos' de Philippe II* (Paris, 1953); and *Une famille de marchands: les Ruiz* (Paris, 1955); V. Vázquez Prada, *Lettres marchandes d'Anvers* (4 vols., vol. 1, Paris, 1960) will also furnish much information about the complexity and wide-ranging affairs of the international merchant bankers.

emperor for loans raised in Spain increased from 9 per cent – an unusually low rate which again points to relative financial stability preceding this period of uncontrolled borrowing – to 31 per cent.[52] In 1554 the regency government reckoned that the average rate was 43 per cent basic and 14 per cent additional to cover delays and prolongation of loan payments. By the end of that year they automatically assumed that a loan would cost twice the capital since they could not keep up with payments and always became liable for the penalty clauses.[53] I have come across examples which exceed this figure, including a loan that cost the government 260 per cent.[54] Further research is likely to demonstrate that this was by no means unique, and may have become the norm during these years.

Apart from basic interest and additional charges for delayed payments, there was hidden interest. It was usual for contracts to incorporate fictitious exchange rates. The most frequent device was to contract the loan in escudos of 350 mvs and demand payment in ducats of 375 mvs; almost as frequent was the practice of paying the crown in escudos of 350 mvs and receiving payment for the same amount but valuing the escudo at 400 mvs. Skilful financiers made some 7 per cent extra by the manipulation of currency and by choosing the right financial fairs for payments. Playing the exchange could be extremely profitable, as was the sale of bullion in markets which – as often happened – were short of it. All this is apart from the brokerage fees that they could charge for their services. These multiple sources of profit must therefore be taken into account, even when they cannot be properly quantified. What we can estimate with some degree of accuracy is how much of the capital and basic interest was repaid and how quickly, although this task does become impossible as the crown continued to default. Table 6 is intended as a rough indication of what the merchant bankers obtained within two years of making the original loan in this first part of the financial crisis. It can be seen that between 34 per cent and 40 per cent of the capital contracted was paid back. It was extremely rare for financiers to disburse the whole sum in one block payment; most contracts specified payment in financial fairs over a period of several years. In other words, although the financial community experienced problems before 1554 as the crown proved unable to cope with the sudden and massive burden of debt, the merchant bankers were able to maintain liquidity, receiving a large part of their investment back from the Spanish government, and they were making vast profits to boot. Later the situation would be more difficult, but the potential for profit was still very considerable.

[52] AGS E. 89 fol. 87. They had not been as low as that for some time, as Carande, *Carlos V y sus banqueros*, vol. 3, pp. 17–20, has demonstrated. Average interest rates in Spanish markets for the period 1520–42 were 18 per cent; 1543–1551 28 per cent, 1552–56 just over 33 per cent. The Genoese charged the highest interest of all other groups, p. 21.

[53] AGS E. 103 fol. 399; and Juana's interesting letter to Charles, 20 December 1554, published by Laiglesia, *Estudios*, vol II, pp. 161–4.

[54] AGS E. 108 fol. 380, loan negotiated in Genoa for 339,000 assigned to Spanish revenues; total repaid 898,000.

Table 6. *Repayment of loans in Spain 1551–4*
(*in ducats*)

Year	Loans	Year	Repayment
1551[a]	1,476,195	1552–4	697,664
[1552[b]	1,769,671]	1552–4	830,997
[1552[c]	2,975,957]		
1552[d]	3,036,772		
1553[e]	2,975,957	1552–4	2,813,404 (may include part of sum above, or all)
1554[f]	2,101,689		

[a] Debts: Carande, *Carlos V y sus banqueros*, III, pp. 335–9. repayments: AGS E 103 (2) fol. 371, 372, 373.
[b] Three sets of figures for amounts borrowed in 1552: AGS E 103 fol. 379.
[c] AGS E 103 fol. 376.
[d] AGS E 103 fol. 377 includes some interest and is the figure used in other documents.
[e] AGS E 103 fol. 369 (23 September 1554); AGS E 103 fol. 376.
[f] AGS E 103 fol. 374; AGS E 103 fol. 369.

Serious problems emerged when the Spanish regency government refused to honour export licences, which it did with increasing frequency from 1552. This meant that ever increasing amounts of capital were retained, if not frozen, in the Spanish realms. This left the financiers little choice other than to continue lending to the Habsburgs and concentrate more of their financial dealings in Spain. Such problems were compounded by the frequent confiscations of bullion which occurred during these years. Charles had helped himself to money arriving in the New World fleets before. It was easy enough to do this since by law all precious metals and stones had to be unloaded in Seville, where they were weighed, inspected and stored in the Casa de la Contratación. Royal officials then checked that all duties were paid on these imports. The crown's share of these riches, one fifth of New World profits, would also be stored here, where it could be collected by those assigned payments of gifts or loans.[55] When the monarch ordered an *embargo* in Seville, that is the confiscation of New World shipments, it usually entailed two things: first, a partial suspension of payments. Assignments due on the crown's

[55] P. and H. Chaunu, *Séville et l'Atlantique de 1504 à 1650* (12 vols., Paris, 1955–60), vol. 1, pp. 70–124, details of registration procedures as well as the more frequent fraudulent practices.

share would be renegotiated and this money was taken by royal officials. Second, it entailed the seizure of money belonging to others, who were compensated with government bonds.

The confiscations had aroused a storm of protest in the past and Charles had promised to avoid them in the future. Since they play such a large part in the financing of the crown's policies in this decade, and have a crucial role in the process of alienation of the Spanish people from their monarchs, it is worth analysing who suffered as a result of these confiscations. My examples are taken from the 1557 *embargo* which is well documented.[56] The sums which ostensibly belonged to the crown were normally oversubscribed, and would include a plethora of officials and individuals expecting to receive gifts, pensions, and payments; merchant bankers would also be affected. Another easily defined category were the 'goods of the dead', *difuntos*, deceased, was how they were known. These were sums or goods sent to heirs and beneficiaries of those who died in the New World. Often they were small, for example, 98 ds for Lázaro Nuñez, 32 ds for Juan de Herrera. Large and miniscule amounts for widows, orphans and charitable institutions formed the bulk of these monies. Those expecting very large shipments, even from inheritance, might find themselves categorised as *particulares*, individual fortunes. This was a loosely defined group which included investors in New World trade, merchants, people returning with fortunes, etc.; among those affected in 1557 we find major courtiers like don Diego de Acevedo, treasurer-general of Aragon, steward of Philip's household; don Diego de Córdoba, and *licenciado* Birbiesca, two other high-ranking officials in his household, were affected as well as those of the regency government, such as Juan Martín de Zarate and Luis de Hortiz. Military commanders, for example, Gonzalo Hernández de Rojas, also lost large sums. Nor were the highest aristocrats spared: Cobos's son-in-law, the marquis of Camarasa, the marquis del Valle and Philip's eldest sister María were among those affected, alongside monastic foundations and other institutions. As for the mercantile community, there was an attempt to divide them into categories so as to ensure that the government did not kill the goose that laid the golden eggs. They might be put under *particulares*, but mostly under *mercaderes*, literally merchants or merchant bankers, and *mercaderes caudalosos*, wealthy merchants. Often the essence of this distinction was between merchants involved primarily in the New World trade and those merchant bankers who had lent the crown large sums and expected payments.

Morally it was impossible to justify seizing money from the *difunto* group since it tampered with the semi-sacrosanct laws of inheritance and affected the most defenceless groups in society, whom the crown had a special duty to protect. Realistically this group was the most vulnerable because it was least powerful so its funds were repeatedly plundered by the crown. Whilst it was hardly wise to deprive nobles and royal officials of their money given the discontent it created at the centre

[56] AGS E. 98 fols. 3, 4, 6–7, 9, 10.

of government, both Charles and Philip tended to trust that the engrained patterns of loyalty would counterbalance resentment. They constantly dipped into these funds too, despite the deleterious effects for monarchical authority. The merchants trading with the Indies got the most sympathy since it was accepted that the trade functioned on a system of credit. If goods or money sent back to Spain were seized, the merchant was either deprived of the means to purchase his next shipment or else prevented from paying back the loans that had made the venture possible in the first place. These considerations were not so influential as to prevent the crown from taking their funds, largely because the group who had the largest share of the Indies shipments – and could have best endured the impact of the confiscations – was also the most powerful and least affected by them. These were the large international financiers who were the crown's chief creditors. Their complaints were far more effective than the cries of widows and orphans.

When he turned his mind to the Parma campaign, Charles could think of no better way to provide himself with ready money than by confiscating part of the New World shipments. Philip dutifully agreed, taking 200,000 ds from the money in the Casa de la Contratación. He was at once confronted by angry merchants facing bankruptcy as a result of his action.[57] He relayed their sorry tale to Charles, but if he expected sympathy and the revocation of the imperial order, he was disappointed. The emperor sent back an angry reproof because Philip had seized so little.[58] In the autumn of 1552 Charles ordered another round of confiscations which highlighted another drawback of this policy. The regency government had hoped to raise money for him by selling 150,000 ds of bonds to those returning with, or benefiting from, Indies monies. The confiscation effectively deprived them of their potential buyers. Would it not have been better to avoid the aggravation and coax these people to invest? After all, their compensation was also in government bonds; so the end result would be the alienation of royal revenues. The answer to this question was negative since those annuities sold bore interest of some 8–10 per cent and those offered in compensation were as low as 3–4 per cent. Nevertheless, the regency officials argued that the saving was not worth the deprivation, anger and distress of those affected, nor the heavy burden to the conscience of the monarch.[59]

In an effort to counter the criticism and opposition to New World confiscations, Charles became increasingly selective. Ordering another round of seizures for one million (ducats?) in December 1553, he tried to assuage Philip's tender conscience by allowing him to restrict the confiscation to the goods of 'wealthy merchants'. For good measure he also reminded his son of the duty to obey and supply the sovereign in this, his hour of need. Philip had been trying to dissuade his father from imposing any further confiscations; having failed, he tried to bring the policy into disrepute by being very selective indeed. He took the full sum from the shipments due to the

---

[57] AGS E. 84 fols. 143–6.   [58] AGS E. 84 fols. 334–6.
[59] AGS E. 99 fols. 80–3; E. 92 fol. 185, E. 109 fol. 240.

Schetz merchant bankers. Quite what the final figure was can only be guessed at: some documents mention 255,000 ds, others, 364,000 ds and in the Netherlands it was said that 600,000 ds of their assets had been seized. There is no doubt that the choice was deliberate. The Schetz were most closely associated with Mary of Hungary, along with the Welser bankers. By striking at them, Philip was undermining Mary's authority and reputation. She certainly took it as a personal insult. She stormed into Charles's rooms and demanded that he order Philip to return all the money. Few could have stood up to Mary in a rage, and Charles did not even try. He promised to do exactly as she asked and duly wrote to his son expounding her arguments and demands. But Charles too was afraid of what Philip might do next. He tended to bend rules for his favourite bankers, the Fugger, and suspected that Philip might remove the threat from one financier and transfer it to another, perhaps the Fugger. He therefore wrote a stringent warning that Fugger assets were not to be touched. Moreover, Philip was to apologise to both Mary and the Schetz and show his contrition by organising and paying the transport of this money to the Netherlands. The wily emperor then confessed that once it arrived there, he intended to confiscate it for himself anyway. Philip refused to cooperate.[60]

This incident neatly illustrates the different attitudes of these key personages towards Spanish finances. Charles was not concerned about the cost in human terms or to his conscience; he just wanted money for his campaigns. Mary was determined to secure money for him but only so long as she could avoid further charges on the Netherlands where, as Eraso aptly put it, no one cared if Spain sank or swam.[61] For his part, Philip was caught in a nasty trap. He needed to show that he was efficient and capable of governing and this meant that he had to raise the money required; but he also had a duty to protect the Spanish realms from the emperor's feckless and profligate policies. His letters became increasingly anguished, full of allusions to the suffering of Spain and exuding his conviction that the area was breaking under the strain. He begged his aunt and father to desist from this spoliation of Spain.[62]

In November 1553 Charles announced his conversion to Philip's viewpoint that the Spanish realms could not continue to fund the war. He proposed a radical, but simple solution: a partial suspension of payments. Philip was told to seize up to 400,000 ds from the next Indies shipment, presumably without offering compensation. Charles estimated that the major financial consortia were expecting a total of four and a half million ducats in that fleet – a staggering sum, and a startling reminder of the size of operations of these merchant bankers. By comparison, taking less than half a million seemed moderate. He wanted rough justice to be meted out.

---

[60] The incident can be pieced together from AGS E. 98 fol. 375; E. 103 fol. 74; E. 808 fols. 106, 110, 114; E. 508 fol. 88.

[61] AGS E. 90 fol. 146, letter to Juan Vázquez.

[62] Some examples, AGS E. 92 fol. 185 (November 1552), E. 98 fols. 88–93 and 99 (March 1553), E. 98 fol. 263 (September 1553).

The financiers who had charged him the highest interest were to be the hardest hit. The most faithful, who had lent in times of need (for this read the Fugger, perhaps the Schetz as well) were to be entirely spared.[63] Put in these terms, the first serious proposal for a suspension of payments sounds reasonable. But the Spanish officials rejected it vehemently. They argued that it would entirely break the emperor's credit. Apart from spelling the end of further loans and advances from the financiers, it would deprive the government of the transfer and exchange facilities on which they depended.[64] All subsequent proposals for a suspension of debt foundered on these fears that the multi-national empire could not marshal its resources effectively without the cooperation of the international financiers.

Philip endorsed their advice but was left with an intractable problem: how to supply his father, finance his departure for the Netherlands and cover Spanish expenditure. He had all but admitted defeat in September 1553 when he had assured Charles that there was no possibility of finding enough money to cover ordinary expenditure for the year, let alone fund a campaign.[65] His distress increased as he acknowledged that Charles and Mary had created exceedingly high expectations of his visit to the Netherlands. A number of leading nobles wrote to him begging for his return and his aid. Philip could not afford to arrive empty-handed – that would be worse than not going there at all.[66]

Trapped by the lack of assets and unable to provide the money demanded by Charles, Philip was vulnerable to his father's persistent arguments that a partial suspension of payments was the only way out of their dilemma. The emperor resorted to making veiled hints in order to procure Philip's cooperation. In a much corrected draft, he settled for such phrases as 'you can see for yourself why I wish to be rid of all these problems'. Eraso was left to enlarge upon these cryptic words: 'Your highness cannot imagine how deeply his majesty regrets the troubled state of affairs there, or the problems he faces here with his debts, that have prompted him to order the suspension'. The secretary added that Charles was now determined to go to Spain as Philip requested. More importantly, 'I believe one of the reasons why he wants to see this matter through successfully', Eraso added 'is because he wants to give up all state affairs'.[67] In the closing days of 1553 when this was written, Philip was motivated less by the obscure offers of future power than by his knowledge that Charles was near death and others were controlling the empire. He must leave for the Netherlands immediately and assert his authority – but where was the money to fund his journey and campaign? The situation was extremely bleak. In Brussels they could at least hope for a remedy; in Valladolid they believed none was available.

[63] AGS E. 90 fol. 132.   [64] AGS E. 98 fol. 352.   [65] AGS E. 98 fols. 263–5.
[66] AGS E. 506 fols. 104–5, letter from the count of Egmont; E. 506 fol. 113, from Adolf of Burgundy; E. 506 fol. 116, from the count of Hoorne. VDK, vol. 2, p. 607, for news of his impending arrival.
[67] AGS E. 90 fols. 147–8, dated 12 and 24 December 1553.

2

On the threshold of power, 1554–5

Depression, disease and death: these three words appear constantly in an account of these years, which mark the emperor's gradual withdrawal from power. It is hard to penetrate through the wall of silence which the court in Brussels created to minimise the impact of his protracted illness and breakdown. Both Mary of Hungary and Philip sought to take the power that Charles let slip from his grasp. This chapter traces their attempts and conflicts as well as the solution Philip found to cover the financial shortage – marriage. The prince's second marriage became a panacea. He saw it as a way to increase his power as well as his credit. Unfortunately for him, Mary also considered it an invaluable expedient and she dealt with it as with others, drawing up the conditions, leading the negotiations and expecting Philip to execute the decision. The struggle for power had now begun in earnest.

THE EMPEROR'S COLLAPSE

There is no doubt that Philip received regular information about Charles, his court, and the situation in the Netherlands. We know that he had made arrangements with Nicholas Nicolay, receiver general of Brabant and a councillor, to send him dispatches in cypher. By the end of 1552 if not before, Eraso was a regular informant too. He occasionally panicked in case he should be found out, but his letters were dealt with in the strictest secrecy by Philip, Ruy Gómez and Juan Vázquez, and they often merited the prince's handwritten replies.[1] Apart from the regular couriers, who were capable of giving an account of what was going on, there were letters from other individuals and extraordinary envoys; all of which added to the store of information available to Philip. It is highly likely, therefore, that he knew of his father's state of health long before the arrival of Francisco Duarte in Valladolid sometime in September 1553. The mission itself is proof that the court in Brussels was deliberately blocking such information; those who felt Philip should know what was afoot considered it necessary to send a secret envoy.

The report presented by Duarte is the most detailed account of Charles's

---

[1] For Nicolay, AGS E. 98 fols. 274–5; only a small portion of the correspondence between Philip and Eraso survives, some examples may be found in AGS E. 89 fol. 120; E. 89 fol. 122; E. 83 fols. 123–4; E. 100 fol. 175; E. 100 fol. 179.

condition to survive.[2] It explains why Mary was so frightened that if Charles led the next campaign as he intended, there would be a repetition of the débâcle at Metz, or worse. Moreover, her insistence on Philip's immediate departure makes a great deal of sense in the light of the details furnished by Duarte.[3] It would seem that Charles was crippled by gout, and beset by catarrh, constipation, and a host of other maladies. Throughout 1553 his health deteriorated steadily. At the beginning of that year, he had suffered from bad attacks of the gout and succumbed to deep depression. There was a temporary respite in April – at least from his physical problems. However, as his depression continued, Charles did not deal with state affairs during this time. Gout afflicted him again so severely during the following months that Charles was unable to use his right hand again until July 1553. By the summer, the emperor's doctors were fully convinced that he would not live much longer. As summer turned into autumn, he improved slightly, but the winter months brought new attacks and ailments. From October 1553 to January 1554, Charles was, by his own admission, once again incapable of attending to anything.[4]

Serious as the physical problems were, it was the mental breakdown which clearly accentuated and extended Charles's illness. His contemporaries invariably described him as phlegmatic and melancholic; he had suffered periods of depression in the past, but never as prolonged or as deep as this. According to Duarte, he was 'constantly sunk in thought, and often he will weep so hard and with such copious shedding of tears, he resembles a child'. When he was like this no one dared to go near him. Besides, as the Venetian ambassador, Damula, informed his government, the emperor would lock himself up in a small house outside the court and spend hours and hours on the balcony, thinking or meditating, sometimes with an astrolabe or a clock in his hand.[5] At times he was occupied reading and selecting for publication books of chivalry and psalms. The situation was grave; what made it dangerous was the combined effects of previous imperial neglect and present international difficulties. Looking briefly at his handling of Spanish affairs, it is evident that during much of 1551 and 1552 he dealt with little other than military or financial business, and that erratically. His excuse was that he was busy with the wars. Later he used his health problems to account for his lack of attention to the multiple problems of his realms; latterly, he had not even proffered an excuse but simply refused to tackle state matters.[6]

Few people were allowed to enter his rooms, and several were sent packing when

2   AGS E. 98 fols. 274–5.
3   AGS E. 808 fol. 108 for example, her letter of February 1554.
4   AGS E. 98 fol. 213; E. 508 fol. 10; E. 508 fol. 116; E. 90 fols. 146, 147–8. It is interesting to note that whilst he admitted to Maximilian in January 1554 that he had been bedridden and close to death for eight weeks, he would only admit to five when writing to Philip. Further details of his health in L. P. Gachard (ed.), *Retraite et mort de Charles Quint au monastère de Yuste* (3 vols., Introduction and vols. I and II, Brussels, 1854–5), Introduction, pp. 5–36.
5   Van Durme, *Granvela*, p. 152, note 21.
6   AGS E. 308 s.f., Charles to Philip, 18 September 1552; E. 100 fols. 171–2, id. July 1553.

they tried to persuade him to attend to important affairs or private requests. Aware that they would seek to draw his attention to these, Charles shunned his leading ministers. Granvelle was repeatedly denied an audience and his enemies were convinced that he had totally fallen from favour. His authority was severely dented by this, and by the public reproof he received from the emperor in one of the rare occasions he was allowed into his presence. Charles dismissed him with clear instructions that he was not to trouble him with matters of state, because he was too busy. Besides, he had no wish to see Granvelle again. Other old favourites suffered the impact of the emperor's mercurial moods. His chamberlain was forbidden to enter Charles's rooms for a week after he urged him to resolve a pressing issue. He was lucky: Mary's leading adviser, the councillor Praet, was told to leave court altogether after making a similar attempt.[7] Only two people still had some influence on the petulant emperor – Mary and Eraso. Eraso lacked the status and patronage network that would have allowed him to exploit the situation; Mary had both and she filled the vacuum of power created by the emperor's withdrawal. She gave audiences to ambassadors, decided what business should be transacted, implemented decisions taken in council – often without consulting Charles. 'The queen does practically everything', Damula commented in May 1553.[8] This was the case for much of 1553 and the early part of 1554. There were few instances when Charles could be roused into action – his intervention on the issue of the Schetz confiscations, for example (p. 71) – but these moments were rare. Not until the spring of 1554 and the opening of the new campaign did he play a more regular role in state affairs. Documents continued to bear his name or stamp, and to all intents and purposes, he was still in command. It is scarcely surprising, however, that Philip should have held his aunt and her advisers responsible for the unpalatable decisions emanating from Brussels, or that he should have been so anxious to go there and seize the reins of government.

Every attempt was made to keep the emperor's condition secret, hoping to minimise the damage of such disclosures. Enough details leaked out to create further instability and uncertainty. Within the Netherlands, the challenge to royal authority was intensified. Already in 1552 Charles had admitted that 'obedience was lacking'.[9] In the aftermath of two disastrous campaigns some Netherlanders were so demoralised they had openly debated what terms of surrender to offer the French in order to avoid further attacks. There were alarming reports that many were considering making a public request for Maximilian's protection. Rebellion was brewing, and neither Mary nor Charles believed that they were capable of coping with it. Within the Italian realms, discontent about the emperor's persistent neglect of their affairs and concern over rumours of his ill-health led to calls for Philip to

---

[7] These incidents were recounted by the well-informed Venetian, Damula, to the Doge, *VDK* vol. 2 p. 617, (9 July 1553); pp. 606–7 (19 May). Duarte reinforces the point that Charles 'abhors all general and particular affairs of all his states', AGS E. 98 fols. 274–5.

[8] *VDK*, vol. 2, p. 606.   [9] AGS E. 98 fols. 136–40.

take over. When he realised what the commanders in Italy were doing, Charles's secretary for Italian affairs immediately wrote to Philip disparaging these appeals and emphasising that they needed him in the Netherlands far more urgently than in Italy.[10] Naturally, the Spaniards were anxious to persuade him to remain with them.

Philip had not been idle during this period. Like Mary he had taken advantage of his father's illness to increase his power. Charles had foreseen the challenge and circumscribed his son with numerous legal restrictions – more than in his previous regencies. Almost at once the two men had come into conflict as a result of the prince's eagerness to exercise power. Soon after Philip arrived, fifteen Spanish vessels were seized by the French off the coast of Italy and further attacks were reported on shipping near Barcelona. Pressed by counsellors in Castile and Aragon, Philip ordered immediate retaliation, seized French vessels and goods in Spain and declared war against France. Unaware of this, Charles had issued a separate order for the seizure of French vessels which arrived weeks afterwards. He was not sorry that it had been anticipated, but he was angry about the declaration of war and repudiated Philip's action.[11] The quarrel continued over the issue of Spanish trade with France. Charles repeatedly ordered all trade to cease; Philip refused to implement this on the grounds that Spain desperately needed certain French commodities. Much ink was spilt on this row over the next two years. The voluminous correspondence does suggest that the issue came to matter less than the mere fact that Philip was challenging Charles on a matter related to the war.[12]

Philip proved even more decisive on matters that related to his inheritance. Charles had entrusted the negotiations with Henry d'Albret to his son, and the latter had dutifully kept his father informed of the most minute details of these talks. But when Albret attempted to take advantage of Charles's weakness and demanded the return of Navarre in exchange for defecting and providing military aid, Philip rejected the proposal outright and almost terminated the negotiations. He did not consult Charles because he feared his father might accept these terms, both out of desperation for support and because he had always been uneasy about Castilian rights to Navarre. Although he was not pleased with his son's action, Charles did not try to force the issue, merely pressing him to continue the talks.[13]

Taking control of Spain's internal affairs was less likely to cause tension (since Charles was not very interested in them) than intervention in foreign matters. But the lack of patronage hampered Philip, and this limitation was only partially solved

[10] AGS E. 508 fol. 12.
[11] AGS E. 84 fols. 183, 389, 351, 185–6, 334–6 and E. 90 fols. 44–59.
[12] AGS E. 84 fols. 334–6, 194–7, 182, 185; E. 89 fols. 36–40; AGS E. 90 fols. 44–59, 109–12; AGS E. 92 fols. 118–20; AGS E. 98 fols. 52–5; AGS E. 308 s.f. (8 September 1552).
[13] AGS E.K. 1485 fol. 55; AGS E. 84 fols. 194–7, 185–6, 348–50; AGS E. 90 fols. 67–70; AGS E. 97 fol. 79.

after he secured Eraso's services.[14] It was not enough to place his men in positions of power, he had to ensure that they acknowledged his intervention. Furthermore, the prospect of Charles's death, or extended incapacity, made it imperative for Philip to secure full control over the regency government before he left Spain. The problem of the new regency appeared to be as intractable as that of securing funds for the war. Yet, as Philip realised in 1553, both could be solved at one stroke.

THE PORTUGUESE MATCH

Philip decided to marry his cousin Maria of Portugal at the beginning of 1553.[15] She was widely regarded as an independent, intelligent woman, a great patron of the arts. Far more important for Philip was the fact that she could offer a very substantial dowry. Her parents had endowed her with 400,000 ds; her half-brother, João III, promised a further 200,000 ds if a suitable husband was found; and on the death of her mother, Leonor, she would receive the lands and revenues that belonged to her as dowager queen of France.[16] Although Maria had no political experience, Philip intended to leave her as regent of Spain, supported by a powerful advisory group. He did not reveal his intentions until the matter was well advanced and an open secret in both Portugal and Spain. Aware of the need to keep up appearances, however, both Philip and Charles made it appear as if he had dutifully left the choice of his next bride to Charles.[17]

There was one major impediment to the match – Philip was unsure whether or not he was bound by the terms of the family compact of March 1551, to marry one of Ferdinand's daughters. Since he was most anxious that the treaty should remain in force, and he knew that if he reneged on any one clause he would invalidate the

---

[14] Eraso was instrumental in putting forward his recommendations for key posts. AGS E. 98 fols. 329–39, 371–2; AGS E. 103(2) fols. 335–6.

[15] King Manoel of Portugal (1469–1521) had married three times, his second wife was doña María, daughter of Isabel and Ferdinand. Of their nine children, two concern use here: João and Isabel. Isabel married Charles V, and was Philip's mother. João III married Charles V's youngest sister, Catalina; their daughter, Maria, married Philip in 1545, but died in childbirth three years later. Documents relating to her married life and death, Fernández Alvarez, *Corpus*, vol. 2, pp. 176–9, 396, 400–1, 408–9. Despite the vast difference in age, Charles forced his sister Leonor to marry the ageing Manoel. The sole surviving child of this marriage was the Maria whom Philip now wanted to take as his second wife. J. Veríssimo Serrão, *História de Portugal*, vol. III *O século de ouro 1495–1580* (Lisbon, 1978), pp. 421–4 for a good, brief guide to the complex genealogy of the prolific Portuguese royal family.

[16] AGS E. 98 fol. 157; E. 376 fol. 89; E. 98 fols. 136–40. Leonor had later married Francis I.

[17] AGS E. 98 fols. 171, fols. 136–40; AGS E. 376 fol. 6. Charles insisted on taking the credit for the choice – AGS E. 376 fol. 89. Even in the private letter he wrote to his son expressing his satisfaction at Philip's choice, he insisted that the draft be altered so that instead of reading: 'I cannot but agree with your decision', it was changed to: 'I cannot but agree to this'. The following account of the negotiations has been taken from the correspondence in AGS E. 98 fols. 136–40, 174, 179–80, 201–3, 226–7; AGS E. 376 fols. 6, 17, 22, 39 (1), 39 (2), 42; AGS E. 100 fol. 170.

rest of the treaty, he consulted with Charles and Mary in Brussels.[18] They advised him to ask for the hand of one of Ferdinand's daughters, demand that the marriage take place immediately, and that the ceremony should be accompanied by the publication of the family compact. Ferdinand was involved in the complex and delicate negotiations that led to the famous Augsburg interim of 1555. If the German princes with whom he was negotiating were to hear the conditions to which he had agreed, it would spell the end of the talks, as they all well knew. The complaints about Habsburg plans to make the empire hereditary would resurface and Ferdinand's credibility would be destroyed.[19] There was no doubt that he would agree to rescind this clause. There is no proof that Philip put this into practice, but no more was heard of the matter and Ferdinand later acknowledged the treaty as valid.

It looked as if the Portuguese match would be quickly concluded, but Philip had not counted on opposition from Brussels. He was ordered to hand over the negotiations to Leonor, ostensibly because the Portuguese would be more generous to the girl's mother than to her prospective husband. A further advantage of using her was that it provided a face-saving device if the proposal met with rejection: Charles and Philip could claim that she had advanced it without their permission. In fact this was a bid for control made by Mary and, perhaps, Charles. Leonor was weak, ineffectual, subservient to Charles and always manipulated by Mary. And the reason why the Brussels government was so anxious to negotiate reflected their awareness that their priorities and Philip's aims did not coincide. Philip wanted the dowry to fund his journey and campaign; he wanted Maria to remain in Spain as head of the regency government. Charles and Mary wanted immediate control of the money and were adamant that Maria must go to the Netherlands with Philip. In 1548, when Charles finally decided that his son would inherit the Low Countries, he stipulated that they must in turn be given to Philip's second child and separated from the Trastámara inheritance. The obsession with providing a 'natural sovereign' for the Netherlands made it imperative for them to have Maria in the area, to give birth to the future ruler of the Netherlands. What they would not admit was their anxiety over the Spanish government. If Maria remained in Spain, she would be subject to Philip's authority, not their own. Philip was told that the dangerous state of the Netherlands required him to give them priority over all other areas; he must sacrifice all other interests.[20]

---

[18] The ambiguity in the treaty was compounded by the fact that Philip was using the Castilian translation rather than the French original. If we compare the French (AGS PR. 57 fol. 121 (1)) 'il traictera mariage et prendra a femme l'une des filles audict sr. Roy' with the Castilian, (AGS E. 649 fol. 181), 'se encaminara entonces el trattado y co[n]sumara el matrimonio', we can see that whilst the first suggests that Philip would not need to set in motion negotiations for the marriage until after becoming king of the Romans, the second assumes that the marriage had been arranged and must be consummated now, if it had not been consummated already.

[19] AGS E. 98 fols. 136–40.

[20] AGS E. 98 fols. 136–40, and Charles's instructions to Philip in 1548 DP, pp. 347–8.

There was no chance of Philip relinquishing control of the marriage negotiations now. He responded to this initiative by dispatching Ruy Gómez to Lisbon with full powers to conclude the match.

João III was no fool and he eagerly sought to capitalise on these divisions and Philip's evident haste to conclude the match. He now offered Maria with only her basic dowry, and as dissent among the Habsburgs continued, he insisted that they should deduct the 180,000 ds Charles still owed for Juana's dowry. Ruy Gómez successfully brought the dowry back up to 400,000 ds, but he could not repair the damage that had been done. Philip admitted defeat; without informing his father, he decided that he would marry Maria anyway. On 8 August 1553, he wrote to the Spanish ambassador in Lisbon telling him to make one last attempt to increase the dowry. Even if this failed, the match was to be concluded immediately. The letter was signed and the courier set to depart; at the last minute, he was recalled and the letter was never sent.[21] Philip had just been informed that another bride was in the offing, infinitely more prestigious – Mary Tudor, queen of England. João was so confident that the match had been arranged, he asked when Maria should depart. In the event, she never did. Philip was deeply embarrassed at the timing of it all, but he nevertheless showed few scruples in ditching Maria, who was already being addressed as princess of Spain.

In order to avoid a full diplomatic rupture with Portugal and to hide the fact that he had come so close to concluding the match, Philip announced that he was suspending the negotiations temporarily, whilst he consulted with Charles over the dowry. He then left a gap of ten days before writing to his father, thanking him for the news about Mary. In this letter he expressed his joy and commented on the excellent timing – just when he had decided to break off the Portuguese negotiations![22] Prudent and devious to the last, Philip did not abandon the Portuguese match until December 1553 when it looked certain that the English marriage would be concluded. The Portuguese monarchs were incensed; insults and recriminations flowed as both sides blamed the other for the failure of the match. As Ruy Gómez put it, instead of nurturing peace and unity, the match had 'bred toads and vipers'.[23]

THE ENGLISH MATCH

As soon as Edward VI's fatal illness was known in the courts of Europe, there had been lively discussions about the succession. Henry VIII's matrimonial affairs had

[21] AGS E. 376 fol. 213. It bears a note in Juan Vázquez's hand explaining this. See note 17 for full references to the various moves in the negotiations.
[22] This letter has long been available in translation, CSP Sp. vol. XI, pp. 177–8, and taken at its face value, thus missing the point about Philip's deception.
[23] AGS E. 376 fols. 39(1) and 39(2), 88, 89, 151, 187; E. Pacheco y de Leyva, 'Grave error político de Carlos I haciendo la boda de Felipe II con doña María, reina de Inglaterra', *Revista de Archivos, Bibliotecas y Museos*, XLII (1921), pp. 59–84, 276–92; see p. 286–9.

left behind a hideous legal tangle. Although Mary Tudor was the eldest surviving child, she had been declared illegitimate after his divorce from Catherine, so her right to the throne was not indisputable, even if widely recognised as valid. Mary was Charles's cousin and had twice been betrothed to him; it was understandable, therefore, that he should help her acquire the throne, protect and advise her, perhaps even choose a suitable husband for her. Mary was politically inexperienced and in need of such support. For these same reasons, Henry II was opposed to her accession. When the duke of Northumberland requested his support in a bid to keep Mary out, he readily agreed. It mattered little that French aid would be used to place a Protestant candidate on the English throne. Henry needed another ally against the emperor, whatever the price. Imperial advisers saw a deeper meaning behind Henry's aid to the rebels. Mary Stuart, queen of Scots, had a powerful claim to the English throne, far superior to that of Northumberland's protégée, Lady Jane Grey. Mary's legitimacy, paternity and Catholicism were beyond question, and her engagement to the dauphin Francis would one day bind France and Scotland into one state. The imperialists feared that once in England, Henry would use his soldiers and the Scottish forces in order to establish Mary Stuart's claim to the throne. If the French ever succeeded in reconstituting the cross-Channel empire of the middle ages, they would threaten the vital communication and trade route between Spain and the Netherlands.

Despite such fears, the imperialists were in no position to help Mary Tudor. It was all they could do to hold the empire together. At most, they offered to organise a show of force in the Channel in order to deter French intervention. Fortunately, Mary was able to benefit from the powerful loyalty for the Tudor dynasty. Her own swift measures to establish her claim to the throne were vital to rally support, and she soon succeeded in gathering a small army. Faced with the prospect of civil war, most of Northumberland's supporters shrank back from confrontation, and the duke himself proclaimed her queen on 18 July 1553. The relief and joy in England seemed boundless.[24] In keeping with tradition and the volatile nature of reputation, Mary's success was considered a great victory for Charles, and a defeat for Henry, although ultimately neither had been involved.

The court in Brussels proceeded with caution, eager above all to ensure that Mary retained her shaky throne. At first they suggested that she might marry an English aristocrat, hoping that this would secure the help of powerful nobles to her cause. Once it was evident that she had established her right to the throne without undue support from anyone or any faction, they hinted that she might consider more prestigious marriages. Mary needed little encouragement. A proud woman, she confessed her preference for Charles. Unfortunately his state of health did not permit them to advance his candidacy. Without knowing whether Philip had concluded the Portuguese negotiations, the emperor's advisers suggested to Mary

---

[24] CSP Sp vol. XL and Weiss, *Granvelle*, vol. 4, have an extensive selection of dispatches relating to Mary's accession. The most recent and fullest account of her reign is by D. M. Loades, *Mary Tudor*.

Tudor that she might consider his son. The opportunity to acquire a new ally and another realm was too good a chance to miss.

It is as well to pause for a moment and assess who was in charge of these important negotiations and what their primary aims were. As suggested earlier (pp. 74–5) Charles was too ill to take much part. In some interesting letters written by Granvelle after the successful conclusion of the marriage, he claimed that throughout the negotiations Charles had refused to read any dispatches or instructions longer than a few pages. He had merely signed some papers without reading their contents. Granvelle alleged that he had personally drawn up all the important documents, with some help from counsellor Viglius, who had been brought in to advise on legal aspects. He also claimed that policy and strategy were worked out by himself and Mary of Hungary, and executed by his protégé, Simon Renard, whom they sent to England. How much Charles ever knew will remain a mystery, but it is worth noting both that he did not contradict Granvelle's statements and that the conditions negotiated fit in with his general notions of strategy and especially the separation of Netherlands from Spain.[25] The most important aspect of the marriage proposal was the decision to create a new northern state out of the Netherlands and England, to be ruled by the heirs of Philip and Mary Tudor.

The imperialists were so obsessed by their concern for the Netherlands during these negotiations that they made some peculiar suggestions. Among the arguments they put forward to convince the principal English nobles of the value of the 'Spanish match', was that the Netherlands would henceforth be able 'to send through England to Spain for help as often as need might arise'. Certainly, but would it have won over many Englishmen?[26] Whilst it provided assurances that England would not become fully liable for the neighbouring province in the short term, this statement also suggested that the ultimate separation of these areas from Spain might be fraught with problems. The defensive advantages of this union strongly appealed to the Netherlands government. It should be remembered that they had pressed Charles in 1551 to seize some of the Channel ports in order to secure this route and ease the problems of maritime communication and trade.[27] The negotiators also saw the marriage as a way to increase honour and reputation. Perhaps one should go further and emphasise that they considered it essential for the survival of the Netherlands. Consequently they were at pains to reassure the English and unhesitant when called upon to give their assent to limitations and constraints upon the future king of England.[28] They were not in the least concerned

[25] Weiss, *Granvelle*, vol. 4, pp. 78, 144, 149–51, 298–300.
[26] CSP Sp. vol. XL, p. 386.   [27] CSP Sp. vol. X, pp. 376–80, pp. 447–9.
[28] Details of the lengthy negotiations can be found in CSP Sp. vols XI and XII, esp. vol. XI, pp. 129–34; vol. XII, p. 204 (marriage treaty) and Weiss, *Granvelle*, vol. 4, pp. 10–11, 56, 71–3, 76–8; in vol. 4, pp. 139 and 157–67 there are good examples of how they responded to and calmed English doubts and demand. Loades, *Mary Tudor*, pp. 109–47; the old article by G. Constant, 'Le mariage de Marie Tudor et de Philippe II', *Revue d'Histoire Diplomatique*, XXVI (1912), pp. 23–73, 224–74 is still of value.

with what Philip thought or felt. They started the negotiations without knowing if he had concluded the Portuguese match, and once assured that he had not, they did not consult with him. Indeed, they deliberately kept the conditions secret because they realised that he would find many of them objectionable, perhaps even unacceptable.

Philip had greeted the news of the English marriage with enthusiasm, as had some of his courtiers. Ruy Gómez ecstatically commented in November 1553, 'now the evil fairies have been dispersed!'[29] But their anxiety increased as the secrecy surrounding the negotiations intensified, and they remained ignorant of the conditions being discussed. Philip gradually adopted a guarded, and even hostile tone. He started to talk of the marriage as if it had been imposed upon him; as if it were yet another duty undertaken for the good of his father and Christendom.[30] Eraso seems to have been of no use to Philip at this point, a strong indication that Charles did not know what was being discussed and decided. At most he could report the obvious events, such as the dispatch of a grand embassy to conclude the marriage, but no more. It is likely that he increased Philip's concern by expressing his own fears. He noted the absence of any Spanish or 'trustworthy' individuals in the embassy, for example, and gloomily forecast that this boded ill for Philip and Spain.[31] Ironically, the same letter that announced this event officially included a reproof to Philip, who had failed to send his opinion on some minor appointments. It must have been galling to be pressed on minor matters and not be allowed to have a say in his own marriage negotiations.[32]

It was not until January 1554, after the match had been concluded by proxy, that Philip saw the treaty. By then the negotiations with Portugal had ended and the hostility which prevailed as a result was much too potent to consider reopening discussion of matrimonial alliances. Nor was there any prospect of renegotiating with the English; he was told quite clearly that these were the only conditions acceptable. He was in a quandary. They were unacceptable to him for a variety of reasons. He would certainly have found it dishonourable to receive only the title of king of England, but no patronage powers. Whilst he was to 'assist his consort in the task of government', he was not allowed to act alone, thus becoming subservient to a woman, indeed a wife. Such things were contrary to pride and honour. Furthermore, his activities were strictly limited internationally as well as internally. He was not to embroil England in the emperor's wars against France. Philip declared that this was impossible since filial duty bound him to help his father against all enemies. Already some Spaniards thought that the only advantage of the match was to score points against France, yet these restrictions amounted to a show of deference towards Henry. Philip allowed himself to question this particular

---

[29] AGS E. 100 fol. 177.
[30] Note differences between his reactions in AGS E. 98 fol. 356, and AGS E. 809 fols. 6–7.
[31] AGS E. 90 fol. 144.   [32] AGS E. 90 fols. 140–1.

clause openly, but none of the rest. Nevertheless he was so opposed to the whole treaty that he secretly repudiated it. In front of witnesses he declared that he had not been a party to the negotiations and found himself committed to conditions which filial duty and circumstances forced him to accept, but which his conscience could not bear.[33] Later evidence suggests that the primary cause for repudiating the treaty was the partition of his inheritance. When he drew up his will in 1557 he clearly stipulated that his eldest son, don Carlos, had a right to succeed to all his father's states, notwithstanding the English marriage treaty. Carlos was explicitly absolved from all duties or debts to any half-brothers or sisters who might still be born out of the union of Philip and Mary. If they were to have a child, the will unequivocally stated that the child would inherit only the English realm and dependencies.[34]

It has frequently been said that Philip was reluctant to go ahead with the 'English' marriage and that he did his best to delay its conclusion. This impression was created by the numerous dispatches sent from Brussels and London during the latter part of 1553 and first half of 1554. They speak of deliberate delays, of his failure to write either to his prospective bride or his father.[35] These complaints were false – a product of the tension, bordering on hysteria, which prevailed in Brussels and London. They knew Philip would object to their negotiations and feared that in the end he might refuse to cooperate altogether. But Philip could think of no easy method to disentangle himself from the proposal without alienating everyone, losing honour and openly defying his father as well as breaking the emperor's word. Having decided upon secret renunciation, he doggedly, if reluctantly, proceeded with the match. Delays did occur, but only a few were due to his actions, and not even these had their origins in his repugnance to the treaty.

His first concern was to avoid loss of honour, consequently he would not go to England until the marriage had been concluded in the most binding manner. When marriages were performed by proxy there were two formulae which could be used: *per verba de futuro* or *per verba de praesenti*. The latter being more definitive, it was favoured by both Philip and the imperial negotiators. The Brussels government had

---

[33] Brief notes of the treaty in CSP Sp. xii pp. 2–4; the repudiation was witnessed by Juan Vázquez, Alba, Ruy Gómez and *licenciado* Minchaca, AGS PR. 55 fol. 32.

[34] AGS PR. 36 fol. 129 (ii).

[35] Tyler, in CSP Sp. vol. xii, p. xii, alleged that Philip had not written to Charles from 16 February 1554 to 11 May, except for a letter of 30 March. In fact Philip wrote at least two long dispatches in February, two couriers are known to have left bearing various letters for the emperor during March, another at least, in April. But the war interrupted communications – one courier was taken by the French, perhaps more. It is true that Philip did not write to Mary directly, despite her desire to correspond with him. He seems to have been most anxious to avoid such contact until he had been declared king of England and would not risk losing face if the negotiations fell through. So he wrote when Charles told him that he had now been accepted as king, and signed the letters to Mary and leading courtiers as Philippus Rex. Renard refused to deliver them, arguing that he could not use the title until after the marriage was consummated, whatever Charles said. CSP Sp. vol. xii, pp. 229, 249–50, 225.

been in such haste to conclude the marriage that the embassy left without the most essential document of all, Philip's assent to the match. Before his authorisation arrived, the Wyatt rebellion broke out in England and the imperial ambassadors fled the country. On their return they found that the English would only agree to a treaty *per verba de futuro*.[36] Renard and Granvelle tried to break the impasse by complying outwardly with the English, but pressing Mary to take part in a secret ceremony using the *per verba de praesenti* formula. In a letter of 12–24 January, 1554, signed by Charles, the prince was told that Mary had agreed to do as they wanted, but in secret. Taken out of context, this phrase has been construed as having a far more sinister meaning. It has been suggested that Mary knew of Philip's reservations to the marriage treaty and had given her assent to his secret repudiation, even to give him power over the realm. Eraso's letter to Philip on this matter, long available in translation, clarifies the issue.[37]

Having accomplished this stage of the negotiations, the English and imperial ambassadors now had to acquire Philip's formal assent to the marriage. They embarked in February 1554, but storms delayed their departure repeatedly; it was not until mid-April that they finally reached northern Spain. The imperial court was so anxious to see the end of these negotiations that they were convinced Philip could have landed in England by this date.[38]

Whilst he had made some preparations prior to their arrival, Philip was hampered by lack of funds. At one stage, he thought that he could get away with a minimal contribution to the forthcoming campaign. Mary was so anxious to conclude the marriage at once, Philip suggested that he should go to England immediately accompanied only by a small retinue. The response from Brussels was rapid and vehement. Much as they liked the idea of a hasty departure and a small train, they were adamant that Philip must bring with him at least one million ducats and substantial military reinforcements. The penalty would be deprivation of the opportunity to lead the next campaign.[39] By January 1554 Philip was reconciled to the fact that he could not leave without these. With great reluctance he ordered the confiscation of 600,000 ds from the latest Indies shipments.[40] At the same time he decided to alter the scale of preparations and to capitalise on the situation by staging a grand entry into his new realm to impress the world and establish his reputation.

The problems were enormous: very few Spanish nobles answered the invitation to accompany him to England, and the number of ships available was small.[41] The prince responded by putting pressure on the nobles and offering them subsidies; he

---

[36] AGS E. 103(1) fols. 72–3; AGS E. 808 fol. 2; CSP Sp. vol. XII, pp. 69–70, 77–82, 85–8. The rebellion has been studied by D. M. Loades, *Two Tudor conspiracies* (Cambridge, 1965).

[37] Eraso's letter, dated 3 January, was published in CSP Sp. vol. XII, p. 71; the original of Charles's letter, AGS E. 808 fol. 12.

[38] CSP Sp. vol. XII, pp. 137–42, 149, 206–7; BPR. II–2251, fols. 255–6, 239–40 AGS E. 809 fols. 105, 180.   [39] AGS E. 98 fols. 356 and 374–5.

[40] AGS E. 103(2) fol.92. He had refused to impose an embargo earlier.

[41] Cabrera de Córdoba, *Felipe II*, vol. I, pp. 18–19.

also ordered ships to be seized from all the coastal areas. Rumours that the French would try to seize him in mid-Channel merely reinforced the wisdom of being surrounded by an impressive fleet. He assured Renard in May 1554 that his own preference was to travel simply, but 'this would have diminished my prestige'.[42] Preparations for a journey of this magnitude took a great deal of time. Over one hundred ships were to set sail in July 1554. The vessels sent from southern waters arrived at Cape Finisterre, only to be driven back by terrible storms. Four thousand soldiers also had to be sent to the appropriate embarkation points, and the nobles too had to gather their possessions and prepare suitably resplendent outfits to honour their prince. The cost was considerable – 220,000 ds in all.[43]

Throughout this hectic period there was a great deal of uncertainty about the viability of his departure to a land seething with discontent. Mary of Hungary and Granvelle had tried to hide the full extent of the problem from Philip by censoring reports and constantly reassuring him that the Wyatt revolt had been a minor affair – a few religious extremists getting out of hand. The French on the other hand had exaggerated the troubles and presented them as a violent rejection of the Spanish marriage. To add to the confusion, Renard, who was a willing participant to the doctoring of information, panicked in March 1554 and wrote directly to Philip giving details of the opposition to the marriage and adding that if the prince valued his life he must not go to England.[44] Philip urgently requested full clarification of these contradictory messages. By March Charles had recovered both health and spirits, and he was personally attending to a few matters of state. He received and read this dispatch, but in spite of the urgency, he refused to answer his son until he had discussed the matter with Mary of Hungary. Mary was ill; the emperor's response was therefore delayed until her recovery and was not finished until 1 April. Philip was then told that the situation was calm and reassured he would be safe; he was also ordered to depart for England immediately.[45] In all probability the prince was less impressed by his father's words than by his steady improvement. After February 1554 the reports on the emperor's health were encouraging and the urgency which characterised Philip's earlier preparations now slackened. In any case, he would not have left Spain until he had settled the matter of the Spanish regency to his advantage.

CONFLICT OVER THE SPANISH GOVERNMENT, 1554

Philip had consistently maintained that if he left the Spanish realms, Charles must replace him. Whilst he accepted the reasons for the request, the emperor refused to

[42] CSP Sp. vol. XII, p. 248; also CSP Sp. vol. XII, p. 143 for confirmation of French intentions.
[43] AGS E. 103(2) fol. 100. Constant, 'Le mariage', pp. 245–6, estimates of the number of ships.
[44] CSP Sp. vol. XII, pp. 173–4, 170–2; examples of censored dispatches in CSP Sp. vol. XII, pp. 94–7, 97–9; BPR. II–2251 fols. 156–7 gives details of French activities.
[45] AGS E. 808 fol. 180, Weiss, *Granvelle*, vol. IV, pp. 234–5.

commit himself, and in January 1554 admitted that even if his health improved, he would not go to Spain.[46] By the end of that month, Ruy Gómez complained wearily that the prospect of a regency under the young don Carlos had provoked jealous quarrels among the most powerful Spanish aristocrats as they vied with each other for power over the regency.[47] Philip had seen it all before, in 1548, hence his anxiety to avert another round of tension and conflict. Moreover, he was convinced that the Spanish realms were much too important and too restive to be left with a weak government torn by faction. He was also eager to capitalise on the situation and used Eraso to suggest to Charles that the choice of regent and government was best left to Philip.

Either the skills of the secretary prevailed or the impatience of Mary of Hungary won the day, since the emperor certainly appreciated that time was at a premium and they could not afford a prolonged debate over who was most suitable for the post. On the other hand, the government in Brussels – it should be recalled that during the closing weeks of 1553 and the first six weeks of 1554, Charles was incapacitated – did not wish to relinquish power over such a vital appointment. They offered Philip a compromise – he was given two names and told to select the one he preferred. The individuals were not named, but there is evidence that Fernando de Valdés, archbishop of Seville and Inquisitor General, was one of them. Valdés had once been president of the council of Castile, and had wide experience of government. The other person was either the constable of Castile, Fernando Enriquez (said to be in line for an 'important post' at the time), or the duke of Alburquerque, governor of Navarre, who was also considered for the viceroyalty of Naples. Expecting no further argument, Philip was sent all the necessary papers from Brussels, signed by the emperor, with the name left blank.[48]

The papers for the regency arrived in Valladolid at the same time as news of a tragic accident: on the second of January 1554, prince João of Portugal died after being thrown from his horse. The news was kept secret from his wife, Juana, until she was safely delivered of a son on 20 January. Philip knew of João's death long before his unfortunate sister.[49] Without waiting to hear whether she had survived the birth, let alone asking if she wished to return to Spain, he began to prepare her succession to the regency. She had been his choice for a successor in 1548, but Charles had rejected the proposal in the strongest terms. He argued that he would never appoint a woman to govern a state unless she was married, widowed or old enough to be widowed and to live in semi-retirement. He hinted that a young woman would be incapable of resisting the multiple temptations of so important a

[46] AGS E. 808 fol. 122. [47] AGS E. 103(2) fol. 100, Ruy Gómez to Eraso, 15 January 1554.
[48] AGS E. 98 fols. 37–45, dated 26 December 1553. This was probably the duplicate since Philip already had the papers at the very beginning of January.
[49] On João's death, BPR. 11–2251 fols. 136–7, 42–3; AGS E. 103(2) fol. 76, Philip to Charles, 10 January 1554.

position.[50] Since she was now a widow, one of Charles's conditions had been met, yet Philip did not believe his father would approve of the proposal, and indeed Charles was to reject it. This suggests that there was something more than her youth which troubled him, and it is likely that her strength of character worried him. It was possible that she might identify herself with Spanish aims and complaints, much in the way that the empress Isabel had done in the 1530s, and so create a powerful source of pressure and resistance.

Philip proceeded cautiously; he eschewed a direct approach, and used Ruy Gómez, Eraso and Luis de Sarmiento, the Spanish ambassador in Portugal, to propose her candidacy.[51] Juana's youth was given as the reason for the emperor's rejection: the draft reads: 'even if she were given a good council she does not seem suitable because she is so young'.[52] Philip was given permission to ask Juana whether she would prefer to stay in Portugal or return to live in Spain, but no more. In order to stress the point, this was followed by a curt request that Philip should inform his father which of the two men he had chosen, and if he had not as yet made his choice, he should do so immediately. The prince would not relent, however. He delayed the appointment, so that by April 1554 Charles felt it was time to make his own choice quite clear. He stipulated a preference for Valdés, but aware of Philip's resistance, he announced his willingness to consider a joint appointment.[53] He failed to grasp that Philip's opposition to his candidates did not stem from his dislike or mistrust of their abilities, but from his determination to eliminate all but Juana.

There was no way out of this impasse; neither man would shift his ground. Unilateral action alone could produce results and with stakes so high, Philip took the initiative. He sent Luis Vanegas to Portugal, asking Juana to come back immediately and take over the government. She probably did not know that the offer came from Philip, not her father. She readily agreed, even though it meant leaving her son behind. It took some time before Charles realised what had happened. Since he did not wish to make public the argument, nor indeed the extent of his capitulation to Philip, he decided to assume credit for the proposal, and sent the necessary validation. The documents arrived only a few days before Juana. Charles had to bear the blame for the secrecy and haste with which Juana's departure had been organised – the Portuguese monarchs were extremely angry and considered the action a further slight from the Habsburgs.

The emperor and his advisers now tried to salvage what they could. Philip had clearly made a bid for independence and control which must be checked; and yet, since he was resident in Spain and determined to impose his will, it was difficult to

[50] Fernández Alvarez, *Corpus*, vol. II, p. 612, Charles to Philip, 9 April 1548; Rodríguez Raso, *Maximiliano*, pp. 11–12.
[51] AGS E. 103(2) fol. 100 Ruy Gómez to Eraso, 25 January 1554; AGS E. 376 fol. 76, Luis de Sarmiento to Charles, 16 January; Rodríguez Raso, *Maximiliano*, pp. 12–14.
[52] AGS E. 98 fol. 113–14.   [53] AGS E. 508 fol. 104; AGS E. 98 fols. 113–14.

oppose him from Brussels. Better to seek conciliation and compromise than to alienate him further. After some discussion, a list of suitable candidates for the all-important regency councils was dispatched from Brussels, with clear orders that Juan de Figueroa was to be appointed president of the council of state. Scenting victory, and determined to leave behind him a government he could control, Philip ignored these orders. He appointed Antonio de Fonseca to the presidency, and filled all other posts of the regency council with the men who had worked closely with him during his regency – the marquis of Mondéjar, Dr Velasco, Juan Vázquez, the duke of Francavila, to name but the most important. Don García de Toledo, another close associate, was given the key post as head of Juana's household, and he soon became her chief adviser. Once he had gone this far, Philip did not hesitate to go further: he made a large number of appointments to vacant legal, fiscal and ecclesiastical posts in both Castile and Aragon. In a laconic phrase, he wrote to his father 'before I left, I made those provisions which seemed to me necessary'.[54]

Charles and Mary must have been deeply shocked by all this, but they could have taken comfort in the fact that they retained the trump card: control of finance. Even here, however, Philip tried to establish a pliable official. He appointed the merchant banker Rodrigo de Dueñas to the council of finance. Charles and Mary demanded his immediate dismissal – there can be no doubt of their alarm. Philip ignored them. For several weeks he devoted himself to the task of instructing his sister and the various officials on their future duties, and the government of Spain in general.[55] He made arrangements with Juana and Juan Vázquez to have copies of all their correspondence with Charles. Without prompting, they were to consult Philip on many issues. It was a successful and thorough operation that left him with the power to influence Spain when his legal links with the realm were severed; and it was all the more astonishing for being kept secret. The main participants maintained the façade of authority and deference to perfection. When Philip set off for England, no one outside the immediate court circles guessed that this quiet and seemingly submissive man had already seized the initiative in the Spanish realms and was determined to wrest control over the rest of the emperor's lands.

'THE QUEEN'S HUSBAND'. PHILIP AND ENGLAND, 1554[56]

Once he had settled the matter of the Spanish government to his own satisfaction, Philip was ready to go to England. Cautious as ever, he sent the marquis de las

54   AGS PR. 55 fol. 27(iii); the struggle over appointments can be followed in AGS E. 103 fol. 14; E. 103(2) fols. 140–2, 143–5, 154–8, 171; AGS E. 508 fol. 104; E. 98 fols. 113–14; AGS PR. 26 fol. 137; Cabrera de Córdoba, *Felipe II*, vol. I, pp. 21–2.
55   AGS E. 103(2) fols. 140–2; E. 107 fols. 15–16; AGS PR. 26 fols. 136, 138, 139, 129; PR. 55 fols. 27(iv), 30.
56   F. Strada, *De Bello Belgico* (Rome, 1632, English edn., trans. Sir Robert Stapylton, London, 1650), pp. 9–10, comments on Philip's annoyance at being called and considered the queen's husband.

Navas to check that it was safe, and on receiving a positive report, he embarked.[57] The English ambassadors were startled by the massive fleet. The German princes were convinced that it was a cover for a major assault against them. The French made no attempt to challenge him.[58] Philip had successfully staged a superb entry into international politics.

As soon as he set foot in England on 20 July 1554, it became apparent that he intended to win over the suspicious and hostile realm by fair means rather than foul. He rode in public with only a small escort to show his trust despite the rebellion. He also dined in public and even drank beer, both activities which he intensely disliked. He received everyone with courtesy and graciousness and showed considerable skill at creating the public scenes so appealing to his contemporaries. There was his well-timed and much-publicised speech to his followers urging them to take his example, forget Spanish customs and 'become English'; and the first meeting with the queen and her ladies, when he charmed them by making his first, awkward attempts to master the English tongue. He dutifully kissed them in the English fashion, despite strong and general Spanish disapproval of the English habit of kissing on the mouth and cheek. Doubtless if the Spanish men had been more impressed by English women they might have found the task more palatable and complained less.[59]

Philip's general demeanour and affability won him adherents, but money had a great deal to do with the apparent transformation of the English mood in favour of the new king. The English enjoyed an unenviable reputation for greed, and those involved in the marriage negotiations were convinced that 'presents and promises', as the count of Egmont put it, were the best ways to win them over. Even Charles admitted to Philip that the total offered in pensions and gifts was 'rather high to begin with'.[60] The accounts of one of his paymasters, Domingo de Orbea, endorse this bland statement. He was in charge of paying twenty-two (of the forty-one) lay members of Mary's privy council. Their pensions were backdated to April 1554 and paid from then to December in a lump sum after the marriage. Orbea also paid half a dozen interpreters and minor officials. He disbursed a total of almost 11,000 ds during August and September. Other pensions and gifts may have been assigned to different sources of payment; churchmen, for instance, were usually given ecclesiastical revenues. Renard, who was in a position to know, estimated that Philip's initial expenses on gifts and pensions came to some 30,000 ds.[61]

[57] AGS E. 107 fols. 15–16; Weiss, *Granvelle*, vol. IV, pp. 267–8.

[58] CSP Sp. vol. XII, p. 311; Constant, 'Le mariage', pp. 245–6; VDK, vol. II, pp. 639–41, pp. 659–60.

[59] A Muñoz, *Sumaria y verdadera relación del buen viaje que el Príncipe don Felipe hizo en Inglaterra* (Zaragoza, 1554; published and ed. by P. Gayangos, with three contemporary letters, Sociedad de Bibliófilos Españoles, vol. XV, Madrid 1877), esp. p. 117 the meeting with Mary. A number of letters by courtiers with Philip have been published in Codoin vol. III, see those of Gonzalo Perez, p. 532, and Juan de Figueroa, pp. 519–25; BPR. II–2286 fols. 59–61; Codoin vol. I, pp. 564–74, account of Juan de Varahona. Loades, *Mary Tudor*, pp. 210–27 assesses Philip's actions as king of England.

[60] Weiss, *Granvelle*, vol. IV, p. 100; CSP Sp. vol XII, pp. 143–4, pl. 149.

[61] CSP Sp, vol. XIII, p. 45; AGS CMC. 1 época 1184 fols. 51–65, Orbea's accounts. I am most grateful to Dr Simon Adams who gave me the reference to these interesting accounts.

Far more important than the leading men of the realm was the leading lady herself. Without her support Philip could do little. From the start his behaviour towards her was correct, chivalrous and — at least according to some Spanish observers — excessively deferential. He took what his followers considered affronts with good grace: for example, Mary apparently sat on a higher throne and was served in more splendid dishes at the wedding ceremony. But as any sign of dissatisfaction would have been exploited by the many hostile observers, Philip chose to let such details pass although he would have been acutely aware of them himself.[62]

Mary Tudor had long been deprived of family, honour and affection and Philip appealed both to her pride and her need for love. By the standards of the time he was also thought physically attractive. Small but well-proportioned, with pale skin, blue eyes and fair hair. The protruding lower jaw of all Habsburgs was ungainly, but he made the best of his looks by exquisite taste in clothes. Whether the attraction was primarily physical or not, Mary clearly responded with alarming speed and passion to her husband's charms. Within weeks she practically made a declaration of love to Philip, which amused Ruy Gómez immensely. Doubtless he enjoyed the spectacle of seeing the reluctant Philip respond 'in a similar fashion'.[63] He could afford to snigger because Philip had arranged for him to marry a vivacious and enormously wealthy thirteen year old the previous year. Mary, at thirty-seven, did not fare well from the comparison. She was by no means ugly, being considered rather pretty in her youth, but by 1554 her small figure and reddish complexion were not altogether tempting. Her large, wide eyes and kindly nature were considered her greatest assets. Spanish observers had hopes of improving her looks (and those of her ladies) by persuading them to adopt better fashions.[64] Whether it was her looks or her character — and more likely a combination of both — Philip never returned her affection. But she was ignorant of his feelings at the beginning, and conscious only of her own. She wrote to Charles expressing her delight and hers were only the most important of many laudatory letters flooding into the emperor's court from England that summer. These missives were clear proof of Philip's success. The emperor had entertained very serious doubts as to how his proud and reserved son would behave in England; in a much quoted letter to the duke of Alba, he had begged him to ensure that Philip behaved properly or else the project would be worthless.[65] Reading these favourable accounts, Charles huffily commented with more surprise than tact, that Philip had evidently changed a great deal since they had last met.[66]

Good relations did not permeate further down the social scale. Most of the king's followers were Spanish and many of them arrived in England with extremely

---

[62] See note 59, accounts of Muñoz and Varahona in particular.
[63] AGS E. 808 fol. 143, letter to Eraso, 12 August 1554.
[64] Muñoz, *Viaje*, p. 106, CSP Sp. vol. XI, pp. 532–3.
[65] AGS E. 508 fol. 107. [66] Codoin vol. III, p. 532.

romantic notions nurtured by their favourite reading matter, the Amadis tales. England was the magical island where their heroes had enjoyed wonderful adventures. Instead they found themselves in a rain-soaked land – typically, it poured on Philip during his first public walk, and he had to borrow a cloak. Bad lodgings, high prices, endless insults were the order of the day and these, rather than the weather, shattered the illusion. Matters were not helped by the fact that Philip had brought his own household and found on arrival that a full English household had also been arranged for him. Philip was highly irritated by the situation. He complained, but did not blame the emperor, believing that this, as so many other problems, had arisen during his father's long illness.[67]

A compromise was eventually found, but the struggle to serve the monarch sharpened the usual rivalry among courtiers. Those who were no longer employed or forced to share their office were angry and disappointed and liable to be factious. Violent scenes disturbed the peace within the court as well as in the city. The Spaniards believed themselves to be under threat of a 'Sicilian vespers' and ascribed their continued survival solely to the supernatural assistance of their favourite saints.[68] Rumours of the intense rivalry and conflicts percolated to other courts. A few weeks after the marriage, the constable of Castile returned home and told such stories that Juana and the council were convinced Philip was in grave danger, probably even under arrest. They decided to fit out a fleet to go and rescue him and the other Spaniards there.[69] The confrontations between the English and Philip's followers persuaded a good many observers that they reflected a basic incompatibility between the different 'nations'. The seeds of doubt whether England could be incorporated with the rest of his inheritance had been sown.

It would not do to overdramatise the situation. The English were considered xenophobic in the extreme, and their hatred of the foreigner had been given an intense focus by the copious and virulent anti-Spanish propaganda that circulated before and after the marriage. It was natural that they should fear domination and a severe reduction in status as well as liberty. But their reaction did not differ greatly from that of the Spaniards when Charles arrived in Castile with a vast Flemish and German retinue. The union of Burgundy and Trastámara had not appeared any more tolerable or possible to maintain, but after terrible violence a *modus vivendi* had emerged. Philip might have been disturbed by the continued clashes, but he thought the situation would soon be eased, if not totally solved, when he and his followers embarked for the Netherlands as they expected to do immediately after the wedding. Indeed, apart from the courtiers and a few servants, most of the passengers, soldiers and the rest, remained on board the ships. They expected to depart within days. The wedding took place on the day of St James, Spain's patron

---

[67] AGS PR. 55 fol. 27 (v) and (iii).
[68] Muñoz, *Viaje*, esp. p. 102; Loades, *Mary Tudor*, pp. 213–16; see also Acts of the Privy Council of England, ed. J. R. Dasent (New Series, vol. v, Kraus Reprint, Nedel-Liechtenstein, 1974), pp. 55, 61–2, for some of these clashes.   [69] AGS E. 103 fol. 289.

saint (25 July 1554); Philip impatiently awaited orders to rejoin his men and sail to the Netherlands.[70]

Henry II was so encouraged by his successes in Italy and along the eastern frontiers of France, that he decided to concentrate his efforts against the Netherlands during the 1553 and 1554 campaigns. He realised it would have been foolish to continue expanding into imperial lands, since this would have brought the German princes into the war against France. Moreover, he fully expected Charles to continue his attempt to recover reputation by attacking French positions. After the uninterrupted victories, however, came the first reverses. In 1553 the imperial general, Lalaing, scored some notable successes, taking both Therouanne and Hesdin. Anticipating a French counter-attack, Charles ordered their fortifications to be destroyed, and this admission of weakness offset the gains made by the victories.[71] Henry was still far ahead in terms of reputation, but he had little to show for the massive effort made during 1553; pressure to produce results during the following campaign intensified as a result.

The French king opted for a three-pronged invasion of the Netherlands, one of the forces to be led by himself. When rumours of these plans reached Charles, he reacted with a mixture of joy and anger, taking it as a personal affront, partly because it was widely bruited that Henry intended to march on Brussels and take him prisoner. The emperor was goaded into action; he decided to leave the city and lead his armies in person. Illness rendered him of little use to his commanders for days at a time, but from the end of July, it is evident that Charles was very much in command of the campaign. Mary of Hungary did her best to dissuade him, but when it came to war, she was powerless to influence her brother. She predicted that Charles would fail and her worst fears were confirmed when the French outmanoeuvred him and took Mariemburg in June. Brabant lay open to the enemy. French soldiers devastated parts of Hainaut and Arras, while Binche, Bouvignes and Dinant fell.[72]

These new reverses wreaked havoc in the imperial council. Granvelle remarked that within the army, discipline was notable by its absence, and the fact is amply supported by Savoy. It appears that the terrible conflicts going on at the highest levels of command had percolated downwards and created a chaotic situation. Heading one group, Charles favoured a new offensive to stop the French. The

[70] Codoin vol. 1, p. 566.
[71] AGS E. 98 fols. 226–7; I. Cloulas, *Henri II*, p. 397; van Durme, *Granvela*, pp. 144–6.
[72] Brief details of the campaign and Charles's gradual assumption of the command can be gleaned from Savoy's diary, E. Brunelli (ed.) *Emanuele Filiberto, duca di Savoia: I diari della campagna di Fiandra* Biblioteca della Società Storica Subalpina, vol. 112, Turin, 1928) especially pp. 6–8; Cloulas, *Henri II*, pp. 406–8.

majority of the council bitterly opposed this, demanding that the remaining forces should be reorganised to defend the Netherlands. They believed they were close to losing control over the whole area and feared that if it fell to France, it would trigger the final dissolution of Charles's empire. Despite his efforts, Charles could not make himself obeyed, a telling instance of the reduced authority he now wielded. Nor could the council force him to take their advice. The result was deadlock, and both the emperor and the counsellors thought that Philip alone could save the situation. The emperor's evident difficulty in maintaining command as much as the fears of his subordinates had led to Philip being called to the front on 9 June 1554. Charles dispatched an urgent letter telling him of the desperate situation and instructing him to consummate the marriage with Mary Tudor and leave after a week or so.[73] As before, Philip was told that this was the ideal opportunity for him to prove himself and gain 'authority and reputation'. But the argument rang hollow now. True, Henry was at the head of his troops and the war was undoubtedly a prestigious one, but the imperialists lacked the resources to make much impact on the French. Charles must have been conscious of this since he issued an order rather than a request, appending a somewhat apologetic sentence at the end to the effect that he did not really think an order was necessary, as he expected Philip to appreciate what needed to be done.[74] Curiously enough, Charles sent the letter to Spain and did not forward a duplicate to England although he knew that Philip was on his way there. Indeed the letter itself assumed that the marriage was about to take place. Less than a month afterwards, on 4 August, Charles dispatched a special messenger to England, contradicting everything he had said earlier. The situation in the camp was still confused and the danger from the French thought to be as great as ever, yet, after consulting with Mary of Hungary, who travelled to the front periodically to discuss matters of state with her brother and the commanders, Charles despatched M. Hubremont to tell Philip that he must remain in England. The king was now told that this was not an opportune moment to initiate his military career. With terms like 'I forbid you' and 'under no circumstances is he to do this', there was no mistaking the emperor's new message.[75]

Philip was extremely confused and very unhappy. His depression turned to anger and acute anxiety when Charles ordered all the soldiers and money in the fleet to be sent to the Netherlands immediately. Ruy Gómez told Eraso that Philip was 'most upset to see his majesty in such a state'. Both he and his advisers deeply lamented that they had been deprived once again of the opportunity to join the war.[76] Philip rightly feared that he would be considered a pusillanimous and ineffectual prince, perhaps even lacking in filial affection. Moreover, he fervently believed that the

---

[73] AGS E. 103 fol. 195 Charles to Philip, 9 June.
[74] AGS E. 103 fol. 195; the fate of the dispatch may be followed in the letters of Juan Vázquez and Juana, dated 3 August, AGS E. 103 fols. 199, 200–1, 202–3.
[75] AGS E. 508 fol. 187, instructions to M. Hubremont, 4 August 1554; Brunelli, *I Diari*, p. 11.
[76] AGS E. 808 fol. 144, 16 August 1554.

money and troops taken by Charles represented his last chance to fund the spectacular first campaign he so desperately needed.

The saga was by no means ended. On the military front, matters were somewhat improved after the French failed to take Renti on 14 August, although it was some time before it was appreciated that they had decided to retreat. It is impossible to say who was advising Charles to send such contradictory orders. On 20 August, Philip was told to set sail for the Netherlands immediately.[77] A week or so later, Eraso was sent with an urgent message: Philip must remain in England after all, and busy himself with the affairs of that realm! It could hardly be a coincidence that Mary of Hungary was once again at the front with her brother – unfortunately it is not clear when she arrived.[78]

PHILIP AND THE GOVERNMENT OF ENGLAND, 1554–5

Inevitably, the insecurity surrounding the length of his residence in the realm affected Philip's attitude towards England. Entirely ignorant of how the government functioned, he realised that it would take time to familiarise himself with its complexities, and he did not know whether that time would be available. Moreover, during his absence Mary and her counsellors would continue to rule as they had done; there was no point in creating dependence upon Philip since he would be unable to spend much time on English affairs in the future. There were also contradictory pressures upon him which limited his range of action. If he did not adhere to the letter of the marriage treaty, he would confirm suspicions that he intended to take over the realm merely to commandeer its resources. But if he limited his activities to the support of his wife, he would tarnish his authority: it befitted his dignity as king and as the queen's husband to take a dominant position in government.

The good relations established between Philip, Mary and the leading councillors made it apparent that he would be able to influence state affairs. The treaty had stipulated that all business must be conducted solely 'in the languages which have been used of old in the kingdom and by natives', yet as early as 27 July, the privy council decreed that 'a note of all such matters of Estate as shuld passe from hence shuld be made in Laten or Spanyshe'. Alba confirms in one of his letters that English affairs were being discussed and dealt with in Spanish.[79] Linguistic problems clearly did not prove a major impediment, since interpreters were available and Latin could serve both sides equally well. Lack of experience and knowledge of English matters was a far more serious drawback. But the alcalde

---

[77] AGS E. 508 fol. 196.

[78] AGS PR. 55 fol. 30, Charles's instructions to Eraso were dated 1 September 1554; Mary's visit, but not the content of her advice, Brunelli, *I Diari*, p. 15.

[79] Acts of the Privy Council, vol. 5, p. 53; CSP. Sp. vol. XII, p. 2; AGS E. 103(1) fol. 9, Alba to Eraso, 13 August 1554.

Birviesca, who was in charge of maintaining order at court and was the major liaison officer with the English authorities, stated that Philip dealt in all state affairs from the beginning, although there were no definite arrangements to delineate his sphere of action.[80]

There were two important matters in which Philip took a prominent part: the reform of Mary's council, and the restoration of papal authority over the realm. The broad outline of his intervention in the structure of the council is well-known. There had been repeated complaints, including some by Mary herself, that the privy council was inefficient and deeply divided. Lord Paget, one of the principal negotiators of the marriage, had long been agitating for a reduction in size, believing that the small councils of Edward's reign, and the latter part of Henry VIII's rule, were better. In fact, whilst Mary's council was large on paper, numbers attending regularly were small. Philip helped to institute the reforms, reducing numbers, but this did not bring a significant improvement, since the problems of the council were twofold: lack of authority and leadership, and rivalry among the courtiers. Paget and Stephen Gardiner were locked in a familiar struggle for ascendancy over the monarch and Philip's arrival probably exacerbated this by providing Paget with his support, whilst Gardiner remained Mary's favourite. The English council, as all others, responded positively to firm handling but became more faction-ridden and inefficient when there was a perceived weakness at the centre. Philip's presence and greater decisiveness, not the size of the council created the impression of greater efficiency. His handling of the council was certainly praised later.[81] The reason why Philip chose to intervene on this matter is to be found in the letters of Renard and the other imperial ambassadors. They had written of the dissent and chaos among the councillors, claiming that Mary was dominated by the council and too afraid to impose her will. Thus in dealing with the council, Philip was going some way towards reducing an alternative source of control over Mary.[82]

The religious situation in England was also of great interest to Philip from the outset, but he left it to his wife to deal with. Mary was deeply committed to the restoration of Catholicism and involved in all aspects of this policy. Philip's contribution was to proffer advice and use his contacts in the curia in order to facilitate the process of restoring papal authority.[83] Mary was being urged by cardinal Pole, the only English cardinal left in the curia to restore Catholicism with a unilateral declaration. The imperialists had advised caution, as had her own ministers, and she agreed to dismantle the Protestant settlement in the same way it had been imposed: by parliamentary consent. Pole refused to recognise the legality

[80] BPR. II–2286 fols. 216–17, letter to Granvelle, 21 November 1554.
[81] Loades, *Mary Tudor*, pp. 136, 227; A. Weikel, 'The Marian council revisited' in J. L. Loach and R. Tittler, *The mid-Tudor polity c.1540–1560* (London, 1980) pp. 52–73.
[82] e.g. CSP Sp. vol. XI, pp. 34, 171, 200–1; CSP Sp. vol. XIII, p. 5, Ruy Gómez to Eraso, 2 August 1555 announcing the king's decision to tackle this matter.
[83] Details of the religious changes, chapter 5, pp. 198–9.

of a secular act of parliament. The pope was in agreement with this principle, but like the imperialists, he was sensitive to the political realities of the time. If Mary attempted to impose these changes without the support of the elites she would provoke such unrest it would lose her the throne, and the opportunity to recover England would be lost too.

The major impediment in the way of England's acceptance of papal obedience had little to do with theology – it was a question of land. By 1553 large areas of the country that had belonged to the English church had been secularised. Those who had bought them, rented them, or seized ecclesiastical buildings and wealth would not give them up, irrespective of their religious proclivities. Almost everyone had expected Mary to change the Edwardian settlement, but many thought she would return to a Henrician church rather than to full subjection to Rome. Once her wishes were clear, the elites had the choice of repudiating the queen or seeking a suitable settlement; they opted for the latter, but would give nothing away. Mary tried to reintroduce papal authority as part of an act of parliament reaffirming her legitimacy, but the ploy failed. Everything now depended on persuading the pope to accept the loss of lands and possessions.

Two things need to be stressed: one, that England was the first important territory to consider repudiating Protestantism and seek to be reincorporated into the main body of the church; two, and consequent upon this, that all those involved sought to take sole credit for bringing about what Juan Manrique de Lara, imperial ambassador in Rome, declared to be 'the most spectacular victory ever achieved'.[84] Honour and reputation were to be gained in quantity by whoever secured England's restoration. The pope was in a difficult position. He wanted to bring England back to his fold, but, with an eye to further reconversions, he did not want to establish a precedent and lose the rights to all former church lands and possessions. Pole was even more determined to recover all the lost possessions; he made it clear he would not consider a compromise. There was a third group involved in all this – the Netherlands government. Their main aim was to ensure that the marriage with Philip was accepted and that the prince would not lose the realm as a result of precipitate action over religion. They wanted a compromise settlement so that royal authority would not be further challenged. However, the imperialists desperately needed a victory, moral or otherwise. Charles had both compromised with and fought against Protestantism without success in either case. Another compromise with the German Protestants was being hammered out in his name by Ferdinand; if he was seen to have engineered England's return, his reputation in Christendom would be greatly enhanced and his bargaining position strengthened. The imperialists therefore refused to let Pole leave Brussels until a settlement had been reached, and undertook to negotiate with the papacy on Mary's behalf. Mary, Gardiner, and the rest of the English counsellors had no control and little influence

---

[84] AGS E. 880 fol. 150.

over the imperial council, and at times their negotiations run counter to these.

At the time of the marriage, the situation was still deadlocked. For Mary, time was running out; she wanted the matter to be dealt with at the forthcoming parliament. Philip could appreciate the advantage of seeing it through whilst he was in England, doubtless hoping to gain from its reflected glory. However, Pole remained obdurate: he would not agree to recognise secular ownership of ecclesiastical possessions. The only concession he made was to promise a review of each individual case. By now Charles had recovered, and took an interest in this affair; his envoys reported that the pope was becoming more pliable and thought they could soon finish the business, particularly if Mary and Philip put their weight behind these negotiations. Charles reported this and told Philip and Mary to send a special envoy to Rome supporting the imperial negotiations, promising a speedy end to them. Philip and Mary thought otherwise. It was probably the queen who insisted that they must win Pole over to the settlement, and they sent their special envoy to him, and letters to the pope, which were entrusted to the imperial ambassador. Aware that time was at a premium, Philip gave strict instructions to the postmaster general to forward these letters to Rome without delay.

This departure from his advice alarmed Charles. When the dispatch arrived within his jurisdiction, he ordered his officials to seize it. He opened and altered the contents of the letters so that they now endorsed his views. He justified his actions saying that he considered it essential to ensure that the two sets of negotiations were fully in accord during this delicate and final stage. He also had to admit that Manrique de Lara was not available in Rome to deliver the message of the English monarchs – Charles had secretly dispatched him to Siena to conclude another set of delicate negotiations, but without Philip's knowledge so that he would not have the chance to oppose his father's action.[85]

Philip was enraged by his unwarranted meddling with their correspondence and negotiations. However close the family links, he was now a sovereign in his own right, as was Mary, and Charles had no right to open, let alone alter, the contents of their dispatches. The matter of Sienna rankled just as deeply. The incident seems to have spurred him to action. Two months previously he had stated that it would be impossible to persuade the English nobles to come to terms without open assurances from the pope that their lands would not be touched. Nevertheless, Philip persuaded them now. The details are obscure, but the agreement clearly entailed a promise on his part to ensure that the pope ratified the existing partition of lands and goods. When papal authorisation finally arrived in England, it appeared to be a result of Philip's successful intervention. And that is certainly the way he viewed the situation. He wrote exultantly to his father: 'no mean honour and glory will accrue to your majesty as a result of my having concluded this matter'.[86] It was

[85] For Siena, see pp. 114–15.
[86] AGS PR. 55 fols. 27 and 27(iii). See also Loades, *Mary Tudor*, pp. 221–2.

no mere boast for him. He remained convinced in later life that God had chosen him to bring about this 'great work'.

Letters of congratulation poured into Rome, Brussels and London. Cardinal Siguenza was not alone in thinking that it was the greatest success the Church had seen since the days of Constantine.[87] In the end, whilst none of the major participants was able to claim full credit, all shared in the success. Philip, who had come at the tail end of the business, rather unexpectedly took the lion's share.

Whilst Philip was far from controlling the English government, these two successful interventions highlight the potential for action. The duke of Alba, who spent several months with Philip in England, was fully convinced that he could take control of the realm, and even become 'the most absolute' monarch the English had known. He simply could not understand why Philip was content to limit his activities and behave as if he were merely 'a poor traveller' just passing through.[88] Alba's vexed comments imply that Philip was not interested in establishing his position within the realm. This is only partially true. That he was preoccupied with his inheritance cannot be doubted; the continuing uncertainty as to the length of his stay was also an important factor, but even more important was his awareness that he would only be able to do what the majority of the nobles and the queen wished to be done. Alba simply ignored the failures, whereas Philip had them very much in mind when he assessed how far he should involve himself with England. The most important failure of all was the matter of his coronation.

Everyone, including the French, had expected that Philip would be crowned king within weeks of his arrival. Doubts existed as to whether Mary could simply order the coronation, or whether it had to be ratified by parliament. It was decided to play safe and secure the symbolic support of the realm in parliament. Mary's pregnancy brought the issue to the fore since it was imperative to make arrangements for a regency in case she died in childbirth. Parliament proved hostile to the coronation. There was even an attempt to subject Philip to a mixed council if a regency was necessary. In the end, his right to rule the realm in his child's name was recognised, but the things that had been said and the rejection of the proposal to crown him revealed the lack of trust of the English towards their new king, and wounded him deeply. Wisely, Philip did not force the issue, although he was to request the coronation subsequently. Later, Mary's own ambivalent position in this matter was to earn her his disdain and reproach.[89] As for the English nobles and councillors, had they supported the motion, it would doubtless have been passed. Philip's evident mistrust and refusal to surround himself with Englishmen had a lot to do

[87] BPR. II–2286 fols. 326–9, to Granvelle.
[88] Alba, *Epistolario*, vol. I, p. 7, letter to Philip, 25 April 1555; p. 236 letter to Ruy Gómez, 29 June 1555.
[89] Loades, *Mary Tudor*, pp. 219, 223–4, 234; CSP Sp. vol. XIII, pp. 124–6, Renard to Charles, 21 December 1554; VDK. vol. II, pp. 660–4, Damula to Doge, 23 October 1554; Vertot, vol. III, p. 170 gives French expectations.

with their dubious religious background, as he explained to Charles, but this matter of the coronation must have played its part too.[90]

How are we to account for the contradictory evidence given by contemporaries about the king's involvement and control over English affairs? Whereas the Savoyard ambassador said that he exercised a powerful influence over state business, the Venetian ambassador denied this. Both had reason to be biased, yet their comments were not entirely irreconcilable. The Savoyard, Stroppiana, furnishes us with a clue to the apparent paradox when he wrote: 'The King hears and despatches almost all state affairs as it befits his dignity and authority that he should'.[91] The king was pragmatic and obsessed with prestige. His aim was to do only as much as he needed to create an impression of authority and honour. In November 1554, for example, the French wanted to know whether England would support the emperor if Philip took part in the next campaign against France. His reaction was not to enquire whether the English would back him. Instead he instructed Mary to give her answer in such a way as to make Henry II understand that as Philip was her husband, she must do what he asked of her. Moreover, since he was king of England, he could dispose of the realm as he saw fit.[92] The refusal to crown him, therefore, did more than hurt his feelings, it threatened to tear the delicate fabric of this illusion of power he was trying so hard to achieve. It also meant that his hold on the realm would remain tenuous and legally insecure.

Insecurity was certainly the hallmark of his English venture. Yet he stayed in the realm for over a year despite expectations to the contrary. The duration of his residence cannot be blamed entirely on Charles. The emperor rescinded his order for Philip to remain in England in December 1554. By January 1555 he complained that his son had refused to obey him, and he continued in this vein for the next few months, heatedly accusing Philip of deliberately delaying his departure for the Netherlands and disobeying a father's command.[93] Philip had longed to leave England from the moment he set foot in the realm, his rejection of such orders is therefore puzzling at first sight. Publicly, he declared that he could not leave until the queen had given birth. Yet the pregnancy had (as all observers commented) created a degree of confidence and quiet in England. If ever there was a good time to leave the realm it was now, when rebellion and unrest seemed but a distant memory. When her unsuccessful confinement ended, he remained, seemingly out of consideration for her mental and physical condition. Mary was devastated by her failure to produce a child. Her sorrow was all the harder to bear when it became apparent that false rumours had spread across the continent that she had given birth to a boy. In Brussels the celebrations went on for some days before the truth was

---

[90] AGS PR. 55 fols 27(v) and 27(iii). See p. 128 for his later attempts to gain the crown.
[91] CSP Sp. vol. XIII, p. 2, Stroppiana to Granvelle, 19 September 1554; CSP V. vol. VI (1) p. 107, Michiel to the doge and senate, 11 June 1555.
[92] AGS E. 808 fol. 54, Philip to Charles, 16 November 1554.
[93] e.g. AGS PR. 55 fols. 27, and 27(iv).

known.[94] The queen was certainly most anxious to have Philip present both during the pregnancy and after, but Mary's wishes were never her husband's commands. The reason why Philip did not sail for the Netherlands until the end of August 1555, as Charles well knew, was money; or, to be precise, the lack of it.

[94] Alba, *Epistolario*, vol. 1, pp. 100–2, Alba to Gonzalo Pérez, Brussels, 11 May 1555. Details of the pregnancy can be followed in the dispatches published CSP Sp. vol. XIII; couriers had already been appointed to take the good news to foreign courts and letters announcing the birth were all ready, leaving only a blank to add the sex of the child, see Acts of the Privy Council, vol. v, pp. 126, 136, 138 and CSP D., p.67. Loades, *Mary Tudor*, pp. 217–20. Charles continued to believe that Mary would bear a child, although most contemporaries doubted this. He believed rumours of a new pregnancy as late as April 1558, see AGS E. 128 fol. 331. His dreams of a separate northern state account for such wishful thinking.

3

The end of an era

Histories of the emperor always dwell on the grand and tearful ceremony of 25 October 1555 when he publicly announced his intention to abdicate. With the awesome trappings of Burgundian ritual and to the sound of muted sobbing, the emperor reviewed his many campaigns, recalled his ceaseless travels and bade farewell to many loyal and long-serving companions.[1] Many contemporaries and most historians regard the spectacular occasion as a reflection of the inner greatness of Charles. Even his evident physical frailty has been used to bring into sharp relief the strength of character that drove the emperor to abandon such great power for the cloister. The heroic image endures, as does the belief that this ceremony was in effect his abdication. In fact it was only the symbolic transfer of power over the Netherlands. The day belonged to Mary of Hungary, who was retiring from the regency, as much as to Charles. This was very much in keeping with the careful exploitation of symbol and ritual which all early modern monarchs used to enhance their prestige. If Philip had obeyed the emperor's orders, each stage of the complex transfer of power would have had its counterpart to the Brussels ceremony. He had been told to organise a grand act in England for the transfer of Naples and Milan and doubtless Charles had similar plans for the rest. To his surprise and disappointment, Philip refused. He appeared to be in no mood to finance impressive ceremonials in praise of his father.

The abdication was indeed an extraordinary action, but stripped of the romanticism it is revealed as the inevitable product of intense political and personal conflict from which no one emerges with much credit. The process took years rather than a day. Properly speaking it started in 1541 when Charles conferred the title of duke of Milan upon his son, and it did not end until his death, when Philip inherited the Franche-Comté. But the ceremonies were no indication of the true state of affairs. For instance, Philip exercised considerable power over Spain long before the formal transfer of power. The abdication might have been avoided if the two men had learnt how to share power. But it was soon apparent that they could not: both were intolerant of any challenge to their authority. Moreover, the situation required

---

[1]. John Mason witnessed the act, his account was printed in RPPB, vol. 1, pp. 1–7; lengthy account, Gachard, *Retraite*, Introduction, pp. 80–105, vol. II, pp. 5–8; brief accounts in Brandi, *Charles V*, pp. 633–5.

unitary command. This chapter will explore the bitter conflicts which predated the emperor's abdication.

CHAOS IN THE ITALIAN STATES

Charles decided to transfer the duchy of Milan and the kingdom of Naples to his son at the time of his marriage to Mary Tudor. The transfer of the latter was ratified at a simple ceremony in Winchester in July 1554. Ostensibly, this gesture was intended as a demonstration of the emperor's favour to his son and new daughter-in-law. Charles stated his desire to give Philip a title commensurate with that of his wife, so that he would not suffer the dishonour of being considered her inferior. Although no one admitted this openly, it was undoubtedly a sop to reconcile Philip to the unfavourable conditions accepted by the imperial negotiators for the English marriage. If these had been the only reasons for the concessions, Charles could have given Philip Sardinia or Sicily and need not have added Milan. Why had he chosen these two states?

Had Charles chosen Sardinia, the poverty of the island would have been such stark contrast to England that it could not give Philip even rough parity with his wife. More importantly, Sardinia belonged to the Aragonese state, and as the threat from Franco–Muslim invasion grew after 1553, it became essential to assign defence subsidies for the island to one of the neighbouring states. Its connection with Aragon meant that Charles charged the three realms with this responsibility. There were many complaints and much resistance. Irregular subsidies were sent, sometimes from Castile; help was dispatched at times of danger from the Italian states, but all complained that the island should be provided by Aragon. Only when it was known that Henry II had proposed to the sultan that they should attack the island in 1557, was serious action taken, however. The Aragonese corts voted an annual subsidy of 20,000 ds from 1558 onwards to subsidise the defence and fortifications of the island.[2] These constitutional bonds between Sardinia and Aragon and the need to marshal help from other parts of the empire ruled out Sardinia.

While England was more powerful than either Naples or Sicily, both had long, proud histories and in terms of prestige, Philip would not be much behind Mary if he had the title to either. Sicily was suffering from constant corsair raids and naval attacks from Franco–Ottoman forces, as well as from the important (and little understood) shortage of grain which struck the island in the mid-sixteenth century. Notwithstanding the cumulative impact of these problems, it was considered to be relatively stable. Juan de Vega was viceroy there and he governed with a firm hand.

---

[2] Philip had pointed out to Charles on several occasions that the island was ill defended and should be helped, e.g. AGS E. 89 fol. 96 Philip to Charles 8 June 1552; AGS E. 809 fol. 33, id 27 June 1555. RAH SC A-60 fol. 40 Alonso de Madrid (viceroy) to Granvelle, 15 May 1557; F. Loddo Canepa, *La Sardegna dal 1478 al 1793*, 2 vols., 1: 1478–1720 (Galizzi-Sassari, 1974), vol. 1, pp. 197, 219.

Although he realised that the emperor was often annoyed by his resistance to orders, Vega stood by his principle that he would rather risk provoking his master than impose policies that would endanger the kingdom. He opposed the orders of Charles and Philip to send grain to imperial allies when the island experienced a shortage of grain and high prices. He resisted their orders to exempt certain powers from the new export dues imposed to raise revenue for defence.[3] On this, as on other issues, he lost the battle; Charles and Philip considered grain an important tool of international politics. They used it to cement the alliance with Genoa and the papacy and to neutralise the Swiss cantons. Vega was not altogether popular in Sicily; he was often in conflict with the local aristocracy. There was no reason to suspect that the island would rebel, however, or prove incapable of defending itself. Naples was different.

As early as 1552 don Pedro de Toledo had complained of the emperor's neglect (p. 51). In April 1554 Charles admitted that he had not written since well before Toledo's death a year earlier. Cardinal Jaén had in the meanwhile sent a string of dispatches with graphic details of the internal troubles and external threats which went unanswered. The very thought of divesting himself of this area, however, prompted Charles into action. That April Charles dispatched orders and decisions on a large number of matters, covering thirty-five closely-written folios.[4] But it would need much more than this to bring stability to the area, and to defend the realm from major attacks. Naples required firm handling which the emperor was not prepared to give; it had the status and was reasonably self-sufficient.

The same may be said of Milan. It is extremely interesting in this respect to note Juan de Vega's remark that Charles had given Naples and Milan 'so that England will now have an obligation and direct responsibility to sustain them. There is no doubt that everything depends on this'.[5] To historians of Marian England, raised on tales of the poverty and chaotic state of the realm at the start of her reign, such expectations may seem extraordinarily naive. To those who knew first hand the burden of debt carried by each of the emperor's dominions, England appeared an unexploited and invaluable resource. There is no proof, of course, that either Charles or Mary of Hungary conceived of the English match as the salvation for the Italian realms, but given the tradition of assigning aid and subsidies for the poorer realms on their powerful neighbours or those who had constitutional links with them, such a possibility should not be discounted. The emperor's anxiety to retain Philip in England and persuade him to assume control of the government could well be related to this.

Charles had already issued patents giving the duchy of Milan to his son in 1541 and 1546, although he had not relinquished control over it. The title issued in 1554

[3] AGS E. 1047 fols. 134–5; AGS E. 1123 fols. 67–8; BPR II-2286 fols. 158–60.
[4] The mammoth document is AGS E. 1046 fol. 138. Some of Jaén's appeals and accounts, AGS E. 1046 fol. 88 (to Philip) and E. 1046 fol. 57 (to Juana).
[5] BPR II-2286 fols. 3–4, to Granvelle, 1 October 1554.

was regarded by Philip as unnecessary and he refused to mention Milan in the ceremony he arranged, arguing that it was already his in title; he wanted it in deed.[6] Apart from these earlier grants, the emperor's concession reflects his awareness that he had lost control of the situation there. In April 1554 he reviewed the imperial position along the war front, the administrative chaos, and acknowledged that he had allowed it to get out of hand. Large sections of the imperial army had mutinied; the rest were threatening to do so. Convinced of the need to provide a radical remedy, and sadly concluding that he could not provide it, he admitted defeat and told Philip to deal with these multiple problems.[7]

This is not, however, the complete story. Behind the decision lay years of acrimonious disputes that led to the paralysis of imperial government in Italy. It was natural that Philip should have shown interest in this, above all areas. Italy was the epicentre of the struggle in Christendom. He had met many of the leading personalities during his journeys to and from the Netherlands in 1548 and 1551, establishing contacts he was later to develop. His first attempts at direct intervention date from 1553, that is the time then Charles was ill and the situation in Italy deteriorating alarmingly as a result of his decision to channel resources to the north. Philip opposed the appointment of Francesco d'Este as commander-in-chief of imperial forces, and supported Ferrante Gonzaga when the latter concluded his unofficial truce with the French. He was alone in this, and Gonzaga wrote gratefully: 'whatever I do, your highness can be sure it is in your service'.[8] But this was also the time when Philip was overwhelmed by requests for direct intervention in Italian affairs, even from Ruy Gómez, who urged him in September 1553 to warn Charles of the terrible dangers assailing the Italian lands. Philip's response was to repeat that he had already done so, to no effect. Ruy Gómez then concluded that Charles lacked willpower rather than the necessary information. He hoped that God would intervene before they lost the whole of Italy.[9]

Ironically, the first victim of Philip's bid for power in Italy was Ferrante Gonzaga. There were two reasons for this: first, Philip's overwhelming anxiety for the Piedmont–Milan front. By the summer of 1553 he was ready to blame the deterioration of the imperial position on the commanders and not just on the dearth of funds. Second, Philip relied heavily on Alba's advice, and Alba was Gonzaga's chief rival. Being of similar rank and experience, the two men were bound to compete. During the siege of Metz their rivalry turned into bitter personal antipathy. Towards the end of 1553 Gonzaga was accused of embezzlement and corruption. The evidence against him had been gathered by three leading members of the Milanese administration: don Juan de Luna, Juan Tavera and Francisco de

[6] Fernández Alvarez, *Corpus*, vol. II, pp. 489–90; AGS E. 808 fol. 30, Juan de Figueroa to Charles, 26 July 1554; AGS E. 808 fol. 32, Philip to Charles, 17 August.
[7] AGS E. 508 fols. 104–6, Charles to Philip, 1 April, 30 April 1554.
[8] AGS E. 1205 fol. 45, to Philip, 24 February 1554; AGS E. 100 fols. 173–4.
[9] AGS E. 100 fols. 173–4, to Eraso, 3 September 1553.

Ibarra. Ibarra was the father of Alba's private secretary, Esteban Ibarra; it later emerged that the duke also had close contacts with the other two.[10] Eraso too had a hand in the unsavoury business – he was instrumental in persuading the emperor, then in the throes of his depressive illness, to raise the matter with Philip, thus giving the latter the chance to put forward his radical proposals for the reform of the administration and government of the Italian lands.

Few details of these initial plans survive. It seems that they assumed Gonzaga would soon be replaced. By December 1553 Eraso was confident that Philip's 'recommendations' would be implemented rapidly. A meeting of the imperial councils of state and war on 22 January 1554 decided that Gonzaga should be recalled under the pretext that Charles needed to consult him in Brussels about the forthcoming campaign.[11] Gonzaga wisely delayed his departure until the emperor's health improved, and on arrival publicly demanded that he should be immediately punished or cleared, and if it were the latter, he demanded prompt reinstatement to his post with full honours. Gonzaga had served Charles long and loyally; the emperor considered him a friend and he was certainly convinced that the charges were malicious and unfounded. In the summer of 1554 he ordered the three men who had made them to come to Brussels to face counter charges. He was too late to save Gonzaga. By then power over Milan had been transferred and when Philip was informed of his father's decision in September, he refused to endorse the order or reinstate Gonzaga. Deeply discomfited, Charles tried to persuade him of the latter's innocence and warned that unless Gonzaga returned to his post at once, the situation along the Piedmont–Milan front would deteriorate so alarmingly, that the French king would soon be making the next appointment. Philip tartly replied that Charles had allowed it to degenerate so badly that it had practically come to this already.[12]

Fearful of provoking an open breach with Philip, the emperor backed down and offered Gonzaga alternative employment as commander of the German cavalry, a post the latter refused because it was not commensurate with his status and experience. Mary of Hungary ardently supported his suit and commended his refusal of the post. She strongly advocated his immediate reinstatement but thought it wise to suggest other posts as well, in case Philip proved adamant. She came up with a surprising alternative: Gonzaga must be appointed as head of Philip's household. It was a prestigious office; doubtless she was also eager to have someone close to Philip whom she could trust. Unfortunately for Gonzaga Philip had already

---

[10] VDK vol. II, pp. 587–9 Damula to the Ten, 23 January 1553 commented on the Alba–Gonzaga rivalry; Maltby, *Alba*, p. 74 on Esteban Ibarra.

[11] AGS E. 90 fol. 147–8, Eraso to Philip, 12/24 December; AGS E. 1205 fol. 162 *consulta*; fol. 103, letter, 26 January 1554; CSP Sp vol. XII, pp. 71–2, Eraso to Philip, 3 February.

[12] AGS PR. 55 fol. 30, Charles's instructions to Eraso, who was sent to England, 1 September 1554; AGS E. 508 fol. 237, Charles to Philip, 7 December; AGS PR. 44 fol. 11(x), Philip's instructions to Eraso (sent back to Brussels), 21 March 1555.

offered the post to Alba. Mary might have known this, for she certainly believed that he would reject the plan if he were given the chance. She advised her brother to offer Gonzaga the post without consulting the king, thinking he would not dare to repudiate the *fait accompli*. Granvelle strongly supported the suggestion, which Charles himself eagerly embraced. However, at the last minute, Charles's courage failed him and he consulted his son, who vehemently rejected the plan. Gonzaga then decided to go to England to plead his case personally with Philip, but to no avail. The king offered him the presidency of the council of war but he rejected it also on the grounds that it befitted neither his status or honour. Charles had now lost patience with his son. In the spring of 1555 he ordered Philip to appoint Gonzaga as head of his household and honour his loyal servant, and offered compensation for Alba in Italy.[13]

This was probably what Philip had been trying to achieve all along. Since the duke of Savoy could not be trusted to command the imperial forces along this sensitive front – he might have used imperial troops to recover his lands – only Alba could have replaced Gonzaga in Piedmont–Milan. The French had recently offered Savoy their friendship and protection as well as ample recompense if he defected. He rejected the proposals, keeping Charles fully informed, but it made it less likely that he would be appointed to an Italian post. Savoy had also been made supreme commander of the forces in the Netherlands in June 1553 and councillor of state and his presence in the north was essential.[14] Besides, ever since don Pedro de Toledo's death in February 1553, Philip had tried to secure the viceroyalty of Naples for Alba. Charles had rejected this but as the time to transfer the realm to Philip was fast approaching, he thought it wise to seek a compromise. Until then he appointed a temporary governor, cardinal Jaén. Charles wanted either the duke of Alburquerque or the count of Benavente to assume the viceroyalty but Philip was adamant that Alba was the most suitable candidate.[15]

Similar disagreements resulted in the appointment of an interim government in Piedmont–Milan. Charles wanted Juan de Vega to leave the viceroyalty of Sicily and take control of the area, but Vega refused.[16] It is possible that his appointment to the presidency of the council of state may have been discussed at this early date. Alternatively, he may have known of Philip's plans and wisely decided not to stand in his way. The king certainly held him in high favour subsequently. Philip put forward his comprehensive plan for the reform of the Italian governments after

[13] AGS PR. 44 fol. 11(v); AGS E. 809 fol. 71.
[14] AGS E. 90 fols. 147–8; AGS E. 1208 fol. 25; Segre, *Emanuele Filiberto*, vol. 1, p. 113; van Durme *Granvela*, p. 148.
[15] AGS E. 90 fols. 147–8; AGS E. 809 fol. 71. The prince of Asculi was a great supporter of the scheme, see AGS E. 1202 fol. 190, and Juana seems to have been delighted when the appointment was eventually made, AGS E. 108 fols. 74–5.
[16] AGS E. 90 fol. 140, Charles to Philip, 8 November 1553; AGS E. 508 fols. 11, 12, 13, Vargas to Philip, 19 January 1554; in the *consulta* of 22 January, Vega and Alburquerque had been suggested as candidates, AGS E. 1205 fol. 162.

Vega's refusal was made public; this could hardly have been a mere coincidence. In the meanwhile, the government of Piedmont–Milan was left in the hands of a mixed council which included the long-time imperial agent in Genoa, Gómez Suárez de Figueroa, handling the financial front; the duke of Sessa took care of the military matters, and the existing council tried to cover the rest.

Philip was convinced that the lack of obedience and loyalty within the emperor's dominions in Italy, as much as the external threats, made it imperative for a man of considerable status and military experience to be given charge of all Habsburg lands in the peninsula. He must be given full powers to deal with the massive backlog of business which had built up over the last few years and restore a semblance of order. Savoy had the status and skills, but could not be trusted. This left only Alba. As he put it some months later, Philip wanted Alba to be given 'el cargo de Italia', to take charge of the Italian states and the imperial war effort in the area.[17] And in order to speed up a process which he thought essential to save the Italian states, he sent his father a set of letters in December 1554 all ready but for his signature, announcing Alba's new charge to the major Italian officials and allies. He made doubly sure of his father's compliance by launching a further attack on Gonzaga, who was told quite bluntly that the only way he could avert further dishonour was by retiring to his estates.[18]

Charles refused to sign the letters, but the new threat to his friend and servant goaded him into action and led to his acceptance of a compromise. On 14 April he reluctantly appointed Alba to an incredible array of posts: captain general of the imperial forces, viceroy of Naples, governor of Milan, general and superintendent of all Italy. But he demanded that Gonzaga's appointment as head of Philip's household should be effective and public as soon as Alba left for Italy.[19] Philip refused and would not let Alba leave England until Charles withdrew this condition. In the end his victory was complete. Gonzaga was forced to retire. Three years later, when Philip mounted a campaign against France, he was recalled and worked closely with Philip for most of the war. There was no personal animosity on Philip's part, only a bid for very high stakes.

Frustrated and angry, Charles sought revenge against Gonzaga's detractors, but he found the way blocked by Philip and Alba. The duke protected them openly, dismissing the emperor's requests as vindictive and silly. Too late, Charles had the courage to put the blame where it was due, and castigated Philip for preventing him from bringing the culprits to heel. His outburst yielded results. Philip forced Alba to send Luna, Tavera and Ibarra to Brussels, but once there he protected them and

---

[17] AGS PR. 44 fol. 11(xi) Philip's holograph note to Eraso, 8 March 1555.

[18] AGS PR. 44. fol. 11(x) Philip to Eraso, 26 March 1555, and fol. 11, id. to Charles, same date.

[19] AGS E. 509 fol. 82, Charles to Philip, 12 March; AGS E. 509 fol. 97, id. 28 March; AGS E. 809 fol. 100, Ruy Gómez to Eraso, 4 April; AGS E. 509 fol. 142, Charles to Philip, 19 May. Alba, *Epistolario*, vol. 1, p. 95 Alba to Lópe de Guzmán, 10 May.

made sure they were not punished. Not only did they keep their jobs, but they went on to hold important posts during Philip's reign.[20]

Charles was not a man to take such a challenge lightly. He dented Philip's victory and marred Alba's life by sending copies of all the Italian correspondence to don Francisco de Toledo, who was used to keep an eye on Alba and restrain him. Alba was much piqued by this but had to learn to live with it whilst Charles remained in power.[21] On the other hand, Philip was not a man to barter royal authority, so he must have had pressing reasons to give Alba such immense power. His view of the situation was passed on to Charles via Eraso in March 1555: he intended to give Alba control of Italy 'for a limited period of time, after which everything can be transferred to me'.[22] In other words, Philip was using the duke to take control of the Italian lands covertly, and ease his way into power later. Ambition was certainly a primary motive; but so was necessity.

After Philip was given the titles to Naples and Milan, the imperial secretary for Italian affairs, Francisco Vargas, commented that he had effectively been given control of Italy, or at least of its most important parts.[23] This was an overstatement. Having given away the title to Naples and Milan, and with it responsibility for these areas, Charles was in no hurry to make the transfer effective in other ways. Despite the fact that it was ratified in July, the emperor did not notify the Italian realms until September.[24] As a result there was considerable confusion among the officials of both realms. Few had any certainty as to whether their appointments or pensions would be ratified by Philip. For once Philip was happy with his father's neglect. Private petitions had simply piled up in the emperor's court for over four years, creating numerous vacancies which his son gladly filled. Charles, however, was under very great pressure from those who had served him loyally (and doubtless were shaken and scared by the fall of Gonzaga), and he was persuaded that he must deal with this backlog. Quite unexpectedly he set about filling all vacant posts after the legal transfer of these possessions. He had all the documents falsely backdated 'so that there will be no impediment'. Rather lamely, he excused his action by telling Philip that many of the posts needed to be filled urgently, suggesting he was doing his son a favour. But this was not all: having seized the reins of patronage once more, he was loath to let go. He had given Philip powers of appointment over these states from the time the concession was made; now he changed his mind. Philip would have no powers of patronage until he had officially claimed Naples and Milan. Since his envoys set out in August and would have to travel, then organise the ceremonies for the official ratification of the transfer, this would mean that he would not be able

20 Alba, *Epistolario*, vol. I, pp. 102–5; 312–13; 318–20; 347–51; AGS E. 809 fol. 709.
21 AGS E. 509 fols. 166–7, Charles to Philip, 16 June 1555; AGS PR. 55 fol. 27(i); Alba, *Epistolario*, vol. I, p. 280.   22 AGS PR. 44 fol. 11(xi).
23 BPR II-2286 fols. 3–4, to Granvelle, 1 October 1554.
24 AGS E. 1046 fol. 57; e.g. of official announcement to Francisco de Toledo, dated 5 September, AGS E. 1046 fol. 91.

to make appointments or grants for months. Philip was incensed by all this.[25] It created a protracted period of instability for all the administration which they could not cope with on top of their many problems.

There were other difficulties impeding a full transfer. Charles did not send Philip the seals which alone authenticated major state documents for these states, nor were the resident agents representing the Neapolitan realm dispatched, depriving Philip of essential advice without which he could not make any important decisions. Couriers were being detained in Brussels, dispatches opened and only those matters which did not interest the courtiers there were being forwarded to Philip. He was uncertain what role Charles had in all this – assessing how far the emperor was in control had been a continuous problem since 1552. But he could scarcely contain his anger. He instructed Eraso to inform his father of the situation, adding: 'since his majesty has put me in charge of this, it stands to reason that his ministers should not deal with matters there but remit them to me'; the officials in Naples and Milan, he went on, were now convinced that Philip 'only possessed the title, and that matters would continue as they were before his majesty made me this gift'.[26] For several months there was nothing but confusion. No one was in charge of these two vital zones. In October 1554 Gómez Suárez de Figueroa wrote a strongly-worded protest from Milan, explaining the desperate straits they were in and declaring it nothing short of a scandal that at a time of war and imminent danger no one had answered his many urgent dispatches. He complained that they had received neither advice nor money since July, that is throughout the campaigning season.[27]

Once Philip wrested control over business and appointments in Naples and Milan, he had to confront other problems, mainly of a legal and military nature. In Milan he found that he could not take decisions beyond those that dealt with local issues. The duchy had not functioned as an independent state for years. It was part of Piedmont–Milan, that conglomerate of imperial and allied territories which were forced to function jointly for the duration of the war. Philip could not make imperial commanders obey him, nor use the resources of the imperial allies. The army encamped and paid by the duchy was not a Milanese but an imperial army. The duchy's finances were in such a state of disarray that they could only survive with the subsidies sent by Naples and Castile. Philip was totally dependent on his father's allies, his father's imperial powers, and his father's authority to send money from Castile. Ultimately this meant that he was entirely subject to his father's policies.

As for Naples it could not survive without the protection of the emperor's

[25] AGS E. 508 fol. 236 Vargas? to Ruy Gómez, 30 November 1554; AGS PR. 55 fol. 27(iii), Philip's instructions to Eraso; AGS CJH. 34 fol. 485, Granvelle to Ruy Gómez, 10 December; AGS PR. 55 fol. 27(iv), Charles's instructions to Eraso (?January 1555).
[26] AGS PR. 55 fol. 27(iii).   [27] BPR II-2286 fols. 41–2.

Mediterranean fleet; its small navy would have been overwhelmed by the corsairs, let alone the French or Ottoman fleets. Moreover, the realm was still technically within the jurisdiction of the council of Aragon, and queen Juana was the rightful sovereign. Only she could give the state away, not Charles. Charles transferred to his son only his own self-appointed regency powers. Although no direct proof survives that Ferdinand set in motion a process to advance his stronger claims to take over the regency of Naples (p. 34), Philip and Charles suspected that he was soon going to challenge the transfer. Even Henry II knew of the legal impediments to this concession, and he galvanised his lawyers into impressing the pope with the illegality of this act, hoping he would refuse to ratify the concession.

Philip responded to these challenges – perceived and real – in a typically direct manner. On the one hand, he strengthened his hold on the realm; on the other, he had formal legal documents drawn up, denying his uncle any rights over Naples and repudiating papal jurisdiction.[28] Queen Juana's death in April 1555 was almost providential. It averted the certain confrontation between Philip and Ferdinand, but it did not save Philip from years of bitter wrangling with papal lawyers over the subservient status of the Neapolitan realm, whose incorporation into the Trastámara inheritance had been ratified by the pope.[29] Months before this, however, Philip had realised that even if he succeeded in getting the seals, advisers and correspondence appertaining to Naples and Milan, he would not be able to control the areas because of their dependence on the other states within his father's empire. Hence his determination to advance Alba and obtain his appointment to a unitary command of Italy. Alba was a cover for Philip; unless he secured control over all the Italian realms, he knew he would have power over none. The logic of the situation, as they all soon realised, was that Philip could not stop at Italy either. Neither Naples nor Milan could survive without Castilian subsidies.

As had been the case in earlier conflicts, Charles and Philip made every effort to keep their disagreement over Italy secret. The whole matter was debated between them in holograph letters or via Ruy Gómez and Eraso, who travelled back and forth, from Brussels to London.[30] But the situation could not long continue; it had been possible to sustain the façade of unity largely because these clashes had been over internal issues, and both Charles and Philip were fortunate to have discreet officials. Nevertheless, as Philip became more eager to establish himself in Italy, he was drawn to intervene in international matters. His assertiveness in Italy would mark his first major moves in the international sphere.

---

[28] AGS E. 881 fol. 49; AGS PR. 42 fol. 12.

[29] Juana informed her brother of the death of their grandmother, AGS PR. 42 fol. 19, 23 April 1555; AGS E. 809 fol. 126, Ruy Gómez explained the relief they all felt.

[30] A holograph note from Eraso in one of Philip's letters suggests that the secretary thought Charles was being less discreet than his son, for he urged Philip to persuade Charles that the matter should be 'pa[ra] sy solo', for him alone. This might also be his effort to keep Mary of Hungary out of the debate, but she was clearly involved in the earlier stages. AGS PR. 55 fol. 27(iii).

PHILIP'S ENTRY INTO INTERNATIONAL POLITICS: CORSICA AND
SIENA, 1553–5

Philip's conviction that the neglect of the Italian front would have serious consequences and must be rectified, drew him inexorably towards intervention. But he was also an opportunist, eager to establish a separate identity and reputation, and the fall of the island of Corsica in 1553 gave him an excellent chance to do both. Corsica was under the control of the republic of Genoa. A poor island, it was of considerable strategic importance, serving as a defensive bulwark for Genoa, and commanding major trade routes from France and Spain to Italy, which became even more important as corsair activity along the southern shores of the Mediterranean increased. Charles had inherited powerful Aragonese claims to the island, which he set aside in order to cement his alliance with the republic and its leading citizens, the Doria family. Together they held the key to the emperor's naval superiority over France in the Mediterranean.

In the summer of 1553, the island was attacked by a powerful fleet of Ottoman, French, and North African corsair vessels. They were guided by Corsican exiles and bandits, and the island was rapidly overwhelmed. When the Muslim forces left for winter quarters, only the town of Calvi was outside Franco–Italian control. Confirmation of the attack reached the emperor's court in August, but Philip did not know until October the full extent of the disaster. Urgent pleas were sent to Spain by the Genoese rulers and by Andrea Doria, who was still commander of the imperial fleet.[31] But they were more like preparatory missives. The Genoese did not expect Philip to respond – such decisions had to be made by Charles. Moreover, relations between Philip and Genoa had been strained for some time. He was suspected of having designs on the republic. This was precisely the reason why he decided that he would take action and so dispel this unfortunate impression. The other reasons he alleged when justifying his independent actions were, first, the strategic importance of Corsica, a key to Italian communications, in his view; second, that he knew the emperor was 'so busy' with other matters, it was unlikely he would attend to this one – a polite if realistic assessment of what would happen. Lastly, he wanted to establish two essential points: his willingness to reward loyalty with aid, and to set aside his own dynastic claims for the benefit of allied states. Offering help to Genoa was an object lesson to other Italian states.

Without consulting his father, and dismissing the protests of leading counsellors, Philip ordered the Spanish fleet to go directly to Corsica with 3,000 infantry which had been raised to relieve the hard-pressed Piedmont–Milan front. Moreover, he offered to cover the cost of levying, transporting and provisioning these troops from

---

[31] AGS E. 100 fol. 182, Juan Vázquez to Eraso, 4 November 1553; brief account of the campaign, Braudel, *The Mediterranean*, vol. 2, pp. 928–9; it was precisely because of its strategic importance that the French were tempted to take it, Vertot, vol. II, pp. 148–55, 177, 207–9, 231. See pp. 260–3 on the Franco–Muslim alliance and campaigns.

Spanish revenues. The Spanish fleet had come back to home waters for the first time in three years in order to get essential repairs, and its commanders were naturally opposed to being sent off again on this mission. Imperial councillors were even more hostile to the prince's actions because they saw it as a diversion of essential resources at a time of grave peril.[32]

The imperial court did respond to Genoese requests for aid, but tardily and poorly, as Philip had suspected. On 30 December a letter was written ordering Philip to send the Spanish galleys to support the Genoese attack, but there was no mention of troops or money. When rumours filtered through to Brussels that Philip was launching a fully-fledged relief operation, they were dismissed, even by Eraso, as false. The secretary thought they must be a clever way of covering up an attack against Algiers.[33] No one had expected Philip to act alone. To the delight of the Genoese, he continued to show further signs of favour: when famine struck in the winter of 1554, he forced the Sicilians to send supplies of grain without paying the new taxes imposed on such exports. The viceroy, Juan de Vega, complained bitterly since the island was also short of grain and desperate for revenue to fund its defence. Both in this and the following year, he sought to dissuade Philip and Charles from giving these important concessions, arguing that the Genoese were merely finding ways to get grain cheaply. Yet the fear of Genoa's defection to France drove Philip to court the republic assiduously. He did not believe Charles was doing enough to deter what would undoubtedly be a catastrophe for them in the Mediterranean.

The difficulty was proving that he was behind these measures. Philip remained convinced of the need to keep all disagreements with Charles secret; moreover, he needed Charles to arrange the grain exports from Sicily, for example. Although he asked his father to tell the Genoese that these gestures were due to his intervention, Charles was unlikely to let pass a chance to earn the gratitude of his old ally. If the emperor could not prevent what he saw as a waste of resources, he might as well get some benefit from it all.[34] In April 1554, a meeting of the emperor's chief counsellors in the Netherlands branded Philip's aid plan for Genoa as ruinous and damaging. They accepted that the area was now in great danger and were willing to condone the dispatch of military aid for Sardinia. The island was poor, ill equipped to counter corsairs, let alone capable of withstanding a major attack. It was also, as they pertinently reminded the emperor, part of the Trastámara inheritance, which Genoa was not. Philip ignored the criticisms and recommendations and continued

[32] AGS E. 100 fol. 182; AGS E. 98 fols. 324–5, Philip to Charles, 11 November 1553; AGS E. 100 fol. 176, Ruy Gómez to Eraso, 12 November.

[33] AGS E. 90 fol. 144, Eraso to Philip, November 1553; AGS E. 98 fols. 329–39, Philip to Charles, 12 November; AGS E. 103(2) fols. 90–1, id., 17 February 1554; AGS E. 90 fols. 131–2, Charles to Philip, 20 November–30 December.

[34] Correspondence between Charles and Philip on this, AGS E. 808 fols. 52 and 35; AGS E. 809 fols. 16, 22 and 49. Correspondence with Juan de Vega, AGS E. 1120 fol. 154; AGS E. 1123 fols. 67–8; BPR II-2286 fols. 158–60; also BPR 11-2286 fols. 183–5, Gómez Suárez de Figueroa, imperial representative in Genoa, to Granvelle.

to send aid to Genoa. By March 1554 Charles admitted defeat and even proffered muted congratulations. He thought his son's prompt measures had assured the Habsburgs of Genoa's continued support. He now agreed to pay half the costs of the campaign to recover Corsica, hoping in this way to deter Philip from diverting military resources.[35] Perhaps the conflict between them would have continued but for the fact that the emperor was seeking to conciliate his son over this issue in the hope that Philip would prove more amenable in another, much more serious disagreement over the fate of Siena.

According to Philip Siena was 'the most important and most direct route leading the French king to the kingdom of Naples, and therefore to be seen as the bulwark for its defence'.[36] The imperial council advised Charles to treat the rebellion there as if it were a French invasion of Milan.[37] Often it appeared as if only Charles recalled that Siena was legally an independent republic and not an integral part of his patrimony. Indeed throughout 1550–1, Ferrante Gonzaga and Diego Hurtado de Mendoza, the most senior imperial military commanders in the area, tried to make it so. They sought to persuade both the Sienese and the emperor to transfer sovereignty and power over the area to Philip. They wanted the leading citizens of Siena to request Philip's appointment as their sovereign, and undertook to secure their petition and Charles's favourable reply. The French-backed revolt put paid to such plans, and was certainly not unconnected to them, or to the imminent conclusion of the huge new fortifications Charles ordered to be built in the city. The loss of their limited freedom fed the flames of rebellion among the Sienese.[38]

Charles balked at the cost of recovering Siena. By June 1553, nearly 540,000 ds had been spent, much of it forced contributions from Naples, which also had to provide additional military forces. When the threat of Franco–Muslim invasion in 1553 halted the flow of subsidies and led to urgent appeals for the return of their troops, the emperor felt he could not deny them. In any case, he had no stomach for the fight; when the Neapolitan soldiers went south in the summer of 1553, Charles drew up plans to withdraw from the conflict.[39] Most of his counsellors opposed his decision. In the imperial councils they drew up three alternatives: one, launch a major invasion and eliminate the problem with a large campaign. This would mean, in effect, making Siena the next military priority. Two, a mixed campaign,

[35] *Consulta*, Brussels 18 April 1554, AGS E. 112 fol. 154; AGS E. 508 fols. 85–6, Charles to Philip, 13 March; AGS E. 103(2) fols. 142–40 [sic], id., 11 May. Details of Philip's aid in 1554, AGS E. 507 fol. 148; AGS E. 1046 fol. 117; AGS E. 1205 fol. 29. R. Ciasca (ed.), *Istruzioni e relazioni degli ambasciatori Genovesi*, (vol. I, Spagna, 1494–1617, Rome, 1951), pp. 148, 150.

[36] AGS E. 808 fol. 54, to Charles, 16 November 1554.

[37] AGS E. 1122 fol. 154, *consulta*, Brussels, 17 April 1554.

[38] E. Spivakovski, 'El "Vicariato de Siena". Correspondencia de Felipe II, príncipe, con Diego Hurtado de Mendoza y Ferrante Gonzaga', *Hispania* 26 (1966), pp. 583–89; J. Hook, 'Habsburg imperialism and Italian particularism: the case of Charles V and Siena', *European Studies Review*, 9 (1979) pp. 283–312.   [39] AGS E. 1045 fol. 242; AGS E. 880 fol. 131.

suggested by Ferrante Gonzaga, who wished to pursue a guerrilla-type war in the winter and follow it with a major assault early in the summer. The third was to transfer the burden of the war to the nearest imperial ally. The duke of Florence, Cosimo de Medici, fitted the bill and had long coveted possession of the republic. He begged Charles to give him charge of the operation, and the emperor agreed. He would subsidise the campaign with 4,000 infantry, 300 horse and 23,000 ds per month. Not long afterwards, the duke persuaded him to increase this: 6,000 men during peacetime, 16,000 for the campaign. The costs of keeping these forces rose accordingly: 33,600 ds in peace, 79,800 ds each month of the campaign. Gonzaga had estimated his plan at 11,300 ds per month in the pre-campaign fighting. He complained that it would have been much cheaper to have followed his advice; furthermore, it would have averted the present situation which made a partition of the area inevitable. The emperor was criticised for making false economies. He had been inveigled into paying for a massive campaign, and lost control both of the expedition and of the area. He made himself doubly unpopular within his realms by denuding Naples and Sicily of troops to make up the number of men requested by the duke of Florence.[40]

All was not gloom for the emperor, however. In the summer of 1554 the French and their Italian allies were ejected from Siena, although pockets of resistance remained in the area. Henry refused to be beaten. Having lost the military conflict, he sought victory by diplomacy. He asked the pope to mediate. The papacy wanted neither great power in an area which bordered on its states; the opportunity to intervene was accepted with alacrity. Julius III proposed that a tripartite government including papal, imperial and French forces, should control the area until the fate of the republic was decided. He urged that the conflict be eliminated by restoring Siena's independence. Throughout the crisis, Charles stood out against the advice of his son and counsellors. He was determined to be free of the problem. His reply was positive: yes, he would be happy to establish a 'free' Siena. Philip was aghast. He believed – or so he pretended – that Charles had failed to understand what Julius was proposing. Freedom for Julius meant 'vera libertà', but surely Charles thought of it in terms of the 'freedom' enjoyed by the republic before the revolt, that is under imperial protection and with an imperial garrison. Until the matter was cleared up, Philip begged his father not to make his reply public. He could not comprehend how Charles would give up an area that had cost him millions of ducats and thousands of lives to seize, defend and recover.

It was Philip who lacked comprehension. Charles was ready to admit defeat and lose Siena. With both France and the papacy determined to oust the imperialists, and without the ample means required to sustain defence against such powerful attacks, his conviction that it was best abandoned in an honourable settlement seems sensible. In November 1554, he instructed the imperial ambassador in Rome,

[40] AGS E. 1045 fols. 88, 57, 90; AGS E. 1047 fol. 219; BPR II-2286 fol. 114; AGS E. 1202 fol. 129.

Juan Manrique de Lara, to speak to Julius on the matter. He was to seek support for the retention of imperial tutelage over Siena, but if Julius refused, Charles was willing to grant 'vera libertà'. He knew Philip would oppose this, so he did not inform his son until it was too late to withdraw the instructions. In the meanwhile, he sought to obtain Philip's assent by reasoning with him. If they did not restore Siena's independence, he argued, 'I would lose – as would you – the good reputation we have earned that we do not take what belongs to others'.[41] Charles was really indulging in wishful thinking if he believed that this was the prevailing judgement of him, but he had a point, as Philip realised. Charles had established himself in Siena by virtue of his imperial power and superior military force; he had no dynastic claims to the area. Philip replied with a repetition of the arguments in favour of retaining the republic, adding: 'I would very much like to justify my actions to the whole world and show that I do not covet lands that belong to others . . . however, I also wish it to be clearly understood that I will defend the lands that your majesty has given me'.[42] For him it was clearly a conflict of two important priorities, and he considered the loss of reputation regrettable but justified by the advantage to be gained from impressing the enemy that he could defend the whole empire. Philip thought Naples could not be held without Siena; furthermore any losses now would convince the enemies of the Habsburgs that the empire would soon break up if only they maintained the necessary pressure.

The emperor ignored his son's arguments and accepted papal mediation and Sienese freedom. But he had forgotton that he could no longer make such decisions alone. He would need to maintain an imperial presence in Siena until the settlement was imposed. As usual he ordered the Neapolitan government to supply the troops and money. Philip blocked this; he reminded Charles that he was now king of Naples and he alone could order what support might be sent from that realm. He instructed the Neapolitans to sell crown lands and revenues and finance the dispatch of a powerful force to the republic.[43] Charles backed down, and in December 1554 withdrew his support for the plan to set up an independent republic.[44]

It was a pyrrhic victory. The man who really did have a say in the future of the republic was the commander of the joint army Cosimo de Medici. Wise enough to realise that he would not get control of the republic if Philip opposed him, he too argued for the restoration of an independent republic. It was preferable to having powerful neighbours wrangling constantly along his borders. Moreover, he would

[41] Charles's views in AGS E. 507 fols. 72–6, 5 November 1554.
[42] AGS E. 808 fol. 54, Philip's views, 16 November.
[43] AGS PR. 55 fol. 27(iii), Philip's instructions to Eraso, *c*. November 1554; AGS CJH. 34 fol. 485, Granvelle to Ruy Gómez, 10 December; These were not the only orders Charles had given to the cardinal of Jaén who was temporarily in charge of Naples, as can be seen in AGS E. 508 fol. 236, ?Vargas to Ruy Gómez, 30 November.
[44] AGS E. 507 fol. 28, Charles to Philip, 10 December.

be able to exert his influence over a weaker neighbour. Consequently, in his negotiations with the rebels in the spring of 1555, he offered them the freedom Charles was willing to give. Charles immediately ratified the agreement before Philip had a chance to intervene. This left the king in an invidious position. If he repudiated the treaty, it would be said (as Alba pointed out) 'that self-interest caused him to have no esteem for his father's oath'. If he invaded Siena, he would be branded as a violent and ambitious ruler, taking all things 'without justice'. Either way the conflict with Charles so carefully hidden until then, would become public, and a breach with Cosimo de Medici would be unavoidable. Yet, if he did nothing, Philip was convinced the safety of Naples was threatened, unrest would follow because they received nothing for the many sacrifices they had suffered in the defence of Siena, and his reputation would suffer. Fortunately for him, Alba was in Brussels at this time, and took it upon himself to represent Philip's views and choices before Charles and the imperial counsellors. To strengthen his case, Alba announced that Philip had rejected every clause in the capitulation, although he had no news of Philip's reaction at all. Philip was delighted at his decisiveness and vigorous advocacy of his case. The duke managed to overawe the imperial counsellors who urged Charles to do something to conciliate Philip. After considerable deliberation, they decided to accept a complex stratagem drawn up by Alba. Charles would send letters repudiating the Siena treaty but delay their dispatch until it was known that there were enough imperial troops in the area to control the situation. Deadlock ensued, because Charles refused point blank to cooperate. His counsellors were now equally resolute that freedom should not be granted and Philip was adamant that Charles must retain Siena or offer ample compensation to Naples.[45]

Once again Philip broke the impasse, and this time he risked an open confrontation: in May 1555 he publicly requested that Charles should give him 'the vicariate of Siena', that is, to transfer imperial powers over the republic. The advantage of this plan was that it would leave the issue of sovereignty open, but Philip would retain control of the area. Charles took refuge in his now habitual practice of delaying all answers until he had consulted with Mary of Hungary on the matter. Granvelle was sent to obtain her opinion; after his return a compromise was drawn up. In June 1555 Charles offered to invest Philip with imperial powers over Siena but not until he arrived in the Netherlands.[46] In the meanwhile he appointed a temporary governor for the area, Francisco de Toledo, knowing full well that Philip wanted Alba to have the job too. Having failed to put his man in, Philip demanded that the governor and troops should take an additional oath of loyalty and obedience to Alba in his capacity as general and superintendent of all the Habsburg

---

[45] Alba, *Epistolario*, vol. I, pp. 72–3, 79–81, 85–6.
[46] AGS E. 509 fol. 166–7, Charles to Philip, 16 June 1555. The discussions can be followed in Alba's correspondence with Philip and Ruy Gómez in May 1555, Alba, *Epistolario*, vol. I, pp. 107–9, 104, 121–2.

Italian lands.[47] Charles was contemptuous of his son's requests. He rejected them, berating him for his willingness to give Alba so much power, and the crass way in which he was demonstrating that he would rule Siena as if it were one of his patrimonial lands.[48] Whether he realised that Philip was using Alba to extend his own power over Italy remains an open question, but by the spring of 1555 control of the Italian possessions was certainly what the two men were fighting for.

Eventually the deadlock proved too much for all involved. Cosimo de Medici was tired of waiting and fearful of the outcome of the negotiations between Charles and his son. He forced the hand of the Habsburgs by cutting off supplies to the imperial troops in Siena and demanding immediate payment of all the money he had spent over the last two years of fighting. The threat of his defection was a further spur to action. Since they could still not find sufficient common ground for an agreement, Charles and Philip resorted to the quite extraordinary expedient of appointing the duke of Alba to make the decision for them. Alba was a cousin of the duchess of Florence and there were long-established contacts between his family and the Italian princes, so the duke of Florence could claim to have some influence over him. Charles still regarded him as his servant, and Philip was convinced of his loyalty, so all agreed he was the best man to negotiate the contentious issue.

Before he initiated the final discussions with Cosimo Charles made it clear that he wanted Alba to ratify the original concession and leave Siena in 'true freedom'. Philip asked him to reject this and requested a settlement that left him power over Siena and excluded the duke of Florence, who, of course, wished to retain control over the area. With many a lamentation, Alba took on the difficult task, and it is to his credit that a settlement was reached in June 1555 which avoided a rupture between Medici and Philip. His solution was to arrange for Charles to transfer imperial powers to Philip, who would be invested with the Vicariate of Siena; Philip would have to sub-infeudate the area to the duke of Florence. Whilst Philip retained the title of the place, Medici controlled it in effect, but was now a feudatory of Philip. The losers were the Holy Roman Empire and Sienese republicans.[49]

The struggle for Siena illustrates the emperor's diminishing interest in Italy, his willingness to cut his losses there, and, by contrast, Philip's growing interest in Italian affairs. Philip saw Italy as the proving ground, the area where he could demonstrate his ability to safeguard his possessions and establish his reputation. He was fortunate that he did not win the battle for Siena – it would have given him a

[47] AGS E. 809 fol. 48, Philip to Charles, 22 May 1555; Charles had already mentioned the matter to Philip, AGS E. 509 fol. 142, 12 May, after Alba had requested the post; Alba, *Epistolario*, vol. I, pp.107–8.

[48] AGS E. 509 fol. 166–7, Charles to Philip, 16 June. He decided the matter was so important, Eraso was sent to persuade Philip to drop his demands, AGS PR. 55 fol. 27(1).

[49] Alba, *Epistolario*, vol. I, pp. 97, 118, 195–6, 206–7, 239–41; AGS E. 809 fol. 48; AGS E. 509 fols. 160, 166–7, 172. Curiously, the transfer of imperial power to Philip in AGS PR. 46 fol. 46 is dated 30 May 1554, but he certainly did not possess them at this date. The effective grant was not until 16 January 1556, when he also received the right to sub-infeudate, AGS PR. 46 fols. 47–8.

reputation for aggression and greed, instead of which he secured the fealty of an important prince and demonstrated his fierce determination to defend his states, thus deterring Italian princes from further aggression. He shrewdly turned failure into success, using Siena repeatedly in his propaganda to demonstrate that even when his lands had made great sacrifices to retain an area, and even when it was strategically desirable to annex it, he would still refuse to do so without a 'just cause'; especially if at the same time he could advance one of his loyal allies. Above all, the conflict highlights the inability of either Charles or Philip to advance an independent policy in a region where both wielded power. They were constantly clashing and blocking each other's policies when a clear lead was most essential. Much the same process was evident in the financial sphere.

THE FINANCIAL MACHINERY: CHAOS AND CONFLICT

Philip had warned his father in May 1554 that he would leave Spain 'without any hope of being helped by further subsidies from these realms'.[50] What he did not know was that Charles had already contracted loans of nearly 636,000 ds promising rapid repayment from the bullion that Philip had been ordered to bring. In other words, most of the money for the campaign had already been spent. Moreover, the emperor had not made any allowance for the cost of Philip's journey, so he found himself short of over 200,000 ds when he finally received the money his son had collected. He solved the shortfall by seizing the bullion shipments which merchant bankers had entrusted to the safety of the royal fleet. But despite the massive subsidies, he found himself in October 1554 with only 300,000 ds left in loans and bullion, to meet immediate demands of over one and a half million ducats.[51] Quite apart from this there were serious problems caused by the suspension of some major contracts by financiers in retaliation for the latest seizure of their funds. The merchant banker who had taken charge of supplying the Spanish fleet was among those reneging on his contract, with disastrous results for the fleet.[52]

Eraso was given the unenviable task of raising money and for a time it looked as if he had succeeded. A consortium of Genoese bankers headed by Alberto Pinelo offered one million ducats, 600,000 to be paid at the delayed October fair 1554, the rest at the Villalon fair of 1555. Astonishingly, they did not want interest; they demanded instead that the emperor should honour all licences given to them to export specie from Spain, and to release the funds he had seized from them which had come with Philip's fleet. They also required repayment of the entire sum in 1556. The recovery of liquidity was clearly far more important than promises of future interest payments; but it was also expected that they would make 7 per cent by exchange speculation, and save 3 per cent since they demanded that the crown

---

[50] AGS E. 103(2) fols. 140–2, 11 May.
[51] AGS E. 103 fol. 43; AGS E. 103 fol. 151; BPR 11-2285 s.f.
[52] AGS PR. 26 fol. 153; AGS E. 803 fol. 66.

must cover the costs of transporting this money. However, rumours that Charles intended to repudiate his debts made the financiers nervous. In October they demanded additional export licences for a million ducats and special collateral – over one million ducats in Castilian annuities, 200,000 ds in Netherlands annuities, and a further 200,000 ds from those of the Neapolitan realm. The papers for the release of the revenues to fund these annuities must be drawn up at once. The merchant bankers would take them up and might negotiate with them *before* the first instalment of their loan was due. Clearly they hoped to raise part of the payment by selling or trading off these government bonds. Their last condition was that Philip should guarantee the agreement – a precaution necessary if the emperor repudiated his debts.

Eraso thought that the loan was no longer feasible. It was impossible to find sufficient revenues for the annuities demanded. But he found himself pressed by both monarchs to finalise the contract. In December 1554 Ruy Gómez told him: 'for the love of God let us get some money, even if we have to pay for it with our own blood. Our lives depend on having the money to make war or peace this summer'.[53] Philip had not counted on Charles's desperation nor on the willingness of financiers at this point to lend in exchange for promises of immediate bullion payments in the Netherlands and Italy. Their assets were frozen in Spain and their own creditors pressing for payment; they had to take risks. Some of them were also victims of the fever of speculation which periodically sweeps through financial markets. Charles borrowed on the security of the Pinelo loan long before it was close to completion! It would never have sufficed to finance the campaign as Philip innocently thought it would. In any case, the governments of the states assigned for repayment failed to supply the required collateral. In Castile, they had been forced to release vast sums of *juros* given as collateral for other loans which the government had been unable to repay as promised. The financiers were busy selling these to recover their capital. Juana offered to pay small sums at the financial fairs of 1556 and borrow the rest. Affected by the general lack of confidence, the Pinelo loan collapsed at the beginning of 1555.[54]

By the end of January 1555 Charles decided that their situation was critical. He faced nearly 600,000 ds of wage arrears, and current expenditure of 100,000 ds per month; this was the end as far as he was concerned. He did not have the means to continue as he was, let alone finance the next campaign, and he was now convinced that only Philip could raise the necessary funds. At last he had acknowledged that he could not survive without Philip's help.[55] Until such time as the Spanish

[53] AGS E. 808 fol. 132; details of the loan, AGS E. 110 fol. 507, AGS PR. 55 fol. 27(v), AGS E. 103 fol. 51.

[54] AGS E. 808 fol. 133; AGS E. 110 fol. 51; AGS PR. 55 fols. 27, 27(iv); an example of sale of annuities recently released to Constantino Gentile, AGS E. 103 fols. 38–9.

[55] AGS E. 809 fol. 37, Charles to Juana, 20 January 1555; AGS PR. 26 fol. 153, his instructions to Juan de Figueroa.

government sent him money, however, Philip could not leave England. But the prospects of sending him the necessary funds were slim until Charles and Philip resolved their differences and restored confidence among the financial community.

The problem, in a nutshell, was that Charles refused to take responsibility for the unpalatable measures required. A suspension of payments, however limited, meant breaking the sovereign's word and brought in its trail important moral as well as financial considerations. Charles openly admitted it was dishonourable, and told Philip that he must put it into effect. Naturally he offered an incentive: if Philip did take responsibility for this unpalatable measure, Charles would reward him by giving him control of finance throughout the empire. Philip could sell revenues, lands, jurisdictions, raise taxation – do whatever was necessary to supply both himself and Charles. The shaky signature on these documents is a powerful reminder of the emperor's ill health and premature ageing.[56]

The proposal put forward on the emperor's behalf entailed a delayed suspension of payments. In January 1555 he ordered Juana to send him 200,000 ds immediately to cover the most pressing needs. Having supplied him with this, she was to suspend all payments assigned on the following revenues: all subsidies granted by the cortes of Castile and Aragon; revenues from the *maestrazgos* (rents of the lands belonging to the Military Orders); from the sale of lands or vassals belonging to the Military Orders; from papal bulls, and from the *subsidio* paid by the Spanish clergy. The much plundered Indies shipments were also affected: 500,000 ds were to be taken, the owners compensated with bonds issued on the revenues hitherto reserved for the upkeep of the households of prince Carlos, queen Juana, and the salaries of leading Castilian officials. No alternative source of supply for these was offered. Charles wanted the suspension to be selective – the goods of merchant bankers trading with the New World were to be exempt. The government must then calculate how much each financier was owed, and when they had lent the money, at what interest, etc., so that the most faithful should be the least affected. The government was to issue more annuities for sale. As the money became available it was to be shared between the two war fronts: 200,000 ds for Italy, 300,000 ds for the Netherlands; the rest he would use to fund the new campaign against France.[57]

Philip eagerly accepted responsibility for the finances of the empire, but on condition that the emperor took full charge – and blame – for the suspension of payments. Having experienced severe difficulties organising direct subsidies in his last regency, Philip did not believe that they could survive without access to credit and the exchange facilities of the bankers. Nor was he convinced that Charles had

---

[56] AGS PR. 26 fol. 149(1); AGS PR. 26 fol. 154, Charles's instructions to the council of finance; PR. 26 fol. 155, his letter to Juana. These powers were revoked later when Philip began to negotiate on his own, see the preamble to the loan in AGS CJH. 27 fol. 82. See also AGS E. 809 fol. 149, Ruy Gómez to Eraso, 25 February 1555; E. 809 fol. 57, *consulta*, London, 2 February 1555.

[57] AGS E. 809 fol. 37, Charles to Juana, 20 January; AGS PR. 26 fol. 153, Charles's instructions to Juan de Figueroa, also documents in previous note.

exhausted all possible means to ride out the crisis. From November 1553 at least, he had urged his father to buy back the Molucca islands, which Charles had sold to Portugal for 350,000 ds. A clause in the contract stated that he could buy them back for the original price, and as they were thought to yield revenues of one million ducats from their spice trade, Philip thought it an admirable way of recovering his patrimony and adding to his future revenues. Charles refused to get into further conflict with Portugal and would not admit that his controversial decision to sell the islands had been wrong.[58]

The king's next suggestion was that Charles should make an agreement with the colonists in the New World. The Castilian monarchs had always claimed full possession of all lands discovered, but allowed first natives, and later their tribute, to be assigned to the settlers in order to provide them with essential labour and support. These concessions were for short periods and from the outset the government had been under pressure to make the grants for life, or in perpetuity. The settlers were prepared to pay for the privilege, with an initial grant and annual taxation. They argued that the concession would prevent undue exploitation of the Indians; short contracts tempted settlers to get the utmost from the luckless natives for the brief time they enjoyed these services. But in the 1520s Charles had become convinced that there were powerful moral reasons for opposing all such contracts. He would gladly have abolished the system altogether but for the opposition this would have caused, and the conviction of all involved that the settlers would never survive without forced labour. Philip urged his father to set aside his moral scruples and exploit this source of revenue which had such great potential. At first Charles was evasive and not altogether discouraging, but as it became apparent that Philip was in earnest, he sharply expressed his determination not to burden his conscience. However, if Philip wished to endanger his soul, the emperor was willing to allow him to put this into effect too. It looked for a time as if Philip would force through this controversial issue, but the council of the Indies strongly argued against imposing such a radical change on colonial government until the rebellion in Peru had been crushed and its causes investigated. The matter was deferred.[59]

There was one final proposal put forward by Philip, more traditional if no less controversial ultimately. He suggested an increase in taxation in Castile. The matter was not easy; opposition from the tax payers apart, there were constitutional barriers against an additional tax burden. The Castilian cortes had agreed to substantial increases in taxation during the 1530s, but in exchange, they had been able to obtain some important concessions. Since 1534 the crown had agreed to settle for a fixed sum which included the expected yield from the two most

---

[58] AGS E. 98 fols. 329–39; AGS E. 103(2) fols. 140–2; AGS PR. 55 fol. 30; AGS E. 809 fol. 37.

[59] J. H. Parry, *The Spanish seaborne empire* (London, 1966, 2nd edn. 1967), pp. 175–86, good summary of the system of *encomienda* and pp. 186–9 *repartimiento*; for the debate between Charles and Philip, AGS E. 89 fols. 52–6; AGS E. 98 fols. 88–93, fols. 136–8; AGS PR. 55 fol. 27(iii); AGS E. 90 fols. 35–6.

important revenues, the *alcabala* and the *tercias*, as well as other less important taxes, allowing the localities to arrange quotas and collection of taxation. The agreement was called the *encabezamiento*. Through this, the crown benefited as it got a fixed sum of money. There were many advantages for the cortes and the cities too, not least the fact that the first agreement, drawn up in 1534, was meant to last for ten years. In 1547 Charles agreed to another five years. The localities were free to raise the money as best they could, and this enabled many of them to dispense with the unpopular *ad valorem* sales tax that Charles sought to impose. In Castile, as in the Netherlands, there was no general acceptance of such modes of taxation, and a marked preference for traditional levies. Freedom of action as well as the prospect of fixing the level of taxation for a lengthy period of time prompted Castilians to submit a proposal for a thirty year *encabezamiento*. To make it more palatable to the emperor, they agreed to a substantial increase in the level of taxation and proposed to use a portion of these revenues to redeem government bonds. Charles had neither accepted nor rejected the plans. He had, however, agreed that he would not increase taxation until making a final decision, which he promised for 1555. As the time for the cortes drew closer, Juana demanded that either Charles or Philip should come to Spain to deal with such an important alteration to the financial structure of the Castilian state.[60] She was ordered to summon the cortes, but when they met Charles refused to have anything to do with the matter, alleging that he had transferred power over the finances to Philip who now had the responsibility to deal with the issue.[61] This was rather disingenuous since as monarch of Castile, he would have to approve and impose any proposal with regards to the cortes.

Philip's advisers came up with a simple stratagem to get more money but avoid commitment over the thirty-year plan. He should refuse to summon the Castilian cortes as was expected. The agreement over taxation would lapse in 1555, technically leaving the crown without these revenues. But Philip should waive legality and continue to collect the taxes. As they had no legal existence, however, none of the assignations on them were valid. In other words, this was a very underhand way of imposing a suspension of payments. Philip rejected it, but the scheme he adopted in February 1555 with Charles's full assent was no less devious. The first step was to summon the cortes as usual. Juana was instructed to do this, but she was neither to commit the monarch to the *encabezamiento* nor to seem discouraging. Once they met she was to request the usual subsidies and when these had been granted, she was to suspend the cortes with no explanation but somehow avoid giving any cause for alarm. Then, seemingly out of the blue, orders

---

60 A useful summary of Castilian finances in Ulloa, *La Hacienda Real de Castilla en el reinado de Felipe II* (2nd edn., Madrid, 1977), pp. 115–18. The *encabezamiento* plans can be followed in AGS E. 809 fol. 57, *consulta*, 2 February 1555; AGS E. 109 fols. 147–8, opinion of the contadores, AGS E. 98 fols. 100–1; E. 809 fol. 37, Charles to Juana, 20 January; AGS E. 112 fols. 48–52, Juana to Charles, 11 February.
61 AGS E. 809 fol. 57, AGS E. 108 fol. 31, AGS E. 109 fol. 147–8.

would arrive from the monarch demanding that they should increase the subsidies. Philip's innate caution is in evidence here: first, assure yourself of the basic taxes, risk a confrontation afterwards.[62]

Great secrecy was enjoined, but some details must have been leaked. In any case, when the cortes opened on 3 May 1555, the deputies expected to discuss the thirty year *encabezamiento* and became highly nervous and suspicious when the royal officials evaded the issue. Within a short time there was much critical discussion of the crown's policies and complaints about inadequate defences and chaotic government. More importantly, the delegates refused to vote any taxes until they were given an unequivocal undertaking that taxation levels would remain unchanged until the king made a final decision over the thirty year plan, as Charles had promised. An acrimonious exchange of letters followed; revenue collection came to a virtual standstill. Philip had provoked a serious confrontation with the Castilian cortes and delayed tax collection, neither of which he had wanted. Worse still, it was to no avail, since the crown had to promise to extend the existing system for another five years.[63] Although Philip did not finally give up hopes of increasing Castilian taxes until the summer of 1555, before then he had realised that whatever expedients might be adopted, they would not yield sufficient money to avert a partial suspension of payments.

Once he had accepted this fact, Philip attempted to distance himself from what he realised would be an unpopular and dishonourable decision. He told his father that it was unfair to burden him with this and tarnish his reputation at the very beginning of his career. But Charles was adamant that he would not incur any further dishonour. When Philip sent Ruy Gómez to Brussels to persuade his father to take responsibility for the suspension, Charles refused to speak to him. Ruy Gómez was told he could speak to Mary of Hungary, Granvelle, or Praet; Charles would not deal with financial issues again. When the Spanish financial official Antonio de Eguino arrived in Brussels with details of Castile's desperate financial plight, Charles refused to see him and dispatched him to England.[64]

It was an astute move. Charles had divested himself of the responsibility to deal with unpleasant issues and avoided direct confrontations, but he did not in fact abandon control of finances as he claimed. Throughout this time he was secretly negotiating with his long-time associate Anton Fugger for a loan of 800,000 ds. Already on 20 January 1555 he had confessed to Juana that the loan he was planning was full of damaging and unpalatable conditions. He had then offered her the chance to avoid these and protect the Castilian realms by providing him with an equal sum of money.[65] Such tactics were unlikely to endear him to the Castilians. Besides, it was an unrealistic request and he should have realised this. Rumours of

[62] AGS E. 109 fols. 134–5; AGS E. 100(1) fols. 22–31; AGS E. 808 fol. 42; AGS E. 809 fol. 37.
[63] AGS E. 108 fol. 113; fol. 254; AGS E. 110(1) fol. 21. The cortes were in session until 28 September 1555. [64] AGS E. 809 fols. 147, 40, 75. [65] AGS E. 809 fol. 37.

these negotiations contributed to the confusion in the financial world. Unable to work out who was responsible for finances – and therefore liable – the merchant bankers wisely abstained from all negotiations. Eraso was at his wits' end. He had been given charge of securing further loans. Unable to find anyone willing to talk to him, he begged Charles to make a public statement explaining who was in charge, in order to infuse some confidence in the market. Unless this was done, he predicted, credit would collapse even without a suspension of payments.[66] The emperor does not appear to have done any such thing. Despairing of his father, Philip decided in March 1555 to go it alone. Using the documents Charles had sent him earlier, he started to negotiate loans and borrow his way out of the crisis. He made a personal appeal to the major banking houses and announced that he now had sole charge of the empire's finances.[67] Very soon, the market picked up and loans were forthcoming, but this had less to do with an increase in confidence than with three other factors: first, the imminent threat of bankruptcy of a number of firms; second, the need to secure royal backing; third, the release of additional revenues for loan repayments.

Deprived of their bullion both from the Indies fleets and from Philip's ships, starved of repayments falling due at the major financial fairs, several leading financiers faced bankruptcy. Tommaso Marino for example, long associated with Milanese finances, came near to collapse at the Besançon fair of 1555. The crown failed to meet contractual commitments and left him with a shortfall of 50,000 ds at the fair. He petitioned Philip, who arranged for the Spanish government to bail him out. Jerónimo de Salamanca and Hernan López del Campo found themselves in a similar situation and turned to Charles instead. The emperor also arranged for their rescue but he demanded in exchange a new loan of 160,000 ds, payable immediately. The unstable consortium decided to link up with other financiers, headed by Ippolito Afetati, and together they offered a loan of 300,000 es in February 1555. Interest rates were heavy: 33 per cent basic with an additional 13 per cent on any delayed payments. The financiers were in the uncomfortable position of being able to attract investment and raise further sums of money, but were increasingly unable to meet the terms of their loans as a result of the crown's constant defaults.[68] They were convinced that the emperor and his son would have to adopt some radical measures and believed rumours of a suspension of payments, but this very fear and uncertainty made them vulnerable to further appeals for aid. They needed to attract the favour of whoever retained control of the empire's finances, so that when the blow came, they would be spared its full effects.

[66] AGS E. 809 fols. 37 and 73.

[67] Among those he approached were the Fugger, the reply can be found in AGS E. 481 fol. 73.

[68] Marin's rescue AGS E. 809 fol. 107 (9 March 1555); Salamanca and López del Campo, AGS E. 108 fol. 35; E. 109 fol. 296. Afetati put in 150,000ds, which should have been repaid by October 1557; in 1569 he complained that the loan – consolidated capital and interest now adding up to 161,500ds – had not been paid.

To encourage further loans, Philip decided to release the revenues in Castile which funded the 200,000 ds annually needed to run his household. Charles heard of this sometime between May and June 1555, and he promptly ordered the council of finance in Castile to arrange a loan of 200,000 ds for him, assigning repayment on these revenues. The result was predictable and lamentable. Philip had released the revenues to fund his own loans. He had just concluded a contract for 300,000 ds and given these revenues for repayment. He was furious when he heard of his father's actions. He informed the Spanish government that since Charles had formally transferred power over the finances to him, they must obey him, not the emperor. His anger was fuelled by the fact that without this money he would not be able to leave England.[69] He was so short of money he could not even afford to stage the funeral obsequies for his grandmother, when queen Juana died in April of that year. He asked Charles to postpone the funeral in Brussels until he arrived so that he would not be accused of failing to pay his respects.[70]

The struggle between Philip and Charles for control over finance deepened as the campaigning season approached. The emperor continued to plan his campaign without reference to Philip, hence his determination to continue negotiating for loans, and the latter was still determined to lead it, whatever the cost. Whoever succeeded in raising money would of course win. Besides seeking credit, both men tried to fund their plans by making direct appeals to Spain. During May and June 1555, both sent urgent and contradictory orders demanding money. Both argued that this was the most pressing situation they had ever faced. In the strongest terms each claimed that only one of them had the right to be obeyed. Charles stated that as sole sovereign of the Spanish realms he took precedence over all others, and he ordered them to send 500,000 ds immediately for the Netherlands, and a further 300,000 ds for the Italian front. Using his father's powers to deal with finances throughout the empire, Philip put in his bid: 600,000 ds at once for Italy. This is the clearest proof of the different priorities and policies which the two men were pursuing in the spring and summer of 1555.

Philip urged the Spanish government to obey him, stressing that 'the enemy, the Italian princes and everyone else is watching me. All must be given to understand that the first provision I have organised is being collected with the urgency required, and is of such quantity as to enable me to preserve and increase the states his majesty has entrusted to me, as well as being equal to my reputation'.[71] Juan Vázquez claimed to have fallen ill with worry when he realised that there were two independent and contradictory demands. The Spanish officials were utterly divided over the issue of who should be obeyed. In the end they opted for a Solomon-style solution that satisfied no one. They divided what little money was available equally

[69] Details of the loans: AGS CJH. 27 fol. 121; AGS E. 809 fol. 110; AGS E. 1322 fol. 144; the reaction: Philip to Juan Vázquez, 3 July 1555, AGS E. 108 fols. 45–6; to Eraso, 18 May AGS E. 809 fol. 98.
[70] Gachard, *Retraite*, Introduction, pp. 63–4.   [71] AGS E. 809 fol. 75, Philip to Juana, 29 May.

125

between Charles and Philip.[72] Clearly the situation could not long continue like this. Confusion and chaos led to a dearth of finance for both men. Unable to make himself obeyed on the financial front, Philip stepped up his attempts to seize political control over the empire. But the meagre results also affected Charles, who was much less in evidence in the financial sphere after this. There would be no major campaign until one of them had successfully taken political and financial control of the empire. Charles and Philip were being inexorably drawn towards a full transfer of power. There was clearly no simple way to divide the empire geographically, and no hope at all of separating its chaotic and insufficient finances. If Charles wished to divest himself of responsibility for part of his inhuman burden, he must allow Philip a measure of power. Perhaps he was too old to allow this, or maybe too proud. He was certainly incapable of accepting a partition that would satisfy his son. Philip too was proud. His thirst for reputation and power combined with his mistrust of his father's policies – which can be largely ascribed to the uncertainty surrounding the emperor's repeated illnesses – made him equally intolerant. Moreover, they all knew that only a powerful, undivided appeal to the loyalty of their subjects could galvanise them into action and save the empire from destruction. Unitary command was imperative. It was against this background of conflict, tension and overwhelming sense of impending disaster, that the notion of honourable retirement resurfaced.

THE EMPEROR'S ABDICATION

Charles explained to his son and his servants that the decision to abdicate had been made without duress or compulsion, and was primarily rooted in three reasons. The first was, quite simply, that he wanted to retire. Secondly, he considered himself unfit to fulfil his duties: 'I realise that I can no longer undertake the tasks I ought to do both to satisfy my conscience and secure the common good of my subjects and vassals'. The third reason he gave was also the most frequently used in official propaganda; his recurrent bouts of ill-health incapacitated him for lengthy periods of time.[73] The fact that Philip was an adult, politically experienced and fully prepared to assume the appalling burdens of empire, was also instrumental in his decision to depart.

Contemporaries were aghast. Julius III thought it 'the strangest thing ever to happen'.[74] He was not far off the mark. Many monarchs had become senile and served out their term nevertheless. Charles, the consummate propagandist, had successfully created a magnificent departure which would continue to enthrall and confuse observers for centuries. He became so anxious to stress the longevity of the

---

[72] AGS E. 108 fol. 47, Juan Vázquez to Philip, 10 August 1555; E. 108 fols. 71–2, id. to Eraso, 13 April.

[73] AGS PR. 55 fol. 30, his instructions to Eraso and through him, Philip; RAH SC A-48 fol. 214, Charles to Juana, 15 January 1556.

[74] AGS E. 883 fol. 15 reported by Manrique de Lara, 23 March 1555.

plan that at least one writer dated its inception to his early childhood.[75] In reality, rumours of the abdication became persistent only after Metz, and especially after Alba returned to Spain with orders for Philip to inspect Yuste and begin alterations to the monastery so that the emperor could have new apartments there. It was not mooted again until 1553 when the first suspension of payments was proposed; it lapsed once again only to be revived when the second suspension was proposed in the summer of 1554. This last bout of intense speculation led Ruy Gómez to write to Eraso, stating that if the rumours turned out to be true, Philip would be extremely angry with Eraso, who had not warned them of the emperor's intentions. Evidently, Charles was either not expressing such feelings openly to his son nor to those close to him; or else Eraso had heard it all so often before he did not consider it serious enough to relate.[76]

The close correlation of such rumours with defeat and dishonourable actions made it easier for those around him, aware of his deep depressions, to consider his words as sheer escapism – the expression of his ardent desire to evade further dishonour and unpalatable decisions. To the world outside the court the appeal of such spectacular events was immense. There was much talk of this in Castile at least. When he sent a monk to Yuste in the summer of 1554, the man found that the news was so widespread it could not have been better known if it had been proclaimed in the main square of Valladolid.[77] The propagation of these rumours was an added cause of instability. Since Charles surrounded his decision with so much myth, it is now impossible to date it accurately. My own view, taking into account the long and painful process of power-sharing on the financial and Italian fronts, is that abdication gradually emerged in the course of 1555 as the most suitable option. Events were to show that Charles took a long time before being fully reconciled to the need to give up all his power.

When Philip was finally reunited with his father in September 1555 – after subsidies from Spain finally arrived – the transfer of the emperor's many titles was already well underway. This is not to say that this stage of the process was rapid or simple. Less than two months after he landed, he received two major titles: master of the Golden Fleece on 22 October, and sovereign of the Netherlands three days later, in the famous Brussels ceremony. Although the Netherlands was among the first states to be bestowed upon him, it was one area in which he had few prior contacts to ease his way to power. Indeed Charles reduced his son's prospects considerably. His departure from power was marked by his decision to make a large number of important appointments to ecclesiastical, military and civil offices. Some of these were for life, others vital for the government of the states – several provincial governorships, for example, and key financial posts. Philip was deprived

[75] BL Add Mss 1054.i.34.
[76] AGS E. 808 fol. 143, 12 August 1554. See also AGS PR. 55 fol. 30, Charles to Eraso; Gachard, *Retraite*, Introduction p. 45, vol. II, pp. 2–3; p. 72.
[77] Gachard, *Retraite*, Introduction, p. 45.

of an excellent chance to establish his men in positions of power. In order to ensure that Philip did not revoke these appointments, Charles had them falsely dated to the 22 October – the day of the transfer.[78] The emperor consulted him only over the position of regent, when it became apparent that Mary of Hungary was determined to resign and join her brother in Spain. The choice was between the prince of Orange, Ferrante Gonzaga and Emanuele Filiberto, duke of Savoy. Philip chose the last. Alba thought him a weakling, but then, as Ruy Gómez remarked, Alba did not consider any man able enough to govern, nor any part of the empire safe unless he was in charge.[79]

Savoy was appointed and given a full council, which included Granvelle, Lalaing, Berlaymont and Viglius. He had been issued with instructions and powers and was opening correspondence relating to the Netherlands, even if addressed to the king, by 24 October, although the appointment was not made public until four days later. In other words, all was settled before Mary's formal renunciation; the only hitch was over the title he could use. The states of Brabant objected to having a foreigner as regent, so he had to accept the title of lieutenant general of the Netherlands.[80] No one has commented on this, nor is there anything odd about the instructions or procedure. Yet it was surely unexpected. It was also another instance of how the fate of England and the Netherlands would be interwoven for a few years, usually (though seldom intentionally) to the detriment of the former. If we consider the background to Philip's arrival in the Netherlands – the insistent cries of disaster, the desperate call for his presence – we would assume Philip to have hastened to take direct control of the northern provinces. The appointment of a substitute with a full council after the campaigning season immediately suggested that Philip did not intend to stay in the Netherlands, and must have realised that they could well survive without his supervision. Philip intended to return to England. He had left his household there and wanted to secure his coronation which he knew would be debated at the forthcoming parliament. Unless he was present, he was certain he would not succeed.[81] The appointment of a regent was to lead to unprecedented chaos for almost a year. Philip was delayed in the Netherlands, as were Charles and Mary. Just where did power reside? All had their adherents and favourites. The struggles at court became immensely complex.

The reason for the king's unexpected stay in the Netherlands was the complexity of the abdication and the emperor's futile struggle to retain power without responsibility. After the official transfer of power in the Netherlands, one observer commented: 'before this weke passe he shall be the lyke of Spayne and Sycille, and then shall he be the greatest prince of seigneuries fallen unto him by right of lyne'.[82]

---

[78] Gachard, *Retraite*, Introduction, pp. 76–8 and Appendix E. pp. 170–83.
[79] AGS PR. 44 fol. 11(ii); Alba, *Epistolario*, vol. 1, pp. 268–72, 318–20.
[80] Brunelli, *I Diari*, pp. 20, 22; RPPB vol. 1, pp. 1–2; 7–8.
[81] Loades, *Mary Tudor*, p. 234; and his *Tudor conspiracies* pp. 179–81. CSP D. p. 70.
[82] RPPB vol. 1, pp. 1–2 John Mason to Sir William Petre.

Mason's remark is particularly interesting in two respects: first, it pinpoints the common expectation that Philip would soon be invested with the emperor's other dominions; second, that he would now become the largest landholder in Christendom, but not its most powerful prince. Unlike later writers, Mason did not allow himself to be dazzled by the sheer extent of territorial holdings, but took into account the many enemies and evident weaknesses of Philip's empire. His opinion was widely shared, yet months were to elapse before Philip was given the Spanish realms, Sicily or Sardinia.

The problem was that Charles realised a man without money and patronage was nothing in this world. In May 1555 he reassured one of his *confidentes* that he would not lose by accompanying Charles to his monastic retreat. No one would, he said vehemently: 'I will be quite capable of granting favours there, because I do not intend to let go of Spanish affairs so far nor in this manner'. The statement was all the more striking for being vague. Alba, who reported it to Philip, dismissed it lightly until another reliable source confirmed that Charles had been persuaded by his old servants to retain considerable control over the Spanish realms; above all, over finance. Philip would deal with routine administration and defence. In August Eraso confirmed that Charles had decided to give Philip the title to all remaining lands, but would maintain considerable financial powers. Ostensibly this was because he wished to discharge his so-called 'debts of conscience' before his death rather than leave it for his successors to do as was usual.[83] Philip had already experienced the qualified nature of the emperor's concessions in the financial sphere. He must have realised that this was the one, indivisible element of government. He evidently disabused his father of the viability of such plans. When the transfer of the Spanish realms and Sicily was accepted and ratified by him on 16 January 1556, there were no restrictions.[84]

Legal problems also contributed to the delay. Curiously enough, the cession of Sicily was drawn up in the names of both Charles and queen Juana, although she had been dead for nearly a year. Perhaps it was necessary to backdate it in order to ensure that appointments made before her death remained valid, or possibly because Sicily and Naples were still regarded as two parts of one realm: Sicilia Citerior (Naples) and Sicilia Ulterior (the island of Sicily) and the transfer had to be made as if for one unit. The problems surrounding the transfer of the Aragonese realms were far more serious. The deputies of the representative assemblies considered the transfer documents inadequate, and they were returned to Brussels for alteration in April 1556. Juan Vázquez warned that in the present mood of the Aragonese and with the plethora of *fueros* which regulated their relations with the

---

[83] Alba, *Epistolario*, vol. I, p. 119, Alba to Philip, 18 May 1555. Unfortunately Eraso's holograph to Juan Vázquez is not very clear. The key word 'ellos' could refer either to the financial returns of the *maestrazgos* only, or to the revenues of the military orders, Aragon, Castile and Sicily. Whatever the exact nature of his reservations they were to prove utterly unacceptable to Philip.

[84] AGS PR. 26 fol. 162(i), the Spanish realms.

crown, it was wiser to meet all their objections. He was worried by rumours that the Aragonese would reject the transfer as illegal. Juana became so alarmed by news of what was being said there that she advised Philip to defer the publication of Charles's abdication and his proclamation until the situation improved. She warned him that he would have to be present in the realms before the transfer could be officially registered. Philip dismissed her appeal for his return and deferral of his claim indignantly, and ordered her to announce the transfer at once. He sent don Diego de Acevedo, recently appointed treasurer of Aragon, to claim the realms and receive the oath of loyalty on his behalf. Charles signed the second renunciation in July 1556. When it arrived the council of Aragon backed Juana's arguments and insisted that it must not be presented in the corts unless Philip was there to take the oath himself. Anything less would contravene the privileges of the realms.[85] Years were to elapse before Philip was able to claim official recognition as king of Aragon – years of rebellion.

One of the titles which Charles tried to give away but could not for several years, was the most prestigious he possessed: that of Holy Roman Emperor. As negotiations between Ferdinand and the German princes took shape, he realised that the settlement was going to result in another compromise, politically and theologically, and he desperately tried to avoid being associated with it. He declared the Augsburg settlement to be dishonourable and a burden to his conscience and refused to ratify the agreement, preferring to give up the title first. Ferdinand had negotiated it on his brother's behalf, and he had no desire to take responsibility for what he considered to be the result of Charles's policies and mistakes. Moreover, like Philip over the issue of a suspension of payments, he did not wish to begin his rule over the empire tarnished with what was clearly a defeat for the emperor and for his faith. Ferdinand thought it unfair of Charles to off-load both the problems and responsibilities to his successors, when he no longer needed prestige and honour quite as desperately as they did. Charles was adamant in his refusal, so Ferdinand called upon his nephew to support his requests. Philip readily agreed. Between them they made sure that Charles signed the treaty of Augsburg, so often praised subsequently but which, at the time, no one wished to be responsible for.

Quite apart from a natural sympathy with a plight that so resembled his own, Philip had ulterior motives in persuading his father to retain imperial powers; soon, in fact, he sought to delay the transfer indefinitely. All sorts of unforeseen difficulties faced him as soon as Ferdinand assumed *de facto* imperial powers, which seems to have happened during the period when the transfer was being drawn up in 1555–6. They became of great importance during the preparations for the campaigns in Italy and the Netherlands. To begin with, Charles had relied very

---

85 AGS E. 113 fol. 206, Juan Vázquez to Vargas, 3 April 1556; RAH SC A-48 fol. 213v., Philip to Juana, 10 June 1556. Acevedo's credentials are in ibid., fol. 211, dated 11 July. New grant AGS PR. 26 fol. 163. See pp. 288–95 for the continuation of the Aragonese resistance.

heavily on German mercenaries and Philip could not replace them, particularly the cavalry, as the alternative were Swiss soldiers already committed to France. Moreover, he could not pay wage arrears to these companies so they had to be employed. In the summer of 1556 Philip asked permission to levy more soldiers in the Holy Roman Empire, and for a muster station in the Tyrol or another imperial possession near Italy as usual. He also counted on using the artillery stored in Innsbruck, much needed in Milan. Above all, he needed the cooperation of the imperial feudatories near the duchy who were refusing to quarter or feed his troops and making difficulties over passage. He asked Ferdinand to order them to comply. He did not get a reply until November of that year, by which time the French attack on Milan was imminent. To cap it all, Ferdinand allowed some levies – but not in the areas Philip had chosen, and refused all other requests. When Philip begged him to reconsider, stressing the great danger he was in, he met with a firm and negative response.[86]

This put the cat among the pigeons. Although Philip had repeatedly stated that he had no wish to make a bid for the imperial title, acknowledging his advisers' dictum that the prestige was great, but the responsibility to cleanse the area of heresy was infinitely greater, he needed it now to withstand the French attacks.[87] He persuaded his father to retain the imperial title for a year or so. Ferdinand's preparations to assume the title were already well advanced, but he showed no resentment. He chose to make the best of a bad job and claimed he was thankful for the delay, since it would allow him to overcome the strong opposition which had been aroused by news of the transfer in Germany and Rome. The electors and the pope both claimed the right to choose Charles's successor, arguing that his abdication would leave the throne vacant.[88] The conflict served as a warning to both Ferdinand and Philip that enmity between the two branches of the Habsburgs was politically unwise as well as morally reprehensible. Whilst retaining full independence, they adopted a guarded, cautious attitude towards each other, straining to maintain the shaky family alliance, seeking a more amicable relationship. Charles successfully unburdened himself of the imperial title just before his death. Philip then offered his uncle powerful support both at the curia and in Germany, and he made sure Ferdinand obtained the necessary ratification of his title.[89]

Another example of the complexities involved in Charles's abdication is the fact that he retained the Franche-Comté until his death. Not out of affection, but because the area was protected by a neutrality agreement signed by Charles and Henry II which explicitly excluded their successors. The French king was in such a

---

[86] The matter can be followed in the copious correspondence printed in Codoin vol. II, pp. 421, 449–52, 453–5, 457–62, 467–9. Fichtner, *Ferdinand I*, pp. 209–20.

[87] AGS PR. 55 fol. 33; E. 521 fol. 45.

[88] Codoin, vol. 2, pp. 471–2, 475–6, 484–6, 502, pp. 505–7; AGS E. 119 fol. 412; AGS E. 120 fol. 65.

[89] BPR II-2291, J. Tassis to Granvelle, 7 January 1559; VDK vol. III, pp. 17–21, 35–8; AGS E. 650 fol. 140; AGS E. 884 fol. 7; AGS E. 885 fols. 135–6; AGS E. 886 fol. 154.

strong position that everyone assumed he would refuse to renew the concession.[90] This area apart, Philip was in possession of his patrimony by the closing weeks of 1556. It was then that he had new seals struck, new cyphers drawn up and confirmed or appointed officials, apportioning grants and pensions.[91] Charles, Mary of Hungary and Leonor finally set sail for Spain on 17 September, thus ending speculation about the emperor's retirement. Philip was at last left alone at the head of the empire.

CHARLES'S ROLE AFTER HIS ABDICATION

During the last few months he spent in the Netherlands, Charles spent most of his time in a small house outside Brussels – perhaps the same place where he had spent such long periods of meditation before his abdication. A certain reluctance to leave is apparent, and understandable. He refused to go without having paid his household, and since there was no money in the Netherlands, months passed until the Spanish government sent enough bullion to cover this and other expenses for his journey. There were times when illness set back the departure as well. Then, at the end, the emperor delayed once more, wishing to see his daughter María and Maximilian before he left; perhaps this was a last minute attempt to patch up relations with his nephew. Most observers could appreciate that once he left, his son would take control of the Netherlands, but there was a great deal of scepticism about Philip's capacity to rule. It was also generally assumed that once Charles was away from the scene of his latest defeats and distanced from his son, he would recover his spirits and exercise the authority that had been his for so long. Few had any doubts that he would guide and control the policies of his son, who was still widely, if erroneously, perceived as an ineffectual and indecisive individual.

Inevitably, Charles will continue to figure in the forthcoming analysis of the French wars and the troubles within the Spanish realms during 1557–8. However, it will be valuable to establish here the nature of his intervention and role in state affairs after his arrival in Spain, since there has been such confusion about it. Interest in the emperor's life in the monastery of Yuste has not been lacking: there have been at least four books in the last century on this theme, none more influential than the three volume work by the great Belgian historian Gachard.[92] By demonstrating that Charles continued to take an interest in state affairs and participated in certain aspects of government, Gachard seemed to furnish proof for the common assumption that he continued to influence, even dictate his son's policies. This is simply not the case.

[90] Gachard, *Retraite*, Introduction, pp. 116–18; Febvre, *Franche-Comté*.
[91] J. de Vandernesse, *Journal des voyages de Philippe II de 1554 à 1559, in Collection des voyages des souverains des Pays-Bas*, (vol. IV, Brussels, 1882), p. 22; J. Dévos, *Les chiffres de Philippe II (1555–1598)* (Brussels 1950), pp. 91–100.
[92] Gachard, *Retraite*; next in importance is W. Stirling, *The cloister life of the emperor Charles V* (London, 1853).

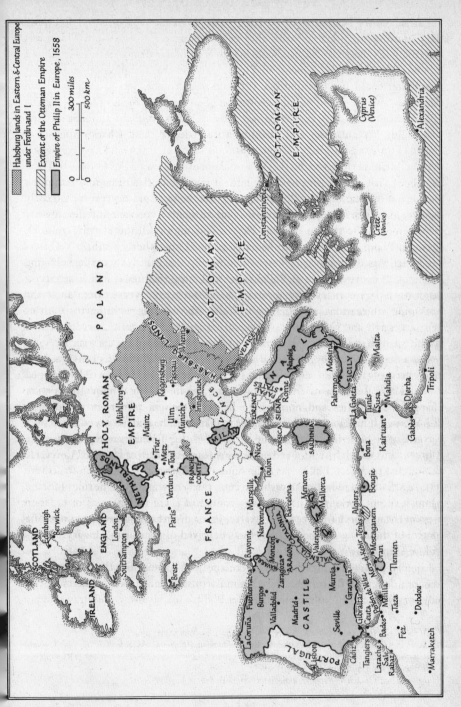

Map 1 Europe and the Mediterranean

Legend:
- Habsburg lands in Eastern & Central Europe under Ferdinand I
- Extent of the Ottoman Empire
- Empire of Philip II in Europe, 1558

300 miles
500 km

Father and son had discussed the latter's role before his departure, and, following the pattern of the previous years, they could not agree. For example, Philip was extremely anxious that Charles should take over tuition of prince Carlos. He wanted his son to live with the emperor in Yuste, knowing that the physical and mental association could not but improve the wild young man, and provide immense symbolic value. It would be a concentration of authority, a focus of loyalty for the Spanish realms. Moreover, Carlos was causing grave problems at Juana's court, challenging her authority and flaunting that of lesser men. Charles must have known of this, and the brief encounters at court on his arrival would have confirmed the fact. Such was his aversion that he would not even allow Carlos to come to Yuste for a brief visit, let alone to live near him. Ironically, Carlos came to worship the memory of his grandfather. Philip repeated his request, and never more urgently than in 1558 when he recalled García de Toledo, Juana's favourite and the only one who seemed to be able to control Carlos's tantrums. Still the emperor refused, although Philip did not give up his attempt until his father's death.[93]

Charles was determined to keep a low profile. He did not want to be in the limelight, at court or even, as Philip requested more than once, in a large city or major town. In February 1557, for example, Philip became very anxious about the worsening international situation and extolled the advantages of having Charles more accessible and visible to all – he would act as a focus of loyalty, serve as a check on the Spanish government, and create an impression that if things went awry, he would assume control over Spain at a moment's notice. Philip was convinced the mere threat of this would serve to deter French attacks.[94] He might well have hoped it would also deter Juana from overstepping the mark. But Philip's pleas went unanswered. Charles had no wish to be seen without power; it would have dishonoured him. However, he did agree to take over the endless negotiations over Navarre after his arrival. Antoine de Bourbon, duke of Vendôme represented the Albret claims which had devolved upon his wife on the death of Henry d'Albret. He also offered to defect. Philip was as anxious as his father had ever been to achieve this. In a distorted reflection of earlier events, Juana now assumed the role of fearful Spanish regent seeking to control the conduct of these negotiations in order to prevent the monarch from ceding Navarre. Juana eventually succeeded in wresting control of these negotiations; Charles was deprived of his role in January 1558 as will be seen later.[95]

Equally protracted and fruitless were the negotiations for the departure of Leonor's daughter, the infanta Maria, from Portugal. Leonor was anxious to see her only surviving child – still unmarried after Philip's unchivalrous withdrawal of his

---

[93] AGS E. 129 fols. 147–8; AGS E. 128 fols. 393, 400; Codoin XXVII, pp. 184–7.

[94] AGS E. 515 fol. 92, his instructions to Ruy Gómez, 2 February; AGS E. 119 fol. 205, Gaztelu (Charles's secretary) to Juan Vázquez; AGS E. 129 fols. 147–8, where it is reported that Ruy Gómez had a five hour audience with Charles.

[95] pp. 214–15; Gachard, *Retraite*, especially letters in vol. II.

proposal. She wished her daughter to come and live with her; doubtless Charles and Philip appreciated the political value of so well-endowed an heiress. The princess could only be persuaded to visit her mother briefly at the Portuguese border; she refused to live in Castile. Despite the inordinate efforts made by Charles, his intervention was a failure.[96] These two were the most important issues he tackled in his retirement. His record can hardly be said to be spectacular.

One other task Philip requested and which Charles undertook with some measure of success, was to keep up pressure on Juana and the regency government so that they would continue to send subsidies. This would lead to grave conflict between the emperor and his daughter, and was to be of great importance in determining the level of influence Charles had over the regency government. As he quickly appreciated, his power to intervene depended both on access to information and the willingness of the regency government to obey him. As early as October 1556 Charles complained that he was not being sent sufficient information.[97] Shortly afterwards, he expressed annoyance because he was not being regularly consulted. He also complained that the regency government was not showing the degree of deference and respect he expected from them. It would be easy to dismiss these statements as mere signs of impatience. Clearly they would all require time and effort to adjust to the novel situation. But there were serious problems to overcome as well. Decisions were seldom made with only one round of consultation; and even if they were, adding Yuste to the long line from Brussels, Valladolid and wherever the problem or letter originated meant extending the process of discussion and the time needed to tackle state affairs. This was hardly desirable at a time of crisis. Nevertheless Charles was right to suspect that the regency government were keeping him in the dark on certain matters and lacking in respect.

To begin with, the regency government must have feared losing power and prestige as a result of the emperor's return. The nature of the illness that affected Charles before his retirement and continuous bouts of ill health must have made them distrustful of his ability to deal with state affairs. Above all, the regency rejected Charles's advice and resented his interventions because he was so out of sympathy with their aspirations and problems. From the moment he set foot in Castile Charles vociferously opposed their most cherished projects – as can be seen more fully in chapter 7. His suspicions proved all too accurate: a man without patronage and power was nothing in this world.

---

[96] Gachard, *Retraite*, Introduction, pp. 105ss, and many of the letters published in vol. II.
[97] Gachard, *Retraite*, vol. II, p. 97.

4

Italy: the tempting prize, 1555–9

The impact of the emperor's illness and the transfer of power upon the international situation has been ignored for too long. Their combined effect was to prompt further attacks upon the scattered possessions of the Spanish Habsburgs. It was no coincidence that the duke of Florence should choose to make his decisive bid for control of Siena shortly after receiving reports from his envoy in Brussels which might be summarised in one of the phrases he used: 'it is not known whether his majesty is Caesar or *nihil*'.[1] The pope thought he knew very well. Charles, he said, was 'a miserable and sorry creature, [a] cripple in body and soul', and the conclusion Paul IV drew from his assessment was this: 'The tyrant, the Emperor, need no longer be taken into consideration, for his possessions are like an old house, which when a single stone is removed, falls to pieces; when we, here in Italy, give him a slight blow, everything will be laid in ruins'.[2]

Paul was sabre-rattling and therefore liable to exaggerate his enemy's weakness in order to heighten his own strength and attract allies. For similar reasons, we have to discount many of the public utterances made by the French king and his ministers as propaganda aimed to bolster up the spirit of the anti-Habsburg coalition.[3] Yet we would be wrong to dismiss their statements entirely. Henry proved by his actions that, like Paul, he was convinced Charles's empire was on the brink of destruction and could be pushed over the precipice if only one state could be isolated and invaded. This accounts for Philip's obsession to defend every inch of his inheritance.

The transfer of power was not thought to have improved the chances of survival of the empire as far as its many enemies were concerned. Once the shock of the abdication was past and the effects of the acquisition of England and Philip's good impression had worn off, Habsburg enemies noted the many disadvantages Philip faced. He was utterly inexperienced in international politics and military affairs. He seemed to them a weak figure whose most notable attribute was his capacity to take orders, first from his father, then from his wife. 'Spiritless', and 'untried' were two

---

[1] Cit by G. Spini, 'The Medici principality and the organization of the states of Europe in the sixteenth century', *Journal of Italian History*, 3 (1979) p. 428.

[2] Cit J. F. von Pastor, *The history of the popes*, ed. R. F. Kerr (vols. XIV–XVII, London, 1951), vol. XIV, pp. 127 and 130 respectively.

[3] See for example Vertot, vol. II, pp. 135, 150–2, 195; 207–9.

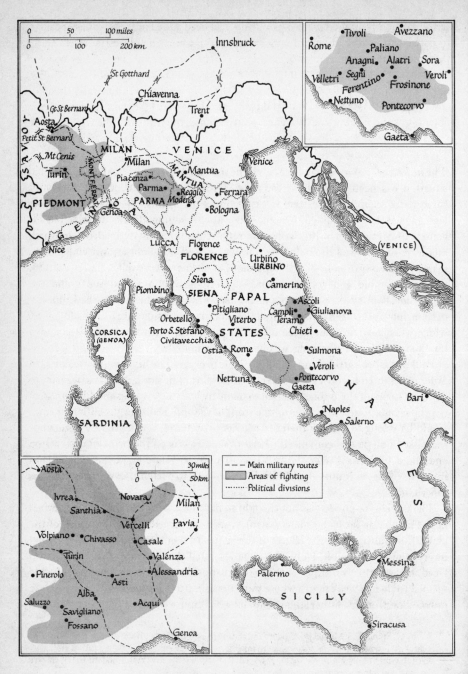

Map 2 Italy in the 1550s

terms frequently applied to him; 'cowardly' had been added in the 1550s as he failed to participate in the great military events of the time. His closest advisers were thought to suffer from similar deficiencies. On the military side he had Savoy, who was considered too young; Gianbaptista Castaldo and the marquis of Pescara were too old. Alba alone had the experience and the right age but was generally thought cowardly. His favourites and political advisers were likewise dismissed as nonentities and lacking in experience. Furthermore, the lands he inherited were all visibly rent by internal divisions, financial problems and unrest. This was hardly a winning combination.[4]

Henry's successful alliance with the German princes had singled out the Netherlands as the most suitable place to attack, and until the inconclusive campaign of 1554 it seemed as if the French would continue to strike until it fell. After that, they reconsidered their strategy. Their troops continued to gain ground in Italy, particularly the Piedmont–Milan front, and it appeared that here perhaps, was the weakest link in the Habsburg chain of states. The advent of a friendly pope in 1555 eager to cement an aggressive alliance with Henry merely reinforced the French move southwards. It became their priority to seize control of the region which still retained the aura of being the epicentre of the Christian world and the base for political and religious dominance.

DEFEAT AND RETREAT IN ITALY, 1555–6

Henry launched his campaign early and met with immediate success. By March 1555 Ivrea and Casale, two important positions which enabled France to dominate Montferrat, were taken. The imperial stronghold of Valenza was now threatened, as were the important routes down to Genoa and across to Piacenza. Worse still, it meant that the French now controlled an area used to quarter the imperial army during the winter. Naturally it was feared that Italian allies would defect to avert a French invasion of their lands. At the time, Charles and Philip were still arguing over the appointments of Gonzaga and Alba. Later, the latter was to accuse Charles of having deliberately stirred up the Gonzaga affair in order to prevent his departure for the threatened front. The accusation is clearly a retrospective attempt to shift the blame for the alarming losses that followed hard on Alba's arrival.[5] All of them bear their share of the blame for the worsening situation in northern Italy, and were responsible for the continuing delays of the duke's departure. The role of Philip and Charles has been touched upon earlier (pp. 104–7). Alba's reason for delaying his arrival at the threatened front once Charles and Philip stopped quarrelling was the shortage of money.

In February 1555 Philip's advisers estimated that more than a million ducats would be necessary to sustain their present position in Piedmont–Milan. A great

4 Cabrera de Córdoba, *Felipe II*, vol. 1, p. 71.
5 Alba, *Epistolario*, vol. 1, p. 319, to Philip, 28 October 1555.

deal more was required to go on the offensive. Wage arrears for the troops had already reached the half million mark. Of course there were mutinies, but relatively few since the men believed that once Philip took over, he would redress the situation and make the required provision. Alba was fully aware that if he arrived empty-handed, these hopes would collapse and large-scale mutinies occur. He wrote in May 'my life and my honour, as well as his majesty's states and reputation, depend on my being sent 600,000 ds from Spain immediately'. This and what might be raised in Brussels would enable him to mount a campaign. Alba assured Philip that the situation in Spain was already so dire it hardly mattered if they made it just a little worse. Although we remain ignorant of Philip's opinion on this, he certainly agreed that his reputation was on the line and urged Juana to furnish him with the required amount, stressing that everything depended on success in this campaign.[6] Alba was confident of his ability to commandeer funds from Spain. He sent Luis Barrientos to demand the money and refused to accept the 400,000 which the regency government, forced to meet the demands of Charles as well, offered instead. It was to prove a serious miscalculation. The regency government did not change its mind.

For months nothing but complaints were heard. Alba reiterated that he was being starved of funds to the detriment of the king's affairs, due to the machinations of Eraso and Ruy Gómez. Impressed by the consistency of Alba's cries and accusations, the Spanish historian Carande came to the conclusion that no money was sent from Spain to the north Italian front from April 1555 to May 1556. He claimed that Alba's suspicions were correct, and that the dearth of funds was due to the malice of his enemies. Maltby recently supported this analysis of the situation.[7] That there was antipathy between the three men cannot be denied, but just who was the victim is questionable. Alba was determined to destroy Eraso and advance Rodrigo Dueñas, for whom he promised to obtain the post of *contador mayor*, one of the most important officers in the Castilian finances. Dueñas in exchange promised an immediate loan of 300,000 ds for Alba and full support in the future. The other candidate for the post was Eraso. When Philip assumed control of the financial machinery in March 1555, Alba told the king that this was the ideal moment to destroy Eraso's power and replace him. By April he was so confident that his campaign against Eraso had succeeded that he informed Dueñas that he was as good as appointed; the public announcement would follow soon. He wished the Spanish financier many happy years in his post. In May, impatient of the delay, Alba recommended Eraso's immediate execution. But the duke had at last found his match: Eraso was just as venomous, and just as good at court intrigue. He

---

[6] Alba, *Epistolario*, vol. I, p. 115, Alba to Antonio de Toledo, 15 May; p. 142, id to Philip; *Consulta* AGS E. 809 fol. 57; AGS E. 109 fol. 350; AGS CJH. 27 fol. 113; AGS E. 108 fol. 41, situation in Italy and Philip's requests. pp. 125–6 deals with the impact of the dual request from Charles and Philip.

[7] Carande, *Carlos V y sus banqueros*, vol. III, p. 441; Maltby, *Alba*, pp. 88–109, esp. 89–90. Alba, *Epistolario*, vol. I, p. 97 original accusation to Philip, 11 May 1555.

discovered what Alba was up to, and rapidly patched up his strained relations with Juan Vázquez. Together the two secretaries secured sufficient incriminating evidence to destroy Dueñas's career as a royal official and discredit Alba, revealing his less than admirable machinations. Charles seized upon the affair in order to lash out at both Alba and Dueñas, whom he hated by now. 'Look my son, what delightful transactions!' he commented, 'Many more like it will occur if you do not keep your eyes wide open'. He warned Philip always to be on his guard against Alba. Realising the game was up, Dueñas withdrew the 300,000 ds offered to Alba. Death saved him from the punishments Charles would have liked to have inflicted upon him.[8]

From this account it is evident that Eraso had good reason to cramp Alba's style and ensure that he was not supplied with money which would enhance his reputation and increase his power. Nevertheless, there was a limited amount he could do. After all he was not the only one assigned to the important task of supplying the Italian front. Philip also ordered Domingo de Orbea, Dueñas (before his fall), Juana and the financial council in Castile to do the same. Eraso and Ruy Gómez could not control these diverse groups. Moreover, all of them were under great pressure from Philip to produce the goods. He made it clear that he meant to make a success of the Italian campaign, and was measuring their efficiency and loyalty by their ability to provide him with what he wanted and needed. With all the good will in the world, however, they could not operate effectively in a financial market suffering from a great dearth of specie and lack of confidence in Habsburg finances. In Brussels they only managed to secure credit notes for 200,000 ds. When Alba, thoroughly irritated, decided to negotiate the loans himself, he found that despite offering his own lands and possessions as security, he could only raise 50,000 ds in cash. He later claimed that the shortage of specie in Italy combined with the reluctance of the financiers to negotiate with the Habsburgs forced him to cash the notes at a discount: he lost 37,000 ds in the transaction. He even had problems cashing in a credit note of 6,000 ds.

In June 1555, amidst loud calls of cowardice and with this paltry financial support, Alba set off for Italy. He considered it imperative to mount a campaign, however late in the year, and relentlessly called for sufficient finance. Spain – as can be seen from Table 7 – did make substantial contributions, whatever historians have said in the past. But the irregular nature of the subsidies and desperate need for money to launch the campaign inevitably led to intense financial demands from the Italian realms. This had been a primary motive for demanding unitary command; the ability to commandeer funds from one area to another was the key to survival. Alba had already sent Bernardino de Mendoza to Naples in April of that year, to investigate the financial situation there. Naples had already made a generous

---

[8] The unsavoury episode can be pieced together from AGS E. 508 fol. 176, Charles to Philip, AGS E. 108 fol. 112, Juan Vázquez to Eraso; Alba, *Epistolario*, vol. 1, p. 119, pp. 70–1. Dueñas's appointment in 1554 and Charles's opposition, p. 88.

Table 7. Piedmont–Milan Front 1553–6

Date	Revenues (Milan)	Amount requested	Loans: assigned on Spanish revenues	Subsidies N = Naples S = Spain	Monthly cost of army	Wage arrears	References
1553	400,000 es[1]			N180,000 es[2]	112,000[1]		1 AGS E 1202 fol. 130; E 1209 fol. 11 2 Chabod, Lo Stato di Milano, p. 128
End of 1553			80,000 es[1] Total for 1553 [418,000 es][2]			c. 247,715[1]	1 AGS E 1203 fol. 165 2 Chabod, Lo Stato di Milano, pp. 132–3
July 1554		100,000 es[1]		N100,000 es[2] (during 1554)			1 AGS E 508 fol. 174 2 Chabod, Lo Stato di Milano, p. 128
October 1554			total for the year 420,000 es			290,000	AGS E 1026 fol. 102; Chabod, Lo Stato di Milano, pp. 132–3
January 1555		600,000 es by Alba					

Date					References
February 1555	100,000 es[1] (for Siena)	200,000 es[2]		400–500,000[3]	1 Ags E 809 fol. 36; 2 E 109 fol. 42–3; 3 E 809 fol. 57.
March 1555	450,000 es[1]	S 200,000 ds[2] N 150,000 ds[3]			1 E 108 fol. 161–2; 2 E 108 fol. 57–8 it was to be shared with the Northern front; 3 E 1048 fol. 5.
May 1555	100,000 es[1]	288,000[3] (n.b. 1st installment of Centurion loan not paid until July)	S 50,000 es[1]	200,000 ds[2] used for payment of arrears	1 AGS E fol. 74–5; 2 Alba, *Epistolario*, I, p. 235; 3 AGS CJH 34 fol. 103.
June 1555	600,000 es[1]	200,000 ds[1]	230,000 es[2]	800,000 ds[2]	1 Alba, *Epistolario*, I, p. 97; 2 id. pp. 190, 238.
July 1555		N 100,000			Alba, *Epistolario*, I, p. 258.
August 1555	1.3 millions[1]	60,000 es[2] S 200,000 ds[1]			1 AGS E 108 fols. 160–6; E 109 fol. 350(3); 2 Donation of Volpiano, Alba, *Epistolario*, I, p. 283.

contribution on hearing of the fall of Casale. The temporary governor, cardinal Jaén, sent 150,000 ds. To cover this loan he had to pledge the last available free revenues in the realm. The Neapolitan government was left with 127,000 ds to cover annual expenditure many times that sum.[9] By then sales and alienation of revenue had built up an annual deficit of 339,000 ds. The Neapolitans did not regard the dispatch of such subsidies as a gift; it was a demonstration of loyalty and cooperation for which they expected due reward in the shape of subsidies from Spain. This view was implicit in the response of the king and Spanish regency government, who occasionally sent them subsidies. That spring 200,000 ds had been sent; Jaén used them to pay off some of the wage arrears, fearing that his troops would mutiny at a time when invasion was anticipated.

When Alba learnt of this, he was beside himself and used choice language to berate Jaén.[10] Ever resolute, Alba used desperate measures to raise the money he needed to launch the campaign. He asked Philip's permission to seize 200,000 ds of the investments held by the *Monte* of Naples – the municipal bank – promising to replace them quickly from the 300,000 ds which he expected soon from Spain.[11] It seems unlikely that this was a banking service for the poor, as were many other of the *montes*. The sums involved are much too large. Nevertheless, Alba admitted that the seizure was morally reprehensible, and politically explosive, which is why he sought Philip's support. If the Neapolitans ever found out that their investments had been seized to fund a campaign to defend Milan, there would be serious trouble. Alba lamented their inability to understand that in saving Milan he was protecting Naples. He also tried to make Philip accept the measure by stressing that no other choice was open to them. Permission must have been given, for Alba used the money; this, together with forced contributions from Milan, such as the 60,000 es he took from Volpiano, enabled him at last to mount a campaign.[12]

At the head of 23,000 infantry, Alba sought to check the French advance and cut their communications by taking Santià, but was forced to lift the siege and retreat, first to Pontesura then to Valenza. The long struggle for Volpiano ended in September 1555 when it fell to the French and, by all accounts, Philip was distraught. Alba by contrast, was defiant and irate.[13] He tried to comfort the king by explaining that the loss of one place in Piedmont was not likely to do irreparable damage to his reputation. After all, he argued, everyone could see the terrible state in which Charles had left the area. In a vituperative attack against the emperor, Alba

[9] AGS E. 1048 fol. 5. Basic interest rate was no less than 41 per cent and Jaén did not think it excessive because the merchant bankers had lent as much as 800,000ds recently and not been paid back at all.

[10] AGS E. 1048 fols. 12–13; Alba, *Epistolario*, vol. I, p. 68, Alba to Mendoza, 7 April; pp. 99–100, id. to Philip, 11 May; pp. 160–1, 235, reaction to Jaén, 'this ancient little turd' ('este cagajón de vejezuelo').

[11] Jaén had also used these funds to anticipate the 150,000ds loan he sent after Casale; AGS E. 882 fol. 126; Carande, *Carlos V y sus banqueros*, vol. III, p. 440; Alba, *Epistolario*, vol. I, pp. 172–3.

[12] AGS E. 1049 fol. 69 – note that he took 100,000ds in July, 100,000ds in August–September and repaid at least half of it soon after. Alba, *Epistolario*, vol. I, pp. 258, 277, 283, 297.

[13] Alba, *Epistolario*, vol. I, pp. 149, 237–8, 279, 303–4.

accused him of wilfully neglecting the Italian realms and behaving in the last few years as if he were determined to do his utmost to help the French take Piedmont–Milan. Alba declared that Charles had only given the area to his son when he realised that it would soon fall to France. He had lacked the courage to stand up and fight. If Philip had proved less decisive, Alba went on, the whole of Piedmont–Milan, and not just Volpiano, would be flying the French flag now. Clearly Alba's attack was a means to transfer some of the dishonour and loss of reputation to Charles. Yet he was right to consider the emperor's decision to withdraw money and manpower from Italy highly damaging. The duke was very bitter that no diversion had been created along the Netherlands frontier to reduce the pressure on Piedmont–Milan, and even more annoyed by the emperor's partisan allocation of funds, allowing the north to get most of the subsidies, while the Italian front bore the brunt of the fighting.[14] The duke's resentment was certainly shared by many of Philip's Italian subjects.

Shortly after the fall of Volpiano, Franco–Italian troops took Moncalvo. Almost all the possessions of the duke of Mantua on the west side of Milan had now fallen to the enemy. This, and the disgraceful treatment of his brother, Ferrante Gonzaga, led to strong suspicions of his defection. Alba was becoming increasingly desperate to find new winter quarters to replace those seized by the French, particularly as imperial feudatories were refusing to cooperate with Philip. Mutiny was also reducing his effective forces: in August he had left his own son as a hostage to mutinous troops, and with wage arrears of 800,000 ds he was genuinely concerned for the safety of his son. By December he was utterly despondent. He told Philip they faced a stark choice: either the king raised money to fund a vast campaign in 1556, or he must seek a truce. Alba assured him that they were drifting inexorably into disaster. Milan would certainly be in French hands in 1556 unless they acted immediately, particularly as Henry was known to be keen to take the field himself in the next campaign. As he put it to Ruy Gómez, 'if we have no money for a war, then let us make peace'. Alba's own preference was expressed in a characteristically forthright and colourful phrase: 'I long for peace more than any nun could'.[15]

Philip was inclined to agree that a truce was their best option by the winter of 1555. Peace was out of the question since his weakness would mean he would be forced to accept unpalatable conditions. His decision to favour a suspension of hostilities was not primarily based on the financial problems of the Italian front, nor the recent losses in Piedmont–Milan, both of which he could reasonably expect to counter in the forthcoming campaign. His fear was for the safety of Naples, now threatened by a Franco–papal alliance. It was imperative to disengage in the north if the threat to the southern realm materialised.

---

[14] Alba, *Epistolario*, p. 319, Alba to Philip, 28 October.
[15] Alba, *Epistolario*, vol. I, p. 207, Alba to don Francisco de Toledo, 21 June; p. 334, to Philip, and p. 341 to Ruy Gómez, December 1555.

Henry had a long tradition of French interest and involvement in Neapolitan affairs behind him, yet he had wisely concentrated on the weakest and nearest Italian sector to attack. Naples became a target by dint of the determined campaign of an octogenarian pope, Gianpiero Carafa, born in Naples and elected on 23 May 1555 to the papal throne. It was usual for the major powers to draw up lists with their preferred candidates for the papacy prior to and during an election. Charles refused to do this in that year, alleging (after a lifetime of intervention) that such practices were burdensome to his conscience. Philip and Mary of Hungary had no such qualms and drew up their lists, which Charles then altered! They had made one unusual addition – specifically excluding one candidate, Carafa. The reason was his well-known francophile sentiments. The instability at the centre of Habsburg government was evident in the confusion and lack of control among the pro-imperial cardinals during the election. The election was a shambles, they were in complete disarray, and Carafa was chosen, taking the name Paul IV. He soon learnt of the exclusion clause, which did nothing to improve his opinion of the emperor or all that was Spanish.[16]

Nevertheless his initial contacts were amiable enough. Paul IV, the once famed ascetic reformer, was transmuted into yet another nepotist once the papal tiara was on his head. His main interest was to advance his dynasty, particularly his nephews: for Carlo Carafa, recently appointed cardinal deacon, he requested the bishopric of Naples; for the duke of Camerino, he demanded Piacenza and other territories. Philip decided to reject both requests. The first, because Carlo Carafa was a rough, licentious soldier, who had served in the emperor's armies until three years previously, when he defected to France. He was far from possessing those theological or moral virtues so highly valued by Philip in all bishops, but particularly those in restive areas like Naples. As for Piacenza, Philip was determined to retain it, and he objected most strongly to Paul's premature investiture of the fief of Piacenza upon his nephew.[17] Having been rebuffed, Paul allowed his hostility to surface with a vengeance. At first his anger was directed against those nearer home – the Roman aristocrats who had become the allies of the Spanish and Habsburg dynasties. Again, it was an obscure, minor incident that sparked off the explosion: the pro-imperialist count of Santa Fiora, head of the Sforza family, along with his brother cardinal Alessandro and Guido Ascanio, persuaded two other Sforza brothers serving in the French fleet to defect with their ships. The defection took place in a papal port and Paul decided that they had breached papal laws and dishonoured him. He demanded the return of the galleys to France and imprisoned some of the lesser men involved. He also threatened to

16 AGS E. 882 fol. 112, AGS E. 509 fol. 111; AGS E. 509 fol. 161; AGS E. 882 fol. 25; Pastor, *History of the popes*, vol. XIV, pp. 65–72, 76–7. Charles had placed great hopes in Carafa's predecessor, Marcellus, see AGS E. 509 fols. 98 and 142.

17 AGS E. 882 fol. 44; Alba, *Epistolario*, vol. I, pp. 194–5; Pastor, *History of the popes*, vol. XIV, pp. 81–7; the fight for Piacenza, pp. 41–2.

incarcerate cardinal Alessandro if his order was not obeyed immediately. The culprits reluctantly agreed to comply but demanded a prior assurance that Paul would not harm Alessandro. The pope at once imprisoned the cardinal to punish their insolence, and did not release him until the galleys had been returned to France and a large sum of money paid to him.

The incident aroused great passions in Rome, and Camillo Colonna was among those expressing strong antipathy towards the Carafa in the heated discussions that followed. He was promptly arrested and the fierce campaign against the Colonna, the most prominent pro-imperial family in Rome, began. Others soon followed. They were asked to surrender their fortifications and many were exiled in August 1555. Some anticipated the orders and fled, among them Marcantonio Colonna and Guido Ascanio. Papal troops seized Paliano, Genazzano and other strong places belonging to pro-imperial families without waiting for legal sanctions, which were only completed in May 1556. Imperial allies were stripped of their offices and possessions.[18]

Soon the attack was directed against Charles and Philip. At first it was purely verbal. In frequent and increasingly vitriolic public speeches, Paul denounced them, but vented his spleen particularly against Charles, whether out of hatred or in the belief that he was the one who really mattered, can only be guessed at. Paul denounced the emperor as an evil man, the perpetrator of atrocities against the papacy and Rome itself, who constantly strove for universal monarchy. On one occasion, he said that Charles had been especially chosen by the devil, a scarcely veiled allusion to the Antichrist which would not have escaped contemporaries. The pope's accusations became increasingly hysterical. He claimed that Charles had 'prompted heresy in order to crush the papacy and make himself master of Rome, that is to say, master of Italy and the world'. But there was more to this war of words than unpleasant and wild messages. Paul set in motion formal accusations of rebellion and felony against both Charles and Philip, explicitly releasing their subjects from the duty to obey them. The excommunication of the two men was intended to increase instability within their realms and tempt foreign powers to join in the affray, in the hope of seizing some territories. Soon, Paul threatened, he would be the protector of all subjects under Charles and Philip, and he would utter 'such a fearful sentence' against them 'that the sun shall thereby be darkened'.[19]

The French were overjoyed to find such a powerful ally. Talks between them were formalised into an offensive–defensive treaty in October 1555, and the duke of Ferrara soon joined them. There were high hopes that the republic of Venice would also join this 'holy league'. The allies allowed for the incorporation of other powers as and when it became necessary, but they did not think it essential. The treaty is

[18] AGS PR. 18 fol. 1, bull Posteaque Divina Providentia; Pastor, *History of the popes*, vol. XIV, pp. 92–6, 99, 102; the Sforza incident, pp. 99–100, 121.

[19] Pastor, *History of the popes*, vol. XIV, pp. 131, 112, 126, 130–1.

ample proof that the pope and Henry believed Philip's position in Italy to be so weak that it would collapse under their joint attack. The fewer the allies, the greater the pickings for the participants. The three signatories agreed that Siena, once it was taken, would be given to the papacy, along with some of the lands now incorporated into the state of Milan. The duchy itself along with Naples was to go to Henry, who would give them to his sons. The only proviso was that the dauphin should not hold the Neapolitan crown as well. Sicily would be partitioned either between the pope and Henry, or else, if Venice joined, between Henry and the republic. When all that was done, the allies proposed to 'liberate' Florence and reinstate a republic. Even if only a part of all this was achieved, it would have been worth the war. Henry seems to have been particularly attracted by the prospect of having an invasion of Naples legalised by the pope. France was to provide a force of 12,000 infantry and supply 350,000 es; the pope would bring 10,000 infantry, 1,000 cavalry and 150,000 es.[20] As Romier noted in his discussion of the 1551 (Parma) intervention, Henry was motivated by his desire to obtain Italian fiefs for his sons, and influenced by the numerous Italian exiles at his court as well as by eager aristocrats like Guise.[21]

Philip tried to avert the attack he could see building up against Naples by urging Paul IV to mediate in his dispute with Henry. By this he hoped to neutralise Paul for a time, but the latter would not take the bait. He made the right noises about the need for peace in Christendom, but he would not put himself forward as a mediator. Philip had no choice but to approach France directly if he wished to divide the two enemies and buy time with which to prepare his defences.[22] The prospects appeared slight. The Franco-imperialist talks in the spring of 1555 had been both unsuccessful and unpleasant. Mary Tudor had offered mediation, and Henry accepted with alacrity, realising that this would neutralise England throughout the crucial period of pre-campaign preparations. He had made his minimum condition the preservation of the status quo; Charles had wanted a return to the status quo *ante bellum*. Philip was not allowed a say in the matter. It was impossible to reconcile these two demands, but cardinal Pole brought the talks to a chaotic close when he suggested that the antagonists should leave the quarrel to be settled by the general council of the Church. The French eagerly agreed, since it effectively meant that the status quo would be maintained indefinitely. No council of the church could take place without their consent and participation – or that of Charles for that matter. The imperialists were bitterly opposed to the proposal precisely for these reasons, and their rejection furnished Henry with admirable propaganda material. Both sides accused England of partiality, and English honour as well as Habsburg

[20] AGS PR. 17 fols. 6 and 41; Pastor, *History of the popes*, vol. XIV, pp. 107–9; Cabrera de Córdoba, *Felipe II*, vol. I, p. 58. Romier, *Les origines*, vol. I, pp. 30–1.
[21] Romier, *Les origines*, vol. I, pp. 173–6.   [22] AGS PR. 17 fols. 64, 66; AGS E. 882 fol. 195.

reputation suffered greatly.[23] Despite these negative indications, the new round of talks between Henry and Philip yielded rapid results.

THE TRUCE OF VAUCELLES, FEBRUARY 1556

This time a suspension of hostilities was made possible by the willingness of both Charles and Philip to lose honour and reputation. They sued for a truce, thus admitting Henry's superior status. They also agreed to his condition that the status quo would remain for the duration of the truce, that is five years. The truce presents the historian with a number of problems. The reasons why Philip wanted a suspension of hostilities are evident. But even after one makes allowances for the personal satisfaction and increase of prestige, Henry's decision to sign the truce remains a puzzle. His own courtiers were aghast and made every effort to press him to repudiate the agreement. He was so close to victory; so fortunate to be offered papal support, why withdraw now? Philip was as incredulous as they were. He did not notify the Spanish regent or his allies until certain that Henry had ratified the agreement and proclaimed it publicly along the borders. Juana and other officials complained that he had kept them in the dark. Others, like Alba, were deeply sceptical. He thought that at best it might last a year, but advised Philip to be realistic and think of it in terms of a one month suspension.[24]

The most likely explanation is Henry's financial plight. The imperial ambassador to the court, Renard, painted a grim picture of France. He spoke of widespread poverty caused by heavy taxation; of churches emptied of chalices and bells to pay subsidies for the war; of bankruptcies among leading financiers as the crown failed to meet debt repayments. All this must have sounded extraordinarily familiar to Philip.[25] In fact, France, like the Habsburg empire, had reached a point of no return. It could not manage the burden of debt accrued during the last wars. The problems were similar; the solutions somewhat different. As one might expect, the French crown anticipated changes less developed monarchies were to impose later.

Henry's success could not have been achieved without the financial reforms he introduced after 1551. He regulated French finances in a series of edicts setting new exchange rates and taxation levels. Nevertheless, by 1555 the crisis struck here as surely as in Spain and the Netherlands. The crown owed over two million écus, and only just over 650,000 of this was secured. Henry needed to find assignments and could not do so unless he rescheduled the debt. He was also desperate to secure

---

[23] Romier, *Les origines*, vol. I, pp. 522–6; Vertot, vol. II, pp. 350–1, 337; Loades, *Mary Tudor*, pp. 229–31; for the row between Charles and Philip over the latter's desire to participate in the talks secretly, AGS E. 809 fols. 70 and 72.

[24] Alba, *Epistolario*, vol. I, p. 388, 28 March 1555; ibid p. 381, Francisco de Toledo's complaint about the lack of information. AGS E. 103 fols. 83–6; Juana's request for clarification from Philip, 26 March, AGS E. 117 fol. 10; AGS E.K. 1643 fol. 3; AGS E. 112 fol. 176; RPPB vol. I, pp. 15–16.

[25] Weiss, *Granvelle*, vol. IV, pp. 556–7. Cloulas, *Henri II*, pp. 415–16.

funds for the campaign. In exchange for a new loan of over half a million écus, he agreed to set his finances in order. A series of edicts followed in March, May and October 1555. Henry consolidated his debts, converting the short-term, high interest loans into a long-term debt bearing a uniform interest of 16 per cent. Moreover, he intended to discharge this debt completely in pre-arranged instalments from the Allsaints fair of 1555 up to 1565. Revenues of 1.3 million livres were to be set aside annually, payable in four instalments coinciding with the major financial fairs. These various measures known collectively as the 'Grand Parti de Lyon' were obsolete almost as soon as they had been published. The demands of war and availability of credit combined to tempt the king and financiers into a new round of massive borrowing. Between April and October 1555 Henry borrowed at least 340,000 écus (792,000 livres). These loans were incorporated into the consolidated debt, throwing existing arrangements into disarray. New revenues had to be assigned to cope with the additional burden; they were added in March 1556, bringing the total revenue set aside for managing the debt to over two million livres (*c.* 870,000 écus).[26] As these figures reveal, the level of debt carried by France was less than that borne by either the Netherlands or the Spanish realms, but action was taken earlier to remedy the situation.

The instability and suspicion caused by the new round of borrowing, and the novelty of the solution deterred some merchant bankers from advancing further credit at the close of 1555. Others tried to make political capital out of financial needs. It was rumoured in January 1556 that the exiled Florentine bankers had offered Henry a loan of 900,000 écus, but only if he attacked the duke of Florence first and made the restoration of the republic his priority in the Italian campaign.[27] Henry could not do this without alienating the pope, and his own interests did not lie in this direction. It may well be that Henry despaired of securing sufficient finance to mount a grand enough campaign, and preferred a temporary truce. Yet we should note that it was not until August 1556 and January 1557 that he was unable to pay the interest due on the newly consolidated debt, and not until April 1557 that the merchant bankers showed real signs of impatience and dissatisfaction, making it difficult for him to secure credit.

Concern over finance may have been compounded by distrust of Paul, or at least of the pope's health. Paul IV was not the first or the last octogenarian elected in the hope of an early demise. In any case, Henry's attachment to the peace was not strong, and Paul was very determined to have war. He had shown his mettle by continuing his anti-Habsburg diatribes and activities despite the truce, offering the strongest provocation. He invested Giovanni Carafa, his eldest nephew, with Paliano and the other Colonna fiefs in May 1556. He accused another longstanding imperial ally, Ascanio de la Cornia, of rebellion and seized his lands and possessions. The special envoy Philip sent to placate the irate pontiff was imprisoned, as was his

[26] Cloulas, *Henri II*, pp. 512–15.   [27] Ehrenberg, *The Fuggers*, pp. 278, 304–5.

master of the post. Soon after this, Philip was formally accused of having attempted to poison the pope and the whole papal palace by placing a deadly substance in their water supply. Paul proclaimed his readiness to undertake any hardship before he would desist from his campaign against Charles and Philip. He would return to Avignon and hand the papal states over to the French even, but at all costs he wanted to free his homeland of Naples from the 'barbarians', here intended to signify solely the Spaniards. After Vaucelles, he sent his favourite nephew, the soldier turned cardinal, Carlo Carafa to negotiate with Henry and organise the next campaign. Whether they received the news with delight or dismay, contemporaries realised this embassy would result in a renewal of the war.[28]

THE WAR AGAINST THE PAPACY, 1556–7

The question that had to be faced in 1556 was as simple to formulate as it was difficult to answer: under what conditions could Philip take up arms against the pope? The problem was to ensure that the king took part in a 'just war', but necessity dictated a pre-emptive strike against the papal states. The theologians he consulted replied almost to a man in the strongest, clearest, most negative terms. By definition, no war against the papacy was just. Even if the pope was at fault, as they were willing to admit, Philip must not fight against him. If he did, he would be accused of being a bad Christian, if not indeed a heretic, which would cause him to lose reputation. Furthermore, if Philip took up arms against the pope it might deal a mortal blow against the papacy which had been so seriously weakened by the onslaughts of heresy and worse might follow. In the words of Domingo de Soto, if Philip attacked Paul, he could inadvertently end up 'eliminating the faith'.[29]

The opponents of war against the papacy found an unlikely ally and leader in Alba. He had no love for Paul nor any scruples about applying sanctions against the clergy at all levels. He wanted Philip to wage an all-out commercial war against Rome, to seize the assets of the church and to imprison any churchman who would not cooperate with the illegal collection of ecclesiastical revenues in Spain. But he felt that it was better for Philip to lose reputation by failing to reply to Paul's constant insults and threats of excommunication, rather than be branded a heretic by taking up arms against the pope. Alba could not see a way to justify the conflict, especially if Philip opted for a pre-emptive strike.

The king, on the other hand, believed that he would be seriously compromised

---

[28] Romier, *Les origines*, vol. II, pp. 44–53, 61–74; AGS E. 883 fol. 15, Juan Manrique de Lara to Juana, 23 March 1556. Cornia's citation, AGS PR. 18 fol. 17; AGS PR. 17 fol. 49, large collection of documents of the growing clashes between Philip and the pope. Alba was convinced Paul was intercepting and reading all his mail, and he thought it wise to warn Philip in February of that year, *Epistolario*, vol. I, p. 367; Pastor, *History of the popes*, vol. XIV, pp. 128–9; Cabrera de Córdoba, *Felipe II*, vol. I, p. 67.

[29] AGS E. 114 fol. 262; the opinion of Silíceo AGS E. 113 fol. 83; Cabrera de Córdoba, *Felipe II*, vol. I, pp. 80–2.

unless he defended his allies against their unjust deprivation. Alba's cousin, don García de Toledo, was married to Victoria Colonna and this might lead one to believe that family ties would predispose him to support the Colonna. A close reading of his correspondence, however, reveals Alba's antipathy for the most important member of that family, Marcantonio Colonna, whom he might have regarded as a potential rival.[30] Rather disingenuously, Alba argued that since the alliances signed by Charles and Philip with these men did not include an undertaking on their part to support the king in a war against the papacy, there could be no reciprocal aid in this instance, and so he was absolved from his responsibility to protect them. It was a specious argument since a 'good Christian' could not sign a treaty with such a clause. Moreover, Alba purported to believe that Paul's attack against Colonna and the rest stemmed from a natural desire to advance his family. Theirs were simply the most convenient lands and titles available; it was not to be seen as an indirect attack against the Habsburgs. This argument too was weak; it was evident that Paul had chosen his victims carefully and intended to fight against Philip. But Alba was ready to use any reasoning, however faulty, in order to avert a general war in Italy at a time when most of his forces were on the verge of mutiny and no money was available.[31]

Ranged against Alba and the theologians were those who believed that defence was always a just cause, and pre-emptive strikes justified under pressing circumstances such as this. Philip would fail in his duty to his subjects if he remained inactive and allowed his enemies to gather their forces and attack his lands. Better keep the fighting away from his troubled and divided states, particularly in areas like Naples where pro-French sentiments endured. It would be cheaper and more effective to attack before the Franco-papal forces had time to coalesce. Such tactical and financial considerations won the day, but they were not the only reasons why Philip eventually attacked. As some of his counsellors pointed out, there was nothing in the military or financial situation of his empire to attract new allies, and little to persuade existing allies to remain within his camp. Philip's sole international success to date had been to cement his friendship with Genoa by offering help to recover Corsica. The reputation he had established as a king willing to back his allies in their time of need was being undermined and would be lost if he failed to help Colonna and the other victims of Paul's aggression. Significantly one of the most difficult tasks that Philip and Alba faced after the war had started, was to explain why the king had delayed for so long before taking up arms to defend his allies.[32]

The protection of his allies became a central feature of the propaganda issued to account for Philip's actions. Indeed it really became the *casus belli*, as much due to

---

[30] Alba, *Epistolario*, vol. I, p. 302, for example.
[31] Alba, *Epistolario*, vol. I, pp. 412–17, 350, 314, 410, 412, 424–5.
[32] A summary of the major arguments can be found in AGS E. 108 fols. 18–20. See also AGS E. 191 fol. 192.

Paul's insistence as to Philip's determination to make some capital out of his war. Paul thought he would seriously dent Philip's reputation if he accused him of having initiated a war against the spiritual leader of Christendom for a paltry and unjust reason – the defence of Colonna and other 'rebels'. This close association of the king with his unfortunate allies served to strengthen Philip's earlier reputation and built up the carefully cultivated image. The end result was so favourable that even Alba was arguing by September 1555 that the protection of Colonna and the others was vital and Philip had no option but to retaliate against anyone who sought to destroy them. The presence of Colonna and other exiles in the duke's camp doubtless helped to change his mind on the issue.[33] Once he had made the difficult decision to go ahead with the war against the pope and France, Philip faced the even more problematic question of how to raise the money to pay for it.

FINANCING THE FRANCO–ITALIAN WAR

It was soon evident that there was little Milan could do to help itself let alone others. The mutinies of 1555 had only been kept under control by raising loans repayable on the *mensuale* of 1556. It seems that Alba secured these by allowing the financiers to collect the taxes before they were officially due, forcing the Milanese to anticipate their payments. This came to light when the government was asked to impose a partial suspension of payments and they had to explain that there were no current revenues to collect, nor for the following year. The government renegotiated the terms of the existing debt in order to stave off bankruptcy. Table 8 shows the figures used by government officials at his point. If anything they were too optimistic, yet they show how desperate the situation was. Debt repayments would take up most of the duchy's revenues, leaving insufficient funds to cover normal administrative costs, let alone fortifications and extraordinary defence expenditure.

Although no one said so openly, the decision to launch a pre-emptive campaign from Naples reflected the conviction that Milan could not be defended. Given his limited resources, Philip ordered the bulk of his forces and channelled most of the money to Naples, where he also sent Alba. Naples was regarded as an integral part of his patrimony, not a land held by right of conquest like Milan; it was also wealthier and more defensible than the northern duchy. Before he left the area, Alba instituted a series of reforms which he proclaimed would make it possible even for a child to govern the area. Don Bernardino de Mendoza was sufficiently quick-witted to refuse the honour of becoming its next governor despite these blandishments. He was the only commander of sufficient standing and experience who could be sent quickly enough to Milan, so his refusal was a serious setback and left Alba no option but to hastily organise a mixed government. The inexperienced marquis of Pescara

---

[33] Paul's accusations AGS PR. 17 fol. 71; AGS E. 191 fols. 192–3; AGS PR. 18 fols. 37 and 41; Alba, *Epistolario*, vol. I, p. 302.

Table 8. *Situation in Milan, January 1557*

Money provided by the Milanese, July 1555 – January 1557		*c.* 700,000 es
		total
Money in hand	125,000	223.556 es needed
Outstanding urgent debts	348,556 es	
Ordinary revenues p.a.	140,000 es	
[Ordinary revenues collected	*c.*125,000 es]	total
Mensuale p.a.	260,000 es	*c.*340,000 es revenue
[*Mensuale* p.a. collected	215,000 es]	
1557 revenues already spent		349,794 es
Payments assigned on 1558 revenues		295,298 es

Reference: AGS E 1209 fols. 11, 17, 18. Monti, 'Filippo II', p. 143.

took charge of military matters with Gianbaptista Castaldo who was too old and too ill to do more than advise him. Don Juan de Guevara and count Ladriano were attached to the military command, making up in quantity what they lacked in quality. Gómez Suárez de Figueroa was once more brought in to deal with finances and cardinal Cristoforo Madruzzo appointed to deal with other aspects of government and vague overall control. Alba thought him 'too partial' in judicial matters, so he insisted on leaving divided command over these too. At a time when firm government was essential to hold the disintegrating state together, further divisions had been created, adding to the confusion.

Apart from the obvious need to cover all spheres of government, this messy partition of power in Milan reflected Alba's own needs and plans. He did not wish to leave a strong governor there to challenge his unitary command over the peninsula. During his months in Milan he had often expressed the view that the duchy could not survive unless its governor had unlimited access to the revenues and soldiers of Naples. By his own admission then, the future governor of Milan would have an indisputable case for demanding control of both this and Naples, thus depriving Alba of his sought-after viceroyalty.[34]

As might be expected, once he set foot in Naples Alba's opinion about the situation of the realm changed radically. Whilst in Milan, his need to take subsidies from the realm for the duchy made him dismiss the reports sent by Bernardino de Mendoza as special pleading. No, he confidently assured Philip at one point, Naples was not poor as Mendoza claimed, it was rich and simply required an efficient governor to tap its wealth. Within days of his arrival he accused Mendoza of

[34] Alba, *Epistolario*, vol. I, pp. 336, 347–8, 356–8; A. Monti, 'Filippo II e il cardenal Cristoforo Madruzzo, governatore di Milano (1556–1557)', *Nuova Rivista Storica* (1924), pp. 133–55.

underestimating the gravity of the situation.[35] In March 1556 Alba reported that he was facing bills of 250,000 ds and had no resources whatever to cover the debts. He ordered the sale of lands belonging to the exiled prince of Salerno to raise some of this. He considered taking the 25,000 ds that remained in the *Monte*, although he knew it would lead to the collapse of the bank. Inevitably a suspension of payments had to be considered. It was suggested that a limited suspension would suffice: if the revenues assigned or sold to the merchant banker Tommaso Marino were seized they could manage for the time being. Alba opposed the proposal for the same reason the king had opposed the general suspension earlier – the chaos it would cause and the withdrawal of the facilities provided by financiers at a time of war. They would consider the attack against any one of their number to be the start of a general repudiation of debts. So a new form of taxation was mooted instead. Alba proposed a Castilian-style sales tax of 10 per cent to the horrified Neapolitans. Although he publicly declared that it would last only as long as the war, in private he admitted it would be necessary to maintain it indefinitely to restore the finances of the realm. There was uproar in Naples where this tax was opposed as bitterly as it would be in the Netherlands years later.

The search for funds had not proceeded very far when French troops crossed the Alps and launched their attacks against Philip's realms and allies. Desperate to get the campaign organised, Alba resorted to blackmail. He threatened to leave Naples to its fate, without making any preparations for the realm's defence unless they provided him with enough money to go on the offensive. Philip also kept up relentless pressure on the Neapolitans, stressing that he expected them to demonstrate their loyalty and love by supplying him with money for this, his first war. Resistance changed to resentful cooperation. Instead of a sales tax Naples agreed to new taxes on meat and bread which would yield one million gold (?scudi/escudos) annually for the next two years. It appears that Philip managed to persuade them to extend it for a third.[36] The realm continued to send subsidies to Milan, albeit small ones.[37]

News of the new Neapolitan taxes was sent to Philip with urgent pleas for help. Revenues had been alienated so far in advance that the future looked extremely bleak and uncertain. Loan repayments would take up most of what revenue could be expected up to 1560, by which time it was estimated that interest payments on loans would have equalled the initial capital invested. As for external threats, Naples was forced to counter the maritime assaults of the Ottoman, French and corsair fleets as well as the landward invasion that would soon come from the papal states. Philip's response to this was characteristic. He outlined his own serious problems to the Neapolitans, and reiterated his appeals to their loyalty. He wanted further sacrifices

[35] Alba, *Epistolario*, vol. I, pp. 362–3, 369, 383.
[36] AGS E. 1049 fols. 24, 69, 72–5; RAH SC A-60 fols. 123–4; Alba, *Epistolario*, vol. I, pp. 369, 383–4, 413–14, 448–9.   [37] AGS E. 1209 fol. 11.

during the war but promised solutions and redress at the end of the conflict. At the same time, he took up all their pleas and complaints and used them to press his other realms to contribute to the war and send subsidies to Naples.

Sicily reacted slowly to Philip's demands and was unable to contribute much. The parliament voted a new grant of 200,000 es in June 1557, but it would be payable over a four year period. They might have responded with greater generosity and promptness if Juan de Vega had remained at the helm, but he had been sent by Philip to Spain to replace Fonseca as president of the council. For four months, until the arrival of the duke of Medinaceli on 25 June, the cardinal of Palermo served as temporary governor. It was not wise to press too hard at a time of instability and weakness at the centre, and attacks from Muslim and French ships.[38]

It was inevitable that Philip should turn to the Spanish realms in order to finance the war. He was lucky to have such an effective and responsive government there; they in turn were fortunate to have some new sources of revenue to draw upon. First, the death of queen Juana left those revenues set aside for her upkeep free.[39] Then there was the seemingly providential discovery of silver mines at Guadalcanal. The mine of Almaguén was especially rich and the government immediately commandeered all of them, delaying compensation for the owners for many years. From November 1555 to June 1556 the mines yielded some 273,000 ds, but the government had already assigned loan repayments far in excess of this to these revenues. As with all sources of bullion, the mines exerted an irresistible attraction for investors which tempted them to further loans and made them put up with the delays caused by over-subscription and dual assignations.[40] But these were far from sufficient. When the Indies fleets approached the Spanish shores and the government realised that little was coming for the crown as local officials had spent most of the royal fifth in quelling the rebellion that had broken out in Peru, Juana reluctantly agreed to new confiscations of Indies goods. Although the sum taken was small in comparison to previous seizures – some 600,000 ds – the opposition it aroused was immense. Philip had ordered his sister to seize all the bullion in the fleet, so far from commiserating with the complaints he received, he angrily demanded why no more had been taken.[41]

The pressure to send money to the Italian and northern fronts forced Juana to resort to blackmail, as Alba had done. At the close of 1555, she threatened to suspend all payments due on the delayed October fair, as well as all those due for

[38] RAH SC A-60 fols. 31–3. Note that the usual parliamentary grants were of 100,000 escudos, and regular extraordinary grants of 125,000 ds, H. G. Koenigsberger, *The practice of empire* (Ithaca, 1969).   [39] AGS E. 112 fols. 3–6.
[40] AGS E. 113 fols. 33, 44, 45; AGS E. 112 fols. 48–52; Ulloa, *La Hacienda Real*, pp. 458–61 for details of what happened to the mines during Philip's reign.
[41] AGS E. 108 fols. 44–6, Philip's order; Juana's letter to him of 10 August 1557 (AGS E. 108 fol. 147) gives the figure. See also pp. 208–13 for the bitter quarrels that broke out over the *embargo* policy 1556–7.

Table 9. *Spanish subsidies for the Italian front 1556–7*

Date	Demand	Subsidy	Confiscation of bullion
January 1556		83,200 es[A]	
June 1556		401,000 es[B]	
January 1557		120,000 es[C]	
May 1557			300,000 ds[D]
June 1557		200,000 ds	
Summer 1557	800,000	550,000 ds (credit)[E]	
		300,000 ds bullion	

[A] AGS E 116 fols. 3–4, date sent.
[B] Alba, *Epistolario*, I, p. 407, date of arrival.
[C] Monti, 'Filippo II', p. 150, date of arrival.
[D] Philip seized the money from merchant bankers, Spain was to repay it. AGS E 119 fol. 226, E 322 fol. 181, E 810 fol. 97.
[E] AGS E 121 fols. 268–9; E 121 fols. 211–12, Alba, *Epistolario*, I, pp. 468–9.

collection from Castilian revenues at the end of the year, unless the merchant bankers advanced 200,000 ds payable in the Netherlands, and 300,000 ds to be paid in Italy immediately. A spate of small loans duly followed, falling short by some 60,000 es of the required sum. The need to finance the journey of Charles, Mary of Hungary and Leonor from the Netherlands meant that the initial distribution of these loans was weighted towards the north: 147,500 ds to Italy's 83,200 es.[42] Table 9 shows the subsidies sent by Spain to Italy during 1556, which provided the bulk of the finance for his Italian wars. The figures reflect both the king's failure to get any more out of his Italian realms and the flexibility of Spanish finances. When these subsidies are considered alongside those which were sent to the Netherlands, Spain's vast contribution to the war can be appreciated.

THE TURN OF THE TIDE

From a military point of view, the first of Philip's many wars was a stunning success, all the more striking to contemporaries because it came after the serious reverses of previous years. Alba set out with only 12,000 men from Naples on 1 September 1556. The late start to the campaign was due to a number of reasons, among which the difficulties of securing sufficient money to provide defence and get the army

[42] AGS E. 108 fols. 230–9; AGS E. 119 fol. 124; AGS E. 116 fols. 3–4; Carande, *Carlos V y sus banqueros*, vol. III, Table on pp. 492–5 shows that the total borrowed was 440,000 ds; by the time it was repaid interest paid was 72.7 per cent.

marching, figure prominently. However, Alba's great reluctance to go to war and his conviction that it should be avoided also contributed to the delay. Colonna and other exiles from the papal states were with the army and doubtless it was their presence which gave such a keen edge to the army's rapid and successful advance. A string of pontifical strongholds fell quickly, and on 16 September Agnani was taken, opening a direct route to Rome for the invaders. Panic spread to a city that retained the scars of the sack of 1527 by the mutinous imperial troops. Unable to reassure his subjects or effectively stem the attack, Paul IV opened up peace talks. This had been the intended effect of that pre-emptive strike; Philip and Alba were jubilant.[43]

Even before the war began, Philip and his counsellors had decided upon what terms they were willing to make peace. The minimum demands were the release of all prisoners, the reinstatement of Colonna and the other imperial–Spanish allies. In exchange, the king was willing to offer lands and revenues in Naples for the pope's nephews. There was no doubt in anyone's mind that Paul was under the influence of his nephew Carlo, the cardinal deacon. It was imperative to offer the Carafa a substantial bribe. Some of Philip's advisers favoured offering them the title and lands of the principality of Salerno.[44] Although Carlo Carafa was convinced that the French would soon arrive, he decided to 'entertain' his enemies. Alba agreed to talks as soon as they were suggested. On 28 November 1556 he also agreed to a forty day truce despite constant warnings that as soon as the French arrived Paul would end the negotiations. Since Monluc and other French mercenaries had already fought on the papal side during the brief campaign, there was no reason why he should have rejected these warnings. His obsession with peace blinded him; he seems to have deluded himself that if Philip was generous, Paul would really withdraw from the war despite French support. But even he must have been taken aback by Carlo Carafa's demand – not Salerno, but Siena.

Alba persisted. He believed that peace with Paul must be made at once whatever the price: 'my opinion about this war' he stated, 'is that we must end it by any means possible'.[45] This is reflected in a discarded set of instructions for his secretary dating from the end of December 1556. Since the papal negotiators made it clear from the start that they would not consider the restoration of Colonna and Cornia, Alba wanted Philip to drop this demand and give them compensation from his own lands in Naples, although he accepted that they must ask for the key Colonna fortifications to be handed over to a neutral power.[46] The degree of desperation in Philip's mind and court can be measured by the fact that he seriously considered these proposals and finally came to the conclusion that, notwithstanding the danger of provoking a breach with the duke of Florence, and the long-term threat of having a semi-hostile power so close to Naples, he would offer Siena to the Carafa. Evidently, the desire to prevent the fusion of the Franco-papal forces and to secure

[43] AGS PR. 18 fols. 14, 15; AGS E. 114 fols. 255–6; AGS E. 883 fols. 46–7; Codoin vol. II, pp. 437–8; Pastor, *History of the popes*, vol. XIV, p. 141.   [44] AGS PR. 18 fols. 43–4.
[45] AGS PR. 18 fol. 45.   [46] AGS PR. 18 fols. 43, 44 and 46.

the restoration of Colonna and the rest overcame these disadvantages. There were some restrictions imposed: Philip would retain a garrison in the city of Siena and other fortifications. Cosimo de Medici would be allotted some Sienese territories and repaid his costs during the campaign.[47] It was as if the spectacular and speedy military victories had never happened. Philip was clearly losing his nerve.

These promises did not deter Paul from dropping the negotiations as soon as he was informed that Henry's troops had crossed the Alps in January 1557.[48] The French have aptly termed this war 'le voyage de Naples'. Cabrera de Córdoba believed that Guise had encouraged Henry by making direct comparisons between him and Charles VIII who had briefly conquered the realm. Henry certainly departed from his father's policy of making the reconquest of Milan his priority. Hipolito d'Este, duke of Ferrara and commander-in-chief of the Franco-papal forces met Guise and tried to persuade him that they should first seize Milan. The place was in shambles, it would almost certainly have fallen to them rapidly. Of course, Ferrara was biased: his share of the eventual conquest of Italy was 50,000 ds annually from Milanese revenues, but his plan was sound. Guise thought it worth consulting with Henry, who reiterated that nothing must deter them from an immediate attack against Naples. Apart from the greater prestige and wealth of that realm, Henry may well have calculated that since Milan could not survive without Neapolitan help, it could safely be left to a future campaign. Ferrara was so disgusted he abandoned the alliance in high dudgeon.[49] In March 1557, the desultory skirmishes along the borders with Naples gave way to a campaign proper.

The Franco-papal attack against Naples was extremely successful at first. Campli fell quickly and Civitella was expected to follow suit. But, as so often happens in war, the unexpected and heroic resistance of a small place bought the lives and freedom of the rest. Civitella held out for weeks, giving the tardy Alba time to gather his troops. He marched at the head of one army and forced the Franco-papal forces back, whilst Colonna and the other exiles, using their lands and allies, directed the main thrust of their attack against Rome itself. They got within sight of Rome, but Alba ordered them to halt and refused to allow the city to be sacked. Once again he insisted on pressing for peace; Paul was unimpressed.[50] The war would have continued but for the fact that Henry recalled his men. In time-honoured fashion, the French had been forced to release their grip over Italy by the successful attack launched against France in the north. Victory in Italy was ultimately won in the fields of France.

[47] AGS PR. 18 fols. 3, 10; Pastor, *History of the popes*, vol. XIV, p. 148.
[48] AGS PR. 18 fols. 18, 27, 45, 48; AGS PR. 17 fol. 69; Alba, *Epistolario*, vol. I, pp. 429–30; Pastor, *History of the popes*, vol. XIV, pp. 134–5; P. Courteault, *Blaise de Monluc historien* (Paris, 1908; and Slatkine reprint, Geneva, 1970).
[49] AGS E. 883 fol. 9; Cloulas, *Henri II*, pp. 440–1; Pastor, *History of the popes*, vol. XIV, pp. 152–4, 318; Prescott, *History of the reign of the Philip the Second, king of Spain* (3 vols., London, 1855), vol I pp. 153ss detailed account of the war; Courteault, *Monluc historien*, pp. 324–30.
[50] Pastor, *History of the popes*, vol. XIV, pp. 158, 161–2; Cabrera de Córdoba, *Felipe II*, p. 117.

Paul IV was at the mercy of Philip's troops and the Spanish government was overjoyed. They drew up a list of numerous important matters which were the subject of conflict and confrontation with the papacy, and they insisted Philip must use his position of power to resolve them in favour of the Spanish realms. It would have been a very practical way to get a return for their massive investment in the war. Instead they received nothing; accusations that Philip had misspent their funds followed suit. The king could have done little, because Alba had pre-empted any such demands. True to his previous view of the situation, Alba reiterated his offers of peace and accepted the pope's conditions in order to terminate the conflict. Philip's stunned supporters had to ask themselves just who had won the war, as Alba humbly knelt before Paul and begged for his pardon in a public ceremony in Rome. Not only had he agreed to this symbolic humiliation of himself and his sovereign, but also assented to the restoration of all papal lands taken in the conflict, and promised compensation for the Carafa brothers in Philip's dominions. Most serious of all, he agreed to leave Cornia out of the settlement altogether, and the Colonna were relegated to secret treaties which left their fate unsettled, and with little hope of their restoration even in the future. The Colonna fortifications in Paliano would be held by a neutral power for the time being.[51] The only thing Philip had gained out of this costly venture was the safety of his southern realm. Alba tried to impress upon everyone that they must look at it from another angle: peace would arrest the loss of reputation. Besides, there was no money to continue the war.

When he heard that substantial parts of the settlement with Paul were contained in secret clauses and separate treaties, Charles V expressed deep misgivings about Alba's activities. Apprised of the full story, he refused to make any comment, but he vehemently repulsed all Alba's attempts to explain his conduct. Whatever Charles had said must have deeply stung the duke.[52] Philip's own reaction can only be guessed at. In view of the speed with which the negotiations were completed, it seems unlikely that he had a chance to see the conditions before Alba accepted them. There may well have been an undertaking on his part to support peace at any price too after the renewal of the campaign.

Philip's attitude towards the war had been ambivalent throughout. He found it abhorrent to take up arms against the papacy, having considerable respect for the institution if not for its incumbents. He was a very traditional man, and it disturbed him to see the world upside down, with the Catholic monarch on one side; the pope, Most Christian king and Ottoman sultan on the other. He was deeply upset by Paul's accusations of rebellion, perhaps because he was terrified that it would deal the death blow to his much weakened authority in some of his troubled states. But he felt very strongly that the action was unjust and dishonourable.[53] From a letter

---

[51] AGS PR. 17 fol. 7; AGS PR. 18 fols. 59, 66; Pastor, *History of the popes*, vol. XIV, pp. 166–71.

[52] AGS E. 128 fol. 326; Gachard, *Retraite*, vol. II, p. 306.

[53] AGS PR. 17 fols. 73, 68, 47; AGS E. 120 fols. 32–4; counter-measures he took, AGS E. 119 fol. 40; AGS PR. 17 fol. 10; Alba, *Epistolario*, vol. I, p. 429.

written to Juana during June–July 1557 it is also evident that he was astonished as well as upset to find himself in this predicament. He thought it inconceivable that the pope should attack him – the man who had so distinguished himself in the restoration of England to the fold. Philip was already presenting himself – and doubtless seeing himself – as a man marked out by God for the extension of the faith. He was confused and concerned that the war would undermine his achievements and reputation. Nevertheless, his victories revealed that God was on his side.[54] Accepting harsh conditions of peace was tantamount to an admission of guilt incompatible with his own conscience and God's judgement of the conflict. Moreover, the conditions of peace, once known, would discredit Philip. They bore no relation to the military victories and most importantly, left Philip's allies in a very precarious position. Colonna, Cornia and their allies had played a key role in Philip's success; they had an indisputable right to expect his protection and favour. Their plight had been the most salient argument in Philip's propaganda: the failure to restore them would make it appear as if he had lost the war. For many years Philip would fight with all the diplomatic tools available to obtain the restoration of his allies, aware that his reputation had been dented. Significantly he refused to ratify Alba's agreement for months. It was not until 28 February 1558, when the loss of Calais made another northern campaign imperative, that he sealed the treaty.[55] A further hint of his lack of satisfaction was the fall of Alba from grace. The duke would be reincorporated to the top rank of advisers months later but he would never regain the power he had enjoyed during these years in Italy.

Surprisingly the loss of reputation was slight, for entirely fortuitous reasons. Philip's victory over France so overshadowed the Italian campaign that few contemporaries could have said who had won in Italy, or under what conditions. Skilful propaganda and the traditions of humanist writers also came to his aid and transformed a diplomatic failure into an admirable demonstration of the Christian principle that a bad peace was preferable to a war among Christians. The papal nuncio in Spain, whose relations with the regency government were often less than amicable, wrote to Philip: 'It has now been proved that your majesty will fight not out of greed for greater wealth, nor out of ambition, nor from any desire to add further territories to your crown, not even out of natural aggression'.[56] Doubtless there was a large measure of flattery in this, but the comment is nevertheless instructive, because it reflects vividly the image which Philip and his advisers had been carefully striving to create.

THE BALANCE OF POWER IN ITALY, 1558–9

For the best part of 1556 and 1557 Philip refused to make an obvious choice as to which war front would take priority. In fact the war was conducted with both fronts

---

[54] AGS E. 119 fol. 40 Philip to Juana; Codoin vol. II, pp. 430–7 to Ferdinand.
[55] AGS PR. 18 fol. 65.   [56] AGS E. 120 fol. 151.

at full strength with disastrous consequences for his finances, but excellent results in military and political terms. By 1558 Italy was clearly of secondary importance. Interestingly enough, unlike the situation six years earlier when Charles had shifted his attention northwards, there were no accusations that Philip had abandoned Italian affairs. This perception of his deep and abiding commitment to the area was extremely useful. Together with the military victories and the reputation so far gained of his readiness to protect his allies, it served to reverse the unfavourable trend away from the Habsburg camp in the previous years. It is commonly stated that Philip's control over the Italian states did not come until he signed a treaty of peace with France in 1559, at which time the French supposedly 'pulled out of Italy' and left him the undisputed master of the area. This view has to be substantially revised, and is probably best discarded.

It is evident that the Italian states were moving towards the Habsburg camp long before Cateau-Cambrésis. The first notable defector from the French camp was the duke of Parma. We left the battle for Parma in chapter one at an inconclusive stage, overtaken by seismic events elsewhere in Europe. The war was short and inconclusive. Ottavio Farnese with French support managed to retain his duchy of Parma but failed to regain Piacenza. Julius and Charles, having lost interest in the conflict, agreed to a suspension of arms during April and May 1552 respectively. For two years desultory fighting continued, but his lack of success made Farnese eager to explore diplomatic avenues. In 1554 he approached Charles and offered to consider an alliance in exchange for the return of Piacenza. Charles needed the prestige of the defection. His anxiety to have the duke of Parma as an ally again may also have reflected guilt. Philip put paid to these discussions by strenuously opposing the return of Piacenza unless Farnese agreed to allow imperial or Spanish garrisons inside the fortifications of both Parma and Piacenza. Ottavio Farnese rejected these conditions.

After the truce of Vaucelles, Henry's financial difficulties led him to reduce pensions, including the money he had been supplying for Ottavio and his wife Margaret. The latter was also embroiled in a battle with Catherine de Medici over the inheritance of Alessandro de Medici, Margaret's first husband. Deeply insecure and desperate for support, Ottavio Farnese came to terms with Philip in October 1556. Once again the king made considerable propaganda capital out of a loss. A great deal was said of his willingness to hand back Piacenza and little mention was made of his garrisons in Parma, Piacenza and 'Placentin'. The return of the duchy was used to underline the general principle that Philip did not wish to enlarge his empire, that he was content to waive his own dynastic claims in order to show favour and give justice to his allies. It was also put about that whilst Philip might have driven a much harder bargain with Farnese, his desire to reduce tension in the area and to restore family harmony had prompted him to be generous. As was expected, the defection enabled him to score points against France; Henry was both shocked and angered by what he described as rank ingratitude on the part of the duke and duchess of Parma.[57]

The Italian princelings had made tentative approaches towards Charles and Philip in the past, especially during 1554–5. The timing furnishes us with a clue to their motivation. It was the nadir of Charles's power; almost unconsciously they moved to redress the balance now so heavily tipped in favour of France. Moreover, at such a time of weakness, Charles might be ready to pay a very high price for an alliance. That was the year many of them felt the pinch from Henry's cost-cutting measures too. There was nothing very surprising therefore about the initial contacts. More striking was the high level of success in attracting new allies. With the examples of Corsica, Siena and Piacenza serving as proof of Philip's lack of territorial ambitions; with his military support of the Genoese and Roman families, Philip appeared in 1557–8 as the most pacific and supportive great power the Italians had had the luck to encounter for nearly a century. Soon he was to advance the idea that he always supported his allies in their struggles albeit within the severe limits imposed by his many commitments and absence of spare funds. After the treaty with Ottavio Farnese small contingents of Spanish troops were sent to support his attack against Guardasone (between Parma and Reggio). Similarly, two years after signing an alliance with the duke of Urbino, Philip helped him to conquer the duchy of Sora, despite having good claims to the area himself.

Urbino's defection was a more spectacular feat than that of Parma. Henry declared it a great betrayal. The duke had been one of those to explore possible conditions for defection in 1555. Philip was very excited by the prospect, believing that with Urbino and Florence on his side he would create a barrier to protect Naples from a French invasion. At the time Philip was still locked in conflict with both Charles and Cosimo de Medici over the fate of Siena: this may have deterred Urbino from defecting, as would the lack of success of the imperial–Spanish troops. He remained faithful to Henry's cause until, prompted by the duke of Florence who negotiated on his behalf, he signed an alliance with Philip in May 1558.[58]

In September of that year, Philip drew up a detailed set of instructions for his new ambassador to Rome, don Juan de Figueroa, which give a clear indication of the king's perception of Italian politics.[59] They are a good starting point for an analysis of the balance of power in the area at that time. Philip acknowledged that he had inherited three powerful allies from Charles: the dukes of Florence and Savoy, and Genoa; of late he had drawn closer to all. He thought them vital for his survival, and

[57] The negotiations can be followed in this correspondence: AGS E. 507 fol. 23; AGS E. 808 fol. 66; AGS E. 1323 fol. 128; the agreement is in AGS PR. 45 fols. 23–7, 42; Romier, *Les origines*, vol. II, pp. 76–88; Courteault, *Monluc historien*, pp. 345–6; Cloulas, *Henri II*, p. 430.
[58] AGS E. 809 fol. 47; AGS E. 1323 fols. 12 and 211; AGS PR. 45 fol. 50 the treaty; Alba, *Epistolario*, vol. I, pp. 99, 409; Pastor, *The history of the popes*, vol. XIV, pp. 97, 105.
[59] AGS E. 883 fol. 104.

told Figueroa to help them whenever possible. Relations remained good with Mantua, despite heavy losses by the duke, who had shown no inclination to defect. This underlines poor French diplomacy in Italy during these years, when several imperial allies were dissatisfied with Charles and feared Philip. Mantua would receive powerful support from Philip in the negotiations with France, and recovered Monferrat and Casale.[60]

Apart from the inherited allies, there were the two new additions of Parma and Urbino. As for Ferrara it had long been closely allied to France, but Philip was confident that he could secure his defection soon, with Urbino and Florence on his side. Ferrara felt encircled and threatened by Philip and his allies, and would soon perceive the wisdom of joining them. There had already been some contacts between them in 1557, when rumours of Urbino's negotiations with Philip tempted Ferrara to investigate. Unfortunately Ferrara's price for an alliance proved too high. He wanted Philip to arrange the marriage of his sister Juana with Alfonso, heir to Ferrara. Juana refused, having sworn never to marry again and made it one of the conditions of accepting the regency that she would not be forced to do so. The dynastic ambitions of Ferrara stood in the way of alliance for some years. Philip was seriously handicapped by his lack of progeny or close relations. Ferrara finally defected some years later, attracted by the hand of one of Ferdinand's numerous daughters.[61] Nevertheless by September 1558 Philip considered Ferrara a potential or near ally rather than an enemy and he instructed Figueroa to treat him as a neutral power for the time being.

The same was to be done with Venice. For a long time, the republic had been considered an inveterate enemy of the Habsburgs. But Philip had been impressed by its refusal to join the league against him in 1556–7 despite the handsome offers from France and the papacy. Apart from half of Sicily, the Venetians had been offered several towns and lands in Naples, as well as the 'protection' of Milan during the minority of Henry's son, yet Venice had resisted temptation and remained apart from these internecine struggles. This, and recent contacts, persuaded him that there was every possibility of improving relations in the near future. In fact this was not to be, for a seemingly minor incident over the precedence of the French and (for want of a better word) Spanish ambassador led to the republic adjudicating in the

---

[60] BL Add 18,789 fols. 6–12; AGS E. 883 fol. 104. When the French seemed to threaten Alva (near Aste) after Cateau-Cambrésis, Philip instructed his governor in Milan to help the duke defend his lands. He also personally warned the French that he would not tolerate the least aggression against his ally. AGS E. 1215 fols. 24, 262, 28; AGS E. 1218 fol. 90.

[61] AGS E. 1216 fols. 97 and 159; AGS E. 1215 fol. 110. Ferrara and Mantua left the choice of their respective brides to Philip, since he did not have any obvious candidates they could bid for in order to cement their alliance and advance their families. The king had to use Ferdinand's and Maximilian's children for this purpose, later even the Portuguese royal family. It was a grave disadvantage, see Codoin vol. xcviii, pp. 60–1; AGS E. 650 fols. 157, 52; AGS E. 652 fols. 205, 1, 19; AGS E. 651 fol. 81; VDK vol. iii, pp. 166, 172–5.

dispute and giving precedence to France. This led to the immediate withdrawal of Philip's ambassador from Venice. Relations nevertheless continued amicably.[62]

In sum, all the major states in Italy were either allied to Philip, in the process of negotiating an alliance, or considered neutral by the king. Even small states like Lucca were in the process of negotiating for his protection by the middle of 1558.[63] All this preceded any suggestion that Philip and Henry would make peace. It was also achieved despite the fact that Philip did not possess Charles's great advantage, imperial powers. He could not legalise the seizure of territory or adjudicate important disputes or give away titles as his father had done. Irrespective of his growing success in Italy, Philip was convinced that he would never gain supremacy over the area unless he secured imperial powers. For a brief period – August–September 1555 – there had been hopes that Charles would transfer the 'vicariate of Italy' to him.[64] It never materialised.

When Ferdinand assumed the imperial mantle, Philip himself became a feudatory of the empire, owing allegiance and subject to the emperor in Milan and Siena. In the spring of 1558, having experienced so many difficulties over the defence of Milan, Philip made up his mind that he could not survive without imperial power over Italy. He sent Alvaro de la Quadra, bishop of Aquila, on a secret mission to Ferdinand, demanding the title and powers of imperial deputy in Italy. He alleged that the position was his by virtue of the agreements signed in Augsburg in 1551. He also pointed out that Ferdinand was so busy sorting out the terrible problems of the Holy Roman Empire that he clearly lacked the time and means to impose himself on Italy. Already the Italian princes had shown that they did not respect Ferdinand's authority and therefore thought that they could do as they liked without risk of punishment. Philip assured Ferdinand that the situation was tense and expressed great fear that it would become increasingly unstable unless one of the great powers with interests in the area wielded sufficient authority to restrain them. In the course of the negotiations, Philip also let slip that he was still deeply afraid for his own lands. He explained that when his territories were attacked it was merely an ordinary infraction, dealt with as and when the emperor saw fit. If Philip wielded imperial powers, any attack against his lands could be defined as rebellion, and so would automatically carry far heavier sanctions – and provide a stronger deterrent.

Ferdinand was deeply affected by this request. On the one hand he was loath to alienate Philip whose help in the curia was vital to him. He also considered himself bound by the treaties, but he argued that such a major reduction of imperial authority would be fatal for him, or any emperor. It would reduce his standing everywhere, and affect his power within the Holy Roman Empire as well as internationally. He finally opted to offer his nephew a compromise: he would give

[62] AGS E.K. 1490 fol. 13; AGS E. 1329 fol. 129; precedence AGS E. 1323 fol. 221–2.
[63] AGS E. 883 fol. 104.   [64] AGS PR. 55 fol. 33.

Philip the vicariate of Italy, but only when Philip was resident in the area, not – as originally agreed – whenever the emperor was away. Philip knew perfectly well that he would have little chance to live in Italy in the near future. The concession was practically of no value to him. Yet he did not wish to reopen the conflict with Ferdinand. He was glad to have secured this confirmation that the treaties of 1551 were still valid and applicable, and comforted himself with this thought. He ordered Quadra to leave in July 1558 and shelved his request for the time being.[65] He was left with the intractable problem of finding quarters for the many companies who had used imperial territories in the past. Alba forecast a grim future for the duchy of Milan if it had to take the burden of the huge army alone. Even then it was appreciated that this was the best place to hold reserves of trained troops who could be sent north or south as need arose.[66]

One of the reasons Philip had been so anxious to secure imperial powers in Italy at this point – aside from the matter of defence – was because he feared he would lose the duchy of Bari. Bari and Rossano belonged to Bona Sforza, dowager queen of Poland, although Charles had some claims to these lands which he recalled, for some reason, in 1552. He ordered Philip to find all relevant documents to prove his claim. Two years later Bona asked Charles and Philip to help her get out of Poland and secure her return to her Neapolitan states. In exchange she promised to cede Bari after her death. Both intervened eagerly on her behalf; Philip even helped to raise the money she needed to make the journey in a style that befitted her status. She was very grateful and subscribed a loan of 30,000 es in June 1556 as a way of demonstrating her pleasure. Shortly after she was safely installed in Bari, and on her death in November 1557, it was disclosed that she had left Bari, Rossano and money to Philip. The will was contested by her son, who denied his mother the right to deprive him of his inheritance, and by Maximilian, who demanded compensation since María's dowry had not been fully paid and her annual support grants were constantly withheld. Both appealed to Ferdinand in his capacity as emperor. Since the king of Poland was simultaneously negotiating a marriage alliance with one of Ferdinand's daughters, it was likely that he would favour his future son-in-law or his son in preference to his distant nephew.[67]

Whilst Ferdinand pondered over the matter, Philip's insecurity mounted. His uncle assured him that he would rather Philip had a thousand Baris than the king of Poland one, but such words did not allay his fears. After considerable thought, Philip decided in November 1558 to annex the two areas. Ferdinand was outraged

[65] Codoin vol. XCVIII, pp. 11–13, 24–8, 36–9; AGS E. 649 fols. 159, 184, 193.
[66] BL Add. 18,789 fols. 6–12.
[67] AGS E. 309(1) s.f., Charles to Philip, 28 March 1552; AGS E. 92 fols. 114–16; AGS E. 97 fols. 119–20; her departure, AGS E. 507 fols. 6–9; AGS E. 808 fol. 43; AGS E. 809 fols. 49 and 20; AGS E. 509 fols. 77 and 111; CSP D p. 85, news of her arrival in Venice; her loan: Alba, *Epistolario*, vol. I, pp. 408–9; her death, AGS GA. 66 fol. 303.

at this open disregard of imperial authority and complained to his nephew. Philip's response was to deny imperial authority over the area, claiming that Bari fell within the jurisdiction of the Neapolitan courts. Ironically, it had not been a petty princeling who had provided the first serious challenge to the weakened imperial power in Italy as Philip feared, but himself. Just as he had predicted, however, Ferdinand was powerless to respond.[68] It might appear obvious to us that, bereft of legal powers, Philip would assert himself in Italy through the use of his superior force, but he had not envisaged the situation in this manner. With his mania for staying well within the law, and his desire to use imperial power for his own protection, it had not been his intention to undermine imperial power.

Despite his success in Italy, Philip did not believe that he had secured supremacy there either before or after Cateau-Cambrésis. It would take many years for his conviction of weakness to be transmuted into a perception of overwhelming strength. Given the terrible situation in which he inherited his Italian states, this is understandable. Peace with France was beneficial to Philip and served to strengthen his position in the area. His allies secured the return of their possessions at his hands: the bonds were thus reinforced. Mantua was given his lands back, as was Savoy; the French accepted the situation in Siena and agreed that Corsica should be left to the Genoese, promising to stop supplying the rebels there and to withdraw their troops.[69] But the peace did not alter the balance substantially; it confirmed the wave of support for the Habsburgs against the Valois which was a salient characteristic of the period preceding the treaty. It is equally wrong therefore, to view it as the withdrawal of France from Italian affairs since Henry was effectively weakened by his failure to retain Italian allies. Although the French withdrew from most of Savoy, they retained fortified places there and the network of alliances built up over decades of occupation and cooperation – not just in Piedmont–Savoy and Milan, but also in Siena and Corsica. Add to this the obvious point that France had not been prevented from invading Italy in the past, even when she had no foothold across the Alps, and the conclusion is that as long as the Italian states remained deeply divided and willing to fight, France would have the excuse to intervene in Italy. As long as there were popes or emperors willing to lend a hand against the 'Spanish' Habsburgs, they would be offered a chance to redress the balance in the area. Whilst the alliance between France and the Muslim powers held, they would have the naval force to match and exceed that of Philip and his allies. Furthermore, the French retained their special relationship with Swiss mercenaries who were ideally placed to threaten Milan, Savoy and Venice.

The peace treaty could never have eliminated France as an alternative source of

---

[68] AGS E. 649 fol. 159; VDK vol. III, pp. 78, 97. Philip came to an understanding with the king of Poland separately, as can be seen from AGS SP I fols. 38 and 130, where the latter complained about difficulties in collecting his share of the revenues of the *douana* of Foggia (customs tolls).

[69] See pp. 310, 312.

influence and power over its divided, weaker neighbour. The situation in Italy in 1559 was best summed up by the Venetian Soriano, who said that no one other than Philip would now dare to begin a war in the area; but Henry would constantly be on the look-out, just waiting for an excuse to intervene again in Italian disputes.[70]

[70] Albèri, *Relazioni*, vol. III, pp. 384–5.

5

The French wars, 1557–9 (1). The northern front

Before the campaign of 1557, the Venetian ambassador Giovanni Michiel reported to the doge and senate that Philip's chances of victory were slight. The extent of his inheritance created an impression of power which could not be sustained if the weakness of his states was taken into account. Michiel isolated four major – perhaps even insurmountable – problems. First, finance: his states were in serious financial difficulties, and as a result of the king's constant pressure for funds, he had become extremely unpopular throughout his possessions. Second, the king had to contend with the resentment and envy of his own family, rather than count upon their help – a clear allusion to his strained relations with Ferdinand and Maximilian. Third, the king and his advisers were untried men, lacking experience of government and war. Fourth, and in retrospect most important, was the general evaluation of Philip's character and capacity. Repeating the common belief that Philip was incapable of waging a successful campaign due to his dislike of military pursuits and lack of experience, Michiel also commented that this perception had greatly encouraged his enemies. Confident that they could obtain 'greater advantage' by fighting against him now, hostile powers vied with each other to attack him. The Venetian did not adduce any evidence to contradict their supposition.[1]

This and similar accounts prove that Philip was right to fear that he would be considered pusillanimous unless he took part in a war. Of course his prevarication in the war against the papacy had done nothing to dispel such perceptions, indeed it had contributed to them. But even if the conduct of the Italian campaign had been more decisive on the diplomatic front and longer lasting, it would not have sufficed to establish Philip's reputation as a military leader. As he was well aware, this could be done only by leading a campaign in person to 'prove himself in these matters' as Ruy Gómez put it; and for that campaign to be against Henry. Philip must 'show the French what we are capable of'.[2] The longer Philip deferred an open declaration of war against Henry II and his personal participation in battle, the less his standing would be among the European powers. He explained in a letter to Juana, 'my states,

---

[1] CSP V vol. 6.(ii), pp. 1062, 1064; vol. 6(i), pp. 106–7.
[2] AGS E. 809 fol. 116, holograph to Eraso, 20 June 1555.

as well as my honour and reputation, which I value above all else', were at stake in the war against Henry.[3] It is very telling that he should so often refer to this as his 'first war'. Equally illuminating is Juana's response. She agreed with his view of the campaign, and added that for too long France had called the tune to which all other powers had danced. It was imperative to regain the initiative and have a say as to whether there would be war or peace in Christendom. She was acutely conscious of the fact that unless Philip recovered the credit and reputation lost in previous years, they would be forced to remain on the defensive, constantly responding to the challenges other powers posed.[4] For his part, the duke of Savoy declared that the whole world would judge Philip's future prospects by the outcome of his first major campaign against France.[5]

The general acceptance of the overwhelming importance of the war largely determined his strategy and the response of his realms. All those areas bordering on France promoted themselves as the ideal base for operations because they knew that Philip would have to be present at the front. When he rejected them, they nevertheless contributed more or less generously, spurred by his reminders of what was at stake. Like Charles, he left them with the clear impression that the size of their contributions and sacrifices would be used as a measure of their loyalty. Since they all needed to win his favour in the hope that he would give them priority after the war, they made a tremendous effort to meet his demands. The strain of financial contributions, as much as the tension which grew out of the irreconcilable needs of the different states, contributed greatly to the king's lack of popularity within his empire and was to lead to rebellion.

In this and the following two chapters, the methods used to raise money for the war and the response of the states will be examined, as will other important sources of tension which created unrest within the empire. The primary object of this analysis is to trace the all-important process by which the king became utterly dependent on his Spanish realms.

STRATEGY

Philip's overriding desire was to inflict the maximum damage against Henry with the minimum cost. He started the war with such acute concern for his limited financial resources that he believed he had only one chance to defeat the French. He needed a spectacular campaign to bring Henry to the negotiating table and force him to accept a 'good peace'. His task appeared all the more daunting as Henry was generally thought to be the most powerful king of France since Charlemagne.[6] Some of his advisers were more optimistic; as the count of Feria put it 'no prince

---

[3] AGS PR. 26 fol. 166.   [4] AGS E. 121 fols. 48–9.
[5] Cabrera de Córdoba, *Felipe II*, vol. 1, p. 161.   [6] RAH SC F. 17 fol. 143v.

ever begins a war with enough money to finish what he has started'.[7] But the notion that the war would consist of one, magnificent campaign prevailed.

In order to gain the maximum propaganda advantage, it was hoped that France would furnish Philip with an excuse to declare war; he could not risk being labelled the aggressor. The invasion of Naples could not be considered a *casus belli* since Henry was acting as a supporter of the papacy, not the main aggressor. But in January 1557, Henry allowed a brief and unsuccessful attack against Douai – perhaps to test Philip's reaction – and this served Philip's purpose. He duly warned Juana that the truce was at an end. His ambassador in France, Simon Renard, thought that war had actually started. Not so; Philip delayed until March before issuing a formal declaration.[8] He knew that the delay would reduce his reputation even further, accentuating his lack of spirit, nevertheless he insisted that he must defer commitment until he was certain that his chances of winning were good. This in turn depended on the availability of a sound strategy and sufficient finance to execute it.

The most obvious place from which to launch a major attack against France was the Piedmont–Milan front, with its large military organization, seasoned commanders and fortified places. Three factors combined to eliminate this area, however. First, it was evident that the most spectacular campaign Philip could mount was a direct strike against France. If this area was chosen, it would be necessary to recover most of Savoy and destroy powerful French positions in the region before being in a position to invade southern France. Second, it was thought difficult to provision a large army in an area devastated by recent warfare. Third, and most importantly perhaps, the Italian front had acquired the reputation of being 'an interminable conflict'. There had been no spectacular victories on the Piedmont–Milan front for more than two decades. Both sides were fairly matched, but the advantage lay with the French. Philip ran the risk of getting bogged down with much effort but little gain at the end of the campaigning season. It was also unlikely that Henry would march to this front and so uplift the status of the war.[9]

The regency government in Spain was eager to prove that if he chose it to launch his major assault, Philip would gain most in terms of reputation and territorial advantage. Already in 1551 the duke of Maqueda thought it possible and desirable to extend the Pyrenean frontier by some fifteen leagues with a small-scale attack.[10] Four years later Juana urged a campaign in Navarre. The continuous negotiations between the Spanish government and the Albret claimants kept their attention firmly focused on this area. In 1556 Antoine de Bourbon, negotiating on behalf of

7 Codoin vol. 87, p. 41.
8 AGS E K. 1490 fol. 16, Renard to Juan Vázquez, 13 January; AGS E. 119 fol. 106, Philip to Juana, 9 & 18 January.
9 The fullest discussion of strategy I have come across is the lengthy document in RAH SC F. 17 fols. 143–153v. It is anonymous, but the authors describe themselves as 'some of the best and most experienced soldiers serving his majesty'.
10 AGS E. 84 fol. 183, Maqueda to Philip, 3–4 September; see also AGS E. 84 fols. 389, 185–6, 351.

his wife, thought Philip so weak he might be forced to disgorge the old Albret lands by negotiation or force. In November, impatient of the little progress made in the talks, he threatened invasion. Far from cowing the regent, this emboldened her and other Spaniards; they asked for permission to launch a pre-emptive strike.[11] This proposal was rejected by leading military advisers as difficult and unrewarding. The mountainous and barren nature of the terrain in the Basque country would make travel and provisioning a nightmare. The absence of sufficient experienced forces required major movements of soldiers and armaments from all corners of the empire to a remote area. Most important of all, there was no suitable French target there. Taking Bayonne would certainly be spectacular but it was likely to prove extremely difficult, since it was so well defended. Narbonne would be easier, but lacked prestige. These arguments were also used to reject plans submitted for attacks from Fuenterrabia, Aragon and Catalonia.[12] Philip did not pursue the 'Spanish' proposals and relegated the area to the role it had played in the past, as supplier of funds and troops. It was a hard, unrewarding task, not much to the liking of the regency government or many within the realms. They appreciated Philip's argument that he was saving them from the damage and cost of war within their lands, but he was also depriving them of his presence and any direct advantages (such as territorial acquisitions or commercial advantages) which they could otherwise have made.

The same group of commanders who rejected all the Spanish proposals argued in the strongest terms for an attack on Brittany. They thought it would bring Spain, the Netherlands and England together, as it had in the past. The three states had supported attempts to maintain Brittany's independence at the close of the fifteenth century, and there were indications that their intervention now would tap strong separatist feelings there. Expecting Philip to find the project too ambitious, they suggested an alternative attack against Boulogne, again recalling the cooperation between Charles V and Henry VIII in this area.[13] The king could not have found their arguments altogether convincing, since he made no allusion to them subsequently, but he did endorse the general thrust of their proposal: the best action was a direct attack against France with English participation as a vital component. The choice of the Netherlands as the base of operations responds to this decision and determination to coordinate an attack with England.

Quite apart from his desire to use English ports and secure financial aid from the realm, Philip was attracted to plans with English participation because he was becoming concerned that he would lose reputation. Renard had advocated joint action against France since 1554. During the Italian campaigns of 1555–6, Alba had been desperate to organise a northern diversion and led a relentless campaign to

[11] AGS E. 120 fol. 170, Juana to Philip, 25 July 1557; see also p. 176 for more details of the Bourbon negotiations.   [12] RAH SC F. 17 fol. 145.
[13] Ibid.; also R. B. Wernham, *Before the armada* (London, 1966) pp. 153ss.

persuade Philip that unless he secured a declaration of war against France from the English, his honour would be seriously affected. There was another advantage Alba stressed – England was the least burdened of Philip's states. Soon the duke of Savoy was arguing with even greater vehemence for English participation. He was convinced that unless England provided money and troops for a major assault against Henry, Philip would never deal a significant blow against France. The key to a 'good peace' with France was full English participation. Philip's confessor, who had remained in England to help with the process of conversion, wearily commented that he could think of no other reason for having acquired this realm if it was not to use its military strength against France. They were unanimous that Philip would also lose honour if he did not secure English support.[14] Seen in this context, Philip's return to England in the spring of 1557 assumes much greater importance than it has been credited with hitherto. Equally, his failure to secure the support he requested had far more serious implications than has been perceived.

According to the terms of the marriage, Philip was not allowed to involve the realm in the emperor's wars. He argued that this was his own conflict; the English council, seeking to avoid commitment at all costs, tried to maintain that it was still Charles's war since the previous hostilities had been ended with a truce and not with peace. They also tried another tack: they argued that the realm was racked with poverty and discontent and further exactions would cause widespread rebellion. And yet, when Philip and Mary pressed the royal council to support the war against France, they offered money and soldiers, but refused to declare war. Had the realm been quite so poor and restive, the reverse would have been the case. Philip found himself in the awkward position of having to diminish the importance of this practical aid and concentrated on securing the all-important symbolic sign of unity; an open declaration of war. After very considerable pressure from both monarchs, the council finally yielded to their request in May 1557, but the formal challenge was not delivered to Henry until June.[15]

Contemporaries believed that England's military potential was considerable. One Venetian report states that the realm could field up to 100,000 men and had a sizeable navy. Philip was less interested in raw recruits than in ships, although he demanded 2,000 sappers and some miners both in 1557 and 1558. He had shown interest in the navy from the start and had a report drawn up giving details of the royal forces and those of the major ports. The crown could lay claim to 30 ships, the city of London had 16 and other ports and individuals had some 36 vessels, making a

[14] Renard, CSP Sp vol. 12, p. 124; Alba, *Epistolario*, vol. 1, pp. 320, 346; Savoy, cit. p. 131 L. P. Gachard (ed.), 'La seconde remontrance d'Emmanuel-Philibert de Savoie', *Bulletin de la Commission Royale d'Histoire* (Brussels, VIII, 1856), pp. 124–32; Fresneda, Philip's confessor, AGS CJH 34 fol. 482.

[15] Loades, *Mary Tudor*, pp. 242–2; Harbison, *Rival Ambassadors at the court of Queen Mary* (London, 1940), pp. 279–329; Weiss, *Granvelle*, vol. 5, p. 71; CSP Sp. vol. 13, pp. 295–6 Henry's counter accusations, claiming that Mary had no grounds for declaring war against him.

sizeable total. Philip wanted the English naval forces to join with ships he was fitting out in the Netherlands. With both navies he would be able to control the Channel and might even launch mixed campaigns which required sizeable naval support.[16] He also hoped that England would help with supplies. The Netherlands were suffering a dearth for the second year in succession and the army's appetite was insatiable. He asked for victuals, but was turned down by the English government on the grounds that a bad harvest had been predicted and all grain produced would be needed internally. The king accepted the refusal with good grace. Shortly afterwards he was informed that a bumper harvest was expected. Although there is no reason to believe that the council's initial assessment of the harvest was anything but genuine, it was easy to interpret this response as another sign of their reluctance to support Philip at what he considered a critical juncture.[17]

The English might have been better disposed to help if they had thought Philip willing to help them. Naturally, Henry had responded to the growing signs of English intervention by encouraging dissent and invasion. In time-honoured fashion he galvanised the Scottish front. A small invasion was mounted in August 1557 along the English East March and the Scots got the better of the skirmishes that followed. The government in London were thoroughly alarmed. Twenty ships had been sent to help Philip, but these were immediately recalled, and Mary added an urgent appeal for Philip to send the rest of his fleet to repel the Scottish invasion. Mary and the council naturally expected Philip to issue a declaration of war against Scotland, thus reciprocating their declaration against France. The count of Feria strongly urged him to do so immediately in order to conciliate the English. It was a forlorn hope. To begin with, Philip did not intend to divide his forces, especially not to send them to the far north. More important still was the king's concern not to damage vital trade links between the Netherlands and Scotland. He told Feria he did not dare to threaten the livelihood of his Dutch subjects, who were already in such dire straits.[18] This lack of solidarity naturally upset Mary and her council, and increased their truculence. To add insult to injury – although he did not intend either – Philip then tried to eliminate the conflict altogether. He sent Christophe d'Assonleville to Scotland in September 1557, hoping to arrange peace between the two realms. He had gone over the head of the English and they resented this.[19]

Fortunately for Philip and Mary, the Scots were – as one contemporary remarked – no more 'French' than the English were 'Spanish'. Much to Henry's disgust they

[16] AGS E. 811 fol. 21, list of ships. I am indebted to Professor David Loades for this reference. Soranzo's assessment of England's military potential in 1554, CSP V vol. 5, pp. 547–9; Michiel's for 1557 in CSP V vol. 6(ii), pp. 1046–9.

[17] AGS E. 515 fol. 92; C. S. L. Davies, 'England and the French war, 1557–9', in J. Loach and R. Tittler (eds.) *The mid-Tudor polity c. 1540–1560* (London, 1980), pp. 159–85, esp. pp. 161–2.

[18] Codoin vol. 87, pp. 40, 57, 58. Details of the clashes along the Scottish borders, Davies, 'England and the French war', pp. 162, 167–8, 179; Loades, *Mary Tudor*, pp. 370–1.

[19] Codoin vol. 87, pp. 57–8; 75–6; CSP Sp vol. 13, pp. 391–2; RPPB vol. 1, p. 234; Rodríguez-Salgado and Adams, 'Feria's dispatch', p. 307 and note 3.

withdrew their forces in October 1557 and refused to launch further hostilities that year. Nevertheless, the English government remained concerned about the northern border, especially after the marriage between the dauphin and Mary Stuart in April 1558 finally bound France and Scotland together. Extra soldiers were levied and new fortifications were started in Berwick. Nor was this the only potential trouble spot. Mary called upon Philip to support the English in Ireland, which they claimed was in great danger. Feria commented that the queen and council were deliberately exaggerating the problems of their frontiers to pre-empt any further demands from the king. The claim rings true. It should be noted, however, that at the time of the marriage negotiations with Mary, the imperial envoys promised the English that Philip would help them regain their ancient possessions in Guyenne and other parts of France, even the whole kingdom.[20] Now he was not even seconding their declaration of war, nor contributing to their defence. The sense of alienation and mutual resentment which soon arose out of the war was a vital element in the growing rift between Philip and his English subjects.

The king was deeply wounded by the poor English response. Moreover, without the English navy, he had no hope of controlling vital trade and communication routes and had to discard certain plans requiring naval diversions. Whilst the war in Italy occupied Henry's forces, the absence of sizeable English contingents was less noticeable since the Italian front acted as a secondary front and kept French forces divided. Because Alba terminated the war rather earlier than expected and French troops hastened back, Philip and his military advisers had to draw up alternative diversions. But they were so committed to a northern strategy devised on the assumption that England would have taken charge of a diversion, that they were distinctly lacking in ideas. Eventually a second invasion of France was organised – an ill-fated and badly planned attack against Bourg-en-Bresse, where baron Polwiller (a friend of Granvelle) had contacts. Philip would never have allowed the attack if he had been less than desperate to create a diversion, since it required passage of troops across the Franche-Comté which was strictly forbidden by the neutrality treaty signed with France. The province was totally defenceless, and a breach of the treaty would allow France to attack it with impunity. Worse still, the contacts in Bourg-en-Bresse failed to materialise. The duke of Guise, on his way back from Italy stationed additional troops in the area. Many of Philip's advisers thought that the only good thing about this episode was its brevity. They were not eager to publicise it.[21]

By now they were clutching at straws. Still convinced that the main thrust of the attack against Henry would not succeed unless the French forces were divided, the search for a subsidiary front intensified. Finally Philip was persuaded to recall Alba, who was ordered to proceed to Corsica immediately, put an end to the rebellion

---

[20] CSP Sp Vol. 11, p. 246, Charles to Renard, 20 September 1553; Codoin vol. 87, pp. 59–60.
[21] Van Durme, *Granvela*, p. 22, note 45; Weiss, *Granvelle*, vol. 5, pp. 84–5; Febvre, *Franche-Comté*, pp. 131–2; Cloulas, *Henri II*, pp. 470–2.

there – French-backed rebels were still carrying out guerrilla-style attacks against the Genoese authorities there – and then launch an invasion of Provence from the island. The plan was soon shelved for lack of money, but the sheer logistical and political problems it entailed should have consigned it to fertile imaginations rather than to concrete proposals. Evidently no one could devise viable alternatives to keep French forces divided.[22]

VICTORY: ST QUENTIN, AUGUST 1557

The area to be invaded was selected long before a specific target had been chosen. It was not until the summer of 1557 that the choice had been narrowed to three places – Rocroi, Peronne and St Quentin. All were well inside France, along major routes, yet close to the king's base in the Netherlands. The dukes of Savoy and Glajon had been asked to reconnoitre the towns and present their recommendations, addressing themselves to the requirements set out by the king. The place had to be of sufficient importance to correspond to the exalted stature of the commander, who was of course Philip himself. Moreover, its loss must be considered extremely damaging to French security. Apart from this, it had to be in a terrain best suited to the king's forces, not least because they must ensure that whatever site was chosen should offer an easy conquest. The need to find food and forage was also to affect, if not determine, their choice.

Rocroi met most of these requirements, but would not have allowed Philip to make good use of his cavalry. Peronne was the best from the point of view of provisions, but it was a harder target because of its good fortifications. St Quentin would be easier to take and allowed the effective deployment of cavalry and infantry, but they warned the king that he would need to take a host of nearby towns in order to have a large enough area to quarter and provision the army. At the end of July Philip opted for St Quentin, and accepted a coherent strategy that entailed the conquest of a well-defined area, not just the town itself. Significantly, he introduced new conditions in the negotiations with Antoine de Bourbon at this point, demanding from him La Fère, Ham, Bohain, Beaurieux – all in the environs of St Quentin. The treaty was not concluded, so Philip was forced to conquer most of these himself.[23]

Unaware of the basic strategic thinking behind these moves, many historians constructed a rather odd sequence of events to account for the king's movements after the victories of St Quentin. Somewhat simplified, their chronology runs something like this: having taken the city, Philip did not know what else to do, since he was hopelessly dependent on his father for advice. He bided his time, taking the odd little place around the area until Charles was good enough to tell him to march

[22] Alba, *Epistolario*, vol. 1, p. 469.
[23] AGS E K. 1490 fols. 43, 47, Savoy correspondence; Codoin vol. 2, p. 384, Philip to Ferdinand; E. 120 fol. 174, Bourbon negotiations.

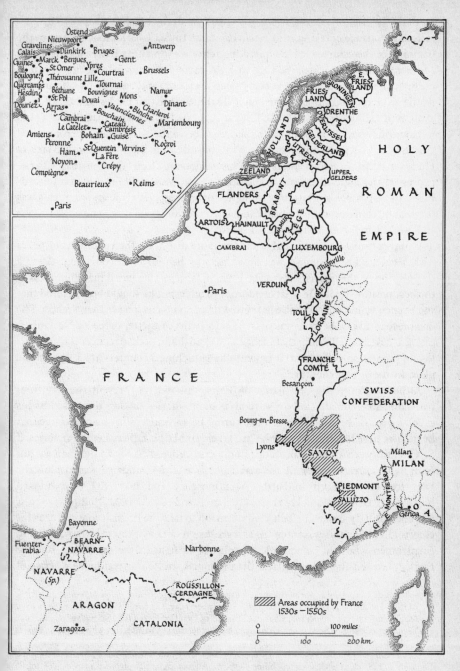

Map 3 France, the Netherlands and disputed frontier area

on Paris. By then of course, it was too late. The French had regrouped and so he missed his chance of taking the French capital.[24] In fact Charles took no part in the planning of the campaign. He limited his activities to writing letters urging Juana and her advisers to furnish the king with the money he required. He first learnt of Philip's victory from a letter sent by Juan Vázquez, and reacted by offering his thanks to God and counselling his son to do the same so that God would continue to show him favour. It was Granvelle who suggested to Charles that Philip would welcome his opinion on how best to follow up the victories, but the emperor replied that he could say nothing until he had consulted on the matter with Mary of Hungary.[25] In a conversation with his confidant, Luis de Quijada, Charles expressed the hope that news would soon reach them of Philip's march towards Paris. Far from being a carefully thought-out strategy, let alone an order, this was the wishful thinking of a man who had longed for similar success against the French and wished to see them reduced to size.[26]

Philip consulted with his father on one issue directly – the conditions of peace with France. The response was anything but helpful or encouraging. After a disquisition on the inconstancy of the French, Charles concluded that Philip was in the best position to decide what conditions to offer, but he should bear in mind that the French would only accept what suited them and for as long as they wished. The one piece of advice he gave was passed on to Juana in a letter dated 15 November. She was asked to tell Philip that Henry would no doubt seek to recover the grievous loss of reputation suffered at St Quentin by launching a counter-attack against the place in the winter months.[27]

Although Philip did not march on Paris, this did not prevent the city from panicking about an attack. Nor were his contemporaries any less impressed by his success because he concentrated on securing his position. What mattered was that he did not have to abandon what he had taken, unlike his father. Yet the victories of St Quentin were a close-run thing. Philip had ordered Savoy to defer an assault until he was present; after all, the major purpose of the campaign was to allow the king to prove himself in battle. Montmorency and his relief force moved northwards far more quickly than anticipated and, by contrast, Philip's progress was enervatingly slow as a result of his decision to take the English contingent as his escort. Doubtless this was intended as a great sign of favour towards the 7,000 or so Englishmen who had come under Pembroke to fight in the campaign. But the English crossed the Channel later than planned, and on arrival made a series of

[24] Cabrera de Córdoba was one of the earliest exponents of this sequence: *Felipe II*, vol. 1, pp. 187–9.
[25] AGS E. 128 fol. 324, Charles to Philip, 17 September 1557; Gachard, *Retraite*, vol. 2, pp. 240–3; AGS E. 128 fol. 326, holograph, Charles to Philip, 15 October; E. 119 fol. 264, E. 119 fol. 218, Juan Vázquez to Charles, 8 September. Of course Philip wrote directly to his father with the good news, as he did to other members of the family.
[26] Letter of 19 September 1557, cit. by Cepeda Adan, 'San Quintin desde Yuste', in *Carlos V*, p. 25.
[27] AGS E. 128 fol. 313, Charles to Philip, 8, 17, 22 August and 15 September 1557; E. 119 fol. 89 Charles to Juana, 15 November.

demands for horses, carts and other essential materials which were simply not available, and had not been asked for in advance. The lack of organisation and parsimonious progress of these forces exasperated the king and his military advisers. Savoy finally had no choice but to give battle before they arrived in order to prevent the reinforcements from entering the town. His victory was spectacular, with much of the French army killed or captured. The king arrived in time to review his victorious forces and take part in the successful siege and assault of the town. His presence at the head of the army when St Quentin, and later Ham fell, sufficed to establish that he was a worthy and successful military leader.[28]

As the king and his entourage caroused, soldiers devastated large parts of northern France. Monluc voiced the fears of many after St Quentin when he said, 'je tenois le royaumme pour perdeu'.[29] Bearing in mind the long spate of disastrous campaigns, Charles's lack of success in previous invasions of France; and the general expectation that Philip would not be able to organise a campaign, it is easier to understand why both sides overreacted. Philip's ecstatic supporters ascribed the spectacular victory to divine favour.[30] Henry did not allow himself much time to mourn. He recalled his troops from Italy and immediately began to plan his revenge. It was quickly realised that it would prove extraordinarily difficult to recover the territory already lost – but there was an alternative way to regain reputation.

DEFEAT: CALAIS, DECEMBER 1558–JANUARY 1559

Calais and the Pale were the last English territories in France. Henry had shown some interest in the conquest of this enclave in the past. Its attraction now was greatly enhanced, first because it was badly defended and certainly unprepared for a major assault that winter. Even more important, it would yield an immense amount of honour and reputation, precisely because it would finally expel the English from French soil. There was a risk involved – it might prompt the English to pursue the war more vigorously and bring them closer to Philip. On the other hand, if Henry was fortunate, the loss of the place would drive a wedge between them which could be exploited. Henry, the duke of Guise and the cardinal of Lorraine planned the campaign meticulously. Nevertheless, the odds against it succeeding in the depths of a severe winter were great; so great a recent historian has declared it nothing short

---

[28] Details of the battle and English intervention can be found in the correspondence between Philip and Savoy, especially AGS E K. 1490 fols. 50, 57. Duplicates of some of their correspondence can be found in BL Add. 28,364 fols. 10–11, 19–20, 26–7. CPS Sp. vol. 13, pp. 303, 317; Loades, *Mary Tudor*, pp. 371–2; Davies, 'England and the French war', pp. 164–6; Cabrera de Córdoba, *Felipe II*, vol. 1, p. 179ss. Romier, *Les origines*, vol. 2, p. 170ss; Vandernesse, *Voyages*, pp. 26–7. Philip's own account of the battle to Ferdinand, Codoin vol. 2, pp. 493–4, another account, pp. 494–6.

[29] cit Romier, *Les origines*, vol. 2, p. 180.

[30] Romier, *Les origines*, vol. 2, pp. 181–3; RAH SC A-60 fols. 166–7.

of suicidal.[31] Naturally, if it could be proved that Henry had inside contacts and knew its defenders would cooperate, the odds would be substantially diminished. For a number of reasons, Philip and his advisers were soon convinced that there had been treasonable negotiations, even perhaps with the commander, lord Wentworth.

Then, as now, Englishmen denied charges of collusion. If it was not treason, it certainly was gross ineptitude and poor leadership that lost the day. Wentworth, for instance, refused to believe that French preparations were directed against Calais, despite repeated warnings from Philip among others. He told the king to look to the defence of Hesdin, which was the real target. He did not ask Philip for help until 31 December, although the king had offered it weeks earlier. By this time, there were some 20,000 French soldiers encamped in the environs of the port. Why or how Wentworth managed to miss the massive deployment of troops on his doorstep continues to puzzle historians. Such a degree of myopia is, as Potter recently put it, 'difficult to grasp'.[32] It is true that the unusually cold weather favoured Henry by freezing up the marshes which had often been seen as the best defences of the area, but the implications of the severe weather conditions should have been as evident to Wentworth as to the French.

The English government was caught totally unprepared by the attack. The king's concern at Wentworth's refusal to take action persuaded him to send a special envoy, Juan de Ayala, to England. Ayala had been in Calais liaising with the English during the campaign; it was hoped that he would prompt the government to take some action. The mission failed since the English government gave greater weight to Wentworth's reports – even after these became increasingly contradictory – than to Philip's warnings. By asking for help and cancelling the request more than once, Wentworth caused considerable confusion.[33] In the end, Mary did order a relief force to be fitted out. The soldiers were already aboard the ships when news came of the fall of Rysbank. The sailors apparently mutinied when it was suggested that they should sail despite this. They had no desire to risk their lives. Instead of asking Philip for a base, the English government disbanded these forces on 12 January, partly because a storm during the night of the 9 January had damaged the fleet. This implied that they had given up Calais for lost, and expected Guisnes and Hammes to hold out until a proper campaign could be organised to recover Calais. Their

---

[31] Davies, 'England and the French war', p. 170.

[32] D. Potter, 'The duc de Guise and the fall of Calais, 1557–1558', *English Historical Review*, 98 (1983), p. 490. Loades, *Mary Tudor*, pp. 375–9 takes the view that the charges of treason were groundless; Cloulas, *Henri II*, avoids the issue altogether in his account pp. 477–81, 484; Davies, 'England and the French war', pp. 168–78, discusses the various charges and concludes that the English (and Philip) were too confident of the strength of the Calais fortifications, and that there was 'a massive failure of nerve' on the part of the English government and defenders, perhaps even 'the chance of treason somewhere among the officers'. Events can be followed in the correspondence printed in CSP Sp vol. 13.

[33] Wentworth asked the English government for aid on 26 December, then cancelled the request on the 29th, they complied. He demanded help again on 31 December.

inability to devise a coherent strategy is clearly reflected in their contradictory orders regarding troop levies. After the order to disband on 12 January, the English council decided to levy troops on the 17th, reduced the number to be levied on the 19th and then decided on 27th to disband these men too.[34]

This contrasts sharply with Philip's prompt and decisive actions. Despite Wentworth's rejection of help, he kept a force of arquebusiers at the ready, so that when the English commander finally asked for soldiers on 2 January, these companies were dispatched the following day. Philip also had ships on stand-by, under the command of Luis de Carvajal. They tried to reinforce Calais by sea, but by the time they had been summoned it really was too late to save Calais. Some of the soldiers in the fleet marched to Guisnes and fought alongside the English in the first and last show of resistance to the French advance. Furthermore, the king had sent a messenger to Spain with orders for a levy of 2,500 men, who were to be kept ready and dispatched immediately if the English asked for further help.[35] It may have been news of the mutiny in the English ships that prompted the duke of Savoy to send some vessels to England to pick up troops. By the time they landed, however, there was not a soldier in sight, and no information could be given by the government as to what they intended to do to reinforce the other positions within the Pale. Savoy was irritated by all this and complained of the ineptitude, unreliability and lack of cooperation from England.[36]

Philip was more inclined to be charitable and put it all down to a lack of organisation and experience. He was under the impression that Mary was levying 10,000 men for Calais, and sent the count of Feria to England in order to provide support and experience, as well as to liaise with Mary, in the forthcoming campaign. He hoped that the queen could be persuaded to raise 17,000 infantry, 3,000 horse and 4,000 sappers; Philip would contribute 32,000 infantry and 11,000 horse. It is interesting to note that when Charles V and Henry VIII planned the Boulogne campaign they agreed to parity of forces: 35,000 infantry and 7,000 horse apiece.[37] As Calais fell in a few days and the English government failed to respond to the crisis, Philip was persuaded of the wisdom of deferring a joint offensive until the campaigning season proper. He was still confident that the English would furnish a powerful contingent and help him to recover the lands and reputation so unexpectedly lost.[38]

[34] CSP D. pp. 97–8; Davies, 'England and the French war', p. 174, thinks that this order was due to the news of the fall of Guisnes, but this makes it no easier to understand the lack of urgency over the levies, and the change of heart over numbers to be sent.

[35] RAH SC A-48 fols. 233, 234; AGS E. 129 fols. 20–1.

[36] CSP Sp. vol. 12, p. 336.

[37] AGS E. 8340 fol. 318, Philip's instructions to Feria, 21 January 1558. I am indebted to Professor Geoffrey Parker for information as to the whereabouts of this document. Wernham, *Before the armada*, pp. 153, 156 gives somewhat different figures for the Boulogne campaign. The exact number is less important than the notion of parity.

[38] CSP Sp. vol. 13, pp. 332–3, Philip's reaction to the loss; AGS E. 128 fol. 355, for that of Charles.

The fall of Calais was also a serious blow to Philip's realms. After St Quentin they expected peace, but Henry's victory turned the tables once again and raised his reputation to new heights. France and her allies were infused with new courage. Significantly, the duke of Guise specifically linked the victory in Calais with the recent defeats in Italy, expressing the hope that this success would lift the spirits of Henry's Italian allies and help to reverse the situation there.[39] In January 1558, Henry told the states general of the realm that he needed their support in order to wage another powerful campaign, 'pour venir à une bonne paix'.[40] Philip made his decision to mount another campaign at the same time. He had forced the English to come into the war and was personally responsible for the losses that might result. He felt this liability deeply, however much he regretted the behaviour of those involved. Much as Juana and the regency government wished for peace, they also spoke of the 'personal obligation' of the king, and recognised their duty to provide aid for the next campaign.[41] Yet they all spoke of it as a shared obligation, especially since they believed the English were largely responsible for the catastrophe.

Feria, now Philip's resident envoy in London, had been forced to delay his return journey to England because he did not wish to arrive there at the same time as news of the fall of Calais. When he met the queen and council shortly afterwards to discuss the necessary measures for its recovery, he was told that England could not afford to launch a campaign of such magnitude. The English councillors claimed that at least 20,000 men would be required, at a cost of £520,000, and they lacked both manpower and money. Much was made of the unrest and the fear caused by the 'sweating sickness' epidemic. The time was not propitious for war. Outside the council chamber, however, a different story emerged. Feria was informed by some councillors that the figures had been deliberately inflated and that a campaign could be mounted for much less. He did not know what to make of all this. Gradually he came to the conclusion that the English council was deliberately falsifying information in order to force Philip to organise and fund the entire campaign on his own. Later he stated that the English government was not interested in recovering the lost colony.[42]

In February 1558 there were some encouraging signs. Mary promised one hundred large ships, with fifty smaller vessels, as well as 10–16,000 men. As spring approached, however, Philip had nothing beyond vague promises and he became alarmed. Despairing of obtaining a strong military contingent, he still hoped he would be able to organise naval aid once more. He summoned the English admiral Edward Clinton to Brussels in May 1558 to discuss the campaign. Clinton delayed his departure, and this alerted the king to the trouble ahead. On arrival, Clinton

[39] Potter, 'The duc de Guise and the Fall of Calais', p. 493.
[40] cit Cloulas, *Henri II*, p. 481.
[41] AGS E. 811 fols. 20–1, Juana to Philip, 14 March 1558; E. 128 fol. 255, Juan Vázquez to Charles, end of January. Codoin vol. 87, p. 48, Feria to Philip, 17 March.
[42] CSP Sp vol. 13, pp. 349–51; Loades, *Mary Tudor*, pp. 378–9; Codoin vol. 87, pp. 41–2.

declared the English navy unfit for a campaign; the only thing they could do was patrol the Channel, or at most mount some minor raids. The English government now offered soldiers again, but constantly altered the figures, ranging from 5,000 to 10,000 men. Feria became increasingly impatient and suspected that such constant contradictions were a cover for their shameful decision not to take part in the campaign to restore Calais.[43]

Philip refused to give up hope. He ordered the English navy to be fitted out. He wanted the ships to be ready for service in July and provisioned (by the English government) until the end of September. Nevertheless, the ambivalent attitude and contradictory reports from England did not allow him to formulate a coherent strategy which included these forces. When hostilities began in earnest he was on the defensive in any case. Guise, the victor of Calais, led the French troops to another important victory in June 1558 at Thionville. The rest of the French forces under Termes led successful raids against Dunkirk, Bergues and St Winocque. Their main task was to prevent the English ships and forces from joining up with Philip. The situation looked extremely bleak for Philip and he was convinced that unless he won the next engagement, the precarious edifice of power over which he presided would collapse. Full of anguish and anxiety, he called the English navy to provide much needed support for an attack against Gravelines at the beginning of July. Everything depended on a successful outcome here.

His reaction to the news that most of the English fleet had been sent off to the island of Alderney without his knowledge – but presumably with Mary's blessing – can only be guessed at. Feria had tried to prevent this and failed. News that the French had attacked the island had prompted the English council to put the defence of their interests in the Channel before Philip's continental campaign.[44] Luckily, the ten large vessels under the command of Carvajal and the troops under the count of Egmont caught Termes and his men in a deadly trap, as the French forces busied themselves sacking Bergues. French losses were high: 1,500 dead, 3,000 prisoners, including their illustrious commander. The two kings had levelled the score once again. Neither could force a 'good peace' upon the other under these conditions, whilst both had made considerable gains in terms of territory and prestige. It was now down to money: whoever could afford to fund a third, massive campaign would emerge as the victor.

ENGLAND'S FINANCIAL CONTRIBUTION

From the moment he set foot in the realm, Philip faced a barrage of complaints and strong special pleading from the English council and courtiers. They informed him

---

[43] CSP Sp vol. 13, pp. 349–51; Codoin vol. 87, pp. 5–11, 45, 47, 48, 60.
[44] Codoin vol. 87, pp. 48, 69–70, 73; CSP Sp vol. 13, p. 403; Cloulas, *Henri II*, pp. 493–6; Davies, 'England and the French war', p. 181, claims that English ships helped to take Gravelines, but the day after the battle Philip was still asking where the fleet was.

that the level of government debt was dangerously high and the realm unstable. The impression of penury has remained to our own day. When Mary came to the throne there was a deficit of *c.* £185,000. She cut down defence costs and expenditure at court in an effort to reduce this. The mood of retrenchment did not last long; the measures were not imposed rigorously or consistently. Government expenditure rose subsequently as would be expected in an age of rapid inflation. At the beginning of the war, the crown's debts stood at *c.* £200,000 – hardly a major increase. In fact it was proof of successful financial management. But this is not how the English government viewed the matter. There was great anxiety over the debt and considerable alarm at the sharp increase in expenditure due to the war. Whereas annual defence costs were £20,000 normally, they rose to £100,000 when war broke out. The navy had been cut down to £14,000 p.a. by Mary; it cost £143,000 to maintain during January 1557 to November 1558. The English council reported a deficit of £100,000 for the year 1557–8 alone and informed Philip that they were close to financial collapse. The speed of change after a period of relative stability added to the general feeling of impending disaster. Set beside the level of debt in Philip's other realms their claim appeared laughable.[45]

Philip expected England to contribute to the war effort along with his other states. He told them that it was a defensive struggle in which his reputation and honour were at stake, and he assumed that they would acknowledge their duty to help him. No one in the English government seriously challenged this much as they might quibble over the size of their contribution. Mary's constant promises of aid showed both her desire to please her husband and her acceptance that he had some claim on the realm, even before the loss of Calais. After that, with proposals for a joint venture mooted, England's duty to find resources for the war could not be doubted.

In England, the usual method of meeting political or military crises was by raising extraordinary parliamentary subsidies. In 1557 neither the council nor the queen was eager to summon another parliament, however. The 1555 session had made its grant of two fifteenths after much bitter complaint; the second instalment of this subsidy was due in May 1557. The government was concerned that political and religious unrest would increase if a new request was made so soon. They delayed a request for parliamentary taxation until 1558. Consequently they had to impose other expedients. The most obvious was the sale of lands and other crown assets. Henry VIII had financed his costly military ventures largely from alienation of royal demesne and secularised lands, and Elizabeth was to use this expedient to fund her wars. Although Mary had given back some lands to the restored Catholic church, she had considerable resources to dispose of, including the forfeited states of condemned traitors such as the duke of Northumberland. She also planned an

---

[45] Loades, *Mary Tudor*, pp. 183–316, 373, 402–23, details of expenditure and cuts. This account has superseded and corrected that of F. C. Dietz, *English government finance* (2 vols., London 1964), vol. I.

investigation into the numerous gifts made by Northumberland, no doubt with a view to recovering the alienated royal properties or fining their new owners. The risks of alienating the nobility deterred her from this course of action. There was still much she could have done to raise funds, and she knew it. She promised Philip to sell crown assets and provide him with 800,000 es. In April 1557 she set in motion a number of commissions which resulted in the sale of small crown properties, but none of this money was sent to Philip.[46]

There were other options available. Mary could have farmed out crown lands and revenues and, since it was usual for the farmer to pay one or more years of revenue on signing the contract, a fair sum could have been collected. The value of crown lands rose substantially during Mary's reign, so it was an attractive form of investment, but she does not seem to have put this into effect. The one expedient used was a forced loan, despite the threat that it would cause unrest. The queen had requested a forced loan in 1556 and was due to pay it back in November 1557; a second request before payment of the first was likely to meet with resistance. Moreover she appointed commissioners to investigate the wealth of important individuals so as to tailor their contributions to their assets. It was an unpopular move. Nevertheless, despite angry protests, some refusals, and the exemption of counties that were paying additional subsidies for their defence, the loan was moderately successful. Instead of using it to pay the long-promised subsidies to Philip, however, the queen used most of it to repay the previous forced loan, and the rest for various items, some (such as the navy) related to the war effort.[47] In a similar vein, Mary asked the London merchants to lend her money. She had called upon them to provide credit in 1553 and 1556; in March 1558 she asked for 100,000 marks. The proceeds were used to cover additional costs, mostly related to naval and military expenditure. It was not set aside to fund the campaign for the recovery of Calais as Philip would have wished.[48]

Even allowing for the brief time lapse between the fall of Calais and the opening of the campaigning season, England could have raised funds to launch a counter-attack by following the example of all major states and subscribing large international loans. By the mid-sixteenth century such loans were probably the only way to fund wars on any but a local scale. At the beginning of Mary's reign, the English government seemed to be moving more closely in line with its continental counterparts. After the extended period of political instability it was natural that the financial machinery should not be functioning smoothly, and that the government should consider anticipating revenue to establish the regime. The prospect of marriage to Philip also opened glowing vistas for the English, who hoped to capitalise on the alliance and gain direct access to New World bullion. The continental banking houses shared these hopes, and declared their willingness to

[46] Loades, *Mary Tudor*, pp. 304–5. It was not a large sum in any case.
[47] Dietz, *English government finance*, vol. 1, p. 211; Loades, *Mary Tudor*, p. 300.
[48] Dietz, *English government finance*, vol. 1, p. 210.

lend the English large quantities of money if Mary took up the money in Spain and repaid in Antwerp or other markets outside Castile. It was a way of getting round the prohibition of the export of bullion. Conscious of their advantage, the English government asked Charles during the marriage negotiations for permission to raise 300,000 ds and export licences for specie up to 500,000 ds. The negotiators were so eager to conciliate the English that they agreed, but they had not reckoned with Philip. He objected strongly and refused to allow the bullion to leave Castile. Bitter dispatches were exchanged between Brussels and Valladolid. Finally Philip was forced to allow the export of 300,000 ds – a sum equal to the money borrowed. Thomas Gresham, chief financial agent for the English government, travelled to Spain to collect the bullion. He was not made to feel very welcome. Philip refused to sanction similar transactions later.

The 'Spanish loan' which had seemed so promising, proved to be less than beneficial. As could be expected, the government did not meet the terms of repayment and accumulated interest grew. Gresham, who looked upon credit with the eyes of a sound merchant, was hostile to the notion of paying high interest or contracting large debts payable over a long period of time. Since he exercised immense influence over English borrowing in Antwerp for several decades, and upon several regimes, his attitude mattered greatly. Opposed to the ruinous policy of extending short-term debts at high interest, which all other governments practised, he tried to raise large sums at low interest on behalf of the government. He was shocked in December 1553 to be offered money at 15 per cent, and furious when the English agent Christopher Dawntesey borrowed *c.* 100,000 ds at 13 per cent. These rates were extremely low when compared with what other states were paying, but high for merchants. Gresham's expectations are understandable because he thought in terms of repaying the loans rapidly and in full. But the international financiers were not interested in making large contracts at low prices, even if the English could be relied on to repay their loans fairly quickly. They could make much larger profits on other state loans. Paradoxically then, the one government which paid off its loans had extremely poor credit in Antwerp.[49]

In March 1558 Mary announced that she would borrow £100,000 in order to fund the war; later she asked Philip to allow her government to float a loan of £200,000 in the Antwerp market. He agreed, despite fears that added demand would push up interest rates. Thomas Gresham was again sent to negotiate the loan but soon reported that he could only raise £10,000.[50] Antwerp had money to lend, but not at low rates. Once again the English government withdrew. In his biography of Mary, Loades concluded that England could not afford a foreign war. Philip and his advisers believed that it could, and so it would have done, if the government

[49] H. Buckley, 'Sir Thomas Gresham'. R. B. Outhwaite, 'The trials of foreign borrowing: the English Crown and the Antwerp money market in the mid-sixteenth century', *Economic History Review*, 2nd ser. XIX (1966) pp. 289–305. See also the financial sections in Loades, *Mary Tudor*, pp. 183–316, 373, 402–23.   [50] Codoin vol. 87, pp. 18, 33–7, 39–40.

adopted the financial measures implemented by the sovereigns of France, the Habsburgs, even the Portuguese. The system of debt financing was not attractive to a nation given to sound finance, but it was the price of great power politics. The crown could have anticipated revenues, alienated demesne and demanded additional taxation. All these measures would have provoked opposition – as they did elsewhere. The rebellions that broke out in Spain, France, and the Netherlands later in the century show the wisdom of avoiding extended wars and excessive financial burdens. On the other hand, these monarchies recovered from and were strengthened by their conflicts. There were gains and losses whatever choice was made. England was not destined to be different, it simply chose a different path.

Mary Tudor was unfortunate, dying before receiving the benefits of the reform of custom dues, which gave her sister considerable revenues. Viewed from Philip's camp, however, the English failure to provide funds for the war was close to betrayal. The notion that England was a financial liability gained ground. It had emerged at the time of the 1553 loan and increased when substantial sums were spent on gifts and pensions to English nobles the following year. Philip softened the English with further gifts in 1557, paying over 25,000 ds during and just after his second visit. Resentment among nobles from other areas increased accordingly.[51] Philip's concern to conciliate the English was shown when he gave preferential treatment to their soldiers when pay fell due. The sappers and miners he requested and used in 1557 and 1558 were paid promptly. This accentuated the different treatment being meted out to the different states in the empire. Savoy dared to complain of unfair advantage. On one occasion he told Eraso that the English soldiers were an infernal nuisance, constantly making demands and capitalising on Philip's generosity. He regretted that the king – and more pertinently his subjects – should have to pay the price of England's interminable requests.[52]

In other words, England was able to resist the pressure for contributions to the French campaigns. Despite the war, the state deficit was £300,000 at the end of Mary's reign. As Loades perceptively argued, this represented a considerable achievement on the part of the queen and her advisers, proving how tightly they had controlled expenditure. Far from praising the results of sound finance, Philip and his non-English advisers thought it rank disloyalty, particularly after the loss of Calais. Even Feria, who frequently supported the English, was struck by their lack of spirit and action during the second campaign. He wrote to Philip in May 1558, 'at a time when all your majesty's states and realms have exerted themselves to the utmost in order to wage this war, (the English) who should have done more than the rest, have done the least'.[53] The hostility caused by the lack of support during the

---

[51] AGS CMC 1ª. ep. 1345 fol. 73; id. 1344 fols. 52–4; id. 1468 s.f.
[52] AGS E.K. 1496 fol. 94; E. 811 fol. 166. The one blot on the king's record was the sum due to 3,000 German soldiers levied by the English government in 1558, which he subsequently used after Feria told him the English government did not require their services. See Rodríguez-Salgado and Adams, 'Feria's dispatch', p. 33, and n. 39, p. 343.   [53] Codoin vol. 87, p. 52.

second campaign erased what good opinions had been gained of English soldiers and ships in 1557. Inevitably, the absence of substantial contributions from England led to further pressure on Philip's other states.

FINANCE AND THE WAR IN THE NETHERLANDS

There was no question of asking the Netherlands whether they wished to embark upon another war, since the sovereign had full power to decide. Nor could they impede the troop levies he thought necessary. Inevitably those areas near the battle zone or involved in the conflict contributed in many ways to the war, often with devastating results.[54] They were forced to offer financial relief to the troops, quarter them, feed them, as well as being made to cope with the disruptions of trade and destruction. It was generally accepted that such areas must be exempt from general subsidies or at least allowed to pay smaller sums over longer periods. Philip had an additional problem to contend with in the Netherlands – his father's last years in power had been characterised by ever heavier and more frequent financial demands, causing widespread resentment as well as gradual impoverishment. In Artois, for example, the sovereigns requested subsidies in September 1554, March, September and November 1555.[55] The states of Utrecht had not finished paying a grant offered in June 1555 before they were asked for another later that summer, which they rejected.[56] For the most part, however, the states had been able to meet their new burdens with apparent ease through the issue of annuities. At times they resorted to propaganda, and had to offer conditions they thought unwelcome to sell their quotas, but on the whole they proved remarkably successful, attracting both private and institutional investment. The disappearance of the system of compulsory purchases of annuities in this period and the over-subscription of some issues confirm the popularity of these investments.[57]

Clearly, the common belief that the Netherlands was the wealthiest of the Habsburg possessions was justified. The problem for its rulers was how to tap that wealth. By the time Philip assumed control of the area, it was seething with discontent and showing great reluctance to provide further subsidies for the sovereign. The level of state debt had increased dramatically while royal revenues

---

54 M. Gutman, *War and rural life in the early modern Low Countries* (Princeton, 1980).

55 Hirschauer, *Artois*, vol. 1, pp. 239–42, 162 and vol. 2, p. 158.

56 S. F. C. Moore, 'The centre and the periphery: Brussels and Utrecht 1550–1559', paper given at the Institute of Historical Research (London, 2 December 1984). I am greatly indebted to Mr Moore for permission to consult and cite this interesting paper.

57 Tracy, *A financial revolution*, stresses the difficulties of the years 1553 to 1556 when rentes had to be offered at 1:6 (16.67 per cent) to attract investors (pp. 92–3, 132–3, 138). He also shows how the cessation of compulsory purchases led to the concentration of annuities in urban areas and among royal officials in particular. Arnauld, in 'Les rentes d'Etat en Hainaut', pp. 167–8, notes that they resorted to pinning up notices of new issues of annuities in church doors so as to attract investment by 'bons laboureurs'. The success of such methods may be seen in the oversubscription of the 1555 issue.

such as the yield from the demesne had decreased. Consequently Philip was more dependent than his father on the subsidies controlled or voted by the states. The combination proved extremely dangerous for the crown. The representative assemblies exploited with relish their power over the sovereign.

Estimates of accumulated debts drawn up by the financial officials show the magnitude of the problem. In November 1556 they announced to the states-general that the state deficit was four million florins. Savoy added the two million owing to the army. A statement of account in August 1557 admitted to a debt of seven million, but Verhofstad has recently estimated that it was nearer nine million.[58]

There are few detailed works on individual provinces, making it impossible at the moment to give an accurate assessment of the distribution of this burden of debt. The evidence for Holland, however, suggests a plausible pattern: a fairly steady level of contributions before the war – 100,000 fl – then rising dramatically and only once dropping below 300,000 fl until 1560. The average contributions for the years 1555–9 was 359,000 fl p.a. Almost half this capital – 41 per cent at least – was raised by the sale of annuities.[59] This was the longest period of war the states in the Netherlands had been asked to fund, and for much of this time they had experienced the devastation as well. Several provinces – among them Hainaut and Artois – asked to be spared any further subsidies on the grounds that they had been impoverished by the conflict and quartering of troops.[60] Philip was sympathetic. He expressed great sadness for the plight of the Netherlands, but he also stated categorically that it was both 'necessary and right' for all his states to contribute to the war as long as it lasted.[61]

The king made his first substantial request for subsidies just after the truce of Vaucelles, in March 1556. Before this he had requested small sums from various provinces, now he asked the states-general for a general subsidy. There were some suggestions of restructuring the tax system of the Netherlands altogether, introducing a sales tax akin to the *alcabala* of Castile. In a country which lived off commerce, a 10 per cent sales tax on transactions was as attractive to the government as it was alarming to all subjects. Philip did not think the time was ripe for such measures and proposed instead a 100th penny (1 per cent) on real estate and 50th penny (2 per cent) on moveable goods. While no one expected the Netherlanders to like the additional taxes, the violent protests took the government by surprise. The bad weather and epidemics, combined with the dislocation of trade as a result of the war, have been advanced as explanations for this powerful opposition.[62] They were certainly contributory factors, but there were other reasons too: these measures provoked the elites in the 1550s as they had in the 1540s because

[58] Tracy, 'The taxation system', pp. 91, 104, n. 145, repeated in *A financial revolution*, p. 100.
[59] Tracy, *A financial revolution*, p. 94 and 'The taxation system', Table, pp. 108–9.
[60] C. Griffiths (ed.) *Representative government in Western Europe in the sixteenth century* (Oxford, 1968), p. 358. Hirschauer, *Artois*, pp. 224–40, esp. p. 237.
[61] Weiss, *Granvelle*, vol. 5, p. 99.   [62] G. Parker, *The Dutch revolt* (London, 1977), p. 39.

nobles and clerics resented further encroachment on their ancient tax exemptions. Some of the newly incorporated provinces such as Gelderland had not experienced this type of taxation and resented the introduction of novelties.[63] Other factors helped to make this demand unpopular. Conflict between the monarchs and provincial states in the Netherlands over the extent and control of taxes was the norm. In many ways this one appears to be a repetition of countless earlier conflicts.[64] Only now the struggle was for control of the subsidy rather than the size of the contribution. Brabant led the opposition because its deputies wanted the king to allow them to assign and control their quota. They had managed to secure this concession repeatedly from Charles; perceiving Philip as a weaker man, they were convinced that they could succeed again.[65] Other states followed suit. Once embarked on this course of action, the deputies became obstreperous and indulged in an orgy of complaints against excessive taxation, provincial problems, poor government and the like. Some states used the occasion to demand specific favours in return for cooperation. Utrecht, for example, secured a promise that they would not be required to make further contributions for four years. They also asked Philip to take the oath to respect their provincial privileges once again – a request probably linked to the fear that these taxes, new to the area, would affect the tax exemption of privileged groups in society.[66]

Philip was not eager to give way on the matter of taxation control in his first states-general, but after months of intensive negotiations he was forced to capitulate. As soon as they were certain of his agreement, Holland, Flanders and Brabant offered contributions amounting to 883,333 fl and other states followed suit. The first of two instalments was due on 1 May 1557, the second exactly a year later. Philip needed the money quickly, however, so he asked the states to anticipate the subsidy because his own credit was too weak to secure the necessary loans. Each state and major city was asked to sell redeemable annuities which would be discharged with the subsidy contributions. There was a mixed reaction: cities such as Dordrecht and Amsterdam, and states such as Utrecht sold their quotas without trouble. Some areas may have experienced difficulties, however, as the severe famine required urban authorities to make large purchases of grain. In order to raise the necessary bullion they had been forced to sell annuities, and the market for the new issues would have been reduced.[67]

[63] J. Gilissen, 'Les Etats Généraux des Pays de Par Deçà 1464–1632', *Standen en Landen*, XXXIII (1965), p. 308. A Friis, 'An inquiry into the relations between economic and financial factors in the sixteenth centuries. 1. The two crises in the Netherlands in 1557', *Scandinavian Economic History Review*, 1 (1953), pp. 192–217. The author argues that the situation was not as grim as has been claimed, and blames the novelty of the taxes for the uproar. Hirschauer, *Artois*, pp. 134, 137–8, 168–9, 242–3 shows the application and implementation of such taxes.

[64] Gilissen, 'Les Etats Généraux'; Griffiths, *Representative government*, p. 298ss.; P. Rosenfeld, 'The provincial governors of the Netherlands from the minority of Charles V to the revolt', *Standen en Landen*, XVII (1959), pp. 1–63.

[65] Schepper, 'Las "finanzas" públicas en los Paises Bajos', p. 12.

[66] Moore, 'Utrecht'.   [67] Friis, 'The two crises in the Netherlands' esp. pp. 215–16.

To encourage further cooperation and reduce the level of accumulated debt in each province, Philip empowered provincial states to reduce the interest payable on existing annuities from 12 per cent to 5 per cent. This is very much in keeping with measures imposed in Spain. Research on the impact of this edict in the Netherlands would very welcome. One suspects that the states received this measure with mixed feelings. On the one hand they would have welcomed the reduction of their burden; on the other they would have realised that it could undermine confidence in their annuities and caused grave problems for the future. Consequently they may not have availed themselves of this edict.[68]

Philip probably used the money anticipated to levy the troops needed to fight against France. But the cost of the war far exceeded what the Netherlands and other areas had provided. Problems with Spanish subsidies and the failure to obtain money from England forced the king to demand further sums from the states of the Netherlands all too soon. Convinced that his situation was critical, he summoned the states-general again in the summer of 1557. War and innovation went hand in hand. Philip did not have the time or the patience to haggle with each individual state as usual, so he ordered all the deputies to meet together as a states-general and vote a general subsidy. In this way he hoped to cut down the time spent negotiating. The symbolic importance of such a meeting did not escape contemporaries and Philip may well have been as eager to have this endorsement of his policies by an assembly representing a united Netherlands, as he was to expedite matters. Despite the legal unity which Charles had imposed upon the Netherlands in 1548 by separating them from the Holy Roman Empire, the provinces were still largely autonomous. The new lands which Charles had brought into the state, Tournai, Cambrai, Gelderland, Friesland, Utrecht, Overijssel, Groningen, the Ommerlanden and Drenthe, still considered themselves separate from the patrimonial states. The full states-general had met only once after 1548, and then for purely ceremonial reasons – to endorse and witness Charles's transfer of power to Philip. Consequently, when all the states met together in 1557 to discuss a general subsidy there was terrible confusion about seating arrangements, precedence, and the more serious business of tax quotas. Philip had foreseen trouble, so he had requested a traditional grant: an eight year *aide* of 800,000 fl p.a. to cover defence expenditure in the Netherlands. Neither the traditional nature of the subsidy, nor the promise that it would be used solely for their protection appeased the representatives of the provinces. From the start they voiced complaints and grievances and refused to discuss the subsidy request.

Behind the truculence of the states lay more than a worsening economic situation. The struggle for control of the subsidy overshadowed other considerations. Brabant

---

[68] Hirschauer, *Artois*, vol. 1, p. 244; Tracy, *A financial revolution*, p. 91 claims that Philip proposed a reduction from 12 per cent to 5 per cent on loans contracted from foreign bankers in the Antwerp market – with the agreement of the states general. This may be as far as the proposal ever went.

once more led the way and their request for control of the subsidy proved more dangerous than in the past because it was made in the general meetings. States that had not yet secured much control over their grants were encouraged by this example and were soon voicing similar demands.[69] The states were conscious of the plight of the monarch – with war raging and the demands of a huge army and navy to be met. They capitalised on the situation and refused his request unless he reviewed the tax quotas of each state and conceded their request for control of the subsidy. Although Philip lived close to where the meeting was being held and maintained personal pressure on the deputies, they were impervious to these pressures. Mortified and distressed, he ordered a recess at the beginning of January 1558. When the states-general reconvened on 7 April, their mood was as hostile as ever. The deputies snubbed Philip's attempts at conciliation and compromise. When he promised to set up a commission headed by Lalaing to investigate and reallocate quotas, they responded by voicing bitter complaints of poverty and impossible tax burdens. Some provinces such as Zeeland refused to contribute any further taxation. The king announced that he would provide the share of this or any other province which refused to contribute their part of the general subsidy – an extraordinary offer. The states vehemently rejected the proposal on the grounds that a general subsidy had to be general: either all paid or none. They realised how dangerous this precedent could be: kings might henceforth impose general subsidies when they had only a majority rather than unanimous agreement.

Months passed and Philip's desperation increased. Since he could not use force against the deputies, he opted for symbolism and ceremonial. In a carefully staged ceremony which owed as much to the French *lit de justice* as to the grand entries of the sovereigns of the Netherlands, he sought to overawe the states-general and remind them of their duty to obey, by appearing before them surrounded by the highest nobles and officials. He made a personal appeal for an urgent conclusion to the business in hand. The move failed. Respect for the monarchy and love for the dynasty were too low in the Netherlands by now. Besides, the prize at stake was very high.[70] Philip finally capitulated, allowing the collection and administration of the subsidy to be organised by the provincial states. The blow to the sovereign's authority cannot be sufficiently stressed. Royal power over taxation was being eroded dramatically.

But why had the king been so obdurate? True, his sovereign powers were diminished as a result, but the complicated negotiations of 1556–7 should have proved to him that he was not in a position to resist requests for provincial control of taxation. It would have seemed wise under the circumstances to capitulate earlier and take as much money as possible. The details of the agreement between king and

---

[69] Griffiths, *Representative government*, pp. 303, 356–69 for an account of the states-general. It had been summoned for 3 August 1557.
[70] Griffiths, *Representative government*, pp. 356–69; Baelde, 'Financial policy', p. 229 AGS E. 129 fols. 178–83, Philip to Juana, 5 June 1558.

states may furnish us with clues to the monarch's aims and actions. The states-general forced Philip to rescind the current ordinary grants that began in 1555 and were due to run until 1560. He had already anticipated 65,000 fl and had to find money from other sources to meet this debt. Nevertheless, they gave him the subsidy he requested and an additional 800,000 fl payable in 1558. In effect the eight year subsidy was converted into a nine year grant, with the added advantage that the king could enjoy the benefits of this substantial figure almost immediately. Even more important, the king secured the agreement of the states-general to anticipate 2.4 million fl by selling their own annuities. A further 2.4 million would be raised by floating loans on the Antwerp market with the collateral of the states. These would be repaid from the yield of the subsidy which would be collected from 1559 onwards.[71] In other words, the long and painful struggle had ended with considerable gains for both sides. Philip obtained a large contribution and was able to anticipate most of it in order to meet his immediate requirements. He could not give up until he obtained both concessions since, unbeknown to the states-general, he had already anticipated and spent 2.5 million florins of this subsidy.[72] Ideally, the king wanted to regain control of the subsidies so as to have the power to anticipate them without revealing the extent of revenue alienation to the states. Moreover, he appreciated that his credit was weak while that of the provinces was strong, and concluded that the key to this was control rather than good management of revenues. He was partly right; in the short term he would have increased his credit by obtaining direct control of revenues, but he would undoubtedly have overburdened these very quickly and so broken his credit anew. The demands of war were not compatible with sound finance.

During the long negotiations between the king and states-general relations soured. The deputies imposed a number of conditions the king considered incompatible with honour and sovereignty, such as the demand that no more than 18,000 foreign soldiers should be paid from the subsidy they voted. When German troops mutinied for lack of pay and Philip asked the states for a loan, he was curtly told to disband them if he could not afford them. In August 1558, with hungry soldiers ravaging his lands, Philip asked the states individually for help once more, arguing that if they advanced him money he could send the soldiers home and prevent further damage to the Netherlands. The patchy response reveals the weariness and temporary financial exhaustion of the provinces.[73]

In conclusion, while the quarrels between Philip and the states-general were bitter and prolonged, we should not see them as an early manifestation of the revolt of the 1560s. Philip secured considerable contributions from them during the war, both directly and indirectly. Yet these were small compared to the total cost of the

---

[71] Griffiths, *Representative government*, pp. 356–9; Tracy, *A financial revolution*, pp. 101–2 and ibid., 'The taxation system', p. 92.
[72] AGS PR. 26 fol. 166, Philip's instructions to Carranza, 5 June 1558.
[73] Hirschauer, *Artois*, p. 245.

campaigns. As in the case of England, there was a substantial difference in the reaction to the first and second campaigns. In effect he did not receive additional support from them for the latter and this forced him to press his other possessions further. He had been right to think that he could only safely demand a massive effort from his empire for one campaign.

Although the Netherlands had successfully resisted the monarch's attempts to gain control of taxation, and were able to curtail his demands by the length of time spent over each subsidy request, Philip did not harbour resentment, let alone hatred for his difficult northern subjects. In a confidential account he wrote for Charles in June 1558, the king described the situation as very dangerous.[74] Indeed, he assured his father, things could not be worse. Ordinary revenues had been anticipated well in advance. The disruption of the war and widespread discontent had made it almost impossible to collect ordinary revenues, exacerbating the problems of repaying the accumulated debt. The serious shortfall meant he could not pay the salaries of councillors, officials or the judges. His northern subjects had good reason to be disgruntled. He spoke of their deep alienation and the growing resistance to royal commands. Yet he voiced great concern and love for the Netherlands, as well as anguish at the thought of losing even a part of them. Philip also admitted that his desire to reduce the burden on the Netherlands had caused him to add to that of Spain. Subsidies from Castile had been used to cover basic items of expenditure in the Netherlands for several years. 'All the expenses of the last war, which were very considerable, as well as the costs of ordinary garrisons, the *bandes*, fortifications, artillery and munitions have been covered from the money sent by the (Spanish) realms and the sums seized from the Fugger and other merchants'.[75] Sadly, his efforts to alleviate the Netherlands succeeded only in alienating both Spain and England without conciliating the Netherlanders.

SOCIAL PROBLEMS AND POLITICAL DIVISIONS IN ENGLAND AND THE NETHERLANDS

It would be easy to conclude that the wars of the 1550s were to blame for the serious social and economic problems affecting England and the Netherlands during this decade. While it is not possible here to go into detail, the degree to which the war created or contributed to these problems should be assessed. Inflation was a major factor, exacerbating the problems of harvest failure. From the moment they set foot in England, Philip's followers constantly complained of high food prices, and the dispatches of French, Venetian and other envoys attest to chronic food shortages and high food prices in London during Mary's reign. There were bad harvests in 1555 and 1556, and for a time famine was forecast in 1557. The weakened population succumbed to a virulent influenza epidemic in 1556–7. The famous

[74] AGS PR. 26 fol. 166.   [75] AGS PR. 26 fol. 166.

'sweating sickness' affected recruitment for the war and created shortages of farm labourers so that the harvest in 1558 was said to have been seriously affected.[76] These natural disasters combined with political and military failure and created an atmosphere of death and decay at the close of Mary's reign. Protestant zealots used the epidemics and dearth to show that God was chastising the realm because it had tolerated an unjust ruler. This explanation conveniently ignored similar scourges affecting all other parts of Christendom.

The Netherlands too experienced bad harvests during these years, and over the winter of 1556–7 there was famine in some areas. Friis has argued that it was the worst winter in a century that experienced a good number of them. As a substantial grain importer even during good years, the Netherlands was vulnerable to bad harvests at home and abroad. Some provinces relied on grain shipments from France, severely disrupted during the war. All major urban centres were well organised, however, and grain supplies from Danzig probably saved many thousands of people in 1557. The period of dearth coincided with the amassing of an army against France, making the situation infinitely worse. Philip was constantly preoccupied with problems of supply. The importance he gave to the issue of commerce during the war years reflects his primary aim of keeping supply routes open. Since England had denied him grain exports, he was forced to rely almost entirely on the Netherlands and their suppliers, and this was to prove of significance in his relations with England. When the commercial interests of the two northern states conflicted, Philip naturally favoured the Netherlands. As mentioned earlier, he refused to declare war against Scotland because it would disrupt Flemish trade with the Scots. Similar considerations underlay Philip's dubious handling of the dispute between England and the Hanseatic League as well as his negative reaction to Mary's demands over trading licences.

The question of the rights and privileges of the Hanse merchants in England had long been debated but it was to loom large during Philip's reign. Mary relied on the credit of the Merchant Adventurers and therefore favoured them at the expense of their foreign competitors. She continued the trend of restricting the favourable conditions the Hanse had enjoyed in the past. By 1557 relations were so tense the English council claimed that the German merchants were about to attack them. They asked for Philip's support. But the Hanse were so important in the grain trade with central and eastern Europe that Philip could not afford to damage his own relations with them, even at the cost of further clashes with his English subjects. The Netherlands councillors were also adamant that good relations must be maintained. Philip was unwilling to reject English requests outright, however, so he took refuge in duplicity. While making sympathetic noises to the English, he also sought to persuade them that the only reason the Hanse had not attacked was

---

[76] F. B. Fisher, 'Influenza and inflation in Tudor England', *Economic History Review*, 2nd ser. XVIII (1965).

because he had intervened on their behalf. There is no evidence of this. Philip repeatedly assured the English that he had their best interests at heart and would deal with their affairs with the same favour and justice as if they were part of his patrimony. Meanwhile he told the Hanse that he was willing to mediate in the dispute, but ordered Feria to indicate to the Hanseatic negotiators in London that he intended to go further, so as to show how greatly he favoured them. Although neither side realised the full extent of his double dealing, there is proof that they did not trust him fully. They seemed more aware than he was of the contradictory nature of his policy. As king of England Philip could not mediate in a dispute that affected his subjects. That he even considered such an ambivalent position shows his own distance and alienation from England. The English became very resentful of his actions over the Hanseatic dispute, rightly believing that their interests had been sacrificed in order to safeguard those of the Netherlands. The conflict with the Hanse dragged on inconclusively, causing much discontent among the English government and commercial world, and adding to Philip's unpopularity in England.[77]

Relations worsened in 1558 as the interests of England and the Netherlands conflicted once more. It was normal to stop all trade with enemy states once war was openly declared, and then issue licences to allow limited trade links. Thus the monarchs sanctioned what they could not prevent and received a useful source of revenue. After 1557 both the English and the Netherlands governments issued general prohibitions of trade with France and licences to selected merchants. The licences sold in the Netherlands specified that the holders could trade anywhere in France. When Calais fell, the French were short of supplies. They then drew up contracts with merchants in the Netherlands to provision their forces in the town. The sight of Flemish ships supplying French soldiers in Calais outraged the English government. In the traumatic aftermath of the fall of the Pale they did not pause to consider whether the licences had been issued before or after the event. They merely assumed that Philip had given in to the requests of his Flemish subjects and sanctioned the supply of the French troops. Feria supported English protests and their demand for the immediate withdrawal of all such licences. In view of the passion aroused by the incident, Philip was tempted to conciliate the English; but in the end he concluded that he could not afford to alienate the Netherlanders. He offered a compromise: he would not issue more permits, but existing licences would be honoured. He explained that he could not revoke them because the ports and maritime regions of the Netherlands had been badly hit by the war and depended for their survival on the continuation of commercial activities. He would not deprive them of their livelihood.[78]

Quite unexpectedly the war had brought into sharp relief the incompatibility of

---

[77] Loades, *Mary Tudor*, pp. 295–6; Friis, 'The two crises in the Netherlands', p. 200; Codoin vol. 87, p. 57; AGS E. 811 fol. 84.   [78] Codoin vol. 87, pp. 16, 24–5, 30.

two areas which had hitherto been considered natural partners. Philip's evident preference for the Netherlands drove a deeper wedge between him and his English subjects. He did not alienate them because he was a Spaniard, but because of his desire to protect the Netherlands.

Dearth, disease and the disruption of commerce were not the only problems assailing these two states. Both were suffering the insidious spread of ideological divisions which flourished in this atmosphere of insecurity and gloom. Religious dissent and political instability went hand in hand. In England, the alliance with the Habsburgs had accentuated existing political problems because it provoked Henry II of France to foment rebellion throughout Mary's reign. The leaders of the 1554 uprising appealed to him for help and received a favourable answer. If the conspirators had not been forced to act prematurely, French subsidies would have sustained them. When the rebellion failed, several of the conspirators managed to escape to France, where they were encouraged to fit out ships and empowered to attack Spanish and Flemish vessels in the Channel as well as English ones. Henry also backed the next major conspiracy, Dudley's plot in 1555, as well as the raid led by Thomas Strafford against Scarborough in the summer of 1557, which served as the *casus belli*.[79] The constant support and encouragement of dissent from a powerful neighbouring state ensured that instability in England remained great.

Not surprisingly, the most enduring impression made by the English on Philip and his court was their propensity for rebellion. In 1557 a group of military advisers treated the king to a summary of England's history since the Roman occupation and concluded that there was nothing the English loved better than novelty. They satisfied their desire by war, rebellion and deposing their leaders. The only way to control the realm, therefore, was to maintain a standing army. They advised him to levy 1,000–3,000 Spaniards, to be supported by 1,500 Spanish veterans and a regiment of German cavalry. Aware that the English would object, they envisaged the inclusion of local troops, but these were never to exceed half the total force maintained, and preferably no more than a third.[80] This radical scheme accurately reflects the mistrust and unease found among Philip's advisers. Yet it was not so much a love of novelty but a reaction against it that prompted much of the instability in Mary's reign. And this instability was not solely, or even primarily, caused by international tensions.

Mary came to the throne after the death of an adolescent king, and this minority, like others, was a period of intense political instability. Because she was a woman and therefore considered inferior to men, no one was very sure how she would fulfil her role as monarch. There were no precedents within living memory and only the vaguest myths about English female rulers. Even before they could adapt to

---

[79] Vertot, vol. 2, pp. 149–50, 315; vol. 3, pp. 14–16, 17–19, 37; Loades, *Tudor conspiracies*, pp. 15–127 for Wyatt's rebellion; other conflicts, pp. 176–217; ibid. *Mary Tudor*, pp. 365–8.
[80] RAH SC F-17 fols. 151v–152v.

the novel situation, Mary's marriage to a foreign prince led to the incorporation of the realm into a large, international state. Equally radical if more familiar, was the queen's determination to alter the religious settlement. The system and the people needed time to adjust to all this. Because these changes all happened at once, it is difficult to say which caused the greatest unrest. Insecurity over one heightened fears of the other; but religion was probably the most frequent source of instability during Mary's reign. It was the one policy that affected the lives of all her subjects directly. Moreover, her decision to destroy the Protestant edicts that had shaped the country's life since the 1530s affected all levels of society. Although the imposition of Catholic conformity was sporadic and patchy, it created confusion, fears and division even in those areas where it scarcely touched the lives of the inhabitants.[81]

Mary's religious policies were also the most effectively pursued and must count as her greatest achievement. We should not be misled by Protestant propaganda, which has left an enduring impression of widespread rejection of the Marian settlement. While neither Mary nor Pole appreciated the importance of propaganda, and concentrated on punishment rather than education and information, they made considerable headway with their conversion policy. Most contemporaries considered them successful enough to wish to take credit for it, especially Philip. If the progress of Marian Catholicism appears slight by contrast to the propagation of Elizabethan Protestantism, this is largely due to the distorting effect of time. It is hardly fair to compare the achievements of her five year reign with Elizabeth's forty-five year regime. While religious changes provoked a good deal of popular unrest in England, there were few major outbreaks of violence and no major rebellion that can be attributed solely to their destabilising influence.[82] This is significant. Historians may continue the controversy over Mary's success or failure for a long time yet, but when set beside the activities of other contemporary rulers, and the fusion of rebellion and religious dissent elsewhere, England's experience is unique.

Ironically, the most disruptive incident in the process of converting England to Catholicism again was caused by the pope, and it had nothing to do with internal dissent, the war or Philip. Paul IV wanted to strike against cardinals whom he considered suspect, and Pole was high on the list. He revoked Pole's legatine mission and summoned him to Rome to answer charges of heresy in 1557. Many Englishmen must have felt as if the world had turned upside down. Who was to be believed? What was the true religion? Worse still, Paul was eager to recover secularised lands. He was thinking of Germany primarily, but his brief ordering their return was couched in general terms and was therefore applicable to England. The agreement between the monarch, the papacy and the English lords was in peril. Mary, the arch-supporter of papal power, found herself opposing him now. She

[81] See Loades, *Mary Tudor*, and his *Oxford martyrs* for a general description of the Marian changes.
[82] See note 79; Loades has studied a few disturbances inspired by religious dissent, *Tudor conspiracies*, pp. 142–50.

tried to retain Pole and knew that without the land settlement the English would not accept Catholicism. Ancient fears about undue meddling by the pope in English affairs resurfaced. More significantly, both Catholic and Protestant owners of ecclesiastical property realised that their titles would only be safe if papal power was abolished in England once more. Only a Protestant settlement after 1558 secured their position; Elizabeth was able to capitalise on the mistakes of the pontiff.

Although the religious changes in England were closely associated with Philip, his role outside of the formal negotiations with the papacy (pp. 97–8) remains a mystery. By the time he arrived with a dozen or so hand-picked clerics, the process of restoration was already under way, firmly directed by Mary, Stephen Gardiner and Edmund Bonner. The Spanish theologians were intended to help with the education of the elites. Men like Juan de Villagarcía and Bartolomé Carranza were to serve in Oxford, Cambridge and London. Nor do English policies reflect Philip's subsequent actions. He believed in converting the leaders of society first, but accepted that this was a slow, long-term process. Moreover, he was not a man to meddle in English politics, unless they directly affected him. From the available documentation it appears that only one Spaniard significantly influenced the course of England's re-catholicisation: Carranza. This was not because he enjoyed Philip's favour, but because of his long-standing friendship and earlier cooperation with cardinal Pole. Later he also won Mary's trust. Most importantly, he was in full sympathy with the repression being practised by men like Bonner, bishop of London. He was involved in the debates that preceded the adoption of burning on a large scale, and may have been one of its instigators. He was also as hostile as Bonner, if not more, to the attempts of his fellow Spaniards to concentrate their resources on securing recantation and the reconciliation of leading Protestants. Carranza thought that men such as archbishop Cranmer should be burnt irrespective of recantation. Later he claimed credit for the rigorous policies implemented by the English government.[83] While this is an exaggeration, he was unquestionably involved in their implementation.

Even a cursory examination of Philip's policies in the Netherlands will highlight the contrast to Mary's decisive actions and the greater cohesion within English society. When Philip inherited the Netherlands, the area was riddled with Protestant groups, especially Anabaptists, Lutherans and Calvinists. His response was to draw up long-term measures to improve the ecclesiastical organisation of the provinces.[84] There had been plans to impose such reforms since 1332 at least.

---

[83] The documents published in volumes 18, 19, 22, 30, 33 of the Archivo Documental Español, *Fray Bartolomé Carranza. Documentos históricos* (Madrid, 1962–81), are invaluable for details on the actions of the Spanish clerics in England. Further material can be found in the articles by Tellechea Idígoras collected under the title *Fray Bartolomé Carranza y el Cardenal Pole* (Pamplona, 1977), esp. pp. 15–118, 257–73.

[84] M. Dierickx (ed.) *Documents inédits sur l'érection des nouveaux diocèses aux Pays-Bas (1521–1570)* (3 vols., Brussels, 1960–2) is an extensive study of the episcopal reorganisation of the Netherlands. See esp. vol. I, pp. 75–80 (1520s), pp. 90–6 (1530s), pp. 102–6 (1551), pp. 171–2 Philip's attempts.

Charles V had shown some interest in the 1520s, 1530s and again in 1551, but his solution to the growing problem of heresy was to proclaim savage edicts which he expected the secular authorities to impose since the ecclesiastical structure was so inadequate. Irrespective of reconciliation with the Catholic church, the accused were burnt or imprisoned. The problem of heresy did not disappear; indeed Alastair Duke has shown that these measures proved counter-productive.[85] There was opposition to the punitive policies in the 1520s and it intensified as the number of offences that were converted into capital crime by decree increased. By 1550 even minor offences such as reading prohibited literature or discussing the scriptures were punishable by death. The growing reluctance of the secular authorities to impose this legislation led Charles to turn to the ecclesiastical representatives. In 1546 he increased the authority of the five active inquisitors in the Netherlands. They were given power to examine and arrest suspects without justifying their actions to the secular authorities of the area. Like so many of the emperor's orders, this decree remained a dead letter. Characteristically, it was Philip who sought to enforce his father's legislation, and allowed the inquisitor in Delft in 1557 to use these powers of arrest.

The reaction was swift. The Dutch immediately cried that the privileges of Holland were being infringed. Here, as in other provinces, citizens of good standing were immune from arrest until the local authorities had checked the charges and weighed the evidence and quality of the witnesses. It was a privilege greatly valued by magistrates and burghers since it protected them from malicious accusations and enabled them to prepare their defence. Other provinces soon joined the outcry, fearing loss of similar privileges.[86] It is in this context that we have to read and assess the powerful surge of protest in the states-general of 1558–9 against the Inquisition – as well as the key role it played in the subsequent unrest. Far from ignoring these protests and imposing measures he thought essential for the prevention of Protestantism, Philip backed down and quietly set to work on plans to create an effective ecclesiastical organisation.

The plan to divide the provinces into fourteen new bishoprics which did not entirely accord with political or cultural divisions was radical in its own way. Each diocese was to have two resident inquisitors, controlled by a central inquisitorial office. They would concentrate on repression, whilst the carefully-chosen and learned bishops would help with the task of education and infusing new life into the Catholic church. Gradual reformation of the structure and revitalisation of the leadership were the salient characteristics of Philip's programme. There was no attempt at rapid or forced change. Until the scheme had been approved by the papacy and the details worked out, Philip did not even announce his intentions

---

[85] A. Duke, 'Salvation by coercion: the controversy surrounding the "Inquisition" in the Low Countries on the eve of the revolt', in P. N. Brooks (ed.), *Reformation in principle and practice*, pp. 137–56.   [86] Duke, 'Salvation by coercion', p. 144.

outside an inner circle of advisers. Although he was firmly committed to the Catholic faith, he was above all a pragmatic man, all too aware of his weakness and limitations. He realised that to achieve religious conformity it was essential to have the support of ecclesiastical and secular authorities. When solidarity against a foreign enemy was required, however, no sensible government would provoke internal confrontation. Whilst the war lasted, the king could not afford to press ahead with highly controversial religious policies; in his empire, religious differences unfortunately divided the elites.

The ability to deal with religious dissent is a sure sign of strength in early modern states. It shows that, whatever the signs of tension, that society remained fairly cohesive and loyal to the sovereign. Ironically then, while religious conflicts caused constant unrest in England, they prove that the Marian government was effective when firmly guided by the queen. The comparison to Philip's reactions in the Netherlands shows how much stronger royal power was in England, thus confirming recent revisionist views of Mary and her council.[87] Nevertheless, this had less to do with the strength of character of the monarch than with the pressures of a long and costly war, as well as the threat of invasion which undermined royal power in the Netherlands. Outside the religious sphere, Mary was often indecisive and hesitant. She would have happily devolved much of the burden of government to Philip. Later she showed the same tendency to rely on Pole, whose preoccupation with religion deterred him from involvement in other aspects of government. She did not trust many of her councillors because they had been implicated in previous regimes. Without her full support, councillors were unlikely to adopt policies that might arouse further unrest or lose them what little favour they enjoyed at court. The queen's immediate household servants, whom she trusted fully, proved as inexperienced in high politics as she was, and were unable or unwilling to take the key positions in the administration. After the death of Gardiner, there was no central figure in the administration who could command the respect of his peers and the trust of the queen.

Despite the wide distribution of pensions in England, Philip never secured enough support within the council and court, as his failure to obtain the crown and the difficulties in securing an open declaration of war against France amply demonstrate. Philip's half-hearted efforts to influence English government made little impact on its composition or decisions. The queen's character was all-important in this respect. If the king had resided in England, there would have been clear leadership, particularly during the war. Instead, for most of Mary's reign, there was no clear policy nor aim in any areas except religion. But without power over patronage, there was little Philip could do in England. He does not seem to

---

[87] Weikel, 'The Marian Council revisited', in J. Loach and R. Tittler, *The mid-Tudor polity c. 1540–1560* (London, 1980), pp. 52–73. John Murphy has also been working on Mary's court and is a forceful exponent of the thesis that Mary and her government have been grossly underrated.

have attempted to influence appointments, with one possible exception. Carranza thought that with Philip's support a 'well disposed' man could be appointed to succeed Gardiner as Lord Chancellor. Unfortunately there is no indication who their candidate was, or whether Philip's intervention was successful.[88] It may well be that he could do no more than this if he were to remain within the bounds of the marriage treaty and avoid giving great offence to the English aristocracy. Of course Philip could have strengthened his bonds with the English nobility by providing them with posts and patronage in his other lands. As early as 1554 Charles advised him to give the governorship of Asti to an English noble. Philip rejected the suggestion, partly because he wanted Alba to take charge of the place. It was an important garrison, mostly full of Spanish soldiers and habitually troublesome. English soldiers were also thought to be of poor quality.[89] Later he opposed the appointment of Netherlanders to Spanish and Italian offices. He believed that reciprocity was essential. It was unwise to appoint English and Dutch nobles to posts there because he could not reward Spanish and Italian nobles with important offices in England or the Netherlands.

War offered the king an excellent opportunity to integrate more closely the elites and finances of his states, and he was quick to grasp it. He gave English nobles employment and favour. Even those involved in conspiracies during Mary's reign were offered pardon and employment in the king's armies.[90] The good relations thus established were offset by the loss of Calais, the clashes over the Scottish front, the Hanse and the deployment of the English navy.

Philip became the scapegoat for England's ills even before Mary's death. The English blamed him for the dearth, suspecting that grain was being exported to feed his armies. They accused him of having bled England dry, taking huge quantities of money to fund the war. Even Elizabeth, on the eve of her accession expressed the common opinion that England's poverty was due to Philip's exactions.[91] Mary did little to arrest this process of vilification. She was bitter at his long absences and as time passed her disenchantment with marriage grew and her general mood of disillusion deepened. She suffered greatly when forced to oppose the papacy. When Calais fell, her hopes of increasing her reputation were dashed. In the midst of these setbacks she persuaded herself that she was pregnant. When she acknowledged that she was not, her sense of personal, political and religious failure was complete. During 1558 Mary sank into depression and the whole court caught the mood of despair.

Philip might have prevented this dangerous despondency and infused some sense of purpose by sending money to bolster his supporters and forge a group that would respond to his orders despite his absence. Better still, he could have returned to

---

[88] See the rather garbled report of Gonzalo Pérez in Tellechea Idígoras, *Carranza y Pole*, p. 107.
[89] AGS E. 808 fol. 66.
[90] Loades, *Mary Tudor*, esp. 266, pp. 368–9, 371–2; Davies, 'England and the French war', pp. 162–3.
[91] Rodríguez-Salgado and Adams, 'Feria's dispatch', p. 333.

England and restored order and confidence. Unfortunately he could not send money until the winter of 1558, by which time both the count of Feria and William Paget judged that he had lost his chance.[92] With Mary's health failing, men looked to the future – and Elizabeth. As for his much-promised return to England, it was out of the question until he could find a suitable substitute for the Netherlands.

When Philip began preparations for a return visit in 1556, Savoy warned him that he was not prepared to remain in the Netherlands without him because he did not believe that the truculent states would provide him with the necessary money and provisions for the army unless the king was present. He also despaired of making himself obeyed unless Philip was there to lend his authority. Believing that he could only preside over the disintegration of royal authority in the Netherlands if the king left, Savoy threatened to resign unless Philip remained.[93] He changed his mind in 1557 because he was convinced that winning the war required English help and realised that it could only be secured by Philip's personal intervention. The brevity of that visit was largely due to Savoy's difficulties in the Netherlands. Neither he nor the king believed that he could remain on his own again.[94] Conflict continued unabated between the leading figures of past and present regimes. Wearily, Savoy reported further outbursts of fighting between leading advisers in July 1557 with the remark that there was nothing more he could say about the constant struggles except that they were as frequent as before and would invariably lead to the diminution of royal authority in the Netherlands.[95] He was right.

The search for another regent for the Netherlands became a matter of urgency in 1558 with Philip's presence urgently required both in England and Spain. Reluctantly Philip concluded that only one person had the authority and character to take control during his absence – Mary of Hungary. Relations between Philip and Mary were as strained as always. During the spring of 1558 they were in dispute over the powers she demanded in her place of retirement. In effect she wanted to assume sovereign powers over the area and Philip was adamant that she must show him due deference and respect and accept that he alone was sovereign. But he set aside personal antipathy in favour of political necessity. He urged Charles and Juana to cajole or pressure her to resume her post in the Netherlands so that he could move freely throughout his empire. Charles sympathised with his predicament and agreed to help. Juana, who found Mary intolerable, was delighted to do so. In addition, the king instructed Bartolomé Carranza to expedite the matter. Carranza, who returned to Spain to take up his duties as archbishop of Toledo, was instructed to press Charles to act more decisively and persuade Mary to return by giving a carefully vetted picture of the situation. Philip instructed him to tell

[92] Ibid pp. 315–16; AGS E. 811 fol. 131; E. 812 fol. 32, Codoin vol. 87, pp. 11, 13–14, 17–21, 91, 96, 98–9, 168, 142–6. Harbison, *Rival ambassadors*, Appendix II, pp. 340–2 (with references to CSP Sp).
[93] Gachard, 'Remontrance', p. 126; AGS E. 128 fol. 349–50.
[94] AGS PR. 26 fol. 166; Savoy's quarrels in the Low Countries are explored in van Durme, *Granvela*, pp. 206–9.   [95] AGS E.K. 1490, fol. 47.

her that things had greatly improved and the states-general had shown great willingness to help him; unfortunately he could not leave Savoy in charge because of his frequent quarrels with the Netherlands nobility. Besides, Philip no longer believed Savoy had the skills to serve as an effective regent there.[96]

Mary was not taken in, although she agreed that the situation had improved and believed that royal authority could be fully restored in a year or two if Philip remained where he was. She argued that Henry lacked the resources to continue the war. During the truce or peace that would soon follow, Philip could do what Charles had done – 'impose his authority' by the 'use of rigorous measures'. But she was adamant she would not resume her old post.[97] Still, Mary thirsted for power and was deeply frustrated in Spain, where most of the nobility seem to have given the three prestigious arrivals a cool reception. She was unable to resist the combination of flattery and power; when Philip finally agreed to ask her personally to help him and offered her wider regency powers, her resolve weakened, but she would only agree to serve as a councillor of state, not as regent. She also stipulated that she would not leave until the Spaniards had given her large quantities of money to take to the Netherlands and made it clear that she would not remain there if Philip left. 'She would not do it, she would rather go to the Indies than the Netherlands because of the difficulties she would encounter there'.[98] This suggests that she was still convinced rebellion was inevitable if the king departed.

Philip reluctantly accepted some of these conditions. He was prepared to give her a role analogous to that of Charles in Spain, but insisted that she must reside in the Netherlands while he returned to Spain for a brief visit. Mary hesitated, but after the deaths of Leonor and Charles there was no reason for her to remain in Spain. She prepared her return journey with many details as to her role still unresolved. Strong financial inducements and considerable pressure from Juana were required before suitable travelling companions could be found among the Castilian nobility.[99] Just as Philip breathed a sigh of relief and prepared to leave the Netherlands, on 12 December 1558 came news that Mary had died on her way to Brussels. Ironically he must have felt her death more deeply than most. Now he had to remain there until another substitute was found.

The pressures of war cast into sharp relief the weakness of each government and the impossibility of reconciling the needs of Philip's many states. But England and the Netherlands enjoyed one inestimable advantage over the Spanish realms: both had resident sovereigns. Serious as their problems were, they had monarchs who could remedy their troubles at hand. These monarchs were the focus of loyalty and

[96] AGS PR. 26 fol. 166. Juana's clash with Mary, and the latter's quarrels with Ruy Gómez's in-laws, Codoin vol. 97, p. 299, pp. 291–2.

[97] AGS E. 128 fol. 337; details of their negotiations and relations also in E. 128 fols. 349–50, 347, 341; E. 129 fols. 125–6, 63–9.   [98] AGS E. 128 fol. 337.

[99] AGS E. 129 fols. 63–9. Juana finally appointed the marquis of Denia and his brother the bishop of Badajoz for the task, but had to provide them with 8,000ds for the journey.

could contain the divisions within the elites, even if they could not eradicate them. Moreover, the actions of Philip and Mary in the two northern realms persuaded their subjects that they were concerned and willing to protect them from the full impact of war and internal dissent. Mary aroused Philip's anger by refusing to press her subjects for subsidies, and he in turn angered her by rejecting appeals to declare war against Scotland or revoke trading licences. Such actions aggravated the divisions between the different parts of the empire, but restrained the unrest. In Spain matters took a different turn entirely.

6

The French wars, 1557–9 (2). Spain

The Spanish realms were as deeply affected by dearth, disease and religious divisions as England and the Netherlands. And yet, their financial contribution to the war was infinitely greater. The king was able to impose his will upon the wealthy Spanish church and to prompt an increasingly resentful regency government to respond to his demands. Whilst Philip realised that his financial expedients were provoking widespread unrest, he was confident that the Spanish realms would remain loyal and that the government would continue to supply him with the necessary funds. He believed implicitly in the loyalty of his sister and the advisers he had appointed for her. Above all, he felt safe because his father was present in the Spanish realms – as if it filled the vacuum of authority created by the absence of the reigning monarch. The initial response to his financial demands and eradication of Protestantism prove that his confidence in the regency government was not unfounded, but the ensuing conflict between them shows that Philip greatly overestimated the emperor's influence; the tolerance of his sister and the Spanish officials; and above all, his own power over the Iberian realms.

THE REGENCY GOVERNMENT AND THE EMPEROR

Philip's supreme confidence in his regency government was amply demonstrated by his refusal to return to Spain, despite alarmist reports of the situation there. For example, in the summer of 1556 Philip was deluged with calls for his immediate return. Juana and many officials were deeply affected by a combination of adverse circumstances: the Aragonese had refused to accept Philip's succession; there was unrest in Catalonia; the threat from the Muslim powers in the Mediterranean was increasing, and the financial situation had worsened dramatically with the increased demand from the Italian front. Philip replied to these requests with an emphatic declaration that his presence was not essential now that Charles was resident in Castile. True, he promised to return later that summer, but he had no qualms about delaying his departure first until January 1557, then to the summer and later indefinitely.[1]

The struggle to secure the king's return was one of the first issues to provoke a rift between Charles and the regency government. The emperor consistently opposed

---

[1]   The continuous calls for Philip's return and his response in these years can be illustrated from the following documents: AGS E. 512 fol. 185(2), AGS E. 120 fol. 170; AGS E. 119 fol. 99.

his son's departure from the north – whether this was out of concern for the Netherlands or awareness of the need for Philip to remain near the war front remains unclear. In the spring of 1557 the regency government decided to send Ruy Gómez back to Brussels much sooner than planned in order to impress upon Philip the need for his presence in Spain. They deliberately withheld this information from Charles, ostensibly because they did not wish to trouble him with such matters whilst he was suffering an attack of the gout, but in reality it was because they knew he would have tried to prevent the dispatch of this embassy and might even attempt to counter the effect of their pleas.[2] Disagreements over major aspects of policy were evident from the moment Charles arrived, and this particular conflict did much to alienate the two sides. However, it was soon overshadowed by a bitter dispute over the *embargo* of Indies money in 1556 which coloured relations among the leading members of the royal family as well as the major officials.

The embargo of 1556–7

The deep unpopularity of this policy has already been discussed (pp. 69–70). Philip's staunch opposition to the forcible seizure of bullion and goods from the Indies, and resistance to Charles's orders during his regency, was to be an important factor in the ensuing drama. The effects of the previous *embargo* also played a part. As a result of the bullion confiscations by the crown in 1555, three major firms in Seville had gone bankrupt. Juana was from the first bitterly opposed to the seizures. She was deeply concerned by the commercial and financial implications, and especially by the plight of orphans, widows and captives who were being unjustly deprived of their funds. Charles proved as deaf to her pleas as he had been to those of his son. Before he relinquished power over the Spanish realms to Philip, Charles had ordered yet another round of confiscations – this time for a total of 800,000 ds. Rumours of the royal decision led a number of shipmasters to dock in Lisbon in February 1556 rather than Seville.[3] Their action served as a warning to the Castilian government that it was likely to lose control of this lucrative trade if this unwarranted royal intervention continued.

The regency government was confident that once Philip assumed power the *embargos* would cease. Furthermore, as the crown's share of the bullion in the 1556 fleet was rumoured to be unusually large, Juana did not take Philip's initial warning that he would need to confiscate part of the shipment in order to pay for the Italian war too seriously. Indeed the regency government responded to this suggestion of further confiscations by reiterating at length the damage which this measure had caused. They were certain that Philip would never implement what he had so fiercely resisted in the past. But they had not reckoned on Philip's radical change of

[2] AGS CJH. 26 fol. 18.
[3] AGS E. 112 fol. 61; Carande, *Carlos V y sus banqueros*, vol. III, p. 237; Chaunu *Séville*, vol. II, pp. 540–7, esp. 542–5.

perspective once he exchanged his post of regent of the Spanish realms for that of sovereign of a large empire. Anticipating resistance, he had secretly paved the way for an *embargo*. He dispatched a special agent to Seville, the *licenciado* Salazar, to spy upon the royal officials and ease the way for the confiscations. Aside from providing information, Salazar told Philip of the traumas following the previous seizure of bullion. A number of merchants had been imprisoned for debt and he spoke in touching terms about the petitions and curses of the women and children who clamoured for justice and help outside his door.[4] Juana's concern about the situation was demonstrated by her support of a proposal to make legal tender the devalued government bonds that had been issued to the previous victims of royal confiscations, or at the very least, to ensure that they would be accepted for the repayment of debts. Philip resisted these plans until 1560.

Since the king persisted in his warnings that the impending war made a partial confiscation inevitable, the regent and royal officials gradually realised that he intended to follow in Charles's footsteps. Their optimism gave way to resentment; there was a sense of moral outrage in the regency's letters and actions. Philip had ordered that all ships and cargoes arriving from the New World should be retained until he decided how much bullion he would need to confiscate. He repeated his order in a letter of 27 September 1556, as ships docked. But his orders were not transmitted for some time. Almost at once there were rumours of irregularities in the handling and unloading of cargo, which the government officials ignored. When the Seville officials sent a confused account of the ships and cargoes expected in the autumn fleets, the council of the Indies simply forwarded it to Philip, noting its lack of coherence without offering to clarify the matter. Salazar reported that he had seen royal officials deliberately destroying licences and accounts to prevent accurate accounting of the fleet. They allowed people to disembark and go home, often with all their goods, on the flimsiest excuses. He reported how they accepted palpably impossible tales of huge losses from gaming during the journey, when individuals unloaded quantities of bullion far less than the amount they had originally registered and paid tax for.

By February 1557 it was widely known that 1.5 million ducats of registered bullion had gone missing. Salazar estimated that goods worth 2 million ducats had arrived unregistered and these too were gone.[5]

Fraud on such a spectacular scale could not have been perpetrated without active government involvement – that was how Charles V put it in a letter to Philip in April 1557. He made the startling claim that the council of the Indies had issued licences signed by Juana and countersigned by the secretary Ledesma ordering the

---

[4] Of course, it should be noted that some of their difficulties were caused by the Peruvian revolt, but royal policy was blamed. AGS E. 109 fol. 318; E. 112 fol. 192; E. 108 fols. 155–9.

[5] The incident can be pieced together from AGS E. 113 fols. 135–7; E. 112 fol. 181, E. 112 fol. 179, E. 112 fols. 207–8; E. 114 fol. 20; E. 112 fols. 19–21; E. 112 fol. 192; E. 112 fol. 181; E. 112 fols. 202–4; AGS CJH. 29 fols. 289–90.

release of bullion and individuals in open contravention of Philip's orders. When Salazar investigated he sent copies of licences issued by the council of finance and duly signed by Juana. But he informed Philip that these had been issued to release named merchants and their goods so that they could fit out the return fleets. He asserted that the licences had then been used improperly by royal officials and masters in Seville, who chose to believe that they now had the power to release all the merchants on the ship named in the licence. Charles rejected this interpretation. He was adamant that the leading officials in Seville and Valladolid – including the secretary Juan Vázquez – were implicated directly in the fraud.[6] He may well have been right. It is certainly odd that the council of finance should have waited until 1 March 1557 – three days before finally admitting to Philip that the money had 'gone missing' – before issuing an unequivocal order that all bullion in the Casa de la Contratación should be retained there pending the king's pleasure. Moreover, when the fraud was too public to be ignored, Juana merely sent a minor official to Seville to investigate the matter, whereas both Charles and Philip thought that, given the gravity of the situation, a senior councillor of state should have been dispatched at once.[7]

The incident touched a raw nerve in the emperor. By his own admission he was so incensed when he heard what had happened that he forced himself to wait for several days before writing to his daughter. He realised that he needed to calm down before committing his thoughts to paper. Yet the tone of his letter was anything but temperate even after this enforced cooling-off period. Charles wanted blood: he told Juana to abandon the path of ordinary justice since the laws of Castile had no punishment harsh enough to fit this abominable 'crime'. He lamented that his health would not permit him to leave at once for Seville. He wanted to show those responsible just how terrifying the wrath of a sovereign could be. Aware of his reaction, some of the Seville officials (on their way to Valladolid to explain what had occurred), begged an audience so that they could put their case to him. He refused; later he regretted his decision, claiming that if he had seen them, he would have extracted the truth from them, if necessary by tearing them to pieces. In strident tones he ordered Juana to deprive of their offices all the royal officials implicated; to have them paraded in chains through the streets of Simancas (near Valladolid) at midday as if they were nothing but beasts of burden, then to confiscate their possessions and imprison them. But throughout this conflict it is clear that Charles did not trust his daughter: he believed that she was implicated too. He came very close to accusing her directly. Aware that she was unlikely to obey

---

[6] AGS E. 120 fols. 201–3; E. 119 fol. 29; E. 120 fols. 258–9.

[7] Government officials accounted for their failure to issue clear orders saying that they were convinced Philip would revoke his order after they had pleaded with him. AGS E. 120 fol. 221; E. 120 fols. 201–3. A note on the back of this document, in Eraso's hand, shows that by now he was convinced Salazar too had been implicated in the events. AGS E. 514 fol. 30, E. 120 fols. 37–42; E. 119 fol. 248; E. 119 fol. 37; E. 119 fol. 43.

his orders, he resorted to threats. But his ferocity was coloured by his impotence. He warned her that if she did not do exactly what he had ordered, he would write to Philip 'in such a way', and tell the king 'things' that would cause Philip to 'reveal his anger' towards Juana far more openly than he had done thus far. He went as far as saying that he would personally undertake to implement whatever Philip ordered, even if he were at death's door, unless Juana punished those involved in this 'crime'.[8]

The similarity to Lear is inescapable: Charles had given away his power and could no longer force his daughter to obey. His fury was now a thing to be scorned rather than feared. After one of his letters to Juana on this matter was read out at a meeting of the council, Gutierre López de Padilla wrote to his friend and fellow contador mayor, Ruy Gómez de Silva. Its contents, he claimed, had made him both laugh and cry. López de Padilla found 'the part where his majesty reprehends [the council of state] because they did not hang the officials of the Casa de la Contratación' very amusing. The passage in which Juan de Vega (who had been recalled from Sicily and appointed president of the council) was strongly criticised on the grounds that he had the means but lacked the will to seize and punish the culprits, caused great general merriment. Vega apparently went round the court making funny remarks about the 'great power' which he now ostensibly wielded. As for Juana, López de Padilla thought that she was right not to taint her conscience by implementing the rigorous measures which Charles dreamed up in Yuste.[9]

Philip was not at all amused. He was no less furious than his father; his language no more restrained. He declared the fraud 'the greatest act of treason that could have been committed against my person'. He accused all those involved of having 'declared war' against him and all his lands. He claimed that they had placed his person, his honour and his states in gravest danger. The reason for his fury was clearly rooted in his inability to seize this bullion, which he had counted on to launch the campaign against France. He had declared war and could not withdraw from the confrontation now without losing credibility. He told Juana that his honour and reputation were in jeopardy as a direct result of the Seville fraud. He would have to initiate the war without funds and would be unable to levy enough troops to win. He wanted her to know that if anything were to happen to him, they would be responsible. In these angry and petulant missives there was heavy emphasis on the personal danger Philip faced. He wrote eloquently of his preference for honour above life itself. As he put it 'honour matters more to me than the threat to my own life which might result from this'.[10]

The very excess of his reaction suggests that there was more to it than wounded

---

[8] AGS E. 119 fol. 21, Charles to Juana, 1 April 1554; see also AGS E. 119 fol. 34; A. Llorente 'La primera crisis de hacienda en tiempo de Felipe II', *Revista de España* II (1868) pp. 317–61, esp. 350–4.   [9] Codoin, vol. 97, p. 336.
[10] AGS E. 810 fol. 141, to Juana; E. 810 fol. 80, to the council of finance. These can be compared to the warm thanks he extended to Charles, commending his actions and sympathy, E. 810 fol. 40.

honour and anxiety about one bullion shipment. A glance at the policies he was implementing reveals the reason for his fury. Philip had decided to re-schedule his debts at the beginning of 1557. This directly affected the situation in two ways: first, it raised the level of tension and conflict as the regency government had refused to ratify the decree (pp. 234–8) and were fighting his policy directives on finance; second, he knew that this action would lead to a breakdown of relations with the merchant bankers; consequently no loans would be available for a time. Therefore, the only way to finance the campaign against France was to obtain cash subsidies from Spain or the Netherlands. In effect the king was not simply reacting to the situation in Seville but making a vehement protest against the conduct of the regency government, seeking to undermine their opposition by castigating them on this particular issue where they were most vulnerable.

Juana and the Castilian officials reacted with mounting anger and resistance to the barrage of abuse and accusations from Charles and Philip. As Juana pertinently reminded the two men, these people had committed no crime: they had taken their own money. It was the crown who had unjustly seized what belonged to others, knowing full well that it did not have the means to offer adequate compensation. Juana concluded that it would be immoral to punish people for having taken what was theirs by right. She decided that it was also foolish to punish the pilots and ship owners since they would merely take service with the French, and only after a great deal of pressure was she willing to summon a few leading officials to Valladolid to answer charges. The royal officials supported her actions in many ways. Most pleasing was the report written by the official originally sent to investigate the matter, licenciado Jarava, an ingenious document devoted to a complex explanation of how all the money could have been legally dispersed in the twenty-four days that elapsed between the issue of the limited licences and the reiteration of Philip's order to retain all goods in the Casa.[11] Although she left Philip in no doubt that the regency government now felt fully vindicated, she agreed to send a senior official to carry out further investigations, because, as Charles soon realised, she saw this as a way to delay an official response. A few leading officials from Seville were summoned to Valladolid and imprisoned, but when one fell ill and died, Juana used it as an excuse to release the rest. She also refused to seize the unregistered money which had been discovered in the fleet. Charles sought to persuade her that this money belonged to the crown, but she would not listen.[12] Neither Charles nor Philip received any satisfaction.

The anger and bitterness generated by this conflict is striking. It drove a deep wedge between Juana and the royal officials on the one hand, and Philip and Charles on the other. Despite Philip's clear indications of his position, none of his appointed officials in Spain backed him or challenged Juana. On the contrary, the regency

---

[11] AGS E. 121 fol. 237–8, the report. Jarava named only two culprits – Francisco Mexía and Salazar.
[12] AGS E. 119 fols. 101–2; E. 119 fol. 104; E. 120 fols. 32–4.

government closed ranks. It was the beginning of a drift away from the sovereign and towards greater independence.

Nevertheless, if Charles failed to provide the focus of loyalty and authority Philip had hoped for, he proved extremely useful in other ways. By applying constant pressure on Juana and leading councillors to prompt them to raise funds; by seeking to intervene in the process of government (as over the seizure of Indies funds), he attracted the opprobrium and opposition of the regency government, deflecting its anger from Philip. Nevertheless his overall influence may have been pernicious. During 1557–8 Charles provoked another conflict with Juana which strengthened her resolve to be free of his influence and, where the regent led, lesser men followed. Far from proving the rock upon which an unstable government was firmly anchored, the emperor's presence acted as a catalyst in the process of gradual alienation from royal authority.

Juana, Charles and the Portuguese inheritance

King João III of Portugal died on 11 June 1557. His successor was Juana's only son, the infant Sebastian, hence the question of the regency immediately arose. In essence it was a straight fight between the dowager queen Catalina (Charles's youngest sister); and João's brother, the cardinal dom Henrique. Juana appreciated that she could not make an effective bid for the regency whilst acting as regent of the Castilian and Aragonese realms, but she wished both to establish her rights to a future regency and make a bid for control over her son's education. The crisis came at an unfortunate time: there was no resident ambassador in Lisbon. The new envoy was on his way, but had stopped at Yuste to receive further instructions from the emperor regarding the visit of the Infanta Maria. Juana dispatched a special envoy to carry out her dual mission but sent him to Yuste first, in case her father wished to add letters of condolence. When Charles learnt of his daughter's plans, he at once determined to foil them. He destroyed her letters and instructions and substituted his own. He ordered her envoy to express her condolences only, and never to mention the regency or to deliver her letters to Portuguese nobles. Charles seems to have been guided by his fear that Juana's claims might prejudice his sister's bid for power and divide the pro-Castilian supporters.

It is not clear why the envoy chose to carry out Charles's instructions rather than those of the regent who had appointed him. Once more the division of authority and confusion as to who was the ultimate power in Castile was evident. Juana appears to have learnt of her father's actions too late to save the mission. Her reaction can only be surmised from her known feelings and her subsequent actions. We know that she still saw her future inextricably bound to that of her son and his realm. We also know that Philip and Charles had promised to release her from her post and allow her to return to Portugal as soon as Charles set foot in Spain – a further indication that neither man initially expected the emperor to retire. They had gone back on their promise and she had good reason to feel that they were to blame for her absence and inability to establish her position in Portugal. She had good cause to feel aggrieved. Moreover, she was intensely proud, and her pride as well as the interests of her son and herself had just been sacrificed by the intemperate action of the emperor.[13]

The incident would have been painful enough if it had ended there, but a few months after aborting her initiative, Charles had changed his mind and urged her to establish her rights to the regency and build up contacts with the leading nobles and officials. This dramatic turn had been provoked by the emperor's encounter with a shady Portuguese character who had requested an audience, been sent away, then summoned back as the emperor developed an interest in his vague warnings of a Portuguese–Jewish conspiracy against the Castilian realms. In the course of their conversation Charles found himself having to argue that don Carlos was now the rightful heir to the Portuguese throne and would remain so until Sebastian produced a male heir of his own. This curious incident and otherwise unimportant conversation, had suddenly opened Charles's eyes to the reality of the situation in Portugal, making him aware of the wave of anti-Castilian feeling that had swept through the neighbouring realm; and especially of the doubts regarding Carlos's rights to the throne. He ordered Juana to send envoys, to establish her rights to the regency and build up a group of well-affected nobles to support her future claims to the regency. His aim was clear: to redress the situation and firmly establish Carlos's claim. He was not at all concerned with Juana's maternal feelings or political ambitions.[14] Still smarting from her father's earlier intervention, Juana was in no mood to cooperate. Moreover, she was aware that Catalina was unpopular and had no wish to be associated with her aunt's regime. Above all, she thought it imperative to wait for another suitable occasion, such as Catalina's death, when her bid for control would be less evident and have a greater chance of success. Although Juana's rejection of Charles's proposals was couched in moderate language, if rather cool in tone, Charles described it as a haughty and disobedient missive. He realised he could no longer force her to obey him, so he appealed to Philip. He asked his son to force Juana to obey his order. But by now it was March 1558, and Philip was having considerable trouble imposing his own will upon Juana. He does not seem to have even attempted to support his father on this issue, and the matter was dropped.[15]

It is hardly coincidental that Juana should have made a successful challenge to her father's authority over the Bourbon–Albret negotiations shortly after the news

---

[13] AGS E. 119 fol. 45, Charles to Juana, 24 June 1557; AGS E. 119 fol. 49, ibid., 5 July; A. Danvila, *Felipe II y el rey don Sebastián de Portugal* (Madrid, 1954), pp. 73–5; Veríssimo Serrão, *História de Portugal* vol. III, pp. 58–60 and also chapter 9.

[14] AGS E. 128 fol. 323; see also Gachard, *Retraite*, vol. II, pp. 216–19; AGS E. 128 fol. 328.

[15] AGS E. 128 fol. 328, Charles to Philip, 31 March 1558; AGS E. 128 fol. 390, Juana to Charles, 22 March.

of what he had done to her original Portuguese embassy reached her, and when the rows over the Seville scandal were still candescent. In the past, she had concurred when officials delayed sending certain information to Charles about the progress of these negotiations, or even retained it. By the beginning of January 1558, she was determined to take control over the negotiations and did so by altering the way they were conducted. Juana informed her father on 3 January that she and the council had decided the negotiations must be speeded up, and henceforth only the duke of Alburquerque (governor of Navarre), Philip and Bourbon himself must be involved, thus reducing considerably the line of consultation and decision-making. Juana had no legal power to impose this, but she did have *de facto* control. Since Alburquerque kept her informed of everything and it was unthinkable that Philip would make a final decision without the advice of the regency government, the only one excluded from the negotiations as a result of this manoeuvre was Charles.[16] In a letter written on 4 January, the day after, Gutierre López de Padilla expressed the council's growing contempt for Charles. In mocking terms he described how the emperor kept showering letters of advice upon them, particularly on Juan Vázquez and García de Toledo. The message was invariably the same: they must think carefully upon all matters of state; they must have due respect for Charles's great experience and prudence – in other words, consult and obey him – they must make sure to keep him informed of everything. But these councillors did not see the point of doing this, because, as López de Padilla explained, they were convinced that Charles did not understand the problems of the Spanish realms, and that he did not care for his Spanish subjects. So they shrugged their shoulders and laughed at the emperor's repeated and increasingly pathetic pleas for consideration.[17]

THE ERADICATION OF PROTESTANTISM

Whilst conflict was the hallmark of relations at the highest levels of government within the Spanish realms, the combination of Charles's presence, Juana's strength of character and Philip's distant support – or constant pressure – could have created firm and decisive government if the issues under consideration had not been so divisive. This can clearly be seen in the prompt and successful action taken to root out Protestantism in Castile, as well as in the financial exactions during these years. However, even in these two instances, the interactions of key personalities and clash of ambitions decisively influenced the formulation and execution of policy.

The rejection of Protestantism in the Iberian peninsula owed little to the distrust of northern ideas – that process was still a generation away. The Catholic kings had initiated a precocious reform programme that set their realms in the vanguard of ecclesiastical reform in the fifteenth century. Erasmian literature found ready acceptance among an intelligentsia long aware of the need to cleanse and change a

---

[16] AGS E. 128 fol. 388.   [17] Codoin, vol. 97, pp. 335–6.

corrupt church. But Erasmus and Luther became increasingly associated in the 1530s, and fears of the disruption and divisions provoked by the latter provoked a reaction which ended in the rejection of both. However, it was inevitable that Charles's Spanish subjects should encounter Protestantism in the course of his reign and his constant travels. Some embraced the new ideas, and not unnaturally, most of these converts had close connections with the emperor's peripatetic court and the international business world. Before the 1550s, the few so-called Lutherans punished by the Inquisition tended to be foreign merchants or travellers.[18] In the autumn of 1557 the situation radically altered: a 'cell' of Lutherans was discovered in the monastery of San Isidro, near Seville. A dozen or so monks had espoused Protestant ideas and collected Protestant literature in Spanish, printed in Frankfurt, which the authorities had no difficulty in identifying as 'Lutheran'. The Inquisition at once demanded a grand demonstration against the 'daring and clever heretics'. Remarkably, the incident made little impact at first.[19]

One possible explanation for the curious lack of reaction is the ambivalent position of the Inquisitor General, Fernando de Valdés, in the regency government. Philip (and Juana) had been attempting to eject Valdés from court, and send him back to his archbishopric of Seville. Since neither threats nor blandishments had secured the desired result, Juana (with Philip's blessing) appointed him to the unenviable task of escorting the body of queen Juana to Granada.[20] Valdés was still at court when news of the arrests reached the regency government.[21] Both supporters and opponents of the archbishop thought that they could use the discovery of Lutherans in Seville to their advantage. Opponents argued that as archbishop of Seville, he must leave at once to deal with the situation in his own diocese. Supporters countered this argument with the claim that, as Inquisitor General, Valdés must remain at court, near the regent.[22] Unable to use the situation in order to force the issue both parties played down the Seville cases. But Valdés realised that he was alienating both Philip and Juana by his constant excuses and refusals to leave for Seville. He finally agreed to go, but was far from reconciled to this. He desperately needed to find a way out and whilst he searched for it, he made leisurely arrangements for his departure. The answer to his prayers was a crisis within the court itself. He had got no further than Salamanca when he was secretly informed that there might be enough evidence to convict some individuals at court

[18] See, for example, the token *Luteranos* punished at an *auto de fé* in Barcelona in October 1552, AGS E. 92 fols. 79–80.

[19] AGS E. 121 fol. 48, E. 121 fols. 165, 162 and other related documents have been published by J. L. G. Novalin, *El Inquisidor General Fernando de Valdés (1483–1568)* (2 vols., Oviedo, 1971), Documents, vol. 2, pp. 181–2 and ss. Erasmian influence and the background to these 'Lutheran' converts has been exhaustively studied by M. Bataillon, *Erasme et l'Espagne* (Paris, 1937; second, Spanish ed., Madrid, 1979).

[20] Gachard, *Retraite*, vol. II, pp. 354–6, reprinted by Novalin, *Valdés*, vol. II pp 184–5.

[21] Novalin, *Valdés*, vol. II, pp. 181–2.   [22] Novalin, *Valdés*, vol. II, pp. 184–5.

of heresy. Using various pretexts to stay in Salamanca, he instigated the hasty but important investigations in Valladolid and nearby areas that led to the really spectacular discoveries of 'heretics' in 1558.

The inquisitors made their move in April with simultaneous arrests in Valladolid, Zamora and other towns. Among the accused were several nobles and a few government officials. Father Domingo de Rojas was the son of the marquis of Poza; don Carlos de Seso an ex-*corregidor* of Toro; the *licenciado* Herrera had been *alcalde de sacas* in Logroño. In view of the serious nature of the charges and the proximity of these 'dissidents' to the court, Valdés had to be allowed back to court where he triumphantly presided over (or even orchestrated) the heresy scare.[23] The enthusiasm of the Inquisitor General for this case accounts in part for the hysteria that ensued – so different from the earlier incident. However, it would not do to imply that the extreme feelings aroused within the Spanish realms were all a plot of the inquisitors. There is no doubt that the high status of the accused was also an important factor, as was the reaction of Charles V and Philip II.

Like so many others, the two men were deeply shocked. They had come to believe that the Spanish realms were among the few areas of Christendom to have remained safe from Protestant ideas. Their response now was based on the alarmist information produced by the Inquisition. Charles in particular seemed stunned by the news. He took it as a personal affront, lamenting that after he had spent 'a lifetime fighting heretics' [*sic*] he should have his final resting place 'defiled' by them. Once again, he told Juana to ignore existing legal practices, and pursue a policy of rigour. He found the Inquisitor's insistence on the primacy of reconciliation of the accused distasteful. Heretics, he declared, should be dealt with summarily through charges of treason, even if these had to be falsified, so that punishment would be immediate execution and confiscation of their possessions. Recantation would lead to lesser sentences, of which he thoroughly disapproved. In his view, God's service and the safety of the realm were at stake; under the circumstances, he did not believe that the sovereign was bound by ordinary rules of conduct. He had not overestimated the problem – he was convinced that swift and brutal reprisals would eradicate it, but if it was allowed to spread it would soon be out of control.[24] In the light of these remarks, Charles's use of secular authorities in the pursuit of Protestantism in the Netherlands becomes more comprehensible, as does his insistence that heretics must be executed regardless of prior recantation. Although the Spanish Inquisition had already acquired an unsavoury reputation for harshness, it was much too lenient for the emperor's liking. Secular justice could be

---

[23] Note that whilst the documents published by Novalin, op. cit. have been used here, this is not his interpretation. Details of the discovery AGS E. 129 fol. 110; E. 128 fol. 361, letter informing Charles; E. 129 fol. 77, the report of the council of the Inquisition to Philip, 12 May 1558.

[24] AGS E, 128 fol. 361; E. 128 fol. 363. He offered similar advice in a letter written to Philip from Yuste on 25 May 1558, AGS E. 128 fol. 1.

manipulated more easily and the charge of treason extended. That is what Charles had done in the Netherlands, and that was what he wanted Juana to do in Castile. Juana and her councillors refused to implement his suggestions and orders.

Philip's reaction to the news was characteristic. Whereas his father wanted heads to roll immediately, he requested information and recommendations. He ordered Juana to summon a select group of theologians and jurists who were to meet with the council of the Inquisition and submit their advice before he would decide on a course of action.[25] He shared with his father the belief that the problem would be eradicated through immediate and resolute action, and he was equally doubtful whether the regent and the councils would act as the situation demanded, especially in view of the exalted status of some of the defendants. Although outwardly he expressed total confidence in his sister and the councillors, in private he voiced deep misgivings, particularly after the death of Charles. The heresy scare had reinforced the trend evident during the conflict over the New World confiscations and drawn the two men closer together, in direct opposition to Juana and the Spanish councillors in Valladolid. Philip had come to regard Charles as the only truly responsive and sympathetic figure in the Spanish realms. On the back of a letter from father Gaspar de Tamayo, in which the latter had expressed his fears that Juana would slacken her efforts to root out and punish the Protestants now that Charles was no longer able to put pressure on her, Philip noted: 'I am deeply pained by all this, particularly because I am so far from being able to set sail and go there immediately. I am even more fearful than this man of what will be done about these matters henceforth'.[26] Other clerics, including his confessor, fuelled Philip's fears, casting doubts on the ability of the regency government to deal with what they considered a major crisis. Fresneda thought it a cruel twist of fate that the man who had 'reduced the English realm to obedience' should now face heresy within his own states. His letter suggests that he viewed the incident as a serious loss of honour for the king.[27]

Philip's reaction reveals how out of touch he was with the mood of the Spanish realms and of his regency government. Far from allowing the noble connections of the defendants to mitigate justice, the government reacted promptly and decisively to punish them. The public outcry against these 'heretics' was such that the prisoners had to be moved at night to prevent enraged mobs from lynching them. Rojas was convinced that his family would have him assassinated before he reached court.[28] Huge crowds, larger even than expected, gathered to witness the *auto de fe* in Valladolid in May 1559, which was also attended by Juana and prince Carlos; smaller but still impressive ceremonies took place in Zaragoza, Murcia and Seville.[29]

[25] AGS E. 129 fols. 178–83.
[26] AGS E. 130 fol. 118, Tamayo's letter was dated 1 November 1558.
[27] J. I. Tellechea Idígoras, 'Felipe II y el Inquisidor General D. Fernando de Valdés', *Salmanticencis* (Salamanca) XVI, 2 (1969), pp. 329–72; Fresneda's letter p. 346.
[28] AGS E. 129 fol. 110.   [29] AGS E. 129 fol. 110; E. 138 fol. 248; E. 137 fol. 4; E. 137 fol. 15.

Unlike Philip's other states, the pursuit of Protestant dissent at this time united the Spanish people and realms – divisions were to emerge as the Inquisition tightened its grip and vigorously pursued Protestants involved in trade with Iberia later in Philip's reign. The importance of this incident, the much vaunted discovery of 'Protestantism' in Iberia, lies more with the impact it had both at home and abroad, than with the problem of repressing it. As in England and the Netherlands, religious dissent was an additional and important source of anxiety for the government. It aggravated the atmosphere of gloom and heightened the sense that society was being assailed on all sides. This mood pervaded both the government and governed during the latter years of the 1550s. Philip's deep despondency over the religious health of the Spanish realms seems exaggerated in retrospect, but his feelings become comprehensible when one considers the cumulative effect of several events and conflicts, and the willingness of those within the regency government to paint the situation in its blackest colours to force him to return or win his favour. For example, Valdés wrote Philip a lengthy report on the discovery of the Protestants at court in May 1558. He also dealt with the uproar caused by the suspension of divine services in a number of sees – a measure taken by the bishops in protest against royal policy (p. 229). Then came bad news about the real problem of dissent in the Spanish realms – the *Moriscos*. There had been trouble in Granada and Aragon. A formal delegation from the kingdom of Aragon had been sent to court to explain the seriousness of the situation, and demand that the Inquisition should reduce its activities against the *Moriscos* until the secular authorities were strong enough to deal with the opposition. Juana was forced to agree to the suspension, but this triggered off similar demands from *Moriscos* elsewhere – including, curiously enough, Valladolid. As if this was not enough, Valdés then related worrying reports from Murcia where large numbers of people had lapsed into Judaism, and he finished with a warning of new discoveries of heresy at the highest social levels in Valladolid, Salamanca, Zamora, Toro, Palencia, Logroño and other unspecified places.[30] As a result, he created an impression of a state in the process of internal disintegration.

SOCIAL AND COMMERCIAL GRIEVANCES

Adverse climatic conditions added to the atmosphere of gloom and decay. Like so many other areas of Europe and Africa the Spanish realms suffered an extremely bad harvest in 1556. Juana reported with alarm the sudden and sharp increase in grain prices – fourfold in many places. The situation was made worse because it proved so difficult to secure grain from the usual suppliers, in particular Sicily, which was itself experiencing similar shortages. Matters reached crisis proportions in certain areas. By February 1557, the Catalan authorities reported that they were

---

[30] AGS E. 129 fol. 129, published by Novalin, *Valdés*, vol. II, pp. 187–91.

dealing with famine and not just high prices and scarcity. They assured Juana that many people were subsisting on roots and acorns. As was usual in such cases, the crisis put great strain on urban areas. The authorities were highly nervous and feared general unrest.

The harvest in 1557 proved to be equally poor, and when plague struck that summer its impact on the starving realms of Catalonia and Valencia was devastating. It triggered off large-scale movements of population away from the coastal areas towards the centre and this in turn exacerbated fears of possible Muslim or French invasion.[31] The shortage of grain was just as acute in North Africa, and, as tended to happen in such situations, the corsairs sought to supply their cities by launching raids against shipping and coastal areas of Spain and Italy, taking any grain and provisions they could find. Under threat of internal unrest and constant attack, centres like Seville and Barcelona sent urgent pleas for aid to the regent.[32] Philip was sufficiently concerned about the situation to give the matter some thought, but his lack of knowledge about North Africa was at once apparent. He believed that the shortages within the Spanish realms might be remedied by imports of grain from the Maghreb. He ordered his sister to negotiate a trade agreement with the sultan of Fez and Morocco which was primarily intended to secure exports of grain to southern Spain, and Seville in particular.[33] Not surprisingly, nothing came of this.

Until recently it was common to think of corsairs as little more than a nuisance – colourful, exotic characters more suited to novels and children's tales than history books. The works of Tenenti in particular have helped to demonstrate that they were far more sinister figures. Even small groups of corsairs could have a devastating impact on the trade and political standing of the most powerful maritime states.[34] The situation facing the Spanish and Italian realms during the 1550s was extremely serious. French corsairs and pirates ravaged the northern and eastern coast and islands, disposing of their stolen goods in both Portugal and France. The Canary Islands were a favoured hunting ground for French and Muslim corsairs; the local authorities, tired of vainly seeking aid from the regency government and king, raised extraordinary taxes and fitted out three vessels to patrol and defend themselves.[35]

---

[31] Details of the situation in Valencia and Catalonia in AGS E. 322 fols. 69, 173, 81, 147. For Sicily, AGS E. 1123 fols. 7–8.

[32] See the previous note; also AGS E. 112 fols. 200–1, Juana to Philip, 1 November 1556, AGS E. 322 fols. 71, 261.

[33] AGS E. 511 fol. 210; AGS GA. 1321 fol. 144. See p. 278 for negotiations with Ash-Shaykh.

[34] The centre of his work was Venice, but many of the experiences of the city-state were shared by other Mediterranean powers. A. Tenenti, *Piracy and the decline of Venice 1580–1615*, English edn. (London, 1967); *Naufrages, corsaires et assurances maritimes à Venise 1592–1609* (Paris, 1959). The colourful, as well as the dangerous exploits of both Christian and Muslim corsairs have been dealt with by Bono, *I corsari*, and P. Earle, *Corsairs of Malta and Barbary* (London, 1970).

[35] AGS E. 376 fols. 65–7; E. 99 fol. 101; E. 89 fols. 52–6.

Quantitatively and qualitatively, the North African corsairs proved the greater danger to the Spanish realms. Unlike their Christian counterparts, they were not dependent on the issue of special licences or letters of marque to legalise their activities. In the Mediterranean, war between Christian and Muslim was a permanent feature of life – indeed it was a duty for members of either faith to annihilate the other. Consequently, whereas French attacks tended to coincide with periods of open war, those of the North African corsairs were constant. The North African corsairs were a motley group of different races and cultures. There were a few native Maghrebians from different tribes and cities; there was an increasing number of Ottoman subjects (especially from the Balkans) after the Barbarossa brothers established their successful base in Algiers during the 1520s. The largest and most important group were the Hispano-Muslims, exiles from the initial expulsion at the turn of the century as well as more recent arrivals. Driven by desperation and an unquenchable thirst for revenge against the Hispano-Christians, they supplied vital knowledge of shipping routes and coastlines and provided fresh information culled from friends and relatives still resident in Spain. Finally, there were the renegades – Christians from all parts, attracted by the many opportunities offered to them by the Maghrebian states and in the Ottoman empire. The policy of toleration and emphasis on merit within the Ottoman administration paid rich dividends.

By their very nature, corsair activities were varied and numbers fluctuated constantly. However, it is still possible to divide them into broad categories although individuals would frequently move within these. At one end of the scale there were countless small, fast craft, which Braudel aptly terms the 'lesser scavengers'. They were most active in the narrow stretches between the southern Spanish coast and Sicily, and their favoured prey were small fishing vessels and isolated coastal settlements. They did not spare the outskirts of the largest cities either: Málaga, Cádiz, Gibraltar, Seville all complained of daring raids by small corsair ships.[36] Larger vessels such as galliots or galleys could aim for other targets too.[37] They frequently acted in groups, thus increasing their range and scale. Assaults on a town or a convoy were usual. Attracted by its legendary wealth, they repeatedly ventured into the Straits of Gibraltar and beyond in the hope of catching the Indies fleet. Or else they stayed around Málaga where ships were fitted out to supply the Iberian bases in the Maghreb. Often these ships were involved in special raids to obtain slaves, who were in great demand in the Ottoman world. The activities and success of such groups can best be illustrated by summarising one

---

[36] Braudel, *The Mediterranean*, vol. II esp. pp. 871, 907; P. de Salazar, *Hispania Victrix* (Medina del Campo, 1570), p. 1a; examples can also be found in AGS E. 476 s.f., e.g. 'El dicho del Turco'; and Cervantes opens up his play *Los baños de Argel* (Biblioteca de Autores Españoles, CLVI Madrid, 1962) with a dramatisation of one such attack on a small settlement.

[37] A useful and brief description of the different types of ships, Tenenti, *Piracy*, p. 154, Bono, *I corsari*, p. 88, n. 19.

expedition for which we have detailed information, although it dates from 1561. The redoubtable corsair Yahia Rais set out with four galliots from the Peñón de Vélez with the usual crew of natives, Turks and Hispano-Muslims. He went to the Straits to look for Indies ships; having failed to find them, he raided the coast and took slaves as well as seven ships at sea. He ran eleven others aground, taking what goods he wanted from them. Only one vessel was destroyed, and this was unintentional; it caught fire in the course of a fierce struggle. All the ships attacked were large, and their country of origin varied – including Castilian, Aragonese, French, Flemish and English crews and cargoes. Ammunition, salt, grain, cloth and iron were, along with slaves, the most valuable items taken.[38] These depredations were not always the most serious consequence of such raids. Larger groups of corsairs could terrorise an area and deter commercial movement for weeks. Not infrequently they blockaded ports and whole coastlines. In 1557 for example, a fleet of fourteen Algerian corsairs virtually closed the Straits of Gibraltar for several weeks by sailing from one end to the other in search of prey. That same year, and at much the same time, another squadron of eleven 'Algerian' ships successfully disrupted trade around Barcelona, preventing part of the royal fleet from sailing to Italy with vital supplies of soldiers and money for three whole months.[39]

Whilst many corsair raids could be dismissed by the government as irritants, the repeated attacks of larger groups represented a serious threat to the security of the Iberian realms, and not just to their commerce – a point that will be examined in greater detail in the next chapter. Indeed the North African corsairs outnumbered the ships of the Spanish crown. Contemporary observers estimated the combined corsair fleets at about one hundred sizeable vessels by 1560. Whenever the Algerian corsairs were involved in joint campaigns with the Ottoman and French fleets in the Mediterranean during this decade, they would contribute twenty-five or even fifty ships, and still send large numbers to attack enemy coasts and shipping. The combined fleets of Charles, Philip and their allies amounted to some fifty ships.[40] When the Castilian cortes stated in 1559 that Mediterranean commerce had all but ceased as a result of these constant corsair raids, they were undoubtedly exaggerating, but they had good reason to protest. Numerous letters from local and urban governments as well as the petitions of the corts and cortes in the Iberian realms testify to the general perception of a rapid and significant (perhaps even catastrophic) decline in the volume of Mediterranean – and particularly Spanish – trade during the 1550s. And this, rightly or wrongly, was blamed on the activities of the corsairs. Consequently, the calls for immediate action against the growing

[38] AGS E. 444 fol. 104. Other examples in AGS E. 322 fol. 118, E. 108 fol. 298 and Braudel, *The Mediterranean*, vol. II pp. 880–1.

[39] Gibraltar: AGS E. 125 fol. 1; Barcelona: RAH SC A. 60 fol. 241; AGS E. 322 fol. 55; E. 322 fol. 118.

[40] AGS E. 481 fol. 8 report of Francisco Hernandez de Peralta, although from the early 1560s, it was common for the figure of 100 to be used a decade earlier. See I. A. A. Thompson, *War and government in Habsburg Spain 1560–1620* (London, 1976) Table H, p. 300, figures for the galley fleet.

Muslim threat multiplied, as did resentment about the way in which the king was disposing of Spain's resources.

FINANCING THE WAR

Before Philip decided to launch a campaign against France, his military advisers warned him that 'everything depends on your majesty's ability to find and raise sufficient funds with which to pay and sustain the army . . . In the words of a Greek adage, war is made up of three elements: money, more money and even more money'.[41] Juana realised that he would seek the bulk of those funds within the Spanish realms. She was in the difficult position of having to persuade her brother that these lands could absorb no further debts. She admitted that in the past similar complaints had been made, yet money had been raised nevertheless. But by the closing months of 1556, all revenues had been mortgaged in advance up to 1560, in order to manage the accumulated debt of 7.5 million ducats. Two million of this remained without assignations. The long-term problem implied by these figures was made all the more acute by the immediate concerns they faced. The regency government needed to raise 4.5 million ducats for payments and expenditure during 1557. This was quite apart from any demands Philip might make – and soon after he demanded 826,506 ds with all haste. Juana replied that he must look elsewhere for money to fund a major war. The Spanish realms would be unable to supply him with substantial funds until radical reforms were imposed and these reforms could not be carried out unless Philip was present in Castile.[42] The emphasis on the need for him to return to Spain, alongside the traditional claims of poverty, persuaded Philip that she was exaggerating in order to bring him back. Instead of accepting her analysis of the situation, he took steps to improve his control over the government by securing Charles's help. The conflict over the Seville *embargo* made him realise that he must restrain the regency government and bring it under more direct control. He sent Ruy Gómez de Silva and Gutierre López de Padilla to Spain to expedite the collection of revenue and discuss various expedients. An overpowering sense of urgency pervaded his correspondence when he realised that he would not be able to seize as much money as he had hoped from the New World fleet. Table 10 shows that Philip had expected to receive nearly two million ducats from Spain at the beginning of 1557, with further direct subsidies of 1.5 million by July of that year. Since the first sum failed to materialise, he desperately sought other means of raising cash quickly. They proved as unpopular and controversial as the confiscation of bullion.

[41] RAH SC F. 17 fols. 143–53.
[42] AGS E. 112 fols. 3–6, Juana's interesting letter to Philip, 13 June 1556. The figures for the accumulated debts and money required: ibid., also AGS E. 113 fol. 69; CJH. 28 fol. 203; E. 120 fol. 308, E. 121 fol. 111; Ulloa, *La Hacienda Real*, p. 138.

223

Table 10. The first campaign

Date	Philip's expectations/demands	Provision from Spain	Money confiscated N=Netherlands I=Indies	Date
Beginning of 1557	Demand 1,650,000 ds. for the Netherlands[a] 300,000 ds for Italy	c. 1.2 million ds[b]		May 1557[c]
28 June 57	In hand 500,000 ds from Caravajal's fleet	did not go		
	Expected: 700,000ds. with Pedro Menendez's fleet 800,000 ds with Ruy Gómez's fleet 500,00 ds. loans being negotiated	only 300,000 sent[e] 585,000 ds loans[f] 300,000 ds bullion sent[g]		July 1557 July 1557 August–September 1557
	TOTAL = 2,500,000 ds[d]	TOTAL = 1,085,000 ds		
	Demand: 400,000 ds for Italy 250,000 ds Philip's household 200,000 ds cash urgently 1.6 million ds for the army (for July–October 1557)			
	TOTAL = 2,450,000 ds[d]			

		Sept. 1557
October 1557	*Demand:* 1.5 million ds from[l] the money in Seville	
	(N) 350,000 ds[h]	From the 1556 fleets
	(N) 650,000 ds[i]	From the 1557 fleets
	(I) 1,756,990 ds[j]	
	(I) 1,000,000 ds[k]	

[a] AGS E 121 fol. 210.
[b] AGS E 120 fol. 275.
[c] AGS CJH 32 fol. 42: note that the suspension of payments occured May–June.
[d] AGS E 810 fol. 21.
[e] AGS E 119 fol. 55. Philip had already borrowed 500,000 ds of this.
[f] 55,000 ds from various financiers, AGS E 121 fols. 209–10, 530,000 ds Daniel Spinola, AGS E 142 fol. 150.
[g] AGS E 121 fols. 268–9; E. 121 fols. 209–10; CJH 20 fol. 23 arrived October.
[h] AGS E 120 fols. 24–5.
[i] AGS E 517 fol. 30.
[j] AGS E 103 fol. 57, they originally planned to take only 800,000ds., E 112 fols. 207–8.
[k] AGS E 103 fol. 57; E 121 fols. 123–4; E 103 fol. 64.
[l] AGS E 121 fols. 98–9.

The forced loan and suspension of ecclesiastical subsidies

When Charles was planning his campaign in 1552, he had resorted to a forced loan from the leading noble, ecclesiastical and commercial figures in the Spanish realms. Five years later, in the spring of 1557, Philip did the same. He personally supervised the compilation of a list of suitable individuals and institutions. The expedient had never been popular, but circumstances conspired to make it less popular now. First, Charles had not repaid the earlier loan. Secondly, Philip decided to employ his father in this task, quite specifically so that the emperor could remind leading ecclesiastics that they owed their positions to him and should respond by showing due generosity in this time of need. Charles displayed renewed vigour and set to his task with enthusiasm. Juana and the councils, by contrast, resisted Philip's requests that pressure be applied to those who refused to contribute. The regency government alleged that the loan was supposed to be a voluntary contribution and not a tax, therefore it was immoral to force people to contribute. Far from being a selfless gesture protecting fellow elites, this attitude reflected the firm opposition of leading councillors to the new demands. A number of them had also been singled out and had refused to pay their assigned contribution.[43]

The king expected the higher clergy to donate the most. As one secular figure after another rejected the request, it appeared as if they might be the sole subscribers. Philip had asked leading bishops and archbishops for sums in six figures: the few who replied offered much less – between 1,000 and 4,000 ds. The archbishop of Seville, Valdés, once more took the limelight, this time unwillingly. Philip had asked him for 150,000 ds. After a great deal of pressure, largely from Charles, Valdés offered 50,000 ds but insisted that the sums owing to him from previous loans should be deducted. In effect, Philip would have received a mere 16,000 ds. To encourage other contributors, and doubtless prompted by his own animosity, the king decided to make an example of Valdés. There is little doubt that he was also influenced by his favourite ecclesiastic, Bartolomé de Carranza. Carranza has been all but canonised by admirers of his lengthy and largely unsuccessful combat against the Spanish Inquisition after 1558. The toughness and determination so evident in his captivity were amply displayed earlier as he furthered his ambitions at court. He was a ruthless manipulator, and eminently successful for a time. Carranza had been involved at least since 1554 in plots to discredit Valdés. Both were aiming for the highest stakes in the ecclesiastical hierarchy and court. Valdés was hardly an attractive character either: a choleric, vengeful individual, he shamelessly exploited his position as Inquisitor General to

---

43 AGS E. 112 fols. 241–2, memorandum of the meeting with Ruy Gómez de Silva, 27 March 1557, to discuss the loan; List of names, AGS E. 127 fol. 4; see also E. 120 fol. 155; E. 119 fol. 226; E. 120 fols. 75–6; E. 119 fol. 55; E. Libro 73 letters sent by Juana requesting the money, dated 21 June 1557; example of Charles's letters for this purpose, E. 119 fol. 35. Other details emerge, p. 288 ns. 93–4 from the Carranza-Valdés conflict.

advance his family and allies, as well as to extend his power at court. Having served as president of the council of Castile in the 1540s, and subsequently in other senior posts, he was one of the most experienced members of the regency government, and had been considered by Charles to be the best candidate for the regency in 1553–4.[44] This point serves to set the ensuing conflict into perspective. Valdés was undoubtedly one of the most powerful men in Castile, yet Carranza advised Philip to treat him as if he were an ordinary Indies merchant. Since the king had not hesitated to confiscate the money of such merchants, why should he be deterred from forcing the archbishop to give up his wealth? Heartened by Carranza's assurances that this action would be both canonically and morally justifiable, Philip ordered his financial officials first to demand 100,000 ds from Valdés; then, if he did not comply at once, to seize control of the archbishopric of Seville and collect its revenues until the full sum had been paid.

This was an extraordinary, indeed outrageous order, riding roughshod over clerical, legal and personal privileges. No one in Valladolid, not even the faithful Ruy Gómez, would implement it. It says a great deal about Philip's desperation to secure funds for the war, but also about his disregard for the political realities of Spain. He was soon to alienate large sectors of society within the Spanish realms with his high-handed and insensitive policies.

In the short term, his ploy was partly successful. The higher clergy were suddenly infused with a generosity so conspicuously absent in their initial reactions to the loan. The bishop of Córdoba lent 100,000 ds, Zaragoza offered 20,000; others followed suit with smaller sums. The archbishop of Toledo, Philip's old tutor, was even pressed to lend 400,000 ds although this had stringent conditions attached, which Philip, typically, ignored after Silíceo's death.[45] But the long-term consequences were also considerable. Valdés would do everything in his power to avenge the slight to his honour and threat to his position.[46] The incident also increased tension between the king and the higher clergy at a time when Philip should have been doing everything in his power to conciliate them.

The Spanish church made substantial contributions to the crown's revenues. A conservative estimate for the years 1552–5 set their contributions in this triennium at 1.2 million ducats, which came from a variety of sources: sales of indulgences and lands were among the most important. These were not taxes in the legal sense of the word, but gifts granted by the church on the orders of the papacy, to reward the Spanish monarchs for the sterling work they were doing to spread and defend the faith. Many of these grants had been specifically designated to fund the war against the Infidel. The monarchy had used them for other purposes in the past. In the closing months of 1554, Juana and the council of finance had assigned repayment of a loan to current and future revenues from the *subsidio*, the most important

---

[44] pp. 86–7.   [45] See pp. 271, 282–3, for his other loans.
[46] ADE Carranza, vol. XVIII, especially pp. 9–10; 202, 238–42.

ecclesiastical contribution. The regency government assumed that the grant would be automatically renewed when the existing three year concession ran out.

The clergy objected to this action because the government appeared to be treating the grants as ordinary taxes. But the main reason for their violent reaction was the emotive issue of Spain's relations with North Africa. Defence against Muslim powers and the demand for an offensive policy in the Maghreb were the most controversial issues in Spain – this will be explored at length in the next chapter. By 1556–7 the call for action was overwhelming but constantly rejected by the king and government on the grounds that there was no money to fund either adequate defence or an expedition. However, as was repeatedly pointed out, if the sovereign used clerical subsidies for the purpose they had been granted, then funds would be available.[47] Much as they approved of such sentiments, the regent and councils upheld the assignation of loan repayments on future *subsidio* grants because the alternative was to offer revenues earmarked for the upkeep of the administration and royal households.[48] The clergy refused to accept the decision and the uproar did not abate.

At this inopportune moment, pope Julius III died, and his successor, Marcellus II, rapidly followed him to the grave. Strictly speaking, all ecclesiastical concessions lapsed on the death of the pope who had granted them. The Spanish clergy took the opportunity to cease paying the *subsidio* and other dues. They were delighted when Gianpiero Carafa became pope, believing that the old reformer would support their case. They lodged a formal appeal against the government's actions. Their hopes were dashed when Paul IV renewed the various concessions in November 1555; yet a few days later he had a change of heart and revoked all ecclesiastical grants in Spain. The regency government had counted on all these dues and assigned them up to and including those of 1558. The revocation left them with a grave problem – finding alternative funds to cover current expenditure assigned on these revenues. Repayments promised on future assignations were now added to the floating debt.[49]

Juana responded to news of the clergy's appeal and papal revocation with characteristic vigour. She summoned a group of theologians and councillors to advise her. She wanted to know whether it was possible to continue collecting these revenues without papal authorisation. The general consensus was negative, but desperation drove the regent and her immediate advisers to continue anyway. Compliant clerics such as the bishop of Lugo and Melchior del Cano willingly participated in the regent's policy. They argued that Paul IV had no right to revoke concessions he had legally granted, since Philip had given him no cause. Yet few secular councillors endorsed the argument. They believed, along with a majority of ecclesiastical advisers, that the pope must be obeyed. The archbishop of Toledo,

---

[47] For a fuller discussion of this, see pp. 230–1, 265.

[48] AGS E. 103 fols. 380 and 399. Details of clerical contributions in Carande, *Carlos V y sus banqueros*, vol. III, pp. 451–2; Laiglesia, *Estudios*, vol. II, pp. 176–8.

[49] AGS E. 883 fol. 9; E. 883 fol. 94; E. 121 fols. 40–1.

not a temperate man at the best of times, was incensed by the regent's decision. He denounced all those who agreed to collect ecclesiastical revenues illegally as heretics and warned Juana that she was risking her soul as well as endangering the empire. He reminded her that her great-grandfather, Ferdinand, had conquered both Navarre and Naples after their respective monarchs had been placed under papal ban. Paul would adopt similar tactics and encourage Philip's enemies to seize his states. Other bishops demonstrated their disapproval in more practical ways. As government officials prepared to collect ecclesiastical dues, the bishops of Segovia, Seville, Badajoz, Córdoba, Plasencia, León, Coria, Cartagena and Avila imposed a *cessatio divinis*, prohibiting all ecclesiastical services within their dioceses. The regent was warned that other bishops were preparing to do the same.

Her reaction was swift. In February 1556 she sent angry letters ordering the resumption of divine services. She sought to convince the higher clergy that the government would only collect revenues to which they were legally entitled. For example, the bishop of Lugo was empowered to preach indulgences for the redemption of captives, and to raise money for the cathedral of Santiago. He continued to do so – but he extended his activities and, contrary to the conditions of these grants, he allowed these contributions to be used for the French war. Juana also encouraged prebendaries, long locked in conflict with their bishops, to resist and challenge their authority especially if they were opponents of the scheme. By April of that year this particular wave of protest had been scotched and divine services resumed, but the clergy had not been pacified, nor had Juana managed to persuade the majority of the secular councillors that her decision to continue collecting ecclesiastical revenues was justified. Some, like Juan Vázquez, were willing to back the regent, even if it meant endangering their souls. Reproached by opponents of the government, he commented that when he weighed the dangers to his soul with the pressing needs of the king, the burden to his conscience and soul was easier to bear. But others would not cooperate, and disliked Juana's tactics of divide and rule.[50]

When Paul IV realised that the Spanish government had continued to collect some ecclesiastical dues, he renewed his injunctions against all those involved. Silíceo took the opportunity of this new papal protest to present Juana with a petition signed by many of the bishops and archbishops formally declaring their intention to disobey her and obey the pope. They confirmed their primary allegiance was to him and not to the sovereign. In June 1556 Juana warned Philip that these new developments heralded the end of ecclesiastical subsidies for the time being.[51] Yet she was far from beaten. She was persuaded that they might still secure a good deal of cooperation – and by extension, revenue – if they detached Silíceo

[50] AGS E. 112 fols. 247–8; 245; 9–10; 161; E. 114 fols. 74, 135; E. 113 fols. 82–90; 70, 131; E. 103 fol. 355; E. Libro 73 (February 1556), letters to the bishops and archbishops; E. 114 fols. 93, 135; E. 883 fol. 94; E. 121 fols. 268–9.
[51] AGS E. 114 fols. 74, 123; E. libro 73; E. 112 fol. 125; E. 114 fols. 186–7; E. 113 fol. 199.

from the rest of the opposition. With the primate of Castile on their side, many others would follow. The archbishop was still eager to extend his power, particularly within central government: Juana suggested to Philip that they should agree to let him play a greater role in exchange for his silence or outright cooperation. With Philip's blessing this was done. Furthermore, Juana and the councils pursued a policy of favouring compliant clergy with higher salaries and gifts, excluding leading opponents from royal patronage.

By the end of July 1556 Juana claimed that all higher clergy and most churches had been persuaded to support the king, and that almost as much revenue was being collected without papal authorisation as before. This was probably an exaggeration, but there is clear evidence that revenues were seized by government officials.[52] Moreover, all payments due to the pope were retained and used.[53] Interestingly enough, however, there seems to have been no support for Lugo's proposal that Philip should impose a straightforward system of taxation over the Spanish church, along the lines of the Gallican model.[54]

In short, the conflict with the higher clergy first delayed, then drastically reduced the revenues available to the government, preventing it from further anticipating ecclesiastical dues in order to settle debts. Philip was just as anxious as his sister to minimise the damage. Apart from supporting her initiatives, he attempted to settle the dispute by offering a compromise. He admitted that the crown had taken liberties with ecclesiastical subsidies in the past, using them to pay for the French wars, but he assured the clergy that their funds had not been misappropriated. He explained that revenues came to court in a haphazard way, seldom when needed. They were used as they were received and allocated to the most immediate needs. Ecclesiastical subsidies might pay for the French war now, but funds meant for this war might be sent to the Maghreb. Nevertheless, he had decided to deal with ecclesiastical subsidies separately in the future to assuage all doubts. He would send all such monies to the college of St Paul (Valladolid?), where they would be stored in a special coffer with three locks. One key would be held by the Rector, one by a special commissioner who would administer the money, and one by the crown's representative. They would ensure that the money was released only for the struggle against the Infidel.[55]

In view of this conflict with the higher clergy, and his need for their cooperation, the king should have sought further means of conciliating them; instead he decided to make an example of them over the forced loan. Not surprisingly, his heavy-handed tactics lost him support, and by 1557 the situation was chaotic. A few ecclesiastical revenues may have been collected during the second half of that year and later. But the majority resisted the government's efforts and their resolve was

---

[52] AGS E. 113 fol. 199; E. 114 fols. 186–7, 174; E. 112 fols. 173–5; E. 112 fol. 161.
[53] AGS E. 112 fols. 9–10; E. 117 fol. 1.
[54] AGS E. 114 fol. 134, Lugo to Philip, 1 October 1556.
[55] AGS E. 114 fols. 178–80, Philip's instructions to Villaroel, 2 July 1556; also E. 112 fols. 141–2.

stiffened by papal support and anathemas. The pope did not renew these subsidies until 1560, and only for a brief period. In 1562 they were all abolished and a new subsidy was granted, specifically designated for the upkeep of a Mediterranean fleet and campaigns against Muslims.[56]

The attempt to re-schedule the debt and restructure the financial machinery, 1557

Philip had hoped that the forced loan and confiscation of Indies funds would provide him with sufficient funds to launch his campaign. But he would also need regular subsidies to fund the armies once they were in the field. He ordered the regency government to retain all the bullion arriving in the 1557 fleets from the New World. He hoped to make the measure a little more palatable by arguing that he intended to use this money in Italy, and specifically in Lombardy, not in the Netherlands. Juana and the officials were not appeased. They deluged Philip with complaints, to no avail. They did not dare to repeat the fraudulent practices of the previous year, however. In the end, just over a million ducats were seized after Philip reiterated his orders with considerable force and clarity. Few of those whose money was confiscated received any compensation, since there were no revenues free for the *juros* Philip offered as compensation. The lucky ones were forced to sell their annuities almost at once, to recover liquidity. As a result, the market – which was already affected by the over-issue of government and merchant banker's bonds – was flooded. Prices slumped dramatically.[57]

Other expedients were put into effect such as the sale of titles, offices and crown assets. But the yield from these sources was relatively small by comparison with the huge sums needed for the war.[58] Consequently, Philip ordered Juana to explore the possibility of increasing taxation in Castile. Undeterred but affected by the acrimonious exchanges with the cortes in 1555, he told her to negotiate directly with the cities who alone sent delegates to the Castilian cortes. A century later, this tactic was successfully employed by Philip's grandson, but the measure was resisted both in the sixteenth and seventeenth centuries. Monarchs and their governments were well aware of the value of such 'representative' assemblies, particularly during royal absences or at times of war and internal unrest. The cortes were still a symbolic forum where monarch and subjects communicated each other's needs and concerns. Juana objected to the king's proposals on the grounds that such novelties would merely result in further disruptions to revenue collection. She also objected to his suggestion that taxes should be increased. To her this represented a rather underhand way to reopen the bitter debates of 1555. She made it clear that Philip

---

[56] Ulloa, *La Hacienda Real*, pp. 128, 571, 595, 597–61, 623–6.
[57] Juros AGS E. 121 fols. 127 and 111; details of the fleets and cargoes, AGS E. 103 fol. 64, E. 130 fol. 57, E. 121 fols. 123–4.
[58] AGS E. 120 fols. 241–2, 217, 142; E. 129 fols. 173, 47–8, fol. 478; CJH. 33 fol. 260; Ulloa, *La Hacienda Real*, ch. 12.

would have to wait until the present term of the *encabezamiento* came to an end in 1561 before attempting to change the tax structure of Castile. With great reluctance Philip had to accept that she would not tackle the cortes on these key issues, and agreed that the *encabezamiento* should be extended to 1561. A more bitter pill to swallow was her rejection of a new tax on wool, and refusal to raise custom dues along internal frontiers.[59] The realm was much too restive to tolerate further tax demands.

Even if Philip had succeeded in raising the sums he demanded from Spain and the Netherlands, he could not have avoided bankruptcy. The revenues of his states were so heavily mortgaged, and so far in advance, that a radical solution was inevitable. The leading merchant bankers were fully aware of this. In September 1556 the Genoese consortium headed by Constantin Gentile, who normally resided at the regent's court, had to be rescued by the same government that had failed to repay outstanding debts and obligations. Gentile had been negotiating for the houses of Centurione and Doria as well as his own. Since the Dorias were the lynchpin of Philip's Mediterranean policy, and Gentile all but dominated Milanese finances, the consortium had to be protected from bankruptcy. The council of finance somehow found enough revenues to assign annuities at 10 per cent with which Gentile paid off some of the most pressing debts. Juana warned Philip that their ability to fund further rescue operations was extremely limited. If he felt compelled to buttress any other banker or company, he must offer them annuities with lower returns – a maximum of 7.14 per cent and preferably lower – since there were no revenues for the near future.[60]

The difficulties of the merchant bankers made them increasingly reluctant to negotiate further loans or offer exchange facilities. Already by the closing months of 1556, Juana found it extremely difficult to arrange credit transfers. Despite her offers of good revenue assignations in return for bullion payments in the Netherlands, few bankers came forward and the sums they covered were small.[61] The need for bullion in the northern front drove the king to seize money belonging to merchant bankers, and to demand direct cash subsidies from the regency government. It was now imperative for the government to free the best Castilian revenues and regain direct access to taxation. Fully conscious of the situation and the limited options facing a sovereign determined to fund a major campaign, some financiers decided to avert the dangers of a royal bankruptcy and minimise the damage to themselves by devising a mutually acceptable solution to the financial crisis. Since the bulk of their assets were now frozen in Spain and there they had access to the all-important bullion, they concentrated on the finances of this area.

---

[59] AGS E. 128 fol. 377; E. 120 fols. 37–42, E. 517 fol. 8. Events in the cortes during the seventeenth century I. A. A. Thompson, 'Crown and Cortes in Castile, 1590–1665', *Parliaments, Estates and Representation*, II, 1 (1982), pp. 29–45; Wool tax, Ulloa, *La Hacienda Real*, pp. 327–46; and p. 244.

[60] AGS E. 113 fols. 58, 56, 51, 55; E. 112 fol. 181.

[61] AGS E. 112 fol. 178; fols. 191, 193, Juana's letters to Philip, 15 and 26 October 1556.

One of the earliest proposals submitted was that of Rodrigo Dueñas. This financier turned royal official was convinced that he could manage the state debt at a profit so long as his company was given total control over the issue and manipulation of crown annuities in the Spanish realms. At the time his suggestion was made *juros* were selling fast and maintaining their value. In April 1556 for example, Juana needed to send Philip 300,000 ds urgently; she raised the money very quickly by selling annuities.[62] Other merchant bankers favoured more cautious solutions. It was suggested that for the time being Philip should pay his creditors only what they themselves owed to others.[63] Philip sent the financial official Eguino with these and other proposals to Spain in November 1556. He was determined to re-schedule his debts and did not give his sister or her councillors a chance to question his decision. He merely asked them to advise him of the best method to secure his goal. The new high-ranking financial officials – Gutierre López de Padilla and Ruy Gómez de Silva – were sent to Castile with full powers to conclude the matter on Philip's behalf. As befitted a man of tender conscience, Philip had secured theological approbation before deciding on so important a matter. The archbishop of Toledo made the sensible point that as the king could order a moratorium on debts when nobles got into financial trouble, he clearly had the power to do the same for himself. Father Joseph de Angulo went further. He argued that the financiers had charged excessive interest rates and were guilty of usury; consequently, the contracts Philip had drawn up with them were invalid in canon law. The king not only had power to repudiate them, but would be party to the sin if he repaid them.[64]

Even before the regency government had time to consider the options Philip had selected, he initiated an exhaustive investigation of all his debts with the intention of settling a sum for the global debt he owed to major companies and individuals, and assigning it. At the same time he announced his decision to re-schedule the debt by converting the capital and interest of all loans assigned to Castilian revenues into a consolidated, long-term debt bearing uniform interest of 7.14 per cent. Both the new interest and the consolidated 'capital' were to be repaid in annuities from Castilian revenues. Philip was convinced that by freeing all these revenues from their present assignations he would be able to manage the debt with *juros* of 14,000/1,000 and still be left with sufficient funds to cover ordinary expenditure and the campaign against France.[65]

[62] AGS E. 112 fols. 95–112. Dueñas was extremely eager to control the market in *juros*. During 1555 he had offered the king 400,000ds in cash in exchange for an equal sum of *juros* which were to be released on signature of the contract. Clearly he expected to make a profit from immediate sale of these annuities. For this and the 1556 proposals: AGS E. 108 fols. 259–60; E. 110(1) fol. 56; E. 110 fol. 44.

[63] AGS E. 114 fol. 301, holograph, contador Eguino, 30 November 1556.

[64] AGS E. 113 fol. 31, Silíceo to Philip, 21 September 1556; E. 114 fol. 267, Angulo's opinion, 18 September.

[65] A brief and clear summary of the conversion plan can be found in F. Ruíz Martín, 'Las finanzas españolas durante el reinado de Felipe II', *Cuadernos de Historia, Anexos de la Revista Hispania*, II (1968) pp. 109–73; esp. 114–18; also Ulloa, *La Hacienda Real*, pp. 138–41; Ehrenberg, *Fuggers*, pp. 114–17; Llorente, 'Crisis de hacienda', pp. 317–61. However, the process was far more complex than these writers allow, as will emerge from the following discussion.

Juana and the regency officials were incredulous. Castilian revenues were substantial but fell far short of such expectations. They immediately warned the king that he had been wildly over-optimistic. Yet they were in favour of radical action and not opposed in principle to the re-scheduling of the accumulated debt. Their initial response concentrated on the need to parcel out revenues in *juros* bearing 5 per cent interest. Ruy Gómez and López de Padilla endorsed their assessment. However, the latter were under strict instructions from Philip to raise money for the campaign whatever the cost. Consequently, although they started from the same premise as Juana and other officials, that is declaring the king's plan to be unworkable, they proceeded to offer very different advice. They told Philip that the financiers could be persuaded to accept the re-scheduling of their Castilian debts if given annuities bearing interest of 10 per cent; they would tolerate an arrangement which offered them interest of 7.14 per cent, but would undoubtedly reject out of hand a settlement at 5 per cent. The two officials therefore suggested in April 1557 that Philip should implement his original plan in the full knowledge that it was unworkable. They were undeterred by the questionable morality of such a move and pragmatic about the chaos that would ensue when the financiers realised this. They reckoned that Philip would have secured sufficient finance before the moment of truth was faced.[66]

The king was certainly eager to secure money for the forthcoming campaign, but he hesitated to commit himself to this scheme. In fact, by the end of April 1557, he had accepted that his original proposal must be altered, and the consolidated debt was now given compound interest of 5 per cent.[67] With this, he hoped that Juana and the Spanish financial officials would be satisfied and implement his orders. After all, they had been the most vociferous supporters of reform and retrenchment.[68] To his surprise and annoyance they refused to cooperate. They complained about the timing. If the measure were imposed now it would entirely break the king's credit; no merchant banker would offer exchange or credit facilities and so the regency government would be forced to supply the king directly at a time of war. They doubted their ability to do this. Philip was philosophical. He candidly admitted that his credit rating was now so low that it scarcely mattered if he broke it altogether.[69] Still they resisted his orders. The reason was only incidentally connected to the details of the conversion plan. Not for the first time, Philip tried to do two things at once and succeeded in neither as a result. Apart from the re-scheduling of his debts he sought to restructure the financial machinery. At stake was control of the monarchy's finances.

The degree of control exercised by the Spanish regents over finances whilst the

[66] AGS E. 120 fol. 142, Ruy Gómez and Gutierre López de Padilla to Philip, 25 April 1557. Opinion of the council of finance in Castile, AGS E. 121 fol. 111.
[67] Philip's response, AGS E. 810 fols. 78 and 80.
[68] Apart from their letters, it is worth noting that Ruy Gómez and López de Padilla remarked on this in AGS E. 120 fol. 142.   [69] AGS E. 114 fol. 301 and E. 120 fols. 37–42.

monarch was resident in the Netherlands had declined ever since the traumatic days of 1552 when Mary of Hungary seized the initiative and largely took over the process of securing funds for Charles.[70] This position of inferiority had irked Philip during his regency and continued to annoy his successor. As the situation worsened, resentment grew and the need for greater local control of finance was evident. The way matters stood, those in the Netherlands had greater power than the rest, but no one person or area had overall responsibility or an overview of the situation throughout the monarchy. A group of Netherlands councillors proposed to bring order to this chaotic situation and at the same time secure their control of the machinery. The plan known simply as *la factoría*, was the brainchild of a special commission set up by Philip in the Netherlands during October 1555. Their charge had been to discuss the financial situation in general and to suggest the best method of reducing the huge debt owing to the armies in the king's service. The commission concluded that the king would have to reform the financial structure of the empire and introduce new management. He must appoint a *factor general*, that is, a general broker with powers to control and coordinate the finances of all the monarchy. He was to be assisted by *factores*, preferably one in each major financial centre. These men would act as a team, responding to the needs identified and negotiated by the *factor general*. They would have the power to transfer funds from one area to another thus freeing the king from dependence on the financiers for credit transfers. Furthermore, they would take advantage of market facilities, earning money for the crown with currency speculation, for instance. They would settle accounts jointly, especially before major financial fairs, persuading financiers to accept repayment of debts in markets where cash was most abundant and exchange rates favourable. The system would thus facilitate the process of settling debts, many of which might be transacted on paper now. The ability to borrow in one market and repay in another without long, formal negotiations was thought advantageous to the financiers as well, since they too could negotiate to transfer payments from one fair or market to another, according to their own needs. Flexibility and rationalisation were not the only merits of this proposal, which was clearly inspired by mercantile organisations. It was intended to restore the king's broken credit. All the brokers appointed were to be financiers in their own right. They would not be allowed to transact business with the crown directly but must offer their names, persons and goods as security for the loans they arranged on the king's behalf. Moreover, they were to use their contacts to secure these loans. They therefore brought much-needed expertise to the monarchy's financial machinery, and a new source of collateral.

On paper the new financial system appeared a great improvement on the existing one. Philip gave it his approval at the end of October 1555, and pressed for its immediate implementation.[71] But rationalisation was anathema to the ram-

[70] See pp. 59–60.
[71] Brunelli, *I diari*, pp. 23–4; van Durme, *Granvela*, p. 205; further details from the letters cited in the following notes.

shackle empire of the Habsburgs. Opposition to the project was violent. It was contrary to the very nature of the loose, federal structure Philip had inherited. The principle that each state retained its independence but supported others in times of danger remained paramount. Although the volume of transfers and transactions between the states had multiplied in the previous years, all were eager to curb it, not to rationalise it. A unitary organisation also undermined the notion that these exchanges were taking place to meet an extended military crisis. It implied that the monarchy intended to pool resources permanently. The regency government in Valladolid at once detected both a general threat and a specific attack. There was great apprehension that the Netherlanders had devised a new way to extend their control of Spanish finances. Since the *factor general* was to be resident in the Netherlands, these fears appeared justified. The immediate appointment of Gaspar Schetz, a man closely identified with the government of Mary of Hungary and thereby with growing Dutch influence over Spanish finances, confirmed their suspicions.[72]

The delay in the transfer of power from Charles to Philip was a setback. Philip could not impose the new system until he had full control over his patrimony. This gave Spanish officials in the Netherlands valuable time to refine the plan to their advantage. Eraso and Bernardino de Mendoza, both newly appointed to senior posts in the Castilian finances, led the campaign.[73] They persuaded Philip that Schetz lacked the required knowledge of Spanish conditions to be given control over this area. Moreover, the volume of work would be too great for any one man to bear. So they proposed a two-tier system: two general brokers would reside in the Netherlands. A Spaniard must deal with loans assigned for payment on Spanish revenues, or any others floated there, irrespective of whether they would finally be assigned for discharge in another state. In effect, this would give the second *factor* greater powers than Schetz. Their suggestion, and their man, Juan López Gallo, were accepted by the king. This was the first victory of 'Spanish' officials over the Netherlands councillors since 1552 and most, like Granvelle and Savoy, rightly interpreted this move as a challenge to their authority and opposed it. Their failure increased tension at court. Indeed, van Durme plausibly suggests that this conflict so alienated Netherlands officials, it directly influenced their attitude to the king's demands for money.[74] It is easy to see how they might interpret Philip's decision as an anti-Netherlands move, particularly after the appointment of Hernan López del Campo as *factor* in Spain, with wide-ranging powers that further removed the financial machinery from their influence. There must have been a great deal of apprehension for the time when the Netherlands would not be able to have direct access to Spanish subsidies or to transfer their burdens. However, this proposal was

[72] His appointment was decided on 31 October, Brunelli *I diari*, p. 23. He was in Brussels by 4 November.   [73] AGS Contaduria General legajo 886 fol. 27, list of new appointments.
[74] *Granvela*, pp. 205–6.

in no way a victory for the Spanish realms – Juana and her advisers were appalled by the whole scheme and had no reason to trust Eraso and his cronies any more than his non-Spanish predecessors. From the start, the regency government was committed to a relentless campaign to revoke the *factoría*.

There was already much dissatisfaction in the financial world of Castile, due to a *visita*, a formal investigation into the organisation of Castilian finances, ordered by the king in 1556. Dr Velasco's findings resulted in reprimands and prosecutions, and the fate of senior officials such as the *contador*, Francisco de Almaguer, hung in the balance for some time. Almaguer had been in charge of preparing the detailed statements of account for the realm; he was now accused of both sloth and senility – charges he heatedly denied. He was quite convinced that it was all Eraso's dirty work and accused him of trumping up charges to get rid of those he opposed or who stood in his way to power, now that he had been appointed as a *contador*.[75] Any change would have been considered disruptive under these circumstances, but the *factoría* created an intolerable degree of instability, particularly as the broker for Spain, Hernan López del Campo, arrived in the middle of the divisive debates over the consolidation and conversion of state debts. He brought with him Philip's latest instructions and orders to implement the re-scheduling of debt at once. Inevitably, the two issues became inseparably linked.

Philip had granted the *factor* power to control revenues currently assigned for debt repayments, and to seize those not yet mortgaged. In other words, the revenues set aside for the administration and royal households were now his to dispose of. As soon as he reached Valladolid, he allocated these, sharing them out between debt repayments, defence, salaries and other basic expenditure. Juana might be regent in name, and the councils of state and finance in theory exercised considerable control over financial affairs, but without revenues, their powers were theoretical rather than real. They could not protect the realms from further exactions, nor challenge Philip's new demands with any hope of success; they would be unable to fund projects which the king did not approve, but which they thought vital for survival, or even indeed ensure that their most basic needs were met. They were now subject to the whims and decisions of a mere merchant banker. Moreover, since López del Campo had the right to appoint a number of lesser financial officials, the whole operation and not just the man at the top would escape the direct control of the regency government.[76]

Juana and the financial officials successfully opposed every effort López del Campo made to negotiate loans or transfer revenues. They ignored his powers and insisted that local officials should not obey him. Soon he complained that he was

[75] AGS E. 103(i) fols. 57–63; E. 113 fol. 209; E. 112 fol. 146. Almaguer had been another of Cobos's protégés.
[76] AGS E. 131(i) fol. 22; E. 114 fols. 9–12; E. 121 fols. 66 and 67–70, instructions and powers for López del Campo; E. 120 fol. 39, E. 114 fols. 5–6, Juana to Philip, 25 July 1557.

incapable of doing anything unless Juana sanctioned it.[77] Worse still, from Philip's point of view, the regency government made the implementation of the rescheduling of debts conditional on his revocation of the *factor*. This forced the king to offer a compromise in April 1557. He ordered that the Spanish *factor* should control only those revenues already consigned to the repayment of debts, and conceded that neither López del Campo, nor López Gallo could shift assignations or use these revenues without prior consultation with Juana and the councils. This failed to satisfy the objections of the regency government. Despite his orders that they must now implement both the *factoría* and the conversion plans immediately, they were determined to settle for nothing less than full restoration of their limited powers.[78]

Finally, Philip's patience ran out and he ordered a decree forcibly converting his debts to be publicly proclaimed on 10 June 1557. The decree followed the basic proposals outlined in February and incorporated the suggestion of the regency government that interest should be reduced to 5 per cent. Whether they liked it or not, the re-scheduling of the state debt was now legally in operation, and further resistance would be exposed to the full glare of publicity. Nevertheless, the regency government were obdurate. Juana refused to publish the edict within the Spanish realms. Considerable pressure seems to have been put upon her before she allowed it to be proclaimed at the end of July 1557. Even so, it remained a dead letter, and the reason, as López del Campo repeatedly told the king, was the government's determination to destroy the *factoría* system. As late as November 1557, he stated that they would not cooperate with the king until he abandoned it.[79] The only way out of the impasse was for Philip to return immediately and personally see to its implementation. For different reasons, Juana echoed the call for his presence. She sent Ruy Gómez de Silva back to Brussels in July 1557 with instructions to impress upon the king that they were deeply dissatisfied with his policies and expected him to sort out the financial chaos he had created in person. It was clear by the end of 1557 that unless Philip took control of the Castilian realms directly, the re-scheduling of the state debt would not be put into effect.[80]

Throughout these tense exchanges, Juana and the financial officials in Castile continued to raise money for the king, but the sums they sent fell so short of royal expectations that his determination to impose the decree in no way diminished. Nevertheless, circumstances were forcing him to reconsider his position. The Genoese bankers spread the rumour that Genoa was considering a change of alliances unless Philip withdrew the decree.[81] In fact it was the Genoese merchant bankers who once more rescued Philip when he was at his wits' end for funds. They suggested that he should do as in 1554 and 1555 and borrow his way out of the crisis. They realised the importance of maintaining Philip afloat until they could

[77] AGS E. 121 fol. 66.   [78] AGS E. AGS CJH. 32 fol. 42; E. 810 fols. 80 and 78.
[79] AGS E. 121 fols. 209–10, letters of 5 and 28 July; E. 121 fols. 211–12, 7 November.
[80] AGS E. 121 fol. 205; E. 119 fol. 55.
[81] AGS GA. 66 fol. 172, Gómez Suárez de Figueroa to Philip, 20 July 1557.

reach a less damaging settlement. Moreover, some of them were again threatened with bankruptcy as the king's latest seizures of their bullion created dangerous cashflow problems for them. Export restrictions continued to impede the movement of bullion from Spain. The need to recover liquidity played a vital part in the reopening of *asiento* negotiations in Castile and Brussels.

After an initial period of confusion and resistance – even López del Campo with all his contacts could only raise loans totalling 55,000 ds in the summer of 1557 – Daniel Spinola and company came forward in July of that year with an offer of 530,000 ds. The interest rate was most reasonable: 9 per cent – although this was still more than the 5 per cent imposed in the financial decree. It was strictly a short-term loan. The Spinola needed the whole sum in the forthcoming fair of Villalon (1558). There were two other noteworthy conditions: first, they demanded that the 170,000 ds the king had failed to repay them recently should also be paid back at the same time. Second, they appear to have obtained a promise that the king would recognise the entire debt owing to the financiers who made up the company. Clearly, they were still afraid that Philip would repudiate his debts or those of his father. Official recognition of their loans also implied the king's agreement to abide by their original conditions, thus releasing Spinola and his associates from the purview of the 1557 financial decree.[82]

Others sought to win Philip's favour and obtain bullion by advancing smaller sums in the Netherlands. Since he was expecting Ruy Gómez to arrive with 500,000 ds in cash, the king was able to persuade financiers to lend him the full sum, promising almost immediate repayment in cash or bullion. Ruy Gómez arrived with only 300,000 but even the partial payment brought the merchant bankers sufficient relief to tempt them to make similar advances on later fleets. Sometimes their contributions were less than voluntary. The Spanish merchant banker Gregorio de Salamanca was told by Eraso that he could either lend the 12,000 ds he was known to have in Santander, or Philip would seize them by force. Military men were also likely to take the law into their own hands. When the marquis of Berghes needed money for his troops, he sent a soldier from one of the starving companies to 'visit' the bankers every day, threatening them with hanging unless they advanced the necessary funds.[83]

With a mixture of promises and threats, the king was able to 'anticipate' a further 650,000 ds by the spring of 1558. This second round of borrowing was undertaken in the full knowledge that the subsidies expected from Spain would be far less than this. Writing in April 1558, Ruy Gómez expressed his joy that only 200,000 ds had arrived in the latest fleet. The discrepancy between what had been sent and what Philip had announced was so great that they would be able to argue that it was the

[82] AGS E. 142 fol. 150. Spinola later extended the terms for repayment, receiving an additional 12 per cent compensation fee. Both debts were settled in full in March 1559. See table 11(1).

[83] AGS CJH. 34 fol. 128; L. P. Gachard (ed.), *Correspondance de Guillaume le Taciturne, Prince d'Orange,* (vol. 1, Brussels, 1847), p. 387.

first of several instalments.[84] Had the sum been larger, the merchant bankers might have realised that the king had deliberately deceived them.

As can be seen from Table 10 (pp. 224–5) the king also impounded money which the merchant bankers entrusted to the safety of the royal fleets. The Fugger and Schetz probably lost all the 350,000 ds they dispatched in September 1557; as much as 650,000 ds was taken from ships sailing with Carvajal, and at least 165,000 ds from those sailing with Pedro Menéndez in March 1558. There may have been other confiscations, and the burden fell unevenly. The Fugger, for instance, claimed that they had lost 600,000 ds in bullion in the various seizures.[85] Deception, force and misinformation were the keystones of Philip's successful policy to finance his campaigns against France.

What had happened to the proposed financial reforms and re-scheduling of debts in the meanwhile? No one knew. In November 1557, the regency government and the *factor* in Spain asked Philip to clarify the matter. They were being approached by merchant bankers with proposals for new loans – perhaps encouraged by the Spinola experience – and wanted to know if Philip intended to set a ceiling of 5 per cent interest on new loans. From these enquiries and the correspondence related to the 1558 loans it appears that the financial decree had resulted in a haphazard moratorium of debts in Castile. A suspension of payments had been imposed at some stage in the autumn and winter of 1557 but it is not clear just how widespread it was. The money thus released from ordinary revenues was used first to supply Philip with direct subsidies – see Tables 10 and 11 (i). The prevailing impression was that the decree had been nothing more than a temporary moratorium and radical remedy to reduce interest rates. Financiers could negotiate with him or his officials and free themselves from the shackles of the decree. Some thought that they need only withdraw from negotiations for a time; sooner or later Philip would give in. He could not dispense with their credit and transfer facilities. Others appreciated the need to buy their way out of trouble.

Juana was happy enough to curb interest rates and so reduce the crippling burden of repayments; but she was realistic enough to appreciate that no new loans would be secured with a mere 5 per cent interest. The demand for credit on the international market was too great and other powers would borrow on more attractive terms. Moreover, she was reluctant to cooperate in the tendentious process of reconciling accounts with the major financiers. The regency officials seem to have appreciated the value of vast indebtedness in a financial market unfettered by national or ideological restrictions. The more the merchant bankers were given, the more they would be available for France or other enemies to borrow. In April 1558, Juana argued that Philip would lose rather than gain from a complete settlement of his debts. The sheer burden of such indebtedness ensured that the

---

[84] AGS E. 119 fol. 55; E. 517 fol. 3, and CJH. 34 fol. 512.
[85] AGS E. 120 fol. 245, E. 129 fols. 178–83, E. 517 fol. 30; E. 131 fol. 111; Ulloa, *La Hacienda Real*, p. 144.

majority of the world's financiers would remain dependent on the Spanish monarch.[86] The regency government concentrated on securing supplies for Philip – that is, on short-term objectives – and did little to implement his orders.

As for the *factor*, they could not get rid of him or the system, so they continued to restrict his activities. López del Campo was allowed to negotiate new *asientos*, and settle old ones, but only after consultation with Juana and the council of finance. He had become yet another official rather than a replacement for the existing machinery. But the most serious blow to the *factoría* system did not come from the hostile Castilian officials. Philip's persistent filching of the bullion shipments organised by the brokers at first damaged, then destroyed them. The financiers soon ceased to put their trust in these new officials and demanded more stringent conditions and additional collateral. Increasingly, the crown brokers had to offer their goods as security. In one instance, Diego Bernui offered to lend Philip 40,000 es if López Gallo underwrote the whole sum. The *factor* refused, fearing that he would be forced to produce the collateral all too soon given Philip's inability to repay any further loans. He suggested that López del Campo should share liability, but Bernui would have none of it. Pressure was put upon López Gallo to underwrite the full sum, but he did so only after he received an undertaking from López del Campo, Tomás de Guzmán and Ruy Gómez that they would pay him 10,000 es apiece if the financier claimed his collateral. However, Ruy Gómez had in turn to offer his pledge to each man that if this unfortunate situation arose, he would pay them the sum they had underwritten![87]

Whilst Juana and her councillors could resist Philip's financial decrees, they lacked the power to force him to withdraw them. The merchant bankers had that power and were desperate enough to propose risky measures in order to break the existing impasse and release the vast assets frozen in Spain. The breakthrough came in February 1558 when a group of Genoese financiers headed by Luciano and Adamo Centurione, and Constantino Gentile made a substantial offer. It had originated with a request from López del Campo to the Centurione for a loan of 200,000 ds. Gentile decided to join forces with them, and they proposed instead to lend 600,000 ds but required five major conditions which are worth noting in detail because this loan was a prototype for others. First, they demanded an explicit, official repudiation of the financial decree, freeing their accumulated debt from the 5 per cent interest restrictions and opening the door to negotiations with the crown. They wanted higher interest and a say in the reassignment of their repayments. Second, they wanted official acknowledgement and confirmation of 'old debts' – in this case amounting to 200,000 ds. In other words, these specific loans were to be repaid by the king according to the original conditions. In later *asientos*, financiers demanded larger sums under this heading, and sought to have their debts confirmed

---

[86] AGS E. 129 fols. 166–7. Mary of Hungary had made much the same point in 1533, cit. Tracy, *A financial revolution*, p. 41. Information on the confused situation in Castile emerges from the documents cited in the following two notes.   [87] AGS PR. 92 fol. 68 s.d.

in their entirety, with interest rates, exchange rates and place of settlement left unchanged. The larger companies could only hope for partial recognition, but they found other means of profiting from this clause. In later contracts, they asked permission to include here the debts of other merchant bankers, thus acting as brokers for others less powerful or more needy than themselves, and doubtless securing handsome returns for this service. Through these agreements, the number of loans entirely escaping the 1557 decree grew considerably. If the financier paid off the original creditor – perhaps at a better rate than the official 5 per cent, but lower than that specified in the original loan – this in no way affected his right to claim the full conditions from Philip. The third major demand was no less extraordinary: they required the first repayment (sic) to be given either in bullion or saleable *juros* and handed over *before* they disbursed their first instalment. If the crown failed to do this, the *asiento* would be automatically forfeit. The sums stipulated in such clauses were often very large – at times as much as half the loan. This was clearly a way to free a part of their assets. The fourth major concession was the demand for licences to export specie from Spain. Usually they requested the full amount and interest, or a greater sum. The government was required to give an additional assurance that it would honour these licences. Lastly, it was stipulated that if the crown chose to make the final payments in *juros*, these would bear a return of 5 per cent or 7.14 per cent, but no less. Evidently, the financial community were not convinced that Philip would stop at 5 per cent. As for interest on the new loans, they requested 9 per cent, a modest sum when compared to the rates before the decree.

Philip was pressing the Spanish government for supplies with all haste in the first months of 1558, eager to organise a campaign for the recovery of Calais. Conscious that they could not ensure that he would get the necessary money as quickly, or in the place where he needed it, Juana and her advisers decided to abandon the attempt to provide Philip through direct bullion shipments and accept the bankers' offer. They empowered López del Campo to conclude the loan with these conditions. It was signed on 11 March 1558 by royal officials and the agents of the consortium.[88]

On March 12, the heads of the consortium, who had secretly been negotiating directly with Philip in the meanwhile, signed a separate agreement with him in Brussels, unaware that their subordinates had completed their transaction first. The conditions extracted directly from Philip were more attractive in several respects. The financiers were allowed to retain the best revenues they had possessed in Castile. They were given *juros* of 7.14 per cent for their cumulative debts, and 18 per cent interest on the present loan. Furthermore, Philip agreed to give them 300,000 ds immediately from the bullion stored in the Casa de la Contratación in Seville. They could use it to pay the first instalment of their loan, if they wished, or

---

[88] AGS CJH. 34 fol. 63; E. 121 fol. 200; E. 121 fols. 233–4; Ulloa, *La Hacienda Real*, pp. 141–3. Note that Ulloa believed this was the first loan to break the conditions of the decree but, as was demonstrated above, the Spinola loan of September 1557 bears that distinction.

settle debts. They were given export licences for specie for the whole sum now borrowed. Finally, the king and the financiers had come to an agreement as to the global debt owed to their companies – 1.3 million ducats – and some measures were taken to discharge part of it, especially the floating debt. The king gave them the town of Estepa with full jurisdictional rights. They were also given back their original revenues to cover the rest of the debt, or revenues of equal value. Philip was perfectly aware of the opposition that this loan would provoke in Spain. He sought to pre-empt their hostility by arguing that the conditions were excessive, but necessary. He needed provisions and the merchant bankers needed to survive the crisis.[89]

News of the Brussels agreement shattered the regent's court. Even López del Campo professed himself incredulous. They argued that if they returned the revenues specified in the contract, there would be very few left to meet government expenditure – which suggests that the moratorium could only have been partial. As for the money in the Casa, this had been allocated to the *factor*, so that he could meet urgent payments at the forthcoming financial fair. If they did not give him this money, the Spanish end of the *factoría* would collapse entirely. Such details apart, there is no doubt that the explosion of anger caused by this agreement had at root the division of power over finances. Juana was powerless when Philip, notwithstanding the unfavourable nature of his own agreement, ordered that it must stand and declared the Spanish loan null.[90] The regency officials refused to accept defeat. They managed to persuade Gentile to come to Castile to deal with the mess. Once he was at court, he agreed to sign a new contract, less attractive than the first loan, but more favourable than the Brussels agreement. Now it was Philip's turn to be stubborn. He rejected the new contract and insisted that the Brussels loan was the only valid one. He was not greatly troubled by the damaging conditions it imposed on the Castilian finances; he was merely interested in an immediate payment, and the one advantage of the Brussels agreement was the promise of the first instalment in May 1558.[91]

Juana and López del Campo reacted violently to Philip's final order. They accused him of having ruined their attempt to impose a new system of negotiating loans. In effect, the only novelty was to ensure that new *asientos* should have low interest rates, but given their perception of Castile's financial problems essentially in terms of excessive interest charges, such a change was highly significant. They railed against the king, who imposed all manner of expedients from afar, eschewing responsibility instead of accepting that it was his duty to impose unpopular measures and novelties personally. They told him in no uncertain terms that henceforth they considered themselves absolved of the duty to impose better

[89] AGS E. 128 fol. 163; AGS CJH. 34 fol. 55, CJH. 34 fol. 125; E. 131 fol. 12. See also the lengthy discussion of both loans and conditions in AGS E. 128. fol. 163.
[90] AGS E. 129 fol. 166, Juana to Philip, 5 April 1558; E. 129 fol. 163 and E. 131 fol. 12.
[91] AGS E. 129 fols. 162, 296–7, 166–7, 232, 234–5; E. 517 fol. 89.

conditions on creditors. They would imitate him – take the easy way out and secure supplies for his campaign by squandering Spanish revenues. By the beginning of May 1558, the regent and chief financial councillors felt free to ignore any limitations imposed by Philip's orders and decrees. By implication, they also refused to accept responsibility for the chaos that would result from unrestrained borrowing.[92]

Recklessness was certainly in evidence in the loan they contracted with Nicolò Grimaldi on May 22 – two days before despatching their angry letters to the king. Some of their righteous anger over his behaviour may have been intended to justify their own actions. However, their sense of grievance was genuine. Grimaldi offered one million ducats. He would be given 300,000 ds in coin or bullion before his first instalment was due. Export licences for 800,000 ds were issued; *juros* of 10 per cent were given to cover 100,000 ds of the loan, and he received unrestricted choice of revenues for their assignation.[93] It was Grimaldi who first asked to include other people's debts under the 'old debt' clause. He was empowered to use 200,000 ds worth of *juros* either to raise money for himself or to transfer them to others. He would pay the crown the interest due on these bonds and give them up as soon as the entire debt had been discharged. Meanwhile, he had obtained access to regular revenue and the potential to help others by giving or selling these bonds. Grimaldi obtained other advantages – hidden interest in the exchange rates stipulated, compensation rates of 12 per cent. No wonder he offered another loan of 500,000 ds in October 1558 on similar terms.[94]

Philip was no less active, negotiating with financiers in the Netherlands, especially with the Fugger. By August 1558 conditions to discharge all but 300,000 ds of the 1.7 million ducats owed to the firm were agreed.[95] He had not consulted the Castilians on this and found them opposed to almost all aspects of the contract. There were no revenues to cover the assignations; above all, they bitterly condemned Philip's grant of the silver mines of Almaguen as part payment. Their opposition was so violent that Philip withdrew the proposal, and even tried to convince them that he had never meant it seriously. But he capitalised on their fear and used the occasion to force upon the realm a new tax on wool which they had resisted for several years. This unpopular measure coincided with an acute shortage of money that forced the regent to delay the opening of the financial fair in May 1558. It did not open until October, and the October fair had to be suspended indefinitely because the government could not find enough money to cover its payments.[96] Already in February of that year López de Padilla had warned the king

[92] AGS E. 129 fols. 234–5; E. 129 fols. 36–9.
[93] AGS E. 129 fol. 233; Ulloa, *La Hacienda Real*, pp. 144–5.
[94] AGS E. 131 fols. 8–10 (5 October 1558) – note he would be paid 250,000ds in Spain two months before his first instalment was due in the Netherlands. AGS E. 130 fol. 72. Grimaldi was still using the export licences granted for this loan in 1561, see AGS CJH. 65 fol. 171.
[95] AGS E. 131 fol. 111.
[96] AGS E. 129 fols. 63–9; E. 130 fols. 216–21, with Eraso's marginal comments.

that the level of discontent throughout the Spanish realms was high – and growing. The administration had become so disillusioned with the king's policies that no future financial demands could be made other than by using 'rigour and force'.[97] But strong-arm tactics were hardly likely to endear Philip to his officials and subjects.

Juana became more resentful and displayed her dissatisfaction by resisting and obstructing her brother. The complex situation can be illustrated by the extended chain of command now necessary to implement financial orders. In 1558 Philip can be found ordering Juana and the council of finance to release specific sums of money to López del Campo, who needed it to pay off debts incurred by the Spanish *factor* in the Netherlands (López Gallo), who had acted for Philip or the general *factor*, Schetz.[98] She continued to fight for greater control of financial affairs, arguing that it was impossible to retain a system whereby vital decisions were made in the Netherlands, by people with scant regard for Spain and even less knowledge about the conditions prevailing in the realm. Philip scarcely bothered to counter these accusations; he simply reiterated that he had no choice but to meet the great demands he was faced with. They, in turn, had no choice but to obey.[99]

The one thing that can be said in favour of this chaotic mixture of conflict, deception and bullying, was that it worked. Although, as can be seen from Tables 10 and 11, Philip's expectations were invariably disappointed, the amounts he obtained were sufficient to fund two vast campaigns that established his reputation and reduced French power.

The first campaign was evidently easier to fund than the second. Of course, the difficulties of the 1558 war can largely be explained by the extraordinary efforts made to fund the first campaign. The regency government had exerted themselves in 1557 and, as Carranza noted, they were convinced that the king's victories heralded the start of peace; after the fall of Calais they were deeply despondent, as they realised that another campaign would be fought.[100] The king had the dual task of finding further expedients and infusing some sense of purpose and determination in his subjects. As can be seen from Table 11, the second campaign was funded almost entirely by the confiscations and ruinous loans of 1558.

Naturally, Indies fleets continued to be a source of supply. The *embargo* of these funds was as conflictive in 1558 as it had been in the past. Notwithstanding the unpopularity of the gesture, Philip had ordered his sister to take everything as it arrived. In open defiance of his order, she released part of these consignments to individuals and merchants. However, since she was committed to give Gentile, Centurione and Grimaldi large sums of bullion in order to secure their loans, Juana

[97] Codin 97, p. 348.   [98] e.g. AGS E. 129 fols. 178–83.
[99] See the exchange in AGS E. 129 fols. 47–8 and E. 129 fols. 178–83.
[100] Tellechea Idígoras, *Carranza y Pole*, p. 269, Carranza to Villagarcia, Brussels 20 January 1558. The financial implications of the second campaign: AGS E. 135 fol. 101 memo sent by Philip; AGS E. 129 fols. 47–8; CJH. 34 fol. 512, CJH. 33 fol. 260.

Table 11. The second campaign (1)

Date	Philip's demands/expectations	Provision from Spain
? 1558	3,000,000ds Believes Spain can supply 2,180,000ds of this[A]	September 1557 to May 1558 instalments of 530,000ds loan from Spinola[B]
Feb/March 1558	3,384,000ds Spain to supply 2,000,000ds[A]	
March 1558	*Revised figures:* demand[C] 3,200,000ds for the Northern front 386,000ds for the Italian front Total = 3,586,000 *Philip expected*[C] 600,000ds with Pedro Menéndez's fleet 300,000 ds embargo of New World bullion 400,000ds from the Centurione–Gentile loan[G1] 600,000 ds (another loan being negotiated by López del Campo[G2]) Total = 1.9 million	200,000ds sent in Pedro Menéndez's fleet[D] 165,000ds taken by Philip from that fleet[E]

| April 1558 | 650,000ds borrowed in the Netherlands payment promised in cash in Pedro Menéndez's fleet[F]. | 600,000ds Centurione–Gentile loan payable May–July 1558[G]. |

[A] AGS E. 129 fols. 47–8, E 135 fol. 101

[B] See p.239

[C] AGS CJH. 33 fols. 260. *Pressing debts* 1,000,000 ds to the German Cavalry; 600,000 ds cash promised to financiers to cover 1557 seizure of bullion. Ulloa, *La hacienda Real* pp. 143–4

[F] Codoin 97 p. 350

[G] AGS E. 517 fol. 3, CJH. 34 fol. 512

E 517 fol. 3

See pp. 241–3. Philip had not realised that these loans (G, G1 and G2) were all one.

Table 11. *The second campaign (2)*

Date	Philip's demands	Loans renewed in the Netherlands	Loans negotiated by the Spanish government	Expenditure on Northern army	Indies fleet (embargo)
July 1558	3,000,000ds[A] (1.5 million from Spain 1.5 from realms other than Spain or the Netherlands)		1,000,000ds[B] (Grimaldi, payable July–December 1558)		
September 1558	2,000,000ds[D] (from Spain)			May–December[C] 1558	
October 1558			500,000es[E] (Grimaldi, Payable November 1558–February 1559)	1,862,105es	
November 1558		150,000 (Centurione)[F] 150,000 (Spinola) 300,000 (Imperiale)			November 1558[G] to April 1559 1,400,000ds taken from fleets in Spain
December 1558			600,000ds[H] (Spinola–Centurione) 800,000ds (Grimaldi)	December 1558[I] to February 1559 1,200,000ds	
January 1559	1,600,000[J] (from Spain)				

A AGS CH 33 fols. 87 and 91, note he ordered the *embargo* of Indies money in June, E 135 fol. 55, and a cash payment of 430,000 ds at once for the Fugger too, E 131 fol. 111.

B AGS E 129 fol. 233 and p. 244. 300,000 ds had to be paid to him before he gave the first instalment in the Netherlands; 200,000 were to be sent to Italy.

C I have obtained this figure from partial accounts of what the Paymaster General distributed, AGS CJH 33 fol. 61; 34 fol. 451 and 36 fols., 241–2, 243, 244, 247, 259. It is probably not a full account of what was spent.

D AGS E 129 fol. 63–9.

E AGS E 131 fol. 8–10 and E 130 fol. 72. He would only give this if given 250,000 immediately.

F AGS E 117 fols. 200, 201 and 202–4 respectively. Since they were re-negotiated loans, probably only a part of the total would have been paid out.

G AGS E 137 fols. 196–7.

H AGS E 130 fol. 240.

I AGS E 137 fol. 196–7.

J AGS E 137 fol. 184, E 137 fols. 109–10.

was forced to impose a limited *embargo*. What angered her most was Philip's failure to accept that Spain could not cover his new loans and provide him directly with bullion: it was one thing or the other.[101]

By the winter of 1558, when the king once again ordered her to take all bullion from the Indies, she had had enough. She took what was needed for urgent payments at the financial fair, and to cover essential items of expenditure – for example, 250,000 ds to improve the defences of the Spanish realms and their North African possessions. But she seized only 100,000 ds to dispatch to Philip. The rest was given to its rightful owners. She informed Philip of her actions on 17 December. She justified her decision not to inform him beforehand as 'right and necessary'. She was convinced – or so she claimed rather disingenuously – that he would endorse her decision since the alternative was to cause grave harm to many people.[102] Of course, as she well knew, this was the least of Philip's worries. He would oppose her, and it was essential to act before he could parry her actions. On receiving her letter he countermanded her orders, insisting that all bullion or goods in the Casa de la Contratación must be retained, and demanding the immediate dispatch of 1.6 million ducats to the northern front. However, he understood the need to change tactics in order to reduce conflict. He decided to give her a choice. If the regent and financial council could find other means to supply him with this money, he would not insist on them taking it out of the Indies fleet.

Eraso read the draft of the letter and advised the king not to send it. He told Philip to face the facts: the regency government would do anything rather than seize Indies bullion. They would search – but they would never find alternative revenues, because Spain had been drained of money. Since Philip needed the money with the utmost urgency, it was pointless to allow this fruitless search and delay provision.[103] Despite this sound advice, Philip sent the letter. As his instructions to Bartolomé Carranza in June 1558 prove, the king knew that he had become extremely unpopular in Spain and felt this keenly. 'My subjects in that realm,' he wrote, 'are in great need and disaffected – not without reason. For many years we have done nothing but take large sums of money from them and send it to other parts'.[104] His longing to win the popularity and the trust of his regency government failed dismally on all counts. Eraso proved an accurate prophet. Juana and the councillors spent much time talking to financiers, dreaming up expedients, stepping up sales of lands and jurisdictions . . . and finally they came to the conclusion that they could not raise the money Philip demanded. In an effort to reduce the confiscation of Indies funds they resorted to another loan, justifying it on the grounds that the war made the dispatch of direct subsidies much too dangerous. They managed to secure 800,000 ds credit from Grimaldi but they still had to seize bullion from Seville. It

101 AGS E. 135 fol. 55, order dated 7 June 1558; E. 129 fols. 63–6, E. 130 fol. 241–2.
102 Details of the fleets; AGS E. 130 fols. 61; 62, 240, 247; E. 137 fol. 274; Juana's initial reaction AGS E. 129 fols. 63–9; her December letter E. 130 fols. 241–2.
103 AGS E. 138 fols. 27–8.   104 AGS PR. 26 fol. 166.

was now April 1559. Juana sent Philip details of this loan and of an extraordinary meeting held with the councils of finance and state. They issued a joint statement of the situation in Castile graphically encapsulated in Juana's words: 'there is no other refuge'. All expedients had been tried, all sources exploited. This was the end.[105] Philip rightly read this as a rejection of all further demands.

In conclusion, the re-scheduling of debts announced in 1557 was never implemented. It had important repercussions, leading to a temporary suspension of payments and a partial moratorium in Castile, but its impact was haphazard and the large Genoese banking houses were able to evade it entirely after the initial confusion, by offering new loans. Other major companies, like the Fugger, also did well, obtaining the confirmation of their debts and assignations for most of them. On the other hand, the smaller companies and individuals were most affected, having to endure a suspension of payments until the king finally returned to Castile and imposed a new regime for the outstanding debts (1560–1). Philip's determination to change the financial structure undermined the limited autonomy of his states and led to grave problems, particularly in Castile where there was strong resistance from the regency government. His inability to resist temptation and repeated confiscation of bullion ruined any prospect of success for the new system. This, combined with local resistance, ensured that it was never fully operative either.

One final question about financing the war remains – did it directly influence the conduct of the campaigns? Given the haphazard nature of supplies, and the way Philip managed to secure substantial advances on slim promises, it is difficult to say how much money he had at any given point. The problem is compounded by the partial survival of records. Nevertheless, three points may be made with some certainty. First, that the original strategy was worked out with honour and the geopolitical situation as the dominant factors. Philip expected to be supplied with the money he required and demanded. Second, Philip would not have marched on Paris in August 1557 even if he had been well supplied. True, Ruy Gómez warned the regency government in September that the shortage of funds was seriously hampering them and might put an end to Philip's success, but the decision to consolidate his position around St Quentin was largely a response to the original strategy.[106] The king knew that without the subjugation of the neighbouring towns his forces would be under-supplied and easily overwhelmed. Moreover, his advisers opposed any further invasion for other reasons: Granvelle, because it was too late in the season; López de Padilla because he could remember all too clearly Charles's disastrous campaign in Provence. For the latter, the annihilation of the French forces and not the taking of St Quentin had been the essence of victory. Philip's

---

[105] AGS E. 137 fols. 139–40, Juana to Philip, 22 April. Details of the money taken from the fleets AGS E. 137 fols. 196–7.

[106] AGS E. 119 fol. 55; E. 120 fols. 24–5, E. 121 fols. 123–4; E. 322 fol. 232.

advisers were cautious. They were acutely aware of Henry's strength and determined not to take any unnecessary risks. Their fear was that Philip would lose everything by making one wrong move.[107]

There was one occasion when we can show that the availability of money significantly influenced the king's strategy. By October 1557, Philip owed the troops stationed in France over 300,000 es. The men were restless, especially the Germans, whose clashes with the local population were getting out of hand. Having decided to consolidate his position, Philip wanted to reduce costs and conflict by disbanding these men. As soon as news filtered through that Pedro Menéndez had set out with bullion for the king, he borrowed and paid off some of these troops. When Calais was attacked in January 1558, Philip did not have sufficient troops at hand to launch a decisive counter-offensive, and required English help. Since that failed to materialise, there was nothing for it but to gather his resources and wait for the season to commence.[108]

The war had cost over eight million escudos by August 1558; several million were required over the next few months to pay and disband the army and navy.[109] Much of this money had been provided by Castile and the merchant bankers, despite the heavy indebtedness of Castile at the beginning of the campaign. The unrest provoked by these financial measures naturally concerned the regency government. What worried them most, however, was the attack on their power and limited freedom. They were acutely conscious of the struggle going on around Philip for control of finances – a struggle that would eventually determine which area would have greater influence on Philip's policies. In 1558 no one had yet secured an overwhelming advantage. Ironically, Castile would emerge the victor not because of its overwhelming superiority when it came to supplying the monarch with funds, but as a result of its refusal to do so any longer. And yet, however dire the situation, financial grievances and struggles for control over money could never have turned the dissatisfaction of the regency government into rebellion. In the early modern world an ideological issue, not just hardship or discontent, was required before different groups and different levels of society could unite and rebel. Granted that the conflicts outlined in this chapter played a vital role in the challenge to royal authority which characterised Castile's relations with Philip. But the heavy burdens imposed upon the realm became intolerable when it was evident that the monarch was not willing to reward these efforts and respond to the needs and desires of Castile. The war against Islam was the catalyst that transformed opposition into revolt here. The difficulties Philip encountered with the regency government were in turn to have a direct bearing on his failure to quell the rebellion in Aragon.

107 Granvelle: Weiss, *Granvelle*, vol. v, pp. 128–9; López de Padilla, AGS CJH. 32 fol. 123; pp. 176–9, strategy.
108 Weiss, *Granvelle*, vol. v, pp. 128–9; BL Add. 28264 fols. 34–5; fols. 37–8; AGS E.K. 1490 fol. 104; E.K. 1492 fol. 114.
109 AGS CJH. 33 fol. 90. I hope to discuss the problems of disbanding the troops and how it was funded in a forthcoming work.

7

Rebellion in the Spanish realms

In September 1556 father Joseph de Angulo wrote to Philip complaining that the Spanish realms desperately needed leadership. There was 'no order', he lamented. The king must return immediately to prevent authority from breaking down altogether.[1] In retrospect it would seem that he was being unduly alarmist. Indeed historians have tended to go to the other extreme and present a picture of relative calm. Yet his view of a steep decline in order and obedience was not far from the truth, so it is striking how little has been known about the events treated in this chapter. At the time, every effort was made to keep them hidden from foreign observers. In this, the regency government and the king succeeded admirably, proving that even large and powerful realms tended to lapse into obscurity when monarchs and more dramatic military events were elsewhere. Nevertheless, the challenge to Philip's authority within the Spanish realms (which later cultivated the myth of their inviolable loyalty so assiduously) was of the utmost importance, and must be examined in detail.

THE SHADOW OF THE CRESCENT: SPAIN UNDER THREAT OF INVASION, 1550-9

The conquest of Granada in 1492 appears in retrospect as the last episode of a long saga. Yet for many contemporary Hispano-Christians, it was only a beginning: the start of the reconquest of North Africa. The Straits of Gibraltar were not seen as a natural frontier but as a passage linking two areas which had long been united. The *reconquista* of Iberia was celebrated with the usual grants and gifts from the crown to the nobility whose efforts had been a key to its success. Apart from the titles and promises of lands within Iberia, the monarchs issued titles to Maghrebian possessions and bishoprics, often in response to appeals from the beneficiaries. Their aim was to recreate the Visigothic empire. The vision of an expanded Hispano-Christian world was expressed in Queen Isabel's last testament, in which she enjoined her subjects to continue the fight against Islam by conquering North Africa. Ferdinand supported this policy after her death, albeit fitfully. The struggle against France and the acquisition of Italian lands competed with Maghrebian

---

[1] AGS E. 114 fol. 267.

expansion for scant resources. In addition to other commitments, the Spaniards still managed to take a long line of towns along the Maghrebian coast, the *presidios* of Melilla (1497), Mers-el-Kebir (1505), Peñón de Vélez (1508), Oran (1509), Mostaganem, Tlemcen, Tenes, Peñón de Argel, and Bougie (1510). These ventures were supported by the crown, but most of the finance came from leading nobles, clergy, and urban areas; they also provided most of the manpower, but the bulk of the armies were unpaid volunteers.[2] These posts were intended to serve as bases for the conquest of the interior. When Charles V came to the throne, however, he consistently diverted money and manpower away from the Mediterranean. The garrisons were far too small to expand, or indeed to withstand a major attack. One by one the Spanish outposts fell to the Muslims. By the 1550s only Melilla, Mers-el-Kebir, Oran and Bougie remained of the original conquests, whilst the Peñón de la Goleta (known simply as La Goleta), had been taken in 1535. The fort on the rocky islet outside Tunis was all that was left of Charles's only successful North African enterprise. His campaign had displeased his Spanish subjects, who considered it an 'Italian' venture. This did not mean that they were allowed to withhold contributions. The Spanish regency government maintained constant pressure for expansion in the Maghreb, but their interests lay within a well defined area of central and western lands. Above all they dreamt of the reconquest of Algiers. Ever since the Barbarossa brothers had expelled the Spanish garrison, Spaniards demanded its reconquest. After nearly two decades of pleading and pressure, they finally obtained Charles's support in 1541. The emperor launched a hastily organised campaign late in the season, but it ended in disaster. In Spain there was much criticism of the emperor and a great deal of pressure for a new expedition. The disaster in no way diminished Spanish desire for revenge: in fact it probably increased it. The corts of Valencia even offered to grant Charles extra subsidies for this purpose – an unheard-of gesture from an area that had strongly resisted all other attempts to increase taxation. They expressed their confidence that Catalonia and Aragon would follow suit if he guaranteed that the money would be spent on a campaign against Algiers. Nor did these proposals fade away: as late as May 1554 Philip was asked to consider an invasion of the city-state with the help of one of the military commanders, Ali Sardo, a renegade who wanted to return to Sardinia in comfort and was willing to negotiate with the Spaniards. But Philip had no

---

[2] Isabel's will can be found in DP, this clause, p. 38. The reign of the Catholic monarchs has been admirably dealt with by L. Suárez Fernández and M. Fernández Alvarez, *La España de los Reyes Católicos (1474–1516)*, vol. XVII of *Historia de España* dir. R. Menéndez Pidal; also J. M. Hillgarth, *The Spanish kingdoms*, vol. II, 1410–1516 (Oxford, 1978); The documents published by L. Suárez Fernández, *Política internacional de Isabel la Católica* (4 vols., Valladolid, 1965–71) are also invaluable. The greatest controversy surrounds Ferdinand's commitment to North Africa, J. M. Doussinague has always maintained that this was his chief ambition; see in particular his books: *El testamento politico; La política internacional*; and *La política exterior de España en el siglo XVI* (Madrid, 1949).

enthusiasm for the venture and advised against it. The conquest of Algiers was to remain a chimera for early modern Spain.[3]

The emperor's failure to attend to North Africa remained a source of conflict and tension with the Spaniards. It is true that many Spanish nobles and commoners gradually associated themselves with his aims and vision of expansion against France and within the Holy Roman Empire. But there endured a traditional view that saw the interests of Spain in the south and its natural expansion in Africa.[4]

During the 1550s such dreams and desires coalesced with basic defensive needs. Changes in the political structure of the Maghreb presented the Spanish realms with immediate dangers that necessitated a radical reassessment of Spain's position in the Maghreb. Charles's lengthy absence from the Spanish realms and his lack of interest in Africa go far in accounting for his inability to perceive the rapid deterioration in the position of the Mediterranean lands, but Philip had no excuse. He was in Castile when some of the major changes in the Maghreb occurred, and the Spaniards had high expectations that he would respond to the challenge. This made his subsequent refusal even harder to accept.

Before analysing the conflict between the monarchs and their subjects, an account of the changing situation in the Maghreb is needed. Iberian successes at the turn of the century had depended on Muslim weakness. The Hispano-Christians had exploited the divisions within the enemy camp. They had been able to ignore North Africa subsequently because it was divided among warring tribal groups, more concerned to fight each other than the Christians. By the mid-sixteenth century the Muslims, though still divided, were regrouping. New political units emerged, and a fundamentalist Islamic movement swept through the area. This so-called 'maraboutic revival' led to the rise of many individual religious leaders or marabouts and the founding of a number of extreme sects. It also provided a powerful element in the creation of new states which could lay claim to represent the traditional ideology of holy war – jihad. It is no coincidence that the two most successful Muslim powers in the area during the sixteenth century – the Sa'di and Ottoman dynasties – were led by men who claimed direct descent from the Prophet Muhammad and embodied Ghazi mentality. They were holy warriors committed to endless strife against the enemies of God. Christian forces found themselves face to face with two Muslim states whose *raison d'être* was ceaseless war against infidels.

Four factors are of particular importance in the changing situation in the Maghreb: (a) the emergence of the Sa'di dynasty, (b) the expansion of Ottoman–Algerian forces into Tlemcen, (c) the steady advance of the Ottomans

---

[3] Jóver Zamora, *Carlos V y los españoles*, especially letters from the empress Isabel pp. 87, 124, 135, 137–8, 403–4; R. García Carcel, *Cortes del reinado de Carlos I* (Valencia, 1972), p. 220; the negotiations between Philip and Ali Sardo can be found in AGS E. 98 fol. 142, and fols. 329–39; E. 508 fols. 85–6; E. 1032 fols. 140–2; E. 90 fol. 144.

[4] J. Sánchez Montes, *Franceses, protestantes, turcos, Los españoles ante la política internacional de Carlos V* (Pamplona, 1951); Vanderlinden, 'La politique méditerranéenne'; Jóver Zamora, above.

into the central and western Mediterranean, and (d) the intensification of the conflict between Hispano-Christians and the newly converted Hispano-Muslims, usually referred to as *moriscos, tagarinos* or *mudéjares*.[5] All these factors came together during the 1550s and spelt the end of the favourable conjuncture in the Mediterranean that had enabled the Iberians to expel the moors and expand in the Maghreb.

The expansion of the Sa'di state

The Sa'di dynasty emerged from the obscurity of southern Morocco to the limelight of international politics in little more than three decades. The Sharif Muhammad ash-Shaykh was instrumental in their transformation from tribe to major state. After 1525, using Marrakesh as his base, he moved steadily northwards. Expansion against both Christians and Muslims was justified by fundamental Islamic values: the smaller Muslim states he annexed were accused of heresy or of failing to fulfill their duty to fight the Christians. The Portuguese were among his first victims, but as he came further north and east, he posed a threat to Spanish bases and the exposed southern coast. By 1549 he controlled Fez and Morocco; the following year he invaded Tlemcen. An English resident reported the great fear that swept through the Spanish realms with news of this feat. They believed that 'he mindeth to passe into Spain'. A new phobia had taken root: the fear of another Muslim invasion.[6]

The Sharifian invasion of Fez and Tlemcen presented Spain with concrete, as well as psychological problems. The most important Spanish base in the Maghreb was Oran. Successive governors had been carefully cultivating the local tribes of Tlemcen in order to create a network of alliances which would serve as a buffer around them as well as a regular source of provisions. The latter was especially necessary since food supplies from the mainland were irregular. The commander of Oran, the count of Alcaudete, had recently accepted this post in exchange for the better paid and more prestigious viceroyalty in Navarre. He believed that expansion in the Maghreb was possible and lucrative. He was instrumental in expanding

[5] *Morisco* denotes a baptised Hispano-Muslim; *mudéjar* was the term used for those Muslims remaining within Christian areas after the conquest, but in this period it was also loosely – or pejoratively – used to refer to *moriscos* especially from Valencia.

[6] SIHM Angleterre, vol. I, pp. 11, 12–13. There is a brief account of the Sharif's exploits in A. C. Hess, *The forgotten frontier: a history of the sixteenth century Ibero-African frontier* (Chicago, 1978), pp. 50–3. Detailed accounts can be found in a number of contemporary narratives, often by captives who spent some time in the Maghreb and with the Sharifian forces, the best is D. de Torres, *Relación del origen y suceso de los Xarifes y del estado de los reinos de Marruecos, Fez y Tarudante* (Seville, 1586), edn. of M. García Arenal (Madrid, 1980). L. del Marmol Carvajal, *Primera parte de la descripción general de Africa* (2 vols., Granada 1573); Salazar, *Hispania Victrix*. Details of his movements can be taken from the excellent collection of documents which I have used extensively, *Les sources inédites de l'histoire du Maroc de 1530 à 1845*, ed. H. Castries et al. *Première série: dynastie Sa'dienne* (SIHM).

Spanish influence in Tlemcen, which had become in effect a Spanish protectorate before ash-Shaykh's arrival. Alcaudete's success was due to his skills as a politician and soldier, and his willingness to adapt his tactics. By dint of constant raiding and punitive expeditions he had emerged as a powerful force in Maghrebian politics. When the Sa'di forces swept into the area, almost all the local leaders fled to Oran.[7] Only a few lesser men sought shelter and aid in Algiers, the city-state which represented the other leading Islamic jihadist ruler, the Ottoman sultan. This fact was carefully noted by ash-Shaykh and Suleiman.

From the tattered remnants of the various states that ash-Shaykh had subjugated, one man emerged as the natural leader, Bu Hassun. He soon took the titles of 'king' of Doubdou, Fez and Badis, the three largest political entities recently subsumed by the Sa'di state. Bu Hassun had also taken refuge in Oran, but he realised that it needed more than letters from a distant land to move Charles out of his usual lethargy. He travelled to the emperor's court in Germany to plead his case personally, and from there he was sent by the emperor to Spain. After Charles chose to leave to Philip the final decision whether to commit Spanish forces to Bu Hassun, the chieftain and his followers travelled with Philip and his train.[8] Their enforced proximity did not make Philip any more sympathetic to Bu Hassun's cause, but he did agree to give Bu Hassun a pension of 3,000 ds on condition that one of the Muslim leader's sons be left as a hostage in Castile. It was not a negligible sum, but Bu Hassun was more intent on securing men for immediate action than promises of future funds. It is notable that he asked permission for his 'numerous friends' in Andalucía to be allowed to support his campaign to recover his lands. Bu Hassun was apparently convinced that large numbers of volunteers would come if Philip gave them licence. Certainly Philip did not like this reminder that many crypto-Muslims still resided in the southern realms, nor could he have relished the prospect of seeing able-bodied men depart from the realm as war broke out in the north. Frustrated by the lukewarm response, Bu Hassun went to Portugal, where he found greater awareness of the Sa'di danger and a government willing to respond quickly. The Portuguese were deeply concerned over Sharifian expansion but had few resources to commit to the defence of their North African bases. They welcomed the prospect of local cooperation and made available five ships. They also offered Bu Hassun some soldiers and money, and allowed volunteers to join the expedition.[9] A joint Muslim–Christian venture to reduce the aggressive, expansionist Sa'di state had materialised. Unfortunately for Bu Hassun, the five vessels were spotted by corsairs under Salah Rais, the beylerbey (to the Spanish and Portuguese,

---

[7] AGS E. 479 fols. 126 and 157.

[8] AGS GA. 40 fol. 26; E. 476 s.f. (20 April 1551); E. 476 s.f. (17 November 1551).

[9] SIHM Espagne, vol. ii, pp. 7–8; AGS E. 477 s.f., s.d.; E. 477 s.f. (27 February 1552), Bu Hassun's petition to Philip; E. 477 s.f., Philip to Martín de Córdoba, 6 March 1552; SIHM Espagne, vol. ii, pp. 11–13, 3–6, 38–40; L. de Marmol Carvajal, *Descripción general de Africa*, vol. ii, p. 260v.; Salazar, *Hispania Victrix*, pp. 21v–24.

king) of Algiers. On one of his frequent raids into Spanish waters, he encountered and seized the whole force near Gibraltar. This seemingly minor incident had enormous repercussions.[10]

Landward expansion of the city-state of Algiers

Salah Rais had a distinguished career as an indefatigable fighter against Spain. As beylerbey he represented Ottoman authority in the Maghreb, and the Ottoman state was actively pursuing jihad throughout the known world. The alliance between Algiers and the Ottoman sultan had been forged in the 1520s, when the Greek Barbarossa brothers took the city from Spain and established a corsair base there. Aware that they could not counter Spanish reprisals alone, they turned to the sultan for support. They accepted his suzerainty and from 1529 onwards Algerian coins bore the sultan's symbols. The beylerbey and higher levels of the administration were appointed by the sultan. In exchange for his protection he demanded a base for his fleet, and naval assistance whenever he launched campaigns in the central or western Mediterranean. Although the corsairs were to prove difficult subjects and often disregarded Ottoman requests, the Algerian state was rightly seen as a forward base for Ottoman expansion.[11]

Salah Rais was one of the most successful beylerbeys of the sixteenth century. His violent anti-Spanish sentiments chimed in well with the sultan's determination to crush the Christians. His first reaction on encountering the joint Christian–Muslim force may have been hostile, but Salah Rais was an opportunist. By the time he captured Bu Hassun, the Sharif was in trouble. Supporters of the regimes he had overthrown had pre-empted Bu Hassun's return and started a number of local rebellions. Ash-Shaykh's forces were over-stretched and his lines of communication endangered. Moreover, the Algerian rulers had been gradually expanding inland themselves: like the Spanish garrisons they needed to secure regular supplies. They had fixed their sights on Tlemcen, but expansion in this area was difficult due to the presence of the Spanish base of Oran and its allies. They did not relish the thought of adding a further obstacle in the shape of this aggressive and highly successful Sa'di state. Salah Rais decided to ally with Bu Hassun in order to expel the Sharif. Naturally, Bu Hassun was forced to break his agreement with Portugal. But his betrayal yielded spectacular results: by the end of the 1553 campaign, their extraordinary army composed of Arab, Berber, Ottoman, Hispano-Muslim and corsair forces, had overrun most of Tlemcen and Fez.[12]

---

[10] See the previous note, also AGS E. 478 fol. 147.

[11] Hess, *Forgotten frontier*, pp. 65, 72 for a brief account of the links between Ottomans and Algerian corsairs.

[12] Apart from the standard accounts provided by Torres, L. del Marmol Carvajal and Salazar – see note 6 – the alliance, battles and subsequent split between Salah Rais and Bu Hassun can be followed in AGS E. 478 fol. 147, E. 477 s.f. (Noticias, 8 April 1552), E. 477 s.f., Ali el Elche to Bu Hassun, GA. 51 fol. 155; GA. 55 fol. 99; E. 477 s.f., E. 478 fol. 71 (printed SIHM Espagne II, pp. 93–4, 36, 128–30, 74–6, 128–30, 146–8, 95–6 respectively); also AGS E.478 fols. 24, and 215–16.

Their success brought a new wave of panic to many areas of Spain. In March 1553 a rumour spread that the sultan had agreed to send Salah Rais sixty galleys to support the next campaign in Fez. The rumour was groundless – the sultan had committed both his ships and those of the Algerians to a joint campaign with France that year – nevertheless it provoked great anxiety. The tide was turning in the Maghreb: during 1554 the Sa'dis recovered sufficiently to make a stand in Fez. The city, like the kingdom, was now divided between the two Muslim groups. Still confident of success, Salah Rais decided to rid himself of Bu Hassun. Unfortunately for the corsair, the assassination attempt failed. Aware of his complicity but unable to retaliate in force, Bu Hassun and his supporters pressed the Algerians to leave. This proverbial falling out among thieves had some startling results: Salah Rais now offered his alliance to the Sharif. Henceforth the Christian forces feared the fusion of the Sa'di and corsair states. They need not have worried, because ash-Shaykh contemptuously rejected the beylerbey's approach, and Salah Rais returned to Algiers. Some two thousand Ottoman mercenaries chose to remain with Bu Hassun, but they were insufficient to prevent a successful counter-attack by ash-Shaykh. In the encounters that followed, Bu Hassun was killed and the Sharifian forces re-occupied Fez and most of Tlemcen: only the strategic position of the Peñon de Vélez remained in Algerian hands. Until 1564, Algerian corsairs used this base to launch devastating attacks against the nearby Spanish coast.

Juana and members of the state councils met to discuss the situation. She forwarded their recommendations to Charles on 3 October 1554.[13] The councils concluded that the Spanish realms faced the greatest threat they had seen for decades. There was still time to act: the Sa'di state had not yet acquired a navy, and the Ottoman–corsairs were still severely hampered by their poor land forces. Ash-Shaykh had once said (and not without contempt), that Suleiman was the sultan of fishermen, since he made war only at sea.[14] The events of 1553–4 had forced him and the Spanish government to reassess their opinion of the Ottoman threat; it was clear now that with local help, the Algerians were capable of landward expansion.

Both the Christian and Muslim leaders reacted in a similar fashion: they immediately identified the Algerians as the most dangerous enemy in the Maghreb – behind Salah Rais they could all see the sultan's shadow. Fear of Ottoman–corsair expansion led both ash-Shaykh and Bu Hassun to turn to Spain for support. The latter warned the Spanish government just before his death that Suleiman had decided to send the entire Ottoman fleet to the western Mediterranean in 1555, where he expected support from the French fleet. His strategy was simple. First he intended to take Fez because he needed a base to launch an invasion of Spain.[15] Even before this warning arrived, Juana and the councillors were convinced that the danger to Spain required immediate action. Unaware of Bu Hassun's death, they asked Charles for permission to conclude an offensive–defensive alliance with him

[13] AGS E. 103(2) fols. 397–8.   [14] Cit. Hess, *Forgotten frontier*, p. 45.   [15] AGS E. 104 fols. 70–1.

or ash-Shaykh. Juana informed her father that they would need one or both Muslim leaders to halt the Ottoman–corsair advance, which had to be stopped in the Maghreb since Spain itself was too weak to withstand an invasion. Letters and the petitions of the corts and cortes paint a grim picture of the landward defences in Spain at this time. Wages were in arrears, soldiers deserted in despair: the permanent garrisons in Spain were dangerously weak. The cortes of Castile had repeatedly asked for improvement of the kingdom's defences. They feared in particular for the coasts of Biscay, Guipúzcoa, and Galicia in the north, which were constantly harassed by French pirates and corsairs; and those of Andalucía (especially Granada) in the south, where Muslim corsairs abounded. The Aragonese knew from bitter experience how vulnerable the Valencian and Catalan coastlines were to corsair attacks.[16] The defence budget had been cut consistently since 1551 as resources were diverted to the northern front.

All this rankled, but even more resentment had been aroused by Charles's decision to keep the Spanish fleet in Italian waters. During his regency, Philip had written countless letters to his father begging for the return of the Spanish galleys, even if they only came to winter in the realm. Their presence for even part of the year was thought to act as a useful deterrent.[17] Juana was not slow to take up the call for the return of the fleet when she took over the regency in 1554. Both she and other officials had high hopes of securing this concession since they expected Philip to support their request. To their surprise and dismay, Philip radically altered his opinion after leaving Spain. Once he had been given charge of Naples and Milan, his primary concern was to protect the Italian realms. He now vehemently opposed the division of Charles's naval forces and insisted that they must be retained in Italy. In general terms, he also subscribed to his father's opinion that the only conflicts that really mattered were the wars in Italy and the north. He did not alter his opinion or seriously consider the return of the Spanish galleys to their home ports until the peace negotiations with France were well underway in 1559.[18] Both Philip and Charles adhered to their belief that the call for stronger defences in Spain was a psychological, not a real need. Neither could be persuaded that a second Islamic invasion was imminent.

The Ottoman advance and the Franco–Ottoman alliance

The one threat that Charles and Philip did take seriously was the Ottoman fleet, and this was largely because it was inseparably linked in their minds with French power

[16] AGS E. 108 fols. 155–9; Carande, *Carlos V y sus banqueros*, vol. III, p. 453. *Real Academia de la Historia, Cortes de los antiguous reinos de León y Castilla* (5 vols., Madrid, 1882) see vol. 5, pp. 627–8 for the complaints in 1555. S. García Martínez, *Bandolerismo, piratería y control de moriscos en Valencia durante el reinado de Felipe II* (Valencia, 1977).

[17] e.g. AGS E. 97 fols. 53–63; many other examples may be taken from the letters published by Fernández Alvarez, *Corpus*, vols. 3 and 4.

[18] AGS E. 104 fol. 92; E. 808 fol. 82; E. 114 fols. 57–60; E. 130 fol. 233.

in the Mediterranean. Contacts between the French and the Ottomans dated as far back as 1525, after the captivity of Francis I at Pavia. They were intensified when the Genoese defected to Charles in 1528, but did not bear fruit until some ten years later. Since Venice refused to join either side, the French had no alternative but to turn to the Ottomans in an effort to redress the balance of naval forces in the Mediterranean in their favour. In 1536 the French king and Ottoman sultan concluded a trading agreement and launched the first of many joint expeditions in the Mediterranean – this time against the Balearic islands. Four years later the Christian world was stunned when Francis allowed Barbarossa, ex-corsair king of Algiers, now the commander of the Ottoman fleet, to winter in Toulon. When Henry II came to power he sought to renew and increase naval cooperation with the Muslims by granting subsidies. In 1551 he proposed a joint attack and the occupation of Mallorca. He hoped to convince Suleiman that a joint base there would enable them to dominate Spain.[19] The Ottoman fleet along with some corsair vessels duly joined the French fleet in 1552. The expedition against Mallorca was a fiasco, however, because the three groups were unable to coordinate their movements effectively. It seems likely that Henry intended to use the combined fleets in Naples that summer, but the revolt so confidently predicted (and promised) by the prince of Salerno failed to materialise. Sinan Pasha, commander of the Ottoman fleet, decided that they could make no major gains and departed, pursued by the irate French commanders who felt that they had got nothing for their money. Bad weather caught up with the French fleet near Chios, and they decided to winter there. The prince of Salerno was on board, and he, along with French and Italian dignitaries, travelled to Constantinople and presented their plans personally to the sultan. According to one spy, Salerno promised to hand over Naples itself. One can only conjecture if memories of the Ottoman occupation of Otranto in 1480–2 had a part in prompting the sultan to cooperate. Suleiman was certainly receptive to their proposals. His ships had taken seven of Doria's galleys that summer in a feat widely acclaimed in the Ottoman world, which now boasted that one Muslim ship was worth at least two Christian ones. The sultan agreed to further cooperation and ordered the corsairs of Algiers and those associated with the Turkish corsair Dragut to join the Franco–Ottoman fleets for the following campaign.[20]

Relations between the Muslims and the French were strained. The former disparagingly referred to their Christian allies as 'new Turks', echoing the Spanish name for newly converted Muslims ('new Christians').[21] There were many sources of conflict. Nevertheless, the two sides could function effectively if pressed by their respective rulers. The real problem was the corsairs, who were rather cavalier when

[19] AGS GA. 40 fol. 46; E. 476 s.f. (16 July 1551), E. 306 fol. 280. A. C. Hess, 'The evolution of the Ottoman seaborne empire, 1453–1525', *American Historical Review*, 75 (1970), pp. 1892–1919; C. Imber, 'The navy of Suleyman the Magnificent', *Archivum Ottomanicum*, VI (1980), pp. 211–82.
[20] AGS E. 478 fol. 93; E. 1042 fol. 75; Braudel, *The Mediterranean*, vol. II, p. 924.
[21] AGS E. 478 fols. 93 and 98.

it came to obeying the orders of their distant sovereign. Salah Rais had been told to present himself and his ships for the joint campaign in 1553. Instead, he indulged in his usual raids against Spain and later launched wars against the Sharif. Dragut, who was eager to establish a rival corsair state and had established similar links of vassalage with the sultan, did appear. But he was determined to use the French rather than obey. Dragut's problem was finding a good base in the central Mediterranean. He had tried Mahdia (see p. 269) but he had been expelled from it, now he wanted Tunis. He proposed a joint attack on the Spanish *presidio* of La Goleta, which dominated the city. The French rejected the proposal; hoping to change their minds, Dragut refused to sail unless they agreed to the attack. In the end, a bribe of some 10,000 es persuaded him to join the Franco Ottoman flect in their attack against the emperor's Italian lands. Dragut's forces employed such brutality in these attacks, however, that the prince of Salerno protested. Since Dragut would not desist and the campaign had yielded little thus far, the joint commanders tried to ease the situation by focusing on another target: Corsica. Corsican exiles led by Sampiero Corso had fled from Genoese domination and taken service with the French fleet. With their help and guidance, the island was overrun in a few weeks, a fine demonstration of what the combined fleets could do when acting in unison. But Dragut's tactics had not changed, and Sampiero Corso was emphatic that the Muslims must not continue to ravage the island and harass its people. Tired of these disputes and restrictions as well as overloaded with more than 4,000 Christian slaves from their raids that summer, Dragut and his men left just before the last town was subdued. The sultan and king of France were inundated with bitter recriminations from both sides.[22]

These problems should not obscure the vitality of the Franco–Ottoman alliance. Both rulers favoured further joint ventures, but their experiences thus far had taught them some unexpected lessons that affected their subsequent cooperation. The Christian forces realised by 1554 that the corsairs were now so powerful that the French did not need the Ottoman fleet to tip the balance in the Mediterranean if the corsairs joined them. The Genoese also informed Charles that the Franco–Algerian fleets could overwhelm their own.[23] In July 1554 a Franco–Algerian fleet mounted a spectacular raid against Veste in which three thousand Italians were seized. The cardinal of Siguenza was so depressed by these raids that he asked the king to pardon the prince of Salerno and allow him to return to Naples, in order to reduce the attacks against the realm.[24] Similarly, the Ottomans became more confident of their ability to act without French support. In

---

[22] AGS E. 478 fols. 98, 100, and 215–16; Braudel, *The Mediterranean*, vol. II p. 928 suggests that the imperialists bribed Dragut and secured his departure, but I have come across no other evidence of this. See pp. 111–13 for the repercussions of the invasion.

[23] R. Ciasca (ed.), *Istruzione e relazioni degli ambasciatori genovesi* (vol. I, Spagna, 1494–1617, Rome, 1951), vol. I, p. 145.   [24] BPR II. 2285 fols. 53–4.

1555 their ships made spectacular raids against Calabria, Messina, Porto Santo Stefano, Piombino and the Stromboli islands. Even the pope was forced to admit that this was novel. He remarked that the Ottomans 'know our homelands and our shores better than we do'. He lamented their regular descent into central and western Mediterranean waters: they were getting too close for comfort.[25] In 1557, Juan de Vega, viceroy of Sicily, eloquently expressed the changing perception of the Ottoman threat when he recalled that in the past people spoke of the Ottomans as if they lived in the Antipodes. In the last thirty or forty years, however, they had become a regular part of everyone's life. They were all but neighbours, and so well informed that they knew what was happening in the Spanish and Italian Mediterranean possessions as quickly as the Spanish government.[26]

Although most of these Ottoman or Franco–Ottoman attacks had been directed against the Italian possessions, the impression prevalent in the Spanish realms was that they were preparatory moves to facilitate the major objective – the invasion of Iberia.

Tensions between the 'Old' and 'New' Christians in Spain

The obsession with a new Islamic invasion of Spain was heightened not only by the parlous Spanish defences, but also by the awareness of how vulnerable the southern and eastern regions were to a simultaneous attack and internal rebellion. Valencia and Granada were particularly exposed since they had the largest *morisco* populations, often settled in areas with few, if any, old Christian inhabitants. Tension between the old Christians and recently converted moors had increased substantially during the first half of the sixteenth century. Not until the edicts of 1525–6 ending toleration in Aragon, Catalonia and Valencia was Spain officially rid of Islam. The Castilian realms had forced conversion somewhat earlier – in 1501–2. Whilst many Hispano-Muslims had chosen exile, the majority opted to remain in their homes and receive baptism. But with few provisions made for teaching or enforcement of Christianity, they remained firmly attached to their old customs and practices. Dissatisfaction with Christian pressure led many *moriscos* to leave in the following years. Charles was accommodating, encouraging flight rather than resistance, and allowing *morisco* communities to evade the unwelcome attentions of the Inquisition in exchange for outward conformity and annual cash payments. But the mood of secular and religious authorities was becoming increasingly hostile to this policy. As the corsair attacks increased, Christians believed that the exiled Spaniards were largely to blame. They realised that there were close contacts

---

[25] AGS E. 882 fol. 44, Paul's conversation with the Spanish envoy in July 1555. The attacks: AGS E. 1123 fols. 4, 37, 48; E. 1208 fol. 20. [26] Weiss, *Granvelle*, vol. 5, p. 165.

between the exiles and *moriscos* still at home. The external threat and internal problem were two sides of the same coin.[27]

Collusion between *morisco* and corsair was real and inevitable. Many of those who had left Spain maintained contacts with relatives and friends and had every reason to seek revenge on their Christian enemies. They were ideal corsairs because they had access to information and could pass as locals when necessary to obtain supplies or news. Most importantly, they knew the coastline. One example suffices to illustrate cooperation between the corsairs and the increasingly marginal *morisco* population. A raid was carried out by two foists in the summer of 1555. They set off from the Peñon de Vélez in ships manned by local moors, a few Turks, and Valencian exiles. They picked up a *mudéjar* in Ceuta who acted as their guide and was probably related to one of the exiles. Together they drew up a battle plan including some five or six isolated hamlets on the Valencian coast, which they attacked in the usual dawn raids.[28] Many local authorities uncovered similar instances of such cooperation and this led them to challenge the emperor's policy of encouraging dissidents to leave Spain.[29] By 1550 there was a widespread belief that each *morisco* who left was a corsair in the making, and each *morisco* who remained was a potential supporter and abettor of corsair attacks. The identification of *morisco* and corsair became axiomatic. The desire to eliminate the corsair threat had severe repercussions for the *moriscos*; but the reverse was also true. Fear of *morisco* insurrection heightened the sense of imminent attack from Islamic powers. Those who hated the newly converted moors on religious and racial grounds focused their attention on the corsairs, on events in North Africa and the Mediterranean at large. Consequently, the frequent descent of the Ottoman fleet added fuel to the fire. According to the inquisitor Gregorio Miranda, who believed himself to be the only man trying to control the *morisco* problem in Valencia, these Ottoman attacks had stiffened *morisco* opposition and made them more determined than ever to hold on to their faith and customs. They had high hopes that they would be able to secure corsair and Ottoman aid and reassert Muslim control over parts of Spain.[30]

As a result of these developments, the *morisco* problem was given far greater prominence during the 1550s. Areas affected by the corsairs became highly sensitive

[27] The experiences of the *moriscos* are dealt with by A. Dominguez Ortiz and B. Vincent, *Historia de los moriscos* (Madrid, 1978); L. Cardaillac, *Moriscos y cristianos. Un enfrentamiento polémico (1492–1640)* (Paris, 1977, Spanish edn. Madrid, 1979), especially ch. 2, pp. 105–18. Hess, *Forgotten frontier*, pp. 129–55; A. C. Hess, 'The Moriscos: an Ottoman fifth column in sixteenth century Spain', *American Historical Review*, 74 (1968), pp. 1–25. E. Belenguer Cebriá, *La problemática del cambio político en la España de Felipe II. Puntualizaciones sobre su cronología* (Bellaterra, 1980), pp. 18–28. M. S. Carrasco Urgoiti, *El problema morisco en Aragón al comienzo del reinado de Felipe II* (Valencia, 1969). The laws against them can be found in the *Segunda parte de las leyes del reino* (Alcalá de Henares, 1567), book 8, title ii, law iiii (sic), fols. 148v–9v. García Martínez, *Bandolerismo, piratería, y control de moriscos en Valencia*.

[28] AGS E. 476 s.f., 'El dicho del Turco', 4 July 1555. Foists were small oared vessels, with about 10–12 benches.

[29] AGS E. 1324 fols. 85–6, e.g., Viaje de Turquía, pp. 451–2.   [30] AGS E. 306 fols. 118 and 120.

to changes in the Ottoman threat and the strength of the *morisco* communities. One other element contributed to the greater attention paid to these issues: during his regency, Philip had shown interest in taking action against the *moriscos*. In 1552 he summoned a group of theologians to discuss the situation in Valencia, still considered the most vulnerable area. Two years later, he gathered leading secular and religious figures in Guadix to discuss Granada. The commissions recommended a radical change of policy to offer equal measures of proselytising and punishment. Their underlying assumption was that the *morisco* problem was getting out of hand as a result of the growing success of the Islamic powers.[31]

In other words, by the 1550s the Spanish authorities – and not just popular opinion – had come to regard the *morisco*, corsair, Ottoman and North African situation as different aspects of the same basic Islamic threat. The one element which was present in all was the corsair. The greater the frequency of their attacks, the more powerfully shame and dishonour took hold of many a Spaniard. As St Tomás de Villanueva once remarked, it was a great dishonour that so large a kingdom should be continually harassed and devastated by a 'petty king', that is the Algerian beylerbey.[32] But, as the inquisitor Corro pertinently stated, the worst of the matter was that the Spanish realms should continue to give the king so much money, and that he should fail to spend even a small part of what was paid in taxes for the defence of the Spanish realms. He begged Juana to persuade Philip to set aside some of this money and use it for the purpose it had been granted: protection against Islamic aggression.[33] Shame, anger, frustration, fear: these were the potent feelings behind the demand for action against Spain's Islamic enemies.

But the world looked very different to Philip's eyes. He was obsessed with establishing his reputation against France, and lacked the interest and proximity to give the Islamic threat much thought. Throughout this decade he continued to regard it as a series of distinct problems all of which required different solutions. He never understood how the Spaniards had come to fuse these elements into one fearful threat. For him the *moriscos* were essentially an internal, religious problem which could be solved by better ecclesiastical organisation and an effective inquisition fully supported by the lay authorities. As for the corsairs, they were primarily a threat to commerce and communications, and Philip felt that the mercantile community had as much responsibility as the government to repel or counter their attacks. He did not see corsairs as a national danger, and like Charles he sought to saddle the merchants and the areas most affected by their attacks with the bill for building watch towers and providing additional defence. The localities and merchants complained bitterly. They argued with some force that they already paid ordinary and extraordinary taxation, which the crown was supposed to use for defence of the realms, not in distant conflicts. The one problem that Philip (and

---

[31] AGS E. 97 fols. 119–20; E. 308 s.f. (Charles to Philip 18 September 1552); see the references in note 27, especially Cardaillac, Belenguer Cebriá and García Martínez.
[32] Codoin, vol. 5, p. 100.   [33] AGS E. 110 fol. 267.

Charles before him) recognised as important to all and therefore the duty of the crown, was the Ottoman fleet. Both believed that the only way to counter this threat was to keep all their ships and allied vessels in Italy to intercept the enemy. The Spaniards complained that this exposed them to countless attacks from the corsairs and North African powers. Philip agreed that this was regrettable, but consistently rejected the Spanish notion that there was a real or immediate danger of invasion from the Maghrebian states, the corsairs, or the Franco–Muslim fleets.

THE ATTACK AGAINST THE SPANISH SETTLEMENTS IN NORTH AFRICA

When the regency government appealed for permission to take action in the Maghreb in 1554, Charles consulted with Philip. Philip expressed his regret at the Sa'di occupation of Fez, and admitted that the recommendations made by Juana and the council of war for immediate military intervention in the Maghreb were sound if viewed in terms of Spanish defence. Unfortunately, other commitments must take priority, namely the struggle against France and in Italy. The Mediterranean states would have to wait until the 'situation was more favourable'. In the meanwhile, he advised Charles to refuse permission for Spanish intervention. Charles clearly liked his son's recommendations since he ordered his secretary to copy most of this letter and send it as if it were his own considered response to Juana in January 1555. In a separate letter, Philip expressed sympathy for their plight and assured Juana that he was aware of the problems, but he reiterated that they must avoid direct involvement in Maghrebian politics for the time being.[34] However, he encouraged the regency government to follow up the unofficial talks that the count of Alcaudete had initiated with the Sharif. This is one of many instances when Philip tried to defuse discontent in his lands and divert pressure for action by allowing them to negotiate an alliance that gave hope for the future.

By the summer of 1555, ash-Shaykh and Alcaudete had hammered out an agreement acceptable to the regency government. Juana at once demanded official recognition of the talks and powers to conclude the alliance. Her request was strongly supported by the Portuguese government. João III was extremely anxious to reduce his commitments in North Africa and stem the danger from the Sharif. He was willing to join the Spaniards in an alliance with his erstwhile enemy in order to avert the greater danger of Ottoman–corsair control of the neighbouring states of Tlemcen and Fez. The Portuguese were not happy with the conditions being offered by ash-Shaykh, but, as the infante Dom Luis pointed out, time was running out. If the Christian powers delayed any longer, the situation would be transformed beyond remedy with Ottoman–corsair forces in control of the two areas.[35] A sense of

[34] Philip's position can be found in AGS E. 808 fol. 82; E. 809 fol. 75; Charles's AGS E. 809 fol. 37.
[35] AGS E. 377 fols. 145–6. The negotiations between Alcaudete and the Sharifians can be followed in SIHM Espagne, vol. II, pp. 191–201, 208–10, 218–19, 270–84 and AGS E. 479 fol. 115, E. 108 fol. 8; the Portuguese position AGS E. 108 fols. 57–8; SIHM Portugal, vol. V, pp. 34–8, SIHM Espagne, vol. II, pp. 253–4, 251–2.

urgency pervaded these discussions as the Iberians appreciated that they had been lucky. Salah Rais had been recalled by Suleiman to Constantinople, thus reducing the danger from Algiers for a time. The sultan was angry because he had failed to obey the summons to join the Franco–Ottoman fleet, and worried that his beylerbey had become involved in a war against a fellow Ghazi leader. But Salah Rais justified his actions so successfully that Suleiman soon restored him as beylerbey of Algiers and sent him back with promises of further aid. The Iberian powers were conscious that they must organise themselves before the Ottoman–corsair forces could regroup.[36] Their efforts were hindered, however, by the determination of both Charles and Philip to stall any action.

Salah Rais returned from his talks with the sultan armed with greater authority and a new strategy. One of its salient characteristics was the emphasis on jihad. No sooner had he arrived than he publicised his intention to lead a holy war and rid the Maghreb of infidels. The call worked as well for him as it had for the Sa'di chiefs. The Ottoman–corsair state had not been popular with local tribes; in fact there had been constant conflict. Now they were joined in a common cause. The new strategy required different tactics. In order to capitalise on the contributions of neighbouring tribes, the campaign would have to be a land war, with the corsair ships providing support rather than being the first line of attack. The war against the infidel thus served two important ends: it would be used to extend the power and influence of the Ottoman–corsair state over the Maghrebian tribes; and it would eradicate the chief impediment to the Algerian conquest of Tlemcen, the Spanish *presidios*.

The Spanish bases were in no state to resist a major assault. The defence cuts had struck them as severely as in the peninsular garrisons, if not worse. It was estimated in 1554 that Spain needed to provide a minimum of 150,000 ds per annum to maintain them, but wage arrears in 1553 had already exceeded 130,000 ds. The impact was uneven: in July 1552, for instance Alonso Peralta, captain-governor of Bougie, reported that the workers in the garrison had not been paid for four years – the soldiers' pay was also several months in arrears.[37] Essential repairs on fortifications had not been carried out for lack of funds. The conditions in the *presidios* were so appalling – Alcaudete himself thought them worse than those of galley slaves – that they did not attract recruits.[38] The fortifications were invariably undermanned and the soldiers of poor quality. Desertion was frequent and morale was low.

Bougie, 1555

All the *presidios* suffered from neglect. Bougie was no worse than the rest in many respects, but it was certainly in a sorry state by 1555. The soldiers had not been

[36] AGS E. 478 s.f. (SIHM Espagne, vol. II, pp. 181–2); AGS E. 478 fols. 215–16; E. 808 fol. 82.
[37] AGS E. 477 s.f.
[38] AGS E. 103 fol. 35; E. 480 fol. 310, E. 481 fol. 252, E. 130 fol. 78, E. 482 fol. 103.

properly paid since 1551. Hunger had driven them to attack neighbouring tribes repeatedly. Most of the garrison had been captured or killed in one raid in 1552. Although some vacant posts had been filled, the government had failed to provide them with victuals in 1554 and 1555. Through a combination of desertion and disease, the garrison was only at half strength when danger struck. Juana was sufficiently worried in the summer of 1555 to dispatch an emergency shipment with soldiers and money. The men arrived ill; the money was insufficient to pay off the soldiers' debts. Salah Rais knew all this. Spies and local merchants kept him informed; but they also traded information with the Christians.[39] Alcaudete told the regency government that Salah Rais was thought to be planning an attack against Bougie, but this was no more than a smokescreen. His real target was Oran.[40] The vehement assurances of each local commander that he alone was in danger made it extremely difficult for the regency government to assess the situation accurately. Alcaudete's pleas were usually taken seriously since they all realised that Oran was the strongest of the Spanish positions and therefore must rank among Salah Rais's most urgent priorities. In this instance they were wrong. Supported by large numbers of local tribesmen and his corsair ships, Salah Rais besieged Bougie by land and sea.[41]

As soon as news of the siege reached court, the government sought to organise a relief force, but the crisis merely highlighted the appalling state of Spain's defences. The most the Spaniards could do in time was to fit out the four galleys maintained by the military order of Santiago. Since no other galleys were available, Juana ordered all foists and brigantines along the southern coast to be seized and prepared for the relief of Bougie. Four thousand men who were ready to go to the Italian front were ordered to new embarkation points for immediate dispatch to Bougie. Further levies were planned. Juana also sent a desperate appeal to the duke of Alba in Naples, asking him to send part of the fleet immediately to relieve the *presidio*.[42] These feverish preparations were to no avail. Before any ships had sailed to its relief, Bougie capitulated. The men had simply refused to fight against such overwhelming odds. The shock in the Spanish realms was immense.

Two major issues were at once raised by this defeat: the weakness of Spanish defences, particularly the absence of her fleet; and the value of the North African bases. The discussion soon extended to a general debate of the Spanish position in the Maghreb and the desirability of intervention there.

[39] AGS E. 89 fols. 50–6, E. 479 fol. 213. Bougie was supposed to have a peacetime garrison of 500 men and required at least 722 men to withstand assault, AGS E. 476 s.f. 'Relacion'; AGS E. 478 fol. 152 (pub. SIHM Espagne, vol. II, pp. 104–6).   [40] AGS E. 480 fol. 119.

[41] An account of the siege may be found in L. del Marmol Carvajal, *Segunda parte de la descripción general de Africa* (Malaga, 1599), II, f. 225; D. Haedo, *Topographia e historia general de Argel* (Valladolid, 1612), 'Epitome' fols. 68v–69. Braudel, *The Mediterranean*, vol. II, p. 934. It can be followed in detail in the official correspondence between the local officials and regency government: AGS E. 479 fol. 224 (17 September 1555), E. 479 fol. 227 (11 September), E. 479 fol. 229 (id), E. 479 fol. 230 (5 September), E. 479 fol. 232 (11 August), E. 479 fol. 233 (11 September), E. 479 fol. 35 (16 October).   [42] AGS E. 1049 fol. 11; Alba, *Epistolario*, vol. I, p. 390.

Once again it was Philip, not Charles who took the important decision. He had never been an ardent supporter of the *presidios*. Indeed, he had led the agitation to abandon Mahdia which was under Habsburg control from 1550 to 1554. Mahdia (or Africa as it was then called), had been taken by Dragut in 1550. The governments of both Sicily and Naples at once expressed grave alarm, since Dragut had already acquired a reputation as a redoubtable corsair. The new base would facilitate his attacks against Italian shores. They were also aware of his contacts with the Ottomans. They appealed to Charles for immediate action and, as the imperial fleet had nothing to do at the time, he allowed them to launch an attack. On 10 September 1550, imperial troops marched into the port. Only then were important questions asked – who would maintain the base and how much would it cost? These questions became all the more pertinent after it was decided that the garrison would need to be around 1,500 men and the annual cost some 88,000 es. This elevated Mahdia to the status of second most important base along the Maghreb. There was no doubt that Mahdia had been acquired to safeguard the Italian states, but Charles believed that neither Sicily nor Naples could afford to maintain it. Spain was simply ordered to take full responsibility for this new base.[43] The decision was heatedly contested by Philip, who was then regent in Spain.

The issue was further complicated by the conflict over La Goleta. Sicily had provided a share of the funds required to maintain this fortification since 1535. However, it had found the burden increasingly intolerable and Spain had been left to shoulder more of it until, from 1552 onwards, it was forced to cover all expenditure.[44] This was resented by the Spaniards, who believed that it was only fair that *presidios* intended for the defence of the Italian states should be financed by them. Unable to reconcile the needs of his states, Charles offered Mahdia to the Knights of St John on the same conditions that he had given them the island of Malta. But they turned it down. The debate over the North African bases intensified as the imperial councillors clashed over the fate of this new conquest.[45] Philip's reluctance to burden the Spanish realms further partly accounts for his vehement advocacy of immediate withdrawal and destruction of Mahdia. Granvelle claimed that his intervention was instrumental in pushing the unwilling Charles to order the town to be razed to the ground in 1554. There was more to this than concern for Spanish finances. But Philip's subsequent actions also show that he failed to appreciate the role played by the *presidios* in Spanish defence.

The advisers of Philip and Charles readily agreed that Mahdia was of considerable strategic importance, especially as a base from which to conquer the

[43] AGS E. 478 s.f. includes an estimate of Mahdia's needs; later it was reduced to 20,000es. per annum. The story of the conquest and fall of Mahdia, A. Paz y Melia, *Series de los más importante documentos del Archivo y Biblioteca del Excmo. Sr Duque de Medinaceli* (2 vols., Madrid, 1922), vol. II, pp. 369–71; AGS E. 476 s.f. s.d. 'Nueba de Berberia' and others. Braudel, *The Mediterranean*, vol. II, pp. 908–10 for a brief account.   [44] AGS E. 89 fols. 36–40, Philip to Charles, 4 April 1552.
[45] AGS E. 89 fols. 36–40, Philip to Charles, 4 April 1552. The various proposals for the future of Mahdia AGS E. 1120 fol. 59, E. 478 fol. 186, E. 1322 fol. 73.

neighbouring states of Kairouan and Tunis. Indeed one group insisted that unless the emperor was ready to finance an expansionist policy in the area, it was pointless to retain the place. Juan de Vega and Sancho de Leiva (an experienced soldier) led those who favoured the retention of the port because they believed in the wisdom and necessity of establishing a protectorate over Tunis and Kairouan. They were supported by others less concerned with Mahdia but interested in having the emperor adopt a more aggressive policy in North Africa. This view received unexpected support when the garrison of Mahdia mutinied. The mutineers, tired of instability and starved of supplies, organised themselves into a disciplined group. They used raids and diplomacy, integrated into local politics, and for the first time the base was properly supplied and able to exert considerable regional influence.[46] The success of the mutineers encouraged the local Spanish commanders who were constantly advocating a more active policy and frequent raids. The government, on the other hand, ever conscious of the need to reduce expenditure and anxious to avoid major conflicts, invariably restrained them.

In other words, a year before the fall of Bougie, leading royal councillors had been debating the role of the *presidios* and the wisdom of taking the offensive in North Africa. Almost to a man they had agreed that these bases served little or no purpose as they were. Opponents of North African intervention included men who thought them a waste of money, a relic of the past, and wished to withdraw from the area. They won the first round of the struggle when Charles finally acquiesced in the destruction of Mahdia. Supporters of North African expansion were more determined than ever after 1554 to arrest this process of gradual disengagement. The fall of Bougie merely confirmed that unless positive action was taken, the other bases would soon have to be abandoned or lost. But it also provided those in favour of intervention and expansion with an admirable opportunity to recover lost ground: they were able to cloak their proposals for intervention behind the call for the recovery of the *presidio*.

The reaction of the Spanish realms to the loss of Bougie has been variously described as a sharp spasm of disappointment and the expression of wounded pride.[47] But it was really a great deal more. Fear gripped Valencia and Catalonia, the areas most likely to be affected by the installation of a major corsair base in Bougie. More widespread was the sense of anger and frustration. The violent reaction suggests that tension had been building up for many years. Many Spaniards still believed that North Africa was their true goal, their natural sphere of influence. Even more thought that the worst threat facing them was an invasion from North Africa. Since the regency government was itself in favour of taking the initiative in the Maghreb, they were quick to respond to the popular outcry. Later they used popular pressure to promote and justify their policy. Their immediate reaction to

---

[46] See notes 43, 45.
[47] Cabrera de Córdoba, *Felipe II*, vol. I, p. 42; Braudel, *The Mediterranean*, vol. II, p. 34.

the rapid fall of Bougie was to make an example of the captain-governor and leading officials. Salah Rais, eager to rub salt into an open wound, had enslaved the common soldiers and workers but sent the leading officials to Spain. On their arrival, without consulting Charles or Philip, Juana initiated legal proceedings against them. The haste with which they had capitulated led to accusations of cowardice and treason. She ensured the immediate execution of Peralta and harsh sentences for the others, ranging from exile to fines and confiscation of property. Juana informed her superiors that if she had waited for the necessary powers, procedural delays would have offended the Spanish people, who wanted to see justice done quickly. Her letters repeatedly referred to the great bitterness and sorrow voiced in Castile and Aragon when news of the tragedy was made public.

More significant than punishment of the Bougie officials was the decision of the regency government to organise a campaign for 'the recovery of Bougie and the conquest of Algiers'. From the very beginning, Juana and the Spanish councils spoke of the two as if they were inseparable.[48] In November 1555 Juana launched a nationwide appeal. She announced the government's determination to organise a campaign in the spring of 1556 for the recovery of Bougie and Algiers. Since the government had no funds, nobles, towns, institutions, and the clergy were asked to contribute what they could: money, soldiers, munitions and victuals. Suitable texts for sermons were also sent to ensure that the people at large were informed and aware of the need for their contributions and cooperation. The response was heartening. Unfortunately only partial accounts survive, and most give details of what was actually collected two years after the appeal. Since the time lapse and the intervening famine reduced contributions, these figures understate the total offered. The government eventually collected at least 150,000 ds in cash; the archbishop of Toledo offered a loan of 300,000 ds, thus emulating his predecessor, who had played a key role in the conquest of Oran. Large quantities of grain, wine, oil and other provisions were given, and 8–10,000 volunteers eventually fought without pay in the Maghreb, most of them providing their own arms and victuals, for themselves and their tenants and friends.[49] The willingness of the Spanish people to provide an additional levy reflects not only their desire to recover Bougie and their military reputation, but also their determination to capture Algiers itself.

Juana had not requested permission to make the appeal, and did not inform her father or brother until it was clear that the response was positive. Nor was this the only factor working in favour of intervention in the Maghreb. Despite Philip's

[48] AGS E. 119 fol. 121; E. 108 fol. 236, E. 119 fol. 117, E. 112 fol. 65, E. 480 fol. 166, E. 113 fol. 108; details of the punishment of officials, E. 480 fol. 129.

[49] See AGS GA. 1321 fol. 35ss; E. 110 fol. 10; E. 101(1) fols. 6–13; E. 109 fols. 218–19; E. 481 fols. 1–5 account of 30 April 1556; E. 114 fols. 251, 211–13, account of September; E. 127 fols. 107–9; E. 133 fols. 45–6. Note that the volunteers were of excellent quality. Silíceo's contribution, AGS E. 109 fols. 83–5; E. 113 fol. 113; E. 483 fols. 263–4; Codoin, vol. 38, pp. 567–74, E. 114 fols. 177–8. Philip seized the money later to pay off debts incurred in the French war, contrary to the archbishop's will, AGS E. 113 fols. 110–11.

refusal to give official sanction to the negotiations with the Sharif, Juana had encouraged them. Ash-Shaykh was convinced that he would soon be attacked by the Ottoman–corsair forces again and he was eager to conclude an alliance. He wanted 12,000 Spanish soldiers and was willing to pay 44,000 es in advance, plus an additional 36,000 es per month during the campaign. Such generosity presented an opportunity too good to miss.[50] When Philip was confronted with details of the appeal and the negotiations he realised that he could not simply reject them as in the past, particularly as he was negotiating a truce with France which deprived him of the usual excuse for deferring action elsewhere. He also appreciated the need to lead rather than counter the upsurge of emotion in the Spanish realms. Philip gave the impression of having changed his views radically. He now urged his sister to conclude negotiations with ash-Shaykh – but he would only agree to a defensive alliance which pleased neither the Sharif nor the regency. Even more striking was his decision to return to Spain as soon as the truce was signed and his promise to lead the campaign in person in the spring of 1556.

The regent and her court were nothing short of ecstatic. They opposed his decision over the Sa'di negotiations, pressing for an offensive alliance, although some found it as distasteful as Philip did to cooperate on an equal footing with a petty Islamic prince in the Maghreb. The weakness of the Spanish realms made such cooperation imperative. As hopes of Philip's participation rose, so did estimates of the cost. An account of 31 March 1556 put the total for a six month campaign to recover Bougie and Algiers at 1.3 million ducats.[51] The regency government was now clearly planning full-scale warfare. But their hopes were soon shattered by new Muslim attacks and endless delays, followed by the cancellation of Philip's journey. The leopard had not changed his spots. The king was no more committed now than before to Maghrebian expeditions.

Oran, 1556

One of the recurring assumptions in Maghrebian politics during the early modern period was that everyone lied. Deception was an integral part of foreign relations. If anyone declared his intention, everyone else assumed that the declaration was a feint aimed to lull the victim into a false sense of security. In 1555 Salah Rais made it amply clear that his next campaign would be against Oran. His victory parade into Bougie was accompanied by wild cries of 'Oran, to Oran!'. He responded by publicly declaring that he would lead his cheering troops against the *presidio* the following year. Tribal leaders in the area were duly informed and advised to prepare for the attack. The beylerbey also requested naval support from the sultan, who was, according to Alcaudete's spies, well pleased and willing to help.[52]

---

[50] AGS E. 108 fol. 8; E. 109 fols. 83–6; E. 114 fol. 69; GA. 1318 fol. 92; E. 113 fols. 144–5; E. 114 fols. 57–60. [51] AGS E. 113 fol. 114. [52] AGS E. 408 fol. 86; E. 480 fols. 129; 40, 7, 293, 233.

The mere fact that it was all so public and open convinced many observers that it was an elaborate sham: genuine plans were kept secret, not broadcast. Neither the regency government nor ash-Shaykh appreciated that Salah Rais needed this publicity to establish himself as a holy warrior (Ghazi), and secure the support of the Maghrebian tribes. Local Spanish commanders were just as ignorant and gripped by panic. Throughout the spring and early summer of 1556, don Alonso de la Cueva wrote increasingly hysterical letters to Charles, Eraso and Juana, seeking to persuade them that Salah Rais intended to attack La Goleta.[53] The authorities of Melilla were certain they were the next target. The duke of Medinaceli, owner of Melilla, decided to abandon the place rather than suffer the dishonour of losing it. He informed Juana that he would willingly cede it to the government if they acted quickly; if not it would be deserted. Juana was loath to take on further responsibilities in North Africa. She tried to persuade the duke to retain Melilla by promising greater government subsidies. She failed; backed by her councillors she then transferred responsibility for the maintenance of the base to Castile. Anything was preferable to relinquishing another position in the area.[54] These pressures made her all the more determined to ensure that the Italian realms should assume responsibility for the North African possessions, particularly La Goleta. But Philip would not support her efforts. He was eager to use Italian resources for the war against the papacy, and later against France. Juana was not alone in accusing him of favouritism towards the Italians.[55]

As the 1556 campaigning season approached, ash-Shaykh, the commanders of La Goleta, Melilla, and Oran all assured the Spanish government that they were the intended victims of Salah Rais's aggression. On the whole the regency government inclined to the view that the Sharif would be the next target. Then, to their immense relief, Salah Rais died before the campaign was launched. Plans for a campaign to take advantage of the interregnum were aired. Since Philip repeatedly delayed his return, it was difficult to proceed to specific discussions of strategy; disappointed, the regency government relaxed their guard. Having thus lulled themselves into a false state of security, they were devastated by the news that Oran was besieged on land and sea. The Muslims had been momentarily taken aback by the beylerbey's death, but since several thousand tribesmen, forty-three Ottoman ships and at least sixteen corsair vessels had arrived at the appointed time for the campaign, Salah Rais's able deputy Hasan Corso persuaded the Ottoman naval commander Ali (a one-eyed Greek renegade), that it would be wasteful to disband these forces. They decided to follow Salah Rais's plan and lay siege to Oran.

Once more the attempt to organise a relief force highlighted the problem of

[53] AGS E. 481 fols. 50–2, 55, 59–62, and 58–6 [sic].
[54] AGS E. 481 fol. 239; GA. 64 fol. 413; E. 113 fols. 50–4; E. 112 fols. 95–102.
[55] AGS E. 112 fols. 115–22, Juana to Philip, 13 June 1556; a typical response from Philip to this sort of accusation, AGS E. 514 fol. 15 (1 & 5 February 1557); AGS E. 120 fols. 37–42 (20 July) a riposte from her.

Spanish defences. Juana had already taken some steps to ensure the safety of Oran. She had allowed one thousand extra soldiers to winter there after the Bougie débâcle – which doubled the usual size of the garrison. This caused problems, since they required twice the normal provisions. She had also requested the return of the Spanish galleys from Italy, only to be told that war was likely in the area, and the king would not split his forces. With no royal warships at hand, all that she could do was to send supplies of grain, gunpowder and men to enable Oran to hold out until a proper relief force was available. In July 1556 the decision was taken in council to send 1,500 men and supplies in whatever ships could be fitted out in time. They would have to run the blockade. One month later, only 400 men had been levied and four galleys fitted out. Whilst this fell far short of the intended force, Juana and her councillors decided that the situation required desperate remedies. They ordered the ships and men to prepare for immediate departure on what everyone recognised was a highly dangerous and probably suicidal mission. Philip was so shaken when he read of their decision that he decided to take radical action. He ordered her to stop at once, arguing that the plan was sheer madness and would merely succeed in giving essential supplies of grain, ammunition and slaves to the Muslims. Then, aware that the regent had no choice but to pursue the risky plan, Philip ordered sixty ships to leave Italy and go to the relief of Oran. The letter informing Juana of his decision was dated 8 September.[56]

If Oran had depended solely on government aid from the regent and king, it would have fallen to the enemy as surely as Bougie. But Alcaudete was a decisive leader who saw attack as the best means of defence, and his men were determined to avoid the fate of the Bougie garrison. The Spaniards poisoned the wells in the vicinity of the *presidio*. They mounted a series of daring raids upon local tribes to deter them from joining the enemy, and constantly harassed the besieging army. The Muslims soon found themselves short of water and decimated by epidemics. Worse still, serious divisions among the leaders weakened the attack. Ali and the Ottoman commanders were contemptuous of the local tribesmen; old suspicions and conflict between Maghrebians and Ottomans resurfaced and led to violent clashes within the Muslim camp. Relations between the new arrivals and Hasan Corso were scarcely better. Mulay Hamet, one of the sons of Salah Rais, had come with the Ottoman fleet and saw himself as the next beylerbey of Algiers. But Hasan Corso himself wanted to claim the post. Despite these difficulties, the Muslim force was still strong. They had conquered one of the outlying forts, and by the end of August the leaders of Oran were convinced that they would soon have to surrender or die. Just as the Spaniards abandoned themselves to despair and debated how many more days they could hold out, the Ottoman–corsair and Maghrebian forces withdrew. The decision was sudden and hastily executed: it remains a mystery.

---

[56] The reactions of king and regent can be followed in: AGS E. 108 fols. 200–6; E. 112 fol. 126; E. 112 fols. 131–7; E. 114 fols. 27–31.

Some said that Suleiman had summoned his forces back to deal with internal strife; others that the Muslims had been frightened by reports of the impending arrival of Doria at the head of a large fleet. Without the Ottomans, the corsair and Maghrebian forces could not finish the assault. In the end, all that mattered to the astonished and jubilant defenders was that 'a great miracle' had happened. They had been saved by divine intervention. Philip immediately countermanded his orders for the fleet.[57]

To the sixteenth-century mind miracles were portents: Alonso de Gurrea (one of the Oran officials) interpreted this one in an instructive way. Gurrea thought that God was telling the Spanish people that this was the time for action, and He expected them to do His work. God had chosen to 'clip the wings' of the Turks so that Spain could deal them a decisive blow before they had time to increase.[58] Few shared the optimism that flooded through the Oran forces in the immediate aftermath of the siege. The regency government was preoccupied with the problem of how to counter further aggression. In August 1556 a Moor confessed under torture that he was an Algerian spy sent with three ships to find out what preparations were being made for the relief of Oran. He also declared that the Ottoman–corsair forces were following a comprehensive plan of action. After the fall of Oran they planned to take Ibiza and Menorca. From here they would proceed to the sack of Cajena (?) before taking up winter quarters in Algiers. Using these as forward bases, further attacks would be mounted against Spain.[59] There were fears that the Algerians and Ottomans might still go ahead with Salah Rais's grand plan. Alcaudete stated that the corsair leader had intended to sail to Valencia to pick up several thousand *mudéjares* to settle in Oran. His arrival would have triggered a revolt in which the *moriscos* would play a leading role. The regent hardly needed Alcaudete to remind her that in this area of Iberia, the *moriscos* were well armed and well trained. He thought they could field up to 80,000 men, so that the rebels and Ottoman–corsair forces might have successfully annexed part of Valencia.[60]

The siege of Oran reinforced a trend already clearly visible at the time when Bougie fell. Imperceptibly the *presidios* in general and Oran in particular had come to represent the first link in a chain of disasters that would end with simultaneous rebellion and invasion. These bases along the Maghrebian coast had to be maintained at all costs as bulwarks to deter invasion. Indeed, in the words of the financial official Luis de Ortíz, they were 'las fronteras' – the real frontiers of the Spanish realms. They deserved as much care, attention and financial support as major fortifications in Valencia or Granada.[61]

[57] The siege can be followed from the correspondence of the Oran officials, Juana and Philip: AGS E. 112 fol. 156; E. 481 fol. 203; E. 482 fols. 196–7; E. 114 fols. 64–5; E. 482 fol. 9; E. 481 fol. 249; E. 481 fols. 212–13; E. 481 fol. 26; E. 112 fol. 162.
[58] AGS E. 112 fol. 249.   [59] AGS E. 115 fols. 230–1.   [60] AGS E. 119 fol. 120.
[61] M. Fernández Alvarez (ed.) 'El memorial de Luis Ortiz 1558'. *Anales de Economía*, XVII, 63 (1957), p. 161.

Throughout 1556 and following the retreat of the Muslim forces, Juana was inundated with letters demanding that she defend Oran adequately. Even Charles V added his voice to the general clamour when he heard that Oran had been besieged. He told her that he hoped he would be neither in Spain nor the Indies nor anywhere on earth where the news of Oran's fall could reach him, because he would feel its loss so deeply. To Charles it would be 'a personal affront'; to the Spanish realms, as he now realised, it was a matter of the gravest danger.[62] No one, however, suggested how she might fund this important project. By 1556 the regency government faced wage arrears of 600,000 ds to the garrisons within Spain, and a further 130,000 for the wages of the Oran defenders alone. Alcaudete reported that the lack of money and provisions had led to massive desertion and the near disintegration of the garrison. It therefore seemed imperative to settle outstanding debts as well as to make new provisions.[63] Philip was equally emphatic that she must ensure Oran was fully defensible before the next campaigning season. He ordered her to provide money for new fortifications to be built immediately. But he took pains to stress that this must not affect the collection of money for the northern front, which was to continue undiminished. His preoccupation with the war in Italy and against France was further revealed when he demanded that all additional soldiers still stationed in Oran should be sent to Italy and the Netherlands at once. Alcaudete refused to obey, stating that he had no wish to end up like the governor of Bougie. Juana was sympathetic and did not press him. She merely reported his decision and endorsed his conclusion that bricks and mortar no longer sufficed to stem the Muslim advance in North Africa. The combined Bougie and Oran crises had turned Juana and the majority of her advisers into firm advocates of an aggressive policy in the Maghreb.[64]

Alcaudete was convinced that taking the offensive was now a cheaper and more effective way of dealing with the Muslim advance than strengthening the fortifications. To prove his point he produced a set of figures the regency government found convincing. The government estimated in 1551 that an annual expenditure of 30,000 to 35,000 ds would suffice to maintain Oran. Alcaudete stated that combined expenditure for repairs to the fortifications and additional men required during the summer months would bring the cost of defending Oran in 1557 to 250,000 ds. So he suggested that the government should spend the minimum on the fortifications and use the rest of the money and the men in an offensive. He thought that 3,000 regular troops supported by a force of 4,000 volunteers would suffice. They should organise the campaign early, emulating Ottoman–corsair tactics. They would seize the harvest and the *garrama* (a tribute paid by tribes to their powerful overlords or neighbours), as the Sharif and beylerbey had done. Helped by this infusion of money and provisions, as well as aid

---

[62] AGS E. 119 fol. 120.
[63] AGS E. 112 fols. 205–6; E. 114 fols. 216–19; E. 103 fol. 35.   [64] AGS E. 102 fol. 23.

from the Sharif, the two month campaign he envisaged would not be costly – at least no more so than static defence. He was adamant that the Spaniards must proceed with caution owing to the great strength of the Ottoman–corsair forces and the present weakness of the Spanish realms. There could be no direct assault against Algiers precisely because of the relative inequality of their forces. Instead, the Spanish should begin by taking the ports of Tlemcen and Mostaganem, establishing a protectorate over the region of Tlemcen. This would provide Oran with a buffer zone and a wide sector for provisions. Then the Spaniards could put pressure on Algiers and eventually attack the city-state. In his view, the conquest of Tlemcen was an essential first step to the recovery of Bougie and Algiers. The strategy he had adopted in the early 1550s was still the right one – indeed even more apt now than before.[65]

Philip was alarmed by Alcaudete's proposals because he was conscious that Juana and some of her advisers found them attractive. He was also extremely irritated by the count's continuing resistance over the dispatch of additional forces stationed in Oran. The king was clearly aware that he must drive a wedge between Alcaudete and Juana in order to prevent further pressure for direct action in the Maghreb. At first he sought to convince the regency government that they and Alcaudete had hopelessly confused two distinct problems and policies: the conquest of Algiers (which Philip conceded ought to be considered jointly with the recovery of Bougie); and the creation of a protectorate over Tlemcen. Whilst he intimated that the first would serve the best interests of the Spanish realms, the second was to advance Alcaudete's ambitions. Over the next few months he reiterated that Alcaudete was not really interested in the recovery of Bougie and Algiers, but only in extending his power over Tlemcen. The king's campaign to denigrate the count by alleging that his proposals were mere self-aggrandisement was unsuccessful; more effective was the pressure to provide for the French war. Philip also used the full range of arguments to show the overriding necessity to concentrate all resources on the northern front, where the king's reputation, realms and even his own person were in danger. The final stage of his offensive was to emasculate the regency government: he refused permission for them to levy money for an African campaign, and he issued an express prohibition regarding the money and provisions that the realms had offered for the recovery of Bougie and Algiers. Philip insisted that no one was to use these until he was ready to lead the campaign against Bougie and Algiers in person. In the meanwhile, he continued to demand subsidies and the immediate dispatch of all additional forces to the northern front, and he ordered Juana to reduce the danger from the Maghreb by concluding a defensive alliance with the Sharif. His views were forcefully expounded in letters, and verbally by Ruy Gómez de Silva who arrived in Valladolid in March 1557.

The combined impact of this pressure and the imminent outbreak of the war

---

[65] AGS E. 482 fols. 65, 66, 93–4; E. 114 fols. 216–19; E. 121 fols. 89–90.

against France served to dampen the ardour of the regency government for Maghrebian ventures – at least temporarily. When Alcaudete's agent arrived at court with a draft of an offensive treaty with the Sharif, the regency government rejected the conditions and dutifully replied that they could not engage in any campaigns in this area whilst Philip was occupied with the war against France. The king must have congratulated himself on the success of his initiative. It seemed as if the regency government had finally accepted his view of the matter and would no longer trouble him with unwelcome pressure for Maghrebian campaigns.[66]

PHILIP OVERRULED: THE REVOLT OF THE REGENCY GOVERNMENT 1557–8

The impression of obedience was illusory. In the same letter informing Philip that the council of war had rejected the proposed treaty with the Sharif, Juana admitted that she had sent 1,000 extra soldiers to Oran and had promised Alcaudete a further 1,500. Granted that the plague that struck Oran in the summer of 1557 weakened the garrison, but this did not justify the large numbers involved. Moreover, she did not mention her decision – taken probably in early June – to allow Alcaudete to levy 4,000 men. These were probably the volunteers he had requested.[67] The regent and her advisers were certain that the grave danger to the Spanish realms required immediate action: this opinion created an unbridgeable gap between themselves and the king. But it would not prove easy for these people, personally chosen by Philip and bound by ties of kinship and patronage to him, to move from passive and reasoned resistance, to open rejection of his authority. These were early signs that the regent would support a campaign in the Maghreb even against the express wishes of the king.

Aside from the pressures outlined earlier, Juana and her council were influenced by reports that the Sharif had been approached by the Ottoman–corsair forces and was contemplating an alliance with them and the French. The Portuguese were thoroughly alarmed by the news. Both Christian powers had suspected all along that the two Muslim jihadist powers would end up fighting on the same side. The rumours were confirmed in March 1557 by the governor of Melilla.[68] It was imperative to act before this overwhelming coalition was formed.

The situation in Algiers itself lent weight to the pro-intervention arguments. Throughout the winter of 1556 and much of 1557 the city-state was paralysed by internal conflicts. The rivalries which had erupted during the siege of Oran claimed

---

[66] Philip's orders AGS E. 119 fols. 12 14; E. 448 fols. 73 4; reaction and details of the draft treaty: AGS GA. 1318 fols. 88, 99; E. 468 s.f. 'La declaración, etc.'; E. 468 s.f., response of the council of war, 26 July 1557; see also E. 120 fols. 37–42.

[67] AGS E. 483 fol. 49 Alcaudete to Juana, 8 August 1557; E. 120 fols. 37–42, Juana to Philip, 26 July; E. 120 fols. 32–4, Juana to Philip, 10 & 18 August; E. 483 fols. 54–5, don Martín de Córdoba to Juana, 17 July. [68] SIHM Portugal, vol. v, pp. 55–7; AGS E. 483 fol. 111.

numerous victims: Hasan Corso, who seized power, was assassinated, as was Mehmet Pasha, the beylerbey sent by Suleiman to replace Salah Rais. Their supporters also died in droves as corsairs fought janissaries and men staked their future on supporting the next successful leader. Once again Alcaudete urged immediate action, sensibly arguing that they must take advantage of this unexpected weakness. He set off for Spain in July 1557 to plead his case and stiffen the government's resolve.[69] Philip was equally true to style: he thought they might benefit by establishing an alliance with a rebel 'king' of Algiers. Two draft letters survive: one addressed to Dragut, the other to Mostafa Arnaut. Both men were potential candidates for the leadership of the city-state. Philip urged them to establish an independent regime, and offered his benevolent 'protection'. But he would neither give them the forces to wrest control of Algiers nor commit himself to specific aid against the Ottomans; he merely stipulated his willingness to support their resistance to the sultan.[70]

Once again, the Spaniards lost their chance. Suleiman appreciated the danger and sent Hassan, one of Kheir-ed-din Barbarossa's sons, as the new beylerbey of Algiers. Hassan could count on the prestige of his father's name and the full backing of the Ottomans. He quickly restored order in the city; to ensure that it would last, he decided to organise a campaign. Relations with neighbouring tribes were at a low ebb; many leaders had challenged Algerian authority during the period of civil strife. Moreover, the campaign had to be organised hastily, and Hassan was under pressure to win support by providing booty for the disaffected Algerians. All these factors influenced his decision to avoid the Spanish bases and launch an attack against the Sa'di state. He may also have been in touch already with the rebels in ash-Shaykh's camp. There is no doubt that he was involved in the assassination of ash-Shaykh (October 1557), which coincided with his successful attack against the Sa'di chief. The Ottoman–corsair forces were in control of much of Tlemcen again by the end of 1557. Instead of returning to Algiers as before, they took up winter quarters in the area: they would be in a position to begin the 1558 campaign at the earliest moment.

Where would they strike? They could continue their advance and take control of Fez, so near to the Spanish coast. Or they might decide to annihilate the Spanish *presidios*, particularly Oran which still stood in the way of full Muslim control of Tlemcen. Whatever Hassan decided, the Spaniards would be in danger. In Spain the shock of the Ottoman–corsair success was compounded by their horror at the prospect of the disintegration of the Sa'di state. Ash-Shaykh had deposed his brother, who was still alive, as were his numerous progeny; his own sons had already started to fight over the inheritance. One thing was clear to the regency government: whether they liked the Sharif or not, they could not face the combined might of the Ottoman–corsair forces alone.[71]

---

[69] AGS E. 483 fol. 49.   [70] AGS E. 483 fols. 258–9.   [71] AGS E. 120 fols. 107, 110; E. 484 fol. 87.

Despair and hope alternated rapidly. News arrived of a devastating epidemic in the city of Algiers. It struck with particular ferocity in the late summer and continued in the winter of 1557. Since the best troops were away and many of those remaining to defend the city had died, Algiers was highly vulnerable. From the plague-ridden city, the redemptionist friar Luis de Sandoval assured Philip in December 1557 that God had arranged this punishment so that the Spanish king could recover Algiers for Christendom. God had chosen Philip as his champion, the man who would rid Christendom of the scourge of these Muslim corsairs. He must launch an immediate attack.[72] The same advice, albeit proffered with a different theological interpretation, came from ash-Shaykh's successor, his son Muhammad Abd Allah al-Ghalib. He had been involved in all the negotiations with the Spaniards, and he could not conceive of surviving without their help. He pressed the count of Alcaudete to conclude an offensive alliance against the Ottoman–corsair state, offering extensive concessions. Alcaudete was inclined to accept because he was convinced that Oran, not the Sharif, would be their next target. He had been informed that several tribes from the Oran area had asked the Algerian leader to attack the *presidio* and offered their support. It was rumoured that Suleiman had promised to send 70 or 80 galleys for the campaign. Alcaudete urged the regency government to take advantage of al-Ghalib's fear and conclude this vital offensive alliance whilst conditions were favourable.[73] There were other reasons for concern in the Spanish camp. The corsair Dragut, in alliance with leaders from Djerba and Tripoli, had attacked Kairouan and was now threatening Tunis. Suleiman was rumoured to have offered his aid here too. Clearly, if Tunis fell, the Spanish outpost of La Goleta could not survive.[74]

Despite the growing panic among local commanders and the Spanish regency government, Philip remained unmoved. He refused to allow them to intervene or to conclude offensive alliances with local Muslim leaders. Events followed their course now as before, with the Iberians as interested and increasingly frustrated spectators. This position was only tenable because the Ottoman–corsair forces attacked the Sa'di leader in the spring of 1558 after all. The Muslim forces clashed on 12 May 1558 near l'Oued el-Leben. Al-Ghalib proved just as decisive and energetic as his father. But he was also fortunate in having acquired a number of close allies before taking control of the state. They moved rapidly to secure his position after ash-Shaykh's assassination. They organised the murder of all adult male relatives of ash-Shaykh who threatened to divide the Sa'di state. When the Ottomans attacked, they encountered a determined and united foe and were decisively beaten. The Spanish officials in Oran reported that scarcely 2,000 men managed to evade death

---

[72] AGS E. 121 fol. 20.
[73] AGS E. 448 fol. 273; E. 484 fol. 36. Juana used the letter in March 1558 to justify her decision to launch a North African campaign, AGS E. 129 fol. 19.
[74] AGS E. 484 fol. 27, reports of spies forwarded by the governor don Alonso de la Cueva to Philip, January 1558; other news and rumours AGS E. 883 fol. 143 and E. 1323 fol. 205.

or captivity. Once again Spain had a chance to attack Algiers, since the remnants of her army were far from home and the city was drastically undermanned. Don Martín de Córdoba, in charge of Oran during his father's absence at court, declared this to be yet another sign from God, telling the Spaniards to act immediately and destroy Algiers whilst it was so weak. The same message was relayed by the Portuguese officials in Mazagan, and strongly expressed by Alcaudete himself in the Spanish court.[75]

The speed of events, combined with the difficulty of pin-pointing exactly when news reached Valladolid, makes it almost impossible to ascertain whether the regency government finally decided to act because they were confident or afraid. In some ways it scarcely mattered, for whether they advocated preventing the advance of the two jihadist states in North Africa, or wanted to recover Algiers and Bougie, they favoured active military intervention.

During October and November 1557 Alcaudete had put before the regent and councils a wide-ranging plan of action which was formally and extensively discussed. The proposals were refined in subsequent meetings, but the essentials were unchanged and formed the basis of subsequent Spanish policy. Alcaudete began from the premise that defence was difficult and costly, and that they had to retain the advance bases in North Africa in order to protect Iberia. He also believed that corsairs could never be entirely eliminated: at best they could be contained by ensuring that they had no access to neighbouring ports. Furthermore, he was certain that if Spain was to be safe, she had to deal with both the Sa'di and Ottoman–corsair states in the Maghreb. His solution to the problem of Muslim expansion and corsair raids was already familiar to the regency government – a campaign in the Maghreb, first attacking the ports of Tlemcen. This would deprive the corsairs of their bases and put pressure on Algiers, which he acknowledged was the ultimate aim of the Spanish conquest. But there was a major impediment: Philip would not support the campaign with his naval forces. It was necessary to devise an alternative strategy with the minimum naval support. In effect, Spain would have to revert to traditional patterns of land warfare against Islam. Victory was possible, but it would take longer. Alcaudete suggested that with 8,000 men and four galleys as back-up, they could make a good start. He was convinced that the Sharif would sign an alliance with Spain and provide food and subsidies as he had promised. He dismissed the fears of some councillors – who showed deep repugnance at the notion of allying and depending on a Muslim princeling – by arguing that once the Spanish troops were in Tlemcen, they would be strong enough to force neighbouring tribes to supply them directly and to control the Sharif. Alcaudete's plan corresponded to the original proposals mooted under Ferdinand: the creation

[75] AGS E. 484 fol. 107, report on Algiers; E. 484 fol. 209, Córdoba to Juana; E. 484 fols. 122–3, Alcaudete's memoranda of 23, 24 and 26 April 1558; SIHM Portugal, vol. v, pp. 73–5; SIHM Espagne, vol. II, pp. 445–8; pp. 454–60 details of the battle.

of large buffer zones around the *presidios* to supply provisions and provide a springboard for further expansion.[76]

Juana and the majority of her councillors accepted the analysis and the plan. They also agreed that it was imperative to act at once. Their financial situation was so dire, however, that even a small-scale enterprise would be difficult. Their only means were the provisions offered for the recovery of Bougie and Algiers, but Philip had repeatedly ordered them not to touch these provisions until he returned. Nevertheless, in January 1558, the regency government decided to launch a campaign in the Maghreb with these provisions, directly contravening Philip's orders. Conscious that he would not endorse their decision, the regency government put the plan into effect 'without waiting to consult your majesty, because we felt that it was necessary'. That was how Juana justified their astonishing decision to flaunt Philip's authority.[77] Charles was not informed either. Interestingly enough, Alcaudete appeared more worried and unhappy than the others at the prospect of acting without royal authorisation. He realised that Philip was already hostile and would lay much of the blame for the decision upon him. He also appreciated that the campaign could encounter all sorts of difficulties without active royal support.[78]

When Philip learned what was happening, he sent a peremptory order telling his sister to stop the preparations for the campaign immediately. By now he realised that it would need more than a written order to stop them. Apart from repeating his earlier injunctions against opening another front, he reminded the regency government of their duty to obey him and respond to his requirements for the war with France. He warned of the risk to his reputation, his empire and his person, if his scant resources were diverted. He realised that the most effective way to prevent the opening of another front was by pressing the regent to use all available resources for the French war. He also reiterated his prohibition over the collection of provisions for the Bougie–Algiers campaign. But he attempted to deflect their anxieties by allowing Juana to send reinforcements to Oran – up to 4,000 men, if she found means to pay for them. All soldiers already levied for the Maghreb were to be dispatched to Italy immediately as he was short of troops in this area. Finally, Philip persuaded the new archbishop of Toledo – Carranza – not to give the 300,000 ds promised by his predecessor to the regency government for the Bougie–Algiers campaign. Having, as he thought, successfully deprived the regent of access to funds and troops, the king then removed all prospects of naval support by refusing permission for any royal ships, including the four galleys of Santiago, to go to the Maghreb, although the latter had been built and were being maintained with ecclesiastical subsidies specifically to fight Islam.[79]

[76] AGS E. 119 fol. 415; E. 129 fols. 8–19.
[77] AGS E. 129 fols. 8–10.   [78] AGS E. 119 fols. 428–9.
[79] I have not found Philip's orders, but the measures he took can be deduced from AGS E. 129 fols. 107–9, Juana's response to them dated 14 May 1558, as well as from subsequent correspondence.

The sharpness and speed with which Philip reacted jolted the regency government. There was a further round of formal discussions between Juana and the various councils, now dangerously circumscribed with strict financial limitations. They could no longer hide behind their initial pretence. If they decided to launch the Maghrebian campaign after receiving Philip's latest letters, they would directly challenge royal authority. There was an unspoken assumption that Philip had drawn a line beyond which they were not to tread. Thus far there had been conflict and compromise, but launching a campaign against his orders would be usurpation of sovereign powers and intolerable to the king. Notwithstanding the enormity of this decision the regency government opted to carry out the plan for a North African campaign in April 1558. Even more surprising, this open defiance was practically unanimous. Juan de Vega, president of the council of state, felt compelled to tell Philip that he had not been in favour of disobeying him, but he fully endorsed the arguments for action in North Africa and approved of the plan which had been adopted. The marquis of Mondéjar did oppose the decision, but this was largely because of his long-standing feud with Alcaudete; besides he no longer believed land-based expeditions would succeed. Mondéjar had become a convert to the large multi-national naval campaigns of the emperor.

The challenge to royal authority could never have taken place without the powerful fear of the Muslim threat, and alienation from the remote and unsympathetic monarchs. There was a strong and widespread conviction that they had wilfully neglected Spain in favour of northern pursuits, leaving the regency government no option but disobedience in order to defend the realms. On 14 May 1558, Juana launched the campaign. The momentous import of her decision must not be underestimated simply because the policy proved a dismal failure. The regency government had not only usurped a sovereign function; they had also put the rest of the empire at risk, since it was likely that an attack on the corsair state would lead to Ottoman reprisals.[80]

The campaign thus began under difficult circumstances. Juana ordered the collection of the supplies offered by the kingdom in 1556, but the intervening famine (1557) made the collection of provisions difficult. Without the 300,000 ds from Toledo, the government had no major source of credit to levy troops and supply them. Without the galleys of Santiago, they had to find and impound ships to take the troops across to the Maghreb. Delays were inevitable. Alcaudete had stressed the importance of an early strike to maintain the element of surprise and to collect the harvest before the enemy. It proved impossible to meet this requirement.

[80] AGS E. 129 fols. 107–9; E. 484 fol. 211; Marmol, *Descripción general de Africa*, vol. II, fol. 197; Cabrera de Córdoba, *Felipe II*, vol. I, p. 232 claims that Charles intervened and gave the regency government the support and courage to challenge Philip and overcome the resistance of the councils of state and war. There is no evidence to support this view and it runs contrary to everything Charles stood for and had done. Moreover, Alcaudete, in his eagerness to convince Philip that he was not acting alone, made much in his letters to the king of Juana's personal commitment to his proposals – e.g. AGS E. 119 fols. 428–9. He would hardly have omitted to mention the backing of the emperor.

Not until 22 August 1558 was the Spanish army gathered in Oran in a position to take the offensive. The Ottoman–corsair forces had been given ample opportunity to prepare and obtain reinforcements. They knew Alcaudete's plans, and they were driven to recover their reputation, so recently mauled by the Sa'di troops. Twenty-five corsair galleys had been sent to harass the Spanish coast during the spring, impede preparations, and take provisions for the Ottoman–corsair war effort. They probably hoped to repeat Salah Rais's coup of 1553 and capture all or part of the expeditionary force.[81] To add to Alcaudete's problems, the Sharif refused to support the Spanish troops, partly in retaliation for their failure to help him when the Ottoman–corsair forces attacked, partly also because he was faced with a number of internal rebellions. Local tribes who had promised provisions for the Spanish troops had been warned by the Ottoman–corsair forces that they would face savage reprisals. They chose neutrality as the better part of valour and remained inactive as the two alien armies clashed.

Alcaudete had decided to begin the campaign with the conquest of Mostaganem, a strategic port. He had to act quickly; to speed up the progress of the soldiers he sent the bulk of their provisions and artillery on board the small vessels that had transported the troops. Unfortunately, the corsair menace once again aborted a promising campaign. Passing corsairs took all the ships and their contents. The Spanish army, which numbered some 10,000 men,[82] was left short of food and with scarcely any artillery. They might still have avoided disaster if they had managed to reach Mostaganem itself but Hassan Pasha caught up with them before they could establish a defensible position.

As was customary in North African wars, the battle lasted over several days. Alcaudete's men were desperately short of food and water, but they fought bravely enough, winning the encounters on 24 and 26 August. Late on 26 August, however, the count was killed. As soon as news of his death spread through the camp, the Spanish army disintegrated. Mass panic seized the men. Many abandoned their weapons in a crazed attempt to escape. Few succeeded: thousands died and many more were captured, including Alcaudete's son, don Martín. The Spanish army had been all but wiped out. The Oran officials reported in awe that they had never before witnessed such a devastating and complete victory.[83]

Ironically, Philip had in the meanwhile accepted that he could not deny the government the use of the Santiago galleys without deepening the rift between himself and the Spanish clergy. He gave permission for them to be sent to the

[81] AGS E. 484 fol. 211; pp. 257–8 for the earlier incident.
[82] The figures vary in all the accounts, ranging from 6,000–12,000. Some 8,000 men crossed over and Alcaudete used most of the garrison in Oran, so 10–11,000 seems a reasonable estimate.
[83] The campaign has been pieced together from the various reports, especially AGS E. 484 fols. 138–9; 136–7; 146; E. 130 fol. 79; Marmol, *Descripción general de Africa*, vol. II fols. 197–8v. T. García Figueras, *Presencia de España en Berbería Central y Oriental*, (Madrid, 1943), pp. 180–1. R. Cornevin, *Histoire de l' Afrique* (vols. I and II, Paris, 1976), vol. I, pp. 412–13. Hess, *Forgotten frontier*, p. 78.

Maghreb to support the Spanish troops. But it was too late; the ships and reinforcements arrived after the campaign had reached its tragic end.[84] Far from earning the gratitude of his disgruntled Spanish subjects, his decision provoked further resentment as people reflected on what might have been if the king had supported the campaign sooner.

There were both immediate and long-term repercussions from the disaster at Mostaganem. The most urgent problem was how to defend Oran. Alcaudete had taken most of the soldiers stationed in Oran and the neighbouring Spanish base of Mers-el-Kebir on campaign, along with some of their artillery. The garrisons were therefore desperately weakened, and short of rations. Reduced to a diet of bread and water they were hardly an effective force. At the same time, part of the town walls of Oran collapsed. Neighbouring tribes were sufficiently emboldened by these tragedies to launch a series of raids, breaking the water mills that served the garrison, and threatening the supplies of wood and bread ovens, which were saved by the timely intervention of a group of arquebusiers. The tribes sent envoys to the Ottoman–corsair camp requesting aid, but Hassan Pasha decided to rest on his laurels and return to Algiers. He promised to lead a campaign against Oran the following year if the sultan and the king of France supported the venture. The Oran garrison was doubly fortunate therefore: first they were spared from immediate attack by the Ottoman–corsair forces, then the four galleys of Santiago laden with provisions for the campaign arrived.[85] But Oran was more vulnerable now than ever. As the marquis of Mondéjar stated, the victory at Mostaganem had strengthened the Ottoman–corsair forces immeasurably. It had increased their reputation; it had provided them with numerous captives, some of whom would be ransomed for cash, others would be exploited as slaves; and it had given them artillery, which they desperately needed. He believed that the hope of gaining honour, glory and riches would bring volunteers from the Ottoman empire in droves to North Africa, further increasing the power of Algiers.[86] Gloom was the order of the day as the regency government discussed how best to counter the attack they expected against the *presidios* in 1559.

In order to appreciate the full impact of the Mostaganem disaster, it should be set in context. So much hope had been placed on this long-awaited offensive! Moreover, 1558 proved a dramatic year for all the Mediterranean realms. Throughout the summer, the inhabitants of the coastline stretching from Gibraltar to Cádiz lived in terror of twenty corsair vessels which attacked them continuously. The Ottoman fleet moved westwards attacking first Sorrento and Massa, then sacked the town of Ciudadela in Menorca. The Catalans were convinced that the

[84] AGS E. 129 fols. 119–24; his letter was dated 6 October 1558.
[85] AGS E. 484 fols. 136, 148, 129, reports on the situation in Oran, 29 August to 3 November 1558; don Francisco de Córdoba bitterly arraigned Philip for not allowing him to take the galleys of Santiago and provisions earlier. He believed at would have averted the disaster: AGS E. 130 fol. 79; also E. 130 fol. 73; E. 484 fols. 155–6.   [86] AGS E. 139 fol. 122, to Juan Vázquez, 2 October 1558.

city of Barcelona was the fleet's main target. They sent panic-stricken appeals for help both to the government in Valladolid and to neighbouring Aragon. These appeals spread fears of invasion to inland areas not directly affected by the naval attacks. Inevitably Spain's failure to arrest the Muslim advance in the Maghreb combined with the proximity and savage attacks of the Ottoman fleet in the Balearics to elevate the hope of the *moriscos* communities. They believed more strongly than ever that the Muslims might yet establish another kingdom in Iberia. It is impossible to prove whether these groups became bolder – as the biased authorities maintained – or were simply more noticeable to a Christian population which was becoming increasingly neurotic about Muslim invasion and insurrection. The regency government received countless letters in 1558 complaining of renewed *morisco* activity and warning of rebellion. To minimise the prospect of an uprising the government agreed to a suspension of inquisitorial activity in Aragon, having already done this in Valencia the previous year.[87] This cautious policy in turn alienated the zealots who felt that radical action was the only way to contain the Muslim menace. They successfully prompted a change of policy in Aragon in December 1558, when the government ordered that all *moriscos* should be disarmed and restricted in settlement and movement. Later edicts followed this pattern. It is unlikely, however, that the government would have imposed these changes but for the fact that the disarmament of the *moriscos* was also a way of reducing the power of the Aragonese nobility.[88]

Philip remained aloof from these fears and untouched by the disaster. His only comment was this: 'there is nothing further to say except that I regretted it as much as you can imagine'.[89] He must have been ambivalent about the defeat. The campaign had attracted little attention, so the defeat was not significant to his reputation. The Ottomans were unlikely to order major reprisals against him since his forces had been so decisively beaten. He glossed over the incident and preferred to forget it. He ordered Juana to provision Oran, Sardinia and the other Mediterranean islands, so that they could withstand further attacks in 1559, and told her to send artillery to Valencia, Ibiza and other exposed areas. He continued to demand large sums for the French war. This indifference to their plight was no longer tolerable to Juana or the Spanish elites. Francisco de Córdoba argued in a letter to Philip in January 1559 that he could not ignore the Maghrebian front. He must either provide sufficient resources to defend the North African bases, or abandon them all now, razing their fortifications.[90] Juana did not believe that there was a choice now. They simply could not continue to drift towards disaster, but must act immediately to strengthen the North African bases. Juana wanted to

[87] Valencia: Braudel, *The Mediterranean*, vol. II, p. 959; J. Reglá Campistol *Felip II i Catalunya* (Barcelona, 1955) p. 66. Aragon: Cardaillac, *Moriscos y cristianos*, p. 117, Novalin, *Valdés*, vol. II, pp. 187–91 (AGS E. 129 fol. 129).

[88] See pp. 288–94.   [89] AGS E. 485 s.f., to Juana, 31 March 1559.

[90] AGS E. 130 fol. 78; E. 137 fol. 161, E. 137 fol. 159.

upgrade the garrisons and allocate realistic sums for their upkeep. In theory, the government would set aside only some 30–35,000 ds to defend Oran, whereas in the 1550s expenditure for the garrison had oscillated between 80,000 and 160,000 ds. Similar increases had transformed the budget provisions for the other *presidios*.[91] Others strongly supported her view. Luis de Ortíz, very much Philip's man and no hysterical xenophobe, nevertheless warned that unless Philip acted now, the whole of the Spanish coast would be made desolate by the Muslims. The kingdoms of Valencia, Murcia and Granada would soon be lost to the enemy. In fact he predicted that Turks, Moors and other enemies would soon be found in the very heart of Castile.[92] Even allowing for rhetorical flourishes, this was a serious indictment of the king's neglect of the Maghreb.

Nothing could persuade Philip to alter his view of the situation. He was obdurate: all resources must be channelled to the northern front. He maintained that there was no immediate danger of invasion from the Muslims, and that the Ottomans, the corsairs, the *moriscos*, and the defence of the *presidios* were all separate problems. Far from changing his policies, he chose to believe that the situation in Spain could be solved by a change of personnel. Don García de Toledo, Juana's favourite, was removed as head of Juana's household and replaced by the loyal and experienced marquis de Sarria, Juan Manrique de Lara. Philip's favourite cleric, the pliable Bartolomé de Carranza, was also dispatched to Spain, and Philip renewed his efforts to drive Valdés out of the court. The marquis of Mondéjar, pressed to relinquish the presidency of the council of the Indies in favour of the more malleable licenciado Vaca, was given a post in the Contaduría Mayor instead. More importantly, Philip ordered Juana to show all the letters and dispatches he sent her to Juan de Vega, Gutierre López de Padilla and Juan Vázquez. He evidently intended power to be shared among these three and thereby to diminish Juana's own freedom of action. It was a bid to isolate the regent, curb her independence and weaken the position of men whom the king considered less interested in advancing his policies than those of their realm and their families.

Juana was unhappy. She was powerless to prevent the departure of don García. She told Philip that she no longer trusted any of the councillors at court. She refused to accept Manrique de Lara as head of her household, arguing that she could make her own choice. Furthermore she refused point blank to show Philip's letters to the triumvirate he had designated. She boldly justified her decision to ignore his orders by saying that this arrangement would merely serve to increase pressure on her when she could do nothing more to respond to the king's incessant demands. In view of their widely diverging positions and increasingly frequent conflicts, Juana decided to resign and give her brother the option of replacing her altogether. Charles was convinced that she meant it. One of the last letters he sent before his death was an appeal to her, urging her to remain as regent, despite the problems she

[91] AGS E. 137 fols. 147–9, 159; E. 112 fol. 202.   [92] Fernández Alvarez, *Ortiz*, pp. 160–1.

faced. Her correspondence in August 1558 reveals that she agreed only with great reluctance.[93]

Apart from Juana, two other individuals merit special mention in connection with the king's government reshuffle of 1558: Carranza and Valdés. Carranza arrived in Spain that August with a brief to speed up the process of Valdés's departure from court. This task was most congenial to the new archbishop of Toledo. As soon as he arrived, he launched vitriolic attacks against Valdés in council meetings as well as in general conversation. Rumours that accusations of heresy had been made against him by the Spanish Protestants captured during 1557–8 in no way deterred him. Carranza trusted that his exalted status and high favour with the king were sufficient protection against such charges. Valdés was out for revenge, however, and his campaign was made easier by the general hostility against the king prevalent at court. The attack on Carranza, and in particular his arrest, were indirect but substantial demonstrations of disrespect for Philip. Everyone knew that the king trusted and consulted Carranza on many issues. Most could guess that he had been sent to Spain to press royal demands, yet only one high-ranking courtier came to his defence in Valladolid: Gutierre López Padilla.[94] Whilst he lived, Charles V also provided protection for the archbishop, and chose to have him by his side as he lay dying.[95] After Charles died, no one was left to prevent the archbishop's imprisonment. In sum, Philip's attempt to regain control of the regency government failed dismally, and he had nearly provoked a worse crisis by driving Juana to offer her resignation.

THE FORGOTTEN REBELLION: ARAGON 1556–9

Philip's failure to impose his will upon the regency government in Castile had dire repercussions for his policy towards Aragon. Behind the rebellion, which lasted for over three years, lie the tensions that were driving Philip and his regency government apart: the Muslim threat, Christian–*morisco* rivalry, and the belief that the monarchs had neglected them woefully.[96] Opposition was also encouraged by the king's absence and the belief that the regent was weak. The greatest grievance, however, was the subjection of Aragon to the old rival, Castile.

---

[93] AGS E. 128 fols. 393, 396, Juana to Charles 8 and 17 August respectively. Details of the government reshuffle also emerge from the Carranza documents, cited in the next note.

[94] *Archivo Documental español, Carranza*, 9 vols.; and the articles of Tellechea Idígoras, 'Felipe II y Valdés'; *Carranza y Pole*; Novalín, *Valdés*. Pastor, *History of the popes*, vol. XIV, p. 315; also AGS E. 129 fol. 110.

[95] Juana informed Charles of the charges against Carranza in a holograph letter – AGS E. 128 fol. 393 – but Charles refused to believe them.

[96] J. Reglá Campistol, *Felip II i Catalunya* (Barcelona, 1955) is one of the very few historians who realised that there had been trouble in Aragon. He puts together some of the facts from documents found at the Arxiu Corona Arago (pp. 17–18); I have been fortunate to find further documentation in the Archivo General de Simancas, Real Academia de la Historia (Madrid) and the Biblioteca Nacional (Madrid).

The marginalisation of the three Aragonese realms had started with the marriage of Ferdinand and Isabel. The long absences and brief visits of reigning monarchs since then allowed factionalism and noble violence that was thought excessive even by the tolerant standards of the sixteenth century. Constant feuding and banditry flourished. During Charles's reign the situation had worsened because he had seldom thought the area sufficiently important to attend to its legal, political or religious affairs. By 1554 Philip was so worried that he warned Charles that something must be done to redress present grievances and past neglect, otherwise his conscience would have to bear the guilt of having utterly failed to fulfil his royal duty towards Aragon. These were strong words, written in Philip's own hand. He pressed Charles to fill vacant posts and solve the most urgent business, but to no avail. Gradually Philip moved in to the vacuum and began putting his own candidates into office and dealing with Aragonese affairs. To his delight Charles endorsed his choice of viceroy in 1554 and accepted Philip's unauthorised appointments. In 1555 Charles once again proved his lack of interest in Aragon by forwarding the requisite powers and telling his son to make whatever appointments and provisions were necessary, expressly waiving any need for further consultation.[97]

Once he had been given power over the rest of his inheritance, however, Philip's interest in Aragon was minimal. The expectations he had aroused made his neglect that much harder to bear. The duke of Maqueda, viceroy of Valencia, eloquently expressed the growing resentment of the three Aragonese realms in a bitter missive he addressed to Philip on 2 August 1557.[98] He was angry that neither Charles nor Philip had deigned to reply to his numerous letters despite the fact that Valencia was devastated by plague and famine, and constant corsair attacks. He appreciated that Philip had so many other concerns that the problems of Valencia might appear small by comparison. However, in Maqueda's opinion, the most upsetting aspect of the king's persistent neglect was his failure even to designate anyone at court to listen and discuss what royal officials *in situ* thought was a very serious situation. The absence of adequate mechanisms to air their grievances directly to the monarch and the absence of any hope of improvement for the future were the aspects he emphasised most.

The gradual subjection of the Aragonese to Castile was even more significant, however. Charles and Philip had appointed successive regents who resided in Castile, but were given powers to deal with Aragonese affairs. The council of Aragon, created to advise the monarch and deal with the problems of the three kingdoms and their dependencies, was resident with the regent in Castile, not with the sovereign. Dissatisfaction was widespread, but it came to a head in the kingdom of Aragon, and specifically in the capital, Zaragoza. The spark that lit the flame was the action of Philip's regent, the duke of Francavila, father-in-law of Ruy Gómez de

---

[97] AGS PR. 55 fol. 27(iii); PR. 55 fol. 27(iv).   [98] AGS E. 322 fol. 10.

Silva. Francavila was an advocate of firm and rigorous government and set about reducing the bandits and restoring a semblance of order to Aragon. When the bandit leaders proved too hard to catch, Francavila decided to make an example of a man accused of complicity with the outlaws. His ruling was immediately declared unconstitutional by the men whose task was to protect Aragon's many privileges. They declared that a Castilian could not order the execution of an Aragonese, irrespective of his office. The dispute soon broadened into a general discussion of privileges (the *fueros*) and the nature of the relationship between Castile and Aragon.

Other sources of conflict merged with the general dissatisfaction. The initial protest against Francavila's sentence was made by a deputation representing the Aragonese corts and the inhabitants of the county of Ribagorza. This, the most important principality in Aragon, was torn by peasant unrest and factional disputes. The count of Ribagorza had been dispossessed of his extensive lands in 1554, a process in which Philip played a major part. Since then riots and feuds had proliferated, some probably instigated by the count. As so often happens, other long-standing disputes were triggered off by the outbreak of violence. The debate over one man's execution became a general expression of dissent. Francavila thought it possible to control the situation in the spring of 1556, as long as the council of Aragon did not issue any provocative orders. He promised to avoid any further irritating actions. But the riots in Zaragoza continued.[99] Deputies from the city were dispatched to the Netherlands in April 1556 to present their grievances directly to Philip. They complained about the powers assumed by the 'regent of Castile' over their kingdom, of the slowness and corruption of the legal system, of the constant and uncontrolled feuds and violence of the nobles. They also presented a host of lesser grievances.[100] The violence finally got out of hand, and Francavila fled the kingdom in the summer of 1556. His departure prompted further riots in Aragonese towns. Juana was powerless to impose a military solution to the crisis since this would have to be organised and funded in Castile. Apart from the difficulties of raising the men and money, it was inevitable that the Aragonese would see this as a Castilian invasion. Royal officials in nearby Valencia and Catalonia dared not intervene either, for fear that the troubles would spread to their states. Nothing was done to restore the viceroy.

Royal authority was not entirely overthrown in Aragon: the governor, Gurrea, held on tenuously as the king's chief representative. Initially he had to lie low, taking no action against the perpetrators of violence. For a long time he did not dare step outside Zaragoza for fear of being lynched.[101] Rebellious spirits were appeased

---

[99] AGS E. 320 fol. 334, Francavila to Juan Vázquez, 6 May 1556; further details of the troubles in Ribagorza and Aragon, E. 308 fol. 26, E. 507 fols. 6–7; RAH SC A. 48 fol. 238; G. Colas Latorre and J. A. Salas Ausens, *Aragón bajo los Austrias* (Zaragoza, 1977) give a summary of the problems in Ribagorza during Philip's reign, pp. 136–41.   [100] RAH SC A. 48 fols. 222–5 (26 April 1558).
[101] Some of his correspondence has been preserved in BNM mss. 784.

for a time by Francavila's flight, and the city was quiet. In the countryside, however, violent feuds were endemic, and little legal action was being taken against malefactors.

Philip was understandably upset and annoyed. He had not yet secured official recognition as king of Aragon. The troubles served to focus attention on this area once more. He sent don Diego de Acevedo to claim the realms and reorganise the government. To minimise opposition and counter the current troubles, Philip had decided to sever the links between the Aragonese and the regent in Castile. The plan did not get beyond the court of Valladolid. The regent and regency councils saw it as another measure aimed to reduce their power, and opposed it. Juana informed her brother that he was being less than wise to deprive her of her powers over Aragon when he had no viceroy there and no guarantee that the new concessions would bring the Aragonese back to obedience. He ran the risk of annulling what little royal authority there was.[102] There was some sense in all this: Gurrea's letters show that he had assumed some of the viceroy's functions after Francavila's flight, but every time he used viceregal powers, he had to obtain Juana's permission. This alone enabled him to act legally. Under Philip's new proposals he would have to obtain the king's permission until a new viceroy was appointed.[103] Plausible as Juana's argument was, it could be countered by the equally sound statement that unless Philip granted the Aragonese demand for separation from Castile, he would not be able to quell the disturbances and establish himself there.

There was more to the crisis than constitutional conflicts and power struggles. The king was determined to make the realms of Aragon contribute a substantial sum to the war. To do this, he had to summon the corts; but the Aragonese corts could only be summoned by the legitimate ruler. Until he was officially recognised as their king, Philip was technically only the heir to the throne, therefore only Charles could do this. Juana and the councils capitalised on this situation. They suggested to Philip that Charles should summon the corts, attend them personally, inform them officially of his retirement, and demand official recognition of Philip as his successor. However, Charles must stipulate that until Philip's return to the peninsula, Juana would remain in charge of both Castile and Aragon. When Charles refused to leave Yuste for this purpose, Juana suggested that he should transfer power over the Aragonese realms directly to her; she could then summon the corts in his name, attend them, and request funds for Philip. This was not as drastic as might first appear. The Aragonese did not recognise the right to the succession of a legitimate monarch until he had claimed the realms in person and swore to abide by their privileges; if the king did not return and Charles would not go there, Juana was the only one who could claim the realms. Philip rejected the proposal out of hand. He would not tolerate any questioning of his right to rule Aragon, nor would he

---

[102] AGS E. 322 fol. 69; E. 119 fols. 19–20.
[103] AGS E. 119 fols. 19 and 20, Juana to Philip, 4 February 1557 – note that she was still using the powers granted to her by Charles in 1554 as the legal base for her actions in Aragon.

consider at so critical a juncture, any proposals that might increase the power of his sister and the regency councils.[104]

The issue remained unresolved when Charles died in September 1558. The situation was now more complex than ever. Technically, there was now no sovereign of Aragon and appointments made by the emperor lapsed. Philip tried to make a legal and reasonable case for claiming the realms *in absentia*. He told Gurrea in November 1558 that he had 'weighty reasons' for remaining in the northern realms and could not leave them. The Aragonese must nevertheless recognise his claim on two grounds: one, Charles had formally renounced his title and transferred it to Philip; two, he had already been sworn in as the legitimate heir in Aragon. No further constitutional proofs of legitimacy could be required. Gurrea must have been puzzled by this letter. Somewhat earlier, he had received two letters from Valladolid on this very issue. Juana had expressed her dissatisfaction and demanded that something be done to restore royal authority in Aragon. The other missive, dated 28 September, was sent in Philip's name. Gurrea was ordered to summon leading men of the realm and canvass their opinion on three issues: first, could Juana continue to rule over Aragon until Philip returned? second, could she appoint a viceroy, and would such a viceroy exercise his office legally until the king came back? third, if the answer to the previous questions was negative, these men were to advise the monarch on proper procedure during his absence. All this had to be done in the utmost secrecy.[105] Gurrea was eager to solve his own confused position; he still relied on Juana's authority to legitimise his actions. If her role was clarified, so would be his own. Gurrea therefore acted upon this letter. But the leading Aragonese he called were loath to address themselves to explosive political issues. They merely reiterated the constitutional position: the corts had recognised Philip in 1542 as Charles's legal heir and so conferred 'authority' upon him. Juana was extremely irritated. She tartly responded that she knew perfectly well what the 1542 ceremony had conferred upon her brother; they must give a straight answer to the questions put before them. Even now the Aragonese resisted. On 15 November 1558 Gurrea reported that the leading men of the realm affirmed that the monarch had to claim the kingdom in person.[106] They refused to commit themselves on the questions regarding her powers.

Not unnaturally, the French sought to exploit the troubles in Aragon. After Philip failed to establish a foothold in Picardy during the autumn of 1557, it was widely believed that the French would counter-attack in northern Spain. Juana tried to anticipate the crisis by sending additional forces to the area, but money was scarce. The wages of the northern garrisons were between fourteen and forty months in arrears, and it was difficult to find recruits. The bishop of Urgel thought the famine that struck that year was providential because it would effectively deter

---

[104] AGS E. 119 fols. 19–20, Philip's holograph.
[105] BNM mss. 784 fols. 52 and 52v.   [106] BNM mss. 784 fol. 67.

an invasion.[107] Henry II could not let such a good opportunity slip, but he was unable to divide his forces until the late summer of 1558. The French aptly call this 'la guerre mouillé.' Torrential rains during September and October 1558 made the routes almost impassable and living conditions appalling. Food was extremely scarce and there was little love for France among the Aragonese.[108] The invasion across the Pyrenees might well have been planned to coincide with a Franco–Ottoman naval attack against Catalonia. The authorities in Barcelona certainly thought so and argued that the city would fall unless supported with extra troops. Their request for immediate assistance from Aragon once again raised the issue of sovereignty. Only the king or his regent could levy troops and authorise their movement across frontiers. But it was the Aragonese deputies who received the request and acted upon it, sending soldiers to strengthen the Catalan defences. Gurrea was not inclined to oppose them, given the grave danger, even if it was an infringement of sovereign powers.[109]

The Aragonese themselves became suspicious at the lack of royal activity, unaware that deep divisions between Philip and Juana had all but paralysed any initiative over Aragon. Rumours spread that Philip had lost patience and intended to empower Juana to summon the corts, despite the absence of formal recognition of his sovereignty. Calls for the defence of privileges immediately merged with another conflict: the Inquisition issued an edict ordering the Aragonese nobles not to give arms to their *morisco* or new Christian tenants. The penalties were considerable – a fine of 20,000 ducats, deprivation of holy offices for the noble or lord, and perpetual service in the galleys for the hapless *morisco*. The recent incidents in which the Inquisition had been challenged and prevented from carrying out its duties were evidently judged too serious to ignore, but this symbolised a significant departure from the government's careful policy thus far. Had it not been for the obvious repercussions of such a move – weakening seriously the power of the nobles, whose private armies were largely composed of *morisco* tenants – the regents might have been tempted to turn a blind eye to yet another display of lawlessness in Aragon. The elites took it as an assault on their powers and privileges. A few days after Christmas 1558 a large group of Aragonese nobles met in Zaragoza and decided to 'call the realm', that is to summon a meeting of the corts of the kingdom of Aragon for 6 January 1559.[110]

The crisis immediately split the remaining royal officials in Zaragoza. Gurrea opposed the meeting on the grounds that only the monarch could summon the corts. The *abogado fiscal* – or fiscal advocate, the most powerful legal official after the

[107] AGS E. 322 fol. 168 Urgel to Alcalá, lieutenant and captain general of Catalonia; AGS E. 322 fols. 134, 136, 118, 108 and 121, details of conditions along the Catalan border 1557.
[108] AGS E. 129 fols. 63–9, Juana's report of the campaign.
[109] BNM mss. 784 fols. 35–6; see also pp. 285–6.
[110] Details of this and the subsequent actions of the deputies can be found in RAH SC A. 48 fols. 242–3, 248–9, BNM mss. 784 fols. 72–81.

governor – decided to negotiate secretly with the rebels. Henceforth it was difficult to know exactly what his intentions were. Juana could do nothing except send a special envoy, Andrés de Ponce, to support Gurrea and keep her informed. Despite their efforts to prevent it, the illegal corts met. The duke of Vendôme, ever hopeful of recovering Navarre for the Albret family, prepared to fish in troubled waters and moved his troops near the frontier. Fortunately for Philip, there was no inspired leader, charismatic figure or leading noble to rally discontent. Moreover, since the king and the regent had done everything in their power to give the Aragonese no further cause for complaint, there was no pressing issue to unite the disparate forces. Urban officials were still at odds with nobles, old Christians against new, family against family. Moreover, the Ottoman and French threats deterred many Aragonese from joining the disturbances: they could see no great advantage in accepting Muslim or Valois rule in exchange for the distant Habsburgs. When the corts were in session two deputies expressed their dissatisfaction with the procedure adopted by their more energetic fellows. The protest led to a brawl in which one of the men was stabbed and seriously wounded. The incident further alienated the moderates and split the rebels. Subsequently the meeting could not agree on anything. Even a motion to send a special envoy to Philip demanding redress of grievances led to bitter disputes. It did not escape some of the deputies that this implied recognition of Philip's sovereignty. The meeting dissolved by mid-February. Passions subsided, nobles disbanded and Vendôme retreated.[111]

By this time Philip was weary of the conflict and frightened by the external threats assailing his recalcitrant realms. He had also learnt his lesson. He conceded that until he returned (or unless he could establish full control over Juana and the regency councils), he would not be able to separate the governments of Aragon and Castile. Assuming the sovereign powers which he believed were rightly his, Philip now appointed Juana as his governor and lieutenant in Aragon, in effect giving her full regency powers and formally announced that although he could not return to claim the crown of Aragon in person, nonetheless he was their rightful king and they must obey him and his appointed representative, Juana. Gurrea was confirmed in his office, but he was ordered to consult Juana on every issue.[112] In other words, Philip had been forced to capitulate: the Aragonese had not recognised him as king, and far from reducing his sister's power, he had been made to reinforce it.

Not until his return was imminent, in the summer of 1559, did Philip make an attempt to restore his honour and authority. The way he chose to do so is instructive. He sent the duke of Francavila to Aragon in an undefined capacity, but instructed Gurrea to ensure that he was received and treated as if he were still the viceroy. The symbolic welcome of the duke with due pomp restored his personal honour and the king's – albeit only partially. His recalcitrant subjects appreciated that this ceremony was a precondition for the restoration of good relations with their

111 As n. 110, also BNM mss. 784 fols. 91v–2.   112 BNM mss. 784 fol. 81.

monarch. The respect they now demonstrated towards the duke was a signal that they would submit to the authority of the king. However, Philip did not get full recognition of his title in Aragon until he travelled there several years later.

In retrospect, the Aragonese rebellion appears a very minor incident. But it had one major repercussion: Philip would not allow his son Carlos outside the Spanish realms until he had been recognised as the legitimate heir to Aragon.[113] Besides, Philip failed to obtain money from Aragon. Philip was greatly annoyed and concerned that his honour was being trampled by his subjects while his possessions were threatened by external attack and internal disintegration. The rebellion was also an additional source of tension between the king and the regency government, who once more stood in the way of his chosen solution to a problem. They had prevented him from restructuring the government of the Iberian realms just as surely as from imposing a new financial settlement.

The word 'rebellion' tends to invoke images of bloody insurrection and the overturning of established regimes. As such it may not seem applicable to the situation in Aragon, where violence was sporadic, brief and uncoordinated, and where the sovereign's rights were not so much challenged as ignored. 'Rebellion' may seem even less appropriate for Castile, where no uprising took place and the government itself led the opposition to the absent king. Yet if one accepts the broader meaning of the word, its use is justified. Philip's authority was repeatedly challenged, questioned and repudiated; his orders were ignored. More importantly, both the regency government and the Aragonese moved from obstruction and disobedience to the usurpation of certain sovereign functions: troop levies and calling of the corts, the formulation and implementation of an independent foreign policy and military campaign.

There were a number of reasons why Castile did not experience widespread violence and open insurrection against the monarch, despite the worsening financial crisis, dearth and dissatisfaction with Philip. First, the Castilians had been eager to prove themselves loyal subjects after the thorough repression of the *comuneros* revolt. The absence of alternative candidates to the throne or issues that would unite disaffected groups against the government has already been mentioned in Aragon, and was equally true in Castile. Similarly, their exposure to dangerous threats from abroad prompted restraint. But the most important factor in the containment of unrest within Castile was the ability of the regency government to sympathise with the plight of the Spanish – and specifically Castilian – realms and lead the resistance. Not that Juana and her advisers were universally popular; they suffered from the general unpopularity of the king's rule, but they did win respect by acting to counter the Muslim threat and because they were seen by the elites at times to

[113] AGS PR. 26 fol. 166, instruction to Carranza, 5 June 1558. I suspect this may be related to Ferdinand's possible claim to the realms if Charles was incapable or unwilling to govern them. If so, it would not be so important beyond September 1558.

protect their interests over such emotive matters as the Indies *embargos* and taxation.

Both Philip and Juana realised that this situation could not go on indefinitely. By the close of 1558 Philip had lost so much authority that he could not rely on any of his orders being obeyed, or his financial demands being met. And here was the crux: the king could tolerate a great deal of resistance from the Spanish realms, but he could not function without their contributions, particularly after the Netherlands had refused to make substantial efforts to fund his wars. At the end of 1558 it was hard to say which of these two states would first fall prey to violence and attempt to secede. It wasn't just his reputation within the Spanish realms that was at stake, but his international status. In December 1558 he wrote plaintively to the count of Feria: 'We must make peace . . . it is the only way we can prolong our lives for more than a week'.[114]

[114] A. Med. s.f. s.d.

8

A time for peace, a time for war

In February 1559, Juana informed the governor of Aragon that Paul IV had conceded plenary indulgence to all those who would go to confession, fast on specified days, carry out works of charity and offer prayers so that God would reconcile the princes of Christendom and bring peace. Thus Christians throughout Philip's lands were encouraged to participate directly in the process of peace, both by requesting divine favour and by making financial contributions that would enable the king to disband his large army.[1] Contributors in the Spanish realms were encouraged to regard the end of war in Christendom as a prelude to the renewal of war against the Infidel. Yet this was far from Philip's mind. In fact, peace negotiations with the Ottoman sultan preceded those with Henry. So little was known about these contacts with Suleiman that few realised then, or subsequently, that they had started before and continued after the peace with France. Nevertheless, Philip's failure to make peace with Suleiman was to prove as significant as his success with Henry. The first removed his final chance to divert demands for action against the Muslims, and the second deprived him of his usual excuse to defer such action any longer.

In the long run, these two sets of negotiations would reinforce the trend away from the north and toward the southern front already apparent to acute observers, but strongly resisted by the king. Philip was no more intent in 1559 than previously on Mediterranean ventures. Indeed his preoccupation with the northern front and specifically with France and England grew after the much-vaunted peace of Cateau-Cambrésis. With hindsight this treaty appears as the single most important event of this period, the final settlement of the Habsburg–Valois struggle; that was not how the protagonists viewed it. There was certainly a great deal of rejoicing as well as pious hopes for perpetual peace, but these were illusory. Dynastic and religious disputes were to bring Philip and Henry into serious conflict even before the ink on the treaty was dry. International tensions therefore continued to determine Philip's reactions to internal demands, until the obdurate resistance of both the Spanish realms and the Netherlands forced him to set aside international commitments and attend to the plethora of problems besetting his multi-national empire. 1559

---

[1] BN (Madrid) mss. 784.

heralded the king's reluctant return to Spain, and with it, a change of priorities and the close of the first stage of his long and troubled reign.

PEACE NEGOTIATIONS WITH THE OTTOMANS, 1558–9

The initial contacts between the two most powerful leaders of the early modern world in 1558 reflect the limitations imposed by traditional concepts of reputation and holy war. Both Suleiman and Philip relied heavily on notions of jihad and crusade respectively, and were extremely touchy about honour. The mere suggestion that they might relent from the eternal struggle against the 'enemies of the faith' would be seen as an admission of failure and inevitably reduce their prestige, as well as undermine their claim to be leaders of their respective religious groups. Thus whilst both sides were eager to suspend hostilities neither had the courage to initiate the process of peace.

Suleiman emphasised that 'it was not proper for the lord of the Turks to be the first to sue for peace'; Philip, for his part, constantly referred to the loss of authority, reputation and prestige – *desautoridad* – that would follow if he were to make the first move.[2] It was left to minor officials and the underworld of renegades and shady merchants to establish the initial contacts. A little-known Genoese by the name of Francesco Franchis was entrusted to express the sultan's desire to arrange a truce early in 1558. He was well received at Philip's court, and was quickly dispatched back to Constantinople to negotiate on Philip's behalf. But the king refused to provide the requisite credentials for Franchis that would have put the negotiations on an official footing, fearing the *desautoridad* that would result from such a move. When Franchis returned, he met with a hostile reception at Suleiman's court and was suspected of spying. Eventually he convinced them otherwise, and was sent back to Philip with assurances that the sultan was willing to discuss a truce. As proof of his good faith he sent a safe conduct for Philip's official envoy. It was a very clever move since it enabled each side to claim that the other had initiated the official talks.

The conditions outlined in Franchis's report, sent from Venice on 21 January 1559 and expanded later, were considered acceptable. There was to be a truce of 10–12 or else 15–20 years; it would include the subject states and allies of both sovereigns. Galley slaves were to be exchanged and corsairs of both faiths suppressed. Commerce between the two empires would be officially sanctioned. The status quo would be maintained for the duration of the truce and complex safeguards for advance warnings and meetings were proposed to ensure that conflict between allies or client-states would not trigger off war between the two leaders. There would be no sudden rupture between the two major signatories. Philip found only one aspect unacceptable – the sultan's demand that the truce be public and

---

[2] AGS E. 485 s.f., Francesco Franchis's report (Venice, 21 January 1559); AGS E. 485 s.f., Philip's instruction to Nicolò Seco, 6 March; these and the king's letter to the duke of Sessa also in E. 485 s.f., dated 6 March, give details of the negotiations.

official, and should be reinforced by setting their future relations on a formal footing, with an exchange of ambassadors. The king had deliberately kept the negotiations secret, and did not wish to make an open declaration of amity with the sultan. Ideally, Philip wanted a general suspension of hostilities without the slightest hint that he had requested it.[3] Suleiman too must have had doubts regarding the public announcement of the peace for much the same reasons. But he must have considered the advantages greater than the disadvantages. He could have gained reputation by claiming that Philip had sued for peace, and he would be left free then to concentrate on the serious unrest within his realms – and his family.

Torn between his desire for peace and his fear of dishonour, Philip admitted to Alba that he was very interested in pursuing the talks but he would defer a final decision until the French negotiations were settled.[4] This did not mean that they were suspended. Philip summoned Nicolò Seco, ex-captain of justice in Milan, to serve as his envoy. Unfortunately Seco had also been summoned by Ferdinand to undertake separate negotiations for peace with the Ottomans on behalf of the Holy Roman Empire. When he realised that Philip had summoned Seco as well, he claimed priority as Charles's successor to the imperial title. Seco had represented the Holy Roman Empire in an earlier mission to Constantinople. Philip argued that Seco was an official in Milan and therefore owed service first and foremost to the duke of Milan. It was not the last such dispute between the two branches of the family; this time Philip won largely, I suspect, because Seco himself chose to serve him rather than Ferdinand. Philip did not reveal why he needed Seco.

Nor is it entirely clear at first sight why the king decided to proceed now rather than wait until peace with France was concluded as he had said. The answer may well lie with the alluring promises made by the grand vizier, Rusten Pasha. Rusten Pasha had offered (via Franchis) to 'dissuade' Suleiman from sending his fleet to the western Mediterranean in return for a bribe of 15,000 ds. Philip accepted the bargain, but for it to be effective, he would have to move quickly. The delay caused by Seco's recall effectively cancelled the prospect of such an agreement for 1559. Notwithstanding this setback, the king decided to proceed; his formal instructions to Seco are dated 6 March 1559.[5] In other words, it cannot be said that the talks were a mere front for a shady deal over the dispatch of the Ottoman fleet. Franchis could have arranged that. Further proof that the king was serious may be afforded by his willingness to spend money on the process of peace. Seco received 7,000 ds for his journey; and 4,000 were spent buying silks and other presents for Rusten Pasha's support of the truce. These would be quite separate from the bribe for diverting Suleiman's fleet. Trifling as these sums were when compared to the huge sums spent on the war, they appeared substantial when the king was cutting all but

---

[3] AGS E. 485 s.f., Franchis's report; another copy in E. 1323 fol. 243. Philip's response E. 485 s.f., instructions to Nicolò Seco, 6 March; and E. 652 fol. 62 (5 March) published in Codoin 98, pp. 53–4.
[4] AGS E.K. 1492 fol. 30.   [5] AGS E. 495 s.f., letter to the duke of Sessa of the same date.

absolutely vital expenditure.[6] More significant, however, is the fact that Philip decided to pursue peace negotiations with Suleiman at a time when the treaty with France was all but complete. Contrary to general historical opinion, Philip did not eschew the proposals as soon as he eliminated the conflict with Henry II.[7] The prospect of peace with France seems to have reinforced his decision to conclude a long-term agreement with the sultan. The reason is clear: his overriding aim in 1559 was to buy time to recover his strength and put his realms in order. He did not wish to end the war with France to get a free hand in the Mediterranean, however ardently his Spanish (and many Italian) subjects may have desired this.

Philip remained uneasy about the talks. At times his fear of losing reputation bordered on paranoia. When an incautious secretary described Seco as an ambassador, Philip ordered all documents to be altered to read 'envoy'. The king repeatedly asked leading advisers for suggestions on how best to reduce the loss of reputation that might result, and how to eliminate the risk of being let down by Suleiman at the last moment. Alba improved his strained relations with Philip – and incidentally, showed again his ability to understand and respond to Philip's preoccupations – by putting forward a plan that satisfied most of Philip's requirements. Seco, the accredited envoy, was to travel with Franchis to Ragusa. There he would remain whilst Franchis continued the journey to Constantinople to iron out any remaining difficulties. Franchis was also instructed to make sure that Suleiman was still willing to proceed with the talks. Only when he received full assurances was Seco to continue with his journey and mission.[8]

At the beginning of April 1559 this seemingly promising initiative was aborted, but for none of the reasons Philip feared or foresaw. The break came when Suleiman refused to include Philip in the truce he had agreed to sign with Ferdinand. This was interpreted by Philip's disappointed supporters as a clear demonstration of Suleiman's bad faith and a full justification of the king's cautious approach. His conduct appeared to have displayed commendable sagacity. Such an interpretation is not borne out by facts: indeed it was Philip who ruined the talks with his inept attempt to conclude a truce with the least cost to himself and his reputation.

As far back as January 1558, Ferdinand had approached him asking for advice whether or not to negotiate a new truce between the Holy Roman Empire and the

---

6 Ibid.
7 Most historians miss out the negotiations between Philip and the sultan altogether; but Braudel, *The Mediterranean*, vol. II, pp. 967–70, dealt with some aspects of the matter. He was aware of the negotiations between Ferdinand, Philip and the sultan and mentioned the instructions to Seco and Cid in March 1559 (pp. 968–9), but he believed that 'in order not to lose face, Philip II, who was now free from troubles in the West, did not pursue his peace moves'. Pierson, *Philip II*, p. 107 and Parker, *Dutch revolt*, p. 43, briefly re-state the point that peace with France prompted him to drop negotiations with the sultan.
8 Alba, *Epistolario*, vol. I, p. 498, Alba to Gonzalo Pérez, 16 February 1559; E. 485 s.f., instructions to Seco.

sultan. This was not out of politeness, but prompted by Ferdinand's lack of resources to face the Ottomans without Philip's backing. The latter had a vested interest in counselling peace, and he urged a speedy end to negotiations even if it meant paying a larger annual contribution for the maintenance of peace than had been offered previously by Charles and Ferdinand. Philip dwelt on the need to offer substantial bribes and gifts to the sultan's wives and councillors pointing out that war was infinitely more costly. He confessed that he could not support further war and assured Ferdinand that there was only one way he could help: by allowing his name to be put forward by Ferdinand as joint negotiator for a truce. He argued that Suleiman would be so afraid of facing the combined forces of the Habsburgs that he would respond favourably to Ferdinand's demands and agree to reasonable conditions. Both at the time and subsequently he reiterated that he was not interested in a truce with the Ottomans but was allowing his name to be used in order to strengthen Ferdinand's hand.[9] His own secret negotiations belie his words. It would have been very convenient indeed if Ferdinand had paid for the truce and openly negotiated with the enemy whilst Philip enjoyed the benefits of the treaty without losing honour or footing the bill.

The vehement refusal of Suleiman and his advisers to include Philip in his uncle's treaty should not be seen as a rejection in principle of a truce with the Spanish king. Philip's emissaries were quite convinced of the sultan's sincerity. Suleiman, however, wished to safeguard and increase his own reputation while his servants wanted to line their pockets. These goals could only be reached if a separate truce was negotiated with Philip. In February 1559, when Suleiman's negotiations with Ferdinand were well advanced, the Sultan suspended talks with the Genoese republic until the negotiations with Philip were finalised – clearly then, he expected them to continue. The Genoese were deeply embarrassed when Philip found out that they too had been secretly negotiating with the Ottomans. They sought to persuade the king that their purpose had been to secure commercial agreements (especially grain), rather than the conclusion of a separate peace. Philip's position in the Mediterranean would have been seriously imperilled by a withdrawal of Genoese naval support.[10] Once Ottoman opposition to include Philip within the imperial truce had been made public, however, he could not avoid accusations of having sued for peace if he continued the talks. Moreover, it might emerge that these discussions had been going on for some time despite Philip's denials. It seemed prudent, therefore to pull out immediately and reiterate his disdain of the Ottomans. Philip boasted that he had nothing to fear from Suleiman, who was old and far too busy with internal strife to trouble his possessions. Seco's mission was

---

[9] AGS E. 649 fol. 161, Philip's instructions to the bishop of Aquila, his special envoy to Ferdinand, 21 May 1558, published in Codoin, vol. 98, pp. 6–10. Since rumours had by now leaked of his talks with the Ottomans, Philip declared that he had been approached by the sultan but had not decided what to do yet.   [10] Ciasca, *Istruzioni*, vol. 1, p. 162.

hastily revoked.[11] This cover-up was remarkably successful and the timing ensured that the end of the Ottoman negotiations were henceforth linked to the successful conclusion of the French peace treaty.

Franchis continued to advocate a renewal of peace talks, assuring Philip in the closing months of 1559 that Suleiman was still interested. Others, including the harassed viceroy of Naples, took up the call for peace.[12] But Philip feared the loss of reputation even more than war. And that was precisely what he had to consider once the peace with France eliminated his main military commitment.

The king had promised to give priority to the recovery of Bougie and Algiers, yet he does not seem to have considered this plan seriously. Instead he chose to throw his forces against Tripoli, and launched a campaign that was to end in disaster at the island of Djerba in 1560. There were cogent reasons for this, other than the fact that Philip did not pay much attention to Spanish demands at this juncture. His main preoccupation was with the fleet, which was extremely expensive to maintain, yet lying idle. He could not dismiss allied ships or put his own in mothballs until the war with France was formally over. Later, he would be forced to retain the ships in order to ensure that Henry did not go back on his word and keep the Italian lands he had granted by treaty. Already in January 1559 Philip had been concerned to devise some enterprise that would employ all his ships.[13] But nothing had been decided when peace with France was concluded, nor did the situation alter substantially as a result of this, save to increase the problem of employing the numerous, unemployed soldiers Philip could not disband for lack of funds. It was sensible under the circumstances to draw up a campaign that would make use of these resources. The shortage of money dictated that such a campaign should be short and, if possible, funded by others. On 8 May the king ordered his fleet to gather in Messina, although no target had yet been chosen. Shortly afterwards he gave his assent to the attack on Tripoli.

Tripoli had been taken from the Knights of St John by the corsair Dragut, with Ottoman support.[14] The Sicilians were particularly affected by the constant depredations of their ships, consequently the most ardent promoter of this campaign was the new viceroy, the duke of Medinaceli. Other Italian states were affected and chorused their approval. From the base of La Goleta, the Spanish commander endorsed their pleas, and the Knights urged Philip to act too, eager to recover their honour. They all considered the time ripe because of recent developments in the area. The perennial tension between the Ottoman–corsair forces and the local

[11] AGS E. 650 fol. 132, Philip to the count of Luna, 8 April 1559 (also in Codoin, vol. 98, pp. 57–9). He did not admit to others that he had even considered talks with Suleiman, only to Ferdinand, and that was because his uncle knew enough for an outright denial to be useless.

[12] AGS E. 1323 fol. 232, Franchis to Philip, 6 December 1559; E. 1210 fol. 126, Sessa to Philip, 1 & 4 December.

[13] AGS E. 1124 fol. 311.

[14] AGS E. 1124 fols. 30–2, Juan de Vega to Juana, 2 August 1556; E. 1124 fol. 134 also.

Muslims had led to war. Local tribesmen led by the 'king' of Kairouan had gained the upper hand and their latest attacks had left Tripoli seriously weakened.[15] With alluring visions of a cheap and prestigious campaign, Philip decided to proceed in June 1559, eager to capitalise on the offers of help from the Italian princes. He instructed an envoy to go to Milan, Genoa, Florence, Naples and Sicily with the news, and to persuade each governor or ruler that it had been their specific advice that had persuaded him to act. Naturally, the Grand Master of the Order of St John and the pope were also given to understand that it was really their influence that prevailed.[16] Clearly, he was making capital of this to reinforce his position in Italy and to establish his credentials as the leading Catholic prince. These elements are evident in the documentation; there is no suggestion that Philip was prompted to act by the desire to take the initiative in North Africa.

Medinaceli was given command of the campaign, partly because he had been a leading promoter, and also because he had promised large sums from Sicily for it. The king made it clear that he wanted a surprise attack to be launched immediately. The viceroy wished otherwise. He demanded more troops, ships and money and was instrumental in transforming the campaign from the quick raid visualised by Philip, to a large, formal operation.[17] The consequences were dire. There was no money to fund such a campaign, least of all in Sicily, where financial officials could not even find revenues to assign repayment of the 1.6 million escudo accumulated debt.[18] It was mid-September before Medinaceli negotiated a loan for 86,000 es – only a third of what was required. He was reduced to begging Philip for 100,000 es to fit out the fleet.[19] Moreover, the king's men in Naples and Milan would not obey his command to release their best troops until the process of exchanging territories with the French was complete, and the Ottoman fleet was back in its home ports. Despite reports that it would not proceed further west, its appearance off the coast of Albania made them highly nervous. Philip believed that it was now too late to send reinforcements from the north, so he ordered new troop levies in Italy. Costs soared and much time was lost.[20]

The leading generals now begged Philip to call off the campaign, even though he had been assured by the Grand Master that the summer in Tripoli lasted well into

[15] AGS E. 485 s.f., letters of Alfonso de la Cueva, governor of La Goleta, to Philip, 31 May, 4 July, 24 July 1559; AGS E. 1124 fols. 278–9.

[16] AGS E. 1124 fols. 278–9, Philip's instructions to the commander of the Order, Guimaran, dated 15 June 1559; letter to the Grand Master, E. 1124 fol. 302, whose delighted reply is in E. 1124 fol. 157, Malta, 20 July; that of Alonso de la Cueva is in E. 485 s.f., 24 July.

[17] The most accessible account of the Djerba campaign is in Braudel, *The Mediterranean*, vol. II, pp. 970–86. A fascinating contemporary account by one of the survivors who was taken to Constantinople as a slave in RAH SC G-64, 'Relacion de las jornadas que hicieron a Berberia (sic) las armadas Catholicas'; Herrera, *Primera parte*, fols. 13–16; Cabrera de Córdoba, *Felipe II*, vol. I, pp. 280–4; there are numerous documents in AGS E. 485 and E. 486. Don Sancho de Leiva's eloquent testimony is in BNM mss. 11085.

[18] AGS CJH. 32 fol. 32.   [19] AGS E. 1124 fols. 20–2; E. 1124 fols. 227–8.

[20] AGS E. 1049 fols. 101, 187–8; E. 1124 fols. 204–6, 165, 330; RAH SC A-64 fols. 55–6.

November.[21] They argued that it was too late in the season. Don Juan de Mendoza had the temerity to withdraw most of the Castilian ships, taking advantage of some confusing instructions. Berenguer de Requesens and Gian-Andrea Doria would have done the same with their Sicilian and Genoese squadrons if Philip had not sent peremptory orders for them to remain. As for the soldiers, Sancho de Leiva also warned of their dissatisfaction and urged the king to suspend the campaign. When rumours spread that Medinaceli intended to attack Djerba as well as Tripoli, these men refused to discuss the expedition with him, and Medinaceli henceforth ceased to consult the leading military and naval commanders on preparations or strategy.[22] Surprisingly, Philip did not impose his authority. He had enough sympathy for the opponents of the expedition to limit his intervention to pleas for cooperation, but he stood by Medinaceli's plan. He was now too deeply committed to the campaign to withdraw without grave loss of prestige. Once again, honour was given greater weight than practical considerations.

Medinaceli's interest in Djerba was influenced by news that Dragut was fortifying Tripoli. The island would serve as an excellent base for the attack, if it should prove long and arduous. Moreover, the local Muslim leader had offered his services to the governor of La Goleta in order to reduce Dragut, who was a frequent, if unwelcome visitor to the island, both in 1554 and again in 1558.[23] As Sancho de Leiva pointed out, however, the Djerban prince would aid the Christians only as long as the Ottoman fleet was absent, and if they looked strong enough to protect him from reprisals. Whilst the Christians slowly prepared the campaign, Dragut launched a punitive raid against Djerba which left its inhabitants in no doubt as to the severity of the reprisals that would follow if they cooperated with Philip. Henceforth they desperately sought neutrality.

Despite these adverse developments, the expedition finally set sail: some fifty large vessels and over thirty supply ships and smaller vessels, as well as 10–15,000 men. Shortly after leaving Syracuse they were dispersed by violent December storms. Some ships were lost, but the majority of the casualties were due to disease and rotten food. Thousands of men died before the fleet set sail again from Malta in February 1560.

The tragic débâcle is well known. Dragut had called upon his ally, and the sultan sent aid. Helped by favourable winds the Ottoman fleet arrived in record time and caught the Christian forces in Djerba. Medinaceli had been warned of their impending arrival, but in order to protect Philip's prestige (and his own honour) he chose to fortify himself on the island rather than retreat. He finally gave in to the

21 AGS E. 1124 fol. 157.
22 RAH SC A-64 fol. 57; AGS E. 1124 fol. 270, Sancho de Leiva to Philip, 30 November; E. 1124 fol. 252, ibid., 19 October.
23 AGS E. 478 fol. 206; E. 1122 fols. 60, 61, 54–6 for the 1554 plans, opposed by Antonio Doria; AGS E. 484 fols. 26–7, the 1558 offers. Medinaceli was so confident of taking both Djerba and Tripoli he wanted prior instructions on what to do with them, AGS E. 1124 fols. 229–30 and 177.

passionate entreaties of the other commanders to withdraw, but insisted that the whole fleet should leave together. The majority of the ships were not even ready to sail when the Muslims arrived. Few Christians escaped; ironically Medinaceli was one of them. For months, the Christian forces took shelter in ships and half-built fortifications. Their capitulation was inevitable and the loss of prestige considerable.[24]

After this spectacular defeat Philip had no option but to avenge his honour. Yet he was left with an enduring impression of his own weakness and this deterred him from taking action. Once in Spain, he concentrated on building up his fleet and strengthened his Mediterranean defences. He even conceded that action was necessary in the Maghreb, and mounted some small-scale operations there. But he continued to deny them the chance to attack Algiers, afraid to face the might of the sultan until, in 1565, the Ottomans attacked Malta and forced Philip to face them once again.

PEACE WITH FRANCE

The obsessive concern with honour and reputation, which overshadowed Philip's negotiations with the sultan, more than once threatened the success of his talks with Henry II. There was no need to worry about the disapproval of fellow Christians since both Philip and Henry would gain honour by making peace. But the potential loss of reputation if he failed was incomparably greater. The strength and reputation of Christian powers were still measured essentially in relation to each other. Victories and defeats against Muslims could clearly affect their status but not to the same degree. It was certainly dishonourable for the Holy Roman Emperor to pay an indemnity to the sultan, but it would have been far more damaging for him to pay it to the king of France. The former was interpreted as a sign of weakness certainly, but essentially as a temporary compromise, whereas the latter would have been tantamount to acknowledging the supremacy of France.

The peace talks of 1558–9 had an even greater importance than was normally accorded to major treaties between the two principal Christian powers. Charles V had been the main contender for supremacy in Christendom against Francis I and Henry II; now that his empire had been divided, could either of his successors hope to maintain his challenge? The peace would finally establish Philip's position in the international order as well as that of Ferdinand. The arrangements would also reveal whether as a result of the partition of the empire France would be able to demand recognition of the superiority she had claimed for decades.

Philip was acutely conscious of what was at stake. His ardent desire for peace frequently found expression in his correspondence during the first years of his reign. Nevertheless he would not buy peace at any price. From the beginning of his

[24] See note 17.

bitter conflict with Henry, Philip qualified the term peace with two words: *buena* and *firme*, literally good and lasting. He never wavered from the position he stated so clearly in June 1557: 'God will help and favour us so that as a result of this war, we will be able to force him (Henry) to conclude and maintain a good and solid peace'.[25] His subjects were wont to echo these words.[26] More than mere platitudes, they actually encapsulate a programme. Philip knew better than to make excessive demands: treaties such as the agreement imposed upon Francis I after the battle of Pavia (1525) brought the victor spectacular prestige but lasted only as long as it took the other side to reorganise and resume the war.[27] These settlements could be termed 'good' in the sense that they were favourable and increased prestige, but they could never be 'lasting'.

Charles doubted Philip's capacity to conclude the peace he wanted. In his reply to the latter's request for advice, the old emperor expressed his deep conviction that the French never agreed to a truce, let alone peace, unless it was inherently favourable to them. Moreover, they never kept it when it ceased to suit them. Charles also reiterated that he had long wished for peace – as all good Christians should – but his earnest desires had always been foiled by the perfidious French, who used war and peace solely to advance their interests. Since he did not believe that the French could make a lasting settlement therefore, Charles was in principle opposed to his son's peace policy, whilst being unable to suggest how he could continue to support the crushing burden of war.[28] Quite apart from revealing the emperor's habit of placing full responsibility for the long wars with France firmly on his opponent's shoulders, this letter is invaluable as proof of the deep pessimism pervading the imperial camp at the close of Charles's reign. It highlights the conviction that the initiative – and advantage – lay with the French.

Philip himself did not despair of achieving his goal, but he concentrated above all on acquiring reputation. This meant in the first instance, holding back and avoiding an open request for negotiations. It was imperative that the French should begin the process in order to boost Philip's prestige. Thus whilst both his private correspondence and letters to the agents designated to make unofficial contacts with the French are redolent with longing for peace 'whatever it cost', no one was allowed to give the slightest hint of this. On the contrary, Granvelle, Alba and the prince of Orange were instructed to impress upon the constable, Montmorency, and marshal St André that Philip was quite capable of continuing the war indefinitely. This obsession with preserving an aggressive front may have contributed to the failure of Granvelle and other officials to appreciate the depth of Philip's commitment to peace.

Philip was fortunate to win the first round. After months of unofficial contacts Henry gave in and officially requested negotiations in October 1558. Only then did

[25] AGS E. 121 fol. 167, to the archbishop of Toledo.
[26] RAH SC A–60 fols. 166–7, archbishop of Zamora to Granvelle, 22 September 1557.
[27] Brandi, *Charles V*, esp. pp. 234–6, 239–40.   [28] AGS E. 128 fol. 313; E. 119 fol. 104.

Philip openly declare his intention to discuss terms for peace, not merely a truce.[29] But this appearance of superior strength should not delude us. Philip appreciated his weakness and the need to buy French compliance with territorial concessions. There could be no peace without the restoration of conquered lands – his own, and even more, those of his allies. Yet he realised that he might have to pay a heavy price, so he empowered his plenipotentiaries to offer the duchy of Milan. As in earlier negotiations, it was envisaged from the outset that the treaty would be sealed with a union between the two dynasties: the duchy would be given to a child of the marriage between don Carlos and Elizabeth of Valois.[30] Cynics might argue that Charles V had made similar promises and always failed to honour them; Philip could have made them in the same spirit. The issue was never put to the test since Elizabeth married Philip rather than his son and new conditions were negotiated. What mattered most, however, was Philip's open acceptance that he would have to make substantial territorial concessions to secure peace. This was a victory for France as much as encouragement to pursue the talks.

The process of peace was complicated by the allied powers. The English were the only ones to be allowed independent representation: other states and individuals were officially represented by the plenipotentiaries of the two major powers. Most visited the negotiators at some stage and kept constant pressure on them at other times through letters and personal envoys. Not surprisingly, the final treaties were wide-ranging, including such items as the return of the silver plate and valuables belonging to the duke of Alburquerque, seized by the French in 1545. There were promises of justice or fair hearing for cases suspended or caused as a result of the conflict: Diane de Poitiers, for example, was offered some hope for lands she claimed in Naples. Numerous other individuals were named in the treaty often alongside the territories, abbeys and inheritances in dispute.[31] A plethora of individual claims thus had to be considered alongside major issues. Amidst this mêlée of petitioners, pressure groups and a bewildering mass of paper, the plenipotentiaries of Henry and Philip set to work in unsanitary and overcrowded conditions at the abbey of Cercamp, where the English envoys soon joined them. It proved a most uncomfortable and difficult autumn and winter for all participants.

Several powers had been willing to act as official mediators. Traditionally the pope and emperor would be given priority, but in this instance Paul was disqualified

[29] L. Romier, 'Les guerres d'Henri II et le traité du Chateau-Cambrésis (1554–9)', *Mélanges d'Archéologie et d'Histoire*, XXX (1910) p. 36; Orange, *Apologie*, p. 57; Weiss, *Granvelle*, vol. 5 esp. pp. 169–70 (9 September 1558), pp. 171–2 (id.), 173 (11 September), 186–91 (12 September), 229–30; AGS E. 1209 fol. 74, Philip to Sessa, 8 October 1558. The plenipotentiaries were: for Philip, the duke of Alba, prince of Orange, Ruy Gómez, Granvelle, Ulrich Viglius, jurist and councillor in the Netherlands; for Henry, the cardinal of Lorraine, Montmorency, marshall St André, the bishop of Orléans, the secretary of finance, Claude de Laubespine; for Mary (and Elizabeth), Dr Nicholas Wotton, the earl of Arundel and the bishop of Ely. [30] Weiss, *Granvelle*, vol. 5, p. 576.

[31] J. Dumont (ed.), *Corps universel diplomatique du droit des gens*, (vol. 5, part 1, Amsterdam–The Hague, 1728), pp. 23–57, for the full treaties; the items mentioned here, p. 45.

because of his war with Philip, and Ferdinand was himself a participant in the peace through his interest to recover the imperial territories seized by France – Toul, Metz and Verdun. The two kings chose Christina, the dowager duchess of Lorraine and assigned her a symbolic rather than active role. The duchy was vulnerable to attack from both parties and the rulers bound by ties of kinship to Habsburg and Valois. The drawback was that she lacked sufficient authority over the warring parties to prevent or pacify disputes when they became so bitter that both sides threatened to walk out. It was necessary for Henry and Philip to keep up constant pressure on their envoys to ensure that the negotiations continued.

Savoy and the Italian lands

From the first two issues dominated the peace process: the restoration of Savoy and Calais. The two were frequently linked, with concessions for one being balanced by resistance on the other. But why these two areas? There were other, equally contentious disputes. For example, one of the first official acts of the emissaries was to attend a formal remonstrance on 9 November 1558 for the 'unjust occupation' of Navarre by the kings of Castile and Aragon. Navarre had been a bone of contention and the cause of several invasions since the 1510s and whilst the dynastic claims of the Spanish monarchs were weak, the influence of the Albret claimants in France was strong. Here was a potential obstacle to peace – yet Henry chose not to make a stand on it. Similarly, the return of the three imperial bishoprics still occupied by France, could have proved gravely divisive. If Philip had chosen to make these a key issue, his standing with the German princes would have risen and his relations with his family could have improved greatly, yet he chose otherwise.

There were many reasons why an Italian principality should have been so important. To begin with both belligerents still believed that Italy was the battlefield where supremacy would be lost or won. Aside from Savoy, the negotiations almost foundered over disputes about Corsica and Piedmont. The island had inestimable value to France as a base to interrupt communications in the Western Mediterranean; besides, it could be used to drive a wedge between Philip and the Genoese, who might change sides. On the other hand, the concentration of fighting in Piedmont–Savoy made it appear the main area of contention between Habsburg and Valois, and by extension, the key to their overall international position. The recovery of an independent duchy of Savoy was imperative for Philip. It was regarded as a barrier to French aggression in Italy, especially against Milan. Moreover, Philip was obliged to prove that he could recover the lands his allies had lost in order to maintain his reputation in Italy and elsewhere. He also owed a considerable personal debt to Savoy, who had acted as his adviser, his governor and leading military tactician. His awareness that Henry would consider the restoration of the duchy a major defeat made Philip even more determined to recover it.

Throughout September 1558, envoys tested the troubled waters. To begin with,

Henry was adamant that he would only restore part of the duchy and offer the duke compensation elsewhere. Philip was equally determined to secure full restoration and on 11 September presented Henry with an ultimatum – either he reconsidered this issue or Philip would not agree to formal discussions of peace.[32] The French prevaricated, then gave ground – literally. Slowly, they agreed to restore the duchy, until by 22 October they were left with ten fortified positions. Alba assured Emanuele Filiberto that they could do no more for him, but the duke refused to accept this partial restoration. Two days and some hard bargaining later, the French agreed to reduce their holdings to four fortified places.[33] The course of the debates was tortuous and both sides despaired of a settlement. Nevertheless, by mid-November the two monarchs were broadly satisfied with the compromise agreement, even if Emanuele Filiberto was less than happy.

The French had in effect restored the duchy but it was far from independent. They retained Torino, Chieri, Pinerolo, Chivasso and later insisted on keeping Villanova d'Asti. In order to weaken the bonds with Philip and infiltrate Savoyard lands, Henry insisted that the duke should marry his sister Marguerite. Whilst this match went some way towards satisfying the dynastic ambitions of the duke, who also received a dowry of 300,000 écus and lands, Emanuele Filiberto staunchly resisted this condition too. He had not given up hope of marrying Elizabeth Tudor, whom he had been courting since 1554. Philip had little time for such doubts. He was convinced that Henry would not give further concessions and considered that he had achieved more than appeared possible at the beginning. By the closing weeks of November 1558 the pressure begun to tell and Emanuele Filiberto acknowledged that further resistance would not be profitable.[34] He realised, however, that he ran the risk of being trusted by neither monarch as a result of these arrangements. Soon enough he had proof of this: in order to counter French influence Philip demanded an equal number of garrisons from the duke. Henry only found out in the second half of March 1559 that Emanuele Filiberto had complied. The news caused an uproar. Whilst the French thought that they alone had the power to intervene effectively in Savoy, the restoration of most of the duchy did not appear a grave threat, but this agreement with Philip checkmated them.[35] Their anger and sense of betrayal was evident in the intense debates over details of the restoration over the following months.[36] Whilst neither side had won, Philip's ability to wrest equal concessions from Savoy turned this into a partial, but nevertheless significant victory.

[32] Weiss, *Granvelle*, vol. 5, p. 173 (11 September), pp. 185–6 (12 September), p. 187 (id.), 244–5 (15 October); Brunelli *I diari*, pp. 77–9. [33] Brunelli, *I diari*, pp. 100–1.
[34] The various stages of the negotiation can be followed easily in the documents printed by Weiss, *Granvelle*, vol. 5, pp. 244–5, 257, 272–3, 274–5, 281–2, 292–3; Romier, 'Les guerres d'Henri II', p. 45; and the treaty in Dumont, *Corps diplomatique*, esp. pp. 38–9.
[35] Brunelli, *I diari*, p. 127.
[36] Cloulas, *Henri II*, pp. 573–7 brief account of the problems after the peace.

Calais

The negotiations over Calais followed a more tortuous course.[37] Henry had made it clear that there were three places he would never relinquish: Savoy, Corsica and Calais. Dr Nicholas Wotton, English representative to Philip's court, was convinced at the very start of the talks that 'the matter whereof they have made the most controversy, is the restitution of Callais'.[38] Consequently he interpreted Philip's call for English plenipotentiaries as a ploy to ensure that if peace was made without its restoration, the English would bear the blame of this diplomatic failure. He was wrong; not only were the Italian issues initially more difficult, but Philip had called for independent English representation because his envoys insisted that since England had entered the war independently, so she must conclude it separately. Henry strongly opposed the inclusion of the English as an equal party in the negotiations but Philip persevered and considered it a victory when the French finally acceded.[39] It was not until the closing days of October that Philip's councillors thought it wise to push the English to negotiate more on their own, 'in case of what might happen in the future'.[40] None of them had appreciated how difficult the restoration of Calais would be until English and French plenipotentiaries faced each other with dossiers dating back to the fourteenth century, with treaties and authorities (including Froissart).[41]

Since Philip's priority was Savoy, he tried to eliminate the problem of Calais altogether by asking for the place in lieu of a dowry for Elizabeth of Valois (later set at 400,000 ds). He was desperate for the dowry to disband part of the army, so the concession should not be underestimated. Given Henry's own financial difficulties the plan had considerable advantages for him – it was also a face-saving solution. There was never any intention of keeping Calais – it would be handed back to the English. When Philip's solution came to the attention of his plenipotentiaries and the English, both opposed it because they thought it called into question English sovereignty over the area. The king had to withdraw the offer, but did so with great reluctance. When the English and French found themselves in total deadlock at the end of October, he repeated it.[42] Once again it was turned down.

This left Philip in an invidious position. He was totally committed to the recovery of Calais for his English subjects. As king of England he considered his reputation

---

[37] J. E. Straukamp, 'Anglo-Spanish relations, 1558–1563', Ph.D dissertation (University of London, 1965), has dealt with the negotiations at considerable length, p. 41ss.; see also Rodríguez-Salgado and Adams, 'Feria's dispatch', pp. 310–13; Romier, 'Les guerres d'Henri II', pp. 46–7.

[38] RPPB vol. I, pp. 245–6, to secretary Boxall, 26 September 1558.

[39] Weiss, *Granvelle*, vol. 5, pp. 221, 236.

[40] Brunelli, *I diari*, p. 102, entry for 26 October 1558.

[41] Weiss, *Granvelle*, vol. 5, pp. 299–30 (24 October 1558), 305–6 (25 October), 307–20 (26 & 27 October).

[42] Weiss, *Granvelle*, vol. 5, pp. 321 (26 October), 327–8 (27 October); Romier, 'Les guerres d'Henri II', p. 45.

and dignity to be at stake. Moreover, he was well aware that failure to restore Calais and the Pale would make him extremely unpopular in England where he could no longer command much support. He appreciated that he would become a scapegoat. The English would blame him and forget that the place had been lost due to their own incompetence. Calais also had strategic value, providing a small buffer zone between Philip's lands and those of France.[43] Perceiving the difficulties he could create between Philip and the English, and deeply attached to what he saw as a glorious conquest, Henry made Calais his minimum condition. On 28 October his envoys declared that no other issue would be discussed until a settlement over Calais had been reached. Two days later, the English plenipotentiaries asked Philip for permission to return home for further talks and instructions, having again turned down Philip's offer of acquiring the place in lieu of a dowry. Unable to break the deadlock, Philip had to let them go. The peace negotiations were briefly suspended and when they reconvened in November it was evident that neither Henry nor Mary were prepared to make concessions. The English responded to the situation by putting even greater pressure on Philip, reminding him that he had brought them into the war and had a duty to recover Calais for England.

There is no doubt that the English made a serious miscalculation. Whilst his own views are obscure, Philip's advisers were certainly convinced that the English would continue to refuse all compromise because they believed that he would secure the return of Calais to England – if necessary by making concessions elsewhere. Although much was said subsequently of Philip's apparent insincerity over this matter, at the time the English were confident of his commitment to their cause and rightly so.[44] The problem for them was that given a choice of Calais or Savoy, Philip would choose the latter. This is not to say that the English council were unanimous in their opinion; it is hard to speak of a coherent English view or policy. Mary's government had been in total disarray over foreign affairs ever since the war. As all early modern regimes, it suffered gravely as a result of having a female leader at a time of war. Not even Elizabeth Tudor could enforce her authority on military personnel once they were out on campaign. Women were thought incapable of understanding war. There should have been fewer problems when it came to peace, but Mary would not give a clear lead, whether through illness or indecision is not clear. Philip was abroad and thoroughly preoccupied with other issues. He was also

---

[43] Weiss, *Granvelle*, vol. 5, pp. 225, 324; Codoin, vol. 87, pp. 102–4.

[44] Rodríguez-Salgado and Adams, 'Feria's dispatch', pp. 312–13. Ruggiero Romano ('La pace di Cateau-Cambrésis e l'equilibrio europeo', *Rivista Stòrica Italiana* (1949),' pp. 538–9) argued that Philip was being a 'machiavellian', letting Calais go in order to create a permanent rift between France and England, and to secure the wool staple for the Netherlands. It is true that Calais would increase tension between the two realms, but a conflict of interests was already guaranteed by the Scottish situation; Philip did not need to create another. As for the second accusation, he made a bid for the wool staple after the loss of Calais, following his earlier determination to extend Netherlands trade by all means at his disposal (see ch. 6, pp. 174, 196); but this is not to say that he was motivated by trading considerations. The disadvantages of losing Calais were of much greater magnitude that these two advantages.

suspect to some of the councillors. The English council tried to fill the void and devise foreign policy, but they were acutely conscious that this was not their brief and did not wish to take responsibility for an unpopular decision, so they sought 'constitutional' support for their actions. They proposed that no major decision could be made on Calais until the matter was discussed in Parliament.[45] No sooner had they informed Philip of this than they changed their minds and declared that it would be decided by a special meeting of selected nobles and commoners. But this suggestion was as fleeting as the first, which they re-adopted now. Mary refused to support or oppose these proposals. She merely insisted that no decision should be made until Philip was consulted. He was more confused than anything else by these contradictory reports and sent the count of Feria to England at the beginning of November to infuse some purpose and clarity into English policy.

Before his departure, the king's plenipotentiaries insisted that Feria must go and see them and receive instructions over Calais. Once again they forced the king to accept their view of the situation. Whilst he was solely concerned to persuade the English of his unshakeable determination to support their cause, the plenipotentiaries bluntly told him (and Feria) that as neither side would compromise over Calais, the English must now be pressed for a clear commitment to war.[46] This was the only alternative.

They were not bluffing, nor unduly exaggerating the sorry state which had been reached in the peace negotiations. Nor were they being entirely honest. From the records of a council meeting that took place on 20 November 1558, it is evident that Philip's leading advisers were convinced the negotiations were indeed on the point of rupture. Several issues had proved contentious, but two were beyond solution: the restoration of Villanova d'Asti, which the French now demanded, and Calais. The main concern of Philip's councillors was to ensure that the break was over Calais. The reason is evident: if Philip could argue that the war had been renewed as a result of French obduracy over Calais, his standing in England would increase and his English subjects would be committed to supporting him in the new war.[47] Henry saved them the trouble. A few days later he announced his willingness to concede almost all outstanding claims over Italy – including the disputed areas in Piedmont and recognition of Genoese rights to Corsica which he had steadfastly denied until then. These concessions were conditional on Philip's agreement that France should keep Calais.[48] It was now evident that the restoration of Calais had become the decisive issue in the peace negotiations.

Philip's advisers were deeply divided over many aspects of the peace, but none more so than Calais. Granvelle had been reluctant to conclude peace from the outset. He used the crisis to reiterate his main contention that Philip had made a serious

---

[45] This is an interesting notion in view of the debates that were to bedevil Elizabeth's relations with Parliament in later years.   [46] Rodríguez-Salgado and Adams, 'Feria's dispatch', pp. 310–13.

[47] Brunelli, *I diari*, pp. 111–12, entry for 20 November.

[48] Weiss, *Granvelle*, vol. 5, pp. 293–6 (Corsica), 362, 365.

tactical error by showing himself eager to make peace. He was convinced that the king could gain more by continuing the war and he was adamant that the English must be supported to the bitter end. No gains in Italy could compensate for a break with England or the loss of Calais.[49] His conclusions, if not his premise, characterised the response of the duke of Alba. Alba did not believe that the French were seriously committed to peace and had all but withdrawn from the negotiations at the end of October over this particular issue.[50] He advised Philip to withdraw from the talks immediately. Should the king consider it absolutely necessary to have a brief respite to raise funds for the campaign, a brief truce would suffice. A leading advocate of the alliance with England, Alba considered English support essential and therefore believed that Calais must be recovered or war renewed. Of course the duke would benefit from a renewal of the conflict, but it is clear that he was under the impression that Philip was close to a decisive defeat of France. His advice was to initiate a new campaign along the Somme, and he enclosed details to tempt his sovereign.[51]

These views were vehemently rejected by men like the duke of Francavila, who knew better than most that Castile was in no state to fund further conflict and Aragon could not long be left to its anarchy. Francavila and the count of Feria urged Philip to make peace immediately, even without Calais, and Antonio de Toledo soon supported their advice. The three men had already stated on 26 October that if Calais were the only impediment to peace, then Philip must let it go. They did not carry Philip's council with them, but when Eraso announced the following day that the infantry was owed over one million escudos and less than 900,000 were available, the Flemish, Spanish and Italian councillors agreed that they were right.[52] Feria had been a staunch advocate of a full-scale campaign to recover Calais in 1558, regardless of cost. His stay in England after its fall persuaded him that the full burden of a new war would fall squarely on Philip's shoulders, and he radically altered his stance. Although the peace with France has long been dubbed an 'Eboli' peace, Ruy Gómez de Silva is the one person who has left no evidence of his views on the matter![53] From Savoy's diary it is clear that he was one of the most active envoys, and – along with Orange – he was used by Philip to assuage the French commissioners whenever Alba and Granvelle pushed them too far or the talks were threatened. The French approached him with important initiatives, such as the marriage of Philip to the French princess. From such indirect evidence one can conclude that he was considered to be deeply committed to the process of peace, not

[49] Weiss, *Granvelle*, vol. 5, pp. 350 (30 October 1558), 351–3; 354–9 (2 November).
[50] Brunelli, *I diari*, p. 105 entry for 31 October.
[51] BL Add. 18,789 fols. 6–12, proposals dating from 15 November.
[52] Brunelli, *I diari*, p. 103, n. 1 and p. 104.
[53] Savoy's report of the *consulta* was cited by Romier, 'Les guerres d'Henri II', pp. 44–5; Van Durme, *Granvela*, p. 28, labelled it the Eboli peace and others have followed suit. Feria's earlier position on the Calais campaign in Codoin, vol. 87, p. 41.

that he was the leading exponent of this policy. That accolade deserves to be shared by Henry and Philip.

Having considered the conflicting views of the plenipotentiaries, the councillors who met on 20 November to discuss the situation – Egmont, Hoorne, Berghes, Antonio de Toledo and Savoy – decided unanimously, if reluctantly, that war was the wisest course to follow if Henry did not agree to compromise over Calais. Although this advice was heavily qualified with reminders that there might not be money to execute such policy, and the king knew other councillors would oppose it, he had to take their recommendation seriously.[54]

As always when he faced very important decisions and a split within the ranks of his counsellors, Philip canvassed opinion beyond his immediate court circle. Not surprisingly, the governors and regents of his Italian lands and officials from the war-weary Netherlands were in favour of peace, and often specifically peace without Calais if need be. One of the most lucid statements of this position came from the duke of Sessa, who was in charge of Piedmont–Milan. He warned Philip that there was no possibility of creating a diversion in Italy, let alone launching an offensive in the area. Consequently, if war broke out again it would have to be waged solely in the north – or in the Netherlands and Spain. Aware that the king's conscience was troubling him, Sessa recommended a little mental arithmetic: let Philip balance his duty to recover a place he had not lost, against the suffering he would cause to his own realms in pursuit of this goal.[55]

It is highly significant that the one group deliberately excluded from this discussion was the regency government in Spain, whose cooperation would be vital in case of a new war. Juana and the regency councils soon realised something was afoot, and rightly concluded that they were debarred from the decision-making process because the king expected them to disapprove of his preferred course of action. In the absence of specific information wild rumours circulated, and not just at court. Juan Vázquez warned that the situation in the Spanish realms was so tense and overcharged that unless something was done to dispel these rumours they would provoke violent uprisings.[56] But the regency government itself was divided on the issue. Some favoured peace at all costs, whilst others thought that it was more important to retain English friendship. The one thing that they could all agree on was the inability of the Spanish realms to fund another war. Collectively they were at pains to disabuse the king of the notion that they would provide funds for a new conflict with France. They decided to send a special envoy to Brussels with their unsolicited advice. The draft of the instructions was repeatedly corrected until all suggestions that the peace negotiations might be broken off had been eliminated. Philip was encouraged to support the English over Calais but only to the extent of

[54] Brunelli, *I diari*, pp. 111–12.   [55] AGS E. 1210 fol. 132 holograph.
[56] AGS E. 137 fol. 239, to Eraso, 17 December 1558; E. 137 fol. 259, to Philip, 4 March 1559.

delaying peace 'by a few days'.[57] Whilst the king could count on their sympathy over this dilemma – no one was intrinsically opposed to the English demands for support – they would not go to war on this issue. The incident further illustrates the breakdown of trust and consultation between Philip and the regency government in Spain. More importantly, it reveals Philip's determination not to allow the aspirations or fears of his Spanish governors to shape his policy or affect his judgement unduly. He cannot be accused of showing partiality for his native land in this period – quite the contrary.

The death of Mary Tudor on 17 November 1558 affected the debate insofar as it persuaded some of Philip's advisers that he no longer had a duty to recover Calais. His commitment as king of England was substantially different from his present position as a mere ally. But for Philip her death – confirmed at the height of the debate, on 30 November – made the recovery of Calais even more essential. He was desperate to preserve English friendship and acted on the assumption that the precarious balance between him and Henry would be shattered if England changed sides. Philip had never been in doubt as to his lack of popularity in England during the latter part of Mary's reign. He was anxious to prevent an increase in hostility and redoubled his efforts to persuade the English envoys and Elizabeth of his commitment to their cause. Indeed he let it be known that the future of the peace negotiations was now entirely in Elizabeth's hands. If no compromise was possible over Calais, Philip accepted that war must be renewed. But he demanded a specific pledge for a joint campaign before declaring his hand and breaking the negotiations. He also reiterated his offer to recover Calais by requesting it in lieu of a dowry for Elizabeth of Valois.[58]

Since the commissions of Mary's plenipotentiaries lapsed on her death, the peace talks had to be suspended again whilst new orders were drawn up by Elizabeth. Anxiety and gloom pervaded Philip's court in this tense period of waiting, especially when rumours spread that Henry was so determined to retain Calais that he had raised loans of seventeen million écus for the new campaign.[59] The mood darkened when news filtered through of the secret negotiations between Henry and Elizabeth. Philip was soon informed that they were discussing a separate deal over Calais as well as longer-term plans for an alliance that would secure Elizabeth's marriage to a pro-French candidate.[60] Elizabeth contributed to the fears of isolation in Philip's

---

[57] AGS E. 8334 fol. 186, note for example the way that this sentence in which they acknowledge Philip's duty to fight for Calais was altered: 1) 'por la onestidad y buen respecto y cumplimiento que se deue tener, no se deue concluyr ninguna cosa no restituyendolo [i.e. Calais], sin voluntad de los Ingleses aunque se dilate algo la conclusion de la paz . . .', to 2) 'por la onestidad y buen respecto y cumplimiento que se deue tener, aunque se dilate algunos dias la conclusion . . .'.

[58] Weiss, *Granvelle*, vol. 5, pp. 371–6; AGS E. 8340 fol. 92; Codoin, vol. 87, pp. 102–3; CSP Sp. vol. 13, p. 440.

[59] Weiss, *Granvelle*, vol. 5, pp. 390–1; Romier, *Les origines*, vol. 1, pp. 29–30.

[60] CSP F., especially the introduction pp. xxviii–xxxiv; Straukamp, 'Anglo-Spanish relations', pp. 60–70; Codoin vol. 87, p. 20, Feria to Philip, 31 January 1559.

court by declaring publicly that the king of France had been at war with her sister rather than herself. Sinister interpretations of her intentions followed after she cancelled Lord Howard's mission to Brussels. Howard should have gone to visit Philip and officially confirm the treaties of friendship between England and the Netherlands. Philip had laid great stress during the preceding months on the mutual obligations which these treaties imposed, and of late he had taken to justifying England's entry into the war and his own duty towards the realm in terms of these specific treaty obligations. Elizabeth's deliberate withdrawal of her envoy thus appeared ominous.[61]

As tension mounted, Philip's depression and indecision increased. He could not make up his mind whether he should keep pressing Elizabeth for a decision on the war, or to leave well alone, since his pressure had yielded no results in the past. In the end Philip left Feria to decide what course of action to take; he did not much care as long as the count obtained a positive response.[62]

At the beginning of February 1559, after much discussion and soul searching, Philip decided that he must have peace. He was now convinced that he had no room for manoeuvre; there was no choice to offer. The situation within his states, particularly the refusal of both Spain and the Netherlands to supply him with money, eliminated the prospect of a new war. When the peace talks resumed in the second week of February, Philip told his envoys that they must conclude peace in all haste, irrespective of what the English decided to do. He was now terrified that Henry would see through his illusion of strength and learn what so many others realised by now, that Philip could not afford another campaign. The rapid disintegration of the army for lack of pay increased the king's anxiety. Both he and the duke of Savoy were convinced that Henry could easily overthrow the fragile military balance and win the next campaign. Savoy's bleak analysis of his master's situation was relayed to the plenipotentiaries in order to prompt them to speed up the process of peace.[63]

Fear of losing English friendship and the need to maintain a façade of power prompted Philip to keep his decision secret from all but a few officials. Feria and his envoys were instructed to behave as if the situation had not changed. They were to repeat his offer – only this time Philip would brook no evasion. Elizabeth must either commit herself openly to a campaign against France or allow Philip to make peace. However, he was anxious that the decision should be in favour of peace, hence his instructions to paint a frightening picture of the expense and risk of another war.[64] Unfortunately for Philip the English called his bluff. When the talks

[61] Codoin, vol. 87, p. 20, p. 97; Straukamp, 'Anglo-Spanish relations', pp. 63–70.
[62] AGS E. 812 fol. 24 (also in Codoin 87, p. 123); E. 812 fols. 7, 8, 9.
[63] Weiss, *Granvelle*, vol. 5, pp. 453–4, Philip to Granvelle, 12 February 1559; p. 459, Savoy to Granvelle; also in this volume, pp. 409–13, 427–30 and 438–45 deal with this stage of the peace negotiations.
[64] Weiss, *Granvelle*, vol. 5, pp. 440–5; Rodríguez-Salgado and Adams, 'Feria's dispatch', p. 312.

reconvened in Cateau-Cambrésis, after the separate negotiations between Henry and Elizabeth had failed, the French made it clear that they would not give up Calais. They even advanced a new argument: since Mary Stuart, dauphine of France and queen of Scotland, had a better claim to the English throne than Elizabeth, it followed that she had a superior claim to Calais.[65] The English envoys had already received Elizabeth's orders to capitulate and secure the best conditions possible. Yet they decided to test Philip's commitment to war before they admitted this. Philip was asked to give specific details of his military contribution to a campaign. His envoys confessed that his financial situation would not permit him to launch a major campaign; at most he could offer a diversionary attack. By comparison to his earlier promises and in view of the constant pressure for a joint campaign, this limited response gave the impression that at the crucial moment, he had pulled back.[66]

Feria was annoyed by these antics. He had been convinced for some time that Elizabeth would compromise despite her theatrical threats to cut off the heads of any subject who made peace without Calais. The council were not in favour of war; she could not persuade them that it was in England's best interest. Feria had advocated increasing pressure for specific commitments to war in order to force her to admit to a compromise. On 20 February he reported Elizabeth's heavy hints about England's poverty and assured Philip they proved her willingness to come to terms.[67] Philip was not convinced and would not risk giving a false answer to the envoys. Once both sides had admitted where they stood, Philip's envoys worked extremely hard to secure good conditions for England. Alba promoted a division of the Pale – leaving the city of Calais to England, Guisnes and the Pale to France.[68] But both Elizabeth and Henry preferred to negotiate a compromise without becoming beholden to Philip. The final settlement which left Calais in French hands for a period of eight years, after which the French would either return it or pay an indemnity of 500,000 crowns, had not been seen or approved by Philip or his advisers. It was proposed by the duchess of Lorraine and took them by surprise. Philip was quick to appreciate the advantages of the French offer, which left the issue of sovereignty open, included assurances of security along the Scottish border and also bound Mary Stuart and the dauphin to the treaty, which strengthened Elizabeth's insecure claim to the English throne.[69] Yet he was worried by this additional sign of England's independence and willingness to agree terms with France.

Granvelle was so far from reconciled to this settlement that he made one last

[65] Weiss, *Granvelle*, vol. 5, p. 468.
[66] Weiss, *Granvelle*, vol. 5, pp. 472–80, 469, 507–9. Straukamp, 'Anglo-Spanish relations', p. 72 states that Elizabeth and Cecil had already drawn up the terms of peace before they had received the final report on their separate talks with Henry.
[67] AGS E. 8340 fol. 92 and Codoin, vol. 87, pp. 125–9.   [68] Brunelli, *I diari*, p. 125.
[69] Weiss, *Granvelle*, vol. 5, pp. 509–13 (26 February 1559), 520 (4 March), 521–4 (5–6 March), 527–8 (11 March), 530–7 (12 March), 538–42; Dumont, *Corps diplomatique*, pp. 28, 29–31, 31–4.

attempt to prevent its acceptance. He tried to persuade Savoy that Henry's sole aim had been to secure Calais and once he had this, he would immediately retract all his earlier concessions, especially in Piedmont.[70] What lies behind this threat is obscure. Savoy refused to be drawn and his trust in Henry's word was fully justified. But the battle was not over. Only days before the treaty was signed it seemed likely that it would never be finalised. The reason was fear of what would happen in England.

England

Quite apart from its involvement over the specific issue of Calais, England more than once threatened to destroy the peace initiatives. To be more precise, conflict over the future of the realm endangered the good relations between Philip and Henry. When Mary Tudor died the succession passed to Elizabeth but there were many who doubted her legitimacy, and some who were willing to argue that Mary Stuart should have acquired the throne. Elizabeth was female, unmarried and politically inexperienced; her realm was visibly unstable. All these factors contributed to the impression of great weakness and encouraged England's enemies. Henry was more interested than anyone else in taking advantage of the situation. He wished to detach the realm from the Habsburg alliance and pave the way for the succession of his daughter-in-law. Aware of her weakness, Philip hastened to reassure Elizabeth of his constant support, but the young queen was determined to make a bid for independence and emulate her father's attempt to become the balance between Habsburg and Valois. In the long term this policy paid off handsomely; but at the time it merely heightened general awareness of her weakness and isolation. Elizabeth played into her enemy's hands. Her prompt response to Henry's offer of separate negotiations increased interest at the French court and excited hopes of dividing England from her Habsburg allies. The eagerness with which Henry pursued the proposal of marriage between his eldest daughter and Philip owed much to his desire to eliminate the prospect of another marital alliance between England and Spain.

Yet for all his skill and sagacity Henry could not have created the favourable situation that existed after February 1559. At the end of that month, the English parliament debated a Supremacy bill which incorporated far reaching changes, ranging from the marriage of the clergy to the full restoration of the Edwardian church as it stood in 1552.[71] With one stroke Elizabeth and her supporters had done what Henry could not have achieved without a great deal of money and trouble, not

---

[70] Weiss, *Granvelle*, vol. 5, pp. 529–30 (11 March 1559).
[71] N. L. Jones, *Faith by statute. Parliament and the settlement of religion in 1559* (London, 1982), examines the settlement in detail. Feria kept Philip informed of all the changes and fears of the Catholics, see e.g. Codoin, vol. 87, pp. 106–8 (29 December 1558), 119–20 (31 January 1559), AGS E. 812 fol. 34.

to mention time. They had prompted the emergence of a substantial opposition group willing to call upon foreign princes for aid. Sooner or later, this Catholic opposition would merge with the supporters of Mary Stuart, who from the start was the most obvious Catholic candidate to the English throne.

As future prospects of French intervention in England increased so did pressure on Philip to counter them. Difficult as relations were between him and the English, it was impossible for him to visualise the survival of his empire, let alone making a bid for supremacy, without England's support. It was not as if the realm had lived up to the expectations conceived in the heady days of 1553–4 when it was said in Castile that as soon as Philip was king of England they would 'lord it over the French'.[72] Henry's skilful use of propaganda and sabre-rattling created an impression of even greater French power after the marriage than before.[73] Nevertheless Philip's conviction of his own weakness and inability to resist the French without English support remained unshaken.

Despite Elizabeth's dealings with France and her deliberate coolness towards him, Philip was hopeful that her gratitude for his support during her unhappy years under Mary's scrutiny would count for something. He also continued to pay pensions and gifts to leading English lords.[74] Above all he put his trust in securing a suitable marriage for her. He revived the proposal to marry her to Emanuele Filiberto as soon as he heard of Mary Tudor's death. His envoy in London, the count of Feria, did so without enthusiasm. He was convinced that Elizabeth would not marry a mere duke whose foreign lands would embroil the realm in wars with France and Spain.[75] Once it was evident that Henry would not accept a compromise over Savoy without neutralising the duke by marriage to a French princess, Philip acquiesced in the withdrawal of his candidacy.

Feria was anxious to secure a long-lasting alliance with England and this, as all knew, could only be done through a second union between Philip and the Tudors. Whilst he pondered on how to broach this delicate question, Elizabeth seized the initiative in a most direct manner. As soon as she came to the throne she coyly asked Philip for his advice on a suitable match. Then her favourite, Peter Carew, asked Feria outright in December 1558 whether Philip intended to consider a match with Elizabeth. Elizabeth was thought to have ordered him to do so.[76]

---

[72] Muñoz *Viaje*, primera carta, p. 108.

[73] Vertot, vol. II, pp. 195, 291, 255–6, 273–5 are all good examples of this.

[74] Rodríguez Salgado and Adams, 'Feria's dispatch', especially pp. 313–14, 316.

[75] For a long time it has been thought that Philip had ordered Feria to propose his own marriage at this point. Matters were further complicated by the fact that his letter to Feria of 25 November 1558, AGS E. 8340 fol. 92 (bis) was wrongly transcribed and published by Kervijn de Lettenhove (RPPB vol. I, pp. 305–6), the king of France was deciphered to read 'the Emperor', Savoy became 'the Archduke'.

[76] AGS E. 811 fol. 101, published by Fernández Alvarez, *Tres embajadores de Felipe II en Inglaterra* (Madrid, 1951), pp. 215–19; Codoin, vol. 87, p. 110.

There was no shortage of support for the match in Philip's court and council. It guaranteed English support in the future and, since Elizabeth was expected to bear Philip children, it would ease the existing concern over the succession. Those who had supported the proposal to create an Anglo–Netherlands state some years previously were gladdened that the prospect had reappeared. Some of his advisers even stressed Elizabeth's personal attractions in order to persuade Philip to accept the marriage. Far more effective were the arguments that dwelt on the dangers that threatened England if the king rejected the match. Philip was told that unless he openly committed himself to Elizabeth, the French would establish Mary Stuart and her husband on the English throne, thus creating a massive new empire that would destroy the Habsburgs.[77]

Philip listened to this advice with a heavy heart. He confided his innermost feelings on the matter to Feria in a series of holograph letters never meant for public consumption. He candidly told Feria that he felt no personal attraction towards Elizabeth. He also concluded at the end of 1558 that he was not sufficiently worried by Mary Stuart to marry Elizabeth out of fear of a Franco–Scottish invasion of England, whatever his advisers might say to the contrary. But there was one argument which he could not reject, however hard he wrestled with his conscience: the defence of Catholicism in England. If it could be proved to his satisfaction that the marriage alone would guarantee the survival of Catholicism, then he would consider it seriously. 'I have offered myself up to God and believe that he will put before me whatever is best for his service', he wrote, in tones far more reminiscent of a monk taking vows than a man proposing marriage.[78] Then, conscious that such sentiments might be construed even by someone who knew him as well as Feria as hubris, the king added a somewhat apologetic sentence explaining that he did not append such expressions to win plaudits but to make it clear that he was extremely reluctant to proceed with the match and would only do so if religion was at stake. Should Feria have any doubts at all on this, the proposal must not be advanced – or, if it had been already made, it must be dropped. On 9 January 1559, convinced at last that unless he married Elizabeth 'the faith would be lost' in England, Philip gave his assent to the proposal. He made it very clear, however, that it could only proceed if two conditions were met: first, an assurance from Elizabeth that both she and her realm would accept Catholicism; second, that the Low Countries would remain Carlos's birthright.[79] The following day he informed Feria of his decision, telling Feria that he felt 'like a man under sentence of death'. Hardly the words of an eager bridegroom![80]

The king's repugnance for the match, so amply revealed in this correspondence, was reinforced by his awareness that there were many reasons why he should avoid it. He had learnt from the mistakes of his second marriage, which appeared in

[77] These arguments emerge from Philip's comments to Feria cited in the following notes.
[78] A.Med. Philip to Feria, s.d.   [79] Brunelli, *I diari*, p. 121.
[80] A.Med., letters of 10 and 28 January 1559; see also AGS E. 812 fol. 15.

retrospect a personal and political failure. He appreciated the need for greater commitment towards England. He warned his advisers to take into account the need for him to reside in the realm for a considerable time after the marriage. He must remain there until the government was on a sound footing and English defences had been overhauled. In effect this would mean deferring his journey to Spain indefinitely – something he initially refused to consider, but conceded later to be of the essence. Both Philip and his advisers therefore had to decide if the benefits of binding England firmly to their side offset the problems that would accrue from cancelling the journey to Spain. Aware of the implications, Juana strongly opposed the match. She laid great stress on the stigma of bastardy which tainted Elizabeth. But she also realised the need for a change of attitude towards England in order to make a success of this marriage: she warned her brother that if he became king of England again he must wholeheartedly commit himself to the full eradication of heresy in that realm. At best she forecast a repetition of Charles's endless struggle against Protestantism in the Holy Roman Empire. Naturally the Spanish realms did not want the king to assume such onerous burdens, knowing full well that they would be expected to finance these policies.[81]

One further objection to the marriage, much stressed by Philip, was the effect it would have on international relations. He argued that an acceptable balance had been established between Henry and himself, symbolised by their willingness and ability to negotiate peace. Both then and in subsequent years Philip was convinced that peace would endure only as long as that balance was maintained. Any change was a threat. His advisers warned that Henry's acquisition of England would tip that balance decisively on the side of France, but Philip believed that the marriage would have the same effect. He argued that the re-acquisition of England would be seen as a provocation by Henry who would have no option but to take up arms. Philip went as far as stating that the marriage would force France to renew the war: indirectly or not, this cast him in the role of aggressor when he was anxious above all to have peace and create an image of a peace-loving monarch.[82]

The debates over a new English marriage were essentially concerned with the future of Habsburg–Valois relations. No one disputed the likelihood of Henry's bid to seize the English throne in the name of Mary Stuart or his good chance of succeeding because of the instability within the realm. But only a few forecast this event as imminent. Whilst images of an awesome empire which included France, England, Ireland and Scotland haunted all Philip's advisers, the impact of such visions of gloom was considerably lessened if projected into a distant future. For the king and some of his councillors at least, there was a choice still: he could pre-empt

---

[81] AGS E. 8334 fol. 186 *consulta*, A.Med., Philip to Feria, 28 January 1559. On a less reverential note, Gutierre López Padilla reminded Philip (AGS E. 137 fol. 283) that his marriage to a saintly English woman had brought him neither peace nor profit; Elizabeth was so far from being a saint that she could only bring him further trouble.

[82] AGS E. 812 fol. 5.

the French bid to control England by renewing the war now, or he could concentrate on recuperating from the previous wars and rely on his future strength to counter any moves Henry might make. Some alarmist voices were already warning that no such choice existed: Philip must settle the English affair to his advantage immediately, through marriage or conquest.

Feria was wholly committed to the new English marriage, but his awareness of the unwelcome ramifications it would have as well as of Philip's reluctance to conclude it, made him as hesitant as Renard had been resolute. He waited until a delegation from both houses of parliament requested the queen to marry before broaching the subject. He allowed two weeks to lapse between meetings with Elizabeth. This is a far cry from the almost daily contact between Mary Tudor and Simon Renard. Of course the situation was far more complex now: Elizabeth's secret negotiations with France for another match made it imperative that Philip's bid for her hand should not be so public as to cause him grave dishonour if she rejected him in favour of his enemy's candidate. A further reason for caution was Elizabeth's own lack of enthusiasm for the match after the initial enquiry by Carew. She told Feria that she had no wish to marry and that she did not consider it necessary to reinforce her present friendship with Philip with a personal union.[83] Officially her coolness towards the proposal was ascribed to the different religious beliefs of the two monarchs, particularly after Feria announced that there could be no marriage unless she fully committed herself to the Catholic cause.[84] Elizabeth strongly affirmed her deep attachment to her father's Protestant settlement. Yet she gave her assent to a far more radical version of the faith and this cast doubts on her commitment to any specific form of Christianity. It was easy to conclude that she was pliable on matters of faith when they conflicted with her personal or political position and prestige.[85] In subsequent meetings Elizabeth and her courtiers reiterated her reluctance to marry and the impossibility of changing England's religion once again. Nevertheless they did not reject the proposal and this gave Feria hope that such impediments could be removed.

The lack of positive response from England left Philip under the impression that he was not irrevocably committed either. It is likely that his hasty assent to marry Elizabeth of Valois owes much to his desire to detach himself from the more unwelcome English match. Unfortunately news of this marriage reached London before Philip's formal announcement, dated 23 March 1559. Feria was unable to warn Elizabeth and pull out gracefully from the diplomatic entanglement. When he next saw her he was treated to a barrage of protest. Elizabeth irately declared that

[83] Codoin, vol. 87, pp. 119, 134.
[84] Alba had predicted her refusal to change religion: AGS E. 812 fol. 22. See also AGS E. 812 fols. 18, 101, published by Fernández Alvarez, *Tres embajadores*, pp. 219–20.
[85] Codoin, vol. 87, p. 137 Feria to Philip, 19 March 1559. Note that these statements run counter to the arguments recently put forward by Jones, *Faith by statute*, that she had always intended to go much further than this.

Philip could scarcely have loved her since he had not waited to receive her answer to his proposal before jilting her. She was furious that Philip had acted before she had the chance to reject an offer which she had been considering for less than four months. Feria could hardly deny any of this. He replied with a lesson in diplomacy: great princes never waited for rejection of their proposals – the loss of prestige would be too great. Her evasive replies had been interpreted as a polite refusal and Philip had duly withdrawn before an embarrassing confrontation could spoil their good relations.[86] It was Philip's turn now to echo general statements of friendship towards Elizabeth.

The imposition of a Protestant settlement was a blow for Philip as well as for Catholicism, but it offered him the prospect of internal support. For the time being, he had the edge on France since he had already established contacts with leading Englishmen. Feria, whose marriage to Jane Dormer made him 'an honorary Englishman' and tied him closely to the Catholic opposition, identified wholeheartedly with their struggle and put great pressure on Philip to support their resistance.[87] As the great Protestant legislation was passed in Parliament, Feria became embroiled in a plan he described as 'the best means ever devised for a prince to win honour in this world and in heaven', which had the added advantage of being 'much cheaper than the marriage'. In frenzied messages he assured Ruy Gómez that 'religion would be lost' if they did not put the plan into operation. He fervently thanked God for having chosen him as the tool by which Catholicism in England could be saved, and dramatically declared that all the water in the Thames could not cleanse the tainted conscience of those who failed to do everything in their power to bring the plan to fruition.[88] Unfortunately Feria considered the proposal so important that he would only impart details to the king by word of mouth. He sent his aide, Quadra, the bishop of Aquila, to report directly to Philip, who immediately sent him to repeat the details to his plenipotentiaries. From the scant information that survives two possibilities can be advanced: one, that this had something to do with the negotiations between Feria and some Catholic Irish lords; two, that he had been won over by the advocates of Catherine Grey and proposed to back her bid for the succession. The latter was suggested a few months later by one Robert Hogan, who told Sir Thomas Challoner that 'the Spaniards' had hatched a plot to abduct Catherine with the intention of arranging a suitable marriage (Don Carlos was among the candidates), and establishing her on the throne with the help of English Catholics.[89]

The exact details of the plan matter less here than the debate that they provoked among Philip's councillors. The collective response of Ruy Gómez,

[86] Codoin 87, pp. 156–7, Feria to Philip, 11 April 1559.
[87] Rodríguez-Salgado and Adams, 'Feria's dispatch', especially pp. 306–7 and note 4, p. 306.
[88] AGS CJH. 34 fol. 477 holograph, Feria to Ruy Gómez, 6 March 1559. Lady Macbeth was not alone in using this evocative image.
[89] M. Levine, *The early Elizabethan succession question 1558–1568* (Stanford, 1966), pp. 13–15.

Granvelle and Alba was to reject Feria's advice. They argued that Philip's priority must be to prevent Henry from gaining a foothold in England. If conflict broke out in the realm, the French would be offered an ideal opportunity to intervene and they were powerful enough to do so successfully. Philip was therefore warned to avoid this and all other plans which entailed open conflict or civil war in England. They stressed the need to keep all options open – by deception if necessary. This entailed giving assurances to both Elizabeth and the English Catholics of his wholehearted support. Feria had asked Philip for a large sum of money to give to the English Catholics: they recommended that he should send 100,000 ds immediately, but should instruct the count that this money must be held in reserve until civil war broke out. This eventuality, which they believed was inevitable if not imminent, would present Philip with an unpalatable choice: should he support the Catholic opposition or the queen? Without hesitation these councillors replied that he must support whoever looked strong enough to counter the expected intervention from France, irrespective of their religious tendencies. They agreed with Feria on only one thing, that the king must defer his journey to Spain and remain in the north to deal with the impending crisis. He should continue to fit out a fleet, so that it could be used to invade England if necessary.[90]

Philip himself evaluated the situation thus: it was likely that civil war would break out in England soon, precipitated either by the frightened Catholics or by disaffected nobles of both religious persuasions who opposed Elizabeth's government. All these groups would be monitored and encouraged by Henry to intensify dissent. Philip was confident that in the event one or both sides would turn to him for help first of all, but neither would hesitate to ask Henry if he was slow in responding or refused his aid altogether. Henry had already proved his willingness to act with Protestant rebels in Germany; he would doubtless align himself with their English counterparts if it served his purposes. To make matters worse, Philip believed that Henry had the military and financial capacity to mount a significant campaign against England. From this he concluded that his best policy was to avert conflict, thus depriving Henry of the chance to meddle in England. Henceforth, Philip was determined to reduce the level of instability in the realm at all costs. In practical terms this meant refusing Feria's request for support of the Catholics. At the end of March 1559 Philip sent 20,000 ds to pay off outstanding debts to his English servants, and a further 40,000 ds which was an emergency fund to meet the initial expenses of intervention if civil war broke out soon. He was adamant, however, that this money should not be used by Feria to encourage or abet Catholic opposition.[91] Nevertheless, he agreed that only the Catholics would be the recipients of this money once war broke out. Despite his lack of sympathy for leading English Catholics, his commitment to Catholicism in the realm was genuine

---

[90] Fernández Alvarez, *Tres embajadores*, pp. 222–3.
[91] AGS E. 812 fol. 34, Philip to Feria, 23 March 1559.

and deep. In another private outpouring to Feria Philip confessed that at times he was overcome with the desire to continue the war and save English Catholicism by force – although he knew it would lead to his own destruction. 'I long to lose everything, and I would consider it well spent if it provided a remedy for the wickedness that flourishes in that realm'.[92] Such quixotic feelings were not allowed to emerge from the realm of wishful thinking. Indeed Philip would have failed in his duty to all his subjects if he had acquiesced in their loss in order to rescue foreigners from their fate.

This feverish debate took place during the closing stages of the peace negotiations. On 21 March Philip confessed that he was in agony over the issue. Should he, as some councillors suggested, abandon the peace negotiations and secure England before the French moved in? He was now prey to fears they had implanted and thought that Henry might have agreed to the peace only to prepare his attack against England. Finally he rejected these arguments and dismissed these suppositions. He concluded that Henry was genuine in his desire for peace, because of the serious internal problems of France, especially that of heresy. Philip's conviction that Henry was committed to a thorough reform of his realm was reflected in his instructions to the duke of Alba: despite his own problems, Philip offered full support in order to cleanse France of heresy.[93] He urged his plenipotentiaries to conclude the peace, and told Feria, 'I tremble whenever I think of something that might break this peace, if it is concluded, because I lack the strength to do anything more'.[94]

THE APPLE OF DISCORD: ENGLAND AFTER CATEAU-CAMBRÉSIS

On 1 April 1559 Ruy Gómez informed Philip that peace was as good as concluded.[95] The treaties were signed on 3 and 4 April. Fireworks lit the skies of Western Europe as the news spread. Numerous Te Deums and services of thanksgiving were offered to the God of the Catholics and the Protestants; the Virgin and saints were duly thanked. Peace was made in heaven just as surely as war was made by men. The euphoria of the moment became in retrospect an expression of enduring aims. The commonplace expressions of joy and pious hopes of eternal peace were given special significance by the absence of large-scale conflict between the belligerents for another half century. But the aftermath of Cateau-Cambrésis was anything but peaceful. Quite aside from the inevitable wrangling as occupied lands changed hands and captives arranged ransoms, there was deep disquiet at the courts of France, England and Spain.

Contemporaries on all sides were far from convinced that the settlement was

---

[92] A. Med. Philip to Feria, 21 March 1559.
[93] This is evident in Alba's letters, especially AGS E.K. 1492 fol. 45.
[94] A.Med., to Feria, 21 March 1559.   [95] AGS E. 518 fol. 84, holograph.

durable or desirable – unlike the unanimously favourable verdict which history has given this peace. The distorting image of hindsight makes the treaty of 1559 appear as a turning point; at the time it seemed at most to be a pause in an unending conflict which was about to enter a new stage. After the treaty was signed, Philip wrote to his uncle Ferdinand announcing the event and declaring that the threat of death and destruction which had hung over Christendom for so long, had at last disappeared.[96] There is no doubt that he ardently wished it so, but Philip was by no means certain that the peace would last the year unless France could be restrained from intervening in England.

The fact remains that both sides had declared their intent to make the peace last. The marriage arranged between Philip and Henry's eldest daughter was highly significant in this respect. It was proposed on 5 February and persistently pursued thereafter. Philip initially rejected it on the grounds of his all-too recent bereavements.[97] There was no hint that he felt any scruples about supplanting his son as a prospective bridegroom. Close dynastic ties were the most binding symbols and best guarantees of close relations and perhaps cooperation. This suggests that both sides considered the settlement so favourable they wished to preserve it. Of course peace offered them the prospect of cutting costs, imposing much-needed reforms in their troubled states and freed them to deal with other pressing dangers, but so could a truce. There has to be more to it than financial exhaustion and internal instability. It is time to weigh up the losses and gains and examine the reaction of Philip and Henry towards this famous treaty.

Philip was delighted with the peace. He informed Juana that he had given and continued to give God his 'infinite thanks' for ensuring that the negotiations had ended so well for him.[98] Alba thought that the principal advantage of the peace was to increase the king's reputation. The treaty was widely regarded as unfavourable – even dishonourable – to France, consequently Philip was seen as having gained the advantage over Henry. The duke was unable to resist a final thrust against Charles V, so recently deceased. He boasted that Philip had successfully recovered the lands and the reputation which his father had lost.[99] Gutierre López de Padilla went as far as saying that France had never been forced to accept a treaty as unfavourable as this. Along with many others, he could only comprehend this diplomatic victory by reference to divine intervention on Philip's behalf.[100] The reactions of Philip's supporters show pardonable excess. Henry had been forced to acknowledge him as an equal; to say more than that is to overstate the case. But it should not lead us to diminish the magnitude of the achievement. It is only by reference to the depressing

---

[96] Codoin, vol. 98, pp. 55–6. That volume, pp. 54–5, p. 56 includes other letters from the king announcing the peace.

[97] AGS E. 137 fols. 112–13, Philip to Juana, 3–4 April 1559; Alba, *Epistolario*, vol. I, p. 501, to Feria 3 April; AGS E. 518 fol. 89, plenipotentiaries to Feria, same date, which all announce and give details of the peace.   [98] AGS E. 137 fols. 112–13.

[99] Alba, *Epistolario*, vol. I, pp. 499, 506.   [100] AGS E. 137 fols. 329–30.

situation preceding the war that the surprise and happiness within Philip's camp can be properly understood. These men had faced countless defeats; they had witnessed multiple attacks and experienced the problems of internal disintegration. No wonder the term miracle was so often on their lips as they contemplated a peace treaty with the greatest power in Europe which was broadly acknowledged as favourable to their monarch.

We are left then with the apparent problem of accounting for Henry's evident joy at the conclusion of peace. At the time it utterly baffled Philip's men. Simon Renard, ambassador in France before the outbreak of war, reckoned that France had spent some fifty million écus during the previous twenty-five years, lost 'an infinity' of nobles and commoners in the wars, and mortgaged royal revenues well in advance. This led him to conclude that they would never surrender gains that had been made with such sacrifice.[101] Similarly, Alba was convinced that Henry would never tolerate a significant reduction of French power in Italy; from this premise he argued that the French king could not be seriously committed to peace with Philip.[102] The greater the concessions made by France on the Italian front, the more suspicious Alba and Granvelle became. They persisted in seeing Italy as the all-important measure of power, consequently, after the peace, the latter expressed complete bewilderment at Henry's delight. He considered the final document to be a victory for Philip and so (rather lamely) concluded that it must be a miracle. God had not merely given them the better of the French, but persuaded the latter that it was to their benefit.[103] It is no coincidence that the most vociferous complaints against the peace made in the French court were from those most closely associated (and committed) to the Italian front – Brissac, Blaise de Monluc, Guise. These men were appalled by the conditions of the treaty, concentrating their attention on Italy. Schooled in the old theories which extolled the overriding importance of Italy, advisers on both sides conceded greater weight to these than to the other aspects of the treaty. Like Renard, Alba and Granvelle, they also shared a bias towards weighing up gains and losses in terms of territory. They showed no appreciation of the diplomatic victories scored by Philip in Italy before the treaty with France; victories which had undoubtedly put him in a much stronger position than his rival by the time they agreed to negotiate. In such circumstances, Henry was wise to shift his attention to those areas where he was likely to encounter less resistance and had greater advantages than his adversary, namely England and Germany.

Both Braudel and Lestocquoy have argued that Henry's motive for concluding peace was specifically to pave the way for the conquest of England.[104] This proposition appears most persuasive to those who continue to doubt Henry's need

---

[101] Weiss, *Granvelle*, vol. v, p. 226.   [102] BL Add. 18,789 fols. 6–12.

[103] BPR II-2230 fols. 6–8, to Juan Vázquez, May 1559.

[104] Braudel, *The Mediterranean*, vol. II, p. 947, calls it a calculated 'manoeuvre against England'. J. Lestocquoy, 'De la prise de Calais au traité du Cateau-Cambrésis', *Revue du Nord* (Lille, 1958), pp. 39–47, especially 46–7.

for peace, and who consider his willingness to cede Italian territory incomprehensible. Yet it is fraught with problems. When peace talks commenced in the autumn of 1558 Philip was still king of England and no one thought Mary's death imminent. Elizabeth might still have married within the Habsburg camp and so reinforced England's bond with Philip. If Henry thought of conquering England, he could only expect to do so in an uncertain (and not necessarily near) future. He was not a man to mortgage the present to such vague hopes. Of course he was keenly aware of the advantages of preparing for intervention on behalf of Mary Stuart, and peace would give him greater freedom of action. Yet the same peace which gave him a chance to recover his strength and prepare for the campaign would bring Philip equal advantages. It is certainly true, however, that England played a central role in his negotiations. He was determined to retain Calais and to separate Philip from the realm. Once Mary's death was known, he redoubled his efforts to isolate England and neutralise Philip. Only now were alluring vistas of expansion possible and the question of England's future absolutely central.

Moreover, it is invariably forgotten that when Henry decided to opt for peace he was dangerously isolated. His envoy to Constantinople explained to Rusten Pasha that he had been constrained to settle with his chief enemy because he had been abandoned by everyone except Suleiman.[105] Henry was not only desperate to restore his finances and impose his authority on the realm, he needed to restore his international relations. Creating deep rifts between Philip and his allies in England and in the Holy Roman Empire and obtaining power over Savoy was a good way to begin the process of redressing the balance in his favour. Henry and those of his advisers who considered the peace a triumph had a more realistic view of their internal strength and of France's position in Italy and the world. They had every right to be pleased with the settlement.

This argument can be reinforced by a study of the other conditions agreed at Cateau-Cambrésis, and equally, by what the negotiators left out. Philip was forced to return all French territory, but he in turn proved unable to recover important areas taken during the conflict – in particular of course, Calais, Toul, Metz and Verdun as well as the Savoyard fortifications. He was lucky, however, that death saved him from the stigma of failure. Mary's death distanced him from the English realm and Charles's death from the Holy Roman Empire. At the end of the process it was said that England lost Calais and the Holy Roman Empire lost the three bishoprics. Even in the case of Savoy, the restoration of an independent state made it seem that the duke had lost, not his ally. But what of the issues that Philip had been too weak even to raise with France? He wanted to settle the problem of the monopoly of the New World, for instance, which the Portuguese urged him to do.[106] More importantly, he had to abandon all hope of settling the vital issue of rights to

---

[105] Cit. Cloulas, *Henri II*, p. 583. Chapter 4, especially pp. 161–8 for a fuller discussion of the balance of power in Italy in 1558–9.

[106] AGS E. 517 fol. 74, Philip to Ruy Gómez, 9 September 1558.

Burgundy. In September 1558 the king and his council had reduced their priorities in these peace talks to three: his rights to Burgundy, the full restoration of Savoy and the return of Calais. Only one of these minimum conditions for peace had been achieved and then only partially.[107]

Posterity and excited men with vested interest had a less clear vision of the balance of power in April 1559 than the respective monarchs or even some of their more detached contemporaries. The best assessment of what the peace of Cateau-Cambrésis signified was also one of the earliest. Soriano, the Venetian ambassador at Philip's court, asserted that there were now only three powers in the world: the monarchies of France, Spain, and the Turks. The treaty confirmed the eclipse of the Holy Roman Empire, now that its ruler was deprived of the resources of the Netherlands and Spain.[108] Of the three great powers, none had managed to establish superiority, but they had raised themselves to a position of rough parity with each other. Their awareness that they might yet secure supremacy over the rest sharpened their rivalry. The fact that Henry and Philip had agreed to a suspension of hostilities did not mean that their conflict was at an end. But war threatened rather sooner than Philip had expected.

He had convinced himself at the closing stages of the talks that the real reason for Henry's peaceful intentions was his need to solve the serious problems within France. Since he considered heresy to be the most pressing, Philip anticipated that the French king would ask him for help. He had already instructed his envoys to respond positively to such requests. In part, this order reflects contemporary convictions that the peace heralded a new era in international conflict, in which Catholic powers would unite against Protestants. The treaty had included the usual clauses about the unity of Christendom and the need to call a council and restore the strength of the faith. There was nothing intrinsically different in these expressions from previous, short-lived treaties between Charles and Francis. Nevertheless, they were considered far more meaningful in 1559 because of the rapid spread of Protestantism. Just as people thought that there was parity between the three largest powers, they were also persuaded that a rough equilibrium had been reached between the Catholics and Protestants within Christendom. Expectations were high in the courts of Henry and Philip.

Whilst the celebrations were in progress, Henry broached the subject of heresy with Alba as expected. But rather than ask for help against heresy in France, he wanted a general commitment for joint action against heresy in Christendom, and against Geneva and Scotland in particular.[109] Decades later, the prince of Orange deliberately and maliciously distorted this, alleging that Henry and Philip had

---

[107] Brunelli, *I diari*, p. 77.
[108] Albèri, *Relazioni*, 1st ser., vol. III, p. 374. This is very much the theme of R. Romano's general article on the treaty, 'La pace di Cateau-Cambrésis', pp. 526–50. It is natural that the Italians should have acknowledged the importance of the Turks.
[109] Alba, *Epistolario*, vol. I, pp. 502–4, where Genova (Geneva) is wrongly printed as Genoa; Romier, *Les origines*, vol. II, pp. 357–60.

decided to join forces in order to destroy Protestantism in France and the Netherlands.[110] Alba had no such brief. He could promise his master's full backing for a campaign within France and no more. In Paris it was widely rumoured that Henry and Philip had agreed to 'dictate the future of Christendom'. The former would allow Philip to become 'master of Italy' whilst the latter would support Henry's bid to incorporate England.[111] Such pronouncements increased tension and expectancy: it was imperative for Philip to give a clear indication of his position over England.

With the prospect of war once again clouding the horizon he had no option but to consult with the regency government in Spain. However, he tried to play down the situation and simply asked them to comment on Henry's suggestion that they should act together against heresy, leaving out any specific details. Juana and her government were not fooled. They were against any joint action until Henry proved his commitment to eliminate heresy by making a significant move against French Protestantism. From the scant resources he had devoted to this they inferred that the French king was merely interested in securing Philip's support for foreign ventures that would increase French power, particularly in Scotland. Juana warned her brother that Henry's aim was to build up a strong military presence in Scotland under cover of destroying the heretics there, thus paving the way for an invasion of England.[112] The last thing Philip should do was to facilitate this process.

Meanwhile, pressure for action increased. In April 1559 Paul IV decided to excommunicate Elizabeth. Philip at once protested. He argued that it would aggravate a tense situation, provoke open persecution against the Catholics and prompt them to resort to arms. It was madness to unleash a conflict in England at a time when Philip was powerless to come to their aid. It is true that at the time of his response Philip did not know that Elizabeth had taken the title of Governor of the Church in England and imprisoned the Catholic bishops who rejected her elevation. But even when he was informed he did not change his mind over the excommunication. He was obsessed with the desire to minimise instability and avert civil war.[113] Of course he was now open to accusations of using his influence in the curia in order to block the succession of Mary Stuart simply because she was allied to France. If Elizabeth was excommunicated this would strengthen the Stuart claim and legitimise a French invasion. Little wonder that 'French' cardinals urged Paul to proceed with the formal declaration.

No one could accuse Paul IV of undue deference to Philip. Their relations had improved greatly since those stormy days of war in 1556, but they were far from

[110] *Apologie*, p. 61. [111] AGS E. 1492 fol. 45, Alba to Philip.

[112] AGS E. 137 fol. 220, to Philip, 13 July 1559.

[113] AGS E. 887 fol. 125, Philip to the cardinals, 24 April 1559. The correspondence between Feria and Philip published in Codoin, vol. 87, especially pp. 152–5 (4 April), 158 (11 April), 167 (18 April), 177–81 (29 April), 181–4 (8 May). There had been great hopes of the public disputation allowed between Catholic and Protestant theologians, but it turned out to have been heavily weighted against the Catholics, see G. Dickens, *The English Reformation* (London, 1967 edn.), pp. 410–11.

close. The pope's decision to delay the declaration must surely respond to his awareness that if he proceeded, two things could happen: Elizabeth might impose reprisals against the Catholics and Henry might invade England. Since Philip would oppose this it would reopen the conflict which had so recently ended. Nevertheless when her excommunication was again debated in the curia in August 1559, Philip sensibly adopted a dual approach. He strongly opposed the measure for the same reasons he had given earlier, but despairing of a second success, he instructed cardinal Pacheco to secure for him the sole rights for carrying out the excommunication and undertaking the reconquest of England.[114] Paul's willingness to delay the inevitable excommunication of Elizabeth was made conditional on Philip taking some action to stem the advance of Protestantism in England, if necessary by threatening reprisals. The only gesture of disapproval Philip allowed himself to make, however, was to replace the high-ranking count of Feria by Quadra as his ambassador in England.[115] The slight to Elizabeth's reputation was not lost on contemporaries, but this could hardly be construed as a significant demonstration. In July of that year Philip responded to renewed pressure from the pope and other Catholic zealots by sending a special envoy, Juan de Ayala, to warn Elizabeth that her measures against the Catholics were likely to cause unrest and therefore she ought to desist from taking further action for her own good. Mild as these expressions were, Philip was anxious that they might be misunderstood, so he instructed Ayala (and subsequent envoys) to ensure that the message was delivered in such a way that it would not be construed as a threat. Aside from toning down his missive so that it became an amicable warning against increasing internal dissent, he sought to make it even more palatable by adding that he had decided to inform Elizabeth of this because her anti-Catholic measures would cause tension and trouble in his own lands.[116]

Afraid to make any moves and bereft of ideas, Philip renewed his efforts to neutralise Elizabeth through a suitable marriage. Soon after his own negotiations had ended, he promised Ferdinand he would promote the archduke Charles. Feria was unenthusiastic: he thought Elizabeth was too much in love with Robert Dudley to marry anyone else. Philip persisted, tempted by the prospect of improving relations with his family. By June rumours were rife that Elizabeth would accept Charles if he embraced the Anglican faith. Few doubted that the archduke would consider the kingdom worth the sacrifice. Philip's deep pessimism at this point led him to conjure dreadful images of open conflict and himself as the recipient of demands for aid from his cousin and the queen on the one hand, and the English Catholics on the other. He also feared the impact of such a conversion on Christendom as it would greatly encourage the Protestants. Furthermore, his fears of Ferdinand or his family making a bid for control of the Netherlands were

[114] AGS E. 885 fol. 156.
[115] Quadra arrived back in London on 30 March 1559, Codoin, vol. 87, pp. 150–1.
[116] AGS E. 812 fols. 79 and 80.

reawakened. Philip knew that they were not yet reconciled to the separation of this area from the Holy Roman Empire or their allocation to Philip's empire.[117] It was natural that Protestants in the Netherlands should look to the neighbouring realm for support and equally inevitable that the Habsburg prince should respond to such appeals.

Just as Philip and his advisers were building up the archduke's marriage into a full crisis, their attention was diverted by a more significant and threatening event. Henry proposed a new initiative over Scotland and England. He was thoroughly alarmed by the situation in Scotland where a group of aristocrats and lesser nobles had banded together to oppose the French regent, Mary of Guise. Politics and xenophobia merged with religious dissent. In December 1557 a group of nobles signed a covenant and committed their movement to seek freedom from France and Protestantism. Throughout 1558 this opposition had grown in strength and pressed Mary for more power and greater concessions to the Calvinists. In May 1559 rebellion erupted. Soon the cities of Perth and Dundee fell to the rebels, and by the end of June, Edinburgh too was in their hands. Contacts were being forged between the rebels and foreign Protestant powers, England especially.[118] Henry realised that he could not defer military intervention there much longer, but he did not wish to arouse Philip's suspicions and so provoke a new war. Ever conscious of the larger price to be won in the area, he retained his ambitions in England and saw no reason to pretend that he had abandoned them. Consequently, when he asked Philip to help him restore royal authority and Catholicism in Scotland, Henry appended a proposal to partition the English realm.[119] The archduke was forgotten as Philip's chief advisers hurried to deliver their opinions on the issues raised by Henry.

A partition of England must have been discussed in Philip's court long before this; it was in many ways an obvious solution. But the failure of the Franco–Spanish partition of Naples had not been forgotten – Alba and Ruy Gómez in their joint response to Philip's request for advice made much of it.[120] In Naples, Ferdinand of Aragon had enjoyed the advantage of dynastic claims that eventually helped him to victory. In Scotland the French held this trump card. Once in England, they would be able to portray Philip as a usurper and unite the realm behind Mary Stuart by declaring war against him. The English Catholics could not be relied upon to support Philip rather than Henry. In the unlikely eventuality of the alliance between Henry and Philip holding firm, therefore, there was still no guarantee that the joint venture would succeed in creating a viable partition. Philip's relations with the English Catholics would also be seriously compromised if they realised that he was willing to consider a partition of their land.

[117] Codoin, vol. 87, p. 180; AGS E. 812 fols. 42, 229; Fernández Alvarez, *Tres embajadores*, pp. 48–5, 74–6. See pp. 35–8 for details of the division of the empire.

[118] C. Read, *Mr. Secretary Cecil and Queen Elizabeth* (London, 1955, edn. 1965), esp. pp. 135–52; Wernham, *Before the Armada*, pp. 247–9.

[119] ADE FR vol. 1, pp. 20–4, Alba and Ruy Gómez reported this on 11 July.

[120] ADE FR vol. 1, pp. 20–4; on Naples see p. 28 and notes.

As for Scotland, Alba and Ruy Gómez dwelt on Philip's dilemma. They acknowledged that he could not refuse Henry's request for aid without being accused of lacking respect for dynasticism and the faith. However, if Mary Stuart's authority was increased it would be tantamount to enhancing French power in Scotland and it was now evident that Henry was determined to use the realm as a base for the invasion of England. Philip was advised to offer aid but delay its departure interminably in the hope that this would ruin the French campaign and weaken them sufficiently to prevent an invasion of England.[121]

Other than this, they could only suggest that Philip should bluff and bully his way out of trouble. He must persuade Elizabeth – if necessary by threats – that she must make no further moves in favour of Protestantism. She must also be pressed to marry a suitable candidate (unnamed), and Philip must 'so arrange matters in England' that the prevailing tension in the realm would not degenerate into open conflict until he was in a position to take advantage of it. They strongly advocated unspecified measures to build up a party of Catholic sympathisers in England. Above all they insisted that Philip should impress upon Henry that he would sustain English independence by force of arms if necessary. He must insist that French soldiers remain in Scotland and threaten war if they did not. Alba and Ruy Gómez were confident that Henry was too weak to call Philip's bluff. The finishing touch to this policy of disinformation was to announce don Carlos's imminent departure for the Netherlands if Philip persisted in his plan to leave for Spain. It was essential to assure the world that his departure in no way demonstrated a lack of affection for his northern subjects, nor a diminution of his interest and commitment to northern affairs.

The vague nature of so much of their advice is striking and highlights Philip's impotence once Elizabeth rejected a close alliance but claimed a vague friendship. It is interesting too that among Alba's papers there is a document which, but for a few minor alterations, could be taken as a copy of that cited above, yet the authorship of this is solely ascribed to the duke of Alba.[122] A mistake by a careless secretary? This is possible, and the issue would not be of the least interest but for the existence of another memorandum which became the key to a major policy review. This uninspired reiteration of vague policies which had already been tried and failed – namely, Elizabeth's marriage or the creation of a Catholic English party – could have been a deliberate attempt to focus the king's attention on that other document to prove that there was no alternative to what was being proposed in that memorandum. It could also be a half-hearted effort by two counsellors who knew that the advice they gave now would be negated by the response to those proposals.

This wide-ranging memorandum was forwarded by Philip to Spain at the end of June 1559 with a request for a clear and detailed response to each of its propositions.

---

[121] My next book on Philip's policies 1559–66 will deal with the tortuous moves that followed when he received calls for aid from both France and England after the Scots rebelled.
[122] BL. Add. 18,789 fols. 13–16, dated 10 July 1559.

He unhelpfully refers to the authors as 'some people'; Braudel, aware of the importance of this proposal, studied it and concluded that it was the work of 'the non-Spanish advisers of the prince'.[123] Internal evidence, however, suggests their involvement: who else would refer to the defences of the Spanish realm as 'home defence' and speak of 'our frontiers' with Africa, to mention but two instances? If we move to an analysis of the policies advanced, it is clear that they, and even the wording, bear striking similarity with memoranda produced by Alba in earlier consultations.[124] As for the non-Spanish presence rightly detected by Braudel, we need look no further than Granvelle with whom Alba was so closely cooperating during the peace negotiations and in their aftermath. Other counsellors may have been involved, but the document most closely follows the recommendations found in the papers of Alba and Granvelle.

The proposal began from the premise that Henry was poised to invade England and had executed his plans with such skill that Philip would be unable to oppose him. They argued that Henry had established contacts with English Catholics, who had despaired of Philip and turned to his rival. They had agreed to launch a rebellion that would coincide with an invasion led by the dauphin in the name of his wife. Henry would declare France neutral in this conflict, thus depriving Philip of a cause and excuse to intervene. If he did move to prevent the invasion, he would be accused of unjustified aggression and support for a Protestant regime. Undeterred by the lack of direct proof of this fiendishly clever plot, and aware that they were likely to be dismissed as overwrought francophobes, the authors pointed to indirect evidence of its existence. To begin with Henry was levying troops, ostensibly to restore royal authority and religion in Scotland, a claim they rejected. They refused to accept that the situation there was serious enough to justify the label 'rebellion' or the number of troops involved. Their second argument was the fact that the dauphin had publicly declared that his wife was the rightful heir to the throne of England. Their third contention was that England's long history of dissent, ill-treatment and deposition of their monarchs made rebellion against Elizabeth all but inevitable. Finally, the authors recounted a conversation between the constable of France and Alba. Montmorency had expressed his determination to make Henry master of England, and had offered to persuade him to withdraw entirely from Italy if Philip in turn offered Henry a free hand in the north.

In their view Philip had to choose between allowing England to fall – after all it was no longer his responsibility – or prevent it by ensuring that Henry did not establish a foothold in the realm. If England fell, they were certain that the Netherlands would soon follow. They could not withstand the inevitable attack from a massive Franco–British state. These counsellors accepted that outside of the Netherlands, Philip's subjects might ask themselves if this mattered. Why not

---

[123] *The Mediterranean*, vol. II, p. 947; The document can be found in AGS E. 137 fols. 95–6; it was sent with Philip's dispatch to Juana of 29 June 1559. See also AGS E. 518 fols. 120–1.

[124] Contrast it with BL Add. 18,789 fols. 13–16, and Alba, *Epistolario*, vol. I, pp. 504–5, for instance.

sacrifice these northern provinces and consolidate power over the south? Their reply was simple: the Valois would never be satiated. Once they had taken the Netherlands, they would want Italy and soon enough they would be 'at home', that is, in Spain. Although the Spaniards would doubtless boast that they could easily deal with a French invasion, these counsellors painted an extremely bleak picture of Spanish defences. Their landward fortifications were so weak that the French would easily overrun them. Furthermore, the very nature of Philip's empire also dictated the defence of each part to ensure the survival of the whole. If he showed that he was too weak to defend one area it would unleash a general attack that would dismember the far-flung, ill-defended empire altogether. Spain is depicted as a realm about to be engulfed by two giant waves: the Islamic powers of the Maghreb and the *moriscos*. Unless Philip gained sufficient time to deal with these pressing dangers, Spain would be engulfed beneath them. The only way Philip could secure this vital breathing space was by 'entertaining' the French in England.

By this rather convoluted reasoning, they concluded that the survival of both Spain and the Netherlands was entirely dependent on Philip's immediate intervention in England. The French must be kept busy there whilst Philip dealt with the Islamic menace in Spain. However, in order to achieve this, he must ensure that there was sufficient opposition within England and this, they candidly admitted, would force Philip to make a decision. He must, since the Catholics were likely to join the French, 'take the wrong side'. In other words, Philip must back the queen and the Protestants. Although these advisers claimed that there was still time to negotiate an alliance with leading English Catholics, and did not despair of persuading Elizabeth to halt her anti-Catholic measures and marry someone suitable, they stated this without much conviction. Everything in their proposal suggests that since Philip had failed to achieve these goals by now there was no alternative to an alliance with Elizabeth and the Protestants.

They were equally emphatic that Philip must remain in the Netherlands. His presence there had deterred Elizabeth from exterminating the Catholics,[125] and the French from invading the island. Moreover, they stressed the need for Philip to stay until the country's defences were in order and the new bishoprics established. They argued that it was imperative for Philip to prove that he loved his subjects in the Netherlands and was ever mindful of their interests and needs. If he left them in the hands of 'an inexperienced duchess' – a veiled reference to Margaret of Parma, who had been suggested as a replacement for the king – at a time of dire peril, his love would rightly be questioned by them. Philip's departure from the Netherlands is portrayed as a dual betrayal. The king was leaving them exposed to attack and sacrificing their interests in the north. Although these counsellors acknowledged that the Spanish realms had serious problems they insisted that those of the Netherlands were far worse. Philip must persuade the Spaniards to send them

---

[125] The French themselves believed this, see Romano, 'La pace di Cateau-Cambrésis' pp. 540–1, n. 6.

subsidies and prove to them that their survival depended on the survival of the Netherlands. His journey to Spain was dismissed – unwisely as it turned out – as a vacation: 'let your majesty forbear from taking this step, which is so out of character, to go there and rest leaving these provinces in certain peril'.[126]

Internal and international policy were now hopelessly entangled. Saving England from a French invasion; saving the Netherlands from internal unrest and external dangers; saving the monarchy as a whole – these were the avowed aims of the king's advisers in this document. It should be appreciated that those who wished to retain Philip in the north and those who favoured an aggressive policy against France there had a vested interest in painting the situation both inside the Netherlands and in England in the darkest colours. Philip found it all so persuasive that he decided to defer a final decision over his Spanish journey until he had weighed up the response of his Spanish and Netherlands states. Was the Muslim threat worse than that of France? Was the situation in Spain better than that of the Netherlands? The bitterness of the debates surrounding England during 1559 owe much to the underlying struggle between the two principal parts of Philip's empire.

As Philip waited anxiously for a reply from the Spanish regency government, an event of momentous importance occurred: Henry II died on 10 July 1559 as a result of a jousting accident. His successor Francis II was fifteen, old enough to dispense with a regency, but too young to rule independently. Philip was devastated, declaring it a disaster. Whilst he had periodic doubts, he remained convinced of Henry's commitment to peace. This could not be said of Francis, now king of both France and Scotland and under the influence of the bellicose duke of Guise. From Paris, Alba and Ruy Gómez reported that Guise and all those who had opposed the peace and considered it dishonourable, were in a position to press for retaliation. The Guise naturally advanced plans for an invasion of England with the aim of putting their kinswoman on the throne. Alba and Ruy Gómez warned Philip to retract the message of friendship and peace which he offered, along with his sincere condolences, to the young monarchs. Notwithstanding their forceful arguments that it would be construed as weakness, as evidence of Philip's desperate need to avoid conflict, and so encourage those who favoured aggression, he insisted that his messages of peace must be effectively relayed.[127] He bargained on Francis's youth and the political instability within France acting as a deterrent unless there was an actual threat to their interests, and his assessment proved accurate.

Granvelle was appalled by what he saw as a supine reaction to an unparalleled opportunity for action – and the pope echoed such sentiments. Whilst both men paid lip-service to peace in principle, and Granvelle at least gave a passing thought to Philip's financial plight, they believed it was sheer madness to let this chance

[126] AGS E. 137 fols. 95–6.
[127] AGS E. 137 fol. 105, Philip's report of Henry's death to Juana; ADE, vol. I, pp. 13–16, 35–6; 30–1, orders and letters to France; see also Romier, *Les origines*, vol. II, p. 388.

slip.[128] Paul IV for one insisted that Philip must not miss this opportunity, because it was his duty to solve 'the English problem', and the only solution was an invasion of England whilst it was weak, and France in no position to challenge Philip. Paul sought to encourage the king by painting glowing vistas of the future: the whole world would tremble at Philip's power once he was in possession of England. Paul even expressed the hope that God would raise the king to a position of universal monarchy (*monarchia del mondo*). The irony was not lost on him. After all, Paul had declared war on him and his father ostensibly because they had tried to gain *monarchia*. Since this tack failed, Paul tried another: from blandishments he moved to offers of substance. Philip was promised investiture as King of England, thus he would be able to conquer the realm legally. To add further encouragement, the pope predicted that the campaign would be easy, successful and most pleasing to God.[129]

The importance of this concession cannot be emphasised enough. Philip would have a legitimate reason to ignore Mary Stuart's unquestionable dynastic claims. Moreover, if the French opposed the invasion, they could be accused of hampering God's work. But he did not trust Paul and probably with reason. Had he replied positively, the pope could have used this to discredit him as an aggressive and unjust power.

Whilst those who supported a northern campaign saw Henry's death as a further justification for immediate action against England, their opponents argued that it had eliminated the threat on the northern front. Whatever Guise might aspire to do, they did not believe that the young king was in a position to declare war against England, let alone challenge Philip directly. In sum, Henry's death intensified the debate without altering the essential arguments of either side. Combined with the pope's pressure, however, it was an added incentive to make a policy decision immediately. None could be made without assessing the degree of support from Spain and the Netherlands. Aware that the king's decision would determine where he would reside and what policies he would adopt in the immediate future, the Spanish realms and the Netherlands hastened to prepare their case and persuade the king to give them priority.

---

[128] BPR II-2320 fols. 54–6 and 42–3 for Granvelle's reaction.
[129] AGS E. 884 fol. 263 Ascanio Caraciolo to Philip, 26 July; fol. 135 id., 1 August; AGS E. 884 fol. 134, don Gonzalo Chacón to Philip, 11 August. Chacón and Caraciolo were acting as Philip's representatives in Rome since Paul had rejected Philip's ambassador, don Juan de Figueroa.

9

Epilogue: Spain or the Netherlands?

All states incorporated into the Habsburg–Trastámara empires of Charles V and Philip II believed implicitly that they had a right to be considered exceptionally loyal and deserving of the monarch's special attention and support. As their finances became overburdened and they withstood invasions, attacks, unrest, the conviction that they had suffered more than the rest deepened. Sicily felt that it was facing the overwhelming might of the Ottoman fleet and countless corsair attacks with scant resources. They took it for granted that the bulk of the fleet should be stationed there and resented not being allocated further aid. Naples always had to contribute more than the other Italian states to northern and Mediterranean wars, particularly in times of crisis, and had long-term responsibilities for the upkeep of important fortifications outside its frontiers. Moreover, they were also frequent victims of Muslim attacks; surely they merited generous subsidies, if anyone did? Milan, turned into an oversized military headquarters, devastated by warfare and underpaid armies, desperately needed help, and thought that long years of suffering as the main theatre of war gave its claim considerable weight. Poor Sardinia had good reason to feel neglected and ignored; its resources could not match those of the enemy and once it became a target for the Franco–Muslim fleets it expected the rest of the empire to provide the defence her inhabitants were unable to provide. Aragon too felt that long years of neglect ought to be rectified, and until that time, they refused to make substantial contributions. The English expressed righteous indignation at the suggestion that they were not as deserving as the patrimonial lands, especially after entering the war against France. They constantly reminded Philip that they had done him a signal favour and ought to receive preferential treatment as a result.

Graver still was the rivalry between the Netherlands and Spain. The two states had contributed more than any others to the emperor's continuous wars, and their perception of what these sacrifices had bought were as irreconcilable as their demands. In 1557 both the duke of Savoy and the count of Lalaing took it upon themselves to explain the bitterness and resentment of the Netherlands. The provinces had faithfully supported Charles through decades of wars which benefited Spain most – for them Charles's wars had been essentially a struggle to establish himself in Naples, Milan and Navarre, all classified as 'Spanish' interests. Their sufferings had been compounded by the wasteful Parma campaign – another

'Spanish' venture. Lalaing even considered Philip's campaign against France to fit this category and was furious at what he considered to be its paltry contributions. If the Spanish realms had contributed but half of what the Netherlands had given, the chaos and suffering of the northern provinces could have been substantially reduced, if not indeed avoided.[1]

Such claims both stunned and appalled contemporary Spaniards, whose unshakeable conviction was that they had been ruined as a result of endless conflicts caused by the emperor's determination to extend his lands and strengthen his claims to northern and central Europe. The defence of the Netherlands and the Franche-Comté; the acquisition of Gelderland, Utrecht and other northern provinces, and the wars in Germany had drained them of funds. To cap it all, the emperor had launched Mediterranean ventures which benefited the Italian states rather than Iberia. The resentment of the Spaniards was great – and growing greater. By 1557 there was an almost universal condemnation of both Charles and Philip for their failure to appreciate Spain's continuing sacrifices. Even Gutierre López de Padilla, a strong supporter of the imperial ventures of the two monarchs, was by then talking of the 'scant knowledge' Charles and Philip had of Spain, and 'the little love they must have for this state'.[2]

Mutual suspicion and antipathy were nothing new. The monarchs of early modern Europe learnt quickly how to deflect such natural discontent – or at least, how to live with it. What made the situation different as the troubled 1550s came to a close was the degree of suffering and misfortune each state had to bear. They were paying the price of many years of war. Disputes over the quartering of troops or naval forces; debates about commercial licences; payment of multi-national loans – all these came to be fought as issues of life and death due to the scarcity of resources and the resentment accumulated after years of supporting the monarchy with loyalty and subsidies. Had Philip been less sensitive, his task would have been much easier. As the war progressed, however, and the discontent in his lands increased visibly, he became acutely conscious of the problems assailing the empire, and convinced that he must deal with them immediately. The vigour and aggression that carried him through these difficult years and protected him against the cries for help from his realms, waned under the combined pressure of the peace negotiations and resistance he encountered from his Spanish and Dutch subjects. Without the all-consuming urgency of the war against France, Philip lost his shield against the protests of his lands. Moreover, having won his wars, he had no excuse, but must set about the arduous task of reforming his empire. For a time, however, whilst he waited for the response to the proposed campaign in England, he was in limbo. Policies of reform and retrenchment did not attract many of his closest councillors, who were eager to continue the march towards international domination. There is

[1] A. Louant, 'Charles de Lalaing et les remontrances d'Emmanuel-Philibert de Savoie', especially pp. 268–9. See also, L. P. Gachard, 'La seconde remontrance d'Emmanuel Philibert'.
[2] Codoin, 97, p. 336.

reason to suppose that Philip to was attracted by the prospect of further prestige. But the king finally accepted, in the months preceding his departure from the Netherlands, that the empire would no longer tolerate the conditions it had endured over the last few years. If he took an inordinately long time to decide how best to tackle the problems of his empire, it is largely because these problems were of such magnitude they defied easy solutions. There was no general agreement as to how he should proceed nor was there a consensus as to which problems were most deserving of immediate attention. Matters were further complicated by the bitter conflict which ensued between the Netherlands and Spain, which he dimly perceived in the spring of 1559 – and fully appreciated by the end of the year. For a long time he would try to avoid making a choice between them; yet the two states were as obdurate and determined to establish their supremacy as ever Habsburg and Valois had been. The crucial question is, did his return to Spain prove that he had capitulated to their demands and given them priority over the Netherlands?

THE CASE FOR SPAIN

The memorandum proposing war in the north could not have arrived at a worse moment in Valladolid. The regency government was in the process of drawing up another statement of the financial situation and the figures were truly frightening. They fanned the flame of opposition to the king's profligate policies. Nothing had been done to improve the financial situation, nor was the government in any position to counter the *morisco* threat or the rebellion in Aragon, let alone take effective measures against the Maghrebian powers.[3] There was also mounting irritation as Philip repeatedly reneged on his promises to return to Spain. He had announced his impending departure after the victory of St Quentin, then he deferred it until peace with France was assured. In January 1559 Juana asked Ruy Gómez to persuade her brother to return forthwith, 'you know how short of money we are here. Press my brother to come soon if he does not want everything to be lost'.[4] Philip reassured her of his determination to leave as soon as peace was signed, but he stipulated that he would not go until he had received money from them for the journey. Juana arranged a loan of 300,000 ds in March 1559 to meet this condition. The contract was in the style of the 1558 *asientos* with all their damaging implications to Castilian finances in the long term, but she thought the price worth paying to bring Philip back.[5] He took the money, but failed to return. Indeed, it was soon clear that despite making a start on the preparations, he was not even fully committed to doing so.

These broken promises increased the frustration and alienation of the regency government. Their patience exhausted and fearful that the king would continue to

---

[3] Details of the problems of the Spanish realms in chapters 6 and 7.
[4] AGS PR. 92 fol. 59 hol.
[5] AGS E. 137 fol. 217; E. 137 fols. 213–14; CJH. 36 fol. 151; CJH. 36 fol. 85.

ignore their warnings, the regency councillors advised Juana to prevent the *factor* or any other financial official from accepting any further loans taken up abroad. She should study each contract and discuss it with Philip before accepting responsibility for repayment. Juana willingly acceded. This measure was meant as more than a delaying tactic; clearly the regency government intended to have a decisive say in any further debts charged on Spanish revenues. It was no more than Philip had wanted in the days when he was regent, but he had not dared to go so far. The prohibition would enable the regent to reject contracts and delay the acceptance of those they were persuaded or forced to admit. Not the least advantage of this measure was that it preserved a façade of obedience. Moreover, it could force Philip's hand – they knew as well as he did that he could not survive without Spanish subsidies.[6]

About this time too, Philip issued orders that the victims of the 1558 seizure of New World bullion be compensated at once, without suggesting where the money could be found. The regency government were all in favour of the principle but lacked the means to put it into practice. Aside from heightening their frustration, this latest order increased their fear that Philip intended to impose a new *embargo* in 1559 and was trying to salve his conscience and appease them before revealing his true intentions.[7] They were right.

Imagine then the impact of a memorandum stating that the problems of Spain were not as serious as those in the Netherlands and requesting the immediate dispatch of subsidies as well as funds for a new war. Philip's covering letter gave further emphasis to the financial points: Spain would have to bear the full costs of the new campaign in England because the Netherlands were incapable of absorbing any further debts.

Officially, the regency government responded to the letter and the memorandum with remarkable restraint. Juana wrote to Philip giving their collective response. The document, they had decided, contained 'certain clauses' which could be termed 'prudent'; nevertheless, they considered its general conclusions unacceptable, primarily because of their implications for Philip's much-awaited return. She hoped that Philip would not mind too much that she had not done as he requested and drawn up a detailed reply to the propositions put forward, but she had thought it best not to waste her time, or that of the councils. They considered that a few general remarks and the enclosed statement of Spain's current financial position would suffice. A glance at the figures would prove why mere words were irrelevant.[8]

The situation can be quickly summarised – fuller details are in Table 12. Annual revenues were estimated at 1.5 million ducats – this erred on the generous side. The regency government needed to provide 4.2 million ducats immediately to cover

6 AGS E. 138 fol. 121; E. 137 fol. 26.   7 AGS E. 137 fols. 196–7.
8 AGS E. 137 fols. 277 (14 July 1559) and 224–5.

Table 12. *Financial situation in Castile 1559*

Estimated revenues[A]	1,538,666ds per annum
Assigned revenues[A]	all for 1559, 1560 and part of 1561/2
	all that had been freed in the moratorium of 1557 reassigned.
Accumulated debt[A]	for the Fugger, 42,666ds assigned on Indies revenues; 3 million more to be shared by Spain and the Netherlands, not yet assigned
	3.7 million for defence expenditure and loan repayments. for the Affetatis and other Genoese firms not yet calculated, but 'very great'
Urgently required[B]	500,000ds cash for Villalon fair.

[A] AGS E 137 fol. 277, Juana to Philip, 14 July 1559, E 137 fol. 224–5, it was rather a generous estimate, with new revenues being given nominal sums that proved too high. Ulloa *La Hacienda Real de Castilla*, p. 130, reckons revenues for 1559 at 1,466,666ds (550 million maravedis) and assignations at 1,447,398ds (c. 543 million).

[B] AGS E 138 fol. 121 (9 July 1559), gives a figure of 370,386 ds for Villalon but the sum of 500,000 was given by López del Campo, E 137 fol. 26 (14 July). Debts of 'the October fair' are given as 605,703 ds, AGS E 137 fol. 142, sent by Juana to Philip with E 137 fol. 220 (13 July).

defence expenditure and manage the government debt. They had already used up all sources of revenue for debt repayment and anticipated revenues to 1561–2. They knew that the king owed the Fugger well over 3 million ducats which would be apportioned between Spain and the Netherlands, but they had not yet calculated the total owed to the Affetati and other Genoese firms. This, they realised, was 'very great'. The inability to calculate the real extent of their indebtedness stemmed partly from the complex nature of the more recent contracts, which included old and new debts and rendered a true account almost impossible. It was also extremely difficult to keep accurate records of the constant defaults and confiscations made by the monarch in numerous fairs across the continent. They were convinced that the investigations in progress to settle an overall figure for Genoese debts would reveal a catastrophic situation. A recent estimate puts the total accumulated debts in Castile at the time of Philip's return to Spain at 25 million ducats.[9] Juana and the councils could see no way to remedy the situation; for them it was the nadir of Spanish finances. Hence their decision to prevent the acceptance of more loans. If the king could not be persuaded of his folly, he must be prevented from destroying them by adding further burdens.[10]

The unofficial reaction of the regent and her court was far from restrained. Philip

[9] Ulloa, *La Hacienda Real*, p. 150.
[10] They had no right to issue the decree without royal authorisation.

was acutely embarrassed by accounts of how they had received the memorandum – they had laughed. The comment that the king would go to Spain 'to rest' was considered particularly amusing.[11] Philip realised that this was not the laughter born of joy, but of derision. The regency government concluded that since the king had seriously considered this proposal, he could not have read or understood the problems of the Spanish kingdoms. Whatever else was said or done at the regent's court stung Philip so deeply that he refused to allow Juana's letter or details of what had happened to be revealed or discussed by his councillors. He gave the following instructions: 'This must not be seen by the council. Do not show anyone this chapter [*sic*] because I do not wish to take advantage of these things, but only to do what I know is best, which is to go without relying on anyone's opinion'.[12] Perhaps Philip had come to understand that it was unwise to make use of comparisons that would increase the antagonism between Spain and the Netherlands. He matched his sister's restraint in his official reply to her letter. Giving no hint of his anger or hurt, he sent a laconic message stating that he 'accepted' their reply and advice.

Relations between the king and the regency government wavered from extreme coolness to heated disputes. During these months conflict was the norm, and most frequently it was because of finance. Philip's desperation for funds increased rather than diminished and he maintained relentless pressure on the regency government to provide the sums he needed to disband the army. But they could not supply him. He empowered Juana and the council of finance to sell more crown assets: vassals, jurisdictions, titles. He hoped that the money they raised would enable him to dispense with further loans. He knew as well as they did that such measures were likely to bring in small sums and piecemeal at that.[13] Both sides were conscious that there was only one way to raise the money Philip wanted – the disreputable policy of taking bullion from the New World fleets. Having dallied with other measures, Philip finally admitted that he wanted a new round of confiscations of New World money. The regency government complained: it was a well-rehearsed ritual by now. Nevertheless, Juana did not disobey after he reiterated his orders. Instead, she was highly selective. Spanish merchants and investors and the Genoese financiers who

[11] AGS E. 137 fol. 227, Philip's holograph note on this document. The comment is extremely difficult to transcribe and the problem is compounded by the lack of clarity of what is being said. It is not surprising that there should be some disagreement over it. My own transcription reads: 'de algunas cosas del memorial se q(ue) han Reydo alla harto, y en algunos han myrado, y vno dellos se me q(ue) era de yo (*sic*) no pensase ir a holgar a casa d(e)sta manera', which translates as: I know that they laughed a great deal over there at some parts of the memorandum, and also discussed some of them; I remember that one of those was the part which stated that I should not consider going to take my rest at home in this manner. Braudel, in *The Mediterranean*, vol. II, p. 965 misquotes it, giving the wrong folio number as well, but rightly identified the 'ellos' as meaning Juana and the councillors; Parker, *Dutch revolt*, pp. 43–4, n. 19, transcribed part of it correctly, but his translation: 'they had a good laugh over there at my expense' is not entirely justified by the context. The reaction is comparable to that described by López de Padilla to the missives sent by Charles V during 1557 – see pp. 211, 215.

[12] AGS E. 137 fol. 227.   [13] AGS CJH. 36 fol. 157.

were still lending were protected. She supplied almost the entire sum requested by the king from the remittances due to the Fugger.

It was Philip's turn to protest and threaten as he took the side of the financiers who were supplying him in the Netherlands with vital sums and credit facilities. He demanded immediate satisfaction of the Fugger payments. Juana refused and allowed other moneys in Seville to be released to their owners thus ensuring that the king could not circumvent her decision. Philip refused to be defeated, although he accepted that he no longer commanded sufficient respect and authority with his officials in Spain to get his way. He arranged a loan of 600,000 florins to cover the shortfall in the Fugger accounts and remitted payment to Spain.[14] To his surprise the battle was not over. By the time the loan was drawn up Juana's order prohibiting the acceptance of loans contracted abroad was in force. Although the king had not as yet endorsed it, and would doubtless order its revocation, the edict was used to justify the rejection of the loan.

Shortly after this, Philip publicly announced his decision to return to Spain. It was difficult for him to persuade Juana and the Spanish officials that this time he meant it – particularly as he made his departure conditional once again on the receipt of further subsidies from them. Somehow, the regency government managed to arrange another loan. Nicolò Grimaldi advanced 100,000 ds but on condition that López del Campo should pledge his own person and all his possessions as additional collateral. That done, López del Campo warned Philip that this was the last subsidy he would obtain from the Spanish realms. The only revenues which had not been committed to the management of debts were those for meeting Juana's personal expenses.[15] No doubt Philip would have seized those as well if he had been able to do so.

Whereas the regency government tended to focus on the ever worsening conditions imposed by the financiers, and repeatedly expressed their conviction that there was no more Spain could give, Philip was struck only by the fact that his promise to return invariably elicited a positive response. These conflicts seem to have strengthened his belief that the problem with Spain was essentially one of personalities. Of course it was fuelled by their different priorities and policies, but by now he was getting used to dealing with irreconcilable demands from the different states. Policies could be forced upon regents, however unpalatable. The real problem was ensuring that the personnel were pliable. Far from accepting their figures and conclusion that no further debts could be added, Philip sought to override the regent's authority. In the summer of 1559, when his own departure was imminent, he sent Ruy Gómez and Dr Velasco to Spain to impose financial expedients that Philip believed would yield very substantial sums. He also sent with

---

[14] AGS E. 137 fols. 196–7; AGS CJH. 32 fols. 31 and 32.
[15] AGS E. 137 fol. 230, Juana to Philip, 20 July 1559; E. 137 fol. 234, ibid., 27 July; E. 137 fol. 57, López del Campo to Philip, 28 July.

them new orders regarding the loan he had contracted to repay the Fugger. He admitted that it would have been cheaper to assign repayment of this loan in the Netherlands, but he insisted that these dominions could not shoulder any further debts. There was no need for him to add that he believed the Spanish realms were capable of taking on further charges.

In other words, the king remained impervious to the central message of the regency government regarding Spain's terminal financial crisis. He was equally blind to their vision of the Mediterranean threat. In July, for example, he ordered the regent to cut down defence expenditure and dismantle some of the coastal defences. He justified this by citing reports which confirmed that the Ottomans would not send a substantial fleet into the western Mediterranean that year. In the aftermath of Mostaganem, with hysteria over Maghrebian attacks still high, such blatant disregard of all their fears and warnings was astonishing. Philip still thought only of countering the Ottoman threat.[16]

This is curious, since Philip showed an ability to sympathise with other areas and could accept that states such as Naples and Milan had reached the end of their endurance and were in need of support and subsidies. In his instructions to the new viceroy of Naples, the duke of Alcalá, Philip informed him that the realm was in a terrible state. No solution had as yet been found to the problem of the ever-growing debts assigned there. Unless some of the revenues mortgaged for repayments could be freed, there would be insufficient revenues to meet basic expenditure for administration and defence.[17] Milan, on the other hand, was in an even worse state. Difficulties with Spain meant that he had little choice but to burden Naples further when the situation in the duchy appeared to bring it to the brink of disaster. Philip appointed a new governor, the duke of Sessa, to restore his authority but he could not take up his post without money. With mutinous and unpaid troops looting and scouring the duchy for sustenance, the prospect of a general uprising of the populace and conflict with the soldiers seemed imminent. Philip pressed Naples to provide 100,000 ds for Milan. Sessa in turn pressed the city of Milan to contribute 200,000 ds and other urban areas were made to add further sums amounting to 300,000 ds. This enabled him to disband part of the army and give some relief to the rest. Everyone realised that it was no more than a holding operation that would last perhaps a couple of months. As letters from beleaguered officials poured into the court, full of doom, Philip responded by promising both Milan and Naples immediate subsidies as soon as he returned to Spain and put his affairs there in order.[18]

---

[16] AGS E. 519 fol. 24, Philip to Juana, 23 July 1559; AGS CJH. 32 fol. 32, 1 August; E. 519 fol. 66, defence.   [17] BNM MSS. 980 fol. 113.

[18] Neapolitan contributions, AGS E. 1049 fol. 70; situation in Milan, AGS E. 1210 fol. 272, Sessa to Philip, 17 January 1559; E. 1210 fol. 51, Philip to Sessa, 15 January. The suspension of payments in Milan had been considered earlier, Monti, 'Filippo II e il cardenal Cristoforo Madruzzo', p. 146; Alba, *Epistolario*, vol. I, p. 414. Details of the situation of the army, RAH SC A. 66 fols. 342, 189, 296.

This peculiarly distorted view of the situation in Spain led him to create such high expectations of what he could achieve, that even if the finances of the Iberian realms had been sound, he could not have fulfilled a half of what he promised. But Philip needed to comfort himself as much as his long-suffering officials. If he had accepted the view promoted by the regency government that they could no longer subsidise him, he would have had to acknowledge defeat: no more war against France, no possibility of holding together an empire rent with discord and financial chaos. Philip's vision of restoring full financial assistance from Spain to the Netherlands and Italy could not have been further removed from the Spanish conception of his return as the beginning of financial healing (they often used the term) and retrenchment. What for them was a cure, for him was the start of a new round of bleeding; a process of timely financial transfusions to save other members of the empire.

When king and country were finally reunited in September 1559, Philip at last appreciated how far his expectations had exceeded reality. Within weeks, this man who had so staunchly refused to believe that his sister and her advisers were giving him a balanced assessment of Spain's problems, exchanged his resentment and rejection for contrition. He blamed them for having painted too rosy a picture, and quickly became an evocative echo for their cries of exhaustion and despair.[19] In the final analysis, the speed of Philip's conversion to their point of view is the greatest tribute that could have been paid to the regency government's efforts. It is also the surest proof that the grim picture they had described during 1559 of realms wracked by poverty, dissent and on the brink of financial collapse, was indeed an accurate depiction of the state of Spain.

THE CASE FOR THE NETHERLANDS

The arguments in favour of Philip's continued residence in the Netherlands also took account of both international and internal considerations. To begin with, much use was made of the former and if the Netherlanders had been willing to fund the campaign against England the king might have been swayed in their favour. It was easy enough to argue that if the situation was as bleak as the promoters of the English expedition claimed, then the Netherlands should feel strongly enough about it to make a further effort for the sake of the king and their own safety. Their refusal to commit their resources to this policy effectively undermined their case. Inevitably, those who wished to retain the king made greater use of internal arguments, even to the point of reiterating the old warnings that there would be a rebellion unless Philip stayed. Aside from this, three issues

In fairness to Philip it must be added that on occasion he did warn Sessa that all other realms were exhausted financially and no further help could be given – e.g. AGS E. 519 fol. 121, E. 141 fol. 142 – but such occasions were rare. The king tended to concentrate on promises of aid from Spain.
[19] Weiss, vol. 5, p. 672.

were repeatedly used: the lack of suitable candidates for the regency; the growth of religious dissent and the urgent need to solve the financial crisis.

Since both Mary of Hungary and Charles were now dead, the most obvious replacements for Philip had gone. Unnamed counsellors, clearly schooled in Charles's court, came up with a proposal reminiscent of his earlier suggestions: as soon as Philip married Elizabeth of Valois, she must be sent to the Netherlands as governor, supported with a strong council that was to include a Spanish grandee. In the meanwhile, the king must take Carlos in hand and groom him for the government of the Netherlands. These men believed that the plan guaranteed Philip's speedy return to the area, since it was most impolitic (as well as unnatural) that he should be away from his new wife for long. The French (and Elizabeth?) would construe it as a lack of affection and respect. They did not envisage that Philip would risk his personal and political relations, and would thus come after a brief visit to Spain. Ideally, they hoped that Elizabeth would later conceive a child in the Netherlands and provide them with the natural prince they had longed for and been promised by Charles. However, they were willing to settle for don Carlos in the immediate future.[20]

There was nothing in this proposal to attract Philip. He resolutely opposed the division of his inheritance. Moreover, he had reason to fear the impact of life in the Netherlands on the young and impressionable Elizabeth of Valois. Her orthodoxy might be endangered in a country and court riddled with dissent; she might fall under the influence of one of the magnates. Worst of all, the French would take advantage of her presence to strengthen their contacts with the Netherlands; they might infiltrate groups already opposed to the monarch and increase instability, perhaps even prepare for an invasion.

The names that were not considered for the regency of the Netherlands can tell us a great deal about the king's relations with some important people as well as his views on the international situation. Apart from Elizabeth of Valois, there was no mention in his letters of don Carlos, or Juana, the two highest-ranking members of his family, both of whom would have been very acceptable to the Netherlanders. There were already some doubts as to the feasibility of putting Carlos in a position of power, given the despotic and unbalanced behaviour he had demonstrated at court.[21] Relations with Juana were strained and Philip clearly nurtured some resentment of her independence and disliked her willingness to challenge him. Nor could he transfer her to the Netherlands at will: he had promised to give her freedom once he set foot in Spain. He knew that she would either retire from public life or return to Portugal. Moreover, he simply could not afford to unleash the political tensions that usually preceded the appointment of a new regent in Spain. Emanuele Filiberto was similarly notable for his absence. Of course he needed time

---

[20] AGS E. 1643 fol. 11, published in A. González de Amezua (ed.) *Isabel de Valois* (3 vols., Madrid, 1949), vol. III(2), pp. 81–2.
[21] See p. 134 for Philip's attempts to force Charles to train the prince.

to go and claim his duchy, and establish his government there. But in all probability his exclusion relates to the countless quarrels with the Netherlands nobility during his spell in the government of the provinces. Nor did Philip consider his imperial cousins, who were in many ways the obvious candidates for the post. Family relations were improving but suspicion of their intention to take the Netherlands remained.

The choice was narrowed down to two other kinsfolk: his cousin Christina of Denmark dowager duchess of Lorraine, and Margaret of Parma, his illegitimate half-sister. Christina had recently mediated the peace with France; she had the political experience, the linguistic skills and capacity needed for the task. Her son's recent subjection to France, and the fact that the duchy of Lorraine was so vulnerable to French attack, weakened her chances. Moreover, she was suspected of having connections and favouring certain members of the high nobility; indeed the ardent support that she received from the prince of Orange, with whom it was said that she was negotiating marital alliances for their children, may well have ruined her candidacy. Philip was concerned to reduce factionalism not to increase it. Margaret was ideal from this point of view: she did not have close contacts with the nobles and she could bring to the job the unquantifiable advantages of being Charles's progeny and being born in the Netherlands. Once she and her husband announced their willingness to allow their only child (and future governor of the Netherlands), Alexander Farnese, to be taken by Philip and raised at court, her appointment was assured. It was a pity that she should be utterly lacking in political experience, but this deficiency could be supplied with adequate counsel.[22]

The king chose Granvelle, Orange, Egmont, Glajon, Berlaymont and Viglius as her advisers and councillors of state. The mixture of experienced and skilled administrators and aristocracy ensured that no one would dominate the central government. The nobles would compete with each other, and would seek to undermine the two non-noble advisers, yet it was to these two, Granvelle and Viglius, that Philip advised his sister to pay particular attention. His dislike of Granvelle had abated and he had come to appreciate the man's value. The nobility, he knew, would be in a position to challenge his regent. Since it was his duty as a good lord to reward them for their services, the months before his departure were spent assessing how best to distribute rewards and appointments. The leading nobles were left as governors of the various provinces, commanders of the *bandes d'ordonnance*, castellans of the chief fortifications and as councillors of state. The most powerful of them all, Orange, was made governor of Holland, Zeeland, and Utrecht; he claimed the right to govern the Franche-Comté as well and, as the most

---

[22] J. Viglius, *Discours sur le règne de Philippe II: la source et le commencement des Troubles*, both in A. Wauters, (ed.) *Mémoires de Viglius et d'Hopperus*, Collection de mémoires relatifs à l'histoire de Belgique. XVIe siècle. (Brussels, 1862), p. 33; van Durme, *Granvela*, pp. 225–30; Cabrera de Córdoba, *Felipe II*, vol. 1, p. 268. Note that the latter claims that Philip tried to leave the count of Feria along with Eraso and Diego de Vargas in charge of the government in the Netherlands, but I have found no evidence to support this.

powerful noble in the province of Brabant, he could dominate the states of that province which was ostensibly ruled by the regent or governor.[23] Far from cutting the power of the nobles, as they were later to claim, Philip was aware of the need to conciliate them as far as possible by honouring them with favours and reinforcing their power.

There were no Spaniards appointed; only minor officials, often left over from Charles's regime, remained. Again, he appreciated the need to minimise conflict between the two areas.[24] Nevertheless, the nobles were not satisfied. At first they adopted obstructive tactics in the hope of retaining Philip in the area; subsequently they concentrated their efforts on securing better rewards. An obscure quarrel at court led Orange and Egmont to threaten to resign. Philip was so irritated by them, his response was to say that if they did not wish to serve him he would be absolved of the duty to reward them further.[25] The situation was certainly tense but Philip was reasonably satisfied that the grants he had made would secure the nobility's support for the regent – at least for a time. Having talked to his half-sister and instructed her on the art of government, Philip proclaimed himself satisfied with her conduct in July 1559. These were not the only preparations he made prior to his departure.

Philip could not have left the Netherlands without taking some positive steps to contain the religious unrest in the area. Granvelle advised him to use the forthcoming meeting of the Order of the Golden Fleece to impress upon the nobles the need to intensify the pursuit of heresy. This and other points were made by the king in his speech to the Order, which contained some additional advice from the monarch. Philip asked the members to take special care of religion. This meant maintaining and protecting the (Catholic) faith in their lands, and punishing heresy. They were also asked that in future only good Catholics should be put forward for inclusion in the Order. Philip's touch can be seen in the injunction to attend mass daily, something he requested all his important officials to do. There was an uproar. The members acknowledged their special duty to support the ruler of the Netherlands, but condemned this unwarranted intrusion into their private lives and rejected the curtailment of their right of presentation. Whilst they accepted that they also had the duty of protecting the faith in their lands, they considered the king's words to imply criticism of their past policies – in this they were not off the mark.[26] Philip's attempt to step up action against heresy was not to the liking of the leading secular members of society.

[23] Van Durme, *Granvela*, pp. 225–30; AGS E. 485 s.f. Philip to Juana, 1 August 1559; Weiss, *Granvelle*, vol. 5, p. 633; Viglius, *Discours*, pp. 15–17; B. Porreño, *Dichos y hechos del Rey D. Felipe II* (Cuenca, 1628; new edn., Madrid, 1942), pp. 228–30. Rosenfeld, 'The provincial governors' for a discussion of their powers.

[24] Lagomarsino, 'Court factions and the formulation of Spanish policy towards the Netherlands (1559–1567)', Ph.D. dissertation (University of Cambridge, 1973), pp. 39–40. Parker, *Dutch revolt*, pp. 44–6.

[25] Weiss, *Granvelle*, vol. 5, pp. 628–30, 631–2. The two would threaten resignation again years later in order to secure further rewards and the sacking of Granvelle.

[26] Weiss, *Granvelle*, vol. 5, pp. 628–30, 631–2.

Epilogue: Spain or the Netherlands?

The expansion of Protestantism continued to preoccupy him. Granvelle constantly harped on the problem, hoping that it would persuade Philip to remain. Following his now usual pattern, the king had instituted a special committee in March 1559 to consider the problem and suggest 'a brief and prompt remedy'. The lack of progress highlighted the difficulties of providing a plan of action in an area where the local secular authorities alone were capable of imposing the anti-heresy laws and reluctant to do so. Had royal authority been less discredited, the king might have persuaded or forced the magistrates and nobles to obey. As it was, not even his warnings of impending disintegration could persuade them to act. Nothing of substance had been achieved by these experts when, in July 1559, religious tensions spilled into open violence in Courtrai.[27] The shock this incident caused at court made the king put even greater emphasis on repression and punishment. He was reluctant to publicise his decision to create a new ecclesiastical structure for the Netherlands which would give them for the first time in their history adequate clerical supervision, until the pope had consented to it. This plan to create fourteen new bishoprics, each with two inquisitors, was the positive side of his religious policy. Philip always believed that the education and cooperation of the elites was the best means to preserve orthodoxy. A man raised in the tradition of Spain, he also considered the existence of a powerful ecclesiastical structure supported with an effective inquisition essential for the preservation of the faith. Once the pope had announced his acceptance of the plan and agreed a price, Philip could persuade himself that the process of recovering the provinces for the faith was now underway and he might safely consider a brief absence – with a good conscience.[28]

The financial crisis was another matter: no restructuring could solve this. By the summer of 1559 the debt assigned to the Netherlands was roughly eight million florins. Immediate problems facing the government centred on the over-subscription of demesne revenues. A total of 173,000 fl was expected from this depleted source; 588,652 fl had been assigned to it before Philip added a further million from the floating debt. Such massive and unrealistic commitments destroyed what little faith there was in the financial community. Despairing of the government, some merchant bankers pressed for the collateral offered by individual cities. The cities refused, pleading poverty and complaining that the government had assured them they would never be called upon to honour these debts. The financiers resorted to law. In June 1559 sixteen cities were facing prosecution for the non-payment of crown debts. Collectively they had stood surety for just over 900,000 florins. Officials considered it imperative to raise the money at once and rescue the cities. Aside from moral considerations, there were sound political reasons for saving the city councils. The worst affected cities were Antwerp, Lille, Ypres and Tournai, but others feared that they would face similar charges. These urban areas played a major role in the states of their respective provinces and could

---

[27] AGS E. 885 fol. 114; Weiss, *Granvelle*, vol. 5, p. 622.
[28] Dierickx, *Documents ... des nouveaux diocèses aux Pays-Bays*, vol. 1, especially pp. 183–6.

henceforth prove crucial in opposition to the government. Moreover, they were still vitally important in the process of anticipating revenue and providing credit.[29]

Philip did not need to be persuaded of this, but he was even more worried by the need to disband his huge army – a task to which he wanted all his states to contribute. He assigned the payment of three German regiments, the Flemish and Walloon troops, and some relief for the Spanish infantry and cavalry to the Netherlands. These commitments, the debts of the sixteen cities and current expenditure put the amount which the Netherlands finances estimated they needed to raise immediately at 1.8 million florins.[30]

Once again the king resorted to a special committee of advisers to debate and advise him on the means to solve the immediate crisis and suggest ways of dealing with the accumulated debts in the long term. This group of experts was no more capable of advancing solutions for the financial problems than those dealing with religious unrest. Annoyed by the lack of progress, Philip suggested to them that he might anticipate the revenues which the states-general had agreed to discharge over the next few years.[31] Granvelle, as their spokesman, bluntly rejected the proposal. Any interference with what little provision had been made to reduce the accumulated debt would rightly provoke an outcry. In spite of Philip's attempts to reassure them that this was a temporary measure and that he would restore these funds, they continued to regard it as another underhand ploy to increase the debt carried by the Netherlands. The committee was even more vehement in their rejection of his next proposal, to summon the states-general and demand a grant of 1.2 million florins. The memory of the lengthy and unsuccessful struggle with the last states-general had left a deep impression upon these men. They warned that it must be avoided at all costs. Even if he had been considering other ways to make the request, the figure was too high. The king was told that by asking for the impossible he would merely succeed in provoking further unrest.[32]

Similar arguments were used to counter the project advanced by Ruy Gómez and Eraso who proposed to raise 720,000 fl by the sale of annuities of 12 deniers. The Netherlands would have to refund the capital (some 60,000 fl worth of revenues), but all interest payments were to be assigned to Spanish revenues. This was an extraordinary suggestion. Although by now loans were being freely raised in one area and assigned or transferred to another, what was proposed here was payment of interest due on annuities issued by another state. The move would undoubtedly be interpreted as another step towards undermining the independence of the separate units of the empire and as such it would have been rejected in principle, never mind

[29] AGS CJH. 35 fol. 171, account of Flemish finances, June 1559, giving details of who was affected and the sums for which they were being sued. Baelde, 'Financial policy', p. 223 and pp. 54, 57 for details of the importance of the demesne revenues and debts. H. C. Koenigsberger, 'The states general before the revolt' in his *Estates and revolutions* (Ithaca, 1971), pp. 128–9 for the role played by the cities.   [30] Weiss, *Granvelle*, vol. 5, pp. 603–5; AGS E. 518 fols. 20–1.   [31] See p. 193.
[32] AGS E. 517 fols. 101, 102, 103. These letters were published in Weiss, *Granvelle*, vol. 5, see in particular, pp. 597–9 Granvelle to Philip, 23 June 1559.

the fact that the Spanish government did not have money to spare. Ruy Gómez and Eraso thought it viable because they believed that there would be a meeting of the states-general soon and they would provide new revenues with which to pay off the capital in three years. But they must have realised that the Spaniards might end up having to pay as much in interest as in capital, given the chaotic financial state of the empire.[33]

The plan proves once again the willingness of Philip and his closest advisers to sacrifice Spanish revenues in an effort to conciliate the Netherlands. It also confirms their habitual overestimate of Spain's capacity and willingness to pay and highlights the impossibility of dividing his advisers into clearly defined Spanish and Dutch camps. Alba was cooperating most closely with Granvelle, and Eraso (a Spanish secretary), with the king's Portuguese favourite. The policies they were supporting would have proved costly and unpopular in Spain. These councillors, as other officials, rightly gave priority to meeting the king's needs whatever their nationality. At a time when a major decision that would affect them all (and the empire) was to be made, they also defended their vision of that empire and pressed for acceptance of their policies.

After months of increasing tension and intense discussions, Granvelle reported the conclusion of the special finance commission on 24 June 1559: the only way to solve the financial crisis of the Netherlands and ensure their preservation was by procuring a substantial infusion of money from outside.[34] The shock of this negative report seems to have confirmed Philip's decision to leave and given him the courage to announce it. On 29 June 1559 he declared his intention to return to Spain.[35]

The length of time and agonising process of consultation attest to the difficulty of Philip's decision. The pressure, combined with the king's despair of securing funds to disband the army, made him ill. He sought to evade these troubles for a time by escaping from Brussels to the monastery at Groendale. He told Granvelle that his health could not withstand such strain.[36] If he hoped to find solace and peace in the cloisters, they eluded him. But he found enough reserves to make a last, despairing gesture: he summoned another states-general despite the opposition of the special financial advisers. His optimism that they would acknowledge his difficulties and respond as loyal, ideal subjects did not endure long. Even before all the summonses had been delivered he finally acknowledged that there would be no miraculous change of heart from the states-general. Only God, he claimed, could save him now.

God, and he should have added, Spain. Far from putting his complete trust in prayer, he reacted to the crisis as before by putting even greater pressure on his regency government. He wrote to them extolling the good will of the Netherlands, the terrible plight of these provinces, and the abysmal fate that would befall him unless Spain provided him with money.[37]

---

[33] AGS E. 138 fol. 124 s.f., in Eraso's hand; Weiss, *Granvelle*, vol. 5, pp. 593–5 Philip to Granvelle, 23 June 1559.   [34] Weiss, *Granvelle*, vol. 5, p. 609.   [35] AGS E. 518 fols. 20–1, Philip to Juana.   [36] Weiss, *Granvelle*, vol. 5, p. 594.   [37] AGS E. 518 fols. 20–1 for example.

Philip's commitment and determination to save the Netherlands runs through this decade as a dominant motif. He told Granvelle that he would gladly supply the needs of the provinces with his own blood if only he could bring them relief by doing so.[38] The words were dramatic but genuine. His sentiments and actions towards the Netherlands are remarkably consistent. Convinced at long last that they would collapse without subsidies and unable to secure that money without returning to Spain, his journey represents a victory for the Netherlands. Not that this was accepted by them. Philip's decision was widely criticised by his northern subjects. While they were glad he appreciated their plight, they were horrified at the end result. This was specially true of some leading councillors, including Granvelle, who tried desperately to persuade him to stay in the Netherlands.

At first he was irritated by their lack of comprehension and refusal to appreciate his dilemma. Their constant use of ever more disparaging comparisons with Spain gradually elicited a more positive response. For instance, Granvelle argued that the Spanish realms had not contributed as much to the war effort as the Netherlands, nor had they suffered as much. As proof he alluded to the fact that the Castilian cortes were not carrying as great a burden of debt as that shouldered by the various states of the Netherlands. Philip denied that there had been an unequal effort and explained that the Castilian exchequer dealt with the massive debts in a different manner from that of the Netherlands, rendering direct comparisons of their accounts impossible. He took the opportunity to say that he would gladly exchange all existing subsidies in the Netherlands for a Castilian-style sales tax. It was Granvelle's turn to explain that the two realms were utterly different. He declared that in the Netherlands they had already imposed sales taxes long ago, and here even the nobles contributed. This had enabled them to finance the war. However, the states would never tolerate the degree of monarchical power over taxation exercised by the Castilian kings. Granvelle reiterated his claim that the Netherlands had contributed far more to the wars than Spain and suffered in many other ways. He mentioned in particular the disruption of trade and devastation caused by fighting in the area.

Although Philip accepted the deep suffering of the Netherlands he adamantly rejected the claim that Spain had not pulled its weight. He reiterated that they had made extraordinary sacrifices and still found ways to provide him with huge sums of money, despite the terrible state in which he had left them.[39] Not since his days as regent had Philip come to the defence of the Spanish realms in this way. Only the vehement attacks of his northern subjects, so disparaging of the efforts made by Spain reawakened his sympathy. This appreciation was not reflected in his correspondence. In his letters to Castile he seldom expressed more than

---

[38] Weiss, *Granvelle*, vol. 5, pp. 606, 612.
[39] Their correspondence is in Weiss, *Granvelle*, vol. 5, pp. 594–5, 600–1, 612–13.

perfunctory gratitude. Instead, he dwelt on the sacrifices of the Netherlands and their sorry plight. Consequently he alienated both groups.[40]

His anxiety to placate the Netherlands was to have severe consequences. He constantly referred to the subsidies he would raise for them in Spain, thus creating very high expectations which, as in the case of the Italian realms, proved impossible to fulfil. It must be realised that he was labouring under the conviction, shared by leading officials throughout the empire in 1559, that it was on the verge of collapse. Of course it is difficult to judge whether their pessimism was worse now than it had been a few years previously. The historian faces formidable problems of evaluation when dealing with unquantifiable issues such as the collective state of mind. The impression given by contemporary correspondence is of a strong conviction that they could not survive much longer. All reported serious challenges to royal authority, crushing burdens of debt, fears of imminent rebellions or invasion. In Philip's court, different groups and individuals exerted their utmost skills and power to control the direction of policy and advanced utterly irreconcilable proposals. They also behaved as if a final and irrevocable step was about to be taken. Their contradictory advice confused the king, who was already depressed by the internal situation and obsessed by the clamour of the commanders seeking pay for the troops and disbandment of their forces. Gradually Philip put all his hope on this journey to Spain until it assumed almost mystical – or should one say miraculous? – proportions. He spoke of it as if it was the only thing that would save the empire from dissolution.

Unlike previous periods of pressure, this one left an indelible imprint on Philip himself. 1559 is a turning point in the sense that it signalled a change of residence, the beginning of a shift in policy, and above all, a change within the king himself. He turned more and more to God. The lengthy period of war, the fears and hope of peace, the terrible decisions which he had been called to make in 1559 forged in Philip a sense of providentialism best illustrated in this extract from a letter written as he waited to set sail for Spain:

Everything depends on the will of God. We must simply wait for Him to show us how we can serve him best. I trust in Him, who has saved me from even worse situations, to save me now. He will give me the means to sustain my states and ensure that I will not lose them through lack of means to preserve them, for this would be the saddest thing that could ever happen to me.[41]

He could not contain his impatience as contrary winds delayed his journey. He was eager to begin the process of regenerating the empire. As this extract suggests, however, he was conscious that he had already achieved extraordinary successes that appeared impossible in the bleak days of 1552. He had helped to sustain his

---

[40] See e.g. AGS E. 518 fols. 20–1.
[41] Weiss, *Granvelle*, vol. 5, p. 643, Philip to Granvelle, 24 August 1559.

father's crumbling authority; he had managed to win the war against the papacy and match the power of France; he had also established a reputation as a great and peaceful prince. He had known that the price would be high in terms of suffering for his subjects but did not anticipate that it would almost cost him his authority and the loyalty of his states. There was no certainty that he would prove as successful in saving the empire from internal disintegration as he had been at preserving them from external attack. In later years Philip and many of his councillors would look back at these years with a sense of awe, as if they had witnessed something of a miracle. Philip already conceived the idea of erecting a spectacular temple to thank God for his survival. Orders for the building of the palace–monastery sited near the Escorial (begun in 1563) specified that the founder was inspired by his intense 'gratitude for the many great favours we have received and daily do receive from our Lord, and because He has guided our actions to do His holy work and preserve our empire in His holy faith and religion'.[42] It was no coincidence that he should choose to dedicate it to St Laurence, on whose feast day, 10 August, Savoy had crushed the French near St Quentin. The Hall of Battles would be illustrated with pictures of ancient struggles against the Moors, and with Philip's battles against the French, notably St Quentin and Gravelines.

Nevertheless, despite the striking impression of power Philip had created, his place at the head of Christian states was based on infirm foundations. No one knew better than he the chasm that separated reality from illusion. In the late summer of 1559, as he prepared to go to Spain, he believed that without God's favour and Spanish funds, the collapse of this sprawling Habsburg empire which had been averted for nearly a decade, might still occur.

[42] Cit. C. v.d. Osten Sacken, *El Escorial. Estudio iconológico* (Bilbao, 1984), p. 15.

Bibliography

NOTE ON MANUSCRIPT SOURCES

Full references to the most important documents are included in the footnotes. The major Archives and Libraries consulted for primary material were as follows:

1 *Archivo General de Simancas, Spain*
   Camara de Castilla (Diversos de Castilla); *Casa Real – Obras y Bosques*; *Consejo y Juntas de Hacienda* (Secretarías de Hacienda); *Contaduría Mayor de Cuentas* (Primera Epoca); *Guerra Antigua* (sometimes called Guerra y Marina, Secretaría de Mar y Tierra; Libros registro); *Mapas, planos y dibujos*; *Patronato Real* (Capitulaciones con Moros y Caballeros Cristianos, Capitulaciones con Pontífices; Cruzada y Subsidio; Concilios, Poderes, Instrucciones y Renuncias; Testamentos Reales; Nápoles y Sicilia; Milán; Diversos de Italia; Tratados con Portugal; Capitulaciones con Inglaterra; Capitulaciones con Francia; Capitulaciones con la Casa de Austria; Bulas y Breves); *Secretaría de Estado* (Corona de Castilla; Corona de Aragón; Despachos Diversos – including the Libros of this section; Armadas y Galeras; Costas de Africa y Levante; Negociación de Portugal; Negociación de Flandes; Negociación de Alemania; Negociación de Francia; Negociación de Inglaterra; Negociación de Roma; Negociación de Nápoles; Negociación de Sicilia; Negociación de Milán; Negociación de Venecia; Negociación de Génova; Estados Pequeños de Italia; Libros; Sueltos de Estado; *Secretarías Provinciales* (Secretaría de Nápoles).
2 *Biblioteca Nacional, Madrid*. Manuscript collections.
3 *Biblioteca del Palacio real, Madrid*. Granvelle correspondence.
4 *The British Library*. Manuscripts and Additional Manuscripts. A very useful guide to Hispanic materials here was compiled by P. de Gayangos, Catalogue of the Manuscripts in the Spanish Language in the British Museum (4 vols., London, 1875–93).
5 *Real Academia de la Historia*. The manuscript collection Salazar y Castro was particularly useful.
6 *Archivo de los duques de Medina Celi*. Although I was not able to go personally, photocopies of letters sent by Philip II to the count of Feria were made available to me. I am deeply indebted to Dr David Lagomarsino and Señor Don Joaquín González Moreno for this.

PRINTED PRIMARY SOURCES

Acts of the Privy Council of England, ed. J.R. Dasent, (New Series, vol. v, 1554–6. Kraus Reprint, Nedel-Liechtenstein, 1974)
Actas de las Cortes de Castilla (Madrid, 1861–1936)

Bibliography

Alba, duke of, *Epistolario del III duque de Alba, Don Fernando Alvarez de Toledo* (3 vols., Madrid, 1952)

Albèri, E. (ed.), *Le relazioni degli ambasciatori veneti al Senato durante il secolo decimocesto* (15 vols., Florence, 1839–63)

Andrada, F. de, *Cronica de D. João III* (Lisbon, 1613, edn. of M. Lopes de Almeida, Porto, 1976)

Archivo Documental Español, published by Real Academia de la Historia, vols. 1–9, *Negociaciones con Francia 1559–1567* (Madrid, 1950–5)

Vols. 18–19, 22, 30, 33, *Fray Bartolomé Carranza. Documentos históricos* (Madrid, 1962–81)

Bejano Robles, F. *Documentos para el estudio del abastecimiento y auxilio de las plazas portuguesas en Marruecos desde el sur de España* (Tangiers, 1941)

Biblioteca de Autores Españoles, vol. XVI: *Romancero General*, ed. A. Duran (Madrid 1945).

Brunelli, E. (ed.) *Emanuele Filiberto, duca di Savoia: I diari della campagna di Fiandra* (Biblioteca della Società Storica Subalpina, vol. 112, Turin, 1928)

Cabrera de Córdoba, L., *Felipe II. Rey de España* (4 vols., 1619; new edn., Madrid, 1876–7)

Calendar of State Papers, Domestic: 1547–1580, ed. R. Lemon, (London, 1856)

Calendar of State Papers, Foreign. Elizabeth I, ed. J. Stevenson (London, 1863)

Calendar of State Papers, Spanish, ed. R. Tyler et al. (London, 1862–1964)

Calendar of State Papers, Venetian, ed. R. Brown et al. (London, 1864–98).

Calvete de Estrella, J. C., *El Felicissimo Viaie d'el muy alto y muy poderoso Principe Don Phelippe . . . desde España a sus tierras de la baxa Alemana . . .* (Antwerp, 1552)

Cervantes, M. de. *Los baños de Argel* (*Biblioteca de Autores Españoles*, CLVI Madrid, 1962)

Ciasca, R. (ed.), *Istruzioni e relazioni degli ambasciatori genovesi* (vol. I, Spagna, 1494–1617, Rome, 1951)

Clifford, H., *The life of Jane Dormer, duchess of Feria*, ed. J. Stevenson (London, 1887)

Colección de documentos inéditos para la historia de España (112 vols., Madrid, 1842–96)

Díaz-Plaja, F. (ed.), *La historia de España en sus documentos. El siglo XVI* (Madrid, 1958)

Dierickx, M. (ed.), *Documents inédits sur l'érection des nouveaux diocèses aux Pays-Bas (1521–1570)* (3 vols., Brussels, 1960–62)

Dumont, J. (ed.), *Corps universal diplomatique du droit des gens* (vol. 5, part 1, Amsterdam–The Hague, 1728)

Fernández Alvarez, M. (ed.), 'El memorial de Luis Ortíz 1558', *Anales de Economía*, XVII, 63 (1957), pp. 101–200

(ed.), *Corpus documental de Carlos V* (5 vols., Salamanca, 1971–81)

Fernández Asis, V. (ed.), *Epistolario de Felipe II sobre asuntos de mar* (Madrid, 1943)

Furió Ceriol, F., *Concejo y consejeros del Príncipe* (Antwerp, 1559, edn. D. Sevilla Andrés, Valencia 1952)

Gachard, L. P. (ed.), *Retraite et mort de Charles Quint au monastère de Yuste*, (3 vols, Introduction and vols. I and II, Brussels, 1854–5)

(ed.), *Correspondance de Guillaume le Taciturne, Prince d'Orange* (vol. I, Brussels, 1847)

(ed.), 'La seconde remontrance d'Emmanuel-Philibert de Savoie', *Bulletin de la Commission Royale d'Histoire* (Brussels, VIII, 1856), pp. 124–32

(ed.), *Lettres de Philippe II à ses filles* (Paris, 1884)

García Carcel, R. (ed.), *Cortes del reinado de Carlos I* (Valencia, 1972)

Bibliography

Garnett, R. (ed.), *The Accession of Queen Mary: Being the contemporary narrative of Antonio de Guaras, a Spanish resident in London* (London, 1892)

González de Amezua, A. (ed.), *Isabel de Valois* (3 vols., Madrid, 1949)

Griffiths, G. (ed.), *Representative government in Western Europe in the sixteenth century* (Oxford, 1968)

Haedo, D. *Topographía e historia general de Argel* (Valladolid, 1612)

Hakluyt, R., *Voyages and documents*, ed. J. Hampden (London, 1965)

Japikse, N. (ed.), *Correspondentie van Willem den eerste prins van Oranje* (vol. 1, 1551–61. 's-Gravenhage, 1934)

Jiménez de Quesada, G., *El Antijovio*, ed. R. Torres Quintero (Bogotá, 1952).

Kervijn de Lettenhove, J. M. B. C. (ed.), *Relations politiques des Pays-Bas et de l' Angleterre sous le règne de Philippe II* (11 vols., Brussels, 1882–1900)

Kossman, E. H. and A. F. Mellink (eds.), *Texts concerning the revolt of the Netherlands* (London, 1974)

Laiglesia, F. (ed.), *Estudios históricos* (3 vols., Madrid, 1918)

Lanz, K. (ed.), *Correspondenz des Kaisers Karl V* (3 vols., Leipzig, 1846)

López de Gomara, F. *Annals of the Emperor Charles V*, edn. of R. B. Merriman (Oxford, 1912)

March, J. M. *Niñez y juventud de Felipe II* (2 vols., vol. 2, documents, Madrid 1941–42)

Marmol Carvajal, L. del. *Primera parte de la descripción general de Africa* (2 vols., Granada, 1573), *Segunda parte de la descripción general de Africa* (Málaga, 1599)

Medina, P. de., *Libro de grandezas y cosas memorables de España* (Seville, 1548, edn. by A. González Palencia, Madrid, 1944)

Mercado, T. de, *Summas de tratos y contratos* (Seville, 1571, edn. R. Sierra, Madrid, 1975)

Monluc, B. de., *The Habsburg–Valois wars and the French wars of religion*, ed. & trans. I. Roy, (London, 1971)

Morel-Fatio, A. (ed.), *L'Espagne au XVIe et au XVIIe siècles. Documents historiques et littéraires* (Heilbronn, 1878)

Historiographie de Charles-Quint. I^e partie, suivi des mémoires de Charles-Quint (Bilingual text, French–Portuguese) (Paris, 1913)

Muñoz, A., *Sumaria y verdadera relación del buen viaje que el Príncipe Don Felipe hizo en Inglaterra* (Zaragoza, 1554, published and ed. P. Gayangos, with three contemporary letters, Sociedad de Bibliófilos Españoles, vol. xv, Madrid, 1877)

Orange, W. Prince of. *Apologie* (Delft, 1581; English edn. *The Apologie of Prince William of Orange against the Proclamation of the King of Spaine*, also 1581, new edn. of this by H. Wansink, Leiden, 1969)

Paz y Melia, A., *Series de los más importantes documentos del Archivo y Biblioteca del Excmo. Sr Duque de Medinaceli* (2 vols., Madrid, 1922)

Pérez, J. (ed.), *L'Espagne du XVIe siècle* (Paris, 1973)

Pérez de Moya, J., *Arithmetica* (Alcalá, 1582)

Reglas para co(n)tar sin pluma, etc. Included in J. de Oriega, *Tratado de Aritmetica* (Granada, 1563)

Porreño, B., *Dichos y hechos del Rey D. Felipe II* (Cuenca, 1628; new edn., Madrid, 1942)

Real Academia de la Historia, Cortes de los antiguos reinos de León y Castilla (5 vols., Madrid, 1882)

Bibliography

Recopilación de las leyes destos reynos (3 vols. Alcalá de Henares, 1581)

Rodríguez Moniño, A. *Diccionario de pliegos sueltos poéticos. (Siglo XVI)* (Madrid, 1970)

Rodríguez Raso, R. (ed.), *Maximiliano de Austria, gobernador de Carlos V en España. Cartas al emperador* (Madrid, 1963)

Rowen H. H. (ed.), *The Low Countries in Early Modern Times* (London, 1972)

Salazar, P. de, *Hispania Victrix* (Medina del Campo, 1570)

Segunda parte de las leyes del reino (Alcalá de Henares, 1567)

Siguenza, J. de, *Como vivió y murió Felipe II, por un testigo ocular*, ed. Apostolado de la prensa (Madrid, 1927–8)

Sleidan, John, *The general history of the Reformation of the Church* (extended English version by Edmund Bohum Esq.) (London, 1689)

Les sources inédites de l'histoire du Maroc de 1530 à 1845, ed. H. Castries et al. *Première série; La dynastie Sa'dienne* (Paris, 1905–   ); Archives et Bibliothèques d'Espagne, vol. I (Paris–Madrid, 1921), vol. II (Paris, 1956), vol. III (Paris, 1961); Archives et Bibliothèques d'Angleterre, vol. I (Paris–London, 1918); Archives et Bibliothèques de Portugal, vol. I (Paris, 1934), vol. II (part 1, Paris, 1939, part 2, Paris, 1946), vol. III (Paris, 1948), vol. IV (Paris, 1951), vol. V (Paris, 1953); Archives et Bibliothèques de France, vol. I (Paris, 1905)

Suárez Fernández, L. (ed.), *Política internacional de Isabel la Católica* (4 vols., Valladolid, 1965–71)

Torres, D. de, *Relación del origen y suceso de los Xarifes y del estado de los reinos de Marruecos, Fez y Tarudante* (Seville, 1586), edn. of M. García-Arenal, (Madrid, 1980)

Turba, G. (ed.), *Venetianische Depeschen vom Kaiserhofe. (Dispacci di Germania)* (vol. II, Vienna, 1892, vol. III, Vienna, 1895)

Vandernesse, J. de., *Journal des voyages de Philippe II de 1554 à 1559*, in *Collection des voyages des souverains des Pays-Bas* (vol. IV, Brussels, 1882)

Vázquez de Prada, V. (ed.), *Lettres marchandes d'Anvers* (4 vols., vol. I, Paris, 1960)

Vertot d'Aubeuf, R. Aubert de, *Les Ambassades de Messieurs de Noailles en Angleterre* (Leyden, 1763)

Viaje de Turquía (first edn., 1555; edn. of F. García Salinero, Madrid, 1980)

Viglius, J. *Mémoires de Viglius et d'Hopperus*, ed. A. Wauters, Collection de mémoires relatifs à l'histoire de Belgique: XVIe siècle (Brussels, 1862)

Weiss, C. *Papiers d'état du Cardinal de Granvelle* (9 vols., Paris, 1841–52)

PRINTED SECONDARY SOURCES

Altamira y Crevea, R., *Ensayo sobre Felipe II, hombre de estado* (Mexico, 1950)

Armstrong, E. *The Emperor Charles V* (2 vols., London, 1910)

Arnauld, M. A. 'Les rentes d'état en Hainaut aux 16e et 17e siècle', *Annales du Cercle archéologique du canton de Soignies*, VIII (1942), pp. 164–82

Baelde, M. *De Collaterale Raden onder Karel V en Filips II (1531–1578)* (French summary pp. 331–5, Brussels, 1965)

'Financial policy and the evolution of the demesne in the Netherlands under Charles V and Philip II (1530–1560)', in H. J. Cohn (ed.), *Government in Reformation Europe* (London, 1971), pp. 203–24

Bibliography

Ballesteros Beretta, A. *Figuras imperiales* (Madrid, 1961)

Barcía Trelles, D. 'Carlos I de España y el problema del equilibrio político', *Archivos del Instituto de Estudios Africanos*, XIII, 50 (1959), pp. 37–53

Bataillon, M. 'Charles-Quint bon pasteur, selon Fray Cipriano de Huelga', *Bulletin Hispanique*, 50 (1948), pp. 398–406

Erasme et l'Espagne (Paris, 1937; second, Spanish edn. Madrid, 1979)

Baumgartner, F. J. 'Henry II and the Papal conclave of 1549', *Sixteenth Century Journal*, XVI, no. 3 (1985), pp. 301–14

Bayne, C. G. *Anglo-Roman relations 1558–1565* (Oxford, 1968)

Beinert, B., 'El testamento político de Carlos V, de 1548. Estudio crítico', in *Carlos V 1500–1558* (Homenaje de la Universidad de Granada, Granada, 1958)

Belenguer Cebriá, E. *La problemática del cambio político en la España de Felipe II. Puntualizaciones sobre su cronología* (Bellaterra, 1980)

Bono, S. *I corsari Barbareschi* (Turin, 1964)

Brandi, K. *The Emperor Charles V* (English edn. Harvester Press–Kraus reprint, 1980)

Braudel, F. 'Les emprunts de Charles-Quint sur la place d'Anvers', in *Charles-Quint et son Temps* (Centre National de la Recherche Scientifique, Paris, 1959), pp. 191–201

The Mediterranean and the Mediterranean world in the age of Philip II (2nd edn., 2 vols., Paris, 1966; English trans. London, 1972).

Braudel, F., et al., *L'Espagne au temps de Philippe II* (Paris, 1965)

Buckley, H. 'Sir Thomas Gresham and foreign exchange', *Economic Journal* (1924), pp. 589–601

The Cambridge Economic History of Europe, ed. E. E. Rich, C. H. Wilson, vol. 5 (London, 1977)

Carande, R. *Carlos V y sus banqueros* (3 vols., Madrid, 1943–67, vol. I, 2nd edn., 1965; vol. II, 1943; vol. III, 1967)

'La gestión del nuncio Juan Poggio colector general de la Cámara Apostólica en España', *Boletín de la Real Academia de la Historia*, CLXXV (1978), pp. 495–532

Cardaillac, L. *Moriscos y Cristianos. Un enfrentamiento polémico (1492–1640)* (Paris, 1977; Spanish edn., Madrid, 1979)

Carlos V (1500–1558) (Homenaje de la Universidad de Granada, Granada, 1958)

Carrasco Urgoiti, M. S. *El problema morisco en Aragón al comienzo del reinado de Felipe II* (Valencia, 1969)

Castillo Pintado, A. 'Dette flottante et dette consolidée en Espagne de 1557 à 1600', *Annales, Economies, Sociétés, Civilisations* (1963), pp. 745–59

'Los juros de Castilla. Apogeo y fin de un instrumento de crédito', *Hispania*, 89 (1963), pp. 43–70

Cepeda Adan, J. *En torno al concepto del Estado en el tiempo de los Reyes Católicos* (Madrid, 1956)

Chabod, F. '"¿Milán o los Paises Bajos?" Las discusiones en España sobre la "alternativa" de 1544', in *Carlos V 1500–1558* Homenaje de la Universidad de Granada (Granada, 1958)

Lo stato e la vita religiosa a Milano nell'epoca di Carlo V (Turin, 1971)

Challis, C. E. *The Tudor coinage* (Manchester–New York, 1978)

Charles Quint et son temps (Centre National de la Recherche Scientifique, Paris, 1959)

Chaunu, P. *L'Espagne de Charles Quint* (2 vols., Paris, 1973)

Bibliography

Chaunu, P. and H. *Séville et l'Atlantique de 1504 à 1650* (12 vols., Paris, 1955–60)

Christian, H., 'L'église selon les Cortes de Castille: 1476–1598', *Hispania Sacra*, XXVII, 53–4 (1974), pp. 201–35

Claretta, G., *Il Duca di Savoia, Emanuele Filiberto, e la corta di Londra, 1554–5* (Pinerolo, 1892)

Clissold, S. *The Barbary slaves* (London, 1977)

Cloulas, I. 'Le "subsidio de las galeras",' *Mélanges de la Casa de Velázquez* III (1967), pp. 289–324

Henri II (Paris, 1985)

Colas Latorre, G. and J. A. Salas Ausens, *Aragón bajo los Austrias* (Zaragoza, 1977)

Coniglio, G. 'La política financiera española en Nápoles en la segunda mitad del siglo XVI', *Moneda y Crédito*, 56 (1956), pp. 37–40

Constant, G. 'Le commencement de la restauration Catholique en Angleterre par Marie Tudor (1553)', *Revue Historique*, CXII (1913), pp. 1–27

'Le mariage de Marie Tudor et de Philippe II', *Revue d'Histoire Diplomatique*, XXVI (1912), pp. 23–73, 224–74

Cornevin, R. *Histoire de l'Afrique* (vols. I and II, Paris, 1976)

Courteault, P. *Blaise de Monluc historien* (Paris, 1908, Slatkine reprint, Geneva, 1970)

Craeybeckx, J. 'Aperçu sur l'histoire des impôts en Flandres et au Brabant au cours du XVIe siècle', *Revue de Nord*, XXIX (1947), pp. 87–108

Daniel, N. *Islam and the West* (Edinburgh, 1966)

Danvila, A. *Felipe II y el rey Don Sebastián de Portugal* (Madrid, 1954)

Davies, C. S. L. 'England and the French war, 1557–9', in J. Loach and R. Tittler (eds.), *The mid-Tudor polity c. 1540–1560* (London, 1980), pp. 159–85.

Dévos, J. 'La poste au service des diplomates espagnols accrédités auprès des cours d'Angleterre et France', *Bulletin de la Commission Royale d'Histoire* (Brussels, C III, 1938), pp. 205–68

Les chiffres de Philippe II (1555–1598) (Brussels, 1950)

Dickens, G. *The English Reformation* (London, 1967 edn.)

Dietz, F. C. *English government finance* (2 vols., London, 1964)

Dominguez Ortiz, A. *The Golden Age of Spain* (London, 1971)

Dominguez Ortiz, A. and B. Vincent *Historia de los moriscos* (Madrid, 1978)

Doussinague, J. M. *El testamento político de Fernando el Católico* (Madrid, n.d.).

La politica internacional de Fernando el Católico (Madrid, 1944)

Fernando el Católico y el cisma de Pisa (Madrid, 1946)

La política exterior de España en el siglo XVI (Madrid, 1949).

Duke, A. 'Salvation by coercion: the controversy surrounding the "Inquisition" in the Low Countries on the eve of the revolt', in P. N. Brooks (ed.), *Reformation in principle and practice* (London, 1980), pp. 137–56

Earle, P. *Corsairs of Malta and Barbary* (London, 1970)

Egidi, P. and A. Segre, *Emanuele Filiberto*, Vol. II, 1558–1580 (Turin, 1928)

Ehrenberg, R. *Capital and finance in the age of the Renaissance. A study of the Fuggers and their connections* (London, 1928)

Elliott, J. H. *Imperial Spain* (Harmondsworth, 1970 edn.)

Escudero, J. A. *Los secretarios de estado y del despacho (1471–1742)* (4 vols. Madrid, 1976)

Evans, R. J. W. *The making of the Habsburg monarchy 1500–1700* (Oxford, 1979)

Bibliography

Febvre, L. *Philippe II et la Franche-Comté* (Paris, 1912)

Fernández Alvarez, M. *Tres embajadores de Felipe II en Inglaterra* (Madrid, 1951)
  Italia en la época del predominio español (Madrid, 1954 also in *Arbor*, CII 1954, pp. 263–73)
  'La paz de Cateau-Cambrésis', *Hispania*, LXXVII (1959), pp. 530–43
  Política mundial de Carlos V y Felipe II (Madrid, 1966)
  Charles V (London, 1975)

Fernández Montana, J. *Felipe II el Prudente y su política* (Madrid, 1914)

Fernández Santamaría, J. A. *The State, war and peace: Spanish political thought in the Renaissance, 1516–1559* (Cambridge, 1977)

Ferrara, O. *El siglo XVI a la luz de los embajadores venecianos* (Madrid, 1952)

Fichtner, P. S. *Ferdinand I of Austria* (New York, 1982).

Finot, J. 'Le siège de Metz en 1552 et les finances de Charles Quint', *Bulletin du Comité des Travaux Historiques et Scientifiques. Section d'Histoire et de Philologie* (Paris, 1897), pp. 260–70

Fisher, F. B. 'Influenza and inflation in Tudor England', *Economic History Review*, 2nd ser., XVIII (1965)

Fischer-Galati, S. A. *Ottoman Imperialism and German Protestantism 1521–1555* (Cambridge, Mass., 1959)

Friis, A. 'An inquiry into the relations between economic and financial factors in the sixteenth centuries. I. The two crises in the Netherlands in 1557', *Scandinavian Economic History Review*, I (1953), pp. 192–217

García Figueras, T. *Presencia de España en Berbería Central y Oriental* (Madrid, 1943)

García Martínez, S. *Bandolerismo, piratería y control de moriscos en Valencia durante el reinado de Felipe II* (Valencia, 1977)

Geyl, P. *The revolt of the Netherlands 1555–1609*, 5th edn. (London, 1980)

Gil Sanjuan, J. 'Malaga y la transmisión de información en la política Norteafricana de los Austrias', *Baetica*, vol. 6, pp. 265–73.

Gilissen, J. 'Les Etats Généraux des Pays de Par Deça 1464–1632', *Standen en Landen*, XXXIII (1965), pp. 261–321

González Palencia, A. *Gonzálo Pérez, secretario de Felipe II* (2 vols., Madrid, 1946)

Griegson, E. *King of two worlds. Philip II of Spain* (London, 1974)

Gutman, M. *War and rural life in the early modern Low Countries* (Princeton, 1980)

Hantsch, H. 'Le problème de la lutte contre l'invasion turque dans l'idée politique générale de Charles Quint', in *Charles Quint et son temps* (Paris, 1959), pp. 51–60

Harbison, E. H. *Rival ambassadors at the court of Queen Mary* (London, 1940)

Hauser, H., 'The European financial crisis of 1559', *Journal of Economic and Business History*, II (1929–1930), pp. 241–55

Headley, J. M. *The Emperor and his chancellor. A study of the Imperial chancellery under Gattinara* (Cambridge, 1983)

Herrera Tordesillas, A. de. *Historia general del mundo de XV años del tiempo del Señor don Felipe II* (Valladolid, 1606).

Hess, A. C. 'The Moriscos: an Ottoman fifth column in sixteenth century Spain', *American Historical Review*, 74 (1968), pp. 1–25
  'The evolution of the Ottoman seaborne empire, 1453–1525', *American Historical Review*, 75 (1970), pp. 1892–1919
  The forgotten frontier: a history of the sixteenth century Ibero-African frontier (Chicago, 1978)

Bibliography

Hillgarth, J. M. *The Spanish kingdoms*, vol. II: 1410–1516 (2 vols., Oxford, 1978)

Hinojosa, R. de. 'Felipe II y el conclave de 1559', *Revista Contemporánea*, no. 72 (1888), pp. 225–36, 466–78; no. 73 (1889), pp. 45–56, 145–53, 360–70, 501–7; no. 74, pp. 68–79, 181–94, 549–60; no. 75, pp. 87–94, 154, 159

Hirschauer, C. *Les Etats d'Artois de leurs origines à l'occupation française 1340–1640* (2 vols., Paris–Brussels, 1923)

Historia de España, dir. R. Menéndez Pidal, vols. XVII and XVIII (Madrid, 1966–9)

Hook, J. 'Habsburg imperialism and Italian particularism: the case of Charles V and Siena', *European Studies Review*, 9 (1979), pp. 283–312

Hurewitz, J. C., *The Middle East and North Africa in world politics. 1: European expansion 1535–1914* (New Haven, 1975)

Imber, C. H. 'The navy of Suleyman the Magnificent', *Archivum Ottomanicum*, VI (1980), pp. 211–82

Inalcik, H. *The Ottoman empire* (New York, 1973)

Iongh, J. de. *Mary of Hungary. Second regent of the Netherlands* (English version, London, 1958)

Jacquot, J. (ed.) *Fêtes et cérémonies au temps de Charles V. vol. II. Les fêtes de la Renaissance* (Paris, 1960)

Jensen, D. L. 'The Ottoman Turks in sixteenth-century French diplomacy', *Sixteenth Century Journal*, XVI, no. 4 (1985), pp. 451–70

Jones, N. L. *Faith by Statute. Parliament and the settlement of religion 1559* (London, 1982)

Jóver Zamora, J. M. *Carlos V y los españoles* (Madrid, 1963)

Kagan, R. L. *Students and society in early modern Spain* (Baltimore, 1974)
   Lawsuits and litigants in Castile 1500–1700 (Chapel Hill, 1981)

Kamen, H. *The Spanish Inquisition* (London, 1965)
   Spain 1469–1714. A Society in Conflict (London, 1983)

Keen, M. H. *The law of war in the late Middle Ages* (London, 1965)

Keniston, H. *Francisco de los Cobos* (Pittsburgh, 1960)

Knecht, R. J. *Francis I* (Cambridge, 1982)

Koenigsberger, H. G., *The practice of empire* (Ithaca, 1969)
   Estates and revolutions (Ithaca, 1971)
   The Habsburgs and Europe, 1516–1660 (London, 1971)
   'The statecraft of Philip II', *European Studies Review*, I (1971), pp. 1–21, now also in his *Politicians and Virtuosi* (London, 1986).

Labande Mailfert, Y. 'Trois traités de paix 1492–1493', *Le Moyen Age*, LX (1954), pp. 379–401

Lapeyre, H. *Simon Ruiz et les 'asientos' de Philippe II* (Paris, 1953)
   Une famille de marchands: les Ruiz (Paris, 1955)
   Las etapas de la política exterior de Felipe II (Valladolid, 1973)
   Les monarchies européennes du XVIe siècle (Paris, 1973)

Laredo Quesada, M. A., 'Les finances royales de Castille à la veille des temps modernes', *Annales, Économies, Sociétés, Civilisations*, III (1970), pp. 775–88

Laroui, A. *L'histoire du Maghreb: un essai de synthèse* (Paris, 1973)

Lea, H. C. *The Inquisition in the Spanish dependencies* (London, 1908)

Lestocquoy, J. 'De la prise de Calais au traité du Câteau-Cambrésis', *Revue du Nord* (Lille, 1958), pp. 39–47

Bibliography

Levine, M. *The Early Elizabethan Succession Question 1558–1568* (Stanford, 1966)

Livermore, H. V. *A new history of Portugal* (London, 1976)

Llorente, A. 'La primera crísis de hacienda en tiempo de Felipe II', *Revista de España*, II (1868), pp. 317–61

Loach, J. and R. Tittler, *The mid-Tudor polity c. 1540–1560* (London, 1980)

Loades, D. M. *Two Tudor conspiracies* (Cambridge, 1965)
The Oxford martyrs (London, 1970)
The reign of Mary Tudor (London, 1979)

Loddo Canepa, F. *La Sardegna dal 1478 al 1793*, 2 vols., vol. I: 1478–1720 (Galizzi-Sassari, 1974)

Longchay, H. 'Étude sur les emprunts des souverains belges au XVIè et au XVIIè siècle', *Académie Royale de Belgique*, XII (1907), pp. 923–1013

Louant, A. 'Charles de Lalaing et les remonstrances d'Emmanuel-Philibert de Savoie (juillet et novembre 1556)', *Bulletin de la Commission Royale d'Histoire* (Brussels), XCVII (1933), pp. 255–69.

Lovett, A. W. *Philip II and Mateo Vázquez de Leca* (Geneva, 1977)

Lynch, J. *Spain under the Habsburgs* (2 vols., Oxford, 1964 2nd edn. 1981)

Maltby, W. S. *Alba. A biography of Fernando Alvarez de Toledo, third duke of Alba, 1507–1582* (Berkeley–London, 1983)

Marañón, G. *Antonio Pérez* (2 vols., Madrid, 1954)

Maravall, J. A. *El pensamiento político de Fernando el Católico* (Zaragoza, 1952)

Mas, A. *Les Turcs dans la littérature espagnole du siècle d'or* (2 vols., Paris, 1967)

Mattingly, G. *Renaissance diplomacy* (London, 1963 edn.)

Menéndez Pidal, R., *Los Reyes Católicos y otros estudios* (Buenos Aires, 1962)
(ed.), see *Historia de España*

Merriman, R. B. *The rise of the Spanish empire in the Old World and the New* (4 vols., New York, 1918–34, vol. IV, *Philip the Prudent*, New York, 1934)

Mesnard, P. 'L'expérience politique de Charles Quint et les enseignements d'Erasme', in *Fêtes et cérémonies aux temps de Charles Quint* (see Jacquot, J.) vol. II, pp. 45–56

Mignet, M. 'Une élection à l'Empire en 1519. Première rivalité de François Ier et de Charles-Quint', *Revue de Deux Mondes*, 2nd ser., XXIV (1854), pp. 209–64
'Rivalité de Charles-Quint et de François Ier', *Revue de Deux Mondes*, 2nd ser., XXVIII (1858), II, pp. 257–305, 618–46

Monti, A. 'Filippo II e il cardenal Cristoforo Madruzzo, governatore di Milano (1556–1557)', *Nuova Rivista Stórica* (1924), pp. 133–55

Motley, J. L. *The rise of the Dutch Republic* (3 vols. edn., London, 1904)

Muto, G. *Le finanze pubbliche napoletane tra riforme e Restaurazione (1520–1634)* (Naples, 1980)

Novalin, J. L. G. *El Inquisidor General Fernando de Valdés (1483–1568)* (2 vols., Oviedo, 1971)

Orveta, R. de *La escultura funeraria de España* (Madrid, 1919)

Osten Sacken, C. v.d. *El Escorial. Estudio iconológico* (Bilbao, 1984).

Outhwaite, R. B. 'The trials of foreign borrowing: the English Crown and the Antwerp money market in the mid sixteenth century', *Economic History Review*, 2nd ser., XIX (1966), pp. 289–305

Pacheco y de Leyva, E. 'Grave error político de Carlos I haciendo la boda de Felipe II con doña María, reina de Inglaterra', *Revista de Archivos, Bibliotecas y Museos*, XLII (1921), pp. 59–84 and 276–92

Parker, G. *The army of Flanders and the Spanish road 1567–1659* (Cambridge, 1972).
  The Dutch revolt (London, 1977)
  Philip II (London, 1979)
  Spain and the Netherlands (1559–1659) (Glasgow, 1979)

Parry, J. H. *The Spanish seaborne empire* (London, 1966, 2nd edn., 1967)
  The Spanish theory of empire in the sixteenth century (New York, 1974)

Pastor, J. F. von *The History of the Popes*, ed. R. F. Kerr, (vols. XIV–XVII, London, 1951)

Pfandl, L. *Felipe II*, Spanish edn. (Madrid, 1942)

Pierson, P. *Philip II of Spain* (London, 1975)

Potter, D. 'The duc de Guise and the Fall of Calais, 1557–1558'. *English Historical Review*, XCVIII, 98 (1983), pp. 481–512

Prescot, H. F. M. *Mary Tudor* (London, 1952)

Prescott, W. H. *History of the reign of Philip the Second, king of Spain* (3 vols., London, 1855)

Ranum, O. (ed.) *National consciousness, history and political culture in early modern Europe* (Baltimore, 1974)

Rassow, P. and F. Schalk. (eds.), *Karl V. Der Kaiser und seine Zeit* (Bohlau Verlag, Cologne, 1960).

Read, C. *Mr. Secretary Cecil and Queen Elizabeth* (London, 1955, 1965)

Reglá Campistol, J. *Felip II i Catalunya* (Barcelona, 1955)

Reivindicación histórica del siglo XVI, published by the Real Academia de Jurisprudencia y Legislación (Madrid, 1928)

Rich, E. E. and C. H. Wilson (eds.), see *The Cambridge Economic History of Europe*

Rodríguez-Salgado, M. J. and S. Adams, 'The count of Feria's dispatch to Philip II of the 14 November 1558', *Camden Miscellany*, XXVIII Camden 4th ser., vol. 29, pp. 302–34

Romano, R. 'La pace di Cateau-Cambrésis e l'equilibrio europeo', *Rivista Stòrica Italiana* (1949), pp. 526–50

Romier, L. 'Les guerres d'Henri II et le traité du Château-Cambrésis (1554–9)', *Mélanges d'Archéologie et d'Histoire*, XXX (1910), pp. 1–50
  Les origines politiques des guerres de religion (2 vols., Paris, 1913–14)

Rosenfeld, P. 'The provincial governors of the Netherlands from the minority of Charles V to the Revolt', *Standen en landen*, XVII (1959), pp. 1–63
  'The provincial governors of the Netherlands from the minority of Charles V to the Revolt', in *Government in Reformation Europe 1520–1560*, ed. H. J. Cohn (London, 1971), pp. 157–64

Ruble, A. de *Le traité de Cateau-Cambrésis (2–3 Avril 1559)* (Paris, 1889)

Ruíz Martín, F. 'Las finanzas españolas durante el reinado de Felipe II', *Cuadernos de Historia; Anexos de la Revista Hispania*, II (1968), pp. 109–73

Rule, J. C. and J. Te Pasque (eds.) *The character of Philip II: the problem of moral judgements in history* (Boston, 1963)

Rumeu de Armas, A. 'Franceses y españoles en el Atlántico en tiempo del Emperador', in *Charles Quint et son temps* (Paris, 1959), pp. 61–75

Ryder, A. *The kingdom of Naples under Alfonso the Magnanimous* (Oxford, 1976)

Salvador Esteban, E. *Cortes valencianas del reinado de Felipe II* (Valencia, 1974)

Bibliography

Sánchez Agesta, L. *El concepto de estado en el pensamiento español del siglo XVI* (Madrid, 1959)

Sánchez Alonso, B. *Fuentes de la historia española e hispano-americana* (3 vols, Madrid, 1952, 3rd edn.)

Sánchez Montes, J. *Franceses, protestantes, turcos. Los españoles ante la política internacional de Carlos V* (Pamplona, 1951)

Schepper, H. de 'La organización de las "finanzas" públicas en los Paises Bajos reales, 1480–1700. Una reseña', *Cuadernos de Investigación Historica*, 8 (1984), pp. 7–33

Shennan, J. H. *Government and society in France 1461–1661* (London, 1969)
The origins of the modern European state 1450–1725 (London, 1974)

Slavin, A. J. (ed.) *The 'New Monarchies' and representative assemblies* (London, 1964)

Spini, G. 'The Medici principality and the organization of the states of Europe in the sixteenth century', *Journal of Italian History*, 3 (1979), pp. 420–47

Spivakovski, E. 'El "Vicariato de Siena". Correspondencia de Felipe II, príncipe, con Diego Hurtado de Mendoza y Ferrante Gonzaga', *Hispania*, 26 (1966), pp. 583–9

Setton, K. M. *Europe and the Levant in the Middle Ages and the Renaissance*, Variorum Reprints (London, 1974)

Stirling, W. *The cloister life of the emperor Charles V* (London, 1853)

Strada, F. *De Bello Belgico* (Rome, 1632; English edition, trans. Sir Robert Stapylton, (London, 1650)

Suárez Fernández, L. and M. Fernández Alvarez, *La España de los Reyes Católicos (1474–1516)* (2 vols., Madrid, 1959), vol. XVII of *Historia de España*, dir. Menéndez Pidal

Tellechea Idígoras, J. I. 'Felipe II y el Inquisidor General D. Fernando de Valdés', *Salmanticensis* (Salamanca), XVI, 2 (1969), pp. 329–72
Fray Bartolomé Carranza y el Cardenal Pole (Pamplona, 1977)

Tenenti, A. *Naufrages, corsaires et assurances maritimes à Venise 1592–1609* (Paris, 1959)
Piracy and the decline of Venice 1580–1615, English edn. (London, 1967)

Thompson, I. A. A. *War and government in Habsburg Spain 1560–1620* (London, 1976).
'Crown and Cortes in Castile, 1590–1665', *Parliaments, Estates and Representation*, II, 1 (1982), pp. 29–45

Tracy, J. D. *A financial revolution in the Habsburg Netherlands. Rente and rentiers in the county of Holland, 1515–1565* (London, 1985)
'The taxation system of the county of Holland during the reigns of Charles V and Philip II, 1519–1566', *Economisch-en-Sociaal-Historisch Jaarboek*, vol. 48 (1985), pp. 71–117

Troeyer, P. B. de., *Lamoreal van Egmont* (Brussels, 1961), Spanish summary, pp. 203–8

Tuchle, H. 'The peace of Augsburg: new order or lull in the fighting?', in *Government in Reformation Europe, 1520–1560*, ed. H. J. Cohn (London, 1971)

Tuñón de Lara, M. (ed.), *Historia de España*, vol. V. *La frustración de un imperio, 1476–1714* (Barcelona, 1982)

Tyler, R. *The Emperor Charles the Fifth* (London, 1958)

Ulloa, M. *La Hacienda Real de Castilla en el reinado de Felipe II* (2nd edn., Madrid, 1977)

Vanderlinden, H., 'Emmanuel Philibert de Savoie Gouverneur-général des Pays-Bas (1555–1559)'. *Bulletin de L'Académie Royale de Belgique*, 28 (1942), pp. 123–39
'La politique méditerranéenne de Charles V', *Académie Royale de Belgique. Bulletin de la Classe des Lettres et des Sciences Morales et Politiques*, XIV (1928), pp. 11–23

Van Der Wee, H. *The growth of the Antwerp market and the European economy, fourteenth to sixteenth centuries*, 3 vols. (The Hague, 1963)

van Durme, M. *El Cardenal Granvela (1517–1586)* (Spanish edn., Barcelona, 1957)

Vaughan, R. *Valois Burgundy* (London, 1975)

Vázquez Prada, V., *Lettres marchandes d'Anvers* (4 vols., vol. I, Paris, 1960)

Veríssimo Serrão, J. *História de Portugal*, vol. III: *O século de ouro 1495–1580* (Lisbon, 1978)

Vicens Vives, J. et al., *Historia social y económica de España y America* (5 vols. Barcelona, 1957–59)

'Imperio y administración en tiempo de Carlos V', in *Charles Quint et son temps* (Paris, 1959)

Wallerstein, I. *The modern world system* (2 vols., London, 1974 & 1980)

Weikel, A. 'The Marian Council revisited', in J. Loach and R. Tittler, *The mid-Tudor polity c. 1540–1560* (London, 1980), pp. 52–73

Wernham, R. B. *Before the Armada* (London, 1966)

White, B. *Mary Tudor* (London, 1935)

Williamson, J. A., *Maritime enterprise 1485–1558* (Oxford, 1913)

Yahya, D. *Morocco in the sixteenth century* (Harlow, 1981)

Zeller, G. *Histoire des relations internationales II: Les temps modernes, I. De Christophe Colomb à Cromwell* (Paris, 1953)

'Le principe d'équilibre dans la politique internationale avant 1789', *Revue Historique*, 215 (1956), pp. 25–37

UNPUBLISHED THESES AND PAPERS

Lagomarsino, P. D. 'Court factions and the formulation of Spanish policy towards the Netherlands (1559–1567)', Ph.D. dissertation (University of Cambridge 1973)

Moore, S. F. C. 'The centre and the periphery: Brussels and Utrecht 1550–1559', paper given at the Institute of Historical Research (London, 2 December 1984)

Riley, C. D. G. 'The state of Milan in the reign of Philip II of Spain', D.Phil. (University of Oxford, 1977)

Straukamp, J. E. 'Anglo-Spanish relations 1558–1563', Ph.D. dissertation (University of London, 1965)

Index

369

CAMBRIDGE STUDIES IN EARLY MODERN HISTORY

For list of current titles please see front of book